Philippines

North Luzon p110

Manila p46 **Around Manila** p92

Mindoro p190 **Southeast Luzon** p163

Boracay & Western Visayas p209 **Cebu & Eastern Visayas** p275

Palawan p378

Mindanao p338

THIS EDITION WRITTEN AND RESEARCHED BY

Michael Grosberg,
Greg Bloom, Trent Holden, Anna Kaminski, Paul Stiles

Contents

MANILA P46

BANAUE P146

Contents

BORACAY P211

CEBU CATHEDRAL, CEBU
P277

KADAYAWAN SA DABAW
FESTIVAL, DAVAO P363

Contents

CHOCOLATE HILLS P315

PALAWAN P378

UNDERSTAND

SURVIVAL GUIDE

SPECIAL FEATURES

Welcome to the Philippines

The Philippines is defined by its emerald rice fields, teeming megacities, graffiti-splashed jeepneys, smouldering volcanoes, bug-eyed tarsiers, fuzzy water buffalo and smiling, happy-go-lucky people.

Cultural Quirks

The Philippines is a land apart from mainland Southeast Asia – not only geographically but also spiritually and culturally. The country's overwhelming Catholicism, the result of 350 years of Spanish rule, is its most obvious enigma. Vestiges of the Spanish era include exuberant fiestas (festivals), Spanish-Filipino architecture and centuries-old stone churches. Malls, fast-food chains and widespread spoken English betray the influence of Spain's colonial successor, America. Yet despite these outside influences, the country remains very much its own unique entity. The people are Filipinos – and proud of it. Welcoming, warm and upbeat, it is they who captivate and ultimately ensnare visitors.

Islands & Beaches

With more than 7000 islands, the Philippines is a beach bum's delight. There's an island to suit every taste, from marooned slicks of sand in the middle of the ocean to sprawling mega-islands such as Luzon and Mindanao. Sun worshippers and divers should head straight to the Visayas, where island-hopping opportunities abound and the perfect beach takes many forms. More adventurous travellers can pitch a tent on a deserted stretch of coastline and play solo *Survivor* for a few days.

Outdoor Adventures

The Philippines isn't just about finding an isolated beach and getting catatonic. From kayaking to kitesurfing to canyoning to spelunking, the Philippines can capably raise any adrenaline junkie's pulse. While surfers are just catching on to the tasty (if fickle) waves that form on both coasts, divers have long been enamoured of the country's underwater charms. Freshwater pursuits include rafting and wakeboarding. Back on terra firma, trekking can be done just about anywhere, while rock climbing is gaining popularity. And the Philippines is also, unofficially, the zipline capital of the world.

Tempestuous Tropics

We've all had it happen: your trip to paradise is ruined by day after day of torrential monsoon rain (in the Philippines that paradise is often Palawan). There are a couple of simple ways to avoid this. One: study the climate charts. The western parts of the country get hammered by rain at the peak of the southwest monsoon (July to September), so go east during this time (unless there's a typhoon brewing). Two: stay flexible. Dispense with advance bookings so you can migrate to fairer climes if need be.

Why I Love the Philippines

By Greg Bloom, Author

With 7000 tropical islands on my doorstep, all ripe for exploration, I find it easy to *like* the Philippines. Love, on the other hand, is borne of subtler things. Love is borne of long rooftop jeepney rides through the mountains of North Luzon; of a frosty San Miguel at sundown on a sublime slab of Visayan sand; of a fresh-fish lunch, followed by a siesta on an interminable bangka journey through Palawan's islands; of friends with names like Bing and Bong; of phrases like 'comfort room'; of – dare I say it – karaoke. Now that is love.

For more about our authors, see page 480

Above: Blue Lagoon (p127), Pagudpud

The Philippines

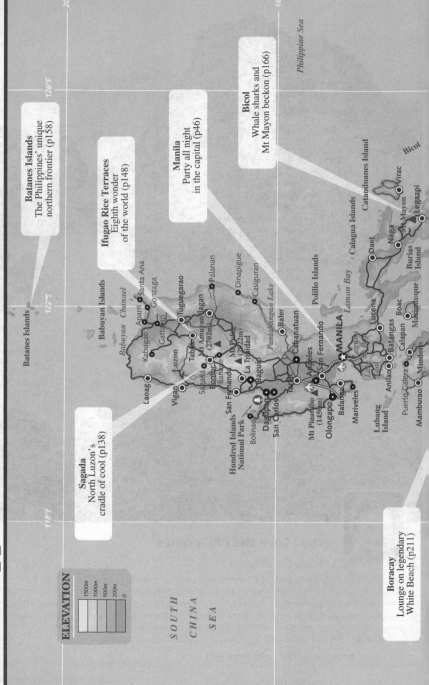

Batanes Islands
The Philippines' unique
northern frontier (p158)

Ifugao Rice Terraces
Eighth wonder
of the world (p148)

Manila
Party all night
in the capital (p46)

Bicol
Whale sharks and
Mt Mayon beckon (p166)

Sagada
North Luzon's
cradle of cool (p138)

Boracay
Lounge on legendary
White Beach (p211)

ELEVATION

1500m
1000m
500m
200m
0

SOUTH CHINA SEA

Philippine Sea

Babuyan Channel

Batanes Islands

Babuyan Islands

Aparri
Santa Ana
Gonzaga
Tuguegarao
Palanan
Kabugao
Gattaran
Tabuk
Ilagan
Dinapigue
Luzon
Casiguran
Laoag
Vigan
Sagada Mt Amuyao (2702m)
Bontoc
Banaue
Mt Pulag (2922m)
La Trinidad
Baguio
Baler
Cabanatuan
San Fernando
Cabarroguis
San Fernando
Angeles
MANILA
Hundred Islands National Park
Bolinao
Dagupan
San Carlos
Mt Pinatubo (1451m)
Olongapo
Balanga
Mariveles
Batangas
Anilao
Calapan
Lubang Island
Puerto Galera
Mindoro
Mamburao

Pantabangan Lake

Polillo Islands

Lamon Bay

Calagua Islands

Lucena
Boac
Marinduque

Catanduanes Island

Daet
Naga
Virac
Bicol
Mayon
Legazpi
Burias Island

20°N
16°N
118°E
122°E
126°E

0 ── 100 km
0 ── 50 miles

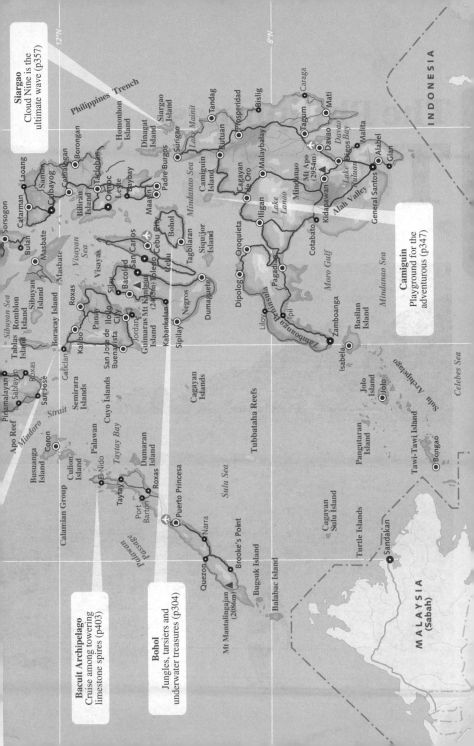

Siargao
Cloud Nine is the ultimate wave (p357)

Camiguin
Playground for the adventurous (p347)

Bacuit Archipelago
Cruise among towering limestone spires (p403)

Bohol
Jungles, tarsiers and underwater treasures (p304)

12°N

8°N

INDONESIA

Philippines Trench

Caraga
Mati
Tagum
Davao
Bislig
Malita
Prosperidad
Tandag
Bunawan
Butuan
Kidapawan
Mt Apo (2954m)
Mindanao
Malaybalay
Surigao
Siargao Island
Dinagat Island
Homonhon Island
Lake Mainit
Lake Buluan
Alabel
General Santos
Glan
Alah Valley
Cagayan de Oro
Camiguin Island
Mindanao Sea
Iligan
Lake Lanao
Cotabato
Pagadian
Moro Gulf
Oroquieta
Dipolog
Mindanao Sea
Zamboanga
Zamboanga Peninsula
Liloy
Ipil
Basilan Island
Isabela
Jolo Island
Jolo
Sulu Archipelago
Pangutaran Island
Tawi-Tawi Island
Bongao
Celebes Sea
Cagayan Sulu Island
Turtle Islands
Sandakan
MALAYSIA (Sabah)

Borongan
Laoang
Catarman
Sorsogon
Santa Calbayog
Catbalogan
Tacloban
Biliran Island
Ormoc
Leyte
Maasin
Padre Burgos
Baybay
Bohol
Tagbilaran
Siquijor Island
Dumaguete
Negros
Kabankalan
Sipalay
Visayan Sea
Cebu City
Cebu
Toledo
San Carlos
Guimaras Island
Mt Kanlaon (2435m)
Bacolod
Silay
Panay
Iloilo City
Jordan
San Jose de Buenavista
Roxas
Kalibo
Caticlan
Boracay Island
Sibuyan Sea
Romblon Island
Tablas Island
Sibuyan Island
Masbate
Bulan
Masbate
Semirara Islands
Cuyo Islands
Cagayan Islands
Tubbataha Reefs

Sulu Sea

Pinamalayan
Sablayan
San Jose
Roxas
Apo Reef
Mindoro Strait
Busuanga Island
Coron
Culion Island
Calamian Group
El Nido
Taytay
Taytay Bay
Port Barton
Roxas
Dumaran Island
Palawan
Puerto Princesa
Narra
Quezon
Brooke's Point
Mt Mantalingajan (2086m)
Bugsuk Island
Balabac Island
Palawan Passage

The Philippines'
Top 15

Bacuit Archipelago

1 Cruising through the labyrinthine Bacuit Archipelago (p403) of northern Palawan, past secluded beaches, pristine lagoons and rocky islets, is an experience not to be missed. Only a short bangka (wooden boat) ride from the easygoing coastal town of El Nido, Bacuit Bay presents a thrilling mixture of imposing limestone escarpments, palm-tree-lined white-sand beaches and coral reefs. Overnight island-hopping trips in the bay or further north through the Linapacan Strait towards Coron offer an opportunity to bed down in remote fishing villages where the daily catch is grilled for dinner.

Ifugao Rice Terraces

2 It's easy to look at a map of North Luzon and assume the Cordillera is all untamed wilderness. And yes – there's rugged jungle. But what really strikes a visitor to Banaue, Batad and the other towns of Ifugao is how cultivated the mountains are. Even the sheerest cliffs possess little patches of ground that have been tilled into rice paddies (p148). Take all those patches together and you get a veritable blanket of upland-tilled goodness, an unending landscape of hills rounded into rice-producing lumps of emerald.

Beaches

3 There's at least one made-to-order beach on each of the country's 7000+ islands. Want to be far away from everybody? It's almost too easy – most of Luzon is ringed by deserted beaches, while your own private island awaits in Palawan's Calamian Group around Coron. Seeking a good dive spot with plenty of additional diversions and a great beach? Dial up El Nido or Sipalay's Sugar Beach. Want action with your beach experience? Take kitesurfing lessons on Boracay or surf lessons in San Juan, La Union. Top: Mona Lisa Point, San Juan (p117)

Fiesta Time

4 The Philippines just isn't the Philippines without the colourful festivals that rage throughout the year. Even the tiniest village holds at least one annually. The grandaddy of them all is the Ati-Atihan Festival (p227) in Kalibo. At Bacolod's MassKara Festival (p243) and Marinduque's Moriones Festival (p189), masked men stir the masses into a dancing frenzy. The Easter crucifixion ceremony in San Fernando, north of Manila, produces a more macabre tableau, with Catholic devotees being physically nailed to crosses. Bottom: MassKara Festival (p243)

JOHN SEATON CALLAHAN/GETTY IMAGES ©

BRYAN L RAPADAS/GETTY IMAGES ©

Southern Negros

5 The 'toe' of boot-shaped Negros (p240) offers a little of everything: World-class diving at Apo Island, trekking on Twin Peaks, dolphin- and whale-watching at Bais and perfect beaches pretty much everywhere. As if that weren't enough, wonderfully quirky Siquijor lies just off the coast. It's all within an hour of Dumaguete, an agreeable city in its own right, with lively restaurants and bars plus an airport. No need to worry about advance planning here. Just parachute in and follow your nose. We guarantee it will lead you to somewhere special.

Manila Culture & Nightlife

6 There's more to this megacity (p46) than traffic and noise. Manila's nightlife is second to none. From the bongo-infused hipster hang-outs of Quezon City and Cubao X to Makati's sizzling bars and chi-chi nightclubs, there's something for everyone. The museums are absolutely world-class, and in contemporary art and design circles, Manila is Asia's rising star. Eternally classy Intramuros oozes history. Even the long-maligned culinary scene is finally emerging, as cutting-edge restaurants open alongside earthy cafes and craft-beer bars.

Bicol Adventures

7 Southeast Luzon, geographically defined by the Bicol Peninsula (p166), is becoming adventure-travel central. Besides boasting some of the best regional cuisine in the islands, Bicol is a top draw for water and adrenaline junkies via the CamSur Watersports Complex, where wakeboarding rules the roost. Daet, Camarines Norte, is a burgeoning surf and kitesurfing destination. To experience a more laid-back connection to the water, head to the edge of Luzon and snorkel alongside the gentle whale sharks of Donsol – an unforgettable highlight.

Above: Whale shark, Donsol (p178)

Sagada

8 Sagada (p138) is the Philippines' cradle of cool, a supremely mellow mountain retreat deep in the heart of the wild Cordillera mountains of North Luzon. It has all the elements of a backpacker Shangri La: awesome hikes, eerie caves, hanging coffins, strong coffee, earthy bakeries, and cosy and incredibly cheap accommodation. Fuel up on granola and head out in search of adventure, or chill out in a fireplace-warmed cafe all day reading books or swapping yarns. There are no agendas when you're on Sagada time. Top: Sumaging Cave (p138)

Boracay

9 It wasn't that long ago that Boracay (p211) was a sleepy, almost unknown backwater. Oh, how times have changed. The world has discovered Boracay, elevating the diminutive island into a serious player in the pantheon of Southeast Asian party beaches. Yet for all that's changed, Boracay remains generally mellower than the likes of Kuta Beach or Ko Samui. And solace can still be found, in particular at the southern end of Boracay's signature White Beach, where the spirit of the old Boracay lives on.

Siargao

10 A chill-out vibe and friendly breaks for both experts and novices make this island (p357) the Philippines' top surf destination. The legendary Cloud Nine break is the hub but waves abound elsewhere; head to tranquil Burgos in the north for an undeveloped experience or take a surf safari to seldom-visited spots. Nonsurfers also have plenty to do, from island hopping to snorkelling to some of the country's best deep-sea fishing. Or just grab a beer at the Cloud Nine pavilion and watch the pros do their thing.

Bohol Nature & Wildlife

11 While most visitors to Bohol (p304) are divers bound for touristy Alona Beach, the real charms of this central Visay-an island lie deep in its interior. Perhaps no island in the country is better suited for a half-week romp by motorbike. Perfectly paved roads lead through jungle to peacock-green rivers, chocolatey hills, dramatically placed ziplines and little tarsiers. The island took a gut-punch with the 2013 earthquake, which toppled many of its centuries-old Spanish churches. But Bohol bounced right back, and is better than ever. Bottom: Tarsier

FARLEY BARIGUATRO/GETTY IMAGES ©

TOMASTDV/GETTY IMAGES ©

The Batanes Islands

12 The Batanes (p158), where women still wear haystack-like headgear and folks live in traditional stone-and-*cogon*-grass houses, are far removed (both geographically and culturally) from the rest of the archipelago. Sample the islands' unique dishes and overnight in simple homestays to experience the daily rhythms of the farming and fishing life. Feeling more active? Cycle the pristine, strikingly beautiful coastlines of Batan and Sabtang islands and hike the hills, rolling pastureland and extinct volcanoes of the interior. Above: Basco (p159)

Climbing Volcanic Camiguin

13 From the northern coastline of mainland Mindanao, the rough-hewn landscape of Camiguin (p347) is camouflaged by its lush silhouette. To truly grasp this island's inspiring topography, veer into the interior on roadways that carve through dense forests and culminate in rocky pathways that trail further up into the highlands. Peaks and valleys offer streams for scrambling, mountains for scaling, canyons for rappelling and pools at the base of thundering waterfalls. Above right: Katibawasan Falls (p349)

Cebu Sand & Sea

14 Cebu (p275) is your quintessential beach lovers' paradise. Around the island, sandy coves and dramatic cliffs abut an unbroken ribbon of turquoise water. Off the west coast, a wall attracts rich marine life and scores of divers to places like Moalboal, where schooling sardines present an umissable spectacle. Offshore, Malapascua and Mactan islands are dive meccas known for thresher sharks and turtles, respectively, while Bantayan is *the* place to get catatonic on the sand. At the heart of it all is the fun and frivolous Visayan capital, Cebu City.

14

Puerto Galera

15 Puerto Galera (p192) on Mindoro is well known as one of the Philippines' dive meccas. Lesser known is that it's also among the most beautiful places on the planet. Serpentine roads leading out of town afford birds-eye views of gorgeous bays and little islands offshore, while jungle-clad mountains provide a dramatic interior backdrop. Trek to isolated hill-tribe villages by day, then return to base and enjoy a sumptuous five course Italian meal by night. It's the perfect 'wow' setting for the must-attend Malasimbo Music & Arts Festival in February.

15

Need to Know

For more information, see Survival Guide (p441)

Currency
Philippine Peso (P)

Language
Tagalog (Filipino) and English

Visas
30 days on arrival for most nationalities. Visas are easily extended for a fee in major provincial centres, or can be requested upon arrival.

Money
ATMs widely available and credit cards accepted at hotels, restaurants and some shops in all but remote areas.

Mobile Phones
Local SIM cards, easy to purchase for a nominal charge, can be used in almost all phones.

Time
ASEAN common time (GMT plus eight hours).

When to Go

■ Tropical climate, rain all year round
■ Tropical climate, wet and dry season
■ Shorter dry season, cooler temperatures all year round

Baguio
GO Feb–Mar

Manila
GO Dec–Jan

Boracay
GO Nov–Mar

El Nido
GO Nov–Apr

Siargao
GO Aug–Oct

High Season
(Dec–Apr)

➡ High season is dry season for most of the country; December to February are the coolest, most pleasant months.

➡ Many resorts triple rates around New Year and before Easter.

Shoulder
(May & Nov)

➡ Rising May temperatures herald the onset of the wet season around Manila and elsewhere.

➡ November sees high-season rates kick in.

Low Season
(Jun–Sep)

➡ Accommodation prices drop 30% in resort areas.

➡ Passing typhoons can cause days of torrential rain.

➡ Eastern seaboard is usually dry, if susceptible to typhoons.

Useful Websites

Philippine Newslink (www.philnews.com) Thorough pile of news, views, links.

ClickTheCity.com (www.clickthecity.com) A great listings site for happenings in Manila and around the country.

Tanikalang Ginto (www.filipinolinks.com) Every topic under the Philippine sun.

Lonely Planet (www.lonelyplanet.com/philippines) Destination information, hotel bookings, traveller forum and more.

MindaNews (www.mindanews.com) Hard-hitting online news site for Mindanao.

It's More Fun in the Philippines (www.itsmorefuninthephilippines.com) Tourism authority site; good for planning.

Important Numbers

Dial 🖉0 before area codes when calling from a mobile phone or a landline outside that region.

Country code	🖉63
Emergency	🖉117
International dialling code	🖉00
International operator	🖉108
PLDT directory assistance	🖉187

Exchange Rates

Australia	A$1	P39
Canada	C$1	P40
Euro zone	€1	P57
Japan	¥100	P41
New Zealand	NZ$1	P35
Thailand	10B	P14
UK	£1	P73
USA	US$1	P44

For current exchange rates see www.xe.com

Daily Costs

Budget: less than P1800 (US$40)

➡ Dorm bed or single room P400–800

➡ Local lunch, dinner and beer P400

➡ Tricycle ride P8

Midrange: P1800–5400 (US$40–120)

➡ Air-con room P1000–3000

➡ Lunch and dinner with drinks in a restaurant P700

➡ Motorbike rental P500

Top end: over P5400 (US$120)

➡ Boutique resort P4000–12,000

➡ Dinner at a resort restaurant P800

➡ Private island-hopping trip P2500

Opening Hours

Banks 9am–4.30pm Monday to Friday (most ATMs operate 24 hours)

Bars 6pm–late

Embassies & Consulates 9am–1pm Monday to Friday

Post Offices 9am–5pm Monday to Saturday

Public & Private Offices 8am or 9am to 5pm or 6pm, with a lunch break from noon to 1pm, Monday to Friday

Restaurants 7am or 8am to 10pm or 11pm

Shopping Malls 10am–9.30pm

Supermarkets 9am to 7pm or 8pm

Arriving in the Philippines

Ninoy Aquino International Airport (NAIA) (p449) Check which of NAIA's four terminals you are arriving in (and, especially, departing from). Public transport into town is complicated and involves transfers, but yellow metered taxis are cheap (P225 average to most hotels) and plentiful at airports. The four terminals aren't particularly close to each other but are linked by shuttle vans.

Mactan-Cebu International Airport (CEB) (p449) There's a rank for yellow metered taxis at arrivals. Public transport requires changing jeepneys three times and isn't recommended when taxis are so cheap.

Getting Around

Air Several discount carriers link a vast range of destinations, primarily with Manila and Cebu.

Boat Bangkas, 'fastcraft', car ferries and large vessels with bunk beds and private cabins link the islands.

Van Often the quickest overland option and generally shadows same routes as buses.

Bus Comfort and reliability runs the gamut from hobbling skeletons way past their expiration date to long-haul, modern vehicles with air-con and even wi-fi.

Tricycle These sidecars bolted to motorcycles, the Philippine version of a rickshaw, are everywhere and will transport you several blocks or kilometres.

Jeepney Workhorse of the Philippines, both within cities and towns, as well as between more far-flung destinations.

For much more on **getting around**, see p449

First Time

For more information, see Survival Guide (p441)

Checklist

➡ Make sure your passport is valid for at least six months past your arrival date

➡ Check the airline baggage restrictions

➡ Inform your debit-/credit-card company

➡ Open up a Paypal account – some accommodation prefers this over credit cards

➡ Arrange for appropriate travel insurance (p000)

What to Pack

➡ Sweater or jacket – for those ridiculously cold air-con buses and ferries

➡ Earplugs – roosters and karaoke operate at full volume

➡ Headlamp – brownouts, blackouts and no electricity are common

➡ Sarong – can act as a beach towel, sheet or shawl

➡ Dry bag – if you plan on doing lots of island hopping

➡ Long sleeve rash guard and reef booties for snorkelling

➡ Sunglasses and plenty of sunscreen

Top Tips for Your Trip

➡ If you're comfortable on a motorbike, it's often the best way to experience ordinary rural life. You'll likely receive friendly smiles, waves and shouts to stop and chat.

➡ Basketball players rejoice. Nearly every village, no matter how small and remote, has a court, although many consist of nothing more than an iron hoop nailed to a palm tree. Call next and be ready to compete.

➡ Schedule at least half a day, preferably a full one, for connecting flights back to Manila or Cebu. Missing that flight out because of domestic delays and cancellations isn't unheard of.

What to Wear

Because of the tropical climate the Philippines by necessity is a casual place. That said, despite the heat most Filipinos look fairly unfazed – they're used to it – and tend to wear long pants in urban areas (offices of course) and to the mall. In villages, rural areas and beach towns, flip-flops or sandals, shorts and T-shirts are all you'll need. For women, outside of beach settings, it's best to avoid wearing revealing clothing that might attract unwanted attention. Otherwise, lightweight and comfortable is the way to go.

Sleeping

During the high season, reservations are recommended, especially at popular tourist areas like Boracay or El Nido.

➡ **Resorts** These range from ultraluxurious to basic fan-cooled nipa huts (dwellings made from the leaves of nipa palm trees). European-owned ones tend to be more sophisticated.

➡ **Hotels** Many cater to the domestic market, which means generic concrete construction and air-con, whereas five-star hotels in Manila are over-the-top palatial affairs.

➡ **Pensionnes** Sort of a catch-all term referring to less expensive, independently-owned hotels.

➡ **Hostels** Those that focus on foreign travelers tend to be more comfortable than ones for primarily young Filipinos; beds in the latter are generally shorter.

Tips for Saving Money

➡ Pack as light as possible since most domestic flights charge extra once you exceed a fairly conservative luggage weight limit.

➡ Some hotels and restaurants provide free purified water; fill up your own bottles when you can.

➡ Hop on 'communal' tricycles for only P8 rather than taking 'private' trips.

➡ Frequent modest restaurants where local Filipinos eat.

➡ Go for instant coffee rather than brewed and certainly not the quality P90 to P110 variety offered at high-end coffee shops.

➡ Always go for the less expensive fan rooms; can be just as comfortable as air-con ones.

Bargaining

A modest amount of negotiating is expected in many outdoor markets, however, prices for some food commodities are usually set. Bargaining is expected anywhere tourist handicrafts are sold. Same applies for hiring motorbikes, taxis for the day and chartering bangkas (wooden boats), though official rates might be posted.

Tipping

➡ **Restaurants** A 10% service charge is automatically added to the bill at some restaurants, but leaving a little extra is always appreciated (perhaps P40 to P50 per person if service is not included).

➡ **Taxis** At minimum, round up taxi fares, but consider tipping more (say P20 to P50). Etiquette

➡ **Transport** Don't lose your temper – Filipinos will think you're *loco* (crazy). It generally takes quite a lot, unless alcohol is involved of course, to rouse someone to anger. Especially for transport frustrations, adopt the Filipino maxim – *bahala na* (whatever will be will be).

➡ **Karaoke** When singing or witnessing karaoke – and you will – refrain from catcalls or disparaging remarks regardless of the timbre of the voice.

➡ **Jeepneys** It's no use complaining when squeezed together with strangers on jeepneys – it's best to grin and bear it instead.

➡ **Restaurants** Filipinos hiss to gain someone's attention, often in restaurants to signal the waitstaff. It's not considered rude.

➡ **Betel nut** Chewing betel nut is common (and subsequent puddles of red spit frowned upon) in places such as the Cordillera.

Language

English is widely spoken in urban centres and areas frequented by tourists. Even in the most rural areas, a few basic expressions might be understood. Along with English, the other official language is Tagalog (or Filipino). The country's unique colonial history means Spanish speakers will recognise many words. While Filipino is the *lingua franca*, there are 165 other languages spoken throughout the archipelago – Cebuano and Ilocano are two of the most widespread. See p000 for more information.

CULTURA RM/CHRISTOFFER ASKMAN/GETTY IMAGES ©

Bus trip, Puerto Galera (p192)

If You Like...

Island Hopping

The world's second-largest archipelago is, naturally, an island-hopper's dream. Clusters of islets abound off all of the main islands, and in any coastal community you'll find a boatman ready to take you exploring.

Bacuit Archipelago This labyrinthine waterworld should be top of the list. (p403)

Calamian Group Isolated fishing villages and mysterious inland lakes abound. (p405)

Siargao The Philippines' surf capital has a dizzying array of idyllic islets to explore when the waves aren't happening. (p357)

Romblon Bouncing around by bangka (wooden boat) is the way to roll in this diverse province in the Sibuyan Sea, north of Boracay. (p270)

Caramoan Peninsula The karsts around this wedge of land in eastern Bicol rival those of the Bacuit Archipelago. (p171)

Zambales Coast Uninhabited islands are dotted off this lonely stretch of coastline within driving distance of Manila. (p111)

Beach Resorts

From empty palm-fringed white strips of sand to others lined with resorts and bars with nary an inch to spare, with over 7000 islands, there's a patch of sand for everyone.

Boracay Most widely known and visited, White Beach is ground zero for the Philippines' beachfront party scene. (p211)

El Nido The mix of exquisite luxury resorts on private islands and down-to-earth backpacker beach bungalows is unprecedented. (p396)

Dumaguete It's not a resort per se, but it's in range of several of the best: Siquijor, Sipalay, Dauin and idyllic Apo Island. (p254)

Mactan Island A host of exclusive self-contained resorts with plenty of activities make Mactan a family favourite. (p289)

Malapascua Island A laid-back diving resort on the verge of big things in northern Cebu. (p292)

Port Barton Ultramellow beach town on Palawan's lonely west coast has affordable resorts both on and offshore. (p392)

Samal & Talikud Islands Sure, Davao is clearly visible, but convenience to tropical beaches isn't to be scoffed at. (p369)

Markets & Shopping

You'll find a dizzying array of souvenirs as diverse as the country's cultural patchwork, from tribal weavings to exotic tropical fruits. Markets are a must-see for their sights, sounds and smells, and of course hulking malls are ubiquitous.

Bait's Friday Market Mangyan tribespeople in colourful tribal dress trek down from the hills to trade vegetables for lowland products. (p203)

Batanes Bring home some awesome raingear – the women's headpiece, a *vakul*, looks like a bad wig. (p158)

Greenhills Shopping Center This massive Manila flea market has quality antiques and even genuine pearls, not to mention a massive amount of knock-off clothing and DVDs. (p86)

Banaue Galleries sell Ifugao hunting backpacks and headgear, and embroidery from different groups in the Cordillera. (p146)

Bicol Look for edible *pili* nut goodies in Legazpi in particular, as well as jars of fiery Bicol express. (p166)

WWII History

Few countries endured more pain, suffering and damage than the Philippines in WWII and sombre memorials across the archipelago commemorate key battles, historic landings and gruesome death marches.

Manila The capital has several poignant memorials, none more peaceful and moving than the American Memorial Cemetery in Fort Bonifacio. (p62)

Bataan Peninsula Kilometre markers trace the route of the Bataan Death March, while the museum atop Mt Samat is a must for military-history buffs. (p106)

Red Beach A quirky statue re-enacts General MacArthur's famous return. (p322)

Corregidor Island Only Bataan is more synonomous with WWII in the Philippines. (p94)

Lingayen Gulf The site of key American amphibious landings. (p115)

Architecture

The Spanish left centuries-old stone churches, European-style homes and mansions that have been turned into lovely hotels, lining cobblestone streets.

Vigan Its Old Town is a remarkably well-preserved district of buildings with Mexican, Chinese, Filipino and Spanish influences. (p119)

Daraga Church The baroque-style church, constructed in 1773 from volcanic rocks, is set on a hill overlooking Mt Mayon and the bustling market town. (p175)

Boac Heavily fortified 17th-century cathedral and narrow streets lined with 19th-century houses whose upstairs verandahs spill over with flowers. (p187)

Intramuros Founded in 1571, this Spanish fortress was erected on the remnants of the Islamic settlement by the mouth of the Pasig River in Manila. (p49)

Manila Cathedral First built in 1581 and rebuilt several times since, it still looks ancient. (p54)

Top: San Agustin Church (p51), Intramuros
Bottom: Diniwid Beach (p211), Boracay

Month by Month

January

New Year is a 'superpeak' period, and hotel rates can quadruple in resort areas. Away from the eastern seaboard, the weather is usually pretty good – relatively cool and dry, although rain can certainly linger into January.

✷ Procession of the Black Nazarene

A life-size and highly revered black image of Christ in Quiapo Church (Manila) is paraded through the streets in massive processions on 9 January and again during the week before Easter (Holy Week). (p66)

✷ Ati-Atihan

The Philippines' most famous and riotous festival is this week-long mardi gras in Kalibo on Panay, which peaks in the third week of January. Other towns in the region, such as Cadiz on Negros and Iloilo, hold similar festivals on the weekend nearest 26 January. (p227)

✷ Sinulog Fiesta

The grandaddy of Cebu's fiestas sees celebrants engaged in *sinulog* dancing, a unique two-steps-forward, one-step-back shuffle meant to imitate the rhythm of the river.

✷ Dinagyang Fiesta

Celebrating the Santo Niño with outrageous costumes and dances, this three-day mardi gras–style party takes place in the fourth week of January in Iloilo City. (p234)

February

It's peak season for foreign travellers, so book ahead. The Christmas winds continue to howl, thrilling kitesurfers, while surf season continues in San Fernando (La Union) and butanding (whale shark) activity picks up in Donsol.

✷ Chinese New Year

The lunar new year in late January or early February is popular even among non-Chinese Filipinos. Dragon dances, street parties and huge fireworks displays take place in Manila.

✷ Panagbenga Flower Festival

In the last week in February, the streets in the northern mountain city of Baguio come alive with song, dance and a grand floral parade with spectacular floats.

April

Everything shuts down during Holy Week, which leads up to Easter, when *sinakulo* (passion plays) and *pasyon* (a recitation of the Passion of Christ) are staged throughout the country. Resort prices again hit 'superpeak' levels.

✷ Lang-Ay Festival

In Bontoc, deep in the heart of the Cordillera, surrounding communities come together for parades decked out in traditional tribal dress.

✷ Moriones Festival

Marinduque's colourful Moriones Festival is a week-long *sinakulo* during which the streets are overrun by masked locals

engaging in mock sword fights and playing pranks on bystanders. (p189)

✦ Crucifixion Ceremonies

The Easter crucifixion ceremony in San Fernando (Pampanga), north of Manila, presents a more macabre tableau, with devotees literally being nailed to wooden crosses. Similar re-enactments of Christ's suffering occur in several towns. (p107)

✦ Lenten Festival of Herbal Preparation

On the 'spooky' island of Siquijor, faith healers and witch doctors gather around a big pot on Black Saturday, chanting and preparing a medicinal concoction some say cures all that ails you.

May

Scorching heat, beaches packed with vacationing locals and light winds can make this an uncomfortable time to travel. Consider highland destinations such as Batad, where the rice terraces are at their greenest. May is the last chance for whale sharks in Donsol.

✦ Rodeo Masbateño

Cowboy up for Masbate's electric week-long rodeo in late April or early May, with bull-riding, lasso contests and other events that will have you clicking your spurs. (p183)

✦ Flores de Mayo

Throughout the country, May sees girls in white

Top: Sinulog Fiesta
Bottom: MassKara Festival (p26)

dresses strewing flowers around an image of the Virgin Mary in a centuries-old custom known as Flores de Mayo. Makati's red-light district hosts a somewhat infamous version.

🎊 Pahiyas sa Lucban

This famous fiesta takes place around 15 May in the town of Lucban south of Manila, where houses are decked out with colourful *kiping* (leaf-shaped rice wafers) decorations, which are later eaten. (p101)

June

The onset of the wet season (and low season) brings welcome respite from the heat. June also marks the onset of typhoon season, so check the radar and re-route if there's a big red blob heading your way.

🎊 Pintados-Kasadyaan

This 'painted festival' in Tacloban on 29 June celebrates pre-Spanish traditional tattooing practices,

albeit using water-based paints for the festival's body decorations.

🎊 Baragatan Festival

In the third week of June, residents of Puerto Princesa, Palawan, flood the grounds of the Provincial Capitol Building in a massive display of merrymaking. (p384)

August

It's the rainiest month (except for on the eastern seaboard, where it's the driest), so you'll get fabulous discounts on accommodation. The end of the month sees durian season begin in Mindanao and surf season launch in Siargao.

🎊 Kadayawan sa Dabaw Festival

Davao's big festival showcases its Muslim, Chinese and tribal influences with parades, performances, and fruit and flower displays. It's held in the third week of August.

WHAT THE FIESTA IS GOING ON?

Nearly every barangay (village) has one. And there's one nearly every day. Fiestas, an integral part of Filipino life and identity, are generally associated with celebrations during the feast of the patron saint. However, like other facets of the culture, some are best understood as the result of syncretism; older rituals and beliefs related to bountiful harvests and abundant seas have been blended into a Catholic architecture, often at the behest of missionaries centuries ago. There are still strictly planting festivities and indigenous, pre-Hispanic traditions. Regardless of the origins, they're jubilant affairs, with entire towns spruced up for loved ones' homecomings.

October

Things start to dry out after the heavy rains of August and September, but typhoons are still common. High-season prices kick in towards the end of the month. Christmas music is already in the malls.

🎊 MassKara Festival

Masked men stir the masses into a dancing frenzy on the streets of Bacolod, capital of Negros Occidental, during the weekend closest to 19 October.

🎊 Lanzones Festival

The northern Mindanao island of Camiguin goes crazy for this small, yellow fruit with parades, dance contests and of course a pageant. (p351)

🎊 Todos los Santos

Families laden with food gather at the local cemetery to spend the night remembering departed loved ones on All Saints' Day (commemorated on 1 November). It's surprisingly festive – check out the Chinese Cemetery in Manila. (p59)

December

The northeast Christmas winds ramp up, launching kitesurfing season in Boracay and surf season in northwest Luzon.

🎊 Shariff Kabungsuan Festival

This festival in Cotabato on Mindanao from 15 to 19 December celebrates the arrival of Islam in the region and includes river parades of decorated boats.

Itineraries

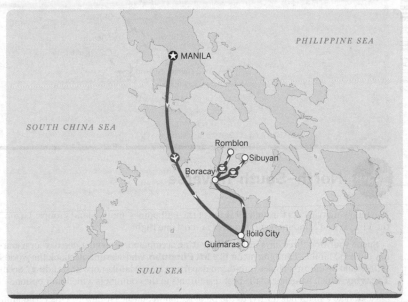

2 WEEKS Manila & Panay

Start off with two days in **Manila** doing a one-day tour of historic sights in Intramuros and nearby museums, and another day in Chinatown and modern Manila as embodied by Makati City. Bars, clubs and all manner of nightlife can keep you busy until dawn if you choose.

Having experienced a little of life in the megalopolis, fly to **Iloilo City** on the island of Panay to experience a more manageable version of urban Philippines. Check out the city's colonial architecture and revitalized Smallville. A short boat ride away is **Guimaras**, a gem of an island for lovers of postcard-perfect low-key resorts, as well as for mountain bikers and mango connoisseurs.

Then bus and boat it quickly to **Boracay**, the Philippines most happening island, and White Beach, the party and nightlife capital. Before long you may be inspired to seek permanent-resident status, but if you find the lifestyle too taxing take a vacation from your vacation by catching a ferry north to the island of Looc and then to either of the island retreats of **Romblon** or **Sibuyan** before returning to civilization via Cebu or Manila.

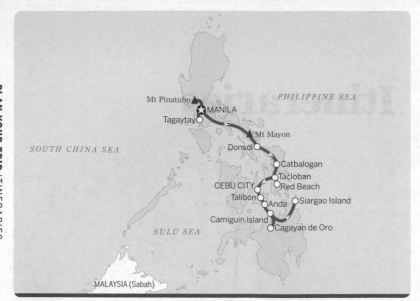

1 MONTH North–South Traverse

The following trip cuts through all three of the Philippines' main island groups: Luzon, the Visayas and Mindanao and requires at most one flight.

Spend your first three days in **Manila** getting acclimated, reserving one day for a journey outside Manila – climbing moon-like **Mt Pinatubo**, whose eruption shook the world in 1991, would be our first choice (pre-dawn departure from Manila notwithstanding). Scenic **Tagaytay**, which has some of the best restaurants in the country, is a mellower option.

Next, take a night bus (or fly) to the Bicol region in Southeast Luzon. This is the Philippines' adventure capital, with surfing, wakeboarding and volcanoes on offer. Around Legazpi you can snorkel with the whale sharks off **Donsol** or climb the symmetrical cone of **Mt Mayon** (if it's not erupting).

Proceeding south, cross the San Bernardino Strait to the rugged islands of Samar and Leyte in the eastern Visayas. Along the way, have the spelunking adventure of a lifetime in **Catbalogan**. Stop off in **Tacloban**, Imelda Marcos' hometown and the city most devastated by Typhoon Haiyan (known locally as Typhoon Yolanda); rebuilding will be well underway. Head to nearby **Red Beach** for a dose of WWII history. Then take a ferry to the Visayas' gritty capital, **Cebu City**, for modern comforts and nightlife.

You'll be approaching week three of your trip by now, and possibly ready for some serious beach time. Take the route less travelled into Bohol, boarding a slow ferry to **Talibon**, then meander down the east coast to **Anda** for some serious chill time on the sand. Once you're sufficiently unwound, move south and catch another classic back-door ferry: 3½ hours from Jagna, Bohol, to **Camiguin Island**.

Camiguin can keep both adventurous travellers and beach bums satisfied for days. Spend at least several here, then hop over to mainland Mindanao by ferry or fly from Camiguin to Siargao via Cebu. This means for your last few days you'll be choosing between **Cagayan de Oro**, a university town with white-water rafting, and **Siargao**, the Philippines' top surf spot and an idyllic island with lagoons and mangroves galore.

Top: Mt Mayon (p176)

Bottom: Children at Malasag Eco-Tourism Village (p346)

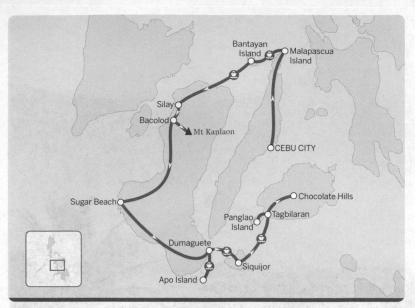

3 WEEKS Voyage to the Visayas

Kick things off in **Cebu City**, soaking up some history during the day before partying it up at night. Then it's time to hit the islands: divers will want to head straight to **Malapascua**, where you've a good chance of encountering thresher sharks; while beach bums can catch some rays on laid-back **Bantayan Island**. A day or three should do you fine, before it's time to skip across to neighbouring island Negros by ferry.

Bus it to **Silay** for a fascinating journey through haciendas and sugar-cane plantations. Spend a night in one of its ancestry homes and dine on Spanish food in the ruins of a grand 1930s mansion. An hour's journey south takes you to **Bacolod**, where you can revel in great food and bar-hopping and go volcano-trekking to **Mt Kanlaon**. Then leg it down the coast for more beach action at the delightfully relaxed **Sugar Beach** – a divine sweep of fine white sand. Continue along the coast to the southeast for the university town **Dumaguete**, which is all about promenading on its scenic boulevard, great seafood and rowdy nightlife. From there you can reach tiny **Apo Island**, one of the Philippines' top underwater destinations.

Say goodbye to Negros, catching the ferry to the mystical island of **Siquijor**. Two or three days here is perfect, allowing you to take in a visit to one of its famed folk healers, laze on some stunning beaches, maybe try a dive or some caving, and absorb its mellow island vibe.

Bohol, a favourite of many travellers, is next. Spend a night in **Tagbilaran**, its lively capital, and take an evening kayak trip to see fireflies, before joining the crowds at **Panglao Island** for fantastic diving and boozy nights on Alona Beach. For a change of scenery take a trip into Bohol's jungle interior. Get an early start to catch the **Chocolate Hills** at dawn minus the crowds. Then of course there's the tarsiers: one of the world's smallest primates, these freaky, adorable critters are best seen at the Tarsier Research & Development Center.

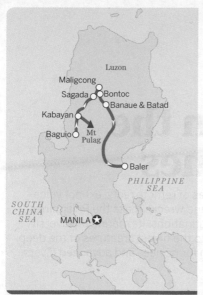

North Luxon
Water World: Palawan

1 MONTH North Luzon

Head north on a non-stop bus from Manila to **Baguio**, the Philippines 'summer capital' and gateway to the Cordillera. A few of the city's museums provide worthwhile introductions to the region's fascinating ethnographic makeup.

From Baguio, take a bus to relatively untouched **Kabayan**, centre of Ibaloi culture and base for hikes in Mt Pulag National Park. Next, **Sagada** beckons. This tranquil, backpacker village has cool temps, a laid-back vibe and top notch hikes.

The amphitheatre-like rice terraces of **Maligcong** are next. Take a jeepney to **Bontoc** and explore on a day trip or overnight in nearby Mainit. Several days can be spent on side trips to Kalinga villages where the contemporary world feels far away.

From Bontoc head to **Banaue** and **Batad**, site of Luzon's most famous rice terraces. Stunning hikes will keep you busy for days. Try to spend at least a night or two in a homestay.

With a little R&R in mind, catch a bus south to San Jose (you might have to overnight here) to connect to another bus to the surfing town of **Baler**.

2 WEEKS Water World: Palawan

Puerto Princesa, the capital and transport hub of this long slender island, is the most convenient place to begin. Spend an evening checking out the city's culinary scene and a day exploring the surrounding countryside on a motorcycle. From Puerto, organise a ride to **Sabang**, a laid-back beachfront village and the base for trips through a darkened riverine cave.

From Sabang, hightail it further north to **El Nido**, a town sandwiched between limestone cliffs and the fantastically picturesque **Bacuit Archipelago** filled with secret lagoons, beaches and rocky landscapes. Several days (at least) can be spent island hopping, kayaking to isolated stretches of white sand and downing drinks at beachfront restaurants at night.

From El Nido, take a boat that winds its way through a maze of islands up to **Coron Town** on Busuanga Island. From here, venture out to the striking lakes of **Coron Island** and some of the best wreck diving in the world. Flights and ferries are available to usher you back to Manila and reality.

Plan Your Trip

Diving in the Philippines

Its varied underwater landscapes of remote reefs, extinct volcanoes, magnificent walls, caves and wrecks make the Philippines one of the world's top diving destinations. Its marine biodiversity is second to none, from sharks to the tiniest creatures of the deep, and there are plentiful sites both for novices and advanced divers.

Best Dives

Best Reef Dive

Tubbataha Reefs (p386) and Apo Reef (p207) are the Philippines' largest and perhaps most unspoiled, though the exceptional reefs of Balicasag (p311) and Padre Burgos (p325) are not to be overlooked.

Best Wall Dive

With so many wall dives to choose from, we can suggest Puerto Galera's Canyons, Camiguin's Jigdup Wall and Samal's Mushroom Rock, but that's just the tip of the iceberg.

Best Shark Dive

Tubbataha Reefs (p386) have a large population of whitetips, grey reef sharks, leopard sharks and rare hammerheads, while Malapascua (p292), off Cebu, is a great place to spot thresher sharks.

Best Novice Dive

There are numerous easy dives off Boracay (p214), Puerto Galera (p193), Anilao (p100) and Cebu (p275).

Best Snorkelling

Snorkelling with Donsol's whale sharks (p178) is hard to beat, though Coral Gardens at Puerto Galera is a fantastic place to see fish.

Planning Your Dive

When to Go

Many parts of the country boast year-round diving, but the Philippines is affected by the annual cycles of the northeast *(amihan)* and southwest *(habagat)* monsoon winds that create a dry season (November to May, with some regional variations), and a wet season (June to October), as well as by typhoons that visit the country periodically from June to December.

Dry Season

The *amihan* winds from November until April dispel much of the remaining rain. The sea can be quite choppy and turbid from late December to early March; many dive centres have alternative sites to visit if weather disturbances are affecting specific areas. Mid-November is generally regarded as the start of the 'tourist season' and Christmas and New Year see most dive centres and resorts overflowing with divers, so reservations are recommended. The *amihan* dies down in late March and the sea becomes flat and calm, with incredible visibility that peaks during April and May.

Wet Season

The height of the rainy season for most of the country (July to September) corresponds with the height of the typhoon

RESPONSIBLE DIVING

Following the points below will help ensure a safe and enjoyable experience.

➡ Be aware of local laws, regulations and etiquette about marine life and the environment, and don't feed fish.

➡ Avoid touching or standing on living marine organisms or dragging equipment across the reef.

➡ Be conscious of your fins. Even without contact, the surge from fin strokes near the reef can damage delicate organisms.

➡ Practise and maintain proper buoyancy control. Major damage can be done by divers descending too fast and colliding with reefs.

➡ Resist the temptation to collect or buy corals or shells or to loot marine archaeological sites.

➡ Ensure that you take your rubbish and any other litter you may find away from dive sites.

season; this results in major tropical downpours. While heavy rain can cause lowered visibility, many of the diving areas have sheltered spots in the lee of the prevailing winds that afford reasonable diving and adequate visibility. Still, remote liveaboard and safari diving are rarely offered from July through to November, and many dive operators close during this period.

What You'll See

The Philippines' amazing diversity of marine life is mostly of the small- to medium-sized variety. Divers who have travelled the world recognise the Philippines as one of the world's best macro (small marine life) diving locations. While big pelagic (open-sea marine) life, such as sharks, turtles and manta rays, can only be spotted at Tubbataha Reefs, Apo Reef and a handful of other locations, the sheer range of marine life and diversity of coral is among the world's best.

Sadly, that coral remains under constant threat, as destructive fishing methods such as cyanide and dynamite fishing are still widely practised. Pollution also takes a toll. The best Philippines dive sites have been given marine-protected status, however, and have thus been spared such ravages.

What to Bring

Dive centres are typically well stocked with a wide variety of well-maintained and reasonably new rental equipment. Technical divers will find what they need at dive centres offering technical diving, including reels and accessories, mixed gas and, in many cases, rebreathers. Many operators also sell equipment, and most internationally recognised brands can be bought and serviced throughout the islands.

Choosing a Dive Operator

The diving environment can often be deceptive in the Philippines. Clear water and great visibility can lead to disorientation and going below the planned depth easily. Currents can be a major factor on many dives, and the sea conditions and weather can change in a matter of minutes at certain times of the year.

Thus it is strongly advised that you dive with a highly professional dive operator. A PADI affiliation can be a good indication of a dive operation's commitment to safety and customer service. In addition, check out an operator's safety procedures and emergency plans. Does the operator have oxygen, is it brought along on dive boats, and are there personnel trained to administer it on board? Is the rental equipment relatively new and well maintained? Finally, as there are hundreds of international dive professionals working throughout the country, find one that speaks a language you are comfortable with.

Certification

All dive centres in the Philippines require that a diver be certified by a recognised international training agency and should ask to see your card. Operators rarely ask to see a log book to assess a diver's experience. Most live-aboard trips require at least an advanced certification, but the good news is that whether you're an entry-level scuba diver looking to learn with a professional dive centre or an experienced technical diver seeking to become an instructor trainer, the Philippines is an excellent place to learn to dive and for ongoing training.

Technical Diving

Technical diving is big throughout the Philippines, and there is no shortage of deeper sites for technical training. The wrecks at the bottom of Coron Bay and Subic Bay make for outstanding technical diving, as do Coron Caves and caves near El Nido.

Qualified technical dive training outfits include **Tech Asia** (www.asiadivers.com), the technical diving arm of Asia Divers in Puerto Galera; **Tech Divers** (www.tech-divers.com), also based in Puerto Galera; Cebu-based **Kontiki Divers** (www.kontikidivers.com); and **PhilTech** (www.philtech.net), based in Makati.

Some live-aboards also offer technical diving, mixed gas and rebreather equipment and training on request to qualified divers.

Costs

Dive prices vary significantly from region to region. If you have a few people along with you, you can expect to pay about US$25 to US$35 per dive with a divemaster, including all equipment and a relatively short boat trip. Prices go down a bit if you have your own equipment, and two- or three-tank dives usually cost less than single-tank dives. PADI open-water certification courses vary widely from resort to resort and can cost anywhere from US$350 to US$500.

➡ Budget destinations include Moalboal, Dumaguete and Padre Burgos in Leyte.

➡ Midrange destinations include Malapascua, Camiguin Island, Coron, Puerto Galera and Siquijor.

➡ Top-end destinations include Anilao, Alona Beach (Panglao Island), Mactan Island and Dauin (Negros).

Dive Sites

Whether you're more comfortable diving on a shallow coral garden or are looking for deep technical dives, the Philippines is one of the world's best diving destinations. It has a profusion of wrecks, walls and reefs, many teeming with marine life ranging from tiny, unique nudibranchs (sea slugs) to giant whale sharks.

Luzon

Luzon is home to the nation's unofficial scuba-diving capital, Anilao, in Batangas Province, with numerous dive sites off Mabini and Tingloy Islands, the Philippines' best snorkelling spot, Donsol, and the country's northernmost (and newest) diving spots off the remote Batanes Islands.

Cathedral A marine sanctuary just off Anilao, with plenty of colourful reef fish.

Mainit Point Off San Teodoro; where whitetips, grey reef sharks and blacktips converge, as well as schools of tuna and jacks.

Sombrero Island Near Anilao; crevices and coral- and gorgonian-covered boulders attract pelagics such as rainbow runners and yellowtails.

Subic Bay This former US Naval Base has several wrecks to dive including the impressive USS *New York*. (p104)

Donsol Swim with whale sharks at the Philippines' top snorkelling-only spot. (p178)

Manta Bowl Commune with manta rays off Ticao Island. (p179)

Ticao Pass Currents attract occasional thresher, whale, hammerhead and tiger sharks.

Batanes Only just opening up to divers; the Kural Marine Sanctuary site consists of coral-covered underwater pinnacles, while Blue Hole is for advanced divers only. (p158)

Mindoro

The Spanish named Mindoro after a gold mine, but for divers, the most exciting treasure is under the water. Puerto Galera (p192) is a major training centre, with a great mix of wall, reef, cave, wreck and drift dives. The Verde Island Passage experiences unpredictable sea conditions and strong currents, so diving with an experienced local guide is an absolute necessity. Two hours off Mindoro's west coast lies Apo Reef (p207); its sheer dropoffs and underwater pinnacles make it one of the Philippines' very best dive sites.

Canyons Advanced dive in Puerto Galera with a strong current and schools of barracuda.

Shark Cave A popular stop full of sharks, octopuses and moray eels.

Fishbowl In the Verde Island Passage; a challenging 40m–50m dive with sharks and huge schools of pelagics.

Top: Diving off
Balicasag Island (p311)

Bottom: Diver and
whale shark, Bataan
Peninsula (p106)

ADRIAN SAMIRO SEE/LONELY PLANET ©

San Agapito Point The sea fans and corals at this Verde Island spot attract schools of jacks, sea snakes and plenty of macro life.

Ranger Station At Apo Reef; consists of coral gardens with plenty of reef fish, turtles and rare pygmy devil rays.

Shark Ridge A great place to spot whitetips, blacktips and occasional mantas.

Hunter's Rock An underwater pinnacle 20km west of Apo Reef; it's sea snake city.

The Visayas

The Visayas is comprised of numerous islands, large and small, encompassing some of the country's most exciting diving, with a practically infinite list of dive sites off Cebu, Bohol and Balicasag. Southern Negros, around Apo Island, and nearby Siquijor are hugely popular dive areas, although the sites are quite spread out. Boracay is a favourite training spot, while Panay and Romblon also offer scores of underwater adventures.

Pescador Island Off Moalboal; has a spectacular wall that starts just offshore, attracting large pelagics and occasional whale sharks. (p298)

Mactan Island Has a hugely diverse terrain of coral mounts, caves, walls and wrecks. (p289)

Kontiki Reef A shallow reef dive teeming with fish.

Gato Island Just off the north coast of Cebu, where a resident shoal of rare thresher sharks patrols the adjacent Monad Shoal year-round and seasonal (June to December) manta rays appear. (p292)

Cabilao Island Its overhanging wall and coral reefs attract schools of barracuda. (p312)

Balicasag Island Its vertical walls and coral gardens are home to plenty of pelagics, with hammerheads spotted in December and January and huge schools of barracuda off Barracuda Point. (p311)

Malatapay Off southern Negros, has steep walls, large fish and great visibility.

Clownfish City Just that – acres of anemones and clownfish at Apo Island. (p253)

Sugar Beach Two sunken islands, four wrecks and good wall dives. (p251)

Dauin The resorts' house reefs here offer amazing muck diving. (p254)

Siquijor The southern end of the island is good for reef-fish spotting. (p261)

Boracay Its best sites include Yapak Walls, with reef sharks, dogtooth tuna and giant trevallies; and Angol Point – a shallow reef that's good for night dives. (p211)

Maniguin Island Off Panay; famous for its hammerhead shark population.

Blue Hole Off Romblon; an advanced diver favourite inside an extinct volcano. (p270)

Alad Marine Sanctuary Its barrel sponges and soft coral fields are home to shoals of colourful fish.

Padre Burgos In Sogod Bay in Southern Leyte; great reef diving and the possibility of spotting whale sharks from February to June. (p325)

Mindanao & Sulu

Mindanao is the second-largest island in the Philippines, and, despite being known for its religious and political unrest, is also home to some excellent diving. The area around Davao, particularly Samal Island, has been a popular dive destination for decades, while Siargao Island is known for its superb visibility. Off the central north coast of Mindanao, Camiguin Island bears reminders of its volcanic origins and more recent tectonic events, and there are some great advanced dives off General Santos (or 'Gensan').

Agutayan Island The marine sanctuary around the island is a spectacular reef that attracts scores of lionfish, angelfish, groupers and occasional hammerheads.

General Santos Sarangani Bay features Gutsy's Reef, a deep reef dive with whitetip sharks, giant trevally and schools of surgeonfish. (p372)

Ligid Cave Its limestone crack is home to spotted reef crabs, anemone crabs and octopuses.

Dakak Island's Mushroom Wall Between Panay, Sibuyan and Masbate islands; a mass of sponges, crevices and ledges that attracts schools of reef fish, while the Caves' numerous crustaceans are particularly impressive during night dives.

Siargao Island The caves and underwater pinnacles here are buffeted by strong currents; Blue Cathedral is particularly beautiful while Shark Point attracts large pelagic life. (p357)

Camiguin The black corals and sponges of Jigdup Reef attract frogfish, occasional manta rays and hawksbill turtles; in Coral Garden you're likely to spot sea snakes, while the pinnacles of Old Volcano teem with batfish, eels and ghost pipefish (p347).

Diving in the Philippines

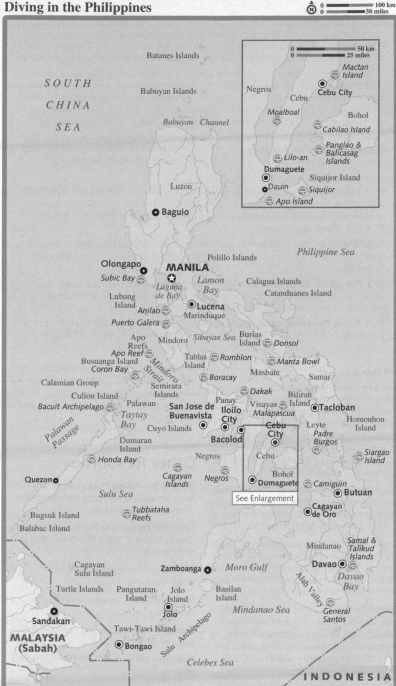

LIVE-ABOARDS

Live-aboards (boats that divers sleep on during dive trips) are a popular way to visit the Philippines' more remote dive sites, or to visit several sites in a week. They range from custom dive boats and yachts to converted fishing vessels and modified bangka boats.

Live-aboard dive safaris depart from and/or are organised by dive operators in Puerto Galera, Boracay and throughout the Visayas and there are new dive safaris in the works from El Nido, Palawan to Coron Bay, perhaps extending as far as Apo Reef. Choosing a live-aboard boat should be as much or more a function of assessing the safety, seaworthiness and professionalism of an operation rather than the price.

An assortment of luxury vessels, from converted schooners and small cruise ships to sumptuous yachts, operating out of Puerto Princesa, in Palawan, are the only way to visit the Philippines' marquee dive site, the Tubbataha Reefs in the Sulu Sea.

Established, recommended operators include:

M/Y Discovery Palawan (www.discoveryfleet.com; 6-day/7-night trip US$2100-2500) A plush dive boat that plies the Batangas–Apo Reef–Calumbuyan–Ditonai route between October and mid-March, followed by seven-day Tubbataha Reefs jaunts from mid-March to mid-June.

Rags II (www.apo-reef-coron-wrecks-liveaboard.com; per day US$240) A large converted bangka specialising in the wreck, reef and cave dives of Apo Reef, Coron Caves and Tablas Strait.

S/Y Philippine Siren (www.sirenfleet.com; 6-day/7-night trip €3150) A luxury live-aboard yacht that runs sailing trips to Tubbataha Reefs, the southern Visayas, Malapascua and Donsol.

M/Y Palau Sport (www.palausport.com; 6-day/7-night trip US$2100) A live-aboard that visits Tubbataha Reefs between April and June and Cebu dive sites in July.

Palawan

The long finger of Palawan points to some great diving whichever way you look at it, from wrecks to outstanding coral reefs, as well as a unique trek-and-dive jaunt. Puerto Princesa (p380) has a few dive sites in Honda Bay, but is chiefly known as the jumping-off point for live-aboards visiting the remote Tubbataha Reefs.

Coron Bay The sunken Japanese WWII fleet beckons advanced divers with the likes of the *Irako* ship and the tuna, lionfish and turtles that live there, as well as the current-buffeted *Okinawa Maru* tanker.

Coron Island A short trek up limestone cliffs leads to a dive in the inland Barracuda Lake. Under the island is the beautiful Cathedral Cave, full of juvenile lobsters, while the pristine corals of Seven Picados Reef attract barracuda and green turtles. (p411)

El Nido The strong currents off Miniloc Island bring schools of tuna, jacks and mackerel to Banayan Point, while the sheltered Biet Point attracts cuttlefish, barracuda and angelfish, and Tres Marias is a great shallow dive reef. (p396)

Tubbataha Reefs The Philippines' remotest dive sites include Shark Airport, a steep dropoff that attracts whitetip and grey reef sharks, leopard sharks, hawksbill and green turtles; Malayan Wall, with occasional hammerhead sightings; and Amos Rock, a gorgonian-fan-covered wall that's another shark hotspot. (p386)

Other Resources

Diving & Snorkelling Philippines (Lonely Planet) A detailed guide to the Philippines' dive sites; secondhand purchase only.

Coral Reef Fishes: Indo-Pacific and Caribbean (Ewald Lieske and Robert Myers) – a useful guide to Philippines' reef fish.

Dive Buddies Philippines (www.divephil.com) All things Philippines-dive-related.

Divescover (www.divescover.com) Dive operators and dive site descriptions.

ScubaBoard (www.scubaboard.com) Global scuba forum.

Green Fins (www.greenfins.net) A conservation initiative.

Plan Your Trip

Outdoor Activities

The Philippines may be famous for lazing on beaches and world-class diving, but its great outdoors span a long way beyond that. From taming volcanoes, catching barrels on Cloud Nine to navigating cave systems in Samar, the Philippines can capably raise any adrenaline junkie's pulse. If that's not your scene, jump on a yacht and raise a glass while cruising tropical islands.

Volcano Trekking

Forming part of the Pacific Ring of Fire, the Philippines is home to around 25 active volcanoes, most of which can be climbed all the way to the summit. Scenery varies from surreal landscapes to verdant jungle, while climbs can be anything from short half-hour jaunts to multiday expeditions. A thrilling prospect to many visitors, some of these volcanoes are active (some more than others), most notably the smoking Mt Mayon, so get in touch with local authorities before setting out. Others have remained dormant for centuries. You'll need to register and obtain permits for many of the climbs.

Where to Go

Mt Mayon The country's most iconic and picture-postcard-perfect volcano, the conical-shaped Mt Mayon (p176; 2462m) is one of the Philippines' most active. It can be tackled in one day, or as an overnight climb with wonderful sunrise views.

Mt Pinatubo Hiking around the bizarre lahar formations of Mt Pinatubo (p108; 1450m) is an experience not to be missed. Its serene crater lake provides a wonderful climax to the trek. The surreal landscape is constantly evolving as the environment recovers from one of the 20th century's most cataclysmic volcanic eruptions.

When to Go

July to October

The wet season may not seem ideal for outdoor pursuits, but if you're a surfer chasing big waves this is the time to head to Cloud Nine in Siargao (Mindanao), when monster off-shore typhoon swells form. The peak of monsoon is also the best time for white-water rafting with faster rapids.

December to March

The *amihan* (northeast monsoon) kicks up stiff, steady breezes from December to March, delighting sailors and turning Boracay into a kitesurfing and windsurfing paradise. There are also some decent waves this time of year on North Luzon's west coast, while December to January is the peak of the kitesurfing season.

March to June

Traditionally the best time to climb many of the Philippines' volcanoes. There's also good hiking weather, with the least amount of rain, though after May conditions can get hot.

ADVENTURE PARKS

Another way to get your thrills is at the growing number of outdoor adventure parks, with their range of ziplines, gorge swings, bungee jumps and canopy walks.

Danao Adventure Park (p317)

Tree Top Adventure (p105)

Makahambus Adventure Park (p346)

Tibiao EcoAdventure Park (p231)

Loboc Eco Adventure Park (p314)

Mt Apo The Philippines' highest peak, Mt Apo (2954m; p371), dominates the horizon in southern Mindanao, tempting climbers to set out from nearby Davao.

Mt Guiting-Guiting Some say this 2058m peak (p272) is the ultimate Philippines climb. The strenuous 10-hour trek to the top takes you through a pristine, prehistoric wonderland of biodiversity on Sibuyan Island, the country's answer to the Galápagos Islands.

Mt Kanlaon One of the Philippines' most thrilling volcano grunts is up Mt Kanlaon (2435m; p247), one of its largest active volcanoes, on Negros. The climb takes you through forests teeming with bird species and wildlife.

Mt Isarog A two-day return trek through pristine jungles and mossy forest landscapes featuring waterfalls and wildlife (p170).

Taal Volcano The most accessible volcano from Manila, Taal (p95) has a spectacular lake location with sweeping panoramas. It's also one of the shortest, easiest hikes.

Caving & Spelunking

Definitely not for the claustrophobic, spelunking is an exhilarating adventure involving a combination of swimming through underground rivers, squeezing under crevasses and over ledges. You'll encounter gleaming formations and breathtaking cathedral-like passages, alit with atmospheric kerosene torches. Levels range from easy walks through to advanced caving with ropes and full equipment.

Where to Go

Langun-Gobingob caves (Samar) The most expansive cave system in the Philippines (p334), including one chamber the size of three football fields. The caves are surrounded by jungle, underground rivers and scores of waterfalls.

Tuguegarao Northeast Luzon's Tuguegarao has several caves worthy of exploration, including Callao Cave (p156), with its seven chambers of limestone formations or the 12.5km-long Odessa-Tumbali Cave (p156), suitable for more advanced cavers.

Sagada Sumaging Cave (p138) in North Luzon is a great place to explore on a four-hour tour that takes you through a labyrinth of passages connecting it with adjoining Lumiang caves through underground rivers.

Puerto Princesa Subterranean River National Park A good option for those not wanting to scramble around or swim underground rivers, the gentle boat cruise (p389) here heads into one of the world's longest navigable, river-traversable tunnels to experience this spectacular limestone cave.

Trekking

The major Philippine islands boast mountainous interiors with forests, birdlife and spectacular views. The rice terraces and mountains of North Luzon are most popular for trekking, but there are also peaks to be bagged across the Visayas, Mindoro and Mindanao.

Where to Go

Rice Terraces Hiking around the ancient trails linking the exquisitely carved rice terraces of Ifugao, Bontoc and Kalinga is one of Southeast Asia's top trekking experiences.

The Cordillera In addition to rice terraces, the Cordillera mountains of North Luzon offer stunning multiday treks around and over several 2500m-plus peaks, including the Philippines' third-highest, Mt Pulag. There's also the Echo Valley trek in Sagada where you'll see the famous hanging coffins (p138). In the area there are also many trails that lead to remote tribal villages.

Mt Halcon More a mountaineering expedition than a hike, Mindoro's Mt Halcon (p201; 2582m) is one of the most challenging peaks in the Philippines.

Around Cagayan de Oro Mindanao has some of the Philippines' best mountain trekking, with summit climbs including Mt Kitanglad (2899m), Mt Sumagaya (2248m) and Mt Balatukan (2450m).

Jungle Treks Lush tropical jungles in Palawan, and around Mt Talinis on Negros, are ripe for exploration. There are also some beautiful forests close to Manila, such as those around Subic Bay, which have good trails and allow you to visit indigenous Aeta groups. Mt Arayat (p108) also provides more trekking opportunities.

Surfing

Stick 7000 islands in the middle of the Pacific and some decent-sized swell is going to make landfall somewhere. The typhoon season in the Philippines occasionally sees giant waves lash the entire length of the eastern seaboard, while west-coast surf hot spot San Fernando reigns supreme in the dry season.

Where to Go

Cloud Nine The name of this legendary right-hander says it all. Despite increasing in popularity of late – some locals dub it 'crowd nine' – Siargao's signature wave remains the country's most awesome break.

Baler The point break made famous in *Apocalypse Now* ('Charlie don't surf') hasn't changed – it's still guarded by palm trees in idyllic Baler and it's still fickle. But when it's on, it's surfing bliss.

The Bicol Coast Majestic (p186) on Catanduanes is the top wave in a region that's rapidly assuming the mantle of the Philippines' adventure-sports capital. Bagasbas is another laid-back surf spot.

San Juan (La Union) Best of North Luzon's more consistent and beginner-friendly west coast. Three- to five-footers pelt the shore November to March.

Calicoan Island, Samar Home to four reef breaks collectively known as ABCD (p337), with both excellent right and left breaks. Otherwise hit the unexplored east coastline of Samar on a surfin' safari.

Rafting, Kayaking & Canoeing

The rugged interiors of larger islands – Luzon, Negros, Mindanao, Panay, Leyte and Samar – feed scores of rivers that seethe with white water during the wet season. Run the rafting routes listed here, or team up with knowledgable locals for a first descent. If you have your own kayak and are into first descents, there are remote, virtually unexplored rivers all over the big islands, especially North Luzon and Mindanao.

MORE RELAXING PURSUITS

There are plenty of ways to enjoy the great outdoors in the Philippines that don't involve risking life and limb climbing volcanoes, flinging yourself down rapids or wiping out in crashing surf.

Views You don't need to partake in long sweaty treks or volcano climbs to catch some of the country's most spectacular panoramas. Iconic panoramas appreciated from a distance include the undulating Chocolate Hills in Bohol, the rice-bowl shaped caldera of Mt Mayon (p176) (from Mayon Skyline Hotel) and outlooks from Tagaytay to Taal Volcano (p95) on a magnificent lake dotted with islands.

Birdwatching Home to around 600 species of birds, 200 of which are endemic, the Philippines is a great country for twitchers. There's abundant birdlife across the islands, including a variety of species of hornbill, birds of prey and kingfisher. Northern Sierra Madre and Mt Kanlaon Natural Parks are great for birds, while the Philippine Eagle Center (p371) has the world's largest eagle.

Fishing The Philippines' waters teem with sailfish, tuna, trevally, wahoo, mahi-mahi and other sportfish, but few organised operators run tours; fishermen can take you out in their bangkas (outriggers). Sipalay in Negros Occidental and Santa Ana on Luzon's northeast tip are particularly fertile fishing waters.

Golf There are several world-class courses in the Philippines. Although many of them are private, you can usually talk your way onto them if you're keen. Some more memorable choices include Manila's Club Intramuros Golf Course (p65), within the old walled city (and it's floodlit at night for an evening hit); scenic Ponderosa (p195), cut into the mountains; or a more laid-back round in Siargao.

Where to Go

Chico River, North Luzon One of the Philippines' best white-water rafting sites, where you can tear down the raging Chico River (p146).

Cagayan de Oro River Take advantage of year-round white water in Mindanao (p346), on rapids ranging from technical to gentle.

Tibiao River, Panay Test the tamer rapids with white-water kayaking in Boracay.

Puerto Princesa Subterranean River National Park Paddle into the depths of this park's river (p389), which twists and turns through a spectacular cave before emptying into a pristine stretch of junglebacked coastline near Sabang, Palawan.

Sea Kayaking Sea kayakers have miles of untouched coastline to explore in Palawan's Bacuit Archipelago, the Caramoan Peninsula, Hundred Islands National Park, and just about anywhere else you can launch a paddle-propelled craft.

Magdapio Falls, Pagsanjan Though your *bancero* (boatmen) will be doing all the paddling on this canoe trip (p101), you'll get to kick back and enjoy the scenery where *Apocalypse Now* was filmed before encountering fun little rapids (best done around July and August when the river is full).

Davao River Fun grade-3 white-water rapids that peak around June, bringing plenty of thrills and spills (p363).

Kitesurfing

The Philippines is home to a world-class kitesurfing scene along with other action-packed water sports, including wakeboarding and windsurfing.

Where to Go

Bulabog Beach With a shallow lagoon protected by an offshore reef, steady winds, and state-of-the-art equipment for hire at low prices, the east coast of Boracay is one of the best places in the world to learn kitesurfing and windsurfing.

Bagasbas Beach, Bicol Excellent kitesurfing conditions from November to March, with winds of 15 to 20 knots, and quality operators offering equipment hire and instruction.

CamSur Watersports Complex *Wake Magazine* calls the home of the 2008 World Wakeboarding Championships, near Naga in Bicol, the best cable wakeboarding park in the world (p170).

Kingfisher Beach, Pagudpud World-class kitesurfing with great waves.

Boating & Sailing

Given the Philippines is a country made up of thousands of islands, it's inevitable you're going to end up out on the water at some point. However, there are more relaxing ways of boating than fast-paced watersports or being crammed into a passenger ferry, so for those who like to take it slow, a boat or sailing trip is the way to go.

Where to Go

Taal The volcano isn't the only reason to visit Talisay, as it's ground zero for the country's Hobie Cat and big-yacht sailors. Taal Lake Yacht Club (p96) rents out catamarans and kayaks, and also arranges sailing lessons. Subic Bay Yacht Club in Subic Bay is also conveniently located close to Manila and is a good place to get out on to tropical waters.

Puerto Galera Sailors in search of good conditions and scenery should head to Puerto Galera Yacht Club (p195) on Mindoro. It's suited for novices wanting to learn how to sail, or more experienced sailors. Each Wednesday it hosts afternoon races.

Boracay One of the best ways to enjoy Boracay's famous White Beach (p211) is to take a relaxing sunset cruise on a *paraw* (traditional outrigger sailboat). There are also luxury catamarans complete with drinks and canapés.

Regions at a Glance

The Philippines consists of three main island groups: Luzon, the Visayas and Mindanao. Between them they offer something for everyone: megacity madness in Manila, hill tribes in North Luzon, indigenous village life in Mindanao, surfing along the eastern seaboard of the entire country, and good snorkelling practically everywhere. The Visayas most embody the defining image of the Philippines: a dreamy desert island festooned with palm trees and ringed by white sand. Palawan is a region apart, a breathtaking water world where small boats navigate through a maze of surreal seascapes.

Manila

History
Nightlife
Food

The steamy, seamy capital is a little in-your-face for many first-time visitors, but if you can get underneath its surface it's mix of fascinating museums, raucous nightlife, varied cuisine and undeniable energy.

p46

Around Manila

Diving
History
Trekking

Names like Corregidor and Bataan evoke WWII like nowhere else. For climbers there's a bevy of accessible peaks to choose from, while the south coast of Luzon has some of the country's best diving.

p92

North Luzon

History
Outdoors
Culture

This region is intimidating in its diversity, with secluded bays where the surf's almost always up, romantic Spanish colonial enclaves and mountains sliced by rice terraces, inhabited by a staggeringly diverse range of indigenous tribes.

p110

Southeast Luzon

Food
Outdoors
Festivals

After searing your tongue on the spicy cuisine of Bicol, cool down by taking advantage of numerous water sports, or heat things up more with a volcano trek. Nearby small islands are perfect for short-hop exploration.

p163

Mindoro

Diving
Cultural Minorities
Remote Places

Diving or snorkelling at Apo Reef can't be beat, while Puerto Galera adds a party element to your diving experience. Elsewhere you can visit lost islands offshore and lost tribes in the impenetrable hinterlands.

p190

Boracay & Western Visayas

Beaches
Diving
Nightlife

Boracay is a powerful magnet drawing international partiers; however, other corners beckon: the less developed Romblon Island, lazy Siquijor and vibrant towns such as Iloilo City and Dumaguete with their historic colonial-era mansions.

p209

Cebu & Eastern Visayas

Diving
Beaches
History

The economic and cultural hub, Cebu is the gateway to diving and beaches galore, mountainous jungle interiors and off-the-beaten track adventures. WWII history has left its mark too through underwater wrecks, museums and monuments.

p275

Mindanao

Hiking
Water Sports
Rural Landscapes

Mindanao's varied topography, including its rugged mountain ranges, is a blessing for thrill seekers, and from its big cities such as Davao to the rural villages it's a tapestry of distinctive cultures and cuisine.

p338

Palawan

Beaches
Island Hopping
Village Life

From chic and exclusive private island retreats to simple beachfront bungalows, Palawan has it all. Get in the water to explore coral reefs and WWII shipwrecks and hop in a bangka to reach remote islands and isolated settlements.

p378

On the Road

Manila

📱 02 / POP 11.9 MILLION

Best Places to Eat

➡ El Chupacabra (p77)
➡ Purple Yam (p76)
➡ Blackbird (p77)
➡ Van Gogh is Bipolar (p79)
➡ Casa Armas (p75)

Best Places to Stay

➡ Manila Hotel (p68)
➡ Luneta Hotel (p68)
➡ Red Carabao (p71)
➡ Y2 Residence Hotel (p73)
➡ Pink Manila (p70)

Why Go?

Manila's moniker, the 'Pearl of the Orient', couldn't be more apt – its cantankerous shell reveals its jewel only to those resolute enough to pry. No stranger to hardship, the city has endured every disaster both humans and nature could throw at it, and yet today the chaotic metropolis thrives as a true Asian megacity. Skyscrapers pierce the hazy sky, mushrooming from the grinding poverty of expansive shantytowns, while gleaming malls foreshadow Manila's brave new air-conditioned world. The congested roads snarl with traffic, but, like the overworked arteries of a sweating giant, they are what keep this modern metropolis alive.

As well as outstanding sightseeing, visitors who put in the effort will discover its creative soul – from edgy galleries to a lively indie music scene. Combine this with a penchant for speakeasy bars, artisan markets and single-origin coffees, and it's clear to see Manila's not only one of Asia's most underrated cities, but one of its coolest.

When to Go
Manila

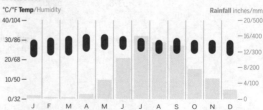

Dec– Feb The coolest, most pleasant months.

Mar–Apr Holy Week is no time to be in packed beach resorts, so spend it in sleepy Manila.

Jul–Aug Some say it rains too much; we say it's the best time to escape the searing sun.

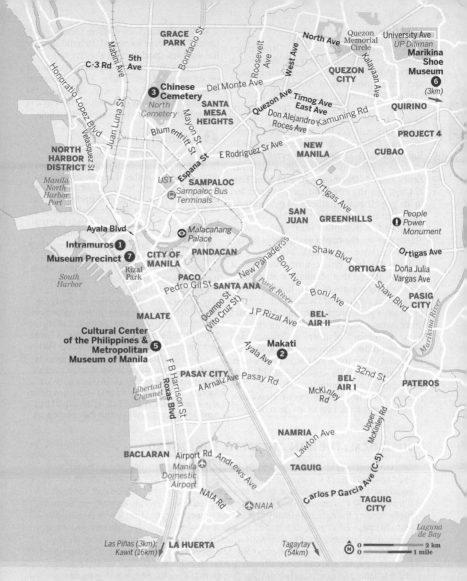

Manila Highlights

1 Hear echoes of a lost past in **Intramuros** (p49).

2 Indulge in the upscale cocktail bars, swanky rooftops and speakeasy bars of **Makati** (p80).

3 Explore the eerie ghost-town–like streets of the **Chinese Cemetery** (p59).

4 Learn about a Manila you didn't know existed on an excellent **walking tour** (p65).

5 Get behind Manila's art scene at the **Metropolitan Museum of Manila** (p58) and **Cultural Center of the Philippines** (p58).

6 Gawk at Imelda's shoes – some 800 pairs – on display at the **Marikina Shoe Museum** (p63).

7 Plunge into the city's culture at its **museum precinct** (p55) for history and art.

History

Early tourists, such as the 19th-century traveller Fedor Jagor, described Manila as a splendid, fortified city of wide cobbled streets and regal town houses. Tragically, most of that splendid city was obliterated in WWII.

Manila was colonised by the Spaniard Miguel López de Legazpi in 1571. Its broad sweep of fertile lands made it more attractive than Cebu, which had been the capital. King Philip II of Spain conferred on the city the illustrious title *Isigne y Siempre Leal Ciudad* (Distinguished and Ever Loyal City), but the city continued to be called by its pre-Hispanic name of Maynilad (presumed to be from *may,* meaning 'there is', and *nilad,* a mangrove plant that grew in abundance on the banks of the Pasig River), which was later corrupted to Manila.

From the late 19th century onwards, it could be argued that Manila was something approaching a Paris of Asia. It was a thriving trading centre and its multicultural mix provided a good entry point into China and other Asian countries. In 1905 Daniel Burnham, the master planner of Chicago, was hired to produce a master plan for the city. His grand vision included Roxas Blvd, which, even today, under its somewhat shabby patina, echoes Lake Shore Dr in Chicago. The streets were lined with grand structures, many reflecting the best of art deco design.

WWII changed everything. Many claim the city has never recovered. Rebuilding after the war was sporadic and the city was never able to reclaim either its regional importance or its sense of self. Many locals complain about the scattered character of Manila; it's true that the various cities within the city feel disunified and there is no sense of a whole.

ⓘ Orientation

Manila can be a very discombobulated place, for it is really just a collection of towns with no definable centre. Rather than seeing Manila as an amorphous mass, focus instead on enjoying its individual areas and you will start to get a feel for the greater Manila, which really is a sum of its parts. The three main areas of interest to tourists are downtown Manila, Makati and Quezon City.

Downtown Manila is the traditional tourist belt encompassing the area immediately south of the Pasig River – specifically Intramuros, where the main tourist attractions are concentrated; and Ermita and Malate, where most tourists still stay. Immediately to the north of the Pasig are the districts of Binondo and Quiapo, gateway to Chinatown. Other districts are Paco, San Miguel, Santa Cruz, San Nicolas and slum-ridden Tondo, near the newly developed North Harbour Port.

Just south of Malate are the adjoining districts of Parañaque and Pasay, which straddle Manila's busy main thoroughfare, EDSA (Epifanio de los Santos). Together, they are best known as a cultural precinct and transport hub, as the airport and many key bus stations lie within their boundaries.

JOSÉ RIZAL: THE MAN, THE MYTH, THE LEGEND

Despite living only to 35 years of age, Dr José Rizal (1861–96) – one of the Philippines' most revered figures – managed to pack a whole lot into his extraordinary life. The genius of the man is showcased at the modern Rizal Shrine (p51) inside Fort Santiago, Intramuros. At this museum you'll learn that beyond being credited as the man responsible for forging the national identity of the Filipino people, in his short life he managed to learn to speak 22 languages; founded a political movement (La Liga Filipina); wrote two novels (most notably *Noli Me Tángere*), as well as being an accomplished poet and essayist; became a doctor in ophthalmology; and gained recognition as an acclaimed artist (painter, sculptor and cartoonist cited as 'the father of Filipino comics'), world traveller and a fencing and martial-arts enthusiast. And if that's not enough – during his time in exile in Dapitan, in between him discovering two species of frog and lizard (both named after him), he also won the lottery!

However it was only in death that Rizal *really* started to add to his extraordinary CV. Not only did his execution by firing squad (p54) in 1896 immortalise him as a martyr that elevated him to the status of national hero, but it allowed him to add 'deity' to his list of achievements – with dozens of cults known as Rizalistas in the Mt Banahaw area still worshipping him today as anything from the reincarnation of Christ, to the messiah himself.

While detractors like to point out that his position as national hero was one bestowed upon him by American colonialists (who wanted the Filipino people to revere someone who preached nonviolence), or that he was an aristocrat who spent more time abroad than in the Philippines – there's not much dirt on the man to take away from his greatness.

MANILA IN...

Two Days

Wander historic **Intramuros** and **Rizal Park**. Head to **Roxas Blvd** (p57) to watch the sun set over Manila Bay and finish the day with some quality hours in the many bars of **Malate**. On your second morning, take an entertaining walking tour around a city neighbourhood, then catch the LRT up to the **Chinese Cemetery** (p59), before backtracking to **Chinatown** for lunch. Spend the evening in upscale **Makati**, where there are oodles of restaurants, bars and nightclubs to choose from.

Four Days

Follow the two-day itinerary, heading back to Makati on the third day for the engaging **Ayala Museum** (p61) and some more good eatin'. On your final day, spend the morning at the museum precinct centered on the **National Museum of the Filipino People** (p55). Explore the camp and classic **Cultural Center of the Philippines** (p58), then take in the sunset at the **Sofitel Philippine Plaza** (p70) or one of many **rooftop decks** (p82).

At the centre of modern Manila is Makati, the commercial centre for the country. Here, in almost orderly surroundings, you can shop, eat and drink to your heart's content. It transcends the generic-mall syndrome by having its own unique vibe that comes from the hordes of locals who come here to work, relax and play. Around 3km to its east is the upscale Fort Bonifacio (aka Bonifacio Global City), a new development on what was a former US and Philippines military base. It's centred on the High Street Mall with high-end shopping, quality restaurants and bars, and affluent residents.

In the north sector of Metro Manila lies Quezon City, about 15km from downtown Manila. It's a sprawling modern city with some three million residents and the largest of Manila's 19 'cities'.

◉ Sights

For a city that's not known as a major tourist draw, Manila sure has a lot to see. Because of its hugeness and its traffic you'll likely never see all of it – the best strategy is to explore one neighbourhood at a time. Much of what's best to see isn't always at a traditional sight, but rather can be found in the life of the varied neighbourhoods.

The vast urban sprawl known as Metro Manila is composed of 16 cities, but its heart and soul remains the City of Manila proper ('downtown' Manila; population 1.7 million). The city was founded here on the banks of the Pasig River; it was here where the Spanish solidified their claim to the Philippines after overthrowing the Muslim rulers of Maynilad; and it was here where the city suffered its darkest hours in the dying days of WWII.

◉ Intramuros

When Miguel López de Legazpi wrested control of Manila, he chose to erect his fortress on the remnants of the Islamic settlement by the mouth of the Pasig River. The walled city of Intramuros, as it came to be called, was invaded by Chinese pirates, threatened by Dutch forces, and held by the British, Americans and Japanese at various times, yet it survived until the closing days of WWII, when it was finally destroyed during the Battle of Manila – with all structures other than the Church of San Agustin flattened.

From its founding in 1571, Intramuros was the exclusive preserve of the Spanish ruling classes. Fortified with bastions, the wall enclosed an area of some 64 hectares. Gates with drawbridges provided access to and from the outside world. Within the walls were imposing government buildings, stately homes, churches, convents, monasteries, schools, hospitals and cobbled plazas. The native populace was settled in surrounding areas such as Paco and Binondo, while the Chinese were kept under permanent supervision in ghettos called *parian*.

While reconstruction began in 1951 to faithfully restore its colonial architecture to how it appeared pre-war, it was the establishment of the Intramuros Administration in 1979 that made it into the tourist sight it is today. The residential areas within the walls have a relaxed friendly feel and provide a nice change of pace from other parts of Manila. Anda St is a good street for a wander; many of the buildings still have Spanish-tile street names.

Greater Manila

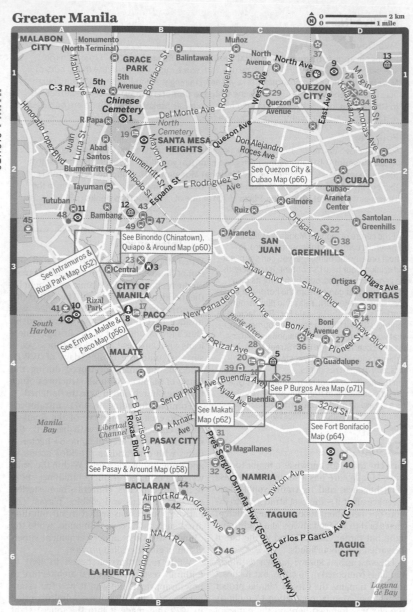

Most of Intramuros' walls, gates and bulwarks are accessible, and you can walk along the top of the ramparts for all or part of their approximately 4.5km length with several places to ascend and descend.

Start your walking tour at the **Intramuros Visitors Center** (Map p52; ☑ 02-527 2961; Fort Santiago; ☺8am-5pm) just inside the gate to Fort Santiago, which hands out an excellent free guided map of the walled city. Next door

Greater Manila

is a cinema inside a bomb-shelter cellar that screens a short film on the history of the area.

Kalesa (traditional horse-drawn carriages) are still a form of transport used in the area and provide an atmospheric way of getting around. They charge a fixed rate of P350 per carriage (good for four) for 30 minutes, or P500 per head for a 1½ hour tour.

Fort Santiago   FORT
(Map p52; Santa Clara St; adult/student P75/50; ⊙8am-6pm) Guarding the entrance to the Pasig River you'll find Intramuros' premier tourist attraction: Fort Santiago. Within the fort grounds is an oasis of lovely manicured gardens, plazas and fountains leading to its arched gate and pretty lily pond. Within is the beautifully presented **Rizal Shrine** (Map p52; admission incl with fort entry ticket; ⊙9am-6pm Tue-Sun, 1-5pm Mon) museum, the building where Dr José Rizal (p48) – the Philippines' national hero – was incarcerat-

ed as he awaited execution in 1896. It contains various fascinating displays of Rizal memorabilia and a recreation of his cell and the courtroom trial.

At the far end of the fort are outlooks over an industrial section of the Pasig River leading to **Baluarte de Santa Barbara**, a restored 18th-century Spanish military barracks where hundreds of Filipino and American POWs were killed in WWII; it's now the **Rizaliana Furniture Hall** (Map p52; P10) displaying Rizal's family furniture. Also of interest are various dungeon cellblocks, including one that Rizal spent his last night in. Brass footprints set into the pavement mark his final steps to the execution spot in Rizal Park.

San Agustin Church   CHURCH
(Map p52; ☑ 02-527 4060; General Luna St) The San Agustin Church was the only building left intact after the destruction of Intramuros in WWII. Built between 1587 and

Intramuros & Rizal Park

MANILA

0 — 500 m
0 — 0.25 miles

Manila North
Harbor Port (1km)

BINONDO

Dasmariñas St
San Vicente St
Juan Luna St
Paredes St

Escolta St

7th St
8th St
9th St
10th St
11th St
12th St
13th St
14th St

Pasig River

Muelle de la Industria

Muelle del Rio

Jones Bridge

18

3 Rizal Shrine
7

22

Bonifacio Dr

Fort
Santiago
Park

42 Santa
Clara St
30

Plaza de Roma

Magallanes Dr
Muralla St

Anda Circle

4
Postigo St
34

9

Beaterio St
Solana St
Legazpi St
Anda St

15th St
16th St
17th St
18th St
19th St
20th St
21st St
22nd St
23rd St
24th St
25th St

Atlanta St
Railroad St
Chicago St
Boston St

Bonifacio Dr

Arzobispo St
General Luna St
41
Cabildo St
Magallanes St

10
5

35
20
Real St
19
31

Casa
Manila
1

Santa Potenciana St

Santa Lucia St
Basco St

Victoria St
40
33
Recoletos St
San Jose St
Muralla St

23
38 Romualdez St

45
46

Baluarte
de San
Diego

P Burgos St
Taft Ave
A Villegas St

South
Harbor

27

Katigbak Dr

14

2 National Museum of
the Filipino People

Parade Ave
Roxas Blvd

21
2GO
Travel
15
6
Manila
Orchidarium

Central
Lagoon &
Fountains

8
16

Parade
Ground

Manila
Ocean Park (20m)

13
43
17 Rizal
Park

M Orosas St

12

11
32
44

US Embassy

26
28

Cortada St
Mabini St

Kalaw Ave

24

Manila Doctors
Hospital

United Nations Ave

Malacañang
Palace (1.4km)

Discovery
Islands

39

Alhambra St
M H del Pilar St
A Flores St
Grey St
Bocobo St

United
Nations
Avenue

Taft Ave
General Luna St

29
36

37 25

Arquiza St

P Faura St

Paco Park (50m);
Oasis Paco Park (100m)

Manila
Bay

Roxas Blvd

Intramuros & Rizal Park

1606, it is the oldest church in the Philippines. The massive facade conceals an ornate interior filled with objects of great historical and cultural merit. Note the intricate trompe l'oeil frescoes on the vaulted ceiling. Be sure to check out the tropical cloisters as well as the slightly shabby gardens out the back.

The present structure is actually the third to stand on the site and has weathered seven major earthquakes, as well as the Battle of Manila. It's an active church and much in demand for weddings and other ceremonies.

To see the interior of the church for free, you must visit during a mass or you can access it through the interesting San Agustin Museum (Map p52; General Luna St; adult/student/child P100/50/40; ⊙8am-noon & 1-6pm), a treasure house of antiquities that gives the visitor tantalising glimpses of the fabled riches of Old Manila. Check out the vaguely Chinese-looking Immaculate Conception statue in ethereal ivory.

★Casa Manila   MUSEUM
(Map p52; ☑02-527 4084; Plaza Luis Complex, General Luna St; adult/student P75/50; ⊙9am-6pm Tue-Sun) This beautiful reproduction of a Spanish colonial house offers a window into the opulent lifestyle of the gentry in the 19th century. Imelda Marcos had it built to showcase the architecture and interior design of the late Spanish period, with lavish features throughout and some interesting items such as a double-seated toilet. The house may not be authentic but the stunning antique furniture and artwork are.

Bahay Tsinoy   MUSEUM
(Map p52; ☑02-527 6083; www.bahaytsinoy.org; cnr Anda & Cabildo Sts; adult/student P100/60; ⊙1-5pm Tue-Sun) The vast Bahay Tsinoy museum showcases the important role played by the *sangley*, as the Spanish called the Chinese, in the growth of Manila (*sangley* means 'itinerant merchant' in the locally prevailing Hokkien dialect). There are

MANILA FOR KIDS

Heading off to Manila with a child or two in tow? Not to worry. The city is home to a number of kid-friendly activities and attractions.

Mind Museum (Map p64; ☑02-909 6467; www.themindmuseum.org; 3rd Ave, Bonifacio Global City; adult/child P600/450; ☉9am-6pm Tue-Sun) This world-class science museum succeeds in balancing education with fun, with plenty of cool interactive exhibits, including a planetarium, life-size T Rex, remote control robots, fossil digs, hourly science experiments and 1980s arcade games.

Museo Pambata (Map p52; ☑512 1797; www.museopambata.org; cnr Roxas & South Blvds; admission P150; ☉9am-noon & 1-5pm Tue-Sat, 1-5pm Sun) Both fun and charming, this hands-on museum has exhibits covering subjects as diverse as the environment, the human body and Old Manila through the eyes of kids.

Manila Ocean Park (Map p50; ☑567 7777; www.manilaoceanpark.com; Behind Quirino Grandstand, Rizal Park; from P400; ☉10am-8pm) Come for its impressive aquarium, shark and ray encounters, or to learn how to swim like a mermaid! If possible, avoid weekends when queues are long.

Star City (Map p58; ☑832 3249; www.starcity.com.ph; CCP Complex, Roxas Blvd; admission P65, tickets per ride from P100, all-you-can ride P420; ☉4pm-midnight Mon-Thu, 2pm-midnight Fri-Sun) A decent amusement park in the heart of the Cultural Centre of the Philippines (CCP) Complex with a good number of kids' rides, playgrounds and other diversions such as ice sculptures. Call ahead to confirm it's open midweek.

Mall of Asia (p85) Head here sunset/early evening to stroll its atmospheric boardwalk lined with carnival rides, including the MOA Eye ferris wheel with amazing views over Manila Bay.

Rizal Park (p54) A large playground, dancing musical fountain and carnival atmosphere will keep the kids entertained.

Repertory Philippines (p84) Respected theatre company that produces child-friendly performances such as *Pinocchio* and *Seussical*.

---

lifelike dioramas depicting Chinese and mestizo (mixed Spanish-Filipino) life in the *parian* (ghettos), old coins and porcelain, and an excellent collection of photos.

Memorare Manila   MEMORIAL
(Map p52; cnr General Luna & Anda Sts) This simple but moving outdoor memorial in a small shady square honours the approximately 150,000 civilian Manileños who perished in the Battle of Manila. Nearby placards contain before-and-after photos of the city.

Manila Cathedral   CHURCH
(Map p52; cnr Postigo & General Luna Sts) First built in 1581 (and rebuilt seven times since, most recently in 1951 following its destruction in WWII), Manila Cathedral's present edifice looks suitably ancient with its weathered Romanesque facade and graceful cupola. Inside are a gilded altar, a 4500-pipe organ and rosette windows with beautiful stained glass. Friezes on its bronze door depict the string of tragic events that led to the cathedral's destruction. The cathedral fronts

Plaza de Roma, which was a bloody bullring until it was converted into a plaza.

◉ Rizal Park & Around

Rizal Park   PARK
(Map p52) Manila's iconic Rizal Park is spread out over some 60 hectares of open lawns, ornamental gardens, ponds, paved walks and wooded areas, dotted with monuments to a whole pantheon of Filipino heroes. It's an atmospheric place to take a stroll, particularly late afternoons, early evenings and weekends.

As the place where José Rizal was executed by the Spanish colonial authorities, it's of great historical significance. Here you'll find the **Rizal Monument** (fronted by a 46m flagpole and guarded by sentries in full regalia), which contains the hero's mortal remains and stands as a symbol of Filipino nationhood.

The park is divided into three sections. At the edge of the middle section is the **Site of Rizal's Execution** (Map p52; Rizal Park; admission P20; ☉7am-5pm Wed-Sun); at the entrance is a black granite wall inscribed with Rizal's 'Mi Ultimo Adios' (My Last Farewell). Eight tableaux of life-size bronze statues recreate the dramatic last moments of the hero's life; at night these statues become part of a **light-and-sound presentation** (admission P50; ⊙7pm Wed–Sun) dedicated to Rizal. It's in Tagalog, but they'll do it in English if you have a big enough group (or pay them enough). At the opposite end of the park towards Kalaw Ave, keep an eye out for the drinking fountain shipped all the way from Heidelberg, Germany, where Rizal spent time studying at university.

Also in the middle is the **Central Lagoon**, a pool lined with busts of Filipino heros and martyrs, and a **dancing musical fountain** that erupts in colourful explosions in the evening.

The long-running **Concert at the Park** takes place at the open-air auditorium; it's free and starts at around 5.30pm on Sundays. At dawn, you'll find various groups gathered to practise t'ai chi or the local martial art of *arnis*, or *arnis de mano*, a pre-Hispanic style of stick-fighting.

Along the north side are several ornamental gardens and the **Chess Plaza**, a shady spot where regulars test each other and look for new blood with shouts to visitors of 'Hey Joe, do you play chess?'

Across Roxas Blvd at the western end of the park is the **Quirino Grandstand**, where Philippine presidents take their oath of office and deliver their first address to the nation.

At the opposite end of the park across M Orosa St where the National Museum is located, you'll find a large statue of **Lapu-Lapu** (16th century national hero famous for slaying the portuguese explorer Ferdinand Magellan), the flower-filled **Manila Orchidarium**, a gigantic three-dimensional **relief map of the Philippines** and an ostentatious **children's playground**.

The new **visitors centre** (Map p52; Kalaw Ave, Rizal Park; ⊙8am-5pm) at the park's Kalaw Ave entrance has a good map detailing the park's attractions and info for upcoming events.

★**National Museum of the Filipino People**   MUSEUM
(Map p52; www.nationalmuseum.gov.ph; T Valencia Circle, Rizal Park; admission adult/child P150/50, Sun free; ⊙10am-5pm Tue-Sun) Within a resplendent neoclassical building, this superb museum houses a vast and varied collection, including the skullcap of the Philippines' earliest known inhabitant, Tabon Man (said by some to actually be a woman), who lived around 24,000 BC. A large section of the museum is devoted to the wreck of the *San Diego,* a Spanish galleon that sank off the coast of Luzon in 1600, with salvaged items such as shell-encrusted swords, coins, porcelain plates, jewellery etc on display.

Other treasures include a large collection of pre-Hispanic artefacts and musical instruments, and extensive displays on the major Filipino indigenous groups. Note that the entry ticket also gets you into the National Gallery of Art.

VIVA MANILA

While downtown Manila has always been the heart and soul of the city, it's never really managed to recover its mojo following its destruction in WWII. The past decade especially has seen it slip, as all investor eyes turn to the shiny high-rise developments of Makati, Fort Bonifacio and Quezon City. Luckily, however, a new wave of young, proud Manileños have brought forward some initiatives that have returned some spark and vitality to the area.

VivaManila (https://www.facebook.com/vivamanila.org) What started off as a Twitter hashtag by Carlos Celdran (of Walk this Way fame, p65) to promote cool things going on in downtown Manila, has since developed into an arts-and-events-based NGO run by passionate hip locals, who are on a mission to revive downtown Manila. Check their Facebook page to find a calendar of upcoming events. Their flagship event is Paysal Sundays, a monthly pedestrianised street market held in Intramuros between September and June. Also keep an eye out for their Sunday brunches.

98b (www.98-b.org; 413 Escolta St, Mezanine Level, First United Building) Based in Escolta St, this collaboration of artists, writers and filmmakers have set up camp in a downtrodden historic locale. They are active in preserving its architecture and host various events and talks. They're most well known for their **Saturday Future market** – a street fair in Escolta St (held at 98b) selling original artwork, magazines, vintage bric-a-brac and the like.

Ermita, Malate & Paco

0 — 200 m
0 — 0.1 miles

MANILA

20 ✕ 34

P Faura St

Paco Park (150m);
Oasis Paco Park Hotel (200m)

36 1 37 35

Santa Monica St

2 ◎

23 ✕

R Salas St

Adriatico St

Mabini St

32

United
Nations
Avenue Ⓜ

Robinsons
Place

Pedro Gil St

9 Filipino
Travel
Center

24 ✕

Bocobo St

M Orosa St

Guerrero St

Vasques St

Hidalgo St

Pedro
Gil Ⓜ

J Quintos Jr St

12 11 28 4 27

General M Malvar St

Alonzo St

6 19 22 31

26 14 25 29 J Nakpil St

10 13

15

18

3 5 21 17 30

Remedios
Circle 8 Remedios St

MALATE 33 ✉

Roxas Blvd

CCP (900m);
Mall of
Asia (4.4km);
Metropolitan
Museum of
Art (800m)

16

M H del Pilar St

Madre Ignacia St

San Andres St

Quirino
Avenue Ⓜ

Aldecoa St

7

Guerrero St

M Adriatico St

President Quirino Ave

Taft Ave

Buendia LRT Stop
& Bus Stations (1.5km);
Pasay Rotunda (3.5km)

Ermita, Malate & Paco

National Gallery of Art   MUSEUM
(Map p52; P Burgos St; adult/student P150/50, Sun free; ⊙10am-5pm Tue-Sun) This proud museum contains many of the Philippines' signature works of art, including Juan Luna's seminal *Spoliarium*, a colossal painting that provides harsh commentary on Spanish rule. It's in the old Congress building designed by Daniel Burnham, across the street from its sister National Museum of the Filipino People (inclusive in the admission ticket).

Museum of Natural History   MUSEUM
(Map p52; www.nationalmuseum.gov.ph; Kalaw Ave) Scheduled to open in 2015, the natural history museum will occupy the neoclassical heritage-listed building formerly used by the tourist office, and feature exhibits of taxidermy and Filipino artefacts.

**Museum of the Philippines
Political History**   MUSEUM
(Map p52; www.nhcp.gov.ph/museum-of-philippine-political-history; Kalaw Ave; donation encouraged; ⊙8am-4pm Tue-Fri) FREE Just next to the Kalaw Ave entry to Rizal Park, this small museum gives a punchy overview of the Philippines' socio-political history from pre-Hispanic, occupation under the Ameri-

cans and Japanese, to 'People Power' under the Marcos regime. Check out the former president's cars parked out front.

⊙ Ermita, Malate & Paco

Baywalk   PROMENADE
(Map p56; Roxas Blvd) Splendid sunset views of Manila Bay can be had from the pedestrian Baywalk that runs along Roxas Blvd.

Malate Church   CHURCH
(Map p56; cnr MH del Pilar & Remedios Sts, Malate) This attractive baroque-style church was first built in 1588; though this version dates from the 1860s. A greatly revered image of the Virgin Mary, called *Nuestra Señora de Remedios* (Our Lady of Remedies), roosts here.

1335Mabini   GALLERY
(Map p56; ☑0917 886 7231; www.1335mabini.com; 1335 Mabini St, Ermita; ⊙2-6pm Tue-Sat, Sun by appointment) Another small step in the revival of downtown Manila is the arrival of this art collective which has set up shop in the colonial Casa Tesoro mansion. It features regular changing shows of experimental art and installations in its ground- and 2nd-floor galleries.

Paco Park
PARK

(Map p50) For those seeking a place of solitude, head to the leafy oasis of Paco Park, where sturdy stone walls surround a picturesque circular park. It's of historical importance too, with its quaint colonial chapel, formerly a cemetery during Spanish times and one of Rizal's favourite places; so much so that he was buried here from 1898 to 1912.

Philippine Kim Luan Temple
TAOIST

(Map p56; 1644 Adriacto St; ⊙9am-5pm) Standing as a beacon of serenity among its depraved surrounds, this Taoist temple is both peaceful and beautiful, and worth popping into for a look.

◉ Pasay & Around

Cultural Center of the Philippines
HISTORIC BUILDING

(Tanghalang Pambansa; Map p58; www.cultural-center.gov.ph; CCP Complex, Roxas Blvd; art-gallery admission free, museum adult/student P30/20; ⊙gallery & museums 10am-6pm Tue-Sun) The centrepiece of the CCP Complex (p69) is this bombastic building designed by noted Filipino architect Leandro Locsin. Inside features a mix of modern art galleries such as the quality Bulwagang Juan Luna gallery with its changing exhibits covering modernist and contemporary painters, and multiple theatres that present performances by the Philippine Philharmonic Orchestra, Ballet Philippines and local and visiting artists. Also here is the Museum of Philippine Culture and Asian Traditional Musical Instruments museum.

★ Metropolitan Museum of Manila
ART GALLERY

(Map p58; ☑02-523 7855; www.metmuseum.ph; Roxas Blvd; admission P100; ⊙10am-5.30pm Mon-Sat, gold exhibit to 4.30pm) Manila's premier modern art museum, the 'Met' is a world-class gallery showcasing Filipino contemporary and experimental art. The ground

Pasay & Around

floor has rotating exhibitions, while its upper floors display a permanent collection of modernist and abstract paintings. There's also a collection of precolonial gold ornaments and pottery in the basement. There are guided tours Tuesdays and Thursdays at 10.30am and 2pm, but you'll need to book ahead.

Museo ng Sining MUSEUM
(Museum of Art; Map p58; GSIS Bldg, CCP Complex, Pasay; ⊙8am-noon & 1-4.30pm Tue-Sat) FREE Another classy CCP gallery housing an extensive collection of contemporary and classic Filipino art.

⊙ Binondo (Chinatown), Quiapo & Around

After centuries of suppression by the Spanish, Manila's Chinese population quickly rose on the economic and social ladder under more liberal administrations. Today the centre of the vibrant Chinese community is Chinatown, which straddles Santa Cruz and Binondo. The teahouses of Chinatown are the big draw in this area, just over the Pasig River from Intramuros. These are some of the oldest parts of Manila, but sadly the few pieces of Spanish colonial architecture remaining are being rapidly torn down. Still, it remains the centre for trading and there are numerous markets, especially in Quiapo.

Bahay Nakpil-Bautista HISTORIC BUILDING
(Map p60; ☑02-734 9341; www.bahaynakpil.org; 432 A Bautista St; adult P80; ⊙9am-5pm Tue-Sun) Built in 1914, this beautiful ancestral home is the former residence of Perona Nakpil, the widow of Andrés Bonifacio – the father of the Philippine Revolution. As well as an insight into the grandeur of pre-war Manila, the museum provides history of the Ilustrados and Katipunan – the anti-Spanish revolutionist movement. It's located in a crowded backstreet accessed across the main road from Quiapo Church.

★**Chinese Cemetery** CEMETERY
(Map p50; Rizal Ave Extension, Santa Cruz; ⊙7.30am-7pm) FREE As in life, so it is in death for Manila's wealthy Chinese citizens, who are buried with every modern convenience in the huge Chinese Cemetery. It's far from your ordinary cemetery and instead feels like a residential suburb with streets lined with mausoleums – some that feature crystal chandeliers, air-con, hot and cold running water, kitchens and flushing toilets (in case the interred are caught short on the way to paradise).

Hire a bicycle (per hour P100) to get around the sprawling grounds and consider hiring a guide for access to the best tombs. Tour guide Ivan Man Dy of Old Manila Walks (p65) does an excellent Chinese Cemetery tour.

Binondo (Chinatown), Quiapo & Around

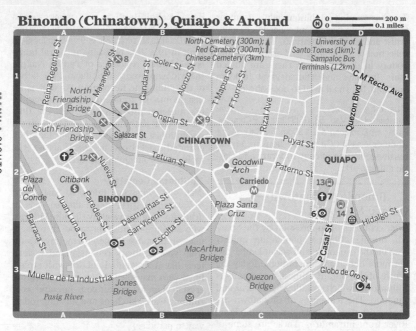

Binondo (Chinatown), Quiapo & Around

To get here take the LRT to Abad Santos then walk or take a tricycle (P25) to the south entrance. While you're out this way, you can also visit the offbeat North Cemetery.

North Cemetery   CEMETERY
(Map p50; Santa Cruz; tour guide approx P300) If you thought Manila's Chinese Cemetery was different, you clearly haven't made it to its abutting North Cemetery. While significant for being the burial place of many notable Filipinos, including numerous presidents and revolutionaries, it's on tourists' radars more so as a place to observe the unique living arrangements of a community of some 6000 people who live here among the dead –

many mausoleums double as houses, small shops and game arcades for kids.

Despite the government considering the inhabitants to be squatters (issuing eviction notices on several occasions), many of the North Cemetery dwellers have jobs within, including those employed by tomb owners to provide maintenance duties and keep their deceased company.

Given it is extremely impoverished, it's essential to come along with a guide who knows the area, either arranged through nearby Red Carabao (p71) hostel or at the cemetery entrance (though with the latter you're not guaranteed an English speaker).

Golden Mosque   MOSQUE

(Map p60; Globo de Oro St) The Golden Mosque was constructed in 1976 as something of a welcoming gift for the late Libyan leader Muammar al-Gaddafi, although his scheduled visit never happened. This is still the city's largest mosque and today it serves the growing Muslim community that has settled by the thousands in Quiapo.

Binondo Church   CHURCH

(Map p60; cnr Paredes & Ongpin Sts) At the northern end of Paredes St stands the attractive granite-stone bell tower of Binondo Church, an unusual octagonal structure dating back to 1596. The rest of the church was rebuilt following destruction sustained by American bombing in WWII.

Seng Guan Buddhist Temple   TEMPLE

(Map p50; Narra St) The Seng Guan Buddhist Temple is the centre of Manila's Buddhist community.

Escolta St   ARCHITECTURE, MUSEUM

(Map p60; Escolta St) While today Escolta St is a fairly gritty and rundown strip, it remains of historical significance as one of the last remnants of swinging pre-WWII Manila, when it was a ritzy strip of upmarket department stores and theatres. Numerous heritage buildings remain along Escolta, including examples of art deco, Beaux Arts and neoclassical design. Opposite the Capital Theatre, pop into the **Escolta Museum** (Map p60; 266 Escolta St, 2nd Fl Calvo Bldg; P100; ☺9am-noon & 1-5pm Tue-Sun) to view its collection of photos and pre-war Manila paraphernalia.

Also visit for the **Saturday Future Market** held weekly by 98b (p55) in the heritage First United buidling.

UST Museum   MUSEUM

(Map p50; http://ustmuseum.ust.edu.ph/; Espana Blvd, Main Bldg, University of Santo Tomas; admission P50; ☺8.30am-4.30pm Tue-Sat) Housed in a superb heritage-listed 19th-century building on the campus of the University of Santo Tomas, this museum lays claim to being the oldest in Asia (its original Intramuros campus dates to 1611). It comprises a mix of taxidermy, coins, religious artefacts and a wonderful visual arts collection featuring Filipino masters and modernist painters. The building also has a grim link to WWII, serving as an internment camp that held 4000 Allied soldiers for three years under Japanese occupation.

◉ Makati City & Around

The towers here house the nation's major corporations and most of the major hotels. Construction started after WWII when the Ayala family seized upon the destruction of the rest of the city as a chance to start building. The heart of Makati was Manila's airport in the '30s and '40s: Ayala and Makati Aves were the runways, while Blackbird restaurant was the terminal.

★ Ayala Museum   MUSEUM

(Map p62; www.ayalamuseum.org; Greenbelt 4, Ayala Centre, Makati; adult/student P425/300; ☺9am-6pm Tue-Sun) This gleaming museum features four floors of superbly curated exhibits on Filipino culture, art and history. At the heart of the collection is a brilliant exhibit consisting of 60 dioramas that succintly, yet effectively, trace the nation's history, which kids will also love. The collection of pre-Hispanic gold jewellery and objects is another highlight with some exquisite pieces. The museum's rotating art exhibits tend to showcase Filipino masters such as Luna and Amorsolo, and occassionally international shows such as Yayoi Kusama.

Guided tours (P100) of the museum are highly recommended; book one week in advance. Audioguides (P75) are also available.

Yuchengco Museum   GALLERY

(Map p62; www.yuchengcomuseum.org; cnr Ayala & Sen Gil Puyat Aves, Makati; adult/student/child P100/50/20; ☺10am-6pm Mon-Sat) A mismatch among Makati's corporate high-rises, this fantastic art and design gallery was established by prominent businessman and former UN diplomat, Alfonso Yuchengco. Set over three levels, its collection ranges from paintings by Filipino masters to contemporary art exhibitions. There's also a display of José Rizal memorabilia (including love letters), and photos of Yuchengco's meetings with a who's who of world leaders.

Museo Ng Makati   MUSEUM

(Map p50; ☎896 0277; JP Rizal St; ☺8am-5pm Mon-Fri) FREE Down by the river, the Museo Ng Makati is a classic old Manila house from the 1800s (look for the capiz-shell windows), with some great photos of old Makati and murals of past mayors, among other exhibits. Closed for renovation at the time of research.

Makati

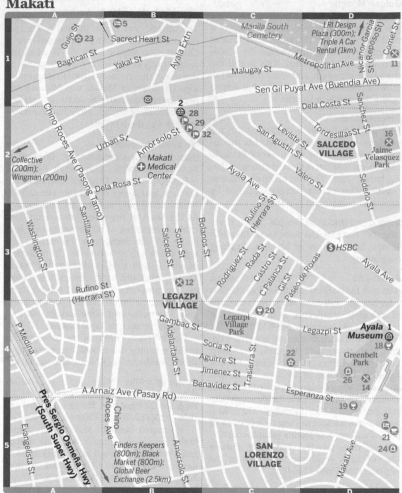

Fort Bonifacio

The up-and-coming Fort Bonifacio area, which lies in Taguig City and is effectively an extension of Makati, does a good Singapore impression. It provides an intriguing insight into how the other half live with designer dogs and Lamborghinis. Like Makati, there are quality restaurants and bars here too.

The interactive Mind Museum (p54) is also worth a look while out this way.

American Memorial Cemetery CEMETERY
(Map p50; Old Lawton Dr, Fort Bonifacio; ⊙9am-5pm) A poignant and peaceful spot, this sprawling war cemetery on a grassy, beautifully manicured plot is the resting place of 17,206 soldiers killed in battle during WWII. In addition to hundreds of rows of perfectly aligned white crosses, there are several excellent open-air galleries with murals and descriptions of key battles.

Quezon City

With about three million people, Quezon City (QC) is the most populous area of metro Manila yet it's overlooked by most travellers. QC is so different from the rest of Manila that you'd do well to look at it as a self-contained

entity. If you have the time, stay for a few days. QC is more about good eating and drinking but there's a few things to see here.

Traffic is the main issue in getting here. Aim to visit on a Sunday when major roads are largely devoid of traffic, otherwise stay well away during rush hour. Better yet, catch the LRT-2 or MRT lines out here. In the heart of QC is chaotic Cubao, a commerical grid that centres on its major bus terminal.

Marikina Shoe Museum   MUSEUM
(www.marikina.gov.ph/#!/museum; JP Rizal St; admission P50; ⊙8am-noon & 1-5pm) A must for Imelda Marcos junkies is the Marikina Shoe Museum. There's footwear of various Filipino luminaries on display here, but it's Imelda's shoes people come for – about 800 pairs of them, in rows behind glass cases. That's

Fort Bonifacio

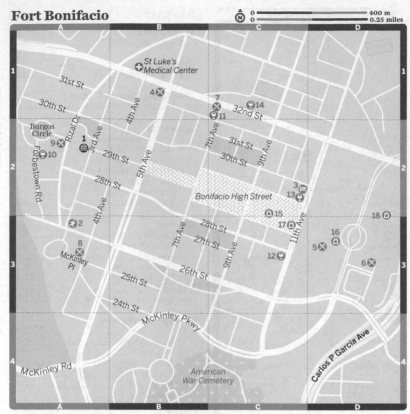

Fort Bonifacio

◉ Sights
1 The Mind Museum A2

✪ Activities, Courses & Tours
2 Neo Spa A3

🛏 Sleeping
3 Seda C2

🍴 Eating
4 Aubergine B1
5 Balducci D3
6 Fiesta Market D3
7 Hungry Hound C1
8 Las Flores A3

9 The Bowery A2

🍸 Drinking & Nightlife
10 Big Bad Wolf A2
11 Niner Ichi Nana C1
12 Skye C3
13 Straight Up C2
14 The Perfect Pint C1

🛍 Shopping
15 Bonifacio High Street C2
16 Echo Store D3
17 Fully Booked C3
18 Market! Market! D2

only about 25% of the horde left behind in Malacañang Palace by the former First Lady.

To get here, take the LRT-2 to its last stop (Santolan) and then a 'San Mateo' jeepney to City Hall on central Shoe Ave, which is a short walk away.

Vargas Museum ART GALLERY
(Map p50; ☎ 02-928 1927; www.vargasmuseum.
wordpress.com; Roxas Ave, UP Campus, Quezon
City; admission P30; ⊙ 9am-5pm Tue-Sat) A won-
derful art museum on the campus of leafy
University of Philippines Diliman (UP), with

a mix of changing modern and experimental art shows, and a permanent collection covering the 19th century to the present day.

Ninoy Aquino Parks & Wildlife Center   ZOO
(Map p50; ☑ 02-924 6031; Quezon Memorial Circle; admission adult/child P8/5; ☺7am-5pm) This park and wildlife rescue centre runs a mini-zoo where injured wildlife are nursed back to life. A few patients who never checked out are on display, including a Burmese python and various birds, reptiles and monkeys. There's also a peaceful lagoon here.

Quezon Memorial Shrine   SHRINE
(Map p50; Quezon Memorial Circle; ☺museum 8am-4pm Tue-Sun) In the middle of Quezon Circle rises this 36m towering art-deco monument topped by three angels above the mausoleum of former president Quezon. There's also a museum here, under renovation at the time of research.

🏃 Activities

Golf

★ Club Intramuros Golf Course   GOLF
(Map p52; ☑ 02-527 6613; Bonifacio Dr; nonresident green fees day/night P1500/2400, club rental P700) Just outside Intramuros, on what used to be the city's moat, you can golf by day or by night at the quirky 18-hole, par-66 Club Intramuros Golf Course. Caddies cost P300, or you can obtain the shady services of an 'umbrella girl' for P350. Green fee is half price for residents.

Spas

It's not hard to find a massage in Manila. Use common sense to avoid getting more than you bargained for – in Malate, that usually means sticking to the nicer hotels. In Makati's CBD they are mostly on the up-and-up (the same can't be said for the P Burgos area).

Touch of Hands   SPA
(Map p56; www.touchofhands.com; 513 Remedios St, Malate; 1hr massages P300-800; ☺1pm-midnight) Good-value, no hanky-panky. Also several branches in Makati.

★ Mandarin Oriental Spa   SPA
(Map p62; ☑ 750 8888; www.mandarinoriental.com; cnr Makati Ave & Paseo de Roxas, Makati; packages from P3400; ☺9am-11pm) At this five-star hotel's recently renovated spa you'll find an array of treatments to indulge in.

The Spa   MASSAGE
(www.thespa.com.ph; 1hr massage from P820; ☺noon-8.30pm) This chain has about a half-dozen

locations, including Greenbelt 1 in Makati and Bonifacio High St in Fort Bonifacio.

Neo Spa   MASSAGE
(Map p64; ☑ 02-815 6948; www.neo.ph; cnr 26th St & 3rd Ave, Fort Bonifacio; 1hr massage P950; ☺1-11pm) A pricier option than many others in Manila, but worth it.

Swimming

You can use almost any five-star hotel pool (which makes a great place to while away an afternoon) but it will cost you P600 to P1000.

☞ Tours

★ Walk This Way   TOUR
(☑ 0920 909 2021; www.carlosceldran.com; adults/students P1100/600) Something of a Manila celebrity, Carlos Celdran is a hilariously eccentric one-man show of Filipino history and trivia. Highly recommended for those with a sense of humour and an open mind. His Intramuros headquarters is in his sort-of souvenir shop, La Monja Loca, opposite San Agustin Catholic Church – Carlos has been at loggerheads with the church over its opposition to the Reproductive Health Bill, even spending a night in jail for the cause in 2010 after disrupting a mass.

Old Manila Walks   WALKING TOUR
(☑ 0918 962 6452, 02-711 3823; www.oldmanilawalks.com; tours from P1100) Tour leader Ivan Man Dy has a deep knowledge of Manila and its history and culture. He's an expert at ferreting out the city's often overlooked secrets, most known for his all-you-can-eat foodie walking tours (P1200, 3½ hours) in his local 'hood Binondo, as well as a Chinese Cemetery tour (p650, two hours).

Also highly recommended are his neighbourhood tours to San Miguel/Malacañang Palace (p75; P1200 including beer and nibbles, 2½ hours) and Intramuros (P1000, 2½ hours) and day trips to Corregidor Island.

Bambike   CYCLING TOUR
(Map p52; ☑ 02-525 8289; www.bambike.com; Plaza Luis Complex, cnr General Luna & Real St, Intramuros; 2½hr tour P1200; ☺10am & 3pm) Set up by the young, laidback entrepreneur Bryan, Bambikes runs guided cycling tours around Intramuros on handmade bicycles constructed using bamboo frames. Pedalling the laidback backstreets of the walled city makes for a great way to cover expansive Intramuros, taking in all the main stops plus some less-visited gems. Prices include entrance fees, helmets and water.

Quezon City & Cubao

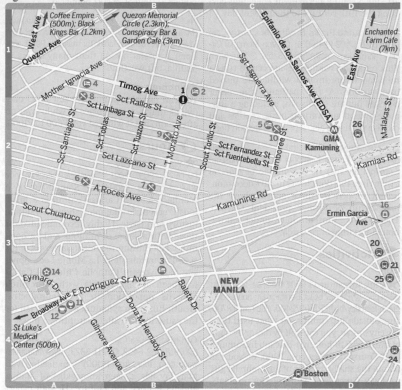

One hour 'express' tours are also available (P600) on demand. The operation is parked next door to Casa Manila (p53), where it also sells its bamboo bikes.

★ Festivals & Events

Black Nazarene Procession RELIGIOUS
The Black Nazarene, a life-size and highly revered statue of Christ in Quiapo Church, is paraded through the streets in massive processions on 9 January and again during the week before Easter (Holy Week). Thousands of frenzied devotees crowd the streets carrying the image, believed to be miraculous, on their shoulders.

Fringe Manila ARTS
(www.fringemanila.com) This arts festival will have its inaugural event mid-February 2015, with three weeks of events showcasing local artists and performers.

Drink Up BEER
(www.drinkupph.com; ⊙ May) This beer festival in Fort Bonifacio showcases Filipino and international craft beers. Check the website for exact dates.

Independence Day NATIONAL DAY
(⊙ 12 Jun) A huge parade in Rizal Park celebrates the Philippines' independence from Spain.

All Saints' & All Souls' Day RELIGIOUS
(⊙ 1 Nov & 2 Nov) What Day of the Dead is to Mexico, All Saints' Day and All Souls' Day is to Manila as hundreds of revellers gather at both the North Cemetery and Chinese Cemetery. The two spots become one big party through the night as Chinese-Filipino families descend to offer food and flowers to their ancestors.

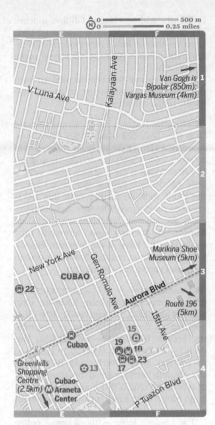

Quezon City & Cubao

◎ Sights
1 Monument to Boy Scouts	B2

🛏 Sleeping
2 Imperial Palace Suites	B1
3 Stone House	B3
4 Torre Venezia Suites	A1
5 Tune Hotel	C2

✕ Eating
6 Chocolate Kiss	A2
7 Greens Vegetarian Restaurant and Cafe	B2
8 Restorante La Capre	A1
9 Uno Restaurant	B2
10 Victorinos	C2

◯ Drinking & Nightlife
11 Big Sky Mind	A4
12 Craft Coffee Revolution	A4
Cubao Expo	(see 15)

✪ Entertainment
13 Araneta Coliseum	E4
14 Philippine Educational Theater Association	A3

⌂ Shopping
15 Cubao Expo	F4
16 Q Mart	D3

ⓘ Transport
17 Amihan Bus Lines	F4
18 Araneta Bus Terminal	F4
19 Cagsawa Cubao Terminal	F4
20 Dagupan Bus Co	D3
21 Dominion Bus Lines	D3
22 Genesis Cubao Terminal	E3
23 Isarog Bus Lines	F4
24 Partas Cubao Terminal	D4
25 Victory Liner Cubao Terminal	D3
26 Victory Liner Kamias Terminal	D2

🛏 Sleeping

Manila has accommodation to suit all price ranges, from P400 dorms in modern hostels to luxurious US$1000 penthouse suites.

🛏 Intramuros

Hotels only recently started opening inside Intramuros' fabled walls. It isn't a bad choice if you want peace and quiet. Intramuros really shuts down after 10pm (or earlier).

Sailor's Inn
HOSTEL $

(Map p52; ☑02-527 6206; 1 Fort Santiago; dm/q/ste P350/1700/2200; ✳) With two huge semi-compartmentalised air-con dorms (100 beds for men, 40 beds for women), this is more like a barracks. Shape up, sailor, you're in the navy now. The cold-water common bathrooms are predictably large. Both private rooms and dorms are ship-shape but basic.

White Knight Hotel Intramuros
HOTEL $$

(Map p52; ☑524 7382; www.whiteknighthotel-intramuros.com; General Luna St; r P1960-3000; ⊖✳@☎) A restored 19th-century heritage building that's part of the Casa Manila complex, White Knight makes a good choice for those wanting to stay within the solitude of the walled city. It has plenty of character though feels a bit overdone with some flowery features.

Bayleaf
HOTEL $$$

(Map p52; ☑02-318 5000; www.thebayleaf.com. ph; cnr Muralla & Victoria Sts; r incl breakfast P3700; ✳@☎) While a boutique hotel within Intramuros' old walls may not suit the area, the Bayleaf is rightfully popular for its rooms decked out in vibrant colour schemes with postmodern design and rainfall showers. It also has a busy restaurant and rooftop Sky Deck bar (p82). Book online for the best rates.

Rizal Park

There are some wonderful historic hotels around Rizal Park.

Casa Bocobo
HOTEL $$

(Map p52; ☎02-526 3783; www.casabocobo. com.ph; Bocobo St; r incl breakfast P1500-3000; ❄❋@☎) A great midrange hotel close to Rizal Park, where classy black-and-white photos and flatscreen TVs adorn the walls, and attractive lamps flank beds draped in soft white linens. Smaller budget rooms are more basic, but great value.

Ralph Anthony Suites
APARTMENTS $$

(Map p52; ☎02-254 7981; www.ralphanthony-suites.com; M Orosa St; studio from P2000, ste from P2400; ❋@☎) It's primarily long-term accommodation but provides good value for short-term guests. Avoid the studios (which are in poor condition) and go for the one-bedroom suites with kitchenettes.

★Manila Hotel
HOTEL $$$

(Map p52; ☎02-527 0011; www.manila-hotel.com. ph; 1 Rizal Park; r from P8500; ❄❋@☎▣) One of Asia's grand and regal hotels, where everyone from General MacArthur to the Beatles to JFK has spent the night. It's more than 100 years old, yet has kept up with the times

brilliantly, adding elegant Filipino touches like capiz-shell dividers and two-poster beds to rooms that include every modern convenience imaginable, such as a flatscreen panel in the bathtub.

You can choose between the modern business rooms in the new wing, or period-style rooms in the old wing.

★Miramar Hotel
HISTORIC HOTEL $$$

(Map p52; ☎02-523 4486, 02-523 4484; www. miramarhotel.ph; 1034-36 Roxas Blvd; d incl breakfast P4480-5600, ste P7728; ❄❋@☎) If you're looking for a classic hotel with a little old-Manila flavour that won't break the bank, look no further than this 1930s art-deco masterpiece. Rooms and common areas are smartly furnished with art-deco features throughout and, although fully modern, still have some pre-war charm. Snare one of the regular half-price promo rates and you've got a great deal.

★Luneta Hotel
BOUTIQUE HOTEL $$$

(Map p52; www.lunetahotel.com; Kalaw Ave; r incl breakfast from P3000, ste from P8800; ❋☎) Just opening its doors at the time of research, the French Renaissance–style Luneta Hotel is symbolic of Manila's shift to return to its pre-war glory. Overlooking Rizal Park, the elegant heritage-listed building is one of few to survive WWII bombings, and the large rooms offer excellent value, some with wrought-iron balconies.

The opulent lobby with gleaming coffee shop adds another layer of class.

WHERE TO STAY IN MANILA?

Being the sprawling megacity that it is, choosing a hotel in Manila can be a daunting task, especially for first-time visitors. The key to accommodation enlightenment is to pick a district before settling on a hotel. A quick rundown of the major sleeping areas:

AREA	PROS	CONS
Downtown (Malate & Ermita)	Traditional tourist belt; close to main sights; 'authentic' Manila; best budget accommodation	Beggars and scam artists; street-level destitution; restaurants are average; nightlife better elsewhere
Downtown (Intramuros)	Quiet, neighbourhood feel; close to sights	Food options limited; nightlife nonexistent
Downtown (Rizal Park)	History, charm	Expensive
Pasay & Parañaque	Close to airport, arts precinct and Pasay bus terminals	Close to busy Epifanio de los Santos Ave; loud; restaurants lacking
Makati	Top restaurants; great nightlife; clean streets; modern hostels and hotels	Lacks character and too 'sanitized'
Quezon City	Less touristy, more local; good restaurants and bars; close to Cubao bus terminals	Far from everything except Cubao bus terminals

CCP & THE COCONUT PALACE

Of all of Imelda Marcos' wacky schemes, the **Coconut Palace** (Map p58; ☎02 832-1898; Pedro Bukaneg St, CCP Complex) may be the wackiest. Hearing that Pope John Paul II was planning a visit to his flock in the Philippines, Imelda ordered that a grand palace be built. And not just any palace either, but one showcasing the nation's crafts and materials.

Huge teams of craftsmen laboured overtime to complete this edifice in time for the pontiff's arrival. As Imelda readied herself to throw open the door to welcome the pope, she got stiffed. After sternly chastising that the US$37 million cost could have gone to better uses, such as clean water for the people, the pope went elsewhere.

These days the palace serves as a vice presidential office and is closed to tourists, although you can still have a look from the outside. It's located in the Cultural Centre of the Philippines (CCP) complex, a pleasant walk from Malate along the Roxas Blvd promenade, or take any Baclaran-bound jeepney on MH del Pilar St.

⌂ Malate, Ermita & Paco

Like a smaller version of Bangkok's Khao San Rd, Malate's Adriatico St is Manila's traditional stomping ground for backpackers. However there's also some classy higher-end and midrange accommodation around too.

Wanderers Guest House　　HOSTEL $
(Map p56; ☎02-525 1534; www.wanderersguesthouse.com; 1750 Adriatico St, 4th Fl, cnr J Nakpil St; dm with fan/air-con P300/350, d with fan/air-con from P700/1200; ❋@🛜) In the heart of Malate, Wanderers knows precisely what backpackers want and delivers beautifully with a mix of clean dorms and private rooms (some with balconies), excellent travel info and cooking facilities. The highlight is its grungy rooftop bar/restaurant/chill-out lounge, perfect for socialising with other travellers. There's also morning yoga and meditation.

V Hotel　　HOTEL $
(Map p56; ☎02-328 5553; www.vhotelmanila. com; 1766 Adriatico St; d incl breakfast P900-2800; ❋🛜⛲) A very well-priced designer hotel in downtown Malate with smart (but boxy) rooms, a vibrant cafe and small roof-deck pool. The cheapest rooms have bunk-beds and shared bathroom, and are a good budget option over hostels.

Where 2 Next　　HOSTEL $
(Map p56; ☎02-354 3533; www.where2nexthostel. com; 1776 Adriatico St; dm with air-con P495, r with fan/air-con P950/1550; ❋@🛜) A slick hostel with sparkling common area full of comfy couches and a glassed-in balcony overlooking Malate's main strip. Well-cleaned rooms are brightened with graffiti murals and there is a full kitchen for self-caterers. Free wi-fi and complimentary continental breakfast and coffee are added bonuses.

Malate Pensionne　　HOSTEL $
(Map p56; ☎02-523 8304; www.mpensionne. com.ph; 1771 Adriatico St; dm with air-con P490, d without/with bathroom P950/1200, with air-con P1100-1600; ❋@🛜) A long-running home away from home (and refuge from Adriatico St's nighttime madness) with old-world architectural details, including dark-wood floors. Management and friendly front-desk staff are attuned to dealing with travellers' questions and concerns. Ask to look at several rooms as some are brighter than others.

Pension Natividad　　PENSION $
(Map p56; ☎02-521 0524; www.pensionnatividad. com; 1690 MH del Pilar St; dm with fan P400, d shared/private bathroom P1000/1100, with air-con P1500; ❋🛜) Inside a beautiful art-deco building, this quiet budget-priced pension is popular with Peace Corps volunteers. Consider staying elsewhere if you plan to party hard – it advertises 'clean guest rooms for individuals, married couples and families'.

Chill-Out Guesthouse　　HOSTEL $
(Map p56; ☎02-503 2660; www.manille-hotel. com; 612 Remedios St; dm P350, d with fan/air-con from P750/1200; ❋@🛜) Newly relocated just off Remedios Circle, this French-managed hostel passes the eye test. It has blissfully air-conditioned and clean dorms and privates, plus an OK hang-out/kitchen area where smoking is allowed. Also has a resto-bar downstairs.

Adriatico Arms Hotel　　HOTEL $$
(Map p56; ☎02-524 7426; 561 J Nakpil St; r standard/deluxe P1650/1850; ❋🛜) A remnant of boutique Nakpil St, Adriatico Arms brings a touch of class to Malate with its lovely and affordable boutique hotel. The charming ground-floor coffee shop, surrounded by wrought-iron detailing, provides a lovely

first impression with an appealing literary vibe. Rooms themselves are dated, but spacious and comfortable. There's a trade-off between street-facing rooms that come with a balcony and rooms away from the street that are quieter.

Oasis Paco Park
HOTEL $$

(Map p50; ☑ 02-521 2371; www.oasispark.com; 1032-34 Belen St, Paco; r from P2000; ◐❋@ 🛜❄) You come here mainly because it's relatively quiet and isolated, and because it's a rare Manila midranger with a pool in a leafy courtyard surrounded by patio furniture. Rooms are generic motel-style; upgrade to a deluxe if you want a window.

Casa Nicarosa
HOTEL $$

(Map p56; ☑ 02-536 1597; www.casanicarosa-hotelmanila.com; 2116 Madre Ignacia St, Malate; d P2000-2400; ❋🛜) Tucked down a quiet residential street, relaxed Casa Nicarosa is a great choice for those wanting to stay away from the chaos of Malate and Ermita, yet remain within striking distance. It's a homely guesthouse, within a fairly grand building that feels like a 1980s mansion with some Victorian-era features.

Lotus Garden Hotel
HOTEL $$

(Map p52; ☑ 02-522 1515; www.lotusgardenhotelmanila.com; 1227 Mabini St, Ermita; s/d from P2000/2200; ❋@🛜) An OK midranger with a glamorous curved staircase and the busy (and smoky) Cilantro Restaurant Bar commanding attention in the lobby. Rooms are nothing special, but as you rise through the price range you gain light, space and amenities. Its jacuzzi is a nice bonus, but the hotel is within a fairly average neighbourhood.

Pan Pacific Hotel
HOTEL $$$

(Map p56; ☑ 02-318 0788; www.panpacific.com; cnr Adriatico & Gen M Malvar Sts; r from P8500; ◐❋@🛜) This luxurious five-star business hotel is Malate's solitary choice for travellers requiring British-trained butler service. The particulars of each stay can be personalised online. Standard rooms include one of the following: free breakfast, free room upgrade or free airport transfer. Some rooms have bay views and TV-fitted bathtubs. Also has a nice pool and swanky rooftop bar (p82).

Hyatt Regency Hotel & Casino Manila
HOTEL $$$

(Map p56; ☑ 02-245 1234; www.manila.casino.hyatt.com; 1588 Pedro Gil St; s/d incl breakfast from US$179/200; ❋@🛜❄) It doesn't get much

more all-inclusive than at the Hyatt, where you can get a haircut, enjoy a foot massage and take a yoga class without ever leaving the building. The high-ceilinged, contemporary styling belongs in a glossy magazine.

🛏 Pasay & Around

Pink Manila
HOSTEL $

(Map p58; ☑ 02-484 3145; www.pinkmanilahostel.com; cnr Bautista & San Pedro Sts; dm fan/air-con P450/570, d P1600; ❋🛜❄) Hidden away on the 5th floor of a nondescript building in a random location lies Pink Manila, one of the city's most sociable hostels. Its rooftop feels like the *Big Brother* household, where bikini-clad, shirtless backpackers laze poolside around hammocks playing guitar. The mix of dorms and private rooms is big and all are swathed in trademark pink linens. There's a bar and kitchen, and its location between Malate and Makati gives guests the best of both worlds.

Manila International Youth Hostel
HOSTEL $

(Map p50; ☑ 02-851 6934; 4227-9 Tomas Claudio St; dm with fan P350, d/tr with air-con P1100/1650; ❋@🛜) This basic hostel has one gargantuan men's dorm (36 beds) and more manageable women's dorms (12 beds). It's more a place for locals than a backpacker hang-out, but it's handy if you want to be close to the airport.

Orchid Garden Suites
HOTEL $$

(Map p58; ☑ 02-708 9400, 708 9414; www.orchidgardensuites.com.ph; 620 Ocampo St; d incl breakfast from P3000; ◐❋@🛜❄) An elegant choice that's also convenient to Malate, guests here stay in a 1980s tower block in huge rooms that have been nicely maintained; go for the upper floor for a view. The lobby and bar are in a 1930s art-deco mansion attached to the building – one of Manila's few remaining pre-war architectural landmarks. We'd like to see more room to hang out by the pool.

Sofitel Philippine Plaza
HOTEL $$$

(Map p58; ☑ 02-551 5555; www.sofitel.com; CCP Complex, Atang Dela Rama St; r incl breakfast from P8000; ◐❋@🛜❄) This five-star masterpiece, with its meandering pool area right on Manila Bay, is the closest you'll get to a resort holiday in Manila. It's the same magnificent hotel that has presided over the CCP Complex for decades now. Other highlights are the library bar and the stupendous buffet meals.

P Burgos Area

Museo ng Makati (300m);
Club Mwah! (2km)

Robelle House (200m)

🛏 Santa Cruz

★ Red Carabao HOSTEL **$**

(Map p50; ☎02-861 6614; www.redcarabaomanila.com; 2819 Felix Huertas St, Santa Cruz; dm P450-500, r per person with fan/air-con P650/1050; ☺2-night min Oct-Mar; ❄@☎; LRTAbad Santos Station) This hipster hostel offers a more authentic local experience in a nontouristy neighbourhood. Set over four levels, it's a social place, with chalkboards promoting interesting events and gatherings, and a cool rooftop spot perfect for house parties. The dorms and private rooms are spacious, comfortable and spotless.

Other perks are its homely lounge and kitchen, gym equipment, free water and coffee. It's a a 15-minute LRT journey into the heart of Manila; visit its website for directions.

WORTH A TRIP

SOCIAL ENTERPRISE AT THE ENCHANTED FARM

Hidden away a 1½ hour's drive north of Quezon City is a small farm that's planted the seeds for some big ideas. Established in 2003, **GK Enchanted Farm** (☑ 02-533 2217; www. gk1world.com/gk-enchanted-farm; day tour incl lunch P850, dm with fan/air-con P500/600, d with air-con P1800) has set itself the goal to wipe out poverty in the Philippines by the year 2024.

Spread over 34 hectares, here local villagers learn new skills and exchange ideas on anything from producing cheese and duck eggs to worm farming. At the time of research, a high school was about to open with the focus of assisting locals setting up their own businesses.

You can come along for a day tour to see a range of demonstrations and what they're doing in terms of permaculture and eco-design etc. For overnighters, accommodation is in comfortable lodgings and there is an infinity pool you can laze around in.

Check the farm's website for directions on how to get here; it involves catching a bus from Cubao followed by a jeepney connection. If you don't make it here, pop into the **Enchanted Farm Cafe** (www.enchantedfarm.com; 463 Commonwealth Ave, Quezon City; ⊙ 11am-8pm Mon-Sat; ❈ 🐾) in Quezon City to sample the organic produce grown on the farm, such as banana blossom veggie burgers.

🛏 Makati City & Around

Modern, air-conditioned hostels have sprung up everywhere these days in Makati, to match the plethora of business and five-star hotels.

MNL Boutique Hostel　　　　　HOSTEL $
(Map p50; ☑ 0917 858 5519; www.mnlboutiquehostel.com; cnr B Valdez & Santiago Sts; dm from P520, r with shared bathroom P1550; ❈ @ 🐾 🖂) Incorporating industrial decor such as polished concrete and colourful plywood doors, arty MNL prides itself on being a stylish, comfy backpackers. While space is squashy and lacks natural light, rooms have character and quality beds. It offers good travel info, a fully equipped kitchen and free filtered coffee. Weekends bring slightly higher rates.

Our Melting Pot　　　　　　HOSTEL $
(OMP; Map p71; ☑ 02-659 5443; www.ourmeltingpotmakati.com; 4th fl, Mavenue Bldg, 7844 Makati Ave; dm P550-750, s/d without bathroom P1050/1500, d with bathroom P1800; ⊜ ❈ @ 🐾) Makati's original backpackers, OMP delivers on minimalist style, friendly staff and a homely atmosphere. Rooms are basic, but it scores points for air-conditioning and curtain dividers between dorm beds. The shoes-off policy (slippers provided) ensures cleanliness, and basic breakfast is included – as are city tours.

The owners have opened a hostel in Tagaytay for those wanting a city escape.

Lokal Hostel　　　　　　　HOSTEL $
(Map p71; ☑ 02-890 0927; www.lokalhostel.com; 3rd fl, 5023 P Burgos St; dm with fan/air-con P450/600, d with fan/air-con P1200/1400; ❈ @ 🐾) In the middle of Makati's tacky red light district, this new hostel offers respite from within, and has spacious dorms with big beds, murals on the walls and a cool roof deck hang-out.

Makati YMCA Hostel　　　　　HOSTEL $
(Map p62; ☑ 02-899 6379; www.ymcaofmakati.com; 7 Sacred Heart St; air-con dm/r from P400/1100; ⊜ ❈) What this hostel lacks in backpacker camaraderie, it makes up for in excellent-value air-con rooms and a quiet barangay (neighbourhood) location only a five-minute walk to Makati's central business district. The dorm is dudes-only, but women can book the private rooms.

Robelle House　　　　　GUESTHOUSE $$
(Map p50; ☑ 02-899 8209; www.robellehouse.net; 4402 B Valdez St; s/d without bathroom P1000/1250, with bathroom P1495/1750; ❈ 🐾 🖂) A brilliant choice for budget travellers who are a bit over the whole backpacker scene, this ancestral house has plenty of character and history. Its chilled-out location down a residential side street is another plus. Rooms themselves are basic, but good value, and it has a small pool.

Hotel Durban　　　　　　　HOTEL $$
(Map p71; ☑ 02-897 1866; www.hoteldurban.net; 4875 Durban St, Makati; r P1600-2550; ❈ 🐾) Makati's best midrange value is a tightly run ship. The immaculate rooms, with fauxwood panelling, are more than adequate for the price. It's popular so book ahead.

Sunette Tower
APARTMENTS $$

(Map p71; ☎02-895 2726; www.sunette.com.ph; Durban St; d/ste from P2500/3000; ❄ @) It's *soooo* '80s, but has a variety of plain studios and apartment suites with kitchenettes.

★Y2 Residence Hotel
BOUTIQUE HOTEL $$$

(Map p50; ☎02-224 3000; www.y2hotel.com; 4687 Santiago St, Makati; r incl breakfast P8000; ❄@☎🏊) With decor influenced by yin-yang balance and harmony, this stylish concept hotel is decked out in black and white throughout. Large, snazzy rooms have Asian-inspired murals, with kitchenettes and big fridges making it perfect for long-term stays. Other perks are the luxurious rooftop bar, plunge pool, gym and spa. Downstairs is an Asian hawker food restaurant and cafe serving artisan tea and coffees. Book online to snare up to 50% discounts.

★Peninsula Manila
HOTEL $$$

(Map p62; ☎02-887 2888; www.peninsula.com; cnr Ayala & Makati Aves; r from P9000; ❄❄@☎🏊) With rooms that highlight the best of Filipino design, the Peninsula is a Makati veteran that nevertheless appears brand new. The cafe in the soaring lobby has a fine Sunday brunch and is a 24-hour destination for the city's business elite. A side note: a tank drove through the front doors here in 2007 during a foiled coup attempt.

★Picasso Makati
APARTMENTS $$$

(Map p62; ☎02-828 4774; www.picassomakati.com; 119 Leviste St, Salcedo Village; r incl breakfast from P9000; ❄❄@☎) Exuding rock-and-roll chic, this suave art hotel has serviced apartments and studios with mounted beds, floating staircases, space-age chairs and bright Picasso-inspired colour schemes. True to its name, the entire hotel doubles as a gallery and it also has a gym and bistro cafe. Promo rates can cut the prices in half.

Makati Shangri-La
HOTEL $$$

(Map p62; ☎02-813 8888; www.shangri-la.com; cnr Ayala & Makati Aves; r from P14,500; ❄❄@☎🏊) With a jaw-dropping main entrance that faces the Glorietta mall, the beautifully done Shangri-La may very well win the award for Makati's most aesthetically stunning interior. The rooms incorporate all the elements you'd expect from these prices. Walk-in guests can use the pool for P600.

Also has a new hotel opening up in Fort Bonifacio scheduled for 2016.

Mandarin Oriental Manila
HOTEL $$$

(Map p62; ☎02-750 8888; www.mandarinoriental.com; cnr Makati Ave & Paseo de Roxas; r from P8000; ❄❄@☎🏊) As with any of the world's Mandarin Orientals, the level of service here will simply astonish those who've not experienced it before. Rooms sparkle and the spa is arguably Manila's finest.

Raffles Makati
HOTEL $$$

(Map p62; ☎02-555 9777; www.raffles.com/makati; cnr A Arnaiz & Makati Aves, Makati; ste incl breakfast from P19,000; ❄@☎🏊) Staking its claim as Manila's most luxurious hotel, Raffles' stunning suites pay tribute to the original Singapore colonial design mixed with contemporary touches. Expect huge rooms, high ceilings, wooden floorboards, standalone bathtubs with city views and on-call butlers. Its opulent palm-lined pool is straight out of a Beverly Hills mansion. Rates includes evening cocktails and high tea at its Writers Bar.

A Venue Suites
APARTMENTS $$$

(Map p71; ☎403 0865; www.avenuehotelsuites.com; 7829 Makati Ave; 1-/2-bedroom ste incl breakfast P7850/9400; ❄❄☎🏊) Here you'll find stylish, immaculate suites in a tower rising above A Venue Mall. It doubles as a long-term apartment complex, so the service and amenities, while good, are not five-star. Online booking sites can get you super deals on this and sister Antel Suites next door.

Berjaya Hotel
HOTEL $$$

(Map p71; ☎750 7500; www.berjayahotel.com; 7835 Makati Ave; r incl breakfast from P4500; ❄❄@☎🏊) This Malaysian-run place just down the street from flashy A Venue mall is very attractive and the service is excellent. It's a pretty big step down from the five-star places and feels a bit like a business hotel, but steep promo discounts are available.

St Giles Hotel
HOTEL $$$

(Map p71; ☎02-988 9888; www.stgilesmanila.com; cnr Makati & Kalayaan Aves; r from P4140; ❄❄@☎🏊) A haunt for business travellers, with a gym, rooftop pool and compact-but-fashionable rooms.

Dusit Thani Manila
HOTEL $$$

(Map p62; ☎02-238 8888; www.dusit.com; cnr EDSA & A Arnaiz Ave; r from P8000; ❄❄@☎🏊) Recent renovations have brought this closer to the big boys.

🛏 Fort Bonifacio

Hotels are very slowly starting to spring up in this development, which is still very much in its infancy. Shangri-La was scheduled to reopen in 2016.

Our Awesome Hostel HOSTEL $
(Map p50; ☑02-804 2013; 5756 Kalayaan Ave, Fort Bonifacio; dm from P450; ❋⊜) A short walk to the Fort, this new hostel has only mixed dorms, in configurations of four to 10 beds. It's a social place with regular parties on its roof deck.

Seda HOTEL $$$
(Map p64; ☑02-588 5700; www.sedahotels.com; cnr 30th St & 11th Ave, Fort Bonifacio; r incl breakfast from P8000; ❋@⊜⊠) One of the few hotel options in Fort Bonifacio, this classy business hotel has large, stylish rooms with jumbo plasma TVs and bench seating. There's a gym, pool and Mac computers in the lobby for free guest use. Weekends bring sizeable discounts. Also has the Straight Up (p82) rooftop bar.

🛏 Quezon City

The most attractive area by far is the T Morato area.

Stone House HOTEL $$
(Map p66; ☑02-724 7551; www.stonehouse.ph; 1315 E Rodriguez Sr Ave, Quezon City; r P1100-2500; ❋⊜) Stone House delivers on price and creature comforts, but you'll need to pay P200 extra to get a window. It's easy walking distance to the T Morato restaurants.

Tune Hotel HOTEL $$
(Map p66; ☑02-426 0567; www.tunehotels.com; 100 Timog Ave, Quezon City; r P1500-2500; ❋@⊜) This ultra-clean chain hotel is a good reliable choice, with quality beds and high-pressure showers. Book online for the best rates.

★Torre Venezia Suites APARTMENTS $$$
(Map p66; ☑02-332 1658; www.torreveneziasuites.com.ph; 170 Timog Ave; r/ste from P4500/5500; ⊜❋⊜⊠) Super-sleek rooms in a towering hotel/residence where beds, furniture and bathrooms all look marvellous. Throw in a gym and decadent spa and you have a gem. Look for big discounts online.

Edsa Shangri-La Hotel HOTEL $$$
(Map p50; ☑02-633 8888; www.shangri-la.com; 1 Garden Way, Ortigas; r from US$200; ⊜❋@⊜⊠) Slightly less impressive than Shangri-La's

Makati branch, yet still a five-star hotel by all rights. The gardens here are truly a sight to behold and the MRT is just steps away.

Imperial Palace Suites APARTMENTS $$$
(Map p66; ☑02-927 8001; www.imperial.ph; cnr Timog & T Morato Aves; d incl breakfast P3700-4875, ste from P8500; ⊜❋@⊜⊠) Well-kept if slightly dated rooms with plenty of amenities, overlooking the Boy Scouts Monument. Has a lovely garden rooftop pool and gym.

🍴 Eating

The downtown area is not the foodie haven it once was, as most of the best restaurants have moved north to Makati, where the average punter has more disposable income.

Self-caterers will find large Western-style supermarkets in the malls, although the many outdoor markets such as Malate's San Andres Market offer more colourful grazing.

🍴 Intramuros

Patio de Conchita FILIPINO $
(Map p52; cnr Cabildo & Beaterio Sts; meals P75-150; ⊙10am-10pm) Within an ancestral house, Patio de Conchita looks fancier than it is, but it's essentially an upscale *turu-turò* (street food vendor), where customers can order by pointing at the precooked food on display.

Ristorante delle Mitre FILIPINO $$
(Map p52; 470 General Luna St; mains P175-400; ⊙8.30am-8.30pm) Here nuns often help cook dishes named after archbishops in this unique and attractive bistro decked out in Catholic paraphernalia – appropriately opposite San Agustin church. The food is a mix of Filipino, Italian and Spanish, and a good place to refuel after a busy day sightseeing.

Barbara's SPANISH, FILIPINO $$$
(Map p52; ☑02-527 3893; www.barbarasrestaurantandcatering.com; Plaza San Luis Complex, General Luna St; lunch/dinner buffet P395/425; ⊙coffee shop 9am-6pm, restaurant lunch & dinner Mon-Sat) In an elegant space within the Casa Manila (p53) complex, Barbara's does a buffet dinner that includes a cultural show (7.15pm) with traditional music and dances such as *tinikling* (traditional dance using sliding bamboo poles). This is white-tablecloth fine dining for the wannabe colonialist in you.

Ilustrado SPANISH, FILIPINO $$$
(Map p52; ☑02-527 3674; www.ilustradorestaurant.com.ph; 744 General Luna St; mains P420-720;

WORTH A TRIP

THE PRESIDENT'S RESIDENCE

The quiet, leafy suburb of San Miguel is famous not only as the birthplace of Philippine's favorite beer (San Miguel Pilsen was first brewed here in 1890), but more importantly as the official residence of the President of the Philippines at **Malacañang Palace** (Map p50; ☑02-784 4286; presidentialmansion@yahoo.com; JP Laurel Sr St, San Miguel; ⊘Mon-Fri).

Perched overlooking the Pasig River, the sprawling palace complex dates to the mid-18th century when it was built originally as the residence of a Spanish aristocrat before becoming the office of the Spanish and, later, American governor-generals. It's been the official residence of the Filipino president since 1935.

Only the **Museo ng Malacañang** is open to tourists and is highly recommended for anyone who's interested in past political history and colonial architecture. It features fascinating displays of memorabilia relating to the 15 Philippines' presidents since 1899. Highlights include president Quezon's office, the room dedicated to the First Ladies and Ferdinand Marcos' original 20-page decree proclaiming martial law (it was here in 1986 that the palace grounds were stormed during the People Power Revolution that overthrew the Marcos' government). The building itself is magnificent with gleaming polished floorboards, high ceilings, sparkling chandeliers, ornate wood panelling and capiz windows.

To visit you'll need to be super organised and book 10 days in advance – which can be done back home before you leave by simply emailng the palace with your contact number, how many people are in your party and attach photocopies of all passports. Otherwise book a tour through Old Manila Walks (p65). Note that the palace is closed on weekends.

⊘lunch & dinner Mon-Sat, lunch Sun; 圏) Set in a reconstructed Spanish-era house, this is fine dining of the stiff-upper-lip variety. Traditional Spanish-Filipino dishes like paella join salmon, duck and lamb chops on the menu. The attached Kuatro Kantos Bar is a less-formal coffeeshop with art posters on its walls.

✗ Rizal Park

Harbor View SEAFOOD $$
(Map p52; ☑02-524 1532; South Blvd, Rizal Park; dishes from P150; ⊘lunch & dinner) This long-standing and popular fresh seafood *in-ahaw* (grill) restaurant juts into Manila Bay. The breezes can be delightful on sweltering days, but check the wind direction as sometimes it sends the bay's insalubrious flotsam into malodorous piles along the piers. The fish is best enjoyed with a golden sunset and some amber refreshments.

Seafood Market SEAFOOD $$$
(Map p52; ☑02-521 6766; 1190 Bocobo St; meals from P400; ⊘11am-10.30pm) The long ice counter here looks much like the seafood tank at a grocery store. Point to your preference, then watch as a team of chefs cooks your meal; just ask for the price when they weigh your fish, lest you be in for an unpleasant surprise later.

✗ Malate, Ermita & Paco

The best restaurants are in Malate around Remedios Circle and J Nakpil St, where there's plenty of neighbourhood colour to observe if you can bag a streetside perch.

Shawarma Snack Center MIDDLE EASTERN $
(Map p56; 485 R Salas St; shawarma P55, meals P100-250; ⊘24hr) It doesn't sound like much, but this streetside eatery serves the richest and most flavourful falafel, *muttabal* (eggplant dip), hummus and kebabs in downtown Manila. The branch across the street has more upscale dining in air-conditioned comfort and upstairs outdoor balcony seating.

Aristocrat FILIPINO $$
(Map p56; ☑524 7671; www.aristocrat.com.ph; cnr Roxas Blvd & San Andres St; meals P150-400; ⊘24hr) This Manila institution began life in 1936 as a mobile snack cart and today has branches springing up all over the country serving delicious Filipino cuisine. This is the original, and the old Ford canteen is incorporated into the front window.

★ **Casa Armas** SPANISH $$
(Map p56; ☑02-523 0189; J Nakpil St; tapas P25-35, mains P300-500; ⊘11am-midnight Mon-Sat, 6pm-midnight Sun) Foodies have been enamoured with this Spanish cavernlike restaurant spot for years, which is best known for tapas favourites such as *calamares a la*

plancha con alioli (grilled calamari with garlic sauce) and *gambas al ajillo* (sizzling prawns in garlic and oil). Also does excellent paellas, and *bocadillos* (baguettelike sandwich) for a cheap eat.

Bistro Remedios
FILIPINO $$

(Map p56; ☑ 02-523 9153; Adriatico St; mains P200-400; ⊗ 11am-3pm & 6-11pm) An excellent place to sample Filipino cooking, with food from Pampanga province a speciality here. The menu includes exotic and healthy dishes such as taro leaf patties in coconut sauce and steamed *bangus* (milkfish). The nicely relaxed ambience mixes traditional Filipino with smart European bistro.

Cafe Adriatico
INTERNATIONAL $$

(Map p56; 1790 Adriatico St, Malate; mains P200-400; ⊗ 7am-5am; ❋ 🛜) Another old-school Malate favourite, this romantic corner bistro is worth a splurge for original multicultural fare with Spanish, English, American and Italian options, and the people-watching on Remedios Circle. It's open till dawn, so it's great for a late-night meal.

Zamboanga Restaurant
FILIPINO $$

(Map p56; ☑ 02-521 9836; www.zamboangarestaurant.com; 1619 Adriatico St; mains P250-500; ⊗ 11am-11pm, cultural show 8pm) The prices here aren't bad considering many dishes feed two and that along with your dinner you get a one-hour Filipino cultural program, complete with colourful costumes and indigenous dances. Food is best described as gourmet Filipino, with seafood specialities.

FOODIE WEEKEND PARADISE

On weekends, those who love artisan food and laidback farmers markets will want to check out **Salcedo Community Market** (Map p62; Jaime Velasquez Park, Salcedo Village; ⊗ 7am-2pm Sat) on Saturday and the **Legazpi Sunday Market** (Map p62; cnr Salcedo & Rufino Sts, Legazpi Village, Makati; ⊗ 7am-2pm) the next day. Close to 150 separate vendors set up shop with a dizzying array of local specialities from food-crazy regions such as Ilocos, Pampanga and Bicol, as well as French, Thai and Indonesian offerings and heaps of organic produce. Several local restaurants are also represented here.

Korean Palace
KOREAN $$

(Map p56; ☑ 02-521 6695; 1799 Adriatico St; mains P200-500; ⊗ 10am-midnight) Still the best Korean restaurant in town; try the stone pot *bibimbap* (rice with meat, vegetables, egg and chilli; P400; vegetarian version also available) or Korean barbecue (P300 to P400).

Kashmir
INDIAN $$$

(Map p56; ☑ 02-524 6851; P Faura St; mains P300-550; ⊗ 11am-11pm) Relatively small but distinctly upmarket, serving Indian specialities and a few Malaysian and Middle Eastern options. Curries are especially toothsome here.

★ Purple Yam
MODERN FILIPINO $$$

(Map p56; ☑ 0926 713 3523; www.facebook.com/purpleyam; cnr Nakpil & Bocobo Sts, Malate; dinner P2500-3500, brunch P1500; ⊗ dinner Fri & Sat, brunch Sun) Bringing fine dining to Malate Purple Yam of Brooklyn, New York fame, has expanded its horizons to open up inside a renovated ancestral home on a boutique strip of Nakpil St. It's an intimate, sumptuous affair with decor of wrought iron, religious icons, wallpapered motif and wood floorboards. Its ever-changing menu features a seven-course degustation of modern Filipino cuisine with pan-Asian influences using seasonal produce. Reservations essential.

🍴 Binondo (Chinatown)

The real reason to come to Chinatown is to eat! Food is Hokkien-influenced, reflecting the origin of where its immigrants arrived from. Foodies should get in touch with Old Manila Walks (p65) for wonderful Chinatown walking/eating tours.

Mei Sum Tea House
CHINESE $

(Map p60; 965 Ongpin St; dim sum from P68, mains from P115; ⊗ 7am-midnight) Superb dim sum and noodle soups in one of the liveliest teahouses in the heart of Chinatown. Great dumplings!

President Tea House
CHINESE $

(Map p60; 809 Salazar St; dim sum P75-120, mains P150-380; ⊗ 7am-10pm) This bright and shiny clean restaurant is the original branch of what has become one of Manila's more popular Chinese chains; it's known for dim sum.

Happy Veggie
CHINESE $

(Map p60; 958 Masangkay St; meals P60-150; ⊗ 9.30am-8pm; ☑) The interior of this place is as brightly coloured as a ripe melon and its name leaves little doubt as to what's on offer here. There's also a few Western dishes to go with scrumptious Chinese vegetarian meals. It doubles as a Chinese health-food store.

Salazar Bakery
BAKERY $

(Map p60; 783 Ongpin St; snacks from P35; ⊘5am-10pm) Experience the singular joys of black mongo beans, sticky mooncakes and all manner of odd and exotic baked goods here.

Sincerity
CHINESE $$

(Map p60; 497 Nueva St; mains P150-200; ⊘9am-9pm) Famous across Manila for its fried chicken and other homestyle Hokkien cooking, run by a third-generation family.

✖ Makati City & Around

The business hub of Manila has also become its restaurant and nightlife centre. Some of the best restaurants in Makati are in the upmarket malls of Greenbelt 2 and 3. These all have outdoor pedestrianised areas lined with restaurants and bars.

★ El Chupacabra
MEXICAN $

(Map p71; 5782 Felipe St; tacos from P95; ⊘8am-midnight Mon-Thu, to 3am Fri-Sun) Bringing the Mexican street-food craze to Manila, El Chupacabra is a grungy open-air taqueria cooking up a mouthwatering selection of soft-corn tortilla tacos. Go the spicy chipotle shrimp or *sisig* (sizzling grilled pork) tacos. It's wildly popular so expect to wait in the evenings (no reservations); they'll call your name, so grab a margarita while you wait in the street with others. During the day you shouldn't have any problems getting a seat.

Ziggurat
MIDDLE EASTERN $

(Map p71; ☎02-897 5179; just off Makati Ave; mains from P150; ⊘24hr; ✐) This culinary gem is one of Makati's best-kept secrets, with an encyclopaedic menu bearing Indian, Middle Eastern and African influences. Ask for the 'not so secret' secret menu for a selection of home-cooked favourites from the Gaddafi family.

Alba
SPANISH $$

(Map p71; www.alba.com.ph; 38 Polaris St; paella from P490, tapas P150; ⊘9am-11pm) Established in 1952, this old-school Spanish favourite is known for its Valencia-style paellas and great-value lunch buffets (P700) from 11am till 2pm.

Som's Noodle House
THAI $

(Map p50; 5921 A Alger St; mains P120-220; ⊘10.30am-10.30pm) Restaurants in the Philippines generally struggle with Thai food but not Som's, which spices staples such as red curry and *tom yum* to your liking. It's a great deal, and it can deliver to your hotel.

Corner Tree Cafe
VEGETARIAN, CAFE $$

(Map p62; www.cornertreecafe.com; 150 Jupiter St, Makati; mains P200-400; ⊘11am-10pm; ✐) A tranquil escape from busy Jupiter St, with quality vegetarian and vegan soups, stews, tofu-walnut burgers, spinach-feta croquettes and smoothies.

Wingman
AMERICAN $$

(Map p58; The Collective, Malugay St; 6/12 wings P180/300; ⊘noon-1am) One of the first establishments to plant its flag at The Collective (p85), Wingman caters to local hipsters with its American diner food, most notably several varieties of buffalo wings – the best in town by far – plus burgers, imported beers and cocktails.

Legend of India
INDIAN $$

(Map p62; 114 Jupiter St, Makati; mains from P250; ⊘11.30am-3pm & 6-11.30pm) One of Manila's best places for Indian food – as evidenced by the local subcontinent community that flocks here – this suavely decorated restaurant does delicious kormas, tandoori and masala dosas, topped off with a cold Kingfisher or cuppa chai.

★ Blackbird
INTERNATIONAL $$$

(Map p62; ☎02-828 4888; Nielson Tower, Ayala Triangle, Makati; ⊘11am-midnight) If its setting is anything to go by, Colin Mackay's new restaurant is special. Blackbird is set up inside the art-deco Nielson Tower, a historic 1937 airport control tower (Makati's only pre-war building), with dining in the old terminal. The menu is international fusion – you can expect the likes of prawn scotch egg served on betel leaf with sambal, gourmet burgers, twice-cooked beef rib or vegetarian lasagne filled with portobello mushrooms, asparagus, fontina cheese and truffle oil.

Sala
FUSION $$$

(Map p62; ☎02-750 1555; www.salarestaurant. com; A Locsin Bldg, cnr Makati & Ayala Aves; mains P1100-1880; ⊘11am-2pm & 6-11pm Mon-Fri, 6-11pm Sat & Sun; ℗) One of Manila's finest restaurants, this refined European bistro is headed by Scottish chef-owner Colin Mackay (who also runs People's Palace and Blackbird). It features A-level service and an ever-changing selection of fusion dishes and creative desserts. The five-course tasting menu (P2100) is a good choice.

People's Palace
THAI $$$

(Map p62; ☑729 2888; www.peoplespalacethai. com; ground fl, Greenbelt 3; mains from P350; ⊙11am-2.30pm & 5-11pm Mon-Fri, 11am-11pm Sat & Sun) This stylish modern Thai restaurant does a mix of classic and envelope-pushing dishes, all with authentic flavours and gorgeously presented. Dine indoors among chic surrounds, or opt for the outdoor terrace on a balmy evening.

La Tienda
SPANISH $$$

(Map p71; ☑02-895 1651; 43 Polaris St; mains P300-700; ⊙shop 7.30am-11pm, restaurant 8am-3pm & 5.30-11pm) As the name implies (The Store), this smart Spanish eatery doubles as a gourmet food shop. The restaurant proper doles out fine tapas such as *patas bravas* in addition to larger plates such as paella and a long list of steaks. Many come just to savour a glass of Spanish red wine.

Filling Station
DINER $$$

(Map p71; ☑02-897 2053; www.fillingstation. com.ph; 5012 P Burgos St; burgers P450; ⊙24hr) Not even in the American heartland itself could there be a diner with as much 1950s pop-culture paraphernalia as you'll find stuffed inside this P Burgos landmark – everything from life-sized superhero statues to vintage motorcycles. Burgers and milkshakes are the specialities.

✗ Fort Bonifacio

Balducci
ITALIAN $$

(Map p64; www.balducciristorante.com; Serendra, Fort Bonifcacio; pizza P350; ⊙11am-11pm) Another reason to come to the Fort, this ristorante cooks up delicious Tuscan dishes, authentic thin-crust woodfired pizzas and handmade pastas using imported ingredients from Italy. It does excellent Negroni aperitifs and has an extensive wine selection. Also a small deli.

Hungry Hound
GASTROPUB $$

(Map p64; www.hungry-hound.com; ground fl, Globe Tower, cnr 32nd & 7th Ave, Fort Bonifcacio; mains P200-600; ⊙11am-11pm Mon-Sat) A classic dark-wood-panelled gastropub with a winning menu of American food and English pub classics. Next door is the classy Niner Ichi Nana (Map p64) cocktail bar, a good choice for serious drinkers.

The Bowery
AMERICAN $$

(Map p64; cnr Rizal & 29th Ave, Fort Bonifacio; mains from P300-500; ⊙11am-2am Mon-Fri, from 10am Sat & Sun) Across from the Mind Museum, this intimate New York-style bistro serves up anything from buttermilk fried chicken and waffles to turkey burgers and mac 'n' cheese (including a posh lobster, shrimp and truffle version!). Its bar has draught craft beer and well-priced cocktails.

Las Flores
SPANISH $$$

(Map p64; ☑552 2815; 1 McKinley Pl, Fort Bonifacio; paella for 2-people P495; ⊙10am-1pm) This trendy contemporary Spanish restaurant impresses with a slick industrial interior and authentic menu of Catalonia-inspired tapas and mains. Serves cava by the glass.

Aubergine
EUROPEAN $$$

(Map p64; ☑856 9888; www.aubergine.ph; cnr 5th Ave & 32nd St, Fort Bonifacio; mains P500-1500; ⊙11.30am-2pm & 6-10pm; ✎) One of Manila's top restaurants, Aubergine lures a well-heeled clientele from all over the metropolis. The service is impeccable and the menu a delight, including a fantastic vegetarian selection. Signature dishes are the porcini leek fondue and Chilean sea bass on risotto. Otherwise indulge in the seven-course degustation menu.

✗ Quezon City

Quezon City has cutting-edge restaurants, excellent coffee roasters and is awash in restobars specialising in Filipino dishes and catering to the university crowd.

Greens Vegetarian Restaurant and Cafe
VEGETARIAN $

(Map p66; 92 Scout Castor St, Quezon City; mains P80-200; ⊙11am-10pm Mon-Sat, noon-9pm Sun; ✆✎) Earthy and laidback, Greens serves wonderful vegetarian and vegan fare, including eggplant parmigiana and delicious logic-defying meatless *sisig* (usually sizzling grilled pork).

Pipino Vegetarian Food
VEGETARIAN $

(Map p50; www.pipinovegetarian.com; 39 Malingap St, Quezon City; mains P120-275; ⊙11am-midnight Mon-Sat, 11am-10pm Sun) Pipino has one of the most creative vegetarian menus in Manila. Here you'll get anything from a watermelon steak with taro miso mash to portobello mushrooms *inasal* (marinated in soy and barbecued). It also serves up dairy-free ice cream using cashew milk and maple syrup. For a drink, head downstairs to the rowdy Pino Bar. There is also a branch of the restaurant in Makati.

Van Gogh is Bipolar
CAFE $$

(Map p50; ☑0922 824 3051; www.vanggoghisbipolar.com; 154 Maginhawa St; ⊘6pm-midnight) Every bit as interesting as it sounds, this chaotic restaurant inhabiting a tiny space packed with curios and artworks, is a delight for the senses. It's run by artist Jetro, who cooks original, delicious food in a riotous atmosphere that'll likely see you dine wearing a flamboyant hat (grab one from the hatstand). The place was set up by Jetro as his sanctuary to assist with nonpharmaceutical treatment of his bipolar condition, and cooking incorporates a lot of natural ingredients (with reputed mood-enhancing properties).

Opening hours are irregular, so call ahead. Reservations are essential. Even if it's closed, it's still worth visiting Maginhawa St, a happening strip with hot new eateries and bars.

Charlie's Grind & Grill
BURGERS $$

(Map p50; Ortigas Ave, Ronac Art Center, Greenhills, Quezon City; burgers from P200; ⊘10am-1am) Charlie's still cooks up Manila's best burgers, with a magnificent menu of American diner food from black Angus and wagyu burgers to pulled-pork sandwiches and duck-fat fries. Choose from its selection of international craft beers to wash it all down. Charlie's is convenient for Greenhills shopping, or otherwise head to its flagship branch in Pasig (Map p50; 16 East Capitol Dr, Pasig City).

Cafe Kapitan
SPANISH, FILIPINO $$

(Rizal St, Marikina; mains from P185; ⊘9am-6.30pm) Just up the road from the Marikina Shoe Museum, this is a good spot for a lunch break within an atmospheric 18th-century building. Food covers a bit of everything, but is heavily Spanish-influenced.

Restorante La Capre
FILIPINO $$

(Map p66; cnr Scout Santiago & Scout Limbaga Sts; mains P190-350; ⊘from 4pm Mon-Sat; 🐾) Tucked away in the quiet streets west of T Morato Ave, this little eatery has Pinoy faves and a host of exotic Pampanga specialities such as sizzling crocodile (P400) and sizzling *kabayo* (horse).

Chocolate Kiss
EUROPEAN $$

(Map p66; www.thechocolatekiss.com; 91 A Roces Ave; sandwiches P150-200, mains P200-300; ⊘11am-10pm Mon-Sat, 9am-2pm Sun; 🐾📶) The continental comfort dishes fashioned by the chefs at this QC favourite might make you nostalgic for home. Chicken Kiev and Salisbury steak are among the surprises. Hit the all-you-can-eat Sunday brunch – just P395.

HEADING OUT TONIGHT?

The following websites are good for up-to-date info on club events, gigs, art shows and new restaurants.

Bandstand (www.bandstand.ph) Great site to tap into Manila's underground music scene with listings of upcoming punk, indie and metal gigs.

Manila Clubbing (www.manilaclubbing.com) Covers the Manila club scene.

Hey Garch (www.heygarch.com) Well-updated site for event listings, gig guide and clubs.

Juice.ph (www.juice.ph) Lifestyle and upcoming events.

Spot (www.spot.ph) Urban guide to Manila, including excellent food reviews.

Good sandwiches and desserts too. There's another branch at UP Diliman.

Victorinos
ILOCANO $$$

(Map p66; 114 Scout Rallos St, cnr 11th Jamboree St, Quezon City; mains from P300; ⊘11am-10pm) With its checkered-tiled floors and antique furniture, there's more than a hint of elegance at well-heeled Victorinos, yet its prices remain very affordable. It specialises in delicious Ilocan cuisine, with its *lechon* (spit-roast pig) being the signature dish. The attached bakery has some of the most delicious cakes in Manila. It also offers cooking classes; visit www.henysison.com for info.

Uno Restaurant
FUSION $$$

(Map p66; ☑02-374 0774; 195C T Morato Ave; mains P300-600; ⊘10am-9.30pm Mon-Sat) A quaint and handsome little bistro serving complex fusion fare whipped up by the talented chef-owner Jose Mari Relucio. The menu rotates quarterly. Enter on Scout Fuentebella St.

Drinking & Nightlife

Downtown Manila

You're rarely far from a drinking opportunity in downtown Manila. The college crowd chug cheap suds just west of Remedios Circle on Remedios St in Malate – dubbed the 'Monoblock Republic' because of the preponderance of brittle plastic furniture. Live-music venues are also great places to drink.

Oarhouse
BAR

(Map p56; www.oarhousepub.com; cnr Bocobo & General M Malvar Sts; ⊙4pm-late Mon-Sat) Around since 1977, the Oarhouse is a Malate treasure, attracting an intelligent, boozy crowd of regulars, comprising students, journalists and foreigners who often linger until the sun comes up. Serves the coldest beer in town and plays great music. Also does pub meals.

Erra's Place
BAR

(Map p56; 1755 Adriatico St; ⊙24hr) In the heart of the main strip, Erra's is your classic Southeast Asian streetside shack serving cheap San Miguel (P30) and luring folk from all corners of the galaxy.

Hobbit House
BAR

(Map p52; www.hobbithousemanila.com; 1212 MH del Pilar St; admission P150-175; ⊙5pm-2am; 🛜) This quality blues bar attracts some of Manila's finest musos. It's staffed by little people, which some people find a delight and others find a bit exploitative. Also has one of the best imported and craft beer selections in Manila.

Silya
RESTOBAR

(Map p56; 642 J Nakpil St; ⊙4pm-late) This side-street outdoor restobar is a great place to kick back and warm up your karaoke skills before hitting the provinces.

Republiq
CLUB

(Map p50; www.republiqclub.com; Resorts World, Andrews Ave, Pasay; cover incl 2 drinks P600; ⊙9.30pm-late Wed, Fri & Sat) Republiq is still Metro Manila's 'it' club, with a mix of local and international DJs spinning hip hop, R&B and party tracks. The strict dress code requires a collared shirt for men and no shorts or caps.

Destination Heaven
CLUB

(Map p56; cnr J Nakpil & M Orosa Sts; entry incl a drink P250; ⊙9pm-5am Wed-Sun) One of Manila's hottest new gay venues, this precinct has four clubs and bars under the one roof, with regular drag shows, go-go dancers and a wonderfully kitschy rooftop cocktail bar.

Makati City & Around

Makati has excellent nightlife, from speak-easys and pumping clubs to swanky rooftop bars and grungy music venues.

Finders Keepers
BAR

(Map p50; www.facebook.com/finderskeepersMNL; La Fuerza Plaza, off Don Chino Roces Ave; ⊙Tue-Sun 8pm-late) One of Makati's hippest bars, this dimly lit speakeasy is hidden within a nondescript warehouse tucked down an industrial sidestreet (look for the 'meat shack' outside). Once you've found it, grab a stool at the long bar for quality cocktails and lounge on a couch. Upstairs is the ultra-cool Black Market (p81) club.

Le Café Curieux
RESTOBAR

(Map p71; www.lecafecurieux.com; Badajos St; ⊙11am-2pm & 6pm-late Mon-Fri, Sat & Sun 6pm-

---

CRAFT BEER

The craft-beer revolution has reached Manila. Visit www.globalbeerexchange.com.ph for the latest craft-beer hotspots and keep an eye out for the Drink Up beer festival (p66) held in May. Here are some places that specialise in Filipino craft beer:

Global Beer Exchange (Map p50; www.globalbeerexchange.com.ph; Unit 103, Tritan Plaza, Makati; ⊙1pm-2am Mon-Sat) Under a highway overpass, Global Beer Exchange is a bottle shop/bar stocking an impressive range of local and international craft beers (both on tap and bottled) to drink here or take away.

Big Bad Wolf (Map p64; www.facebook.com/bigbadwolfph; Forbestown Rd, Burgos Circle, Fort Bonifacio; ⊙11am-3pm Mon-Sat) Reminiscent of a hipster bar in Portland, Big Bad Wolf is split over two levels with comfy couches, wooden floorboards and chalkboard menus with an excellent selecton of beers from Negros, Palawan and Mindanao.

Perfect Pint (Map p64; www.facebook.com/theperfectpintph; Crossroads Bldg, 32nd St, Fort Bonifacio; ⊙11am-late) A big player in the Philippines' craft-beer scene, this pub has multiple mircrobrews on tap, including its home brew. Does beer-and-food pairings too.

Bravo (Map p50; 1331 Angono St, Makati; 1lt beer P200; ⊙11am-11pm Mon-Sat; 🛜) Home to the Pivo Praha microbrewery, which has been producing Czech-style pilsens, dark and wheat beers since 2001. Tastings are available and it also does cracking woodfired pizzas and Czech food. Roasts its own coffee on site.

MANILA'S THIRD-WAVE COFFEE

Coffee is something Manila's new generation likes to take seriously and Quezon City is leading the way with several serious coffee roasters. All of the following source single-origin beans from Luzon, as well as Asia, Africa and Latin America, and roast on site.

Craft Coffee Revolution (Map p66; 66c Broadway Ave; ☺8am-11pm Mon-Sat, 11am-8pm Sun; 🛜) Next door to Big Sky Mind, Craft Coffee Revolution is everything a coffee house should be, with wooden-crate furniture for patrons to enjoy single-origin espressos, 45-hour cold drips or siphon coffee.

Coffee Empire (Map p50; www.coffeeempire.com.ph; 74 West Ave; ☺6am-1am) A chic industrial open-plan warehouse setup with roaster and hessian sacks of green beans on display. It serves a range of excellent single-origin coffees and the baristas are happy to share info and demos. It also does cuppings (check the website) and excellent food.

EDSA Beverage Design (Map p50; www.edsa-bdg.com; CLMC Bldg, 209 EDSA, Mandaluyong City; ☺7am-11pm) Set up as a shared collaborative space for creative types, this bar-cafe has baristas working away on fancy equipment to produce some of Manila's finest caffeine concoctions.

late) A welcome addition to P Burgos's otherwise seedy scene, this French-owned bar and bistro distils its own rums in a range of infused flavours. Grab a stool at its grungy front bar or head back to the open-air space to feast on delicious French cuisine; Monday is all-you-can-eat *moules frites* (mussels and fries) night (P500).

Salon de Ning BAR
(Map p62; cnr Ayala & Makati Aves, The Peninsula; ☺7pm-2am Tue-Sat) Hidden away inside the luxurious Peninsula hotel, this drinking den is inspired by a 1930s Shanghai nightclub and one of Manila's most atmospheric bars. Its adjoined rooms are decked out in themes ranging from a Bohemian lounge room and an air zeppelin cockpit to glassed displays of women's shoes.

Attached is **The Bar** (Map p62; The Peninsula), a pub known for its all-you-can-drink evenings (P1280) on Thursday, Friday and Saturday from 7pm to midnight; cocktails and spirits included!

Black Market CLUB
(Map p50; www.blackmarketmnl.com; La Fueza Plaza, off Don Chino Roces Ave; ☺Wed-Sat 9pm-3am) Upstairs from Finders Keepers (p80), this industrial-chic club has DJs spinning quality electronic music and hip hop, minus the cheese. Has P600 all-you-can-drink rum and cokes.

Commune CAFE
(Map p62; www.commune.ph; cnr D Costa & Valero Sts, Salcedo Village, Makati; coffee from P90; ☺8am-11pm Mon-Sat; 🛜) One of Makati's best

places for coffee, Commune sources its own beans from around the Philippines and does good espressos, aeropress and cold drips. It's a nice place to hang out with quality reading material on hand and aesthetically pleasing pop art splashed on the walls. You can also order food and craft beers.

The Curator BAR
(Map p62; 134 Legazpi St, cnr C Palanca St; cocktails from P400; ☺bar 6pm-2am, cafe from 7am) The place for those who take their alcohol seriously, the Curator serves up an ever-changing menu of original cocktails made by mixologists who know their stuff. Drinks are pricey, but use quality ingredients. It's an intimate sit-down affair in surrounds resembling a concrete bunker. As with Makati's other speakeasys, the bar has no signage and is hidden behind what seems like another decoy bar you'll need to walk through.

During the day it takes on a totally different persona and serves up artisan coffee; another reason to pop in.

71 Grammercy CLUB
(Map p71; www.facebook.com/71Gramercy; 71st fl, Grammercy Residences, Kalayaan Ave, Makati; ☺6pm-4am Mon-Sat) Soar up to the top floor of the Philippines' tallest building (302m) to hang out with the beautiful people at this rooftop club where DJs spin house and electro from 10pm. This is definitely a place you'll need to dress up for.

Museum Café LOUNGE BAR
(Map p62; Ayala Museum, Greenbelt 4) Much more than a simple refuelling stop for

MANILA'S BEST ROOFTOP ESCAPES

To get a different perspective on Manila, head up to one of the city's rooftop bars to escape street level chaos and enjoy some great views.

Sky Deck (Map p52; http://www.thebayleaf.com.ph/restaurants/sky-deck-view-bar; Muralla & Victoria Sts, Intramuros; ⊗5pm-1am; 🛜) One of Manila's best open-air rooftop bars, this is the perfect place to finish up in Intramuros after a busy day sightseeing with 360-degree views, live acoustic bands and a selection of classic cocktails. It's above the Bayleaf hotel.

71 Grammercy (p81) Swanky A-list restaurant-nightclub atop the Philippines' tallest building, with an Astroturf terrace and fine city views.

Pacific Lounge (Map p56; 21fl Pan Pacific Hotel, cnr Adriatico & M Malvar Sts; cocktails incl nibbles P250; ⊗6am-11pm) Hidden 21 floors above Malate, this five-star hotel's rooftop bar is open to nonguests. Hang out in its garden oasis (complete with gazebo and footbridge) or head indoors for suave city views; also good during the day for panoramas of Manila Bay from its restaurant.

Skye (Map p64; W High St Bldg, 28th St, Bonifacio Global City; ⊗5pm-2am Tue-Sat) This Fort Bonifacio roofdeck is a great space to party with regular DJs, a giant marquee, Astroturf and a live green wall full of tropical plants.

Straight Up (Map p64; cnr 30th St & 11th Ave, Seda Hotel, Bonifacio Global City) Another classy Manhattan-style roof bar in the Fort, with great city views and two-for-one cocktails from 5pm to 7pm. It's above Seda hotel.

museum patrons, 'M Café' is a magnet for Manila's chi-chi class. It's usually more of a place to warm up for the evening, either inside or outside, but on Thursday nights the beats are thrown down and M Café becomes the party. Has a menu focusing on light bites and sandwiches (P400 to P600).

Writers Bar   CAFE, BAR
(Map p62; cnr A Arnaiz & Makati Aves; Raffles Makati; high tea for 2 people P995; ⊗2.30-5.30pm; 🛜) Though British rule in Manila was short-lived (1762–64), you can still get a taste of colonialism with a spot of high tea at Raffles. Based on the original Singapore hotel bar, here you can partake in cucumber sandwiches, scones and pastries served on three-tiered platters and, of course, drink cups of tea.

A Toda Madre   BAR
(Map p71; www.atmrestaurant.com; gr fl, Sunette Tower, Durban St; ⊗5pm-2am Mon-Sat, from 11am Sun) One of the few decent bars in the area, this snazzy tequila bar has a selection of 85 different types, plus mescals, Mexican beers and margaritas. Bar food is good too, with hand-pressed soft corn-tortilla tacos and corn chips with a selection of imported hot sauces.

Time   CLUB
(Map p71; 7840 Makati Ave; ⊗from 5pm Tue-Sat) Thumping beats inside, mellow patio overlooking Makati Ave outside.

Palladium   CLUB
(Map p62; New World Hotel, Esperanza St; admission incl drink P500; ⊗Wed-Sat) A consistent club, descending into the depths beneath the five-star New World Hotel.

Bed   CLUB
(Map p50; www.bed.com.ph; Mayflower St, Ortigas, Pasig; admission incl some drinks P350; ⊗6pm-2am Sun-Thu, to 5am Fri & Sat) A club with rare staying power, Bed has gone through many incarnations over the years but is still throwing its infamous gay and straight parties until the wee hours.

H&J's   BAR
(Map p71; www.hnjbar.ph; 5781 Felipe St; ⊗2pm-5am) For anyone needing to escape the debauchery of nearby P Burgos St, this simple and generally well-behaved pub is one of the area's best options and a good spot to watch live sports on TV.

Beers Paradise   BAR
(Map p71; cnr Polaris & Durban Sts; ⊗5pm-4am) Belgian beer is the speciality at this spartan drinkery. Most varieties pack quite a wallop.

🍷 Quezon City

⭐**Cubao Expo**   BAR PRECINCT
(Map p66; Gen Romulo Ave, Cubao; ⊗5pm-late Tue-Sun) A precinct of cool bars, cheap eats and boutiques, Cubao X is a must for anyone

interested in Manila's underground scene. Venues come and go, but ones to check out include **Vinyl on Vinyl** dive bar which mixes booze, vinyl records and live bands; **Fred's Revolución**, a boozy Communist-themed bar; or more refined **Humidor** with its Cuban cigars and single malts.

Big Sky Mind   BAR
(Map p66; cnr E Rodriguez Sr Ave & 14th St, New Manila; ⊙9pm-5am Tue-Sun) A long-time favourite with Manila's indie crowd, this dive bar has tables propped up with bricks, second-hand couches and works by local artists on its walls. Come for the cheap beer (P30), cool playlist and tasty bar food.

☆ Entertainment

Live Music

Live music is the focus of Quezon City's student-driven bars.

★ SaGuijo   LIVE MUSIC
(Map p62; ☑02-897 8629; www.saguijo.com; 7612 Guijo St, Makati; admission after 10pm incl a drink P150; ⊙6pm-2am) A wonderfully decrepit dive bar with a jam-packed roster of indie, punk and new wave bands that kick off at 10.30pm.

★ 1951   LIVE MUSIC
(Penguin Cafe; Map p56; 1951 Adriatico St; ⊙from 6pm Tue-Sat) This legendary bar-cum-gallery is a magnet for bohemian types and lovers of live music, with some of the finest musical talent in the Philippines having graced its stage. The official name is now 1951 but everybody still calls it Penguin Cafe.

B-Side   LIVE MUSIC
(Map p58; www.facebook.com/thecollectivemanila; The Collective, Malugay St, Makati; ⊙varies) This is the bar that makes the artsy Collective (p85) tick. It tosses a live band or two into the Collective's central courtyard on

weekends and on some weeknights, and the whole complex gets jumping – especially on reggae Sundays, which start up late afternoon. As with other places in the Collective, its location remains uncertain, so check the Facebook page for updates.

Sev's Cafe   MUSIC
(Map p58; ☑02-239 2327; www.sevscafe.com; cnr Roxas Blvd & Ocampo St, Legaspi Towers; ⊙7am-9pm; 🛜) In the thick of Manila's cultural precinct this basement venue is where Manila's intelligentsia hang to catch poetry slams, live bands and open mic nights. Also does healthy food options. It's owned by re-knowned journalist Howie Severino.

Black Kings Bar   LIVE MUSIC
(BKB; Map p50; ☑0917 8432 708; www.bkbmusic.com; 107 West Ave, Quezon City; ⊙6pm-late) A great place to catch Quezon City's rock scene, with a regular roster of punk, metal and blues bands kicking out the jams on its dark divey stage nightly. Serves cheap whisky and cokes (P70).

'70s Bistro   LIVE MUSIC
(Map p50; www.70sbistro.com; 46 Anonas St, Quezon City; admission around P150; ⊙7pm-late Mon-Sat) A long-running Quezon City bar, '70s Bistro is known for getting some of the best reggae acts in the country, plus classic Pinoy rock bands that have been around almost since the 1970s, such as the Jerks. It draws a reliable crowd every night.

Conspiracy Bar & Garden Cafe   LIVE MUSIC
(Map p50; ☑453 2170; www.conspi.net; 59 Visayas Ave, Quezon City; admission P100-150; ⊙5pm-2am Mon-Sat) This is a long-standing character-filled venue attracting an older, sit-down crowd for more acoustic-oriented gigs. The garden is a good place to chill with a dark San Miguel. Gigs start around 10pm.

THEY'RE HERE, THEY'RE QUEER & THEY LOOK STUNNING!

Bangkok may have invented the concept of transsexual and transvestite variety stage shows, but Manila may do it better.

The best of the city's transvestite stage shows take place at the opulent **Club Mwah!** (Map p50; ☑02-535 7943; www.clubmwah.com; 3rd fl, Venue Tower, 652 Boni Ave, Mandaluyong City), an incredibly shiny, sparkly and fabulous place with obvious Las Vegas interior-design influences. Manila's gay expats give it a huge thumbs-up.

In the hearl of the Cultural Centre of the Philippines (CCP), the Manila Film Center building stages performances of the **Amazing Show** (Map p58; ☑02-834 8870; www.amazing-show.com; Manila Film Center, CCP Complex; admission P1300; ⊙8pm Mon-Sat). The one-hour revue-type shows and beauty contests star all manner of transpeople.

Route 196   LIVE MUSIC
(☑439 1972; 196 Katipunan Ave, Quezon City; ◎6pm-late Mon-Sat) Another well-loved Quezon City indie-music venue with quality local original bands.

The Library   COMEDY
(Map p56; ☑02-522 2484; www.thelibrary.com.ph; 1139 M Orosa St; shows P100-500; ◎shows from 9pm) In the heart of Malate's gay district, the Library has nightly comedy shows (at 9pm) that are popular with both gay and straight audiences.

Araneta Coliseum   LIVE MUSIC
(Map p66; ☑911 3101; www.aranetacoliseum.com; Araneta Center, cnr EDSA & Aurora Blvd, Quezon City) The place for touring international bands, including a lot of washed-up rock acts from the '70s and '80s. Boy George, the Eagles and Duran Duran are among those to have landed in Manila in recent years. It's also popular for PBA (Philippine Basketball Association) games.

Performing Arts

Cultural Center of the Philippines   PERFORMING ARTS
(Map p58; ☑02-832 1125; www.culturalcenter.gov.ph; CCP Complex, Roxas Blvd; performance prices vary; ◎box office 9am-6pm Tue-Sat, 1-5pm Sun performance days) Manila's major cultural guns perform here, including Ballet Philippines, the nation's premiere dance troupe; Philippine Philharmonic Orchestra, the nation's main classical orchestra; and Tanghalang Pilipino, a theatre group that performs classic and original local work, often not in English.

Theatre

Repertory Philippines   THEATRE
(Map p62; ☑02-843 3570; www.repertoryphilippines.com; Onstage Theare, 2nd fl, Greenbelt 1, Makati; tickets from P420) Professional group that performs plays (some in English) at the OnStage Theatre.

Philippine Educational Theater Association   THEATRE
(PETA; Map p66; ☑02-725 6244; www.petatheater.com; 5 Eymard Dr, Quezon City; ◎shows 10am, 3pm and/or 8pm Fri-Sun) This 'open' theatre group does both comedy and tragedy, most of it original. Arguably Manila's best troupe, though check performances are in English.

Sport

Cuneta Astrodome   BASKETBALL
(Map p58; ☑02-831 4652; Derham St) Popular venue for professional basketball games

managed by the PBA (Philippine Basketball Association), the Philippines' equivalent of America's NBA.

Cinemas
Manila's malls boast hundreds of cinemas, many of them state of the art. Hollywood blockbusters are often shown in the Philippines at the same time as their US release, yet it costs only P120 to P180 to watch a movie here. There's an IMAX at Mall of Asia (p85).

🔒 Shopping

The largest variety of stores is in the shopping malls (most prominently Robinsons and Mall of Asia) which have the added advantages of being air-conditioned and full of other diversions such as restaurants and movie theatres. Market lovers should head to the Quiapo Church area. In Ermita a stroll along Mabini St will often yield authentic old textiles and other antiques.

🔒 Downtown Manila

⭐**The Manila Collectible Co.** SOUVENIRS, FOOD
(Map p52; www.manilacollectible.com; Villa Blanca Bldg, cnr Cabildo & Beaterio Sts, Intramuros; ◎10am-6pm; ☏) Head upstairs to this funky Intramuros shop to pick up handspun textiles and accessories produced by indigenous groups across the Philippines. It also sells fairtrade organic coffee, Filipino cigars, local 'wines', flavoured pilinuts and pure cacao, all of which make fantastic souvenirs. Kids will love it too, with pottery painting (P100) they can take home. Also has a lovely rooftop overlooking Manila Catheral, with plans for a cafe.

Silahis Arts & Artifacts   SOUVENIRS
(Map p52; www.silahis.com; 744 General Luna St, Intramuros; ◎10am-7pm) This is almost more of a cultural centre than a store. Intricately woven baskets, wooden Ifugao *bulol* (rice guard) statues, textiles and other crafts from around the country are sold next to beautiful antiques.

Tesoro's   SOUVENIRS
(Map p56; www.tesoros.ph; 1325 Mabini St, Ermita; ◎9am-8pm) The speciality here is woven *pinya* (fabric woven from pineapple fibres) products, but there are also lacquered coconut-shell products, baskets, bags, coffee, dried mangoes and a few rare books on Philippine culture.

Also has several branches in **Makati** (Map p62; 1016 A Arnaiz Ave, Makati) and the airport too (Terminal 1 and 3) for last-minute gift shopping.

San Andres Market   MARKET
(Map p56; San Andres St, Malate; ⊙24hr) Malate's main market looks like one big cornucopia of fruits including exotic *guyabano* (soursop) and durian. It's a dark warren of treats ripe for exploration.

Hiraya Gallery   ART
(Map p52; www.hiraya.com; 530 United Nations Ave, Ermita; ⊙9am-5pm Mon-Sat) This long-established commercial gallery has a museum-quality selection of Filipino contemporary art. Names to look out for are Leonard Aguinaldo, Norberto Carating and Eric Guazon.

Maria Closa   ANTIQUES, ARTS
(Map p56; www.mariaclosa.com; 1335 Mabini St, Ermita; ⊙9am-6.30pm) Sharing the same building as 1335Mabini (p57), this high-end gallery is one for serious collectors with quality handcrafted furniture, sculpture and artefacts from around the country.

Solidaridad Bookshop   BOOKS
(Map p56; 531 P Faura St, Ermita; ⊙9am-6pm Mon-Sat) Owned by the Filipino author F Sionil José, this fantastic shop has a masterfully edited collection of both Western and Eastern nonfiction, international magazines such as the *New Yorker,* and hard-to-find Filipino history titles and documentaries.

Tradewinds Books   BOOKS
(Map p52; 3rd fl, Silahis Arts & Artifacts, 744 General Luna St, Intramuros) Inside Silahis Arts & Artifacts, Tradewinds stocks a varied assortment of books on the Philippines and Asia, including out-of-print or hard-to-find volumes, Filipino cookbooks and cool postcards by local artists.

Mall of Asia   MALL
(Map p58; www.smmallofasia.com; Manila Bay; ⊙10am-10pm) One of the top 10 largest malls in the world, with all the usual retail shops plus an Olympic-sized ice rink and an IMAX theatre. Come early evening for its oceanfront carnival rides.

🏠 Makati City & Around

Central Makati can seem like one big upscale mall – you might find yourself shopping against your will. Greenbelt and Glorietta malls both sprawl over several precincts.

★LRI Design Plaza   DESIGN, ART
(Map p50; www.lridesignplaza.com; 210 Nicanor Garcia St; ⊙10am-7pm Mon-Sat) A conglomeration of art galleries and contemporary furniture showrooms under one roof showcases all that's chic in the capital's art and design world.

★The Collective   VINTAGE
(Map p58; www.thecollectivemnl.com; Malugay St) A hive of creative energy and cool, this co-op brings together a collection of urban galleries, vintage shops and boutiques along with a few bars and restaurants. It doesn't really wake up until early evening. Many of the stores were in the process of relocating to another venue at time of research, so check website for updates.

Balikbayan Handicrafts   SOUVENIRS
(Map p62; www.balikbayanhandicrafts.com; 1010 A Arnaiz Ave; ⊙9am-8pm Mon-Sat, from 10am Sun) Set over three levels this is the kind of place that pulls in tourists by the busload. The merchandise is of a surprisingly good quality, considering how much of it they have, and the speciality is beautiful glazed coconut dishware and decorative balls, among many other products.

Greenbelt   MALL
(Map p62; Ayala Centre) This is the high end of the Ayala Centre, with scores of swish cafes and restaurants around a central park area. There are five sections (Greenbelt 1 to Greenbelt 5) each with its own character.

🏠 Fort Bonifacio

Bonifacio High Street   SHOPPING ARCADE
(Map p64; btwn 5th & 11th Aves, Fort Bonifacio) Two adjoining upscale, open-air strip malls with loads of good restaurants and upmarket fashion labels. It leads to the **Fiesta Market** (Map p64; Bonifacio Global City) with open-air eateries and regional cuisine.

Echo Store   HEALTH, FOOD
(Map p64; www.echostore.ph; Serendra Piazza McKinley Parkway, Fort Bonifacio; ⊙9am-9pm) ✑ Specialises in fairtrade, locally sourced products (including coffee and handicrafts) and chemical-free beauty/health items. Its cafe serves tasty organic and sustainable dishes.

Fully Booked

BOOKS

(Map p64; www.fullybookedonline.com; 902 Bonifacio High St) Manila's most comprehensive bookstore, with a great travel section and an outstanding selection of fiction and nonfiction (all in English). There are branches in most malls across Manila, but fans of Tintin will want to check out this one in the Fort.

Quezon City

★ Cubao Expo

VINTAGE, ANTIQUES

(Map p66; Gen Romulo Ave, Cubao) Uber-hip assortment of kitschy shops and galleries selling everything from old LPs to retro toys and housewares.

Greenhills Shopping Center

MARKET

(Map p50; www.greenhills.com.ph; Ortigas Ave, San Juan; ⊙10am-8pm) Somewhat like an indoor/outdoor flea market, Greenhills has stall after stall selling DVDs and brand-named clothing of questionable legitimacy. But snoop around here and you'll find quality antiques and the best selection of genuine pearls in the country.

Human Nature

COSMETICS

(www.humanheartnature.com; 463 Commonwealth Ave, Quezon City; ⊙9am-6pm Sat-Mon) 🖉 The flagship store of this social enterprise selling all-Filipino, chemical-free beauty and health products. Also sells local coffee beans, with free cups of brewed coffee. Does excellent work in helping poorer communities.

Q Mart

MARKET

(Map p66; Ermin Garcia Ave) If you want to have a truly local experience – or buy a goat – stumble over to this sprawling covered bazaar not far from the Cubao bus terminals along EDSA.

ℹ Information

DANGERS & ANNOYANCES

Manila is probably no more dangerous than the next city, but it can still be dodgy. As in any big city, crime is a part of life, with foreigners sometimes targeted by petty criminals and carjackers. Be on your guard if walking around on your own at night, especially in deserted places and in rough districts such as Tondo. When riding in taxis, do as your driver does and lock your doors. Pickpocketing is rampant on the MRT/LRT (always put valuables in your backpack worn on your front) and on major bar strips where drunk tourists make easy prey.

Traffic is the big annoyance in Manila; you'll probably spend half your time either stuck in it or talking about it. Leave extra time to get to airports, bus stations and dinner reservations. Noise, crowds and air pollution are the major annoyances.

Rigged taxi meters are becoming more common, although most taxi drivers are honest.

EMERGENCY

In case of emergencies call ⏍117 for police, ambulance and fire.

INTERNET ACCESS

Malls such as Robinsons Place have internet cafes; there are also a few along Adriatico St, in

---

QUIAPO MARKET FERVOUR

Lovers of markets and mayhem should cross the Quezon Bridge over the Pasig River to Quiapo Church (Map p60; Quezon Blvd), home of the Black Nazarene (p66).

The main reason to go to Quiapo, however, is not to see the church but to witness what's happening on and around the church square, Plaza Miranda. Here and in the surrounding markets every manner of product is sold to a throng of humanity.

Most notorious are the dubious apothecary stalls selling herbal and folk medicines, as well as amulets (carved stones and medallions believed to have magical powers). Showing admirable initiative, vendors will tell you that the 'Pampa Regla' potion is good for everything from weight loss to curing erectile dysfunction, depending on how you look. Langis Ng Ahas is snake oil – maybe.

Particularly colourful are the stalls around Carriedo St, which sell thickly padded bras, hardware, porn DVDs and just about anything else. Nearby, under Quezon Bridge, the area known as Ilalim ng Tulay (literally 'under the bridge'), you can find really cheap junk for tourists. Across the road, at Quinta Market, you'll find vendors boisterously pedalling fish, meat, vegetables, fruits and other foodstuffs.

The action is particularly feverish at weekends, when half of the population not in malls is shopping here. As in other crowded areas, don't carry valuables in your pockets and wear your backpack on your front.

Malate, and Makati Ave near the corner of Jupiter St. Rates vary from P30 to P60 per hour.

MEDICAL SERVICES

Metro Manila has several large, private hospitals that are gaining traction for medical tourism.

Makati Medical Center, Manila Doctors Hospital and St Luke's Medical Center are all modern and conveniently located to the primary tourist zones of Malate and Makati.

Makati Medical Center (Map p62; 📞 02-888 8999; www.makatimed.net.ph; 2 Amorsolo St, Makati)

Manila Doctors Hospital (Map p52; 📞 02-524 3011; www.maniladoctors.com.ph; 667 United Nations Ave, Ermita)

St Luke's Medical Center (Map p64; 📞 02-789 7700; www.stluke.com.ph; 32nd St, Fort Bonifacio) Metro Manila's most modern hospital. Also in Quezon City (📞 02-723 0101, emergency 02-725 2328; 279 E Rodriguez Sr Ave, Quezon City).

MONEY

The three main Philippine banks with ATMs that accept Western bank cards – Bank of the Philippine Islands (BPI), Metrobank and Banco de Oro (BDO) – have scores of branches across the city, including in all major malls. They usually have a limit of P10,000 per withdrawal. Citibank allows P15,000 while HSBC allows up to P40,000 per withdrawal. The **Citibank main office** (Map p62; 8741 Paseo de Roxas) and **HSBC main office** (Map p62; 6766 Ayala Ave, Makati) are in Makati's central business district.

Malate and Ermita are peppered with money changers and there are places all over the city where you can change foreign currency into Philippine pesos, but take care to count the money to ensure you haven't been short-changed.

POST

Ermita Post Office (Map p56; P Hidalgo St, Malate) Most convenient to Malate's tourist belt.

Makati Central Post Office (Map p62; Sen Gil Puyat Ave, Makati; ⊙ 8am-5pm Mon-Fri) Located near the corner of Ayala Extension.

Manila Central Post Office (Map p60; Magallanes Dr, Intramuros; ⊙ 6am-6.30pm Mon-Fri, 8am-noon Sat) This beautiful post office building is a landmark; offers full services.

TOURIST INFORMATION

Department of Tourism Information Centre (DOT; Map p62; 📞 02-459 5200; www.visit-myphilippines.com; JB Bldg, 351 Sen Gil Puyat Ave, Makati; ⊙ 7am-6pm Mon-Sat) Recently relocated to Makati, the tourism office has helpful staff, city maps and information for trips around Manila. There are also smaller DOT offices at the various Ninoy Aquino International Airport (NAIA) terminals.

TRAVEL AGENCIES

There are travel agencies everywhere in Ermita, Malate and Makati, but most specialise in outbound tourism. Most hotels can arrange excursions outside Manila.

Filipino Travel Center (Map p56; 📞 02-528 4507; www.filipinotravel.com.ph; cnr Adriatico & Pedro Gil Sts, Malate; ⊙ 8am-6pm Mon-Fri, 9am-5pm Sat) Catering to foreign tourists, this helpful and knowledgeable agency organises city tours and day tours around Manila and beyond.

Discovery Islands (Map p52; 📞 02-523 8541; 2nd Fl, Swagman Hotel, 411 A Flores St, Ermita; bus/boat tickets to Puerto Galera P880; ⊙ 9am-6pm Mon-Sat) Helpful agency inside Swagman Hotel that can arrange visa extensions.

USEFUL WEBSITES

There are a number of websites focusing on Manila's culture and nightlife that are a good place to look for upcoming events (p79).

Click the City (www.clickthecity.com) Manila's online directory of businesses contains vast listings of telephone numbers and addresses that are mostly up to date, plus food and venue reviews too.

Explore BGC (www.fbdcorp.com) Handy website providing an overview of everything Bonifactio Global City (aka Fort Bonifacio) on where to sleep, eat and things to do.

Make it Makati (www.makeitmakati.com) Excellent website with listings of accommodation, restaurants and upcoming events in Makati City area.

ℹ️ Getting There & Away

AIR

All international flights in and out of Manila use one of the three main terminals of Ninoy Aquino International Airport (NAIA; p449) in Manila's south, while many domestic flights use a fourth, domestic, terminal. The four terminals share runways, but they are not particularly close to each other. 'Airport Loop' shuttle vans (P20, 7am to 10pm) link the four terminals, but it's slow and sporadic, so take a taxi if you're in a hurry.

International

At the time of research the P550 departure tax for international departures out of NAIA was set to be integrated into the airfare, so you won't have to pay at the airport.

Take note that several Asian discount carriers fly to Clark International Airport (Diosdado Macapagal Airport, DMIA) in the Clark Special Economic Zones, a two-hour drive north of Manila.

Domestic

The main domestic carriers are PAL Express (PAL) and low-cost carrier Cebu Pacific. Tigerair Philippines and AirAsia Zest are also popular.

One-way flights cost P1000 to P3000 (including taxes) on most routes, provided you book in advance. Flight times range from 45 minutes for short hops such as Manila to Caticlan, to 1½ hours for flights from Manila to southern Mindanao.

The following airlines fly domestically in and out of Manila. All have ticket offices at their terminal of departure or around town.

AirAsia Zest (www.airasia.com; NAIA Terminal 4) Flights to Cebu, Boracay (Kalibo), Puerto Princesa, Tagbilaran, Davao, Iloilo, Bacolod and Cagayan de Oro.

PAL Express (☑ 02-855 8888; www.philippine-airlines.com; NAIA Terminals 2 & 3)

Cebu Pacific (Map p50; ☑ 702 0888; www.cebupacificair.com; NAIA Terminal 3)

ITIAIR (Map p50; ☑ 02-851 5664; www.itiair.com; ITI Hangar No 5-03-127, Andrews Ave, Pasay) Serves El Nido from Manila; primarily for guests of the offshore El Nido Resorts. Note its termnial is located in Pasay City, not NAIA.

Tigerair Philippines (☑ 02-7020 888; www.tigerair.com/ph/en/; Terminal 4) Recently taken over by Cebu Pacific.

BOAT

The flashy **Manila North Harbor Port** (Map p50; www.mnhport.com.ph; Piers 4 & 6, Tondo), northwest of Binondo, is the new departure and arrival point for all domestic ferry travel. The South Harbour is now used for cargo and international cruise ships.

It's best to take a taxi to North Harbor, as Tondo district isn't a place for a foreigner to be wandering around with luggage.

2GO Travel (Map p50; ☑ 02-528 7000; http://travel.2go.com.ph; Pier 4, Manila North Harbor Port) The major shipping lines handling inter-island boat trips from Manila. It has an excellent website for checking schedules and reserving tickets. Tickets can be purchased online, through travel agents, major malls or its main branch in Rizal Park (Map p52; The Hub @ Kilometer Zero, Rizal Park).

For ferries to Boracay, you'll need to head to Batangas pier.

Moreta Shipping Lines (☑ 02-359-6568; www.moretashipping.com; Pier 6, Manila North Harbor Port) Sails every five days to Caticlan (for Boracay) via the town of Roxas; Puerto Princesa on Palawan twice a week; and also has services to Bacolod on Negros, and Kalibo and Dumaguit on Panay.

Romblon Shipping Lines (☑ 243 5886; www.romblonshippinglines.com; Pier 8, Manila North Harbor Port) Sails weekly to Mandaon, Masbate and several ports on Romblon.

BUS

Getting out of Manila by bus is harder than you might expect, as there is no central bus terminal.

Instead, myriad private operators serve specific destinations from their own terminals.

The two main 'clusters' of terminals are known as **Cubao**, which is in Quezon City near the corner of EDSA and Aurora Blvd; and **Pasay**, which is along EDSA near the LRT/MRT interchange (Pasay Rotunda).

Two harder-to-reach clusters are **Sampaloc**, north of Quiapo near the University of Santo Tomas (UST); and **Caloocan** in the far north of Metro Manila.

If heading north, try to get buses that say 'SC-TEX', as these shave up to two hours off any trip by taking the new Subic–Clark–Tarlac Expressway.

Bus Companies

Amihan Bus Lines (Map p66; ☑ 02-387 1790; www.amihanbuslines.com.nu; Araneta Bus Terminal, Cubao)

Cagsawa Ermita (Map p56; ☑ 02-525 9756; P Faura Centre, P Faura St); Cubao (Map p66; ☑ 02-998 9050; Araneta Bus Terminal)

Ceres (Map p58; cnr Taft & Sen Gil Puyat, Pasay, Buendia Terminal)

Dagupan Bus Co (Map p66; ☑ 727 2330; cnr EDSA & New York Ave, Cubao)

DLTB (Map p58; ☑ 986-2771; www.dltbbus.com.ph; cnr Taft & Sen Gil Puyat Aves, Pasay, Buendia Terminal)

Dominion Bus Lines (Map p66; ☑ 02-727 2350; cnr EDSA & New York Ave, Cubao)

Fariñas Transit (☑ 731 4507; cnr Laong Laan & M de la Fuente Sts, Sampaloc)

Five Star Bus Lines (Map p58; ☑ 853 4772; Aurora Blvd, Pasay)

Florida Bus Lines (Map p50; ☑ 781 5894; cnr Extremadura & Earnshaw Sts, Sampaloc)

Genesis Pasay Terminal (Map p58; ☑ 02-853 3511; www.genesistransport.com.ph; Pasay Rotunda) Cubao (Map p66; ☑ 02-709 0545; www.genesistransport.com.ph; cnr New York Ave & EDSA)

Isarog Bus Lines (Map p66; ☑ 02-925 6835; Araneta Bus Terminal)

Jac Liner (Map p58; ☑ 02-404 2073; www.jacliner.com; cnr Taft & Sen Gil Puyat Aves, Pasay, Buendia Terminal; ☎)

Jam Liner (Map p58; ☑ 02-425 5489; www.jam.com.ph; cnr Taft & Sen Gil Puyat Aves, Pasay, Buendia Terminal; ☎)

Ohayami (Map p50; ☑ 02-516 0501; www.ohayamitrans.com; cnr Fajardo St & Lacson Ave, Sampaloc)

Partas Pasay Terminal (Map p58; ☑ 400 5115; Aurora Blvd, Pasay) Cubao (Map p66; ☑ 400 5115; cnr Aurora Blvd & Bernadino St)

Philtranco (Map p58; www.philtranco.com.ph; cnr EDSA & Apelo Cruz, Pasay)

RRCG (Map p58; ☑ 0932 741 9885; cnr Taft & Sen Gil Puyat Aves, Pasay, Buendia Terminal)

RSL (Map p56; ☑ 0917 593 6024; Padre Faura Center, P Faura St, Ermita)

San Agustin (Map p58; Pasay Rotunda, cnr Taft Ave & EDSA)

Victory Liner Pasay Terminal (Map p58; ☑ 02-833 5019-20; cnr EDSA & Taft Ave, Pasay) Cubao (Map p66; ☑ 02-727 4534; cnr EDSA & New York Ave); Kamias (Map p66; ☑ 02-920 7396; cnr EDSA & East Ave, Kamias, Quezon City); Sampaloc (Map p50; ☑ 02-559 7735; www.victoryliner.com; 551 Earnshaw St, Sampaloc)

North Luzon

Comfortable 27-seat 'deluxe' express buses are well worth the extra coin to Baguio and Vigan.

It's recommended to book these, and the direct night buses to Banaue, a day or more ahead.

To Baguio, Ilocos & Zambales

Several bus lines run 27-seat 'deluxe' overnight express buses to Vigan and Laoag. It's recommended to book these a day or two ahead.

Mindoro

For Puerto Galera on Mindoro, several companies (including Discovery Islands (p87) at Swagman Hotel) run combination bus/boat services, leaving around 8am from Ermita. These take about four hours and cost roughly P350 more

BUSES FOR MANILA

DESTINATION	DURATION (HR)	PRICE (P)	COMPANY	FREQUENCY
Baguio	5-7	air-con–deluxe 445–760	Genesis, Victory Liner, Dagupan	frequent
Baler	5	fan–deluxe 450–700	Genesis	morning buses
Balanga	3-4	210-400	Genesis	frequent
Banaue	8½-10	450-550	Florida, Ohayami	2-4 night buses
Batangas	2-2½	120-167	Jam Transit, RRCG, DLTB, Ceres	every 20min
Bolinao	7	350–470	Victory Liner, Dagupan, Five Star	6-7 buses
Clark Airport	2-3	450	Philtranco	6.30am, 11.30am, 8.30pm
Dau (Angeles)	2-3	139-150	Victory Liner	frequent
Iba	5-7	367	Victory Liner	6-7 buses
Laoag	8-12	750-850	Fariñas, Partas, Florida	frequent
Legazpi	10-12	air-con–deluxe 850–1100	Isarog, Cagsawa, Philtranco, DLTB, Amihan, RSL	frequent
Lucena	4-5	210	JAC, DLTB, Jam	frequent
Naga	8-10	air-con–deluxe 670–900	Cagsawa, Isarog, Philtranco, DLTB, Amihan, RSL	frequent
Santa Cruz (for Pagsanjan)	2½-3	140	DLTB, Greenstar	frequent
San Fernado (La Union)	6	378–436	Dominion, Partas	hourly
San Pablo (for Mt Banahaw)	2½-3	127-150	Jam, DLTB, Jac	hourly
Solano (for Banaue)	8	320	Florida, Victory Liner	frequent
Subic Bay (Olangapo)	3-4	air-con–express 207–235	Victory Liner	frequent
Tagaytay	2-3	114	San Agustin	hourly
Tuguegarao	12	650	Victory Liner, Florida	evening buses
Vigan	7-12	air-con–deluxe 580–680	Florida, Partas, Dominion	hourly

than going the individual route and taking a bus to Batangas pier, then a boat to Puerto Galera.

Si-Kat (Map p56; ☎ 02-708 9628; Citystate Tower Hotel, 1315 Mabini St, Ermita) Tickets to Puerto Galera P800. Departure at 8.30am.

To Southeast Luzon

The hub for Bicol-bound buses is **Araneta Bus Terminal** (Map p66; btwn Times Sq & Gen Romulo Aves, Cubao) with myriad 'ordinary' (non-air-con) buses and pricier deluxe buses with three fully reclining seats per row. Otherwise Cagsawa and RSL have coveted overnight buses departing straight from Ermita.

Clark Airport

For Clark Airport, take the Philtranco shuttle, which stops to pick up passengers at Mega Mall in Ortigas on the way out of town. Or just take any northbound bus to the Malabacat terminal in Dau (near Angeles), a short taxi ride from Clark.

LONG-DISTANCE BUSES

Philtranco and a few other bus companies run a masochists-only trip along the so-called 'Nautical Highway' to Davao in Mindanao (fan/air-con P1185/2445) via Samar, Leyte and Surigao City (two days, three daily).

CAR & MOTORCYCLE

If you are driving, the North and South Luzon Expressways are the quickest ways to disentangle yourself from Manila. They are relatively expensive tollways (pricey even by Western standards) but that just serves to cut traffic significantly.

TRAIN

Philippine National Railways (PNR; Map p50; ☎ 02-319 0041; www.pnr.gov.ph) wasn't running its long-distance trains heading to Bicol in Southeast Luzon at the time of research, but there were plans to resume the service. It runs from Tutuban Station in Tondo to Naga (prices approximately seat/sleeper/executive P600/1000/1500, 10 hours) with five quick stopovers in Lucena, Hondagua, Tagkawayan, Cagay and Sipocot. Trains leave at 6.30pm from both stations.

ℹ Getting Around

For many, the worst part of Manila will simply be getting around. Like many Asian metropolises it has enormous traffic problems. Add in rush hour, rain or both and you've got a quagmire. Fortunately there's one thing local transport isn't: expensive. Even a cab will seldom cost more than P250 for the longest journey.

Even cheaper are the jeepneys, which go everywhere in a confusing muddle, but also find themselves stuck in the same traffic despite the best kamikaze-like efforts of the drivers.

The LRT and MRT trains are an excellent way to soar over and past traffic. The only downsides are the lack of comprehensive coverage of the city and the mobs using the trains at rush hour.

TO/FROM THE AIRPORT & BOAT DOCKS

As there are no direct public transport routes from either of the four terminals to Malate or Makati, bite the bullet and take a taxi, especially if you have a bit of luggage. Ninoy Aquino International Airport (NAIA) is quite close to the city and, barring traffic, you can get to Malate or Makati by taxi in 20 minutes.

There are ranks for yellow airport metered taxis, which have a flagfall of P70 (regular metered taxis on the street have a P40 flagfall) just outside the arrivals areas of the three international terminals. Your total bill to Malate should be about P200; closer to P250 if you're travelling to Makati.

Option one is the white, prepaid 'coupon' taxis that charge set rates of more than P440 to Malate and P530 to Makati. These can be found just outside the arrivals area at all four airport terminals.

To save a few pesos you can walk upstairs to the arrivals area of any of the terminals and angle for a regular metered taxi on a drop-off run. These will save you P70 to P100 to either Makati or Malate.

The domestic airport has an easy-to-find taxi rank with regular metered taxis outside.

Braving public transportation from the airport is tricky and involves several changes. It probably isn't worth the trouble, given how cheap taxis are, but if you insist, walk out to the main road and hail any 'Baclaran' jeepney. In Baclaran you can get on the LRT or switch to a Malate-bound jeepney.

At NAIA's Terminal 3, an 'Airport Loop' shuttle bus (P20) runs every 15 minutes from 7am to 10pm straight from the terminal to the MRT/LRT exchange at **Pasay Rotunda** (Map p58; cnr EDSA & Taft Ave), where public transport is readily available to take you to Malate or Makati. Walk out of the terminal and go right – don't confuse this with the other 'Airport Loop' shuttle that connects the four terminals. The van operates from Pasay Rotunda to the airport according to the same schedule.

If you arrive in Manila by boat, you're also better off catching a taxi into town, as the harbour is a pretty rough area and public transport routes are complicated.

TAXI

Taxis in Manila are cheap and plentiful. Flagfall is a mere P40 for the first kilometre, plus P3.5 for every 300m (or two minutes of waiting time) after that. A 15- to 20-minute trip rarely costs more than P150 or so.

Most taxi drivers will turn on the meter; if they don't, politely request that they do. If the meter is 'broken' or your taxi driver says the fare is 'up to you', the best strategy is to get out and find another cab (or offer a low-ball price).

Rigged taxi meters are becoming more common in Manila. If you see the meter changing within the first 500m and/or racing up suddenly, you're being had. The first five minutes in a properly metered taxi in normal Manila traffic should not bring the meter past P50 to P60.

JEEPNEY

For the uninitiated, Manila jeepneys can be a challenging experience. The long-wheel-base jeeps offer a bewildering array of destinations and, though these destinations are written on signboards stuck in the window, few people arrive exactly where they intend to on their first jeepney ride. However, if you stick to the more common routes, you shouldn't go too far astray.

Heading south from Quiapo Church, jeepneys to 'Baclaran' pass Ermita/Malate along MH del Pilar St, continue close to the CCP, cross EDSA and end up at the Baclaran LRT stop. From Quiapo Church you can also take 'Kalaw' jeepneys to Ermita.

Heading north from Baclaran, jeepneys pass along Mabini St or Taft Ave, heading off in various directions from Rizal Park:
➡ 'Divisoria' jeepneys take Jones Bridge, passing close to the office of the Bureau of Immigration, and end up at Divisoria Market.
➡ 'Monumento' jeepneys pass the Manila Central Post Office and roll over the MacArthur Bridge before passing the Chinese Cemetery and the Caloocan bus terminals.
➡ 'Quiapo' and 'Cubao' jeepneys take Quezon Bridge, passing Quiapo Church. 'Cubao via España' jeepneys continue to the Cubao bus stations via UST and the Sampaloc bus stations.

LRT & MRT

Manila's metro system is a good way to avoid Manila's notorious traffic in air-conditioned comfort during off-peak hours. However it's best to avoid during rush hour when huge crowds make it virtually unusable due to long queues.

The LRT (Light Rail Transit) has two elevated lines. The LRT-1 runs from Monumento in the north to Baclaran in the south, interchanging with the MRT at the corner of EDSA and Taft Ave near Pasay Rotunda. The LRT-2 runs from Recto in the west to Santolan in the east, interchanging with the MRT in Cubao.

The MRT (Metro Rail Transit) travels a south–north route along EDSA. It is handy for getting to and from the Ayala Centre in Makati and to Quezon City.

Electronic farecards are usually good for one trip only; a disingenuous system that produces huge lines at ticket booths during rush hour. Fares (P12 to P15) are dependent on distance. Some stations sell 'stored-value cards' worth up to P100, which are good for three months, but these can be hard to find.

FX/UV EXPRESS

Manila has numerous white air-con Toyota UV Express vans that follow similar routes to the jeepneys, picking up and setting down passengers en route. The fare is P30 for long rides and P20 for shorter hops.

FERRY

At the time of research the **Pasig River Ferry** was in the process of resuming its water bus service, which will provide a novel way of getting to Intramuros from Makati and Pasig.

TRICYCLE

Motorised tricycles are useful for short hops around town. Short journeys should cost anywhere from P40 to P50, depending on how well you bargain. Push tricycles, or pedicabs, are a cheaper alternative in a few areas, such as Malate.

BUS

Local buses are only really useful to get to places on the main roads such as Taft Ave, España Blvd, Buendia (aka Sen Gil Puyat Ave) or EDSA, as they are prohibited from most streets in the centre of town. Depending on the journey, ordinary buses cost from P10 to P15; air-con buses cost from P10 to P25.

Like jeepneys, buses have their destinations written on signboards placed against the front windshield, for example 'Ayala' (for Ayala Centre) and 'Monumento' (for Caloocan).

CAR & MOTORCYCLE

Because of traffic and unorthodox local driving habits, renting a self-drive car or motorcycle to get around Manila is not recommended. On the other hand, a rental car is a great way to visit the attractions outside Metro Manila, many of which are hard to reach by public transport.

Your best bet is to arrange a taxi and driver through your hotel (or trustworthy source), which will you set you back anywhere from P2000 to P4000 per day.

Otherwise if you want to drive yourself, international car-rental companies have offices at the airport terminals and some major hotels. Rates start at about P3000 per day. Local car-rental companies tend to be cheaper.

Avis (Map p62; ☑ 02-462 2881; www.avis.com.ph)

Nissan (☑ 02-854 7099; www.nissanrentacar.com)

Triple A Car Rental (☑ 0920 926 5750, 895 4382; tr-a@pldtdsl.net; 1158 Antipolo St, Makati) Hires out vehicles from around P2000 per day, plus P500 for a driver (mandatory). Good, honest service.

Around Manila

Why Go?

After the urban joys of Manila have exhausted you, you'll probably be ready for some fresh air. Believe it or not, it's in ample supply in the hilly regions surrounding Manila.

The area south of Manila is home to a clutch of interesting military history sights and some of the most dramatic landscapes you'll find anywhere. Volcanoes are the speciality, with some impressive sea- and townscapes thrown in.

Head north and you'll run square into the most notorious volcano of them all, Mt Pinatubo, in the underrated Zambales Mountains. It overlooks the twin ex-military bases of Subic and Clark, now struggling to become tourism hubs.

Though it's possible to visit these places as day trips, getting out of Manila can take the bulk of the morning, so it's better to do overnight stays.

Best Places to Eat

➜ Antonio's (p98)
➜ Kinabuhayan Cafe Bed & Breakfast (p102)
➜ Josephine (p98)
➜ Feliza Café y Taverna (p99)
➜ The Castle (p106)

Best Places to Stay

➜ Kinabuhayan Cafe Bed & Breakfast (p102)
➜ Arthur's Place Dive Resort (p100)
➜ Villa Severina (p99)
➜ Sonya's Garden (p97)
➜ Alvin's Mt Pinatubo Guesthouse (p109)

When to Go

Manila

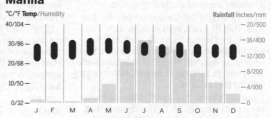

°C/°F Temp/Humidity — Rainfall inches/mm

Dec–Feb The coolest months are particularly welcome.

May Local peaks become places of refuge in the height of the hot season.

Aug–Oct Some surf on the Zambales Coast within range of Subic.

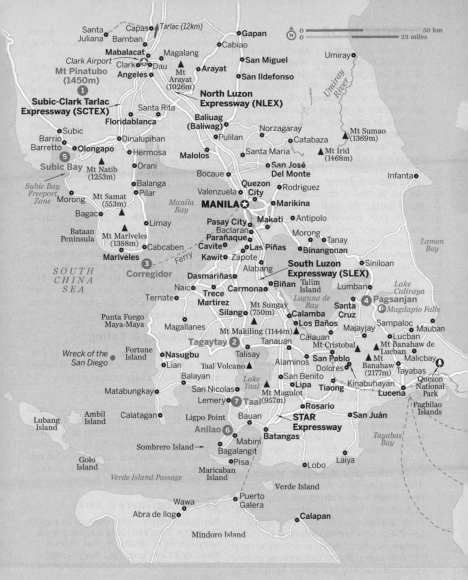

Around Manila Highlights

1 Journey to volcanic drama on **Mt Pinatubo** (p109).

2 Enjoy sumptuous views of Taal Volcano and sumptuous cuisine in **Tagaytay** (p95).

3 Immerse yourself in WWII history on a day trip from Manila to **Corregidor** (p94).

4 Paddle along the heart of darkness in **Pagsanjan** (p101).

5 Go to extremes amid the virgin forests and sunken wrecks in and around **Subic Bay** (p104).

6 Spend a weekend in **Anilao** (p100), offering the best diving close to the capital.

7 Wander the relaxed streets of **Taal** (p98), lined with heritage ancestral houses.

CORREGIDOR

The island of Corregidor (Corrector), 48km southwest of Manila and often referred to as 'The Rock', is a popular day trip from the capital. In the decades after WWII many of the visitors were history buffs and veterans, but now it's mostly locals who venture out here to enjoy the scenic island and its sweeping views.

The Spanish were the first to exploit Corregidor as the ideal first line of defence against trespassers. It was the scene of fierce fighting during WWII, and became the last bastion of resistance by American forces during the Japanese invasion of Luzon in 1941. General Douglas MacArthur holed up here until March 1942, when he fled to Australia. His successor, General Jonathan Wainwright, finally surrendered to the Japanese in May 1942. Huge numbers of American and Filipino prisoners of war died on the Bataan Death March from Mariveles to the concentration camp in Capas.

Corregidor was occupied by the Japanese until January 1945, when MacArthur returned. The second battle for the island was no less bloody than the first, and thousands died.

◎ Sights & Activities

There are, as you'd expect, numerous war monuments and ruins on the island. Significant sights include General MacArthur's HQ, the mile-long barracks, various gun batteries and the Spanish lighthouse, which offers good views over Manila Bay. Also worthwhile is the Japanese Cemetery, which is understated and formal.

Admission to all of the above is included in the packages run by Sun Cruises (☑02-831 8140; www.corregidorphilippines.com; CCP Complex jetty, Pasay; ferry only weekday/weekend P1300/1400, excursion incl lunch weekday/weekend P2250/2500, walking tour without lunch P1700), Corregidor's main tour operator. Tours are conducted on open-air buses modelled on the electric trolleys used by the Americans. Otherwise there are walking tours (P1700 not including lunch), though you won't cover as much ground.

If you opt to take the ferry but not join the Sun Cruises tour, you can sign up for a more engaging, personalised tour with Old Manila Walks (p65) led by WWII-buff Ivan Man Dy.

Malinta Tunnel BUNKER

Completed in 1932 after 10 years of construction, the Malinta Tunnel complex is built into the side of a hill and was used by the Americans as a bombproof bunker, for ammunition storage, and also as a hospital. The tunnel spans 250m, with numerous laterals branching off, one of which was used as General MacArthur's HQ. At times there is a sound-and-light show, in case you need audio and visual cues to imagine the drama here in 1941–42. Some areas still have typewriters and other furnishings sitting untouched from that time.

Pacific War Memorial MEMORIAL

The American-built Pacific War Memorial, at the island's highest point (210m), is a shrine to the thousands from both sides who died in the conflict. There's a symbolic metal flame and an open-topped dome that catches the sun on 6 May, the day on which the island fell. Also here is a small museum with photos, medals, gas masks, samurai swords and Japanese pistols.

🛏 Sleeping & Eating

The only restaurant on the island is Corregidor Inn, where a buffet lunch is served as part of the package tour, or you can order à la carte.

Corregidor Inn INN $$

(☑0917 527 6350; www.corregidorphilippines.com; s/d incl breakfast P1500/2000; ❄ ≋) An attractive hotel with wood floors, fine coastal views, rattan furniture and capiz windows. Has a swimming pool too. Book through Sun Cruises.

❶ Getting There & Away

Sun Cruises has the market cornered for trips to Corregidor. It loads up 100 to 200 passengers every morning at 7.30am; you shall return to Manila by 3.45pm, unless you stay overnight. The price includes lunch and a comprehensive tour of the island.

The only other way to get to Corregidor is to charter a bangka (wooden boat) from Mariveles (P2500 to P3000, two hours).

SOUTH OF MANILA

There is a range of short-trip options south of Manila. The most popular attractions fill up with crowds from the capital on weekends, so visit on a weekday if possible.

Las Piñas

🗺02

The once-tiny village of Las Piñas, 5km south of Pasay (Manila), has long been swallowed up by metro Manila, but the centre has a bit of a village atmosphere and many of its buildings have been restored using traditional methods.

The principal attraction here is the bamboo organ in the attractive San Joseph Parish Church (🗺825 7190; www.bambooorgan.org; Quirino Ave; admission incl tour P50; ☺8am-noon & 2-6pm Tue-Sun, by appt Mon). The famous organ was built between 1816 and 1821, a particularly lean period, by the Spanish priest Padre Diego Cera, who instructed bamboo to be used instead of the more expensive metal for the majority of the organ pipes. The horizontal trumpets are, however, made of metal.

A short organ concert is included in the price of admission. In the second week of February, organists from around the world gather here for the Bamboo Organ Festival.

To get to Las Piñas, take a Baclaran–Zapote–Alabang jeepney from the Baclaran LRT stop and have the driver drop you off at the church.

Kawit

🗺046 / POP 76,000

History buffs should venture 20km south of Manila to view the Aguinaldo Mansion (www.nhcp.gov.ph/baldomero-aguinaldo-shrine; Tirona Hwy; admission free; ☺8am-4pm Tue-Sun) FREE in the town of Kawit. Here the revolutionary army of General Emilio Aguinaldo proclaimed Philippine Independence on 12 June 1898 – a triumph soon quashed by the Americans. The alluring mahogany-and-*nara*-wood house, built in 1849, is now a shrine, and you can tour Aguinaldo's private rooms and see his much-loved bowling alley. The general died in 1964 after a very long life that included a period of chumminess with the Japanese occupiers.

Pick up buses and jeepneys to Kawit at the Baclaran LRT stop or along Roxas Blvd in Pasay.

Calamba

🗺049 / POP 360,300

Calamba, southeast of Manila on the shores of the Laguna de Bay, was the birthplace of Philippine national hero José Rizal. The Rizal Shrine (cnr Rizal & Mercado Sts; admission free; ☺8am-4pm Tue-Sun) FREE is in the rebuilt (in the 1950s) Spanish colonial house where Rizal was born. On display are numerous items of Rizal memorabilia.

For Calamba, take either DLTB or Greenstar buses (P100, one hour).

Tagaytay, Taal Volcano & Lake Taal

🗺046 / POP 62,000

On a clear day, Lake Taal is truly a marvel to behold. From Tagaytay you can peer straight down into the simmering, multiple craters of active Taal Volcano – also known as Volcano Island – rising out of the middle of the lake 600m beneath you.

Lake Taal and Volcano Island lie within a massive prehistoric volcano crater measuring roughly 75km around. This ancient crater forms Tagaytay Ridge, upon which sits the town of Tagaytay. Like a set of Russian matryoshka dolls, Taal Volcano in turn encircles its own little crater lake, itself containing a small island.

Tagaytay is a relaxed town that seems to meander forever along Tagaytay Ridge. Lying just 60km south of Manila, it is everything the capital is not: cool, clean, gorgeous and oxygenated. The Tagaytay area is also known as something of a foodie haven.

The nature of the town changes dramatically on weekends, when the Manila hordes arrive and traffic jams appear.

Sitting directly down the hill from Tagaytay is the small lakeside town of Talisay, where bangkas depart for the volcano.

Tagaytay Rotunda, at the intersection of the road to Silang, is a useful landmark that separates the eastern and western halves of Tagaytay Ridge. Just off the rotunda is the main commercial centre, Olivares Plaza.

◉ Sights & Activities

Taal Volcano   HIKING, VOLCANO
(entry P50) Once you've enjoyed the sight of mist tickling Taal Volcano from afar, it's time to get up close and personal. Notoriously dusty and hot, it's neither a difficult climb nor a particularly rewarding one.

By far the most popular of several possible hikes is the well-worn trail up to the main crater overlooking an evil-looking sulfurous pool. The walk takes about 35 minutes (or you can hire a tired old horse for

DETOX AT SAN BENITO

The Philippines' signature wellness and detoxification centre is the **Farm at San Benito** (☑02-884 8074; www.thefarm.com.ph; r from P6300; ❊ @ ❂ ❈), a peaceful paradise hidden in the jungle less than a two-hour drive south of Manila, near Lipa City. Besides a bevy of detox and spa treatments, the resort has a mouthwatering vegan restaurant, tropical hardwood and bamboo suites and luxurious villas.

This is a great place to try therapeutic coffee scrubs and traditional Hilot massages or gorge on the restaurant's surprisingly filling five-course raw-food meals. The suites are lovely, while the villas are as plush as you'll get, some with private pools and beautifully landscaped gardens. The place occasionally draws A-list international celebrities.

P500); guides charge around P200, but it's easy enough to go alone.

The bulk of Volcano Island emerged from the lake during a savage eruption in 1911, which claimed hundreds of lives. Since then frequent eruptions have sculpted and re-sculpted the island's appearance. With more than 47 craters and 35 volcanic cones, Taal Volcano remains one of the world's deadliest volcanoes.

The main Taal crater is in the middle of the island (the obvious cone visible from the ridge is Binitiang Malaki, which last erupted in 1715). The most active crater is Mt Tabaro, on the west side, which saw dramatic lava flows in the late 1960s and mid-1970s.

The launch point for bangkas out to Volcano Island is the lakeside town of Talisay, where dozens of operators vie for the attention of arriving tourists. Depending on where you hire them, bangkas to the island (20 minutes) cost P1200 to P1800 for the whole boat. The best place to arrange this is one of the many ramshackle resorts that line the lakefront west of Talisay proper.

More adventurous hiking options on Volcano Island include rigorous all-day treks up Mt Tabaro or the south ridge of Taal's main crater, from where there's a trail leading down to the crater lake. Only a few guides make these trips; they charge around P500, plus a bit extra for a bangka ride around to the south side of the island (P3000 for up to six people).

For all the walks bring plenty of drinking water and a hat, as there's little shelter from the relentless sun.

The **Philippine Institute of Volcanology & Seismology** (Philvolcs; ☑773 0293; Barangay Buco, Talisay; ☺24hr) **FREE**, on the lakeside 3km west of the junction (where the road from Tagaytay terminates) houses a monitoring station, with on-site museum detailing previous eruptions and seismographs of recent events. If the door is locked just knock and somebody will materialise to let you in.

Taal Lake Yacht Club   SAILING
(☑773 0192; www.tlyc.com; Barangay Santa Maria, Talisay; ☺8am-6pm) Here you can arrange Hobie 16 catamarans (P3800 per day), single-sail Toppers (P1800 per day) or tandem sea kayaks (per hour/day P400/1200) for a unique way of getting out on to the lake. It also arranges sailing lessons, and can guide you up and down a 'secret trail' on the back side of Volcano Island (P3350 for the boat and guide). It's located 1km west of the Tagaytay road junction.

People's Park in the Sky   VIEWPOINT
(admission P30; ☺7.30am-6.30pm) Improbably perched on a towering mound of earth at Tagaytay's eastern end, this is Ferdinand Marcos' unfinished summer home. It remains a crumbling yet appealing ruin, with a decrepit Greek-style amphitheatre and a smattering of tourist attractions on the grounds. A newly constructed weather tower looms over everything. The 360-degree view of the area is indeed spectacular. Try the doughy rolled coconut snacks sold by vendors in the parking lot. It's 8.5km east of the Tagaytay Rotunda. Jeepneys go out here from Olivares Plaza.

🛏 Sleeping

Visitors have the choice of staying in Tagaytay overlooking the lake and volcano, or directly on the lake itself in Talisay. While Tagaytay is much further from the lake, it has the advantage of stunning panoramic vistas, an excellent choice of restaurants and better quality, more affordable accommodation. Tailisay meanwhile is perfect for those seeking a sleepy getaway, but hotels are a bit rundown.

Tagaytay

Our Melting Pot
HOSTEL $

(0917 400 0960; www.ourmeltingpottagaytay.com; 75 Smokey Hill; dm P400, r with shared/private bathroom from P800/1050; 🛜) Brought to you by the team that runs the popular Makati hostel (p72), OMP is hands down Tagaytay's best budget option. It's a homely retreat with a peaceful location down a quiet residential street. There's a good selection of sparkling, bright-blue private rooms and dorms to choose from, a homely lounge, a rooftop area and a kitchen for guests' use. Rates include a simple breakfast.

Keni Po
HOTEL $$

(483 0977; www.keniporooms.blogspot.com; 110 Calamba Rd; d P1200-1500; 🅿🛜❄) This valleyside place, 3.5km east of the rotunda, is the best of the lower midrange hotels, with small, well-kept doubles that include minibars, cable TV and shared balconies. The small pool out back is a nice touch.

Tagaytay Econo Hotel
HOTEL $$

(483 4284; Calamba Rd; r incl breakfast P1500-4480; 🅿@🛜) This well-maintained place, 2.7km east of the rotunda, is great value, although the budget rooms are somewhat dark. It overlooks the lake but sits on a busy intersection, so noise is a potential problem. Pricier rooms are further from the road and have lake views.

★ Sonya's Garden
B&B $$$

(0917 533 5140; www.sonyasgarden.com; Barangay Buck Estate, Alfonso; cottages: s/d incl breakfast & dinner P5000/6000; 🅿🛜) Alongside its lovely restaurant, Sonya's runs an exquisite B&B set among a beautiful flower garden. Rooms are attractive and rustic with thick rugs, and no TV to detract from the tranquility. Yoga, meditation and a full range of spa services are on offer. It's a way out of town; look for the well-marked turn-off before MC Mountain Home Apartelle, 13km west of the rotunda. Rates for doubles rise on weekends.

Joaquin's
B&B $$$

(483 0463; www.joaquinsbedandbreakfast.com; Aquinaldo Hwy; d incl breakfast Sun-Thu P4800, Fri & Sat P5800; 🅿🛜) A lovely rustic-style B&B where all rooms have sublime views of the lake and volcano from private balconies. Some of the common areas could do with a bit of maintenance, but rooms open up to high ceilings, and there are polished floorboards and arty touches throughout.

Taal Vista Hotel
HOTEL $$$

(413 1000; www.taalvistahotel.com; km 60 Aguinaldo Hwy; r from P5525; 🅿🅿@🛜❄) Faded no more, this 1970s relic has been smartly renovated and now boasts king-sized beds, downy linens and fancy bath products to complement outstanding views. Generous weekday promo rates are usually available. Wi-fi costs extra. It's 4km west of the rotunda.

Estancia
RESORT $$$

(413 1133; www.estanciatagaytay.com.ph; nipa hut/d incl breakfast from P4000/5100; 🅿🛜❄) There's a huge variety of rooms at this resort 1.3km east of the rotunda, but the rooms you want are the stilted stand-alone bamboo nipa huts in the back, which are set unobtrusively amid the jungle with balconies overlooking the lake.

Talisay

San Roque Paradise Resort
RESORT $$

(773 0271; Barangay Buco, Talisay; r P1500-2500; 🅿@🛜) Just east of the Philippine Institute of Volcanology & Seismology, in a well-kept compound in Talisay, this is by far the best option down by the lake. The 11 rooms are clean and the friendly family management will happily organise both local and out-of-town excursions. There's a swimming area on the lake. Meals cost P200 to P350.

Talisay Green Lake Resort
RESORT $$

(773 0247; www.taal-greenlakeresort.net; Barangay Sta Maria, Talisay; d/tr/q P1500/2000/2500; 🅿🛜❄) A solid choice on the lake, but mainly because of the decent swimming pool. Rooms themselves could do with a refurb. It's a good place to arrange transport for onward travel.

✗ Eating

Tagaytay features some of the Philippines' best restaurants; though many of them are located nowhere near the volcano but, rather, are nestled in secluded gardens north of the ridge road.

Java Jazz Cafe
CAFE $

(442 Calamba Rd; sandwiches from P65, mains P100; ☺9am-9pm Mon-Sat) Part coffee house, part gallery, this vibrant little cafe does good breakfasts, Filipino coffee and light lunches. Also has very basic rooms (from P980).

Mushroomburger
VEGETARIAN $

(Aguinaldo Hwy; burgers from P67; ☺6am-11pm; 🖉) A Tagaytay institution known for its incredibly cheap and tasty eponymous burgers (as well as your usual beef burgers etc). It's 300m west of Taal Vista Hotel.

★ **Josephine** FILIPINO $$
(www.josephinerestaurant.com; Km 58 Aguinaldo Hwy; mains P195-520; ⊙8am-9pm Mon-Fri, 7am-10.30pm Sat & Sun) Views don't come better than at Josephine, a long-running favourite that serves some of the best food on the ridge. Enjoy spectacular lake panoramas while feasting on anything from lavish seafood platters to Filipino classics. Does excellent cocktails too. It's 3km west of the rotunda.

Bag of Beans BAKERY $$
(www.bagofbeans.com.ph; 115 Aguinaldo Hwy; pies from P115, mains P200-500; ⊙6am-10pm; 🐾) Dine among hanging angel's trumpets, begonias and other exotic flowering plants on the garden patio of this superb bakery-restaurant specialising in English meat pies (they do a veggie one too), breakfasts, quality coffee and scrumptious desserts. It's 6.5km west of the rotunda.

Leslie's FILIPINO $$
(☎483 4271; Aguinaldo Hwy; mains from P200; ⊙8am-10pm) The central portion of Tagaytay ridge (around Starbucks) is dominated by several large Filipino *inahaw* (grill) restaurants where you can sample *tawili*, a tiny fish found exclusively in Lake Taal. Leslie's is the most famous of the lot, with some truly outstanding views of the lake. It's 1.8km west of the rotunda.

★ **Antonio's** INTERNATIONAL $$$
(☎0917 899 2866; www.antoniosrestaurant.ph; Barangay Neogan; set meals from P1500; ⊙11.30am-1.30pm & 5.30-8.30pm Tue-Sun; 🐾) One of the finest restaurants in the country, this upscale eatery offers the chance to rub elbows with politicians and oligarchs over delicious and delightfully presented dishes – if you can get a reservation. Seating areas include some lovely tables in elegant dining rooms overlooking lotus ponds and a lush tropical garden. The turn-off is 7.6km west of the rotunda.

Also has a superb garden cocktail bar. Book months ahead for weekends. Antonio's has two satellite restaurants along the ridge in Tagaytay proper that, while good, should not be confused with the original.

Sonya's Garden ORGANIC $$$
(☎0917 532 9097; www.sonyasgarden.com; buffet P683; ⊙11am-7pm) 🍃 One of Tagaytay's most beloved restaurants serves up famous buffet set-menu lunch and dinners. It features homemade pasta and produce grown organically in a sprawling garden that practically envelops diners. Reservations are essential.

ℹ Information

There are several internet cafes around Olivarez Plaza as well as banks and ATMs.

Talisay Tourism (☎773 0238; www.talisaybatangas.gov.ph/tourism; 2nd Fl, Municipal Office, Talisay-Tanauan Rd; ⊙8am-5pm Mon-Fri) Has a map and basic information on surrounding sights.

ℹ Getting There & Away

San Agustin buses from Pasay Rotunda in Manila rumble through Tagaytay (P114, two hours) on their way to Nasugbu or Calatagan. To return to Manila, hail a bus from the streetside shed at Olivarez Plaza or Mendez Crossing in town.

For those wanting to stay in Talisay you can also catch a bus heading to Batangas City and jump off at Tanauan (P95, 1½ hours) and get a jeepney/tricycle.

ℹ Getting Around

Frequent jeepneys traverse the ridge road from one end of town to the other.

To get to Talisay from Tagaytay take a jeepney (P35, 25 minutes, hourly) or tricycle (P300, 30 minutes) straight downhill from the Talisay turn-off, 4km east of the rotunda.

Taal

☎043 / POP 51,500
Not to be confused with Lake Taal or Taal Volcano, this charming township is instead famous for its heritage-listed colonial buildings. Its relaxed streets are lined with ancestral houses, and it makes a lovely overnight escape from Manila.

Having been awarded the status of a heritage-listed town ensures Taal's magnificent 19th-century buildings remain intact, and a current trend has seen a number of owners convert their homes into museums, B&Bs and restaurants.

Visit the **tourist office** (☎0917 501 8060; www.taal.gov.ph; ⊙8am-5pm) at the basilica for a map of where to find them, or better yet sign up for a walking tour (P500 per group) led by architect Robert Arambulo, the tourist officer and owner of Villa Severina B&B.

Many shops sell the town's famous embroidery and *balisong* (butterfly knives); be aware the latter is illegal in many countries.

Check out the excellent website www. taal.com.ph for a comprehensive overview of things to see, and places to eat and shop.

◉ Sights

Galleria Taal
ARCHITECTURE

(60 Agoncillo St; admission P70; ⊙8am-5pm) The stunning Galleria Taal is a good example of a well-preserved ancestral house, now converted into a fantastic vintage camera museum.

Basilica of St Martin de Tours
CHURCH

Originally built in 1759, before being destroyed and rebuilt between 1849 and 1865, this truly massive baroque-style basilica is one of the largest and oldest Catholic churches in Asia. It dominates Taal Park at its base.

🍽 Sleeping & Eating

★ Villa Severina
B&B $$

(☑0917 501 8060; villa.severina@yahoo.com; 55 JP Laurel St; r incl breakfast P2000; ❋ 🛜) A stunning ancestral house, built in 1870, with four rooms decked out in period features, each of different configurations and themes pertaining to French colonial cities (Pondicherry, Hanoi, Martinique) and to Paris itself. Styles vary so check them all out if you can. It has lovely common areas, hardwood floors, a well-equipped kitchen and breakfast included, served on its attractive outdoor terrace.

Don Juan BBQ
FILIPINO $

(www.donjuanbarbeque.wix.com; Calle Diokno St; mains from P75; ⊙9.30am-8.30pm Mon-Fri, from 7.30am Sat & Sun; ❋🛜) Don Juan sticks with the theme of the town with its replica ancestral-style building, and is well known for its Taal regional specialties such as *sinaing na tulingan* (native mackerel in banana leaf), *tawili* (freshwater fish endemic to Taal lake) and *boodle* (shared banquets) if you're in a group.

★ Feliza Café y Taverna
FILIPINO, SPANISH $$$

(☑740 0113; 6 F Agoncillo St; mains from P300; ⊙11am-10pm Tue-Thu, 10am-10.30pm Fri-Sun; ❋🛜) The former residence of Marcela Agoncillo – the seamstress who made the Philippines' first national flag – this superbly converted ancestral home has opened as a restaurant and B&B. The beautiful dining room has capiz windows and is full of antiques and memorabilia. There is also a lovely rear courtyard garden. The food is top-notch Filipino-Spanish, mixed with local specialities.

It's also a good place to pop in for a coffee and one of its delicious cakes. The charming rooms meanwhile are excellent value (rooms including breakfast P1000).

ℹ Getting There & Away

The town is 3km off the main road between Batangas and Tagaytay. From Manila or Tagaytay take the Jam bus from Cubao to Lemery (P150, three hours), from where you can take a tricycle.

Batangas

☑043 / POP 295,000

The busy industrial port of Batangas holds little appeal to travellers but is the jump-off point to Puerto Galera and a few other ports on Mindoro and Romblon.

🛏 Sleeping

There's no need to stay overnight unless you are unfortunate enough to miss the last ferry.

Travellers Hotel
HOTEL $$

(☑733 2309; New Access Rd; s/d P850/1050; ❋🛜) A comfortable and reasonably priced option with clean and colourful rooms fitted with wi-fi, cable TV and air-con. It's 1km from the terminal.

ℹ Getting There & Away

BUS

Most Batangas-bound buses from Manila go to the pier but double check with your driver. Make sure you get on an express bus to the pier via the speedy SLEX and STAR expressways (P180, 1½ hours). These are signboarded 'Batangas Pier' and/or 'derecho' (straight). Pick up buses to Manila right at the pier.

BOAT

Super Shuttle Roro has long-distance boats to Masbate (P800, 12 hours), Cebu (P1200, 24 hours) and Cagayan De Oro (P1400, 72 hours).

Boracay

2Go Travel (☑043-702 5525; www.travel.2go. com.ph; Terminal 2) Sails daily to Caticlan (P1300, nine hours) at 9pm.

Abra de Ilog & Calapan (Mindoro)

Several other companies also have car ferries to Calapan and Abra de Ilog.

SuperCat (☑723 8227; www.2go.com.ph; Terminal 3) Nine daily fastcraft to Calapan (fan/aircon P280/360, one hour) from 6.30am to 7pm.

FastCat (☑043-702 6983; www.fastcat.com. ph; Terminal 2) Eight boats per day to Calapan (P300, 1½ hours).

Montenegro Lines (📞740 3201; www.montenegrolines.com.ph; Terminal 3) Car ferries to Calapan (P192, 2½ hours) departing every four hours. Also six daily car ferries to Abra de Ilog (P260, 2½ hours).

Panay Island & Romblon

Montenegro Lines (📞740 3201; www.montenegrolines.com.ph; Terminal 3) Departs 5pm daily to Odiongan (P762, eight hours) daily. Monday, Thursday, and Saturday the same boat continues on to Romblon town (P954, 12 hours).

Navios Shipping (📞0908 146 2243; Terminal 3) Heads to Romblon (P900, 10 hours) on Tuesday, Friday and Saturday at 5pm.

Puerto Galera (Mindoro)

From terminal 3, speedy bangka ferries to Puerto Galera town (P230, one hour), Sabang (P230, one hour) and White Beach (P270, 1¼ hours) leave regularly throughout the day until about 5pm.

The boats usually sail unless there's a tropical storm brewing, but be prepared for a rough crossing. If it looks nasty, you might consider a sturdier car ferry to Calapan.

Anilao

📞043 / POP 650

Anilao, 30km west of Batangas on a small peninsula, is where the Philippines' first scuba-diving operators started back in the 1960s. While it has since been overtaken by places like Puerto Galera and Alona Beach (Bohol), it remains an extremely popular weekend destination for Manila-based divers.

The area empties out during the week, when resorts will be understaffed (so don't expect high levels of customer service). If you're not a diver, there's not a whole lot to keep you entertained, although the fine views and midweek solitude might appeal to some.

Anilao is the generic tourist name for the 13km peninsula that extends south from Anilao village (a barangay of Mabini). The dive resorts are strung out along the rocky western edge of the peninsula, linked by a winding sealed road.

🏃 Activities

Anilao is famed for its colourful corals and rich species diversity, which yield excellent macrophotography. There are good dive sites scattered around Balayan Bay and around the Sombrero and Maricaban Islands. Most resorts offer diving and some form of certification program; expect to pay around P800/1300 per dive with/without equipment.

🛏 Sleeping

Most Anilao resorts are isolated from each other and you may face 100 or more steps getting down to the resort from the road – two reasons people tend to stay put.

⭐**Arthur's Place Dive Resort**   RESORT $$
(📞0919 716 7973; www.arthurs-place.com; d without meals & fan/air-con P1250/2275; ❄) One of the few dive-oriented places that approaches the budget category, Arthur's has very liveable rooms with little patios around a grassy courtyard. To treat yourself, splash out on the family room (P3620) directly on the waterfront. It's 9.5km south of the turn-off in Anilao village.

Ligaya   RESORT $$
(📞02-553 7564; www.philtech.net/VillaLigaya; dm/d incl 3 meals per person from P2000/2700; ❄🛜) Ligaya has long been among our favourites for both the quality of the dive instruction – the owner is one of the country's top technical divers – and the backpacker-friendly dorm-style rooms. The accommodation is understated but comfortable.

Dive Solana   RESORT $$
(📞0908 876 5262; www.divesolana.com; r per person incl 4 meals from P3600; ❄@🛜) A good choice for those seeking some R & R, this reliable old-style resort is just the place to sit back and enjoy calm views overlooking the sparkling water. It's 10km south of the turn-off.

Dive & Trek   RESORT $$
(📞0910 936 4556, 02-851 8746; www.diveandtrek.com; r incl unlimited diving per person from P3850, non-diver per person P3000; ❄@🛝) Accessible only by boat, this is the place to really get away from it all. The unlimited diving and snorkelling on the house reef doesn't hurt too. The simple but comfortable rooms are in a pair of hillside bamboo-and-nipa complexes. Call ahead for a free boat transfer from the Dazu by Dazi resort, 1.5km south of the Anilao turn-off.

Pacifico Azul   RESORT $$
(📞0917 577 9270; www.pacificblueasia.com; r per person without meals, without bathroom P1600, with bathroom P2600-3600; ❄) The newly renovated budget rooms here are quirky but accommodating tree houses, or spend a little more for the well-appointed air-con rooms. The restaurant and common area, under a soaring canopy, is great; too bad there are no views. It's about 200m south of Ligaya resort.

❶ Getting There & Around

To get to Anilao from Manila take a bus to Batangas pier and get off just before the bridge leading over to the pier. From here frequent jeepneys head west to Anilao proper (P30, 30 to 45 minutes).

From Anilao proper, tricycles cost P40 for short trips, or P150 to P200 to the far resorts. The little **tourist office** (☑ 410 0607) on the pier in Anilao can help you get a good price.

Pagsanjan

☑ 049 / POP 35,900

The town of Pagsanjan (pag-san-*han*), 100km southeast of Manila, is where the popular canoe trips up the Pagsanjan River to Magdapio Falls begin. The town itself is fairly gritty with not much going on.

🏃 Activities

Magdapio Falls   CANOEING

The sole reason to come to Pagsanjan is for the river trip to Magdapio Falls, where some of the final scenes of Francis Ford Coppola's epic Vietnam War movie *Apocalypse Now* were filmed. Two *bangcero* (boatmen) paddle you upriver for 1½ hours through a dramatic gorge hemmed by towering cliffs and vegetation. At the top, the *bangcero* will take you under the 10m-high falls on a bamboo raft, an exhilarating moment as you pass directly through its high-pressure cascade.

From here, you let the water do the work, on the fast and exciting downstream return. The height of the wet season (August to October) is the best time to ride the rapids. At any time of year it's best to avoid weekends, as half of Manila seems to descend on Pagsanjan. Bring a plastic bag for your camera, and prepare to get wet.

To arrange your falls trip, secure a canoe from the **tourist office** (☑ 501 3544; ⊙ 8am–5pm) in the centre of town next to the plaza. A minimum of two people is required (boats fit three passengers); if you're travelling solo the tourist office will do its best to pair you with another. Only *bangcero* licensed and employed by the town government are allowed to operate boats, so be wary of the touts that stand along the highway offering boat trips to arriving tourists. Avoid paying more than the going rate for a boat (P1250 per person at the time of research).

It's customary and expected to tip your *bangcero*; P100 per person is suggested.

🛏 Sleeping & Eating

Sleeping options are decidedly simplistic, otherwise there's a few overpriced resorts near the falls launching point.

La Vista   GUESTHOUSE $

(☑ 501 1229; Garcia St; d without bathroom P450, with bathroom & air-con P1200; ❉ ❧) Right on the river in town, 150m west of the bridge, friendly, family-run La Vista has six clean doubles and is all up a good choice. There are an additional six passable budget fan rooms in a house across the street.

Willy Flores Guesthouse   GUESTHOUSE $

(☑ 0948 601 2086; Garcia St; r with fan P400) A basic, fairly rundown option that's more homestay than guesthouse, it's cheap and run by an affable family with heaps of knowledge of the area. Breakfast is P60 extra. It's 400m west of the bridge in the centre of town.

★ **Aling Taleng's Halo Halo**   FILIPINO $

(☑ 0916 309 3683; 169 General Luna St; halo-halo P65, meals for two P200-300; ⊙ 9am-8pm) What's better after a hot day on the river than a cup of sugary, milky *halo-halo,* the national icy treat? This simple place right by the bridge has been making dreams come true since 1933. Also does hearty homestyle meals.

Calle Arco   FILIPINO $$

(National Hwy; mains P120-300; ⊙ 10am-9pm) Easily the best restaurant in town, atmospheric Calle Arco adds uniquely Pagsanjan touches to Filipino fare. Try the chicken *sisig* (spicy and sour pork) fajitas (P120). Also has an attached Parisian-themed cafe.

❶ Getting There & Away

There are no direct buses to Pagsanjan, but regular DLTB and Greenstar buses link Manila (P140, 2½ hours) with nearby Santa Cruz. The Santa Cruz bus terminal is on the highway, about halfway to Pagsanjan; there are frequent jeepneys to/from Pagsanjan (P10).

Pick up jeepneys to Lucena and Lucban heading east along the main road in Pagsanjan.

Lucban

☑ 042 / POP 45,500

Hidden away in the foothills of Mt Banahaw, the quiet mountain town of Lucban comes alive on 15 May for **Pahiyas**, the harvest festival and feast of San Isidro Labrador. Locals compete for a prize by covering their houses in fruit, vegetables and wildly elaborate decorations made from multicoloured rice-

MISTY, MYSTIC MT BANAHAW

Descriptions of the vast dormant volcanic cone of Mt Banahaw (2177m), which looms over the entire southwest Luzon region, are almost always accompanied by the term 'mystic'. The mountain is said to be inhabited by a host of deities and spirits – most famously Filipino revolutionary hero and poet José Rizal, who was executed by the Spanish in 1896. A group called the 'Rizalistas' believe that Rizal was the reincarnation of Christ. No less than 75 cults have taken up residence on the mountain's lower reaches, living their lives dedicated to the spirits of Rizal and others that supposedly dwell in Banahaw's crater.

Though Mt Banahaw offers some of the most impressive hiking in southern Luzon, its summit is off limits to trekkers (until at least 2016) to prevent environmental damage caused by unchecked trekking and mass pilgrimages up the lower slopes of the mountain. You should contact **Protected Areas and Wildlife Bureau** (PAWB; ☑ 02-928 1178; www.pawb.gov.ph) in Manila to see if it's open, and obtain a permit to tackle it from trails from Tayabas and Lucban.

A trip to the Banahaw area is worth it whether you plan to climb the mountain or not. The long drive around the base of the mountain via San Pablo, Tiaong, Tayabas and Lucban is one of the prettiest in the country, with the misty mountain and its foothills – Mt Banahaw de Lucban (1875m) and Mt Cristobal (1470m) – constantly looming.

You can also visit the religious cults on Banahaw's lower slopes. One such group, the Suprema de la Iglesia del Ciudad Mistica de Dios, maintains a rather impressive compound on Mt Banahaw. A brief word of warning: always ask for permission before photographing cult members, and never pull out your camera inside their places of worship.

The ideal base for trips to Mt Banahaw is the town of **Dolores**. From Dolores a rugged dirt road leads you through several cult villages to the village of **Kinabuhayan**, home to the obscure Tres Persona sect, which worships 'the three personalities of God'. The main trailheads for both Mt Banahaw and Mt Cristobal are near Kinabuhayan.

Besides Mt Banahaw, Mt Cristobal and Mt Banahaw de Lucban, another good hiking option in this mountainous region of southwest Luzon is flora- and fauna-rich Mt Makiling near Los Baños. Leeches are rampant on all of these peaks in the wet season.

Sleeping & Eating

Kinabuhayan Cafe Bed & Breakfast (☑ 0916 221 5791; http://kinabuhayancafe.multiply. com; Dolores; r incl 3 meals P2250; ☎) The sleepy town of Dolores is home to one of the Philippines' most memorable guesthouses with open-air tree-house bamboo cottages resting in the canopy of a sprawling tamarind tree. Run by charismatic owner Jay Herrera, there are touches of genius throughout, from its bamboo bathroom with fish-pond bathtub, to the eccentric bar with full-size pool table.

Above all though, the main reason to visit is to gorge on Jay's exceptional cooking – his surprise dishes are among the tastiest, most creative in the country (snacks P100 to P200, large set meals P750). He also mixes delicious Lambanog-based cocktails (fermented coconut alcohol). Be sure to call ahead.

Bangkong Kahoy Valley (☑ 0929 819 8537; www.bkvalley.webs.com; Kinabuhayan; camping P100, r incl breakfast from P2000, chateau P25,000; ☎) In a spectacular natural setting between Mts Banahaw and Cristobal, this fantastic ecoresort consists of a range of open-air nipa cottages and hotel-style rooms, while for bigger groups (and honeymooners) there's a luxury chateau (sleeping 12) – with outdoor Jacuzzi to enjoy the Banahaw backdrop.

It's run by a passionate environmentalist who can arrange a number of walks, birdwatching and other activities, including a 120m-long zipline. The resort grows its own organic vegetables, has a clay tennis court and a rustic self-service bar.

Getting There & Away

Buses from Manila to Lucena pass through San Pablo (P130, 2½ hours), where you can pick up a jeepney to Dolores (35 minutes, frequent during daylight hours) at the public market. From Dolores there are infrequent jeepneys to Kinabuhayan village, or you can hire a tricycle (P300 return); to Bangkong Kahoy Valley you're looking at P350.

starch decorations called *kiping*. Giant papier-mâché effigies are marched through the streets to the church. It's a great festival and, best of all, locals are delighted to have foreigners join them in the bounty (if you want a room, book six months in advance).

At other times of the year, Lucban is pleasant enough, with narrow backstreets lined with old Spanish townhouses, and views of Mt Banahaw to the west. The attractive colonial **San Luis Obispo Parish Church**, dating from 1595 and rebuilt in 1737 after being destroyed by fire, is worth a visit. The tourist office is in the plaza here.

Pick up regular jeepneys to Lucena (P30, 45 minutes) and Pagsanjan (P44, one hour) from central Rizal St.

🛏 Sleeping & Eating

Lucban Summer Capital Inn GUESTHOUSE $
(☑ 042-540 3421; Racelis Ave; r with fan/air-con P500/950) A basic, but ultra friendly and homely budget choice; rooms 306 and 307 both look out to San Luis Obispo church.

Patio Rizal Hotel HOTEL $$
(☑ 540 2107; 77 Quezon Ave; d P2100-2600; ❋ 🛜) Situated in the centre of town, this colonial-style hotel is Lucban's best and has an excellent cafe overlooking a small plaza.

Mama Lydia's Special Siopao CHINESE $
(A Regidor St; dumplings from P80; ⊙ 7am-9pm) A Lucban institution, famous for its doughy pasty-shaped dumplings.

Cafe San Luis FILIPINO, ITALIAN $$
(cnr San Luis & Regidor Sts; mains from P190; ⊙ 8am-midnight) Attractive open-air bistro in Lucban's backstreets serving Filipino dishes, pizza and cold beers.

Lucena

☑ 042 / POP 236,500

Lucena, the capital of Quezon Province, is the departure point for passenger boats to Marinduque. We advise avoiding this gritty, tricycle-mad city, but if you get stuck for a night, there are a few OK sleeping options. Stay outside the centre if you value sleep.

🛏 Sleeping

Fresh Air Hotel & Resort HOTEL $
(☑ 710 2424; Tagarao St, Isabeng; r P325-1025; ❋ 🛜 ≋) Not even Hitchcock could dream up something this creepy, but at least it's cheap (and an option only really suitable for genu-

ine shoestringers). There's a run-down pool complex popular with families. It's out of the centre on the road to Batangas.

Sulu Plaza Hotel HOTEL $$
(☑ 660 5400; Diversion Rd; r incl breakfast from P1475; ❋ @ 🛜 ≋) A convenient location across from the bus station just outside the bustling town, with clean rooms and a massive pool – complete with a wave machine!

❶ Getting There & Away

BOAT
Boats to Marinduque depart from Dalahican port, which is 5km south of the huge Shoe Mart at the east end of Lucena. Dalahican port is not only a major port for travellers, but also for fishing. There's a P30 terminal fee.

Starhorse Shipping (☑ 0948 548 0767) has several departures to Balancan (P260, 2½ hours) in Marinduque, as does **Montenegro Lines** (☑ 047-373 7084), who also have a RORO (Roll on/Roll off) car ferry to Cawit at 4pm. **Kalayaan Shipping** has two weekly ferries to Magdiwang on Sibuyan Island in Romblon Province (P700, 17 hours) via Banton Island and Romblon town.

A tricycle to the port from Lucena costs from P50 to P75.

BUS & JEEPNEY
JAM Liner buses meets ferries to Manila's Buendia LRT stop in Pasay (P175, 3½ hours).

Otherwise from Grand Central, 5km north of town on Diversion Rd (National Hwy), **Lucena Lines** (☑ 0922 852 2096) heads to Manila (Pasay, P210, four hours) every 20 minutes. There's also frequent buses to Bicol (P420) and Legazpi (P450, eight hours).

Jeepneys connect Grand Central with Lucena's centre, from where you need to catch another string of jeepneys via SM Mall to Salahican port.

On the road to Batangas (near the Fresh Air Hotel & Resort) you can flag down frequent ordinary Supreme Lines buses to Batangas.

NORTH OF MANILA

The Bataan Peninsula north of Manila is the destination for those wishing to recall the fateful 1942 Death March. Otherwise the big draw is the Subic Bay area, with its nascent resort centre and many activities. Angeles remains unreformed and unreconstructed, although nearby Clark Airport is now home to a growing number of bargain airlines.

Looming over it all, and easier than ever to access, is volcanic Mt Pinatubo in the Zambales Mountains.

Olongapo & Subic Bay

🖉 047 / POP 227,300

Until 1992, Subic Bay was the base for the huge 7th Fleet of the US Navy – the largest outside the USA. The adjoining town of Olongapo was known for its sex industry, and not much else.

Though the US Navy has recently returned to Subic Bay on a semipermanent (and small-scale) basis, these days authorities are busy trying to remould the Subic Bay Freeport Zone (SBFZ), as the former military base is now known, into a legitimate business hub and family-friendly tourist destination.

The main attractions are a gorgeous bay, renowned wreck-diving, large tracts of pristine jungle and a smattering of beaches and amusement parks for kids. The Freeport Zone has a relaxed feel devoid of jeepneys and tricycles, and a pleasant waterfront strip of restaurants, bars and hotels. The same can't be said for the busy hub of Olongapo, which other than to catch a bus, offers no reason to hang about. The pungent canal divides Olongapo and the Freeport Zone, which feeds a slow-and-steady stream of raw sewage into Subic Bay. The Americans dubbed it 'Shit River' and it still goes by that moniker today.

◉ Sights & Activities

There's plenty for families in Subic Bay with several popular wildlife-themed parks south of the Freeport Zone.

Diving

Wreck diving is one of the big adventure draws in Subic. Of the seven wrecks commonly visited by divers, the USS New York (at a depth of 28m) is probably the most impressive. The battle cruiser was built in 1891 and was scuttled by American troops in 1941 to keep it out of Japanese hands. The New York wreck is penetrable, but this is a huge ship and it is easy to get fatally lost in the endless corridors and passageways. Appropriate training and an experienced guide are vital.

Other wrecks in the harbour include El Capitan (20m), a well-preserved site favoured by photographers for its general intactness, penetrability and prolific marine life; and the San Quintin (16m), home to larger fish such as wrasse, tangs, glasseyes and sweetlips. Both El Capitan and San Quintin are suitable for beginners. Advanced divers might try the LST (Landing Ship, Tank), an American landing craft at 37m.

The Oryuku Maru (20m), or 'Hell Ship', in which 1600 US prisoners of war were imprisoned and mistakenly killed in an air attack, was off limits to divers at the time of research.

Visibility in Subic is not what it is elsewhere in the country. The best time for water clarity is from February to April. Dive prices aren't bad – P1000 to P1500 for a dive, and P16,000 to P18,000 for an open-water course.

Brian Homan is an experienced wreck diver and a good source of information for advanced divers; find him at Vasco's bar.

Boardwalk Dive Center DIVING
(🖉 252 5367; www.boardwalkdivecentre.com; Waterfront Rd) Professional outfit with a technical-diving arm.

Subic Scuba 719 DIVING
(🖉 252 9428; 664 Waterfront Rd) This friendly and laid-back place has heaps of knowledge about the wrecks and good dive prices.

Ecotourism

Illegal logging was nonexistent in the Freeport Zone during the American years and as a result the area has some fantastically pristine jungle trekking. The Subic Bay Tourism Department (🖉 047-252 4123; www.sbma.com; 2nd Fl, Subic Bay Exhibition & Convention Center, Efficiency Rd, SBFZ; ☺ 8am-5pm) can help steer you to walks in the large rainforest south of the SBFZ (you'll need a private vehicle to reach these). which also has excellent .

A unique activity in Subic Bay is the opportunity to learn jungle survival skills from the indigenous Aeta ('Aeta' is the term given to the indigenous Negrito population in the area), who were employed to teach US service officers how to survive in the jungle.

The Cubi district (near the Subic airport) is home to the biggest known roosting site of the world's largest bats: the Philippine fruit bat and the golden-crowned flying fox. Dubbed the 'Bat Kingdom', the roosting site moves around from year to year but it isn't hard to find; just follow your ears around dusk as hundreds of bats take to the sky.

Pamulaklakin Forest Trail ECOTOUR, TREKKING
(🖉 0921 682 7175; from P150; ☺ 8am-5pm) A more grassroots option compared to the commercial JEST Camp nearby; follow an Aeta guide from the Pamulaklakin trailhead into the forest to learn fire-making and other handy jungle survival techniques. Ask about longer ecology tours and overnight trips (P500).

Jungle Environment
Survival Training (JEST) Camp
ECOTOUR

(☎047-252 1489; www.jestcamp.com; from P200; ⊘8.30am-5pm) If you can gather a group of five people, JEST Camp can arrange a number of different activities, ranging from basic demonstrations to hardcore multiday survival courses where you build your own shelters and gather water from vines. You'll also find a bird park and zipline here too.

Tree Top Adventure
ADVENTURE SPORTS

(☎047-252 9425; www.treetopadventureph.com; entry P50, activities P200; ⊘8am-4.30pm Mon-Fri, to 5pm Sat & Sun) The mix of tree-top activities offered by this organisation, such as obstacle courses, rappelling, ziplines and freefalls, are a great way to get intimate with Subic's beautiful forest.

Beaches
Most of Subic's beaches just south of the SBFZ such as **Camayan Beach Resort** (www. camayanbeachresort.com; adult/child P300/250) and **All Hands Resort** (www.allhandsbeach. com; P500) are developed resorts with entrance fees and popular with rowdy daytrippers on weekends, but are decent enough if you want to laze on a beach close to Manila. The Boardwalk Beach along the main strip of the SBFZ isn't recommended for swimming.

Barrio Barretto (northwest of the SBFZ) has a nice stretch of sand, but as a sleazy sexpat hangout it's best avoided. There are some nice **beaches** further north in Zambales, best reached by rented car.

The palm-lined stretch of sand that runs along Waterfront Beach isn't considered suitable for swimming due to pollution from the nearby port.

Horse Riding
El Kabayo Stables
HORSE RIDING

(☎047-252 1050, 0906 453 1175; horse riding 30min/1hr P370/770; ⊘8.30am-5pm) People with equestrian instincts make the trip from Manila just to go here. It has plenty of horses, and riding options around Subic are legion. Rates include a guided trip to a nearby waterfall. It's in Binictican Heights.

🛏 Sleeping

The Cabin
GUESTHOUSE $

(☎250 3042; www.thecabinsubic.com; Schley Rd, SBFZ; dm P430, s/d P700/900) In a town of pricey accommodation, this cosy faux-log lodge comes as a welcome surprise, as does its location down a quiet backstreet (just near the Spanish Gates). Dorms and private rooms are cramped but modern, clean and all-round top value.

Subic Park Hotel
HOTEL $$

(☎252 2092; www.subicparkhotel.com; Waterfront Rd, SBFZ; r incl dinner P2250-3500; ❊@🛜🏊) Near the far end of Waterfront Beach, Subic Park is looking a bit tired these days, but remains a solid choice among the bayfront hotels and has a good pool. Upgrade to the 'Oceanfront' rooms, with sea-facing balconies and king-sized beds.

Herbie's Mansion
HOTEL $$

(☎047-252 7350; Waterfront Rd, SBFZ; r from P1500; ❊🛜) It certainly ain't no mansion, but Herbie's offers family-friendly well-priced no-frills rooms in the heart of the Waterfront.

Sheavens Seafront Resort
BEACH RESORT $$

(☎223 9430; www.sheavens.com; Barrio Barretto, Olongapo; d P1250-1850, deluxe P2950-4800; ❊🛜🏊) While not a family place, Sheavens is at least somewhat removed from Barrio Barretto's sleazier side. It's a sublime location over the rocks on the far southeast end of Barretto's signature Baloy Long Beach, and has a huge variety of rooms, including some with sea views.

Lighthouse Marina Resort
HOTEL $$$

(☎252 5000; www.lighthousesubic.com; Waterfront Rd, SBFZ; r incl breakfast from P6000; ❧❊@🛜🏊) Miles ahead of anything else in Subic Bay in terms of comfort, design, service – and price. The spacious rooms are truly luxurious, with supersized flat-screen TVs.

🍴 Eating & Drinking

The restobars along Waterfront Rd are popular and often host live music. There's also a few upmarket places in the SBFZ's backstreets.

Vasco's
PUB FOOD $$

(☎252 1845, 047-252 1843; www.vascosresort-museum.com; Lot 14, Argonaut Hwy, SBFZ; mains P200-300; ⊘24hr; 🛜) Popular with the older expat community, this 'pirate' bar and restaurant has a prime spot over the bay near the port. Aussie owner Brian Homan is an accomplished shipwreck explorer who has been diving in the Philippines forever. It's a wonderful place for a breezy breakfast, and there are also a few rooms for rent (from P2800).

Some of the porcelain, WWII relics and other treasures salvaged by Homan are on

BATAAN PENINSULA

For WWII veterans of the Pacific campaign, few places have such bitter associations as the Bataan Peninsula. Both sides saw some of their darkest moments in the jungles around Mt Mariveles.

Few are left who experienced the Bataan Death March first-hand, a grisly affair that began when 70,000 US and Filipino troops surrendered to the Japanese in April 1942. The victors marched the prisoners, many sick and diseased from months of fighting, 90km from Mariveles to San Fernando, Pampanga, where they were loaded into box cars and brought by train to the Camp O'Donnell POW camp (now the Capas National Shrine; p109). Along the way some 15,000 to 25,000 American and Filipino troops perished.

For history buffs, Bataan has a smattering of sites that make for easy day trips from Clark or Subic Bay (or even Manila at a pinch). Poignant 'Death March' markers appear along the national highway at 1km intervals starting in Mariveles and ending 102km away at the train station in San Fernando. Annual commemoration events on or around Bataan Day (9 April) include an organised walk along part of the route, and an ultramarathon along the entire route.

The peninsula's most interesting site is the **Dambana ng Kagitingan** (Shrine of Valor; P20) on Mt Samat near Balanga. Atop the mountain is a 90m-high **crucifix** with battle scenes carved around its base. You can take a **lift** (P10; ☉8am–noon & 1-5pm) to the top of the cross, where there is a long viewing gallery with great views out over Mt Mariveles, Manila Bay and the South China Sea.

From the base of the cross, steps lead 50m down the hill to the shrine proper, where the stories of the Battle of Bataan and the ensuing Death March are carved into a marble **memorial wall**. In a bunker beneath the shrine is an excellent **museum** (P20; ☉8am–noon

---

display in a small museum. To get here from the CBD take an 'Airport-Cubi' Winstar (P9).

Gerry's Grill
FILIPINO, SEAFOOD $$
(www.gerrysgrill.com; Waterfront Rd, SBFZ; mains from P200; ☉11am-11pm; 🐾) Head to the waterfront to dine on delicious grilled seafood dishes with the sand between your toes at this popular Filipino chain. Come for sunset.

Rachi Curry Corner
INDIAN $$
(☑047-250 2855; Santa Rita Rd; meals P200-375; ☉10am-10pm) Jovial Nepalese owner Ram serves up large portions of delicious South Asian specialities at this intimate Indian restaurant in a residenial street. There's also a small branch in Harbor Point Mall.

The Castle
FRENCH, BELGIAN $$$
(☑047-250 0540; www.thecastlesubic.com; Sampson Rd, SBFZ; mains P500-1400; 🐾) Subic's best place for fine dining with exquisite traditional French-Belgian cuisine, homemade gelati and a selection of 50 Belgian beers at its front bar. It's next to the historic Spanish Gates.

Roofdeck
BAR
(Terrace Hotel, Waterfront Rd; P300; ☉10am-midnight) Head up to the Terrace Hotel's rooftop bar for ocean vistas, a dip in its infinity pool and a cocktail. The P300 entrance is redeemable against food and drinks.

❶ Information

VisitSubic (www.visitsubic.com) has some useful travel information for the area including accommodation, theme parks and transport.

❶ Getting There & Away

If you're heading to/from Manila try to take **Victory Liner** (☑222 2241; cnr W 18th St & Rizal Ave) express buses with 'via SCTEX' placards to shave at least an hour off the trip (P245, 2¼ hours), departing every hour till early afternoon. Otherwise there are slower (but cheaper) buses to Manila hourly (P218, 3½ hours). There are also frequent buses north to Iba (P139, two hours) and Baguio (P449, six hours). Victory Liner is a 10-minute jeepney ride from the SBFZ.

❶ Getting Around

'Winstar' buses are unique to the SBFZ and perform the role that jeepneys perform elsewhere. They leave from the Transport Terminal near the SBFZ main gate and travel only within the Freeport Zone.

In Olongapo, blue jeepneys for Barrio Barretto and Subic town are signboarded 'Castillejos'.

Taxis operate along Waterfront Rd, and while pricey for individual trips (around P400), for the day it works out to be around P300 per hour – so P2400 for eight hours to explore the Subic region.

& 1-5pm) FREE, with an impressive range of weaponry on display, battle scenes depicted in drawings and in dioramas, and a brilliant relief map of the Bataan Peninsula.

Every 9 April, relatives of American and Japanese veterans of the battles and Death March (plus a few last remaining veterans) gather at the shrine proper and pay tribute to the thousands of their comrades who fell in the surrounding jungles.

The **Bataan Tourism Office** (☑047-237 4785; www.bataan.gov.ph; Capital Compound, Balanga) has an excellent website on where to find historical WWII sites and other places of interest.

Getting There & Away

To get to the shrine you must first travel to Balanga, linked by Genesis and Bataan Transport buses from Pasay Rotunda in Manila (P210, three to four hours) via Angeles' Mabalacat/Dau bus terminal. You can also take a Victory Liner bus to/from Olongapo (P70, 1¾ hours).

From Balanga head south a few kilometres then turn right (west) off the highway toward Bagac. From the turn-off it's 4.5km to the Mt Samat turn-off, then another 7km up a steep but well-paved road to the cross. Tricycles wait at the Mt Samat turn-off (P200 round trip). You can also reach the Mt Samat turn-off from Balanga on a Bagac-bound jeepney.

Hiring a van in Balanga for a half-day trip to Mt Samat costs P1500. The **Gap Plaza Hotel** (☑047-237 6757; www.gapplaza.com; cnr Capitol Dr & Sampaguita St; d incl breakfast P2300-3000; ❋❋☎) can get you sorted and also has the best rooms in the area – the priciest include a free Mt Samat tour.

At the time of research there was discussion of resuming a ferry service from Manila to Bataan, which would cut travel time to 40 minutes.

San Fernando (Pampanga)

☑045 / POP 269,400

The industrial town of San Fernando – not to be confused with San Fernando (La Union), northwest of Baguio – is the capital of Pampanga province. About the only reason people come here is to see devout Christians taking part in a **crucifixion ceremony** every Easter. At noon on Good Friday, in barangay San Pedro Cutud, volunteers with a penchant for pain are nailed to wooden crosses and whipped till they bleed.

Victory Liner has buses to San Fernando from its Cubao terminal in Manila (P102, one hour, every 30 minutes). Be aware that buses from Manila to points further north take the NLEX and bypass San Fernando.

Clark & Angeles

☑045 / POP 314,500

Located 80km northwest of Manila, Clark is the former site of the US Air Force's base, in use since 1903 until the eruption of Mt Pinatubo forced their hasty departure in 1991. Since then the base has been developed into the site of an international airport and the Clark Freeport Zone – a somewhat refined enclave comprising a business district, estates, duty-free shops and upcoming restaurants. It's also used as a base by the Philippine Airforce.

Unless you have a flight or a bus transfer at Mabalacat terminal in Dau there's no reason to visit Clark or Angeles itself, the latter is synonymous with the sex industry in the Philippines. The 10,000 girls and women working the strip of tacky clubs and bars are only the vestiges of the time before the closure of the airbase. It's a grim scene that caters to old sex tourists, and if you've got a flight from here it's better to hang out in the Clark area.

◉ Sights & Activities

★**Clark Museum**   MUSEUM

(Clark Parade Grounds; admission P50; ☺8am-5pm Mon-Sat) On the edge of the former American parade grounds, this delightful museum details the history of Clark from 1901 up to its development of the Freeport Zone. It includes some great military memorabilia, photos and displays on Mt Pinatubo's dramatic eruption (perhaps best seen *after* you've climbed it!). There's also interesting info on the indigenous Aeta, the earliest inhabitants of the area who still live in the region.

While you're here take a stroll around the peaceful **Parade Grounds**, ringed by historic barn houses built in the early 20th century that served as residences of US soldiers.

Mt Arayat National Park
TREKKING

(admission P50) While it feels a bit neglected, the volcanic cone of Mt Arayat (1026m) is still a great trek that's do-able in a half-day. Take a jeepney at the Mabalacat/Dau terminal heading to Arayat town, then take a tricycle to the park entrance, where you pay your fee and pick up a mandatory guide.

Angeles City Flying Club
SCENIC FLIGHTS

(☑ 802 2101, 0918 920 3039; www.angelesflying.com; 10/20min flight P1650/2900) For sublime views take an ultralight flight over Pampanga, taking in its verdant rice paddies and Mt Arayat, with this well-established company located 25 minutes' drive from Angeles in Magalang. It offers free morning pick-ups.

🛏 Sleeping

Tune Hotel
HOTEL $

(☑ 045-459 0888; www.tunehotels.com; Don Juico Ave, Angeles; d from P900; ❋❀🌐) A reliable chain hotel with comfy beds and professional staff. Prices fluctuate dramatically, so book online to ensure the best rates.

Holiday Inn
HOTEL $$$

(☑ 045-599 8000; www.holidayinn.com/clark; Mimosa Dr, Freeport Zone; r from P5750; ❋🌐🏊) Only a five-minute drive from Clark Airport, this sprawling hotel with leafy views and a sparkling pool to relax by is the perfect place to rest up before a flight.

🍴 Eating

Yakiniku Kosyu Japanese Grill
JAPANESE $$

(Santos St, Clark Freeport Zone; mains from P160; ◷11am-10pm) Overlooking the Parade Grounds, this Japanese restaurant is set inside a converted historical barn house with decor mixing a traditional *izakaya* (Japanese pub-restaurant) with colourful kitsch. It does excellent sushi and barbecue dishes.

Iguana's
MEXICAN $$

(☑ 893 3654; Don Juico Ave; mains from P160; ◷11am-10pm Tue-Sat; ❋) Located about halfway between Clark Airport and Angeles (in the Freeport Zone), Iguana's is one of the Philippines' best Mexican restaurants with great margaritas and beer-battered fish tacos.

Cottage Kitchen Cafe
AMERICAN $$

(☑ 893 2599; 582 Don Juico Ave; mains P200-800; ◷10am-11pm Tue-Sun; ❋) Cooks up cajun and creole-style cuisine, from St Louis-style pork ribs to Southern fried catfish.

ⓘ Getting There & Away

AIR

Clark Intrernational Airport (www.clarkairport.com) is in the Clark Special Economic Zone and used by Asian low-cost airlines, which serve the following cities, among others: Bangkok (Tigerair), Hong Kong (Cebu Pacific, Tigerair) and Singapore (Cebu Pacific, Tigerair).

In theory air-con shuttles meet all flights and drop passengers off either at the Clark Freeport Zone main gate (P30) or the Mabalacat (Dau) bus terminal (P50). If these aren't around, look for a jeepney to the main gate, or take an overpriced fixed-rate taxi (P450/500 to Mabalacat/Angeles).

BUS

The cheapest way to get to Manila is to head to the main Mabalacat bus station in Dau around 3km from Clark Freeport Zone main gate, where you'll find scores of buses heading to Manila (fan/air-con P114/150, 1½ hours). There are also buses to Olongapo (P140, one hour) and just about anywhere else in North Luzon. Most depart only when they're full.

Otherwise Philtranco and Partas each run four daily direct trips from Clark to Manila, usually stopping in both Cubao (P400, 1½ hours) and Pasay (P450, two hours).

Getting to Banaue is trickier. If you're comfortable changing buses, the recommended route is Dau–Cabanatuan–Solano–Lagawe–Banaue. The alternative is to backtrack to Manila and get the direct night bus to Banaue.

A constant stream of jeepneys connects Dau and Angeles, a five-minute journey.

Mt Pinatubo & Around

For centuries, the residents of Angeles took the nearby volcanoes of Mt Pinatubo and Mt Arayat for granted. That changed suddenly on 15 June 1991, when Pinatubo, the larger of the two volcanoes, literally blew itself apart, sending a column of ash and rock 40km into the air. The mountain lost 300m in height, and fine dust and fist-sized fragments of rock rained down on nearby Angeles, Clark Airbase and Subic Bay. Compounding the catastrophe, a savage typhoon chose this moment to lash northern Luzon, turning the ash into lethal lahar (mobile volcanic mud), which flooded downhill from the volcano with dire consequences. In Zambales Province to the west of Mt Pinatubo, lahar flows rerouted rivers and sank entire villages under newly formed Lake Mapanuepe.

While the journey up Mt Pinatubo (1450m) is one of the country's most accessible adventures, be aware it's closed off in inclement weather. Given the fragility of the lahar cliffs it's prone to landslides; it shouldn't be attempted if conditions aren't favourable. Flash floods during the remnants of a typhoon in 2009 swept away a convoy of jeeps, killing seven, including five European tourists.

After the accident, the mountain was closed for a spell, and when it reopened new rules were enforced ensuring excursions to the summit begin by 7am or 8am (heavy rains are more frequent in the afternoon). In the height of the dry season that might be extended to 10am. All of this means that organised excursions to Pinatubo start at a ridiculously early hour – pre-dawn in Manila and just a little after that in Angeles.

It's only possible to climb Mt Pinatubo with a guide and 4WD. While many choose to go on organised excursions with Angeles- or Manila-based tour companies, it's easy enough to spend a night in Santa Juliana and arrange it all independently – giving you the advantage of staying at the foot of the volcano to avoid the super-early wake-up.

The main point of contact for the climb is Marisa at the **Sta Juliana Tourism Council** (✆0906 462 3388) or Alvin's Mt Pinatubo Guesthouse, who can advise you on bookings, logistical and safety matters. Call in advance to make sure they're allowing climbs on the day you want to go up.

Costs vary according to group size, but if you arrange it independently a group of four or more can expect to pay around P2000 per person (including lunch). The tourist office and Alvin are both good at matching independent travellers with other groups. Otherwise if you want to go alone, expect to pay around P4000 to P5000. For Manila- and Angeles-based tour companies you'll pay significantly more.

◉ Sights & Activities

After climbing Pinatubo, there are also some interesting Aeta villages in the area you can visit; get in touch with Alvin at Alvin's Mt Pinatubo Guesthouse.

Capas National Shrine　　　MEMORIAL
(admission P10; ⊙8am-5pm) This former Camp O'Donnell POW camp was where the American and Filipino soldiers who endured the notorious WWII **Bataan Death March** were transported: their final destination. It's now a 22-hectare memorial park, centred by the Capas National Shrine, a 70m needle-shaped

obelisk standing solemnly at the end of the flag-lined boulevard.

Also here is one of the 'death box cars' used to transport up to 100 prisoners at a time to Camp O'Donnell in unventilated carriages (resulting in many deaths), plus a small museum. It's located halfway between Capas and Santa Juliana; keep an eye out for the Bataan Death March markers along the way.

Mt Pinatubo　　　HIKING, VOLCANO
The jumping-off point for the volcano climb is Santa Juliana, near the base of the mountain's north slope, from where you take a memorable 4WD journey across an eerie, lunar-like landscape involving action-packed river crossings. From here you walk the final two hours to Pinatubo's crater, with its tranquil lake and sandy beach. While swimming in the crater lake was prohibited at time of research, it's likely to be relaxed in the near future – bring your swimsuit in case.

The easily eroded lahar flows have created a stunning landscape around the volcano that only now is starting to recover some of its vegetation. The Abacan and Pasig-Potrero Rivers have both cut channels through the sediment, which has led to the formation of towering pinnacles of lahar, hanging valleys and canyons.

Other than the sweaty, steep climb towards the end, it's a largely non-taxing trek, though be prepared: your feet may get wet when navigating small river crossings. Pack plenty of water, a hat and sunscreen.

🛏 Sleeping

★**Alvin's Mt Pinatubo**
Guesthouse　　　GUESTHOUSE $
(Bognot Homestay; ✆0919 861 4102; www. mt-pinatubo.weebly.com; Sta Juliana; r incl breakfast P500; ❄) Run by superfriendly Alvin and Angie, this laidback guesthouse is the place independent travellers head to arrange their volcano trek. It's a relaxing spot set among fruit trees in a rural village, with basic, clean rooms (a mix of bunks and doubles) and delicious homecooked meals (P100).

❶ Getting There & Away

To get to Santa Juliana from Manila take any North Luzon–bound bus heading to Capas (fan/ air-con P139/180), from where you then take a tricycle direct (P300); otherwise from Capas you could try for a jeepney to Patling (P28), and then a tricycle to Santa Juliana (P6). Regular buses to Capas also leave Mabalacat bus terminal in Dau, Angeles (P50, 45 minutes).

North Luzon

Why Go?

North Luzon, a region that invites intrepid exploration, encapsulates a nation in miniature. Machete-toting mountain tribes who are quick to smile and quicker to share their rice wine. Surfers racing waves onto sunny beaches. White-sand beaches lapped by teal waters. Impenetrable jungle hiding numerous endemic critters. Spanish colonial cities where sunlight breaks through seashell windows. Far-flung islands whose pristine landscapes greet very few visitors.

For many travellers, the main lures are the emerald rice terraces of the Cordillera, a mountain range that hides hanging coffins, mummified ancestors and the old ghosts of the forest. Trekking is a prime activity in this wild frontier, but caving, mountain biking and rafting are other adrenalin-fuelled activities that shape the experience of exploring North Luzon. Culturally, this is the Philippines at its most diverse, as the peoples of the mountains, Zambales, Ilocos and Batanes are notable for a mind-boggling melange of language and ritual.

Best Off the Beaten Track

➜ Sierra Madre (p155)

➜ Babuyan Islands (p160)

➜ Itbayat Island (p162)

➜ Adams (p128)

Best for Indigenous Culture

➜ Kalinga Province (p144)

➜ Sabtang Island (p161)

➜ Timbac Caves (p137)

➜ Echo Valley Hanging Coffins (p138)

➜ Bontoc Museum (p142)

When to Go

Sagada

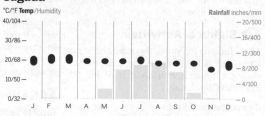

°C/°F **Temp**/Humidity Rainfall inches/mm

Nov–May A nice time to experience the best weather the Philippines has to offer – you won't be alone!

Apr–Jul The heat is on but the crowds are down.

Jul–Oct Rice terraces are green, but typhoons can be a problem.

Language

Myriad languages are spoken in North Luzon, including dozens of dialects in the Cordillera alone. The language jumble is most confusing in Kalinga, where just about every village has its own dialect. In the Cordillera, people are far more likely to understand Ilocano or English than the national language, Tagalog.

In the lowlands, the principal languages are Tagalog and Ilocano, which is the predominant language not only in Ilocos but also in Cagayan, Isabela and La Union. Other common dialects include Pangasinan and Sambal, the language of the Zambales people, while the people of the Batanes speak Ivatan.

❶ Getting There & Away

Regular flights connect Manila with Laoag, Tuguegarao, and Basco (Batanes); Tuguegarao with Basco, Palalan and Maconacon, and Cauayan (Isabela Province) with Palalan and Maconacon. Air-con buses link Manila with the major North Luzon cities, including comfortable deluxe buses to Laoag, Vigan, Pagudpud and Baguio.

Luzon's more remote regions, such as the Cordillera and the northeast part of the island, are also very reachable by an assortment of reasonably frequent public transport. If driving off the beaten track, keep in mind that you'll need a pretty good 4WD, and some of the roads that cut through the Kalinga Province are not for the faint of heart. Lack of parking spots and traffic jams are a common problem in most cities and towns. You can rent cars in Manila.

ZAMBALES COAST

The Zambales Coast lies between a rock and a wet place. The rock? The angry massif of Mt Pinatubo. The wet? Well, the sea of course, with some fine surfing (especially around Pundaquit and Liwa), and often as not the rains that unrelentingly lash this 100km of coastline every summer. Outside this season you'll find uninhabited offshore islands and beach resorts, popular as offbeat weekend getaways with folks from Manila.

Pundaquit, Capones Island & Liwliwa

☏ 047 / POP 2670

Just a three-hour drive from Manila you can sleep under the stars on hourglass-shaped Capones Island, a 20- to 30-minute bangka (outrigger canoe) ride from the small fishing village of Pundaquit. During the rainy season boats can't land, so you have to be able to swim to shore and then back to the boat to get picked up. Hiring a bangka for a day of island-hopping is around P1300.

July to October are the peak months for surfing, but decent swells linger into February. March to May is the flat season. The best spots are the south side of Capones Island, Anawangin Cove (south of Pundaquit) and San Narciso (7km north of San Antonio). Anawangin Cove is accessible only on foot or by boat. Part evangelical retreat, part surf camp, **Crystal Beach Resort & Campsite** (☏ 047-913 4309; www.crystalbeach.com.ph; d from P1550) in San Narciso has Zambales' steadiest waves, boards for rent (P200 per hour) and surfing instruction (P200 per hour).

Another wonderful spot for surfing is Liwliwa, a beautiful stretch of volcanic-pumice-strewn beach just south of San Felipe, which is 5km north of San Narciso, and a corner of Luzon that still very much retains a chilled out backpacker vibe.

🛏 Sleeping & Eating

Beach resorts in Zambales go into hibernation during low season (June to October), while the basic surfer digs come into their own during that time.

★**Circle Hostel**   HOSTEL $
(☏ 0917 861 1929; www.zambales.thecirclehostel.com; tent P300, hammock P350, dm P450) This original, colourful backpacker/surfer hostel in Liwliwa is a great place to connect with a young crowd of fellow wave riders and make friends with the lovely staff. Lodgings consist of varying levels of shoestringiness, with the thatch-walled, breezy dorms being the upmarket option. Lockers are available and the vibe encourages lingering, in and out of the sea.

Kilabot Surfing   BEACH RESORT $
(☏ 0930 509 5122; huts P800) If you've come to Liwliwa to surf but want your own space, these basic beachside *kubos* (thatched huts) are the answer.

Norma Beach Resort   BEACH RESORT $$
(☏ 0910 948 8607, 0918 361 5924; d from P1650, huts P750; ✳✳) Norma's is a collection of thatch-roofed beach huts behind a bamboo stockade. The small cheapies are seriously basic. Located on lovely Anawangin Cove on the far side of Pundaquit; speak with the owners about arranging bangka transport.

NORTH LUZON PUNDAQUIT, CAPONES ISLAND & LIWLIWA

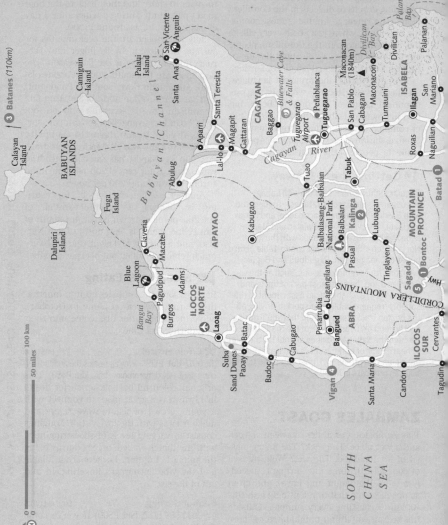

North Luzon Highlights

1 Feast your eyes on the awesome rice terraces around **Banaue** (p146) **Batad** (p149) and **Bontoc** (p142).

2 Hobnob with former headhunters in the **Kalinga Province** (p144).

3 Explore the end-of-the-world **Batanes islands** (p158).

4 Step back in time in the lovely **Mestizo District** (p121) of Vigan.

5 Hike and cave in **Sagada** (p140), aka backpacker HQ.

6 Take in the music, fine food and cool mountain air of **Baguio** (p128).

7 Get up close and personal with the

Jomalig Island

Patnanungan Island

Polillo Island

POLILLO ISLANDS

PHILIPPINE SEA

Pollilo Strait

Infanta

QUEZON

Northern Sierra Madre Natural Park

Dinapigue

Dilasag

Casiguran

Dinalungan

Maria Aurora

Baler Bay

8 Baler

AURORA

Dingalan

Dingalen Bay

RIZAL

METRO MANILA

North Luzon Expressway

MANILA

Maldos

Balanga

BULACAN

Cauayan

San Mateo

Alicia

Echague

Caburreguis

Santiago City

Madella

Nagtipunan

QUIRINO

Bagabag

Solano

Capisaan

Kasibu

SIERRA MADRE MOUNTAINS

Bongabon

Pantabangan

Rizal

Santa Rosa

Cabanatuan

Gapan

Palayan

San Fernando (Pampanga)

PAMPANGA

BATAAN

Subic Bay

Banaue

IFUGAO

Lagawe

Kiangan

Mt Pulag National Park

Abaguio

Ambaguio

Bambang

NUEVA VIZCAYA

Aritao

Santa Fe

San Jose

NUEVA ECIJA

Pantabangan Lake

SCTEX

Angeles

Aglao

Aglao

Subic

Olongapo

Halsema

BENGUET

Kabayan 7

Mt Pulag (2922m)

Binga Lake

Ambuklao Lake

Baguio

La Trinidad

6

Abatan

LA UNION

San Fernando (La Union)

8 San Juan

Bauang

Agoo

Damortis

Rosario

San Fabian

Urdaneta

Villasis

Dagupan

San Carlos

Bautista

Aguilar

Mt Tapulao (2037m)

ZAMBALES MOUNTAINS

Mt Pinatubo (1450m)

Capas

Tarlac

TARLAC

Castillejos

San Marcelino

San Antonio

San Narciso

Mapanuepe Lake

Cabatuan

Botolan

San Felipe

Liwliwa

Pundaquit

Capones Island

Anawangin Cove

Iba

ZAMBALES

Masinloc

Palauig

Santa Cruz

Infanta

Dasol

Tambobong

Hermana Mayor Island

Hermana Menor Island

Dasol Bay

Bolinao

Patar

Alaminos

Hundred Islands National Park

Lingayen

PANGASINAN

Lingayen Gulf

Bacnotan

Bautista

LAKE MAPANUEPE

When Mt Pinatubo erupted in 1991, lava flows dammed the Mapanuepe River flowing out of the Zambales range. Slowly rising floodwaters forced residents of Aglao and Bajaoen to flee to higher ground. Unfazed, locals rebuilt their villages on the shores of newly minted Lake Mapanuepe, nestled in the Zambales Mountains about 15km east of San Marcelino.

These villages are only accessible only by boat and remain quite primitive – the Aeta people wearing their indigenous G-strings (loincloths) are still a common sight.

In the middle of Lake Mapanuepe is the **sunken church** of Bajaoen, easily identifiable by its maroon cross sticking out of the water – an unsettling sight.

There are one or two jeepneys per day to Aglao from San Marcelino (45 minutes), but the last one from Aglao is at noon. A bangka to the sunken church from the 'port' in Aglao should cost about P800.

All buses travelling between Olongapo and Iba stop in San Marcelino.

Mommy Phoebe's Place   FILIPINO **$**
(mains P80-220; ⊙ 5.30am-late) Mommy Phoebe can stuff you full of her delicious *pansit* (stir-fried noodles), *bagnet* (deep-fried pork) and whatever else she's got cooking that day, and sell you quality surfing supplies.

ℹ Getting There & Away

From Olongapo or Manila, take any bus heading towards Iba, get off in San Antonio, then take a tricycle 4.5km to Pundaquit (P80). For Liwliwa, continue to San Felipe and take a tricycle to Liwliwa (P50).

Iba & Botolan

♩ 047 / POP 101,195

These neighbouring towns, about 45km north of San Antonio, make convenient bases for hikes in the Zambales Mountains or make a decent enough place for an overnight stopover.

🏃 Activities

Mt Tapulao   HIKING
The main trek around here is the ascent up mist-shrouded Mt Tapulao (High Peak; 2037m), the highest mountain in the Zambales range. You can walk or take a sturdy 4WD most of the way up the mountain along a mining road that terminates about an hour's walk from the summit. The 18km mining road originates in barangay (village) Dampay, a 40-minute tricycle ride (P170) from the small town of Palauig, 14km northwest of Iba.

🛏 Sleeping & Eating

If driving south to north along the Zambales Coast, this is where the mass of beach resorts begins to pop up.

🛏 Botolan

Botolan Wildlife Farm   GUESTHOUSE **$$**
(☑ 0917 829 5478, 0917 734 2206; www.botolan-wildlifefarm.com; s/d P1500/1800) Located at the foot of the Zambales Mountains and run by Swiss zoologist Martin Zoller, this is a humane sanctuary for an array of rescued beasts, with guest rooms overlooking the animal pens and the mountains. To get there, take a tricycle (P80) 4km east from a well-marked turn-off on the National Hwy, just south of Botolan centre. The star of the zoo is an immense Amur tiger called Ramses.

Rama Beach Resort   BEACH RESORT **$$**
(☑ 0918 910 1280; www.ramabeach.com; d P1600, cottages from P800; ❋ 🏱) There's pretty accommodation and a nice restaurant with a library and pool table at this Australian-owned resort, on a quiet stretch of beach 8km south of Botolan proper. Turtles nest here from October to February and owners arrange trips to nearby caves.

🛏 Iba

Iba's beach resorts are clustered in barangay Bangantalinga, 3km north of Iba proper.

Palmera Garden Beach Resort   BEACH RESORT **$$**
(☑ 0908 503 1416, 047-811 1886; www.palmera-garden.com; r from P1600; ❋ 🏱 ➰) This Swiss-owned resort, 2km north of Iba, is the most service-oriented in the area, its restaurant serving the likes of currywurst alongside Filipino standards. The rooms are clean, air-conditioned and utterly unmemorable, but there's access to a pleasant stretch of beach and a pool surrounded by blooming flowers.

ⓘ Getting There & Away

Victory Liner has frequent buses (hourly from 5am to 6pm) from Iba south to Cubao and Pasay in Manila (P389, five to six hours) via Olongapo (P154, two hours), plus departures every 30 minutes north to Santa Cruz (P111, 1½ hours).

North of Iba

If you're into island-hopping and beach camping, head to the border of the Zambales and Pangasinan provinces. Off Santa Cruz, **Hermana Menor Island** is fringed by a post-card-worthy white beach with decent snorkelling just offshore. The island is privately owned, but bangka excursions there and to neighbouring **Hermana Mayor Island** are possible through SeaSun Beach Resort.

Just south of here, **Potipot Island** is more accessible and more popular. It has a white beach where you can camp. SeaSun Beach Resort can arrange trips out here for P800.

Danish-owned **SeaSun Beach Resort** (☑0917 409 3347; www.seasun.com.ph; barangay Sabang; d/f P2000/4000; ✸) in Santa Cruz fronts a pleasantly secluded sliver of beach in view of Hermana Menor and Hermana Mayor. Rooms run the gamut from bare-bones fan cells (P600) to fancier digs with minibars and satellite TV. The resort is 1.5km off the main road – spot the well-marked turn-off 2km south of Santa Cruz.

Victory Liner has frequent buses south to Iba and Olongapo and north to Alaminos and Lingayen. Local (non air-con) buses run up and down the same road through the day.

LINGAYEN GULF

This pretty pocket of water, a scattershot of emerald islands in azure and turquoise, dominates the coastline of Pangasinan Province.

Conservation efforts are underway to restore the coral reefs that have been severely damaged by dynamite and cyanide fishing. There is no shortage of beach resorts scattered along the coastline from Bolinao to San Juan (La Union), a popular surfer hangout.

Bolinao & Patar Beach

☑ 075 / POP 74,545

Bolinao has a palpable end-of-the-road feel to it – unsurprising, as it is basically located at the end of everything. Depending on your point of view, local beach resorts can feel romantically isolated or a bit forlorn.

Patar Beach, a long stretch of narrow sand linking Bolinao with barangay Patar, situated 18km to the south, is popular with weekenders from Manila and makes for a relaxing stopover. The best beach for swimming is White Beach in Patar proper, overlooked by the towering Spanish-built Cape Bolinao Lighthouse.

The 17th century **Church of St James** in the town plaza is notable for the rare wooden *santos* (religious statues) on its facade, and it's well worth paying a visit to the **University of the Philippines Marine Science Institute** (☑075-554 2755; www.msi.upd.edu.ph/bml; admission P15; ☺8am-5pm Mon-Fri) if you have any interest in the fragile marine ecology of Lingayen Gulf. Researchers cultivate coral-producing giant clams and transplant them to Hundred Islands National Park and as far away as Australia and Malaysia.

If staying along Patar Beach, **Treasures of Bolinao** (☑0921 564 2408, 075-696 3266; 2-person villa P4000; ✸✷), 17km away from Bolinao along a partially paved road, is a luxurious option, with posh villas and upscale coconut cottages with ocean views.

Frequent buses (P55), jeepneys and vans (P65) shuttle to Alaminos (one hour).

A tricycle to the resorts on Patar Beach should cost around P175 one way, depending on how far you are going.

Hundred Islands National Park

☑ 075

This small **national park** (☑075-551 2145; www.hundredislands.ph) off the coast of Alaminos, 35km southeast of Bolinao, actually consists of 123 separate islets. Over the centuries the tides have eaten away at the bases of some of these limestone islands, giving them a distinctive mushroom-like appearance.

Unfortunately, the Hundred Islands may be too popular for their own good. Visitors and fishing have taxed the local ecology. Thus it can be difficult finding the right island where the coral hasn't been damaged by dynamite fishing or typhoons. While many visitors 'do' the islands in a day, the Hundred Islands reward more patient exploration.

Environmentally, the situation has improved since the Alaminos city government took control of the park in 2005. Speedboats patrol in search of illegal fishers, while the University of the Philippines Marine Science Institute in Bolinao has been repopulating the decimated giant clam population, which has helped coral recovery.

◉ Sights & Activities

To reach the park, you first have to get to the town of Alaminos and then take a tricycle (P50) to Lucap Wharf to pay the park entrance fee at the tourism office.

The Islands ISLANDS

Of the scattering of 123 limestone islets and islands shrouded in greenery, some are craggy and cliff-y, and others have pleasant stretches of beach (though litter is a problem on the most popular islands), calm waters for snorkelling, caves to explore and plenty of avian life. The only three islands with facilities are Quezon Island, Governor's Island and Children's Island; the rest are uninhabited and you can have them to yourself, as domestic tourists make a beeline for the former.

The beaches on Quezon, Governor's and Children's Islands are nothing special, although **Governor's Island** has a nice lookout point and the calm, shallow waters surrounding **Children's Island** are ideal for children.

One of the remotest islands, **Cathedral Island** is known for its variety of seabirds; on **Marcos Island** you can practise cliff-diving from a 20m rock tower; **Cuenco Island** is bisected by a cave that passes right through it and tiny **Martha** is picture-perfect beautiful – the beach between the two tiny islets is only reachable during high tide.

⊨ Sleeping & Eating

You can camp anywhere in the national park for P200. Quezon Island has six simple,

two-person nipa huts (P300 to P1100) with no electricity. Governor's Island has a guesthouse (P5000) that sleeps eight to 10 and has air-con when the electricity is working (from 6pm to 6am). Bring your own food and supplies. Make reservations and pay at the Hundred Islands National Park office in Lucap.

Visitors not overnighting on the islands tend to make Lucap their base; there are several guesthouses and hotels with adjoining restaurants spread along the coastal road by the wharf.

Island Tropic HOTEL $$

(☑ 0906 469 7888, 075-551 4913; www.islandtropichotel.com; d/f P1600/2400; ✳🛜) Motel-style accommodation with a breezy restaurant upstairs and a block of seriously spacious, studio-apartment-style rooms (minus kitchenette). Wi-fi only works in the restaurant.

Maxine By the Sea HOTEL $$

(☑ 075-696 0964; www.maxinebythesea.com; d/f P2110/4020; ✳🛜) Maxine is hard to miss, thanks to its chunky exterior that juts out into the sea, but inside you'll find some pleasant, understated rooms, reliably hot showers and cable TV. The restaurant is the best along Boulevard St; steer clear of the overly ambitious dishes and go for the signature squid and the catch-of-the-day *kinilaw* (ceviche).

❶ Information

BDO (Banco de Oro), BPI (Bank of the Philippine Islands) and Metrobank have ATMs in Alaminos, and there are a couple of internet cafes.

Hundred Islands National Park Office
(☑ 075-203 0917, 075-551 2505; www.hundredislands.ph; ⊙24hr) The office is near the pier in Lucap. It collects the park entrance fees (P40 day entry or P80 overnight) and camping fees, arranges boats, kayaking, 'snuba' diving (diving with a 40ft hose attached to a tank on the surface) and parasailing and publishes official rates for bangka hire.

❶ Getting There & Around

Five Star and Victory Liner have frequent departures from Alaminos to Pasay, Manila (ordinary/air-con P380/490, 5½ hours), and to Santa Cruz (P180, two hours), where you transfer to Olongapo. Victory Liner also has buses to Baguio (P230, four hours, three daily).

It's a 10-minute tricycle ride (P50, 5km) from Alaminos centre to Lucap's resorts.

Bolinao is reachable by frequent jeepney (P45), bus (P55) or air-con van (P65).

---

❶ BOATS TO HUNDRED ISLANDS

A regular boat to the islands costs P800 for up to five people and takes you to Quezon Island, Children's Island and Governor's Island only; you choose the island on which you'd like to spend the most time and get to visit the other two briefly. Hiring a service boat (P1400) gives you free reign as to which islands you get to visit and how long you'd like to spend on each one.

Boats run between 6am and 5.30pm.

San Fernando (La Union) & Around

☑ 072 / POP 114,963 / TRANSPORT HUB

If you travel up the west coast of Luzon, you will invariably pass through San Fernando (La Union), a compact, traffic-blighted grid of streets where there's little to detain travellers.

❶ Getting There & Around

Partas (☑ 072-242 0465; Quezon Ave) serves Manila (P550, seven hours, hourly), Pagudpud (P620, seven hours), Laoag (P420, five hours) and Vigan (P280, three hours). Cheaper, more frequent ordinary buses head to Laoag and Vigan from the Quezon Ave stop in front of the town plaza.

Minibuses to Baguio (P80, 1½ hours) leave twice hourly from Governor Luna St.

Jeepneys to Bauang and San Juan (P18) can be picked up along Quezon Ave.

If heading towards Dagupan/Lingayen/Zambales Coast, your best bet is to take any Manila-bound bus to the Damortis turn-off towards Rosario, get off and either wait for a passing bus or hire a loitering tricycle to get you as far as Dagupan (P350 to P400).

San Juan (La Union)

☑ 072 / POP 35,098

Surfers, look no further. Most travellers heading here are bound for barangay Urbiztondo in San Juan, an unassuming beach town 6km north of San Fernando that gets the country's most consistent waves from November to March. During the season a legion of bronzed instructors offer beginners some of the world's cheapest surf lessons (P400 per hour) on the perfect learners' waves that stroke the shore.

Surfing instructors are easily found through the Urbiztondo's lodgings, which also rent boards (P200 per hour). The best beginners' break is usually at the 'cement factory' in Bacnotan, 6km north of San Juan. Urbiztondo's main beach break and neighbouring Mona Lisa Point tend to get bigger waves. Cartile Point and Darigayos are other favourite local breaks that are further out.

⮔ Sleeping

Most surf-inclined travellers stay in barangay Urbiztondo, a stretch of coast 3.5km south of San Juan proper, while tiny barangay Montemar, 1km north of San Juan, is where you'll find some of the more upmarket options.

⮔ Brgy Urbiztondo

★**Circle Hostel**   HOSTEL **$**
(☑ 0917 832 6253; www.launion.thecirclehostel.com; hammock P350, dm P450) Staying at this colourful, chilled out hostel is kinda like staying at a friend's place: you come, you surf, you relax with your fellow wanderers on beanbags in the common area, you befriend the wonderful staff and end up lingering for days. Bed down in the breezy thatched dorms with mozzie nets or sleep in a hammock. The staff organise surfing lessons, rent boards and do occasional hiking trips and waterfall jaunts.

★**Flotsam and Jetsam Hostel**   HOSTEL **$**
(☑ 0917 802 1328; www.flotsamandjetsamhostel.com; ✸❄) Artistic touches abound at this surfboard-strewn beachfront hostel; it's the kind of place where guests spontaneously jam on guitars and the thatched-roof bar heaves with bronzed young surfer bodies even in the off-season. Choose between rooming in a thatch-walled, fan-cooled dorm, a 'sea suite' or a converted RV. The 'spicy Nikki' by the resident 'alcohol alchemist' will lay you flat.

Little Surfmaid   BEACH RESORT **$$**
(☑ 072-888 5528; www.littlesurfmaidresort.com; r/ste from P2500/P3900; ✸❄) Danish-owned hotel that sits right above the most popular surf break, offering a high level of service and one of the best restaurants on the beach. The two-room beachfront suites with balconies facing Mona Lisa Point are worth the extra expense. The same can't quite be said for the standard doubles. Practically dead in the off-season.

San Juan Surf Resort   BEACH RESORT **$$**
(☑ 072-687 9990, 0917 887 5470; www.sanjuansurfresort.com.ph; d/q with air-con from P1800/2600, 2-person villas P1800; ✸❄) Run by Aussie Brian Landrigan, a 25-year veteran of the area, this place has upgraded to an upmarket surfers' village, with spartan standard rooms and multi-person 'villas' to the spacious 'de luxe'. There's a popular thatch-roofed restaurant overlooking the sand and the professionally run multiday surf-school packages come highly recommended.

⮔ Brgy Montemar

Final Option   BEACH RESORT **$$**
(☑ 072-888 2724, 0929 448 5505; www.finaloptionbeach.com.ph; r/ste P2200/3800; ✸❄✉)

San Fernando (La Union) & Around

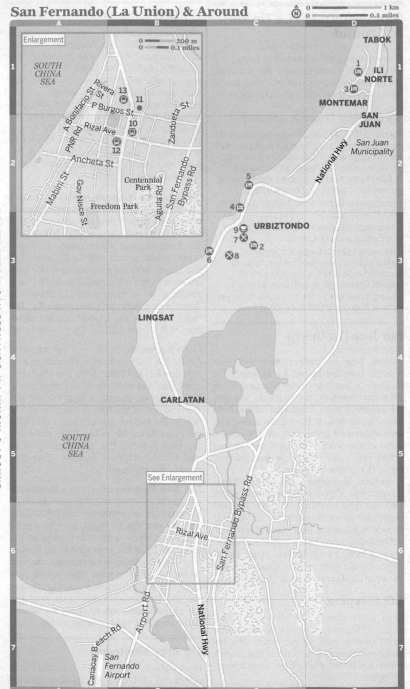

San Fernando (La Union) & Around

While the name of this resort is oddly ominous, the place itself – a German-run collection of clean apartments and bungalows north of San Juan – is anything but. There's a light-hearted, summery vibe here, plus an impressive swimming pool and decent German food (pork schnitzel, Vienna sausage, potato salad...) to boot.

Awesome Hotel HOTEL $$$
(319 Eagle St; r from P4000; ❄ 🛜 ❇) We don't usually trust establishments that blatantly blow their own horn, but in this case the name is largely deserved. David and Grace are gracious hosts, the bathrooms are modern and spacious, rooms are tastefully decked and feature firm queen-sized beds, and the sea views from the top floor are gorgeous.

✖ Eating & Drinking

All resorts have on-site restaurants, generally of decent quality. A few independent eateries are scattered around Urbiztondo.

★Angel & Marie's FILIPINO $$
(📱0920 836 4232; mains P80-199; ⊘6-9pm Mon-Fri, 7.30am-9pm Sat & Sun) Run by a friendly pair of locals, this great little thatched restaurant in the middle of Urbiztondo has a loyal following thanks to its banana pancakes, and tuna *kinilaw* (ceviche). If the place is closed on the weekend, it means that the surf's up!

Gefseis GREEK $$
(mains P140-300; ⊘10.30am-10.30pm Tue-Sun; 🍴) Genuine Greek tavern tempting surfers with such delights as moussaka, pastitsio and generous souvlaki platters.

El Union CAFE
(coffee P90; ⊘1-9pm Tue-Fri, 8am-9pm Sat & Sun) Thimble-sized cafe that takes care of surfers' caffeine-related needs, with chunky sandwiches and the awesome skillet cookies being an additional bonus.

ℹ Getting There & Away

Air-conditioned, northbound Partas buses pass through several times daily en route to Laoag, Vigan, Pagudpud, while the southbound ones head for Manila and Baguio. Regular jeepneys run between San Juan and San Fernando (P18).

ILOCOS

Vigan

📞 077 / POP 49,747

One of the oldest towns in the Philippines, Vigan is a Spanish-colonial fairy tale of dark-wood mansions, cobblestone streets and clattering *kalesa* (horse-drawn carriages). The truth about this Unesco World Heritage site is a little more complicated. Yes: Vigan is the finest surviving example of a Spanish colonial town in Asia. But outside of well-restored Crisologo St (closed to vehicular traffic) and a few surrounding blocks, it's a noisy Filipino town like many others. You may find it easier to appreciate the places where history is alive, where you can smell the aroma of freshly baked empanadas wafting past antique shops, pottery collectives and capiz-shell windows.

History

Located near where the Govantes River meets the South China Sea, Vigan became a convenient stop on the Silk Route, which linked China, the Middle East and Europe, and a thriving trading post where gold, logs and beeswax were bartered for goods from around the world and where Chinese settlers intermingled with the locals.

In the year 1572, Spanish conquistador Juan de Salcedo (the grandson of Miguel Lopez de Legazpi, one of the first conquistadors) took possession of the bustling

Vigan

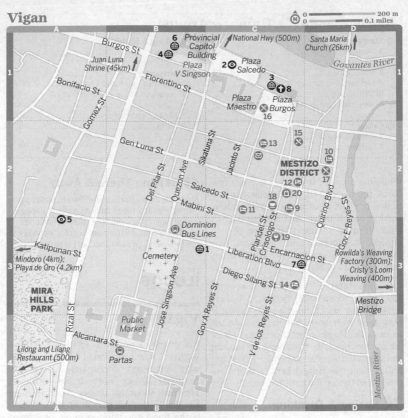

Vigan

◎ Sights
1 Crisologo Museum		B3
2 Magic Fountain		C1
3 Museo San Pablo		C1
4 Padre José Burgos National Museum		B1
5 Pottery Factories		A3
6 Provincial Jail		B1
7 Quema House		C3
8 St Paul Cathedral		C1

⊜ Sleeping
9 Gordion Inn		C2
10 Grandpa's Inn		D2
11 Hem Apartelle		C2
12 Hotel Luna		C2
13 Hotel Veneto de Vigan		C2
14 Villa Angela		C3

⊗ Eating
15 Cafe Leona		C2
Cafe Uno		(see 10)
16 Street Stalls		C1
17 Uno Grille		D2

⊙ Drinking & Nightlife
18 Coffee Break Vigan		C2
19 Legacy		C3

⊜ Shopping
20 Rowilda's		C2

ⓘ Information
Ilocos Sur Tourism Information Centre		(see 15)

international port. Juan de Salcedo became the lieutenant governor of the Ilocos region, and Vigan became the centre of the political, religious and commercial activities of the north. The rise of the mestizos led to considerable tensions, and Vigan became a hotbed of dissent against the Spanish when, in 1762, Diego Silang captured the city and named it the capital of Free Ilocos. He was eventually assassinated (the Spanish paid Silang's friend, Miguel Vicos, to shoot him in the back), and his wife, Gabriela Silang, took over. The first woman to lead a revolt in the Philippines, she was eventually captured and publicly hanged in the town square.

The city avoided destruction in WWII when Japanese troops fled the city just ahead of American carpet bombers, who aborted their mission at the last second.

◎ Sights

Vigan has two main squares located near each other at the north end of town: Plaza Salcedo, dominated by St Paul Cathedral, and the livelier Plaza Burgos, where locals stroll and hang out. The historic Mestizo District is centred on nearby Crisologo St. The main commercial drag is tricycle-congested Quezon Ave, which runs south to the public market.

★ Mestizo District   HISTORIC SITE

The Mestizo District, or Kasanglayan ('where the Chinese live'), is a grid of streets hemmed in between Plaza Burgos and Liberation Blvd and bisected by the beautifully preserved Crisologo St. You can wander in a daze among ancestral homes and colonial-era architecture. The mansions are beautiful and architecturally unique, marrying two great aesthetic senses: Chinese and Spanish. The latter were once Vigan's colonial masters; the former were merchants who settled, intermarried and, by the 19th century, became the city's elite.

In fact, Spanish and Chinese are themselves limiting terms when it comes to describing Vigan architecture. Spain itself has either influenced or been influenced by Mexico, the Caribbean and North Africa, and these regions make their presence known in the form of airy verandahs, leafy inner courtyards and wrought-iron balconies. At the same time, Asia also makes an appearance with dark wooden accents, polished floors, sliding capiz-shell windows and *ventanillas* (ventilated walls).

In most mansions, the ground floor has stone walls and is strictly for storage and/or work, while the wooden 1st floor, with its large, airy *sala* (living room), is for living. The capiz-shell windows are as tall as doors, while the wide window sills are good spots for a siesta. The capiz is a flat bivalve found in the coastal waters of the Philippines. It came into fashion in the 19th century be-

cause it was cheaper than glass and sturdy enough to withstand typhoon winds and rain. Light shines through capiz in a particular way that is almost impossibly romantic.

While a couple of mansions have been converted into B&Bs or museums, most are private homes. Two houses to look out for are the Quema House, with original furnishings and decor, and the Syquia Mansion on Quirino Blvd, the former holiday home of Vigan native Elpidio Quirino, the Philippines' sixth president, who was born in the nearby provincial jail. This is one of the best-preserved historical homes, and a good place to get a sense of the traditional interior of a Chinese-Spanish mansion at the end of the 19th century.

St Paul Cathedral   CHURCH

(Burgos St; ◎6am-9pm) This church was built in 'earthquake baroque' style (ie thick-walled and massive) after an earlier incarnation was damaged by two quakes in 1619 and 1627. The construction of the original wooden, thatched church is believed to have been supervised by Salcedo himself in 1574. The brass communion handrails were made in China, and faint Chinese characters can be seen where they connect to the building. The octagonal design of the church is supposedly rooted in feng shui design principles.

Museo San Pablo   MUSEUM

(admission P15; ◎9am-noon & 2-5pm Tue-Sun) The Museo San Pablo, inside St Paul Cathedral, is a good place to see old *santos* (religious statues). Make sure to have a look at the wonderfully aged photo collection of a German pharmacist who lived in Vigan for a number of years in the late 1800s.

Magic Fountain   FOUNTAIN

(Plaza Salcedo; ◎7.30pm) During peak tourist season, every night at 7.30pm the fountain in the middle of Plaza Salcedo bursts into a music and light show. You can almost hear Freddie Mercury and Montserrat Caballé bursting into 'Barcelona'.

Padre José Burgos National Museum   MUSEUM

(Ayala Museum; Burgos St; admission P20; ◎8.30-11.30am & 1.30-4.30pm Tue-Sun) Built in 1788 the Padre José Burgos National Museum is in the ancestral home of Father José Burgos, one of the three martyr priests executed by the Spanish in 1872. It houses an extensive collection of Ilocano artefacts, including a series of 14 paintings by the locally famed painter Don Esteban Villanueva depicting the 1807 Basi Revolt. Weavings, Tingguian (Itneg) jewellery, musical instruments, pottery, photos of Easter processions and elaborate furniture are also on display.

Pottery Factories   CRAFTS

(Gomez St) Prior to the arrival of the Spanish, Chinese settlers pioneered a still-active pottery industry. You can visit a couple of pottery factories on Gomez St, near the corner with Liberation Blvd. The 50m-long kiln at RG Jar, which was made in 1823 and can hold nearly 1000 jars, is a wonder to behold. Local potters are happy to let you create misshapen ceramics of your own at the pottery wheel. Be nice and buy a small clay souvenir afterwards.

The *burnay* (earthen jars) that you find here are used in the fermentation of *basi* (sugar cane wine) and *bagoong* (fish paste), but you are more likely to see them scattered about in homes and gardens.

Weavers   CRAFTS

Vigan weavers are known for using *abel*, a locally produced cotton fabric, to handweave shawls, tablecloths, napkins and *barong* (traditional Filipino shirts). In barangay Camanggaan, just a 10-minute tricycle ride southeast of Vigan, you can watch *abel* handweavers in action at Rowilda's Weaving Factory, which is actually just a house, or its neighbour, Cristy's Loom Weaving.

High-quality *binakol* (blankets), including some antique blankets from nearby Abra Province, are for sale at Mira Furniture and at many shops lining Crisologo St.

Crisologo Museum   MUSEUM

(Liberation Blvd; entry by donation; ☺ 8.30-11.30am & 1.30-4.30pm) The Crisologos, Vigan's most prominent political dynasty, have converted their ancestral home into this strangely compelling family shrine. In addition to the mildly interesting family photos, personal effects, period furniture and impressive collection of indigenous Filipino headgear you may spot the bloodstained pair of trousers from Floro Crisologo's assasination in 1972 and the old Chevy that Governor Carmeling Crisologo was in when she was (unsuccessfully) ambushed by gunmen in 1961.

🎎 Festivals

Vigan Town Fiesta   CULTURAL

Held in the third or fourth week of January, the fiesta commemorates the town's patron saint, St Paul the Apostle, with a parade, musical performances, beauty contests and cultural shows.

Kannawidan Ylocos Festival   CULTURAL

This festival at the end of January celebrates the best of Ilocos Sur culture, from traditional dress and folk dance to tribal rituals and marching band contests.

Viva Vigan Festival of the Arts   CULTURAL

A grand celebration of the town's cultural heritage takes place in the first week in May. There is street dancing, a fashion show, a *kalesa* parade and, of course, lots of food.

🛏 Sleeping

Rates decrease by about 20% from June to October.

Hem Apartelle   GUESTHOUSE $

(☑ 077-722 2173; 32 Governor A Reyes St; d P700; ❈ 🤶) No heritage-style lodging here: the Hem is just an air-conditioned guesthouse that's cheap cheap cheap like the birds. Rooms are tiled and characterless, but there are TVs, clean sheets, clean floors and clean toilets you can sit on – win!

★ Villa Angela   HISTORIC HOTEL $$

(☑ 0919 315 6122, 077-722 2914; www.villangela. com; 26 Quirino Blvd; d/q from P2000/3200; ❈ 🤶) This hotel is more than 130 years old and retains every morsel of its old-world charm. The spacious rooms, fabulous antique furniture, which includes wooden harps and king-sized *nara*-wood canopy beds, and colonial-style lounge were good enough for Tom Cruise and Willem Dafoe during the filming of *Born on the Fourth of July* in the vicinity in 1989.

Grandpa's Inn   HOTEL $$

(☑ 077-674 0686; 1 Bonifacio St; d/f from P750/2680; ❈ 🤶) With an impressive array of rooms, Grandpa's is solid value, and the fan-cooled doubles cater to shoestring travellers. All rooms have brick walls, capiz-shell windows, wooden beams, antique furnishings and rustic flavour; there are a couple of rooms where you can sleep in a *kalesa*. Drawbacks include thimble-sized bathrooms and street noise; ownership of ear plugs is a boon.

Gordion Inn   HOTEL $$

(☑ 077-674 0288, 077-722 2526; reservation@vigangordionhotel.com; cnr V de los Reyes & Salcedo Sts; s/d/ste from P2500/2800/7000; ☺❈🤶)

DON'T MISS

NORTH & SOUTH OF VIGAN

Santa Maria Church Thirty-eight kilometres south of Vigan, this massive baroque structure built in 1769 – a Unesco World Heritage site – is unique. It has an imposing brick facade and sits alone on a hill – rather than in the town square like most Spanish churches – overlooking the town of Santa Maria, giving it an Alamo kinda vibe. It's not hard to see why it was used as a fortress during the Philippine Revolution in 1896. Take any Manila-bound bus to Santa Maria.

Juan Luna Shrine (www.nhcp.gov.ph; ⊘ 8am-5pm Tue-Sun) It's worth stopping in Badoc, halfway between Vigan and Laoag, for a peek inside the restored ancestral home of Juan Luna, arguably the Philippines' greatest painter. The knowledgeable curator will introduce you to the history of the Luna family and tell the stories behind the paintings. All Laoag-bound buses pass through Badoc and the museum is near the Virgen Milagrosa church.

This bright blue-and-yellow B&B offers smart, spacious rooms (though would it kill them to put up some shelves and clothes' hooks?) and the breakfast buffet is a good introduction to Filipino favourites.

Hotel Veneto de Vigan HOTEL $$
(☑ 077-674 0938; www.hotelvenetodevigan.com; cnr Bonifacio St & Governor A Reyes St; d/f from P2410/6900; ▧ ◉) The renovated exterior of this historical wooden building hides light, bright, modern rooms with particularly comfortable beds and polished floors. Some of the stairs are break-neck steep, but the staff are wonderfully friendly and helpful and we love the colourful mural in the lobby.

⭐ **Hotel Luna** BOUTIQUE HOTEL $$$
(☑ 077-632 2222; www.hotelluna.ph; cnr V de los Reyes & General Luna St; d/ste from P5000/11,000; ▧ ◉ ☷) Vigan's most striking hotel is a 19th-century mansion that's all exposed stone, wooden floors and crystal chandeliers, with original paintings and sculptures of Filipino artist Juan Luna throughout. The standard rooms are compact, carpeted and quiet, and we love the split-level loft suite with a free-standing tub and rain shower. The elegant Comedor restaurant serves fantastic Ilocano dishes.

✖ Eating & Drinking

The Ilocos region is known for its food, and local specialities include *pinakbet* (stir-fried mixed vegetables), *bagnet* (deep-fried pork knuckle) and *poqui-poqui* (a roasted eggplant dish).

⭐ **Lilong and Lilang Restaurant** ILOCANO $
(☑ 077 722 1450; www.hiddengardenvigan.com; barangay Bulala; mains P40-120; ⊘ noon-9pm) Nestling at the heart of what appears to be a garden centre crossed with a very short nature trail, this thatched-roofed, plant-festooned restaurant is a great bet for Ilocano dishes such as the Vigan empanada, *poqui-poqui*, *warek-warek* (pork innards with mayo) and the more conventional *bagnet*, *pinakbet* and mega fruit shakes.

Street Stalls STREET FOOD $
(Plaza Burgos; snacks P50) For quick, cheap Ilocano fare, check out the collection of street stalls that lines Florentino St along Plaza Burgos. They specialise in local empanadas filled with cabbage, green papaya and *longganisa* (Chinese sausage), *okoy* (deep-fried shrimp omelettes) and *sinanglao* (beef soup).

Uno Grille BARBECUE $$
(Bonifacio St; mains P120-220) Run by Grandpa's Inn across the street, this courtyard restaurant caters to the discerning carnivore, with grilled meats hogging the lion's share of the menu. We're still salivating at the memory of the melt-off-the-bone-tender baby back ribs with a touch of Chinese five spice.

Cafe Uno ILOCANO $$
(1 Bonifacio St; mains P90-150; ⊘ 9am-11.30pm; ▧ ◉) Attached to neighbouring Grandpa's Inn, this cafe has a loyal local clientele, largely thanks to its take on the Vigan *longganisa* and *bagnet*. Its shakes and cakes are worth a stop, too.

Cafe Leona FILIPINO, INTERNATIONAL $$
(Crisologo St; meals P120-290; ⊘ noon-10pm) This popular eatery that spills out onto Crisologo St tries to be all things to all people with its eclectic menu of Italian, Chinese, Japanese, and Filipino specialities, though its forte is Ilocano dishes such as *bagnet*. We're less than impressed with the plastic

patio furniture and the loud adjoining open-air karaoke bar, though.

Legacy
CLUB

(Crisologo St; ⊙ 7pm-late) Legacy is conservative Vigan's concession to nightlife. On the inside it resembles a New York lounge misplaced in Ilocos. Thumping bass and electronic music reverberate through the walls; Wednesday is ladies' night (one free beer, girls), and the local DJs get the crowd moving on Fridays and Saturdays.

Coffee Break Vigan
CAFE

(3 Salcedo St; ⊙ 10am-10pm) Cute little cafe that makes for an excellent, frappuccino-fuelled respite from the heat. Its pesto pasta also hits the spot.

🏠 Shopping

Antique and textile shops line the sides of Crisologo St. Bargain hard and you can score some pretty decent deals out here.

Rowilda's
CRAFTS

(Crisologo St) Woven *abel* goods produced in barangay Camanggaan can be found in many of the souvenir and antique shops that line Crisologo St. This place has a particularly good selection.

❶ Information

Plenty of internet cafes and banks with ATMs are clustered on Quezon Ave.

Ilocos Sur Tourism Information Centre
(☑ 077-722 8520; www.ilocossur.gov.ph; 1 Crisologo St; ⊙ 8am-noon & 1-5pm) In the ancestral home of poet Leona Florentino, the highly informative staffers here give out maps of Vigan.

Post Office (cnr Bonifacio & Gov A Reyes Sts)

❶ Getting There & Away

Buses to Manila (P700, nine hours) are plentiful. Try **Dominion Bus Lines** (☑ 077-722 2084; cnr Liberation Blvd & Quezon Ave) to Cubao and Sampaloc, or **Partas** (☑ 077-722 3369; Alcantara St) to Cubao and Pasay. Partas has three nightly 29-seat deluxe express buses (P850, eight hours), as well as frequent buses to Laoag (P265, two hours), a daily bus to Pagudpud (P370, five hours) and buses Baguio (P390, five to seven hours, three daily).

Many more buses bound for Laoag and Manila stop at the Caltex Station on the National Hwy just outside Vigan. Southbound buses go via San Fernando (P235, 3½ hours), with departures roughly every two hours.

❶ Getting Around

Vigan is one of the few remaining towns in the Philippines where *kalesa* are still in use (P150 per hour). Whole day tours will cost you around P1000, but pick your driver wisely, as English is not always strong. A tricycle ride should cost P11 within town (more at night).

Laoag

☑ 077 / POP 104,904

Like nearby Vigan, Laoag is a town with some history behind it. Unlike Vigan, said history is only evident in a few locations, and Laoag largely comes off as a noisy step to something better. This is still loyal Marcos country, and around here the old dictator is still referred to somewhat reverently as 'President Marcos'.

◉ Sights

◉ Laoag

Museo Ilocos Norte
MUSEUM

(www.museoilocosnorte.com; General Antonio Luna St; admission P30; ⊙ 9am-noon & 1-5pm Mon-Sat, from 10am Sun) Housed in the historic Tabacalera warehouse, the snazzy Museo Ilocos Norte is one of the better ethnographic museums in the Philippines. It houses a large collection of Ilocano, Igorot and Itneg tradtional clothing, household utensils, ceremonial objects and more. At the end of the hall is a split-level replica *ilustrado* (19th-century ancestral house).

Sinking Bell Tower
LANDMARK

(Bonifacio St) Laoag's main architectural attraction is the Sinking Bell Tower with what is presently a hobbit-sized doorway. Built by Augustine friars to accommodate men on horseback, it is gradually sinking into the soft riverside loam.

St William's Cathedral
CHURCH

This immense Italian Renaissance–style St William's Cathedral was built in 1880.

◉ Around Laoag

Sand Dunes
SAND DUNES

Located along the coast near Laoag, the seemingly endless sand dunes sprawl south all the way to Paoay. Access is easiest to the La Paz stretch, only 15 minutes from the city, whereas the Suba dunes near the Fort Ilocandia resort is where scenes from *Mad Max*

LEAD-ING THE WAY: ECOTOURS IN ILOCOS

Laoag Eco-Adventure Development Movement (LEAD; ☑077-772 0538, 0919 873 5516; http://leadmovement.wordpress.com) The good people of LEAD are all about facilitating journeys into Ilocos Norte that are environmentally friendly and sustainable. LEAD is also the first bona fide sandboarding (like snowboarding, only down sand dunes) operator in the region, and is actively engaged in sustainable eco-tourism ventures in the village of Adams.

Wen! Travel & Tours (☑077-770 3420, 0917 511 1050; wentravelandtours.tripod.com) The LEAD-affiliated Wen! Travel & Tours arranges treks, rafting and other eco-adventures across the whole of Ilocos Norte; rates run around P2800 for groups of up to four people.

and *Born on the Fourth of July* were shot. Fort Ilocandia rents out ATVs, but we much prefer the eco-friendly sandboarding tours with the folks from the LEAD Movement.

Paoay Church　　　CHURCH
Nineteen kilometres southwest of Laoag is North Luzon's most famous church. Unesco World Heritage Paoay Church was built in classic earthquake-baroque style, with a towering belfry and massive brick reinforcements running along its sides. Begun in 1704 and finished 90 years later, it's architecturally unique: an incongruous yet beautiful blend of Gothic, Chinese, Japanese and even Javanese influences (notice how the layered profile bears resemblance to the famous stepped pyramid of Borobudur). Take a jeepney from Laoag to Paoay via Batad.

🛏 Sleeping

Laoag Renzo Hotel　　　HOTEL $
(☑077-770 4898; www.laoagrenzohotel.tripod.com; F Guerrero St; r from P900; 🕸🛜) With a surprisingly grand lobby full of woodcarvings, Renzo is Laoag's best bargain. Its lemon-scented ensuite rooms are spacious, cool and quiet. If you've got a lot of luggage, the trudge to the top floor is a good thigh workout.

Isabel Suites　　　HOTEL $$
(☑077-770 4998; www.isabelsuites-laoag.com; General Segundo Ave; s/d/tr from P850/1450/1950; 🕸🛜) A study in austerity, the rooms at the Isabel are generally of the swing-a-cat variety, but the beds are comfy and the tiled floors sparkle. The soundproofing is quite good for a central hotel on the main street, which means you might be able to sleep until 6.30am instead of 6am.

Java Hotel　　　HOTEL $$
(☑077-770 5596; www.javahotel.com.ph; General Segundo Ave; r/ste from P2180/4160; 🕸🛜🌊) The petrol station in the parking lot isn't exactly in keeping with the 'Balinese-Moroccan' theme, and the spacious rooms are decorated in warm ochres and yellows; the only concession to the theme being the wicker furniture. Ilocano dishes and sushi grace the menu at the thatch-roofed restaurant.

🍴 Eating & Drinking

Dap-ayan ti Ilocos Norte　　　FOOD COURT $
(cnr Rizal Ave & V Llanes St; mains from P50; ⏱11am-9pm) An outdoor food court, this is a great place to sample local fare such as *bagnet*, bright orange empanadas filled with green papaya, *longganisa*, egg and bean sprouts, and the legendary Ilocos *longganisa* (sausage) on its own.

La Preciosa　　　ILOCANO $$
(☑077-773 1162; Rizal Ave; mains P120-160; ⏱8am-11pm) Laoag's best-loved, homey restaurant is highly recommended for its large portions of delicious Ilocano specialities like *pinakbet* (veggies cooked in fish paste), crispy yet tender *bagnet, poqui-poqui* and *dinardaan* (offal simmered in pig's blood gravy). The sweets don't let down the side either: go for the carrot cake or the decidedly non-Ilocano velvet cupcakes.

Saramsam Ylocano Restaurant　　　ILOCANO $$
(cnr Rizal Ave & Hizon St; mains P75-220; ⏱11am-11pm) Surrounded by the owner's antique collection, you can sample the superlative *pinakbet* and *poqui-poqui* pizza (which we suppose can be loosely classed as fusion), as well as the restaurant's unusual signature pasta with mango. Portions are sizeable, so come ravenous.

ℹ Information

The big banks all have branches around the intersection of General Segundo Ave and Rizal Ave, Laoag's main commercial thoroughfare. General Segundo Ave and Primo Lazaro Ave contain many internet cafes.

ⓘ Getting There & Away

PAL Express and Cebu Pacific fly daily to Manila from the airport 7km west of town. Airport jeepneys (P20, 15 minutes) leave from Fariñas St; most say 'Laoag-Gabu'.

There is no shortage of buses to Manila (from P650, nine to 11 hours). Companies include **Partas** (☑ 077-771 4898; Gen Antonio Luna St) and **Fariñas Trans** (☑ 077-772 0126; www. farinastrans.com; FR Castro Ave), the latter also running to Baguio (P600, eight to 10 hours). The super-deluxe express buses to Manila (up to P965) tend to run overnight.

Partas has frequent buses to Baguio (P550, seven hours) and Pagudpud (P120, 1½ hours). All buses going south stop in Vigan (P175, two hours).

GMW/GV Florida (☑ 077-771 7382; Paco Roman St) has several daily buses to Tuguegarao (P550, seven hours) via Pagudpud (P120, 1½ hours) and Claveria (P270, three hours). Minibuses to Pagudpud (P90) leave every 30 minutes from behind the Provincial Capitol Building.

Laoag–Batac–Paoay jeepneys leave from Hernando Ave. Laoag–Nagbacalan–Paoay jeepneys take the coastal road to Paoay (45 minutes) via the Fort Ilocandia turn-off and Malacañang of the North (30 minutes). They depart from Fariñas St.

Jeepneys bound for Fort Ilocandia (25 minutes) say 'Calayab' and depart from in front of St William's Cathedral.

Pagudpud & Around

☑ 077 / POP 21,877

Pagudpud (and Blue Lagoon in particular) is the stuff of glossy postcards: white-sand beaches, swaying green palms, water that shimmers through every cool shade of blue. Singing frogs at night, friendly locals by day. Plus: a clutch of stylishly renovated hotels and 'next big thing on the surfing circuit' street cred have put this lonely stretch of coastline on the tourist map, although it mercifully remains sleepy compared to the likes of Boracay.

⊙ Sights

Pagudpud actually consists of three vast beaches, strung along Luzon's northern edge and hemmed in by headlands. Coconut-palm-backed **Saud Beach** is where most resorts are to be found. Idyllic Blue Lagoon is a few headlands east. Deserted

---

THE MARCOS LEGACY

Many Filipinos equate the 20-year rule of Ferdinand Marcos with martial law, repressions of civil liberties, imprisonment and torture of opposition, and embezzlement of public funds on an epic scale. In spite of that, the Marcos family continues to be very popular in this part of Luzon, with Marcos' legacy 'enshrined' in several locations.

Marcos Mausoleum (barangay Lacub; ⊗ 9am-noon & 1-4pm) The embalmed body of Ferdinand Marcos (1917–89) is laid out on a mattress and lit by floodlights in an otherwise dark sepulchre at the Marcos Museum & Mausoleum. Full creepiness is achieved by eerie choral music played on a continuous loop. The mausoleum is located in Batac, a town where Marcos spent his childhood, 15km south of Laoag; take a jeepney from Hernando Ave.

It's a sign of the family's continued political influence that the body was allowed to be returned to his boyhood home. And it's testament to the ambivalence (and often outright hostility) to Marcos' legacy that prompts many Filipinos to suspect the body is simply a wax figure, one last-ditch con by the master puppet master.

The impressive Marcos ancestral home is next door (but closed to the public), with some reverential displays out front.

Malacañang of the North (admission P30; ⊗ 9am-noon & 1-4pm Tue-Sun) In a peaceful location next to the scenic **Paoay Lake**, the opulent former estate where the Marcos family spent their holidays is open to the public. The impressive house, with its cavernous *sala* (living room), capiz-shell windows and other colonial touches, provides a glimpse into the family's lavish lifestyle; the golf course where Marcos used to play now belongs to Fort Ilocandia.

Marcos Museum (entry by donation; ⊗ 8am-6pm) The former home where Ferdinand Marcos was born on 11 September 1917 takes pride of place in the small village of Sarrat, 15km east of Laoag. The displays embellish the former dictator's legal career, and the nearby Santa Monica Church hosted the wedding of Marcos' youngest daughter in 1983 – at a price tag of over US$10 million.

Pansian Beach is still further on, near the border of Cagayan Province.

Blue Lagoon   BEACH
At Blue Lagoon, Luzon's whitest sand and deep blue water conspire majestically to compete for a place on your desktop screensaver. There's terrific snorkelling here and despite the recent opening of a few resorts, the beach is rarely crowded. It's 16km from Saud to the beach turn-off, then another 4km down a sealed road. Tourists heading to Blue Lagoon must pay a P30 'environmental fee'.

Kabigan Falls   WATERFALLS
Kabigan Falls, located in the interior jungle, is 120m of crashing white water and a cool, clear pool to swim in, accessible via group tours by all hotels or private tricyle hire (around P700 return). It's a 30-minute walk from the highway turn-off if you don't want to be driven all the way.

Stingray Memorial   MEMORIAL
A minor road branches off the highway towards the secluded Caunayan Bay where the Stingray Memorial commemorates the mission of American submarine USS *Stingray*. The submarine delivered weapons to the Ilocano guerrillas, thus playing a decisive role in the eventual Japanese defeat. Tricycles will take you here for around P1000 return.

Lovers' Rocks   LANDMARK
Near barangay Balaoi you can spot **Dos Hermanos**, a pair of inaccessible offshore islands that local legend claims are the remains of two sibling fishermen lost at sea. Past here are the most Freudian geographical formations in Pagudpud: **Bantay-abot** ('Mountain with a hole'), an offshore hole in a rocky islet, and **Timmangtang Rock**, a stubby lump of rock and jungle. Collectively, the two formations are known as the Lovers' Rocks. Don't make us spell out why.

⚡ Activities

Many resorts rent out **mountain bikes** and Terra Rika Beach Resort has a dive centre.

Pagudpud is growing in popularity as a **surfing** spot – some real giants occasionally form at Blue Lagoon, while Saud and the more isolated barangay Caparispisan also gets well-shaped if fickle waves. The peak surf season is August to October. Boards (P200 per hour) and lessons (P400 per hour) are available at Kapuluan Vista Resort.

Reliably strong winds make the exposed parts of the west coast ideal for **kitesurf**ing and **windsurfing** between October and March. Kingfisher Resort offers instruction.

🛏 Sleeping & Eating

Accommodation rates drop precipitously in low season (June to December). A lot of basic homestays have opened in the village that abuts Saud Beach (follow the road past the big bend near Saud Beach Resort). The going rate at the time of research for fan/ air-con rooms was P650/1100.

🏖 Saud Beach

Evangeline Beach Resort   BEACH RESORT **$$**
(☑0908 863 7564, 077-655 5862; www.evangelinebeachresort.net; d/q P2600/3700; ❀🛜) Evangeline's rooms are Bali-chic-style accommodation, complete with a small pool. The suites tend to be the best deal on the property, the beds strewn with rose petals, though bathrooms are thimble-sized. Evangeline's has an excellent beachfront restaurant that particularly excels at seafood dishes.

Northridge Resort   BEACH RESORT **$$**
(☑0921 415 9545; r with/without air-con P1650/1300; ❀🛜) As close as it gets to a backpacker option, with clean, well-kept doubles at the south end of Saud Beach and helpful staff who are happy to arrange bicycle rentals and transportation.

Apo Idon   BEACH RESORT **$$$**
(☑0917 510 0671, 077-676 0438; www.apoidon. com; r/ste from P4800/7200; ❀🛜🏊) The fanciest resort along Saud Beach, all bright colours and wood carvings, with nicely designed rooms featuring Ifugao art, capizshell windows and Western-style mod-cons.

Terra Rika Beach Resort   BEACH RESORT **$$$**
(☑077-676 1559, 0918 951 5250; www.terrarika. com; dm/d/ste from P1550/3850/6550; ❀🛜) Almost on the beach, Terra Rika sports brightly painted but otherwise rather spartan rooms. The somewhat disingenuously dubbed 'deluxe' rooms are not worth the price, but more expensive dark-wood cottages are a solid bet. Has diving instruction (P3000 for introductory dive) and snorkelling gear (guests only).

🏖 Caparispisan

★Kingfisher Resort   BEACH RESORT **$$**
(☑0927 525 8111; www.kingfisher.ph; tiki hut P2500, casita P7000, ste P12,000; ❀🛜🏊) In splendid isolation 16km along a partially

ADAMS

This former rebel stronghold nestles between jungle-covered mountains and is reachable via a rough 14km road that starts near Pansian Beach, off the coastal highway. All dirt trails and rickety bridges, Adams offers some good trekking, including a popular two-hour hike to the 25ft **Anuplig Falls** with a wonderfully clear pool beneath, and a stretch of the Bulu River open for inner-tubing.

Adams still gets few visitors, in spite of the spectacular location, but you can inquire about homestays at the Municipal Hall and camping is also possible. Local food delicacies include deep-fried frogs and *buos* (boiled fire ant eggs). You can get out to Adams on motorbikes from Pagudpud (around P250), or leave the organising to Wen! Travel & Tours (p125).

paved road from Saud Beach, Kingfisher caters to active travellers, with kitesurfing and windsurfing available between October and March, and paddleboards and kayaks for rent when seas are calmer. Lodge in basic tiki huts or treat yourself to a deluxe casita. The chilled beach party vibe makes it difficult to leave. Three-night minimum stay.

Blue Lagoon

Kapuluan Vista Resort   BEACH RESORT $$
(☎077-676 9075, 0920 952 2528; www.kapulanvistaresortandrestaurant.com; dm/d from P650/P2700; ✳☎) This urbane resort, around 7km west of the Blue Lagoon turn-off, was conceived as a surf resort but now caters to all types. It's an excellent all-round option, with stellar food and a good variety of attractive rooms set around a swimming pool in well-kept grounds. Surfboards (P200 per hour) and surfing instruction (P400) available.

Hannah's Beach Resort   BEACH RESORT $$$
(☎0928 520 6255; www.hannahsbeachresort.com; dm/d/f/ste P1200/3300/5750/16,500; ✳☎) Hannah's is a high-end slice of heaven, overlooking a beautiful cove, sprinkled with plush little cottages and villas. The dorms are bare-bones and prices too high, but all lodgings are served by a huge menu of tours and activities, with banana boats, jet skis and even guitars for rent. You can zipline

down to Hannah's, Superman-style, from the Blue Lagoon viewpoint.

❶ Getting There & Away

The highway around here is spectacular in spots. If you're coming from Laoag, get a seat on the left side of the bus.

Frequent buses travel the coastal road to Laoag (P120, two hours) and Claveria (P85, 1¼ hours).

There is also now a daily Partas bus from Pagudpud to Manila.

THE CORDILLERA

To many travellers, North Luzon is the Cordillera. These spiny mountains, which top out at around 2900m, are beloved, worshipped and feared in equal doses by those who witness them and those who live among them.

The tribes of the Cordillera, collectively known as the Igorot, have distinct traditions that have survived both Spanish and American occupation and that add a culturally rich dimension to the already bounteous attractions of the region. Banaue's renowned rice terraces have been dubbed 'the eighth wonder of the world', while lesser-known but no less spectacular terraces exist throughout Ifugao, Mountain Province and Kalinga. Rice terraces aside, the mountains throw down the gauntlet to hikers, bikers, cavers and other fresh-air fiends.

Baguio

☎074 / POP 318,676 / ELEV 1450M

Every country in Southeast Asia has an upland, pine-clad retreat from the heat and dust of the lowlands, and Baguio (*bah*-gee-oh) is the Philippines' exemplar of the genre. Like other hill stations, Baguio is a university town that boasts one of the Philippines' largest student populations (a quarter of a million!), and is also a crossroads between hill tribe culture and lowland settlers. For most travellers, Baguio serves as the primary gateway to backpacker bliss up north in Sagada, Banaue and Kalinga.

Sadly, thousands of jeepneys, taxis and tricycles are responsible for almost unbearable levels of smog in the city centre. Away from the traffic-snarled city centre, Baguio is airy and pleasant. If you're returning from the mountains, the small-scale urban mayhem, nightlife and burgeoning restaurant scene are actually refreshing.

The Cordillera

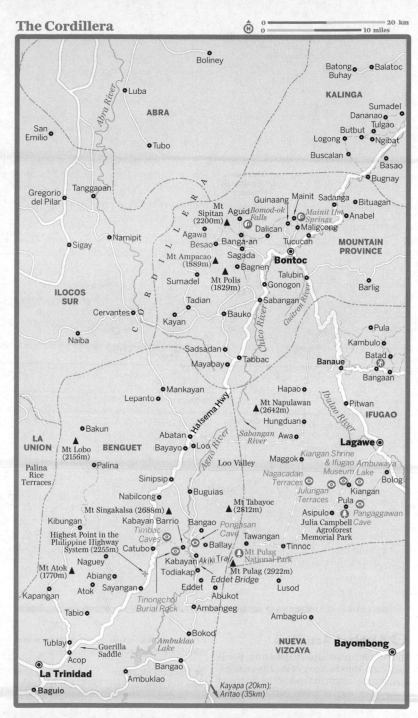

Baguio

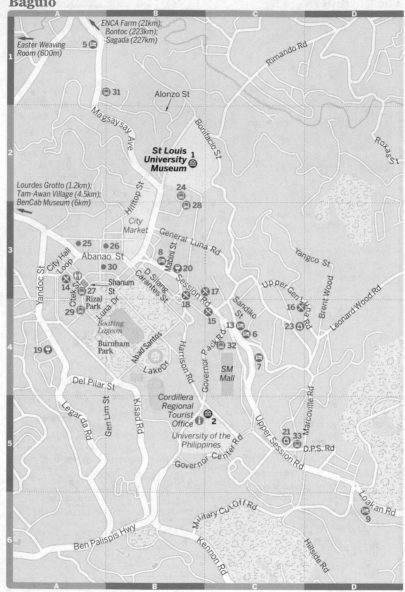

◎ Sights & Activities

The city radiates in all directions from Burnham Park. The character of the city changes dramatically south and east of the centre as chaos gives way to green parks, towering Benguet pines, lavish summer homes and winding roads with spectacular views.

★ **BenCab Museum** MUSEUM
(www.bencabmuseum.org; Km 6, Asin Rd, Tadiangan; adult/student P100/80; ☺ 9am-6pm Tue-Sun)

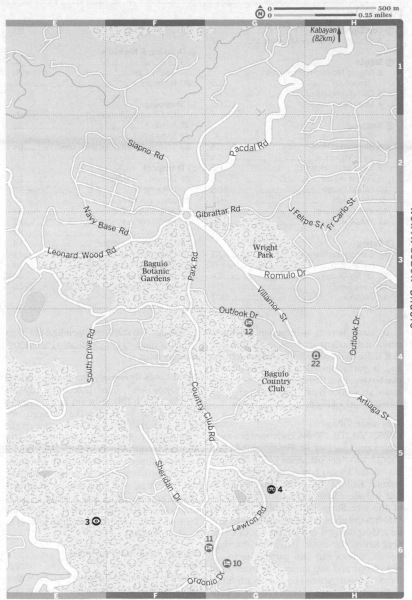

This superb museum dedicated to the life, times and work of Benedicto Reyes Cabrera (BenCab) is as fascinating as the man who is its subject. The gallery is a mix of high glass panes slanting light into modern art colonnades offset by walls of traditional animist wood carvings, *bulol* (rice guardians), psychedelic works by Leonard Aguinaldo and ceremonial *hagabi* (carved wooden benches). Take a jeepney to Asin and ask to be let off at BenCab, or hire a cab (P150).

Baguio

To come here is to experience Filipino crafts and modern art displayed in tandem, in a space that evokes both ultramodernism and is partly modelled after a traditional rice terrace. Plus, there's a wonderfully saucy erotic art section downstairs and a great little cafe overlooking actual rice terraces.

Tam-awan Village   MUSEUM
(☑ 0921 588 3131, 074-446 2949; www.tam-awan-village.com; Long-Long Rd, Pinsao; adult/student P50/30, workshops per person P450) 🥢 Eight traditional Ifugao homes and two rare octagonal Kalinga huts were reassembled at this hillside village on the northwest edge of the city. Steep paths thread their way through the greenery between the huts and on a clear day you can see the South China Sea, hence the name Tam-awan ('vantage point'). Guests can also participate in art workshops and see indigenous music and dance demonstrations (arrange in advance).

To get here, take a taxi (P70) or a Tam-awan–Long-Long jeepney (P15).

The Chanum Foundation, headed by contemporary artist Ben Cabrera ('BenCab'), developed the project in line with its mission to preserve and teach the art and culture of the Cordillera people.

You can also stay here; spending the night in one of the huts (single/double P500/1000) is a rare treat.

⭐ **St Louis University Museum**   MUSEUM
(Magsaysay Ave; ⊙ 8am-12.30pm & 1.30-5pm Mon-Sat) **FREE** This museum in the campus library is run by Isekias 'Ike' Picpican, one of the country's foremost authorities on the history and culture of the Cordillera people. You can spend hours examining the scores of weapons, funeral artefacts, tribal costumes, musical instruments such as the nose flute, woodcarvings, and photographs of various rituals and sacrifices, but it helps if Ike is around to explain their context. Leave some form of ID with the front security folks at St Louis University.

Baguio Mountain Provinces Museum   MUSEUM
(Governor Pack Rd; adult/student P40/20; ⊙ 8am-5pm Mon-Sat) This thorough museum is a great introduction to the Igorot ('mountain people') of the Cordillera and also the harmful 'savage highlander'/'cultured lowlander' divide, introduced by the Spanish. Each display focuses on a separate indigenous group, and you may spot the spears, *bolos* (machetes) and colourful clothing of Kalinga headhunters, accounts of Ibaloi mummification

practises and a Kabayan mummy, the beaded headgear of the Tinguians, photos of Ifugao Imbayah ceremonies and a compelling exhibition on the history of Baguio.

Lourdes Grotto   MONUMENT
Established by the Spanish Jesuits in 1907, the Lourdes Grotto sits at the top of 252 steps in the hilly western part of town. From the top, there's a nice view of the city's rooftops, but even better views are to be had from the top of Dominican Hill, a short walk from the grotto up Dominican Hill Rd.

Camp John Hay   MOUNTAIN RESORT
A Japanese internment camp for Allied prisoners of war, and then a US military rest-and-recreation facility, 246-hectare Camp John Hay has been reinvented as a mountain resort with restaurants, hotels, shops, a fantastic golf course and a handful of scattered sights sprinkled amid rolling hills and stands of Benguet pines. Camp John Hay is very spread-out, and jeepneys are not allowed in, so your best bet is to commandeer a taxi.

The Historical Core – with the attractively landscaped Bell Amphitheatre and some walking trails – incorporates the site where General Yamashita surrendered to the Americans, Tree Top Adventure zipline and the Cemetery of Negativism (9am to 5pm), a twee but entertaining graveyard that's supposed to boost your positive thinking. There's also a nice panorama from the Mile High viewpoint.

🛏 Sleeping
Consider staying out of the centre to escape Baguio's notorious noise and air pollution. Be sure to ask for the 'promo rate' (or just a discount) in the off-season.

The most unique budget choice is Tamawan Village, but note that it's at least a 15-minute ride from the centre.

Baguio Village Inn   GUESTHOUSE $
(☑074-442 3901; 355 Magsaysay Ave; s/d from P400/750; ☎) Close to the Slaughterhouse Terminal, this pinewood backpacker special has swing-a-cat rooms with narrow beds. An ensuite room is worth the splurge; request a room at the back unless you're a heavy-duty sleeper.

YMCA Hostel   HOSTEL $
(☑074-442 4766; Post Office Loop; dm/d P375/1200) The 'Y' boasts huge, bright dorm rooms and colourful private rooms with soft beds and flat-screen TVs – pretty good value. It's cheap, it's central and you can hardly miss the giant 'YMCA' sign.

Mile Hi Inn   HOSTEL $$
(☑074-446 6141; Mile Hi Center; dm/d/tr P600/2100/2350; ☎) Its motto is 'clean, cosy, comfy', and frankly it would be hard to argue with that. Located in Camp John Hay's duty-free shopping centre, it has simple tiled four-bed dorm rooms and golden-hued doubles. Staying here with your sweetie *does not* qualify you for the Mile High Club.

City Center Hotel   HOTEL $$
(☑074-422 3637; www.baguiocitycenterhotel. com; cnr Session Rd & Mabini St; d/f P2100/3200; ❄☎) Though modest in furnishings, these rooms are brand new and in a you-couldn't-be-more-central-if-you-tried location. Perks include power showers and cable TV.

Casa Vallejo   HOTEL $$
(☑074-424 3397; www.casavallejo-baguio.com; Upper Session Rd; d/f from P2700/4500; ➲❄@) Situated in a classic historical building that harks back to the turn of the (20th) century, this understated hotel boasts a grand dining area with dark wood accents and attentive staff. The rooms don't quite fulfil the promise of the exterior, but they are comfortable, carpeted and come with reliable hot showers. Ask for a room away from the road.

Bloomfield Hotel   HOTEL $$
(☑074-446 9112; www.bloomfieldhotel.com; 3 Leonard Wood Rd; d/ste from P2140/3750; ➲❄☎) This snazzy spot near SM Mall has tastefully austere rooms with inviting beds, polished wooden floors and colourful prints. The suites, with king-sized beds, are worth the splurge.

Forest Lodge   HOTEL $$
(www.campjohnhay.ph; Loakan Rd; d/tr P2400/3950; ☎) The spacious, wood-panelled interior of this large lodge at the heart of Camp John Hay leaves you with a vague feeling that there ought to be a ski slope nearby. Instead, you have pine-scented air that's lacking in Baguio proper, spacious, business-traveller-oriented rooms with full amenities and access to the gym and spa that Forest Lodge shares with Manor Hotel.

Villa Cordillera   LODGE $$
(☑074-442 6036; www.villacordillera.com; 6 Outlook Dr; d/tr/q P1600/2400/3200; ☎) There's a cabin-in-the-woods feel to this lodge overlooking Baguio Country Club. Well removed

NORTH LUZON BAGUIO

DON'T MISS

ORGANIC FARMING IN BENGUET

ENCA Farm (☑0919 834 4542, in the US 425 698 5808; www.encaorganicfarm.com) Fulfil your farming fantasies as a WWOOF (World Wide Opportunities on Organic Farms; www. wwoof.com.ph) volunteer on the Cosalan family's organic ENCA Farm in Acop, Benguet, 21km north of Baguio. Marilyn Cosalan's family has been farming for generations using indigenous Ibaloi methods and both short-term visitors (P50) and volunteers are highly encouraged to check the farm out.

Contact Marilyn or take a Baguio–Acop jeepney from the Dangwa Terminal to Acop (one hour); it's a 3km walk to the farm.

The Cosalan family lost its original *kintoman* (red) rice farm in nearby Itogon to unchecked copper mining, which destroyed hectares of farmland and killed several rivers in southern Benguet in the Marcos era. Having won back their land in legal battles, the family now grows beans, lettuce, broccoli, carrots, radish and coffee. Volunteers usually do about eight hours of farm work per day. Accommodation is in rustic but cosy lodging on-site and is very cheap – P250 a night; visitors can also camp overnight (P150).

from the centre, it's so quiet (unless the live band is playing) you'll hardly realise you're in Baguio. Rooms are spiffy with wood floors, walk-in wardrobes and spacious bathrooms (that can use a facelift). Make sure to sample the scrumptious raisin bread.

Forest House   BOUTIQUE HOTEL $$$
(☑074-447 0459; www.foresthouse.ph; 16 Laokan Rd; d/tr from P3700/4950; ☎) Consisting of just four rooms named after the owner's children, this boutique spot is faux-rustic without getting tacky and offers either mountain or garden views from its windows, and the wood-panelled rooms don't lack for luxurious touches (we particularly like Kahlil's Room). The excellent on-site bistro serves superlative *bagnet*, *pinakbet* and other classics and a generous breakfast is included.

✗ Eating

Baguio has arguably the best dining in the Philippines pound-for-pound. The Mile Hi Center in Camp John Hay has several good eating options, plus there's the usual cluster of fast-food joints near SM Mall, and Kisad Rd is lined with Korean restaurants.

Oh My Gulay!   VEGETARIAN $
(La Azotea Bldg, Session Rd; mains P110-140; ☺11am-8.30pm; ☑) After you climb to the 4th floor of La Azotea Bldg, you step into an enchanted, multilevel garden, with wooden carvings, plants, bridges, water features and little nooks to hide in. The all-vegetarian menu tempts with tofu *lumpia* (small spring rolls) salad, pastas, filled crepes and more. Expect some strange flavours.

Volante Pizza   INTERNATIONAL $
(82 Session Rd; 6-/10in pizza from P69/210; ☺24hr) Catering to night owls, revelers with post-drinking munchies and a loyal lunchtime crowd, this informal spot serves surprisingly good pizza, fried chicken and heaped po'boy sandwiches.

★ Cafe by the Ruins   FUSION $$
(25 Chuntug St; mains P200-340; ☺7am-9pm; ☎☑) The thatched-wood interior of Baguio's most beloved restaurant is awash in foliage and sculpted wood and its wide-reaching menu is equally appealing, from the homemade 'breads and spreads (pates)' to organic salads, imaginative sandwiches and superlative dishes such as the shrimp and mango curry and Baguio *bagnet*. The *suman at tsocolate* (hot chocolate and sticky-rice cake) is a wonderful treat.

Solibao   FILIPINO $$
(www.solibao.com; Session Rd; mains P75-270; ☺noon-10pm; ☑) The casual Session Rd branch of a venerable Baguio institution provides a belt-loosening course in Filipino classics such as beef *kare-kare*, crispy *dinguan* (pork fried with chilles and pig's blood) and *pinakbet*, as well as its signature *palabok* (noodles smothered with shrimp and meat sauce), green mango salad and more.

Rose Bowl   CHINESE $$
(General Luna Rd; mains P140-850; ☺10am-10pm) A local institution for decades, the Rose Bowl serves the best Chinese food in town. Its extensive menu runs the gamut from chop suey to expensive delicacies featuring abalone and lobster. Bring friends, as portions are meant for sharing.

Hill Station
FUSION $$$

(📞 074-424 2734; www.hillstationbaguio.com; Upper Session Rd; mains P180-450; ⏰7am-10pm; 🍴) The menu at this ambitious, refined restaurant reads like a foodie's fantasy tour of the world: crispy slow-cooked duck flakes, beef stewed in cinnamon and oregano, five spice tea-rub fish. Some dishes work better than others; the breakfast maple sausages are worth a try and custom cocktails hit the spot, along with the moreish dark chocolate and lemon pie.

🍷 Drinking & Nightlife

Beans Talk
CAFE

(cnr Session Rd & Mabini St; ⏰7am-10pm) Inside City Center Hotel, this bright, canteen-like cafe is a favourite with students, with good coffee, cakes and smoothies and chilli cheese fries coexisting happily alongside lasagne and *lechon kawali* (crispy fried pork).

18 BC
BAR

(16 Legarda Rd; ⏰6.30pm-late) A local favourite for live music, with reggae nights, alternative nights and local bands. Always crowded and fun on weekends.

Rumours
BAR

(56 Session Rd; cocktails P85-130; ⏰11am-11pm) A mellow place that draws its fair share of tourists, expats and local students. Some of the bar's speciality drinks will, in no uncertain terms, lay you on your arse.

🛍 Shopping

Baguio is a shopping mecca where you can pick up all manner of indigenous craft, from antique *bulol* (rice guardians) that are strictly for collectors due to prohibitive prices, and vintage items such as Ifugao headgear to all manner of traditional weavings, baskets, silver, Kalinga spears and mass-produced, glossy woodcarvings.

There are numerous woodcarving workshops along Asin Rd, 7km west of the city centre, right near the BenCab Museum.

★ Sabado's
HANDICRAFTS

(16 Outlook Dr; ⏰8am-5pm) Though nondescript from the outside, Sabado's is an Aladdin's Cave of genuine indigenous treasures. Poke around in the semigloom and you may find Kalinga spears (P2000), Ifugao headgear (P2500), hollow sticks used for carrying water in the jungle, a plethora of woven containers and wood carvings, as well as antique *bulol* (P6000 to P10,000).

Easter Weaving Room
TEXTILES

(📞 074-442 4972; www.easterweaving.com; 2 Easter School Rd) Easter Weaving Room makes genuine Igorot weavings and traditional garments, as well as contemporary men's and ladies' wear. It sells everything from hand-woven bookmarks to *tapis* (woven wraparound skirts). In the basement factory, watch women hard at work on their looms.

Narda's
TEXTILES

(www.nardas.com; 151 Upper Session Rd; ⏰8am-7pm) Started by Bontoc weaver Narda Capuyan, this flagship store carries a broad selection of high-quality, locally made items, from traditional *barongs* (Filipino shirts) to bags, blouses, scarves and table runners. These threads recently wowed the audience at the New York–held World Eco-Fiber Textile fashion show.

Mt Cloud Bookshop
BOOKS

(Upper Session Rd; ⏰9am-7pm) Arguably Luzon's hippest bookstore, with a fantastic selection of Western and Filipino titles, and a trend towards historical and ethnographic nonfiction, although there are plenty of novels also. Located below Casa Vallejo.

Teresita's Antiques and Furniture
HANDICRAFTS

(📞 074-442 3376; 90 Upper General Luna Rd; ⏰9am-6pm) Teresita's largely caters to serious collectors, with antique *bulol* out of financial reach of casual shoppers. There's also a good selection of Igorot textiles and beads, carved wooden items, vintage offering boxes and wooden lime containers that used to be part of betel-nut chewing paraphernalia. There's another outlet at Mines View Park but that one sells mainly mass-produced contemporary carvings.

ℹ Information

Banks and ATMs are all over the centre. Session Rd and its arteries are flooded with internet cafes.

Cordillera Regional Tourist Office (📞 074-442 7014; Governor Pack Rd; ⏰8am-5pm Mon-Fri) Has information on tours and treks throughout the Cordillera and maps of town.

ℹ Getting There & Away

The quickest, most comfortable buses to Manila are the nonstop, 29-seaters run by **Victory Liner** (📞 074-619 0000; www.phbus.com/victory-liner-bus/; Upper Session Rd) to Pasay (P715, five hours, five daily). Many buses take the comfortable, fast SCTEX (Subic–Clark–Tarlac

Expressway), but at the time of research only Victory Liner offers nonstop service. Reserve bus tickets ahead of time. Victory also has slower buses to Manila every 20 minutes (P445, 6½ hours); it accepts credit cards. Victory Liner also runs to Iba and Zambales (P347, five to 4½ hours, four daily) from its other Governor Pack Rd terminal.

Partas (☑ 074-410 1307, 074-725 1740) has hourly buses to San Fernando (La Union; P110, 1½ hours) and to Vigan (P370, five to seven hours) from 8am till about 6pm, with some buses continuing to Laoag (P466). Minibuses to San Fernando (P80) leave frequently from the Plaza jeepney area east of Rizal Park.

Lizardo Trans (☑ 074-304 5994) has hourly trips to Sagada (P220, five to seven hours) departing 6am to 1pm from the **Dangwa Terminal** (Magsaysay Ave), and to Baler via San José at 10am and 2pm (P312, eight hours). **D'Rising Sun** (☑ 0910 709 9102), based at the **Slaughterhouse Terminal** (Magsaysay Ave) on Slaughterhouse Rd, has buses to Bontoc (P240, six hours) hourly from 6am to 4pm. Also at the Slaughterhouse Terminal you will find A-Liner, which services Kabayan (P180, four to five hours); there's a daily bus at 7am and a minivan that typically heads to Kabayan around 4pm (but not to be relied on).

Ohayami and KMS each have daily trips to Banaue (P520, nine to 11 hours) along the paved southern route, via San José, running at about 7am and also overnight from 6pm or 7pm. Their terminals are near each other on Shanum St. A faster way to Banaue is to take a direct air-con van from the Dangwa Terminal (seven hours) via Ambuklao Rd.

> **ⓘ FINDING A GUIDE**
>
> While you can visit most of Kabayan's attractions with little chance of getting lost, local guides are professional and courteous and can clue you in on cultural background that would otherwise go over most travellers' heads. At research time, guides were arranged either by Pine Cone Lodge or enthusiastic tourism officer Berry Sangao at the **Municipal Hall** (☑ 0917 521 5830; ⊙ 8am-noon & 1-5pm Mon-Fri) and fees were standardised: Tinongchol Burial Rock P500; Pongasan Cave P800; Timbac Caves P1500; Mt Pulag via Akiki P2400.
>
> The first three can also be reached by 4WD, for P1000, P1000 and P3500, respectively, and if you're hiking up to Timbac Caves with all your gear, guides can share your burden for P500.

Kabayan

☑ 074 / POP 1389 / ELEV 1200M

Nestled amid dramatic, rice-terraced slabs of mountain terrain and watched over by its world-famous mummies, Kabayan remains an appealing, refreshingly untouristed spot, where villagers get up at dawn and silence falls when the evening darkness.

Even if mummified mortal remains aren't your thing, Kabayan is a nice place to hike around the dramatically sloped rice terraces and marvel at the star-filled sky at night. Kabayan is also the centre of Ibaloi culture, and many Ibaloi traditions and animistic beliefs linger, especially in the surrounding hills. The area is also known for strong Arabica coffee and tasty *kintoman* (red rice).

◎ Sights & Activities

Kabayan National Museum   MUSEUM
(admission P50; ⊙ 8am-noon & 1-5pm Mon-Fri) This compact museum is a good introduction to indigenous culture in this part of the Cordillera. Ask the friendly curator to explain the difference between traditional rich and poor clothing, show off a backpack used to carry pigs and the female mummy, explain local death rites and point out the Kankanay and Ikalahan ritual artefacts and plants used in the mummification process.

Bangao Mummy Caves   CAVES
(admission P30) Although the forests around Kabayan are said to hide dozens of mummy caves that only Ibaloi elders can locate, the nearest site where you can see some (not terribly well-preserved) mummies is *sitio* (small village) **Bangao** in the foothills of Mt Tabayoc (2812m), 7km north of Kabayan. The most interesting is the **Pongasan Cave**, a half-hour climb straight up from Bangao, where you'll find five coffins with mummies. Bangao is two hours' walk from Kabayan.

Tinongchol Burial Rock   CAVES
(donation P30) About 3km northwest of Kabayan, near barangay Kabayan Barrio, is the Tinongchol Burial Rock, where several coffins have been leveraged into cut holes in a boulder. It's a one-hour walk along a footpath that starts behind Kabayan's national museum through stunning mountain scenery. After crossing the river, ascend the paved road; the Rock is signposted off to your left. Either get the gate key from the barangay captain or stop by with a guide en route to the Timbac Caves.

MEETING TIMBAC'S MUMMIES

The centuries-old mummification procedure practised by the Ibaloi is different from that of the nine other cultures that have practised mummification worldwide, because here the internal organs were left intact. According to Ibaloi oral history, the corpses were dried using the heat and smoke of a small fire, then meticulously bathed in herbal preservatives. Tobacco smoke was periodically blown into the abdominal cavities to drive out worms and preserve the organs. The whole process took up to a year. The curator at the University Museum in Baguio disputes this, saying that the process, as remembered by the Ibaloi elders, didn't work when it was attempted in 1907 and that no family could have afforded not to work for an entire year, which the death rites would have demanded.

The Ibaloi stopped mummifying their dead by the 20th century because the practise was discouraged by the Americans as unhygienic. The mummies have been frequently stolen and vandalised over the years, so the main caves are now under lock and key.

The best-preserved Ibaloi mummies are found in the **Timbac Caves** (admission P100). Located about 1200m above Kabayan proper, these are Kabayan's most sacred caves, and locals customarily make offerings of gin before entering them.

The most rewarding and culturally sensitive way to experience the unique folkways of the Cordillera is to hike from Kabayan with a guide. It's a strenuous, beautiful four- to six-hour hike that follows the 4WD track (though your guide will take a steep shortcut through the rice terraces).

When you reach the caves themselves, your guide will get the key from the caretaker, who lives above the caves, and then open the coffins to let you see the mummified mortal remains. The mummies, ranging from adult to small child, are entombed in the traditional foetal position and the sight is vaguely unsettling.

Some travellers bypass the Kabayan hike by taking a Baguio–Sagada bus, getting off at the signposted turn-off for the Timbac Caves and walking 3.5km along the paved road. This is an easier way, but by going without a guide, you risk offending local sensibilities and there's no guarantee that the caretaker will be in.

NORTH LUZON KABAYAN

Opdas Mass Burial Cave CAVE
(suggested donation P50) On the southern edge of town (indeed, in someone's backyard) is this spooky charnel house with hundreds of skulls and bones between 500 and 1000 years old lined up on the stone ledge. It's suggested that they either died during a smallpox epidemic brought by the Spanish or were entombed en mass through the years due to their low social status. Go down a tiny footpath and ask for permission to visit at the green house on the left.

🛏 Sleeping & Eating

Stores along the main road sell basic food supplies, but the dining scene is yet to develop. When we visited, the Coop Lodge had closed down but was due to be rebuilt in 2015.

Pine Cone Lodge GUESTHOUSE $
(☑0929-327 7749; r P250) Currently the only place to stay in town, this friendly guesthouse at the end of the village, overlooking the river, offers spacious wood-panelled rooms and shared bathroom with bucket showers. They can also whip up a meal of roast chicken and French fries on request.

Rockwood Cafe FILIPINO $
(mains P70-100; ⊘7am-6pm) Tastefully done up with pinewood and stone, this cafe (only open during peak season) serves organically grown coffee and vegetables and sells locally produced souvenirs such as lemongrass oil, tea and shoulder bags woven by nearby Kabayan Weaving.

❶ Getting There & Away

Kabayan is linked to Baguio's Slaughterhouse Terminal by bus (P135, four to five hours) that departs Baguio at 7am and Kabayan at around 8.30am daily. The paved winding mountain road up to Kabayan is absolutely gorgeous but very prone to landslides. The road north to Abatan is slowly being paved, but you currently need a good 4WD with high clearance.

For a more adventurous escape, hike to Timbac Caves and walk out to the Halsema Hwy, where you can flag down a bus going south to Baguio or north to Bontoc or Sagada.

Mt Pulag National Park

Mt Pulag (2922m), sacred to the Ibaloi and Kalanguya, is the highest peak in Luzon and anchors the Cordillera's largest national park. The **Protected Areas Office** (PAO; ☑0919 631 5402) in Ambangeg, 1½ hours south of Kabayan, doubles as the park's visitor centre. There's a hefty P950 entrance fee for nonresidents, payable here or at other points of entry.

To get to the PAO office/visitor centre, jump off the A-Liner Baguio–Kabayan bus in Ambangeg. If coming by bus from Baguio, you'll arrive too late to launch an assault on Mt Pulag, as it's often raining by 2pm, so plan to sleep a night in the PAO or in Kabayan and start early the next morning.

From the visitor centre a rough road climbs 11km to the start of the Grassland Trail near the Department of Environment & Natural Resources (DENR) ranger station, where you must hire a guide (P600), or else bring one with you from Kabayan to navigate the final three hours to the summit. About 30 minutes beneath the summit is the 'grassland' campsite.

A more interesting two-day hike is the Akiki Trail – also known as the 'killer trail' – which starts 2km south of Kabayan in Todiakap, a *sitio* of Duacan. From the trailhead it's two hours to Eddet River and another six hours to the 'cow country' camping site. You can camp there or continue on another four hours and camp at the 'saddle grassland' campsite. It's just 30 minutes from there to the summit. A guide for this route costs P1200 per day.

There are still-longer routes up Mt Pulag that take you around the back of the mountain through Tawangan or Lusod, home of the Kalanguya. Call the PAO or ask guides in Kabayan for details. Visibility is best in March and April, and the area sees regular heavy downpours from June to November.

Sagada & Around

☑074 / POP 1674 / ELEV 1477M

Sitting among mist-shrouded mountains, tiny Sagada is the closest thing the Philippines has to a Southeast Asian backpacker mecca, yet it's possible to find tranquility along its many hiking trails and adrenalin-pumping adventure in the depths of its caves. There's a mystical element to this former refuge of dictatorship-fleeing intelligensia: the centuries-old coffins high up along limestone cliffs, since traditionally the spirits of the dead liked to be close to the sky.

Try to time your visit for a *begnas* (traditional Kankanay community celebration), when women wear *tapis* and older men don G-strings and gather in the *dap-ay* (outdoor patio); chickens are sacrificed, gongs are played and general merriment ensues. Sagadans are of Applai (northern Kankanay) ancestry and their native language is Kankanay.

◉ Sights

★ **Echo Valley Hanging Coffins**   COFFINS
Sagada's most popular attractions are the hanging coffins of Echo Valley: some are centuries old, others were put there recently. Most are high up the sheer rock face, leading you to wonder how it was originally done. It's a short trek (P300); it takes less than half an hour to get down to the coffins via the overgrown trail that runs by the cemetery, but people do get lost without a guide.

The chairs, also attached to the rock face, are the funereal chairs that the bodies were originally strapped to during a traditional burial; the smallest coffins are the ones which accommodated the bodies laid out in foetal position.

Lumiang Burial Cave   CAVE
Lumiang Burial Cave is a 10- to 15-minute walk south of the main village, towards Ambasing, and it's well-signposted along the left-hand fork in the road. Steep steps lead down to an enormous, lichen-furred cave where over 100 coffins are stacked in the entrance, the oldest believed to be about 500 years old. Many are carved with images of lizards – symbols of long life and fertility. Across the road from the steps, peer down at another cave featuring more coffins. Animistic Applai elders continue to be entombed in the caves surrounding Sagada – if they can afford it. The gods demand the sacrifice of more than 20 pigs and three times as many chickens for the privilege of being buried in the caves.

Sumaging Cave   CAVE
The exhilarating Sumaging Cave, or Big Cave, is the most popular of Sagada's caves, its immense chambers home to otherworldly rock formations with such fanciful names as 'the King's Curtain' and the more literal 'the Cauliflower'. You'll need a guide (P500) to tour the cave (roughly two hours); the guide will provide a gas lantern. It's quite slippery in parts and you'll get wet; wear

Sagada

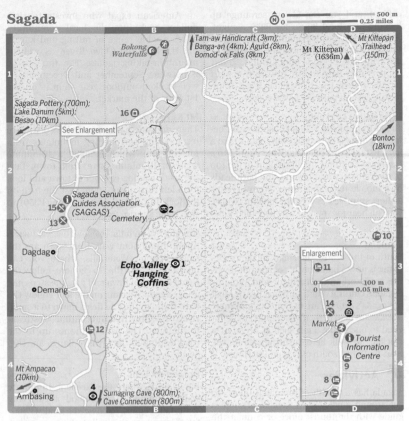

Sagada

river sandals or other shoes with nonslip soles. It's a 45-minute walk south of Sagada.

Ganduyan Museum MUSEUM
(admission P30; ⊙ 8am-7pm) This small museum is packed with sculptures, jewellery and Kankanay artefacts. Be sure to chat to owner Christina Aben, who is full of information about local culture and history. Ganduyan is the traditional Kankanay name for Sagada.

Besao VILLAGE
Hikes originating in nearby Besao are as good as those around Sagada (minus the

coffins), and you can always scrounge up lodging in a local house for P250 a night. Jeepneys and buses bound for Besao pass through Sagada throughout the day, but the last trip *from* Besao is midmorning, so day trippers may have to hire private transport for the return trip to Sagada. It's a 10km journey over a partially paved road.

Echo Valley Lookout   VIEWPOINT

To get to the Echo Valley Lookout, walk behind St Mary's Episcopal Church and take a hard left on a dirt road that winds uphill to a cemetery. Continue uphill straight to the top of the cemetery and beyond; the path leads by a mobile telephone tower. From here it's a short stumble down to the lookout, where you can hear for yourself why it's called Echo Valley.

Demang   VILLAGE

South of the centre, the small village of Demang is now a barangay of Sagada but it was the area's original settlement and remains Sagada's cultural and traditional heart. Most of Sagada's *dap-ay* are in Demang and most *begnas* are held here. If you happen to be invited to one, bring a gift such as bread or a chicken. To walk here, turn right along the road that's just south of Lemon Pie House.

🏃 Activities

Sagada has a wealth of top-notch hikes. To get around anywhere in Sagada, arrange a guide with the tourist office or contact the rival Sagada Genuine Guides Assocation (SAGGAS) (p142); the latter in particular takes trekking and customer service seriously. Their livelihoods rely on tourists, and they do their best to take care of each and every one of their charges.

★ Cave Connection   CAVING

The king of Sagada's cave adventures, suitable for the reasonably fit and courageous, is the Cave Connection, an underground passage that links Sumaging and Lumiang Caves. This three- to four-hour tour (P800) is definitely not for the claustrophobic: it involves crawling through a series of tunnels, some vertical descent that requires jamming your limbs into the rock, and swimming through some underground pools. Trekking sandals are a good idea, as are waterproof torches, though your guide will carry a lantern.

Sagada Outdoors   RAFTING

(☑0919 698 8361, 0919 671 9875; www.luzonoutdoors.com) This excellent outfit, run by an American expat who invests tourism dollars back into the local community, offers a wide range of rafting and kayaking trips up the Chico River, as well as mountain-biking jaunts. The time to go is between September and December. Its well-stocked outdoor gear shop is on the 1st floor of the market.

Mt Kiltepan   HIKING

There are superb panoramic views of the rice terraces and surrounding mountains from Mt Kiltepan, which is about a 40-minute walk (or 10-minute drive) from town. Take the road heading east out of town and look for a left turn about 500m past the turn-off to Rock Inn, or go with a guide (P350) to watch the sunrise from the peak.

Bokong Waterfalls   HIKING

About a half-hour walk from town are the small Bokong Waterfalls, where you can take a refreshing dip. To get here, follow the road east out of town and take the steps just after Sagada Weaving on the left. Follow the path through the rice fields down to a small river. Cross the river and continue upstream to the falls. The path continues up to the road leading to the town of Banga-an, 4km away.

Bomod-ok Falls   HIKING

Banga-an is where the excellent 45-minute walk to the impressive Bomod-ok Falls (Big Waterfall) begins. You'll need a guide (P600) for this one, as the walk traverses rice terraces and access is sometimes restricted because of traditions associated with the planting and harvest seasons.

Two daily jeepneys go from Sagada to Banga-an, but they aren't much use to day trippers as they both depart midafternoon. Walk or hire a jeepney instead. Jeepneys from Banga-an to Sagada depart early in the morning.

Mt Sipitan   HIKING

You can bag a few peaks around here, including Sagada's highest mountain, Mt Sipitan (2200m), although it's said to be rife with hunters' booby traps; don't try it without a guide. The majority of this rigorous, full-day hike, which starts near not-quite-idyllic Lake Danum on the way to Besao and ends in Banga-an, is through mossy forest. **Mt Ampacao** (1889m), 10km south of town beyond Ambasing, is a much easier conquest via a dirt road with a guide (P800).

🛏 Sleeping

Accommodation in Sagada is exceptional value. Many common bathrooms tend to have cold water only. There are at least a dozen guesthouses in this tiny village but book ahead for New Year and Holy Week.

Sagada Homestay   GUESTHOUSE **$**
(✆0919 702 8380; sagadahomestay@yahoo.com. ph; s/d from P350/650; @🛜) Funny name considering it is not a homestay (it's a guesthouse), but it's nonetheless friendly, affordable and loaded with character born of polished pinewood. It also has righteous views.

George Guesthouse   GUESTHOUSE **$**
(✆0920 948 3133; s/d from P300/500) The George is located in a brightly tiled building and while its rooms are simple, the doubles come with TV and there's reliable hot water in the showers – a huge boon for chilly nights and post-hike-stiff muscles. Wi-fi in the restaurant only.

Treasure Rock Inn   GUESTHOUSE **$**
(✆0920 0272 5881; r P250; 🛜) 'Aunty Mary' runs this small, spick-and-span guesthouse with killer views from the simple rooms. There's a cosy local bar where you can be introduced to the joys of videoke (but only before 9pm) and the path to this place runs through a gnarly-treed, Brothers-Grimm-fairytales-like copse; carry a torch at night.

Canaway Resthouse   GUESTHOUSE **$**
(✆0918 291 5063; r per person P300; 🛜) You'll find exceptional-value rooms here, with friendly service, clean sheets and reliable hot showers. Wi-fi comes and goes.

Masferré Inn & Restaurant   GUESTHOUSE **$$**
(✆0918 341 6164; http://masferre.blogspot.co.uk; d/tr/q/ste P1800/2500/3000/4500; 🛜) Sagada's most upmarket option is adorned with the awesome, powerful prints of the late Sagada-born photographer Eduardo Masferré, who recorded the lives of the Cordillera people. As for the lodgings, the rooms are well-appointed, the views are stellar, the water is hot, and the restaurant (open for breakfast, lunch and dinner) makes excellent use of the superb local vegetables.

Rock Inn   HOTEL **$$**
(✆0928 213 1149, 0905 554 5950; www.rock-farmsagada.com; dm/tr/q P450/1500/1800; 🛜) If you don't mind long walks, consider this option in a citrus grove 2km from the town centre. It has a huge, beautiful banquet hall

and top-notch doubles overlooking a tranquil rock garden and *dap-ay*. Bare-bones shoestringers can opt to stay in the attic (P300) like Mr Rochester's mad wife.

🍴 Eating & Drinking

Thanks to the cool mountain climate, Sagada grows an incredible variety of delicious vegetables that feature prominently on restaurant menus. We've never been so excited about broccoli.

★ Yoghurt House   FUSION **$**
(mains P70-180; ⊘7am-8.30pm; ✍) We don't usually rave or fawn, but we can say with absolute certainty that this lovely eatery's tangy yogurt sauce is the best thing ever to happen to (locally grown, succulent) vegetables. Take your banana pancake out on the balcony for breakfast, get an oatmeal cookie to go, or linger over pasta, sandwiches or beef cutlets.

Lemon Pie House   FILIPINO **$**
(pie slice P30; ⊘8am-8pm; ✍) Filipino standards are well represented, and this cafe makes brave stabs at international dishes. The eponymous lemon pie is where these guys really shine.

Sagada Brew   FUSION **$$**
(meals P200; ✍) All clean lines, floor-to-ceiling glass and blond-wood furnishings, Sagada Brew strives to be the most sophisticated cafe in the village, which it does well, with stuffed peppers, rosemary pepper chicken and waffles on its diverse menu. Linger here over a freshly brewed coffee or beautifully steeped wild herb tea – it's that kind of place.

★**Log Cabin** INTERNATIONAL $$$
(📞0920 520 0463; mains P170-250; ⊗6-9pm)
One of Sagada's many wonderful surprises is this aptly named eatery that feels like a cosy ski lodge, with a roaring log fire and a fleece-clad foreign crowd. Treat yourself to the likes of roast meats with local veggies, pasta or even fondue, complemented by a wine list that spans the world. Place your order before 3pm during peak season.

🛍 Shopping

Sagada Weaving CRAFTS
(⊗7am-6pm) Produces backpacks and money belts, as well as traditional loincloths, table runners and more, all in the traditional patterns of the region.

Sagada Pottery POTTERY
On the main road to Besao is Sagada Pottery, which creates labour-intensive earthenware pottery that takes 30 hours to fire. Potters can show off their skills for a small fee (P100 or so) and you can try your hand at the craft. It's 1.5km north of Sagada.

ℹ Information

There's an ATM next to the tourist centre that only works half the time; bring plenty of cash.

Several internet cafes are clustered around the municipal building.

Sagada Genuine Guides Association (SAG-GAS) (📞0916 559 9050; www.saggas.org) Well-organised local guide association that rivals those at the tourist information centre.

Tourist Information Centre (⊗7am-5pm) The tourist information centre in the municipal building is the dispatch centre for half the guides in Sagada. Fixed rates provided for all treks, caving and private jeepney hire.

ℹ Getting There & Away

Jeepneys run hourly to Bontoc (P60, one hour); the last one is at 1pm. GL Lizardo has hourly buses to Baguio (P250, seven hours) until 1pm.

For Manila you have to backtrack to Baguio and transfer there. Transfer in Bontoc for Banaue.

Bontoc

📞074 / POP 3795 / ELEV 900M

Bustling Bontoc is one of the most important market towns and transport hubs in the Cordillera, and you'll find yourself spending a day or two here if you're looking to get out to the rice terraces of Maligcong and Mainit or stay in the former headhunter villages of Kalinga, as it's an excellent place to arrange a guide. Today, you still glimpse an occasional old woman with tattooed arms and snake vertebrae headgear or an old man in a G-string, particularly during the **Lang-Ay Festival** in the first week of April, when locals parade through the streets wearing traditional clothing.

◉ Sights

★**Bontoc Museum** MUSEUM
(admission P60; ⊗8am-noon & 1-5pm) At this wonderful museum, powerful black-and-white photos and indigenous music accompany the exhibits – one for each of the region's main tribes. You may spot Kalinga headhunter axes, *gansa* (gong) handles made with human jawbones, and *fanitan* (baskets used for carrying severed heads), as well as delicately etched nose flutes, snake-spine headdresses of Bontoc women, bark raincoats of the Ifugao, traditional woven loincloths worn by men from each Cordillera group, and bamboo pipes used as containers for rice wine offerings.

☞ Tours

Raynoldo 'Kinad' Waytan TOURS
(📞0929 384 1745) Kinad is a hugely experienced guide who is a treasure trove of local knowledge (and a former candidate for town councillor). He tailors trips to Maligcong, Mainit, the Kalinga Province and further afield for around P1000 per day for groups of one to four, excluding food. If Kinad's number isn't working, you can find him through the municipal tourist office.

🛏 Sleeping

For a bit of comfort, cross the bridge to the quiet eastern side of the Chico River.

Churya-a Hotel & Restaurant HOTEL $
(📞0927 449 6779; http://churyahotel.bolgspot.com; Halsema Hwy; s/d/tr P250/500/800; 🛜) A will-do guesthouse that's showing its age, with a tastefully adorned common area and cafe overlooking the main street. If you're taller than 5ft 8in, you may have to sleep in a foetal position.

Archog Hotel HOTEL $$
(📞0920 607 2126, 0921 456 3166; d/ste P1000/1800; 🅿🛜) The closest thing Bontoc has to a business hotel. The clean doubles without bathrooms are a decent deal. It's a P8 tricycle ride across the bridge from town.

Bontoc

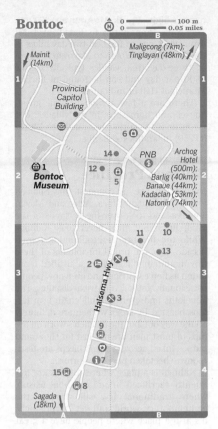

Maligcong (7km);
Tinglayan (48km)

Mainit
(14km)

Provincial
Capitol
Building

Archog
Hotel
(500m);
Barlig (40km);
Banaue (44km);
Kadaclan (53km);
Natonin (74km);

Bontoc
Museum

Halsema Hwy

Sagada
(18km)

NORTH LUZON BONTOC

ket dishes up Filipino favourites with unlimited rice for the extra-famished.

Cable Cafe FILIPINO $
(mains from P80; ⏱7am-3pm & 6-10pm) This dimly lit bar serves large portions of *lechon kawali*, chicken wings and other local faves, alongside nightly live music – OK, it's mostly '80s pop and Pinoy love songs – and beer.

🏠 Shopping

Mountain Province Trade Centre TEXTILES
(⏱8.30am-6pm) Woven materials from Sagada, Sadanga and Samoki, all with their own distinctive styles. Located on the 2nd floor.

ℹ️ Information

There are several internet cafes on the main road.
Municipal Tourism Office (☎ 0949 623 4913; Halsema Hwy; ⏱8am-5pm Mon-Fri) Hugely helpful tourist office, with wall maps of the surrounding area and staff who can suggest hiking itineraries and round up reliable local guides.
PNB The only ATM in town that accepts foreign cards (Visa only).

🍴 Eating & Drinking

Dog meat is consumed widely in the Cordillera (and Bontoc). Most foreign travellers will probably want to avoid it, but we're sure you can find some if you bark up the right tree (sorry, had to). At the market you may also spot bundles of frogs, ready for the *adobo* (meat stewed in vinegar and garlic) pot, alongside the fruit and veg.

Goldfish Cafe INTERNATIONAL $
(Halsema Hwy; mains P65-120; ⏱8am-9pm; 📶) Goldfish takes a decent stab at 'cosmopolitan', with French toast and omelettes sharing the menu with pesto pasta, (rather sweet) pad thai, and fancy coffees in hip, brightly lit surroundings with prints of Lang-Ay Festival on the walls.

Lucky Three FILIPINO $
(Halsema Hwy; mains from P90; ⏱10am-9pm) This informal local favourite inside the mar-

❶ Getting There & Away

Vonvon bus makes the trip to Banaue (P140, 1½ hours) at 10am and 2pm. There is a jeepney to Banaue that leaves when full, usually around noon (P170).

D'Rising Sun has hourly buses to Baguio (P250, six hours) from 5.30am until 4pm.

Jeepneys depart every hour to Sagada (P60, one hour) from 8am to 5.30pm (that last trip may or may not go, so we suggest getting here a little earlier). There's at least one bus and one jeepney every day to Tinglayen (P120, two hours); the best option is usually to catch the 9am bus, which continues to Tabuk (P240, five hours). Maligcong is served by jeepneys (P25, 30 minutes) at 8am, noon, 2pm and 4pm, the return journeys being at 7am, 2pm and 4pm.

Jeepneys tackle the rough roads to Mainit (P50, one hour, 7.30am, 4pm, 5pm), Barlig (P110, 1½ hours, 1.30pm) and Kadaclan (P130, four hours, 11am, 1pm, 3pm). Jeepneys head to Natonin (P170, six hours) via Barlig and Kadaclan at 11am, as does an early-morning Dadance bus.

Around Bontoc

Maligcong & Mainit

The towering, sprawling stone-walled rice terraces of Maligcong rival those of Banaue and Batad, but draw only a fraction of the tourists. Mainit has some scalding hot springs that periodically pop up in random places, several interesting ato *(dap-ay),* and backyard mausoleums adorned with carabao horns – a symbol of the deceased's wealth.

Maligcong to Mainit is a steep two-hour grunt up and down a 300m spine. You can also hike to Bangaan, near Sagada, from Mainit via Dalican (six hours over very steep terrain). Both hikes require a guide; Kinad from Bontoc can arrange both hikes.

If you need to overnight, rudimentary guesthouses are popping up all over Mainit. Geston's (r P250) and Terraces View (r P250) are both good options off the main road a short walk from Maligcong; you'll find clean rooms, hard beds and, in the case of Geston's, a couple of hot-spring-fed swimming pools.

Barlig, Kadaclan & Natonin

East of Bontoc, the secluded, rarely visited villages of Barlig, Kadaclan and Natonin have magnificent rice terraces. From Barlig it takes only about four hours to summit this region's highest peak, Mt Amuyao (2702m). The walk from Barlig to Batad, over Mt Amuyao, is one of the best two-day hikes in the Cordillera. Natonin to Mayoyao is a two- or three-day trek. Guides typically charge P800 per day and can be found in Barlig's Municipal Hall or in Bontoc.

There are a few *extremely* basic guesthouses and homestays in the villages; our favourite is the curiously named Sea World (r P250) in landlocked Barlig.

Kalinga Province

During the age of conquest, the Spanish toppled the mighty Inca, Aztec and Mayan empires, and took over the lowlands of the Philippines. But they never took Kalinga. While the practice of headhunting ceased decades ago, the proud inhabitants of these tiny mountain villages have a justified reputation as fierce warriors and even now people occasionally get killed in tribal disputes. The loincloths and even the full-length arm tattoos boasted by older women are definitely on the way out, but the machetes worn on the hips of most men are not just for show, and tattoos inked across a man's biceps are testimony to his taken part in a skirmish.

Kalinga is a place where animals are frequently sacrificed in *cañao* (ritual feasts), where traditional law still trumps the contemporary world and yet, surprisingly, it's also a place where people have a great fondness for American country music. You'll dwell amid free-ranging livestock in villages with no plumbing, sleep on floors of traditional huts and hike along ancient mountain trails to villages enveloped in rice terraces as spectacular as those in Bontoc and Ifugao.

Tinglayen

📍 074 / POP 1097 / ELEV 900M

The best starting point for treks in Kalinga is Tinglayen, 2½ hours north of Bontoc on the Chico River. Victor Baculi, the barangay captain of Luplupa (just across the hanging bridge from Tinglayen), can set you up with guides; look for him at the Luplupa Riverside Inn, which is run by his son. Enquire at the excellent Municipal Tourist office in Bontoc and with any guide organisations in Banaue or Sagada. Guide rates average P1000 per day.

🏃 Activities

Kalinga's main attraction lies in the scenic treks among the steep rice terraces between its numerous indigenous villages and in interaction with the locals. There are several exceptional routes in the Tinglayen area – some are half-day forays into nearby villages, others are several-day grinds terminating as far away as Tabuk or Abra Province. Local guides will arrange accommodation and transport to the trailhead where necessary.

Headhunting has died out, but you hear rumours of the practice continuing every now and then. Occasionally, you'll see staunch traditionalists, distinguishable by elaborate chest tattoos, and if you see men with tattoos snaking across their biceps, it's a sign that they've taken part in a skirmish. Of the Kalinga women, it's mostly the elders who have elaborate arm tattoos, as the practise is slowly dying out. Among villages where you can still encounter the traditional way of life are Sumadel, a nine-hour hike from Tinglayen, and Dananao, a three-hour hike from Sumadel which is best combined with another three-hour trek to Tulgao, near where you'll find hot springs and a 30m waterfall. One early-afternoon jeepney goes most of the way to Tulgao (40 minutes).

Another excellent one-day hike southwest of Tinglayen is Ngibat–Botbot–Logong–Buscalan; alternatively, your guide can arrange motorcycle transport from Tinglayen to Tulgao, with the walk between Tulgao and Buscalan via Botbot and Logong taking around four hours. You have to be in reasonably good shape and prepared to negotiate a few short, steep sections on most trails. Botbot's blacksmith can supply you with machetes in wooden scabbards, while Buscalan is a beautiful village with pretty stone-walled rice terraces, a few traditional houses, a locally famous tattoo artist and a tiny guesthouse.

East of the Chico River, Tanudan municipality sees fewer visitors than the villages west of Tinglayen. This is extremely isolated and rugged terrain.

For a shorter walk, try the Tinglayen–Ambuto–Liglig–Tinglayen loop. It leads through some small rice terraces, and villages where a few indigenous houses remain.

🛏 Sleeping & Eating

Most of the villages around Tinglayen have a multipurpose cooperative or modest homestay.

ℹ TRIBAL WARS

Tribal wars occasionally break out between villages in Kalinga, Bontoc, and Mountain Province. The Philippine government leaves it up to the tribal elders to resolve the disputes, some of which go back centuries and are over water rights, hunting rights and so on. The last thing mountain tribes want to do is involve tourists in their internal quarrels; still, going with a local guide is essential, because they're tuned in to the local grapevine and can help you avoid trouble spots as well as prevent you from offending the local sensibilities.

Gifts go a long way in Kalinga. Your guide will stock up on matches and, if you really want to be popular, live chickens.

Luplupa Riverside Inn & Restaurant   GUESTHOUSE $
(r per person P250-300) Hard to miss due to the giant sign on its roof, this basic guesthouse is used to hosting international travellers. Meals available on request. It's across the bridge from the main road.

Sleeping Beauty Resthouse   GUESTHOUSE $
(r per person from P200) Tinglayen's swishest option, a short walk east of the main village, has ensuite rooms with hot water, as well as basic digs with shared facilities.

Friendly Guest House   GUESTHOUSE $
(r P200) With an abundance of witch-doctor-style paraphernalia (feathers, skulls, fish traps, stuffed Tweety Bird...) dangling from the rafters, Friendly Guest House in Buscalan village consists of a single room that accommodates two. Owner has an actual toilet.

Good Samaritan Inn   FILIPINO $
(mains P50; ⏰11am-7pm) Buses between Bontoc and Tabuk pause here, in the middle of Tinglayen, for a meal stop. Expect large helpings of dish-of-the-day and a very crowded dining room.

ℹ Getting There & Around

The daily Tabuk–Bontoc bus passes through at around 11am heading north (to Tabuk) and around 10.30am heading south (to Bontoc). Two buses run each way during peak season. There is also at least one daily jeepney heading to both Bontoc and Tabuk. For the best views, sit on the roof.

POT-BELLIED PIGS & PLUMBING

If staying in Kalinga villages, you may notice that a) there's no plumbing and b) the villages don't have that pungent aroma normally associated with lack of plumbing. The secret? Lots and lots of Vietnamese pot-bellied pigs. More than one foreign visitor has been surprised by a prod in the derriere with a snout while taking care of their business amid the rice paddies.

Tabuk

074 / POP 103,912 / ELEV 200M

The capital of Kalinga Province is a flat, dusty, sweltering university town on the banks of the Chico River. There's not much happening here, but **Chico River Quest** (0920 237 8802, 0920 205 2680; www.chicoriverquest.com; lower/upper Chico River trips incl transport & accommodation P4000/7000) runs rafting trips from Tinglayen from June to early January. The lower Chico River Ullalim run is a straightforward Grade III, while the upper river Mataguan run passes through the Chico River gorge, with some challenging Grade VI rapids.

The best hotel in Tabuk is the altogether lovely **Davidson Hotel** (0926 412 6018, 0917 579 7110; Provincial Hwy; d/tr from P1050/1400; ✳🛜🏊), with immaculate doubles and a sense of colonial hill station chic.

Victory Liner has a daily bus to Manila (P750, 12 hours), but you're better off taking one of the frequent vans to Tuguegarao (P100, 1½ hours) where onward connections north or south are plentiful.

A morning bus to Bontoc (five hours) and jeepneys to interior Kalinga villages originate in barangay Dagupan, 7km north of town.

Banaue

074 / POP 2834 / ELEV 1200M

Hemmed in on all sides by dramatic rice terraces, Banaue is directly accessible from Manila and, as such, can sometimes feel a little overwhelmed by visitors. It's hard to blame them: the local mud-walled rice terraces have a pleasing, organic quality that differentiates them from the stone-walled terraces in most of the Cordillera. World Heritage listed, they are impressive not only for their chiselled beauty but because they were introduced around 2000 years ago by the Chinese.

The Ifugao, once headhunters, built the terraces and were as skilled at carving wood as they were at carving terraces. Their carved *bulol* statues are a Philippine icon, albeit a misunderstood one: *bulol* are rice guardians, not rice gods, as many would have you believe.

While Banaue remains the centre of the rich Ifugao culture, tourism now shapes the town. Fortunately, it's easy to leave much of the crowd behind by escaping to remote villages like Kambulo and Pula, which have their own incredible rice terraces.

☉ Sights & Activities

Viewpoint LANDMARK

It's a 10-minute tricycle ride up to the viewpoint (return P220), which is the best place to observe Banaue's terraces. The 'viewpoint' actually consists of four viewpoints lining the road to Bontoc at 200m intervals. Old, yet oddly regal, Ifugao and Bontoc women decked out in full tribal regalia congregate at one of the viewpoints and you can photograph them for around P20 per subject.

★Museum of Cordillera Sculpture MUSEUM

(admission P100; ⊙8am-6pm) This museum showcases a collection of Ifugao woodcarvings, and what a collection it is! Ritual objects and antique *bulol* line the vast hall, among displays of weaponry, fertiltiy carvings and smoked human skulls attached to carabao horns. There are also some fascinating old books that you can read here, including a 1912 *National Geographic* on Ifugao headhunters. An absolute must for anthropologists, it's a 10-minute tricycle ride from the centre (P70).

Banaue Museum MUSEUM

(admission P30; ⊙8am-5pm) The Banaue View Inn runs the Banaue Museum, which contains books written decades ago by anthropologist Otley Beyer and Igorot artefacts collected by his son William, with jewellery, weaponry, traditional dress and headgear and photos of Banaue in the early 20th century spread over two floors. Beyer's massive ethnography of the Igorot is a must-peruse for anyone with an interest in anthropology.

Tam-an, Poitan, Matanglag & Bocos HIKING

The hikes between these villages traverse rice fields in the immediate vicinity of Banaue and make for an easy half-day's walk. They

Banaue

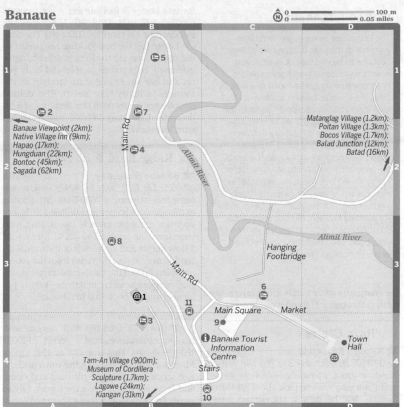

Map scale: 0 — 100 m / 0 — 0.05 miles

Matanglag Village (1.2km);
Poitan Village (1.3km);
Bocos Village (1.7km);
Balad Junction (12km);
Batad (16km)

Banaue Viewpoint (2km);
Native Village Inn (9km);
Hapao (17km);
Hungduan (22km);
Bontoc (45km);
Sagada (62km)

Alimit River

Main Rd

Hanging Footbridge

Market

Main Square

Banaue Tourist Information Centre

Town Hall

Stairs

Tam-An Village (900m);
Museum of Cordillera Sculpture (1.7km);
Lagawe (24km);
Kiangan (31km)

can be done without a guide, provided you frequently ask for directions. You'll see traditional Ifugao houses in all of these villages.

The 45-minute hike from Tam-an to Poitan starts near Banaue Hotel's swimming pool and follows a century-old irrigation canal. At Poitan, ascend to the road, go left towards Banaue, then hang a right at a staircase a few minutes later and start climbing. In 30 minutes you'll reach Matanglag, where a few bronzesmiths work. From here it's another half-hour to Bocos, known for its woodcarving. Along the way you'll pass the waterfall visible from Banaue. From Bocos you can descend to Banaue or head north across more rice terraces and end up at the viewpoint.

🛏 Sleeping & Eating

Bear in mind that none of the guest rooms in Banaue guesthouses seem to have sockets, so you'll be charging your electronic equipment in the common areas.

The best guesthouses double as the best restaurants; we prefer the Sanafe. In general, mains range from around P70 to P150;

IFUGAO'S TERRACES

The Ifugao rice terraces are incredible any time of the year, but they are at their best one to two months before harvest, when they become bright green before gradually turning gold. Around planting time, the terraces take on a barren, naked look that is also appealing. In Banaue, the best viewing period is from June to July (before harvest) and February to March (cleaning and planting time). In Batad, which has two plantings a year, the fields are greenest from April to May and October to November. This is no longer set in stone: with the weather patterns changing over the past few years, the best time for planting has become less predictable, so make enquiries in advance if you have your heart set on watching the lifeblood of the Philippines grow.

the more expensive meals are Western fare pushed through a Filipino mould press.

Town Centre

★ **Randy's Brookside Inn**   GUESTHOUSE $
(0917 577 2010; r from P200; 📶) Not only is Randy a great, knowledgeable host whose brain you may wish to pick about all things Banaue, but he runs a ship-shape guesthouse with the cheapest rooms in town and throws in a free breakfast. A win for backpackers everywhere.

Uyami's Greenview Lodge   GUESTHOUSE $
(0920 540 4225, 074-386 4021; www.ugreenview.wordpress.com; s/d from P300/550; 📶) The Greenview is one of the most popular places in town, which is unsurprising since it covers all the usual backpacker bases: a decent restaurant, mostly functioning wi-fi, transport info, guides loitering on the doorstep. The cheapest rooms are windowless cells; opt for a 'deluxe' with own bathroom and partial view of the terraces. It's a good spot to meet other travellers.

People's Lodge   GUESTHOUSE $
(074-386 4014; s/d from P300/550; 📶) Sharing its space with a woodcarving store, this friendly guesthouse has instantly unmemorable, swing-a-cat rooms (some sans window), and a very busy restaurant looking over the terraces.

Sanafe Lodge & Restaurant   GUESTHOUSE $$
(0939 939 0128, 0918 947 7226; www.sanafelodge.com; s/d from P850/1100; 📶) The Sanafe Lodge has the best-looking restaurant in the centre, serving the likes of fried bangus, extremely cosy rooms, a splendid leafy patio and bar stools that stare straight at the terraces (a happy-hour must). The 'deluxe' doubles are pretty posh (for Banaue), if a bit overpriced, but they do have mini-balconies with terrace views.

Ridge Road & Elsewhere

★ **Banaue Homestay**   GUESTHOUSE $
(0920 278 7328, 0929 197 4242; www.banauehomestay.weebly.com; d P600-1200; 📶) Staying at this spotless, homey guesthouse a little way up from the main town is like staying with your favourite auntie. You get to know your fellow guests and get plenty of individual attention and advice, the views from the rooms are splendid and the meals rival anything you may sample elsewhere in Banaue. Very popular year-round; book well in advance.

Banaue View Inn   GUESTHOUSE $
(074-386 4078, 0916 694 4551; www.nativevillageinn.com/banaueview.html; d/tr/f P1000/1200/1500; 📶) This inn sits at the top of Magubon hill, overlooking the town and the rice terraces. Rooms are pleasant and clean, and service is friendly. Ask the owner, Lily, to regale you with stories about her grandfather, renowned Yale anthropologist Otley Beyer, who wrote extensively about Ifugao culture, or her father, William, a swashbuckling antiques dealer who sired 16 children.

Native Village Inn   HUTS $$
(0908 864 6658, 0916 405 6743; www.nativevillage-inn.com; 2-person huts from P1200) These lovely Ifugao huts, situated 9km out of town, offer incomparable views of Banaue and the surrounding rice terraces. The road to the inn is almost completely paved; arrange pick-up logistics with the owners before you arrive. Guests have access to the mini-museums inside two huts, with extensive collections of *bulol* and smoked Japanese skulls tied to carabao horns.

🛍 Shopping

If you're looking for vintage Ifugao woodcarvings and antique *bulol,* you're likely to be disappointed, as the shops around town mostly stock generic carvings of animals, wooden bowls and kitchen utensils.

You may find a genuine Ifugao hunter's backpack if you poke around; it's worth looking around Batad for some genuine craftsmanship.

ℹ️ Information

Stock up on pesos as there are no international ATMs in Banaue and exchange rates at lodges are poor. Most lodges have wi-fi of varying quality.

The main **post office** is near the entrance to Banaue Hotel.

Visitors to Banaue are supposed to pay a P30 environmental fee at the Banaue Tourist Information Centre on arrival. Batad has its own network of guides.

Banaue Tourist Information Centre (📞 074-386 401; ⏰ 6am-7pm) Manages a network of accredited guides, sells a map (P20) and maintains the definitive list of guide and private transport prices to selected locations. Guides average P1200 for full-day hikes.

ℹ️ Getting There & Away

Ohayami runs a 7pm bus between Banaue and Sampaloc, Manila (P470, nine hours) via Cubao. In the peak season buy your tickets well ahead of time. It's a P20 trike ride from the **bus station** to the town centre.

If you prefer daytime travel, no problem: take a frequent jeepney to Lagawe (P40, 50 minutes), then another to Solano (P80, 1¼ hours), and catch a frequent Manila (Sampaloc)-bound bus there (P350, seven hours).

KMS (three daily) and Ohayami (three daily) run mostly night buses (5pm) to Baguio (P515, nine to 11 hours) via Solano and San José; Ohayami also has a 6.30am departure. Vans also run to Baguio from the main square at around 7am (P415, eight hours).

The least complicated way to Vigan (at least 12 hours) is to take one of those buses, get off in Rosario, La Union, and transfer to a northbound bus. Buses also run to Tuguegarao the long way round (though it takes approximately the same amount of time as the more direct Banaue–Bontoc–Tabuk–Tuguegarao route.

A bus to Bontoc (P170, 2½ hours) leaves at noon and a couple of additional buses pass through. A jeepney to Bontoc (P80) departs at 8.30am. Connect to Sagada in Bontoc.

Most jeepneys leave from the main square.

Around Banaue

Five Ifugao rice terraces are included on the Unesco Word Heritage list: Batad, Bangaan, Mayoyao, Hungduan and the Nagacadan Terraces near Kiangan.

Of those, Batad's are the most famous, but Mayoyao gives Batad a run for its money. Mayoyao is accessible from Banaue (three hours) or Santiago (five hours) in Isabela Province.

Batad & Around

📞 074 / POP 1152

Given the proliferation of hugely picturesque rice terraces all over the Cordillera, winning the 'best terrace' competition is no mean feat. While we don't think these particular rice terraces are necessarily the most beautiful, it's difficult not to gawp in awe when you reach the ridge overlooking Batad's 'amphitheatre' of rice, because as far as stages go, it's certainly very dramatic.

This backpacker hotspot is still only accessible on foot (hence the lack of crowds from Manila), but this may soon change, as

Around Banaue

the road towards the village is being paved as we type. Batad too 'on the beaten track' for you? Escape to remoter surrounding villages such as Pula and Kambulo.

◉ Sights & Activities

There are many hikes in the area and the Banaue Tourist Information Centre or any guide can recommend longer treks. Batad has a network of guides called the Batad Environmental Tour Guides Association. Twenty per cent of all fees these guides collect goes towards restoring the rice terraces. Not all hikes around Batad require guides, but most do, and besides, you'll find their local knowledge a huge asset, especially for locating local craftspeople.

Tappia Waterfall   WATERFALL

It's a 40-minute hike across the terraces and a steep descent to the 21m-high Tappia Waterfall, where you can sunbathe on the rocks or swim in the chilly water. *Do not attempt to swim under the falls;* the waterfall has claimed several lives. To get here from the main guesthouse area, walk down to the village and then up to the promontory, just to the left of the Waterfall Side Lodge.

Batad–Bangaan   HIKING

This 2½-hour hike is a recommended route out of Batad or, if you prefer, in, taking in the tiny village of Bangaan and some fantastic vistas en route. From Batad, take the path behind Rita's guesthouse down to the small river. Cross to the other side, then head across the small bridge to the left and pick up the path. When it forks after 10 minutes go right. From there it's smooth sailing, so you can relax and enjoy the stunning panoramas of the mountains and rice terraces, bisected by a river hundreds of metres below. Eventually you'll walk through a rice terrace and hit the main road, from where it's 2km to Bangaan Family Inn overlooking Bangaan, and another 1.5km from there to Batad junction.

**Banaue Viewpoint–Pula–
Kambulo–Batad**   HIKING

This is a reasonably strenuous hike that passes through jaw-droppingly impressive rice terrace scenery. Most people tackle it over two days, with an overnight stop in Pula, and a guide is mandatory. From the viewpoint overlooking Banaue to Pula it's a four- to six-hour hike, from Pula to Kambulo it's two or three hours, and another two hours from Kambulo to Batad.

The path to Pula from the viewpoint cuts through jungle, which is the only part of the trail that doesn't involve rice terraces. Pula itself is a tiny collection of Ifugao houses on a hilly outcrop. Just outside of Pula, heading towards Banaue Viewpoint, there's a waterfall and a deep swimming pool under a bridge. The trail from Pula to Kambulo follows a winding river, with terraces carved high into the mountains.

If you take this route, you might plan on spending a night in Pula, where the simple Pula Village Inn will put you up for P200 per night; overnight stays are also possible in Kambulo. Some trekkers do this hike in reverse order, but that entails more uphill sections.

Pula–Mt Amuyao   HIKING

From Pula it's a taxing, seven-hour climb up the region's highest peak (2702m). You'll need a guide (P800 to P1000 per day) and have to be in seriously good shape. Be prepared to sleep at the radar station on the top. Amuyao is much easier to scale from Barlig, near Bontoc, which is a three-hour hike from Pula.

🛏 Sleeping & Eating

Mobile phone reception barely reaches Batad, and most of its guesthouses usually cannot be contacted by phone. This normally isn't a problem, but from March to May, many Filipinos arrive on tour groups, and accommodation can fill up. If you visit during this period, get in early in the morning.

Most lodgings are on the ridge overlooking the main village and the rice terraces and are, on the whole, nicer, breezier places to stay than a couple of very basic options in the village proper. All accommodation is very similar: basic wood-panelled rooms, (usually) shared bathrooms and an on-site restaurant serving Filipino and Western fare (mains P50 to P80). Room prices are per person.

Hillside Inn   GUESTHOUSE **$**

(☑ 0936 131 1724; r per person P200-250) The Hillside has clean rooms, hot showers and a lovely verandah on which to eat your *malawach* (Yemeni flatbread), *shakshuka* (eggs scrambled with tomatoes) and Filipino mains. You can even splurge on a double with private bathroom (P900)!

Ramon's Place
GUESTHOUSE **$**

(r per person P200-300) More characterful than most, Ramon's offers lodgings in an Ifugao hut for P500/800 for one/two people, as well as basic rooms of varying sizes. The gregarious host will dress you up in traditional Ifugao clothing, give you a rice-wine-making demo and feed you curry, salads and pizza at his terrace restaurant.

The second Ifugao hut on the property was built by Ramon's grandfather and is adorned with the skulls of deer, monkeys and pigs. Inside you'll find an anthropologist's dream: a mini museum of spears, rice-wine barrels and traditional carvings; the place looks like a set piece from an *Indiana Jones* movie. If you're not staying here but would like to visit, it'd be nice to make a donation (say, P40).

Simon's View Point & Pizza Restaurant
GUESTHOUSE **$**

(r per person P250) Green building with 16 rooms, 24-hour power, a large terrace overlooking the valley and a restaurant that really does serve pizza (along with *malawach*, a Yemeni flatbread).

Batad Guesthouse & Pension
GUESTHOUSE **$**

(☑ 0918 964 3368; r per person P250) Eight little rooms are on offer here. There's reliable hot water in the shared bathrooms, and the small, friendly guesthouse is decorated with the works of the skilled woodcarver whose children now run the place. You can also pick up some traditional cloth, wood carvings and rice wine at the little shop.

Rita's
GUESTHOUSE **$**

(☑ 0910 842 3076; r per person P200) Rooms here might be pokey, but they come thoughtfully equipped with mozzie nets, and chirpy Mr Romeo, with his red betel-nut smile, is quite a character.

ℹ Getting There & Away

From Banaue, it's 12km over a partially paved road to Batad junction, where a beautifully paved 3km stretch runs right up to the 'saddle' high above Batad and continues beyond towards the village. From the 'saddle' it's a 40-minute hike downhill to Batad. By mid-2015 there will be a paved road running halfway to the village, which will cut that hiking time in half.

From Banaue, three or four jeepneys per day pass by Batad junction (P100, one hour). From there you'll have to walk to the saddle or hire a private jeepney (return P2500) or tricycle (return P1000) to take you up there.

To return to Banaue, either arrange transport in advance, walk (taking one of the hikes outlined earlier), or catch a passing jeepney anywhere along the main road to Banaue (traffic heading back is 'heaviest' early in the morning).

Hapao & Hungduan

Spread out over the valley floor, the rice terraces in Hapao and Hungduan are dazzling.

To walk to a small **pool** beside a river in Hapao (population around 2200), a barangay of Hungduan 17km northwest of Banaue, take the concrete steps behind the viewpoint in Hapao and turn left at the bottom. Follow the paved irrigation canal for about 10 minutes until you reach a small group of houses. It's another 15 minutes to the river, where you can cool off in the refreshing water.

Five kilometres beyond Hapao is Hungduan *poblasyon* (town centre; population around 1500), the site of the spectacular **Bacung spider web terraces** and the jumping-off point for the six-hour climb up **Mt Napulawan** (2642m), the final hiding place of General Yamashita at the end of WWII.

You can enquire about more hikes at the Hungduan tourism information centre, a few kilometres from Hapao. You can secure guides at the Hungduan Municipal Hall, where there's also a guesthouse. Guide rates start at P800 per day.

Jeepneys to Banaue leave Hungduan (P80, 22km, two hours) and Hapao (P70, 17km, one hour) around 8am and return between 3pm and 5pm. There is at least one jeepney per day to/from each town. Hapao is within tricycle range of Banaue (return P800, 1½ hours) and it's a 45-minute ride between the two.

Kiangan

☑ 074 / POP 1689 / ELEV 1200M

Kiangan is where Ifugao and American troops helped force General Yamashita, the 'Tiger of Malaya', to make his informal surrender in WWII.

◉ Sights & Activities

To secure guides or discuss more ambitious hikes in the area, talk to tourism council head Ani Dumangeng at the **Kiangan Municipal Hall**. Another great source of information is Ibulao, Ibulao Bed & Breakfast (p152), which organises rafting trips on the Ibulao River via an operator in Tuguegarao and guides overnight treks to caves in the area.

OF CIVETS & COFFEE KIANGAN

In the Pula barangay of Asipulo town, the 48-hectare organic coffee farm, **Bantai Civet Coffee**, is a WWOOF (World Wide Opportunities on Organic Farms; www.wwoof.com.ph) project that specialises in a rare and expensive type of coffee derived from the excrement of the coffee-bean-eating civet. The farm is part of the **Julia Campbell Agroforest Memorial Park** (☑ in the US 512-305-3367, in the US 210-859 4342; www.bantaicivetcoffee.com), named after the US Peace Corps volunteer who was murdered locally. Volunteers and visitors can stay in a small Ifugao village (P300).

Jeepneys to barangay Pula (P80, two hours) run from Lagawe via Kiangan.

Whereas most commercial coffee plantations are on clear-cut plots, here trees have been planted amid natural forest. It is precisely this natural environment that draws shade-loving civets, which means the farm has an economic, as well as ecological motive for preserving native forest.

War Memorial Shrine   LANDMARK
(P30) A short ride up from the village proper, a pyramid-shaped War Memorial Shrine marks the spot where Yamashita surrendered on 2 September 1945, to be hanged for war crimes shortly afterwards.

Ifugao Museum   MUSEUM
(P20; ☺8am-noon & 1-5pm Mon-Fri) Across the lawn from the War Memorial Shrine is the Ifugao Museum, which houses an absorbing collection of Ifugao artefacts, from household utensils and headhunting *bolos* (machetes) to intricately carved *pakko* (wooden spoons). The centrepiece is a huddle of *bulol* (rice guardians).

Nagacadan Terraces   RICE TERRACES
The World Heritage–listed Nagacadan Terraces and **Julungan Terraces** are about 10km west of town, accessible by tricycle. You can hike up into the Nagacadan Terraces and then descend to Maggok village (three hours).

Pangaggawan Cave   CAVE
Pangaggawan Cave is a three-hour hike from Kiangan; there are other caves in the vicinity.

Ambuwaya Lake   SWIMMING
Ambuwaya Lake, 3km east of town, is a good spot for a swim.

Mt Kapugan   HIKING
From town, a classic (ie steep) Igorot trail leads 1½ hours straight up Mt Kapugan, from where there are exceptional views of the surrounding terraces.

✿ Festivals

Bakle'd Kiangan   CULTURAL
If you arrive here around the last weekend of August, you may be able to participate in the Bakle'd Kiangan, a local festival that celebrates a bountiful rice harvest; during this time, locals don traditional dress and consume plenty of *binakle* (rice cakes) and *baya* (rice wine).

🛏 Sleeping

Kiangan Youth Hostel   HOSTEL **$**
(☑ 0910 324 3296; dm/d P250/400) Has passable rooms if you don't mind the Dickensian orphanage vibe.

⭐**Ibulao, Ibulao Bed & Breakfast**   B&B **$$**
(☑ 0917 553 3599, 0917 553 3299; totokalug@yahoo.com.ph; treehouse P600, dm/s/d P500/1600/1800; ☺✳🛜) Roberto Kaludgan and his wife Teresa, both practising doctors, have built a house fit for the pages of *Architectural Digest* at the junction of the Lagawe–Kiangan road. The vast, beautiful family room with native hardwood accents is built right into the rock foundation, and guests can choose between a treehouse, Ifugao hut, and comfortable air-con rooms. No walk-ins; book ahead.

Meals are available upon request and rafting trips can be arranged between October and February.

ℹ Getting There & Away

Kiangan is an easy jeepney ride from Lagawe (P40, 25 minutes, every 20 minutes until 4pm), where there are onward connections to Manila and Banaue.

THE NORTHEAST

Get yourself to northeast Luzon and you're deep in the Filipino frontier. Hill tribes, huge swathes of forest, small towns connected by smaller lumber tracks – you won't find many Filipinos, let alone foreigners, out this way, with the exception of hip surfing town/ weekend getaway of Baler. The Cagayan River, the country's longest inland waterway, cuts a swathe through this famously fertile region. East of the river are the Sierra Madre, among the country's most impenetrable mountains and home to wild and woolly Northern Sierra Madre Natural Park.

Baler & Around

☑ 042 / POP 36,010

Baler (bah-*lehr*) has never needed city walls for protection; the Sierra Madre and the Philippine Sea cut the capital of Aurora Province off from the outside world effectively enough. Today Baler is best known as the location of the surfing scene in *Apocalypse Now*. The minuscule waves on display in that scene are a testament to the area's fickleness, but the surfboards that were left here, post-filming, have kick-started a lively surfing scene.

◉ Sights & Activities

Most lodgings rent boards (P200 per hour) and offer surfing instruction (P350), as do the little surf shops that line Sabang Beach.

Sabang Beach SURFING
The town hosts the Aurora Surfing Cup every February on Sabang Beach, an endless strip of fine dark sand extending north from Baler proper to Charlie's Point, the river-mouth break that spawned the famous 'Charlie don't surf' line in *Apocalypse Now*.

Dicasalarin Cove HIKING
Five kilometres south of Cemento wharf is Digisit, where a hiking trail through the jungle leads south to an isolated white-sand beach at Dicasalarin Cove. It is a two- to three-hour hike (take a guide), or hire a bangka (P1300 return) near the San Luis River mouth at Sabang Beach. A nonmotorised bangka (P5) crosses the river to barangay Castillo, from where you can walk to Cemento wharf. Otherwise take a tricycle from Sabang or Baler centre (P140 one way).

Ditumabo Falls HIKING
Ditumabo Falls (Mother Falls), which drop 15m into a small reservoir above an unfinished hydroelectric dam, are easily accessible from Ditumabo, around 12km west of Baler. Walk or take a tricycle (P100) 2km along an unpaved track to the trailhead, from where it's a straightforward 30- to 45-minute hike to the falls up a creek bed next to a water pipeline. The deep, clear pool under the falls makes for a refreshing swim.

🛏 Sleeping

Most of Baler's accommodation is along the beach in Sabang. Even in low season Baler is not a place to turn up without a reservation, as the place floods with Manila weekenders. Budget accommodation leaves a lot to be desired, but this should all change when the Circle Hostel opens a bona fide backpackers' near the police station sometime in 2015.

Elaine MM Lodge GUESTHOUSE $
(☑0919 537 9405; r P800; ❋) Beachfront cheapie with colourful, basic, fan-cooled rooms and a 2nd-floor balcony that wraps around the building (so hope you get on with your neighbours). Toilet seats appear to have gone AWOL and there are handy buckets and scoops in the bathrooms to shower with.

Aliya Surf Resort HOTEL $$
(☑0929 758 6005, 0939 939 0929; www.aliyasurfcamp.com; tr/q/f from P2100/3200/3600; ❋❂❀) This three-storey concrete building by the sea offers bright rooms, lit by stained-glass windows, with modern clean beds, hot water and working internet, with an on-site surf gear rental shop, lively beachfront cafe and an infinity pool that's not completely full, making it just a pool.

NORTH LUZON BALER & AROUND

DON'T MISS

SURF'S UP!

Baler gets some of the biggest waves during the September–March season (though it's possible to surf year-round, particularly if you're a beginner). Here are our top five breaks:

Sabang Beach Left and right breaks and no reefs to snag beginners

Dicasalarin Point Consistent reef breaks for pros and left and right beach breaks for newbies

Cemento Reef Powerful right reef break for pros, used for surfing competitions

Lobbot's Point, Dipaculao Left and right beach breaks suitable for beginners and intermediate surfers

Dalugan Bay, San Ildefonso Shallow left-hand reef break best for pros

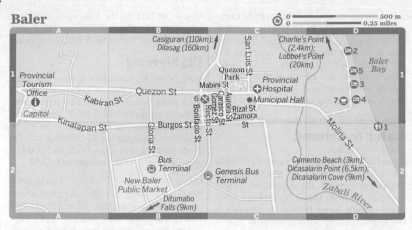

Baler

Bay's Inn HOTEL **$$**
(📞 0908 982 3509; d with fan/air-con P1200/1600; ❄️ 🛜) Bay's has a lively beachfront location and its restaurant does a reasonable job of capturing the surfer ethos, with yummy fish tacos and loud music. The rooms are clean but uninspiring, unlike the bay views from their windows.

Costa Pacifica HOTEL **$$$**
(📞 0917 857 4424, 0917 853 6040; reservations@costapacificabaler.com; d/ste from P3000/5500; ❄️ 🛜 ⊠) With its twin swimming pools, manicured grounds and hammocks strung between the palm trees, this immense waterfront hotel is by far Baler's fanciest, its well-appointed rooms complete with coffee-maker. The chic Beach House restaurant serves everything from excellent fish tacos and ribs to Filipino favourites. The service is inconsistent, however, and woe betide if you need an extra towel.

✖ Eating & Drinking

Most of the beachfront hotels have restaurants and rumour has it that an authentic Indian restaurant is due to open by the end of 2014.

Gerry Shan's Place FILIPINO, SEAFOOD **$$**
(Quezon St; buffet P199; ⊙11am-11pm) Gerry's place is famous for its buffet, which is particularly seafood-heavy, with touches of Chinese cuisine and a welcome bit of spice.

Charlie Does CAFE
(⊙10am-5pm) Opposite the Costa Pacifica hotel at Sabang Beach, this groovy little place is a surfing fashion boutique combined with a book exchange (you're welcome to chill out and read), hip gallery vibe, and coffee counter serving large frappuccinos.

ⓘ Information

Bring cash as the local banks do not accept foreign cards.
Provincial Tourism Office (📞 042-209 4373; off Quezon St; ⊙8am-noon & 1-5pm Mon-Fri) The friendly Provincial Tourism Office, part of the Provincial Capitol Compound, has maps of the area and can help you find a bangka or hiking guide. It also has information on exploring the scenic Aurora coastline north of Baler around Casiguran and Dilasag.

ⓘ Getting There & Away

Buses to Baler, both from Manila via Cabanatuan and from Baguio via San Jose, take the sealed road via Pantabangan. If you have your own 4WD, you can take the more direct and more scenic unpaved road out of Palayan (though it's prone to landslides). **Genesis** (📞 042-421 1425) has hourly air-con buses to Manila until 3pm (P580, six to eight hours) as well as a nonstop, deluxe night bus (P750, five hours). Buses from Manila typically leave for Baler early in the morning.

If you're heading for the Cordillera or Zambales, your best bet is to take the 4pm Baguio-bound (eight hours) Lizardo Trans bus to San Jose (3½ to 4½ hours, P180) and change there.

Vans to Cabanatuan (P270, four hours) depart from the main bus station near the new public market. Also at the bus station, D'Liner has a rickety mid-morning bus that tackles the mostly paved road to Dilasag (P450, five to six hours), the jumping-off point for boats to Palanan, via Casiguran.

San Jose

While San Jose is little more than a crossroads town with no discernible attractions, it's a connection point between the Cordillera, the west coast, the east coast and northeast Luzon, with numerous buses passing through. If coming from Banaue, you can catch one of the three daily Lizardo Trans buses heading to Baler (P140, three to four hours) along main Bonifacio Ave. If you're coming from Baler and want to head up to Tuguegarao and the north coast, hop on a north-bound bus along the north–south National Hwy that intersects with east–west Bonifacio Ave. ATMs and fast-food joints line the National Hwy. If you must overnight here, well-run **Hotel Francesko** (✆ 044-958 0988; r from P1200; ❋ 🛜) offers bland ensuites at the north end of San Jose along the National Hwy and its restaurant whips up great sizzling dishes and Filipino standards.

Northern Sierra Madre Natural Park

The vast expanse of mountainous, dense rainforest that dominates North Luzon's east coast is the island's final wild frontier. Shielded by the mountains, as yet untamed by roads and accessible only by tiny plane, boats dependent on the mercy of the sea, or on foot – it's the most pristine and naturally diverse part of the island.

The Northern Sierra Madre takes up a whopping 3600 sq km (which makes it almost the same size as Switzerland) and incorporates the longest mountain range in the Philippines. It's a hugely exciting area for naturalists, since more than 60% of the country's plant species are found here, as well as 29 threatened species of animal, including the critically endangered Philippine eagle, the country's national bird; the largely harmless Philippine crocodile, a freshwater reptile that is the world's most endangered crocodile; and the Northern Sierra Madre forest monitor lizard, which can grow 2.2m long and dines exclusively on fruit.

The park is mostly uninhabited, with the exception of the unspoiled coastline that is home to the Dumagats, a seminomadic Negrito group whose lifestyle has been relatively unchanged for millennia. This region was also a refuge for the last remaining rebels during the Philippine Revolution – American-led forces captured General Emilio Aguinaldo in the coastal town of Palanan on 23 March 1901.

With a capable guide you can trek through the heart of the park to **Palanan** from **San Mariano**, about 30km east of Naguilian. The going rate is around P1000 per day and a guide can be arranged through the Palanan Wilderness Development Cooperative and possibly through San Mariano's mayor's office. Before entering the park, contact the tourism officer in Palanan so that she can inform the Development of Environment and Natural Resources (DENR) that you'll be trekking there, as the park falls under its jurisdiction.

If you want an encounter with the world's most endangered crocodiles, the **Cagayan Valley Program for Environment & Development** (CVPED; ✆ 078-622 8001; www.cvped. org/croc.php), at Isabela State University in Cabagan, has a crocodile conservation project and arranges guided observation treks for visitors.

There are no guesthouses and only a few basic eateries in Palanan, a sleepy town with an end-of-the-world feel to it; Dumagat men set up thatch lean-tos on the beach, Aeta tribespeople sell monitor lizards for lunch and, in general, there's a sense you're far removed from civilisation. There are beaches in **Dicotcotan** and **Didadungan** that are isolated and pristine, and you can get a guide to take you to the beautiful **Disadsad Falls**, deep in the jungle, along the Palanan River.

ⓘ Information

Palanan Wilderness Development Cooperative
(✆ 0928 341 5375; amgpalanan@yahoo.com) Palanan-based organisation that can help arrange a guide if you're looking to trek in the park.

Tourism Officer (☎ 0906 721 1016) Based in the town hall in Palanan, Myrose Alvarez is the super-helpful tourism officer who has plenty of info on the park in general and can assist with organising a homestay in Palanan where there is no commercial accommodation.

ⓘ Getting There & Around

AIR

Palanan, the main gateway to the park, is connected to Cauayan by daily **Cyclone Airways** (☎ 0915 387 3048, in Cauayan 078-652 0913; www.cyclone-airways.com) and thrice-weekly **Sky Pasada** (☎ 02-912 3333; www.skypasada.com) flights, while **Northsky Air** (☎ 078-304 6148; www.northskyair.com) flies to Palanan from Tuguegarao on Wednesdays and Sundays. All three airlines also serve Maconacon (daily except Thursdays). Flights tend to leave early in the morning, take around 30 minutes to either town and cost around P2000 one way.

BUS & BOAT

There are two boat routes into the park. One involves taking a weekly boat from San Vicente port near Santa Ana (10 hours, P500) to Maconacon and then a second boat from Maconacon to Palanan (four to five hours, P500). Alternatively, take a bus to Dilasag either from Baler (seven hours, three daily) or from Santiago (10 to 12 hours, daily around 5am) and then catch a boat to Palanan from there (P500, one daily, six to eight hours). There are a few simple guesthouses in Dilasag if you need to spend the night. Boat routes are notoriously weather-dependent.

ON FOOT

From San Mariano, reachable by direct Victory Liner bus from Manila, it's possible to trek all the way to Palanan. It's only 45km, but due to trail conditions the trek typically takes at least five days; arrange a guide via the Palanan Wilderness Development Cooperative.

Tuguegarao

☎ 078 / POP 138,865

The only thing that puts the 'wow' in Tuguegarao (too-geg-uh-row), the political and commercial capital of Cagayan Province, is the country's largest cave system 25km east of the city. Otherwise, most travellers take one look at the tricycle-asphyxiated streets and head for Pagudpud and Saud Beach to the northeast or the Kalinga Province out west.

◎ Sights & Activities

More than 300 caves have been discovered in the municipality of Peñablanca, about 40 minutes northeast of town. Some caves suffer flooding during typhoon season (from August to October).

★ Callao Cave   CAVE

(P20) The most accessible part of the immense limestone cave complex is the seven-chambered Callao Cave. Callao Cave is reached by walking up 184 slippery steps. Several sinkholes illuminate the cavernous chambers, the largest of which houses a little chapel. Compulsory guides (P100) are supposed to protect the cave from vandalism. To get here, catch a jeepney (P50) from Don Domingo Market, just north of the city, or get a tricycle (P500) return trip (with waiting time).

A must-do excursion if you're in the area is to hire a bangka (P700) near Callao Cave and head 15 minutes upriver to watch the exodus of tens of thousands of bats as they pour out of the caves for a flight over the Pinacanauan River at dusk. If it's raining, the bats won't come out. You can rent kayaks (P200 per hour) from Callao Caves Resort, across the Pinacanauan River from Callao Cave.

Odessa-Tumbali Cave   CAVE

Estimated to be at least the second-longest cave system in the country at 12.5km (it still hasn't been explored to its terminus), Odessa-Tumbali Cave is for advanced cavers only and can only be visited with permission from the tourist office in Tuguegarao and a guide. Access requires a 7km hike from Callao, followed by a 30m rappel into a sinkhole.

ⓒ Tours

Adventures & Expeditions   NATURE

(☎ 078-844 1298, 0917 532 7480; 29 Burgos St) Run by veteran guide Anton Carag, the company offers kayaking trips on the Pinacanauan, where clean green waters cut through the limestone cliffs. This involves taking a bangka 5km upstream, then navigating the return trip via no-flip kayaks over light rapids. Adventures & Expeditions also organises multiday caving, kayaking and rafting trips on the Chico River in nearby Kalinga Province.

ⓘ Sleeping & Eating

Many hotels here are attached to good restaurants. For something more downscale just roam along Bonifacio St, loaded with fast food and street food. Numerous hole-in-the-wall joints serve the local take on *pansit* (stir-fried noodles).

Hotel Joselina   HOTEL $
(☑ 078-844 7318, 0917 553 7930; http://hoteljoseli-na.com; Aguinaldo St; s/d/f from P750/900/1000; ✳ ☎) Remarkably good value for a central, efficiently run business hotel, Joselina clearly employed better interior designers than most: its compact, unfussy rooms are decorated in warm yellows and browns with a little flair, good beds and various comforts.

Hotel Carmelita   HOTEL $
(☑ 0917 572 2777, 078-844 7027; 9 Diversion Rd; s/d/f from P350/600/1030; ✳ ☎ ☎) Pros? This hotel is close to the main bus terminals, has a pool for guest use, and its restaurant serves some of the best pizza and coffee in town. Plus, the rooms are cheap as chips. Cons? The bathrooms need a facelift and the air-con in the budget rooms is reminiscent of a jet taking off (pack earplugs).

★**Hotel Lorita**   HOTEL $$
(☑ 078-844 1390; www.hotellorita.com; 67 Rizal St; s/d from P1000/1700; ✳ ☎) Tuguegarao's best deal, especially if you bump up to the huge, rear-facing 'matrimonial deluxe' rooms. Rooms are surprisingly modern and well kitted out, and quiet. The downstairs restaurant serves delicious Ilocano and Chinese dishes and there's a trendy cafe attached.

ℹ Information

Tuguegarao's main thoroughfare is Bonifacio St. It has plenty of ATMs and internet cafes.

DOT Region II Office (☑ 078-373-9563, 0918 909 2326; www.dotregion2.com.ph; 2 Dalan na Pavvurulun, Enrile Ave; ☺ 9am-6pm) Inside the Regional Government Centre, this office is an excellent source of information for Tuguegarao, Cagayan, the Batanes and Babuyan island chains, Nueva Vizcaya and Northern Sierra Madre Natural Park. Book your caving permits, guides and trips to the Northern Sierra Madre Natural Park here. It's off Enrile Ave, 4.5km north of the city centre.

Sierra Madre Outdoor Club (SMOC) (☑ 0917 272 6494) The SMOC (that's pronounced 'smoke') guys have up-to-date info on caving, climbing and other adventurous activities. You can also arrange a caving guide for around P1000 per day.

ℹ Getting There & Away

PAL Express and Cebu Pacific have daily flights to/from Manila (one hour) from the airport, 2km north of the city centre. There are also **Sky Pasada** (www.skypasada.com) flights to Basco, Batanes and Maconacan (Northern Sierra Madre Natural Park).

Victory Liner (☑ 078-844 0777), **Baliwag** (☑ 078-844 4325) and **Florida Liner** (☑ 078-846 2265; Diversion Rd) are the most comfortable options to Manila (P750, 12 to 13 hours), with twice-hourly departures. GMW has buses to Laoag (P550, seven to eight hours) via Claveria and Pagudpud. Florida also runs super-deluxe 10-hour night buses (P950). Afternoon Dangwa and Dalin buses serve Baguio (11 to 12 hours).

From the Tuguegarao van terminal, 2.5km north of the centre, air-con vans run regularly to Tabuk (1½ hours, P80), Santa Ana (P180, three hours), Santiago (P160, three hours) and Claveria (P180, 3½ hours).

Santa Ana
☑ 078 / POP 30,458

Near the eastern tip of the infrequently visited part of the north coast, the fishing town of Santa Ana acts as a gateway to the Northern Sierra Madre Natural Park and also as one of the jumping-off points to the equally remote Babuyan Islands. While there's little to detain you in the town proper, **Anguib Beach** is as pristine as they come and easily reachable by bangka from the port of San Vicente (P1500 return), 6km north of Santa Ana. Also accessible via a 15-minute bangka ride is **Palaui Island** (P800 return), with a sedate pace of life, no lodgings and a beautiful three-hour walking trail from the village of Punta Verde to Cape Engaño and its still-functioning Spanish lighthouse.

Santa Ana is a big name in game-fishing circles, with Babuyan Strait rich in marlin, dorado and sailfish. The fishing season is between March and June and you can arrange sport fishing trips through the **Philippine Game Fishing Association** (☑ 0927 320 7261; www.pgff.net). Between February and May the Babuyan Strait is also a good place to spot all manner of cetaceans, from humpback, pilot, and pygmy killer whales to spotted dolphins and bottle-nosed dolphins.

The best place to stay is the **Jotay Resort** (☑ 0906 478 1270, 078-372 0560; www.jotayresort.com; r/ste from P1000/2500; ✳ ☎ ☎) with clean, stylish rooms and an atmospheric restaurant that specialises in seafood dishes, particularly its signature chilli crab. Owner Trevor can arrange boat trips along the coast, whale- and dolphin-watching jaunts, hiking in the Sierra Madre and all manner of water sports.

Located in the municipal hall, the **tourist office** (☑ 078-858 1004; ☺ 8am-5pm Mon-Fri) has info on the area and can arrange homestays on the Babuyan Islands.

NORTH LUZON SANTA ANA

ⓘ Getting There & Away

Lal-lo International Airport is expected to be operational in early 2015.

Large pumpboats leave weekly for Maconacon in the Northern Sierra Madre Natural Park from San Vicente pier.

Direct Guardian Angels buses connect Santa Ana to Manila (14 to 15 hours, two daily), while GMW Trans runs to Vigan (12 to 13 hours, two daily) via Laoag. Frequent air-con vans head south to Tuguegarao (P180, three hours).

BATANES

You can't get further away from the Philippines without leaving the Philippines than Batanes: a group of 10 islands near Taiwan. Only three of these specks are permanently inhabited: the main island, Batan; tradition-rich Sabtang; and remote, northernmost Itbayat. Island landscapes alternate between greenery-clad extinct volcanoes, rugged cliffs, rolling hills, verdant pasture-land and turquoise-wave-fringed white slivers of beach.

Batanes gets battered by typhoons on a regular basis. The locals, most of whom are of indigenous Ivatan stock and converse in their native Ivatan tongue, build their traditional houses typhoon-tough, positioned slightly underground with metre-thick limestone walls and bushy roofs made of *cogon* grass.

That bushy headpiece that some Ivatan women wear is called a *vakul*. It is made from abaca and the fibre of the *voyavoy* palm, found only in Batanes; the men wear a *kanayi* (vest made from *voyavoy*). Both protect the wearer from the sun and rain.

The best time to visit is between March and May, when the weather is relatively dry and typhoons are unlikely.

ⓘ Getting There & Away

Northsky Air (✆ 078-304 6148; www.north-skyair.com) Small plane (Cessna 402 and BN Islander) flights from Tuguegarao to Basco and

Batanes

Itbayat on Mondays, Wednesdays and Fridays only; same day return.

PAL Express (www.philippineairlines.com) Flights from Manila to Vasco (1¾ hours), daily except Mondays and Fridays, returning to Manila daily except Mondays and Sundays.

Skyjet Airlines (www.skyjetair.com) The only jet flights between Manila and Basco (1¼ hours). Mondays and Fridays only.

Sky Pasada (www.skypasada.com) Three weekly flights between Tuguegarao and Basco.

Batan Island

📞 078 / POP 7907

Virtually all visitors to Batanes enter through Batan, the commercial centre and site of the provincial government. You'll want to spend at least a day circumnavigating the island, taking in the fabulous scenery, navigating its hilly roads, and visiting its villages. Batan is blessed with ample natural beauty, but for raw Ivatan culture, Sabtang Island is a better bet.

ℹ Getting Around

There are several ways to negotiate the island.

Most lodgings have sit-up-and-beg bicycles for rent (P20 per hour) or you can hire mountain bikes from Dive Batanes Lodge (P250 per day) or from **Mabino Bikes** (📞 0939 643 9472; Lopez St; P500/day; ⊙ 9am-7pm). Riding the southern loop takes around six hours, not including stops; you have to be in decent shape and carry plenty of water.

Several lodgings have scooters or motorbikes for hike (P150 per hour); if yours doesn't, try the Petron petrol station or the tourist office.

From Basco's tricycle stop, tricycles offer loops around the north part of the island (P1000) and the southern half (P1500).

You can walk stretches of the southern loop, catching the infrequent jeepneys that connect the coastal settlements; hitching might be possible. Some lodgings offer jeepneys and vans for hire (from P2500 per day).

Jeepneys regularly ply the road between Basco and Itbud from around 4.30am to 8.30pm. In Basco, wait for jeepneys in front of ShaneDel's.

Basco

With a wealth of accommodation options and a few decent restaurants, Batanes' compact capital makes an excellent base for exploring the rest of Batan Island. Awash with bougainvillea and shrouded in greenery, Basco's streets are a pleasure to walk. Abad St is the main drag; it really comes to life

in the evenings with fragrant smoke rising from half a dozen streetside grills.

🏃 Activities

The main activity involves getting out of Basco and exploring the rest of the island.

Mt Iraya   HIKING

North of Basco, Mt Iraya (1009m), a dormant volcano that last erupted in AD 505, can be climbed in about five hours and descended in three, though the summit is usually obscured by clouds. Your hotel can help you find a guide (P1200).

🛏 Sleeping

Batan Island's lodgings are located either in central Basco or along Chanarian Beach, 2km to 3km south of town.

Time Travel Lodge   GUESTHOUSE $

(📞 0939 623 8979, 0929 166 9838; r per person from P400; ❋ 🛜) Half-hidden behind a bamboo stockade and blooming shrubbery, this small guesthouse has three rooms, a spacious kitchen, an immaculate front lawn and thatch-roofed open-air dining/hanging out area. Just north of central Basco. Excellent value.

Crisan Lodge   GUESTHOUSE $

(📞 0915 849 0178; www.crisanlodge.com; Dita St; r per person from P400; ❋ 🛜) Run by friendly Mon and Crisan, this very central guesthouse above a grocery store offers rooms of the swing-a-cat variety, guest kitchen and a small restaurant.

Dive Batanes Lodge   HOTEL $$

(📞 0939 922 4609; www.divebatanes.com; r P1700-2700; ❋ 🛜) The rooms at this diving lodge are all warm hues and floral-patterned linens and there are numerous activities on offer, from diving trips off the south end of the island to snorkelling outings and mountain biking. Dive Batanes is located just off Chanarian Beach, 3km south of Basco. Cheapest rooms share facilities.

Octagon Bed and Dine   HOTEL $$

(📞 0917 552 6684, 0939 925 5166; National Hwy; r from P2500; ❋ 🛜) Overlooking the sea, a five-minute walk south of Basco, Octagon is a fussy yet comfortable trio of spacious rooms, all bright floral patterns and miscellaneous collection of wicker furniture. The restaurant menu is a happy coexistance of Ivatan dishes alongside pasta and soup.

OFF THE BEATEN TRACK

BABUYAN ISLANDS

Clearly visible from the mainland but oh-so-inaccessible for much of the year, the Babuyan Islands are 24 volcanic creations, some of which sport rugged cliffs and caves, while others are fringed with white-sand beaches and the most achingly blue, crystal-clear waters imaginable. Only the five largest islands are inhabited: Fuga, Dalupri, Calayan, Babuyan and Camiguan, and their residents lead quiet, pastoral lives, with limited electricity and little contact with the mainland. Braving a wild bangka (outrigger) ride out to this remote quintet of islands, 30-something kilometres off Luzon's northern tip, will certainly win you instant bragging rights in traveller circles.

Volcanic **Camiguin** is also known for its hot springs and has a homestay. The undeveloped islands of **Fuga** and **Dalupiri** have beautiful white-sand beaches but no electricity or accommodation. Ask around for a homestay or just camp. Homestays are readily available on the most developed Babuyan island, **Calayan**, which boasts an incredible natural cover.

April to June is the best time to visit. The Babuyan Channel is generally too rough for crossings from December to March and during peak typhoon season (August to October); April is traditionally the calmest month.

Passenger ferry **MV Eagle** (☎0906 8356 715, 0939 921 6181) sails from San Vicente to Calayan (P750, four to five hours, three weekly) via Camiguin (P400, two to three hours), weather permitting.

Otherwise, bangkas head out to the islands from Claveria and Aparri several times weekly. You can also either hire a private bangka in San Vicente, Aparri or Claveria (around P7500 return) or try to snag a space on a *lampitaw* (cargo boat) from one of the three ports for around P600; prepare for exposure to the elements and a potentially hairy crossing. Irregular bangkas link Calayan with the other inhabited Babuyans or you can hire bangkas to jump between the islands.

★Pacita Batanes HOTEL $$$
(☎0917 855 9364, 0939 901 6353; www.fundacionpacita.ph; ste P6500-13,500;) You pay the price of luxury here, but you're rewarded with a quirky, bohemian arts mansion perched on a bluff over a stormy ocean. Think bold colours, stone walls, luxurious bed linen and carved wooden features. The hotel was under renovation when we visited but will reopen in late 2014 with a new Italian restaurant.

Eating

An abundance of fresh seafood and unusual vegetables makes for good eating in the Batanes. *Tatus* (coconut crabs), the islands' tastiest delicacy, are becoming increasingly rare, but large ones can still be caught and eaten legally. Lobster is also popular.

Ela Food House FILIPINO $
(National Rd; mains from P60; 7am-10pm) Basic little eatery on the corner of National and Lopez. The mother-daughter team cooks up classics such as *lechon kawali* and crispy *pata*, as well as fresh fish and Ivatan dishes.

★Pension Ivatan FILIPINO, IVATAN $$
(Reyes St; mains P80-150; noon-10pm;) Yes, this may look like a nondescript eatery with a blaring TV in the corner, but don't let the interior fool you: this is, hands down, the best place in town to sample Batanes' specialities – from coconut crab and *kinilaw* to *uved* balls (banana root balls with bits of garlic and fish) and *vunes* (fried-up gabi stalks).

Casa Napoli ITALIAN $$$
(cnr Abad & La Fuente Sts; pizzas P280-340; noon-2pm & 5.30-10pm;) With its chequered tablecloths and generous helpings of the ol' pizza pie meant for sharing, this is Basco's answer to a trattoria.

Information

There are a couple of internet cafes along Abad St but the uber-slow connections will remind you of dial-up internet of the long-forgotten '90s.

Batanes by Bike (☎0917 827 4225, 0917 535 3807; www.ironwulf.net) These guys offer downloadable guides to the three islands, complete with cycling routes, and can help with organising a cycling tour of Batanes.

Municipal Tourism Office (☎0929 846 8395; www.batanes.gov.ph; National Rd) Helpful tourist office on the ground floor of the Municipal Hall compound. Can help arrange guides around the island and has info on Sabtang and Itbayat also. There's a small information point at the airport.

PNB (cnr Cagpo & Hordoñez) Bank with a bona fide working ATM (Visa only).

The Northern Loop

OK, this is a figure-of-eight rather than a loop. First, head north of Basco to the **Basco Lighthouse** (1.2km); it's possible to climb it for stellar views of the coast. Further north, there is a short walking path up the crest of one of the **Vayang hills**, with Itbayat and Dinem islands on the horizon.

Retrace your steps to Basco and head southeast up to the **Tukon Chapel**, an appealing stone church built by the Abad family. Further uphill it is **Radar Tukon**, an abandoned weather station on a hilltop with great 360-degree views, reachable via a 1½-hour walk or a tough 30-minute bike ride from Basco.

About 500m downhill beyond Radar Tukon is the **Fundacion Pacita** (www.fundacianpacita.ph), a magnificent stone house perched on a bluff overlooking Marlboro Country. The artist Pacita Abad lived and painted here until she died in 2004. Further east, towards Valugan boulder beach, are the **Dipnaysupuan tunnels**, built deep into the rock face by the Japanese using forced local labour; you can explore them with a torch.

The Southern Loop

The island's main road, National Hwy, hugs the twists and turns of the coastline south of Basco.

Just south of Mahatao, with its cluster of traditional houses, you'll find **White Beach**, a cove that's generally considered safe for swimming. Continuing south, you'll pass through Ivana, the jumping-off point for Sabtang Island, and home to the Unesco-listed **House of Dakay** (1877), the oldest stone house in the Batanes. Right near the pier is the **Honesty Coffee Shop** (⊙ 8am-6pm), a great little place where you drop your money in the box and help yourself to drinks. The road flattens out on the way to southernmost **Uyugan**, where there are a few traditional houses.

The road then turns north, passing a sweeping, wide bay and the **Songsong ruins** of stone houses demolished by a tidal wave. Passing through Itbud and Imnajbu, the road climbs to green, rolling pastureland populated by undomesticated carabao and cattle. This is Racuh Apayaman, better known as **Marlboro Country**. From here there are fantastic views of Batan's eastern coastline and Mt Iraya. You then reach the intersection, with the left fork leading to

Mahatao (3km) and the right taking you to the dorado-fishing village of Diura (1.5km), where you pay P50 to register and there's a 20-minute walk to the refreshing **Spring of Youth**.

Sabtang Island

🔊 078 / POP 1637

Travelling to Sabtang from Basco increases the feeling that you've left the Philippines. Ivatan culture survives virtually intact here. Women still work in the fields in their *vakul* and, unlike on Batan, the traditional limestone houses (*vahay*) and their bushy roofs have been well preserved. Dramatic headlands, white beaches and a striking mountainous interior round out the feast for the eyes that is Sabtang.

On arrival, visitors must pay a P200 fee at the **Municipal Tourism Office** (🔊 0918 488 2424; ⊙ 8am-5pm).

DIY travellers can ask at the Municipal Tourism Office about hiring a motorbike (P800 to P1000) or bicycle (P200) to explore the island, or be prepared to do a lot of hiking; otherwise, the unique, *cogon*-grass-covered Sabtang tricycles can take you around (P800/1500 for half/whole day). A 30km, paved coastal road links the island's six villages.

From **Centro**, where the ferry docks, head south on the road to **Savidug** (6km). Just south of Savidug look for a grassy *id-jang* (fortress), which dates to pre-Hispanic times; there is a great hilly viewpoint overlooking a pristine cove, too.

It's another 4km from Savidug to picturesque **Chavayan**, which the local authorities have nominated to be a World Heritage site because of its exceptionally well-preserved traditional Ivatan architecture. Handwoven *vakul* and *kanayi* can be bought at the **Sabtang Weavers Association**, along the main road.

The road ends in Chavayan, but a two-hour walk through the interior brings you to **Sumnaga**, where there are more stone houses crammed up to the shoreline and flying fish hang out to dry on clotheslines. There are plans to connect Chavayan and Sumnaga by road by 2017. From Sumnaga a paved road leads north to **Nakanmuan**, around the northern tip of the island, and back to Centro via pretty **Morong Beach** and **Malakdang**, with incredible coastal vistas en route. An interior walking trail also connects Nakanmuan and Centro (45 minutes). It's worth stopping at Morong Beach to check out the Mayahaw Cave, a Japanese hideout during WWII.

There are two sleeping options in Centro. The Municipal Tourism Office runs a guesthouse (twin with bathroom per person P300). Next door, the School of Fisheries (dm P150) offers dorm beds. There are also homestay options in Chavayan (P150 to P300 per person, excluding food).

A few *sari-sari* (small neighbourhoods) in Centro have canteens and will cook up whatever is available; with some advance warning, the Municipal Tourism Office can arrange for you to have a delicious meal consisting of a full spread of Ivatan dishes at one of Centro's dining joints for P300. Nights are quiet on Sabtang, as the electricity is shut off around 8pm.

Weather permitting, round-bottomed boats (*falowa*) make at least one daily trip between Ivana on Batan and Centro (P75, 30 to 45 minutes), the first departing from Centro around 5am and Ivana around 7am. There's usually a 1pm boat from Centro and sometimes another afternoon trip is added. If you get stuck on Sabtang you can stay the night or hire a *falowa* to make a special trip (at least P3000). Be warned: this crossing can be rough.

Itbayat Island

☑ 078 / POP 2988

It's a thrilling 15-minute plane ride from Basco to Itbayat, the Philippines' final inhabited frontier. Unlike its siblings, this platform of an island has no beaches; it rises vertically out of the depths, cliff-fringed all the way around.

Trails criss-cross the centre of the island, making for good trekking. There are nice views from Mt Riposed (231m), east of Raele; the hike is a fairly strenuous three or four hours return trip. It's a beautiful half-hour walk from the main town, Mayan (Centro), to Paganaman Port, where at dusk you'll see farmers returning from the fields, and fishers with their day's catch. If you arrive at low tide, you can soak in a little natural swimming pool in the rocks next to the port.

The towns of Raele and Yawran are well worth visiting for a glimpse of traditional thatched houses topped with *cogon* grass,

a design that precedes the stone-and-thatch construction of the neighbouring islands.

In the northern part of the island, the viewing deck at the pinnacle of Ibayat's highest mountain, Mt Karoboban (278m!), is reachable by truck for superlative views of Taiwan.

In the southwest part of the island, Torongan Cave is believed to have been used for human settlement as early as 4000 years ago. The cave mouth is a short hike up the hill where there are barely visible, ancient, boat-shaped graves and fine views across the water.

The mayor, who can be found at the municipal building, will let you stay in Mayan's Municipal Hall Guesthouse (dm P150), with access to a kitchen. Visitors to the island have to pay P90 at the Municipal Treasurer office. A homey place to stay is Cano Homestay (☑ 0919 300 4787; P200), run by Mrs Faustina Cano, the former tourism officer with a wealth of knowledge about the island.

Most places to eat in Itbayat are canteen-style, with irregular opening hours. However, the Itbayat Caterer Cooperative (meals P200) can take care of your daily dining needs by delivering ready-made Ivatan meals to your homestay.

Like Sabtang, Itbayat has electricity between 6am and midnight. If the weather acts up you could get stranded on Itbayat for a few days, so build some flexibility into your schedule.

Northsky Air usually has eight-seater flights between Basco and Itbayat (P1875, 15 minutes) on Mondays, Wednesdays and Fridays at 11am. The landing strip is near Raele, 10km south of Mayan. From there you will be transported to Mayan in a dump truck.

M/B Ocean Spirit (☑ 0920 664 0137) and M/B Itransa (☑ 0908 502 2814) *falowa* ferries depart Basco for Itbayat around 6am and 7am (P450, three to four hours), landing at either Chinapoliran Port (halfway along the west coast) or Panenbatan Port in the southwest, and then turn around and leave Itbayat around noon. This is a rough crossing at the best of times and may be cancelled altogether when seas are particularly perilous.

There's no public transport on the island, so you can either hire a tricycle for the whole day (P1500) or to select destinations, catch rides in pickup trucks, or walk.

Southeast Luzon

Best Places to Stay

➡ Pacific Surfers' Paradise (p186)

➡ Residencia de Salvacion (p171)

➡ Balai Tinay Guesthouse (p173)

➡ Victoria's Guest House (p180)

Best Outdoor Adventures

➡ CamSur Watersports Complex (p170)

➡ Bicol Adventure ATV (p173)

➡ Majestic (p186)

➡ Mt Isarog National Park (p170)

Why Go?

Looking rather like a seahorse that's headbutting a football, Southeast Luzon is one of the less-explored parts of the Philippines. More's the pity, since it's a wildly varied and weird part of the country, where travellers are likely to encounter anything from creatures of the deep (in Donsol and Ticao) to Eastertime Romans and self-flagellation (Marinduque) and cowboys rounding up both steers and crabs (Masbate).

Travellers who do make it down here tend to be surfers, drawn to the waves whipped up by the fierce winds in Southeast Luzon's outer reaches, and those who favour uncertainty and adventure over infrastructure and well-beaten tourist trails. Studded with some of the country's most active volcanoes, Southeast Luzon also attracts fresh-air fiends who come to scale these magma pressure cookers simply because they are there. Last but not least come the foodies; appropriately enough for this volatile land of fire, Bicolano cuisine brings some very welcome heat to the otherwise bland Filipino table.

When to Go
Naga City

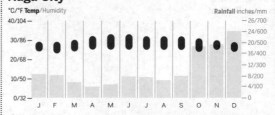

Apr & May Cheer at the rodeos involving bulls and crabs.

May–Jul Sunny (and hot!) time of year, ideal for island-hopping and diving.

Aug–Nov Surf's up in Catanduanes and Bagasbas; kitesurfing also takes off.

Southeast Luzon Highlights

1 Snorkel alongside Bicol's gentle giants, the **whale sharks** of Donsol (p178).

2 Ride an ATV (quad bike) on the old lava trails of **Mt Mayon** (p176), Bicol's prettiest volcano.

3 Sample the best of Bicol's fiery cuisine in **Legazpi** (p166).

4 Watch the cattle hustlers round up some doggies at the **Rodeo Masbateño** (p183) in Masbate.

5 Ride the Catanduanes' legendary **Majestic surf break** (p186).

6 Explore the uninhabited islands and beaches of the pristine **Caramoan Peninsula** (p171).

7 Dive with manta rays in the **Manta Bowl** at Ticao Pass (p179).

8 Wakeboard, wakeskate, kneeboard and waterski at **CWC** (p170) near Naga.

9 Make like a Roman legionary at Marinduque's wild **Moriones Festival** (p189).

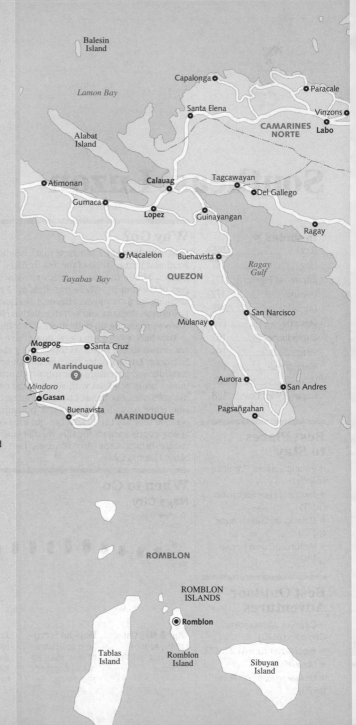

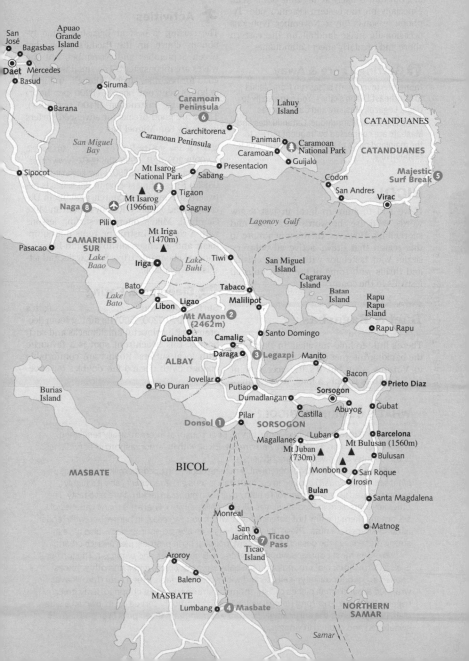

Climate

Southeast Luzon's wet season is a little later than in Manila and the rest of Luzon. It kicks in around late August and lasts until February, but rain is likely at any time of the year, especially on the eastern (Pacific) side. Typhoon season is July to November. Typhoons occasionally make landfall on the eastern shore and regularly affect Catanduanes.

ⓘ Getting There & Away

Numerous (overnight) buses run from Manila to Southeast Luzon's cities. You can also fly to Naga, Legazpi, Masbate and Catanduanes.

The islands of Marinduque, Catanduanes and Masbate are connected by frequent ferries to the mainland ports of Lucena, Tabaco and Pilar, respectively.

BICOL

If we had to sum up Bicol in just a few words, we'd use the words surf, spice and snorkelling. However, there's much more to this region that draws active adventurers, sizzles your tastebuds with its fiery cuisine and thrills with some of the most unusual festivals in the country.

Daet & Bagasbas

☑ 054 / POP 95,572

There's little to hold travellers in Daet once the banking/internet chores are done (head to Vinzons Ave), but it's the access point for **Bagasbas Beach**, a long, white strip of sand 4km north of town that draws surfers with its temperamental waves and kitesurfers with its consistent winds. The laid-back, ramshackle bar strip at Bagasbas morphs into one big videoke joint on weekends.

☂ Activities

The surfing is best at Bagasbas when typhoons churn up the Pacific's waters between September and November, but the waves are inconsistent. The small waves are good for beginner surfers, though, and most lodgings rent out boards (P200 per hour) and arrange instruction (P400 per hour). There are good breaks for advanced surfers in nearby San Miguel Bay.

Mike & Joy's Kite Bar   KITESURFING
(☑0919 209 9191, 0999 458 0902; www.mikes-kites.com; 2hr intro US$60, 1-day kiteboard rental US$20) Kitesurfing season in Bagasbas is between November and March, peaking in December and January. Run by American Mike Gambrill, Mike's offers kitesurfing lessons with a certified instructor, rents out equipment and arranges surfing, island-hopping and wakeboarding trips. Sea kayaks and jet-skis also available.

🛏 Sleeping & Eating

Surfers Dine-Inn   HOTEL $
(d/tr/q P1000/1200/1500) Its dining room decorated with colourful knickknacks and surfboards, this beachfront spot is a favourite with local surfers. Rooms are comfortable enough (with cheapo fan doubles for shoe-

---

WHAT'S COOKIN' IN BICOL?

Filipino food is roundly vilified as the bland, poor cousin of internationally renowned Asian cuisines such as Thai and Vietnamese. Bicol, with its smorgasbord of fiery dishes, is the country's answer to that criticism.

Coconut is a key Bicolano ingredient. Anything cooked in coconut milk is known as *ginataán*. Squid *(pusít)* cooked in coconut milk is thus *ginataán pusít* (and it's highly recommended). *Ginataán santol* (a pulpy fruit) and *ginataán* jackfruit are also tasty. The other key ingredient in Bicol cuisine is *sili* (hot chilli pepper). There are many varieties of *sili*, among them the tiny but potent *labuyo*, which you can order in bars mixed with tender, almond-shaped *pili* nuts. These ubiquitous nuts – an alleged aphrodisiac – also have a strong presence in the dessert department, popping up in pastries, pies and ice cream.

Two of the most popular savoury delights are Bicol *exprés* and *pinangat*. The former is a spicy mishmash of ground pork, *sili*, baby shrimps, onion, garlic and other spices cooked in coconut milk, typically served with rice. *Pinangat* is green *gabi* (taro) leaves wrapped around small pieces of fish, shrimp and/or pork, and a chopped, leafy green vegetable known as *natong (laing)*, which is also commonly served on its own as a side dish. Lastly, there's the surprisingly palatable *candingga* – diced pork liver and carrots sweetened and cooked in vinegar.

stringers – P500) and the friendliness of its young owners goes a long way.

Mike & Joy's Bar
HOTEL $$

(📞0919 209 9191, 0999 458 0902; www.mikes-kites.com; Bagasbas Rd; air-con/fan bungalow P1400/800, s/d hut P300/500; 🅿🛜) The bar-restaurant is a good spot for Western and Filipino food, beer and the chance to meet fellow surf bums. Dedicated surfers are known to linger in the beachfront native huts for weeks on end, with air-con bungalows available for those a step up the creature-comfort ladder. Mike's is north of the main strip, by the big green house.

Bagasbas Lighthouse
RESORT $$$

(📞0917 510 1856, 054-731 0355; www.bagasbaslighthouse.com; dm/d/q from P550/1750/3950; 🅿🛜🏊) At this nautically themed resort hotel, shrouded in vegetation at the south end of the strip, we particularly like the funky converted trailer rooms (even if the beds take up most of the narrow space). Backpackers are well catered for, with spartan, en suite six-/eight-bedder dorms (breakfast not included); the more luxurious of the rooms look out over the waves.

Kusina ni Angel
FILIPINO $

(mains from P60; ⊗8am-9pm) Run by the charming Angel de la Cruz, this local institution has a creative menu specialising in seafood and noodles. It's near the junction where you pick up tricycles.

★ Catherine's
FILIPINO, SEAFOOD $$

(mains P155-450; ⊗8am-10pm) Attached to the Bagasbas Lighthouse hotel, this is by far the snazziest restaurant in Bagasbas, with catch of the day sizzling on the grill, Filipino and Bicolano classics well represented (think crispy *pata*, Bicol *exprés*), guest stars in the form of Chinese dishes and 'exotic and native' duck and goat creations to tempt foodies: goat *kinilaw* (Filipino-style ceviche) is strangely superb.

❶ Getting There & Away

Tricycles from Daet to Bagasbas cost P50.

Philtranco air-con buses (P800) typically leave from Pasay, Manila at 8am, 8pm and 9pm for Daet (nine hours). From Daet, DLTB buses run frequently to Manila from their own terminal along the Mahalika Diversion Rd and include daytime air-con departures.

There are frequent morning minivan services to Naga (P170, 2½ hours) from the Central Terminal along Vinzons Ave.

Naga
📞054 / POP 174,931

Students are ubiquitous in this busy town, home of the oldest university in Bicol, as are the services that follow students: coffee shops with wi-fi, cheap restaurants and raucous nightlife. Of far greater interest to visitors is the volcano-related hiking, biking and climbing in Naga's vicinity, or else taking to the water on a wakeboard or exploring beneath the waves with a scuba tank.

In September, thousands of devotees come to Naga for the **Peñafrancia Festival** in celebration of the Virgin of Peñafrancia, Bicol's patron saint. Book accommodation at least two months in advance.

◎ Sights

Naga City Museum
MUSEUM

(Burgos St; ⊗8am-noon & 2-5pm Mon-Fri) FREE This small museum, located on the 3rd floor of the campus of the University of Nueva Caceres, is ethnographic in focus, filled with crafts, tools and other artefacts of pre-colonial Bicol and covering the history of the Philippines as a whole. Get the enthusiastic curator to show you around.

Holy Rosary Minor Seminary Museum
MUSEUM

(off Elias Angeles St; ⊗9am-noon & 2-5pm Mon-Fri, 8am-noon Sat) FREE If you can't make the Peñafranica festival, this little museum may be the next best thing. Located in the city-dominating St John Cathedral, the exhibits here consist of pictures and glass displays of religious pageantry and some entertaining dioramas of the main procession.

🏃 Activities

Kadlagan Outdoor Shop & Climbing Wall
ROCK CLIMBING

(📞0919 800 6299; kadlagan@yahoo.com; 16 Dimasalang St; ⊗shop 9am-7pm, climbing wall by appointment) For gear rental, guides and tips on hiking and climbing, this is the place to go. Owner Jojo Villareal knows all the local rocks and the best routes and is usually here in the evenings. He organises guides for hikes up Mt Isarog, canyoning and waterfall-rappelling trips and takes groups on multiday adventures to the Caramoan Peninsula.

Steady Eddie
DIVING

(📞054-811 2664, 054-472 7333; www.steadyeddiedivecenter.com; Peñafrancia Ave; ⊗8am-7pm) Divers should head for the 2nd floor of the

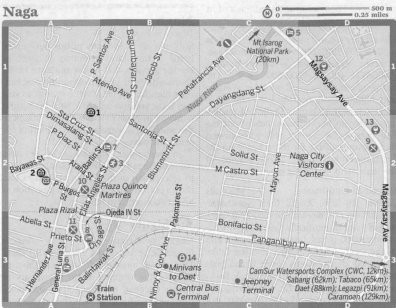

Naga

Naga

◎ Sights
1 Holy Rosary Minor Seminary
   Museum A1
2 Naga City Museum A2

◈ Activities, Courses & Tours
3 Kadlagan Outdoor Shop &
   Climbing Wall B2
4 Steady Eddie C1

◔ Sleeping
5 Avenue Plaza Hotel C1
6 Eurotel Naga A3
7 Hillary & Andrew Hostel B2
8 Naga Regent Hotel A3

◉ Eating
9 Bob Marlin D2
10 Geewan A2
11 Naga Restaurant A3

◔ Drinking & Nightlife
12 Lolo's Music Bar D1
13 San Diego Jazz Bar D2

◔ Shopping
14 SM City Mall B3

Edventure Building. You can call a few days ahead and try to join one of the weekend dive expeditions to the islands of Caramoan,

wreck diving in Santo Domingo, or the Manta Bowl in Ticao. Costs run from US$150 for three dives. Provides open-water and advanced levels of diving instruction.

⊨ Sleeping

Naga's budget and midrange options are found in the city centre, while the more upmarket lodgings are found on and off Magsaysay Ave, a 10-minute tricycle ride north.

Hillary & Andrew Hostel   HOSTEL $
(☑ 0943 709 7118, 0917 558 3347; 32 Barlin St; s/d from P600/900; ❄ 🛜) It's more of a budget hotel than a backpackers' joint with a genuine hostel vibe, but the staff are helpful, there's a popular cafe on the premises serving Bicolano dishes and its location is super central. Cheapest rooms are ensuite but windowless and utterly unmemorable.

Eurotel Naga   HOTEL $$
(☑ 054-472 5321; www.eurotel-hotel.com; cnr General Luna St & Riverside Rd; d/ste from P1500/2350; ❄ 🛜) Spotless business hotel in a central location overlooking the river. Expect funky wall-to-wall prints of famous European landmarks, stuccoed ceilings in the suites and compact twins and doubles with mod cons aplenty.

Naga Regent Hotel   HOTEL $$
(☑054-472 2626; http://nagaregenthotel.com; Elias Angeles St; dm/s/d/ste incl breakfast from P400/1100/2000/3000; ❄@🖥🛜) This newly re-furbished business-class hotel has the goods, from enormous suites with polished wooden floors to spacious dorms with sturdy bunks. All beds (and bunks) feature orthopaedic mattresses and breakfast is included for all guests, making this a perfect catch-all option.

Avenue Plaza Hotel   HOTEL $$$
(☑054-473 9999; www.theavenueplazahotel. com; Magsaysay Ave; r from P4400; r from P7500; 🅿❄🛜🏊) Still the best hotel in town, with wonderfully accommodating staff to match the top-notch facilities. Rooms are spacious, with properly comfortable beds, flat-screen TVs, a downstairs coffee shop, a gym and a big infinity pool with sundeck and loungers.

✗ Eating & Drinking

Come evening you'll find a good crop of food stalls popping up around the squares that dot downtown. A good cluster of vendors collects near the San Francisco church off Peñafrancia Ave, but otherwise the central dining scene is largely limited to the likes of the food court at SM Mall. North of the centre there's a couple of clusters of trendy bars, clubs, restaurants and coffee shops centred on the Dayangdang St end of Mag-saysay Ave, and at Avenue Sq, which shares the same space as the Avenue Plaza Hotel. Bars are generally open from 4pm to 1am.

✗ Centre

Geewan   BICOLANO $
(Burgos St; mains P65-135; ⊙9am-9pm; ❄) This Bicolano cafeteria-style joint is justifiably pop-ular with locals thanks to its extensive menu of dishes such as *lechón* (spit-roasted pig) and *pinangat* (taro leaves wrapped around pieces of fish, shrip or pork), *candingga* (diced pork liver and carrots) and *bangus* (milkfish) with *laing* (a leafy green vegetable), all consumed on genuinely comfy seats in an arctic air-con environment. Remind the staff to heat your food properly, though.

Naga Restaurant   FILIPINO $$
(40 General Luna St; mains from P100; ⊙4pm-1am) Long-standing, informal joint with a loyal local following, thanks to its tasty toasted *siopao* (steamed buns) and simple *pansit* (stir-fried noodles), *adobo* (meat in vinegar and garlic) and other Filipino standards.

✗ Magsaysay Avenue

Bob Marlin   FILIPINO $$
(Magsaysay Ave; mains P160-300; ⊙11am-11pm) Bob Marlin is locally renowned as the best spot in town for crispy *pata* (deep-fried pork knuckle). Other Filipino dishes also hit the spot and, most importantly, soak up the booze during the bouts of live music.

San Diego Jazz Bar   BAR
(Magsaysay Ave) This lounge singing and smooth jazz bar is a good alternative if you're not into the get-blasted-and-sing-karaoke scene popular with so many Naga students.

Lolo's Music Bar   BAR
(Magsaysay Ave; ⊙4pm-1am) On the 2nd floor of Avenue Sq; a cool bar with plenty of room to breathe, and live music from 9pm. It ca-ters to an over 30s crowd, serves Bicolano dishes and has a smart-casual dress code.

ℹ Information

All the major banks are well represented.
Downtown Post Office (University of Nueva Caceres)
Naga City Visitors Center (☑054-473 4432; www.naga.gov.ph/tourism; cnr Miranda Ave & Maria Cristina St; ⊙8am-noon & 1-5pm Mon-Fri) Tourist office inside the City Hall complex.

ℹ Getting There & Away

AIR
The airport is in Pili, 14km south of Naga. Cebu Pacific and PAL Express fly daily (one hour) between Manila and Naga.

BUS & JEEPNEY
All bus services use Naga's **central bus termi-nal** (cnr Ninoy & Cory Aves), just south of the SM City Mall. Cagsawa and **RSL** (☑054-472 6885) bus lines have air-con night buses that

---

> ℹ **NAGA'S TRICYCLES**
>
> One of Naga's little quirks is the prolifer-ation of slightly larger tricycles designed to carry up to five passengers. These tricycles tend to be packed in the eve-nings and they also tend to be unwilling to deviate from certain routes, so if you want to head up to Magsaysay Ave from the centre, you'd best position yourself along Peñafrancia Ave to catch one. Rides within town are P8, or P40 if you want the tricycle all to yourself.

WORTH A TRIP

WAKING UP TO WAKEBOARDING

CamSur Watersports Complex (CWC; ☑054-477 3172, 054-475 0689; www.cwcwake. com; ⊙8.30am-7pm Mon-Thu, to 9pm Fri-Sun) At the CWC, complete with surfer dude music, restaurants, a waterpark and much more, wakeboarders whizz around the obstacle-strewn lake, performing flips and tricks. It's heaps of fun for experienced riders and beginners alike, with a plethora of accommodation options to linger in.

It's 12km south of Naga in Pili; a tricycle from Naga costs P500 return, including waiting time.

No idea what we're talking about? Wakeboarding is essentially snowboarding on water. Your feet are strapped to a board and you're pulled around a watercourse on a cable. Sound easy? Wait till you see the pros do their thing! There's a separate beginners' track where you gain confidence by riding back and forth across a stretch of water. Kneeboarding, waterskiing and wakeskating are also on the menu.

For those who just want to watch the action, there's a big swimming pool, a restaurant and a coffee shop near the water and a waterpark nearby. Prices depend on what you want to do: an hour/half-day on the water, including helmet, vest and board, will cost P165/460.

Building the CWC was a huge gamble but it's paid off, with wakeboarders coming here from all over the world, some staying on-site for weeks. Accommodation ranges from the Mansion Suites (double/suite P1750/2000), private villas for two (P3500) and family trailers (from P2850) to the budget options such as the two-person tiki huts (P1000) and cosy cabanas (from P1250).

go directly to Ermita in Manila, while **Isarog** (☑054-478 8804) and Amihan go to Cubao and Philtranco goes to Pasay. Most air-con and deluxe services are at night (air-con/recliner P650/750). Raymond bus services run daily to Caramoan at 2pm (P250, five to 5½ hours).

Jeepneys and air-con minivans leave from the **jeepney terminal** (Waling-Waling St) 200m east of SM City Mall, while **minivans to Daet** (cnr Ninoy & Cory Aves) leave from a stand next to the mall in the mornings (P170, 2½ hours). There are frequent minivans to Legazpi (P170, 2½ hours), Tabaco (P160, two hours) and Sabang (P100, 1½ hours). Jeepneys head to Panicuason (P25, 30 minutes) and Pili (P15, 20 minutes).

Mt Isarog National Park

Dominating Camarines Sur's landscape is Mt Isarog (1966m), Bicol's (dormant) second-highest volcano. From Panicuason (pan-ee-*kwa*-sone), a steep, half-hour walk along a rough road (passable if it's dry, but a regular car will struggle) leads to the entrance of **Mt Isarog National Park**. There is an admission fee (P100) at the base of the mountain. To the right, a short walk leads down some very steep stone steps to **Malabsay Falls**, where you can swim with a view of Mt Isarog – the experience is amazing. At Panicuason, **Mt Isarog Hot Springs** (admission P100; ⊙7am-6pm) has five natural hot-to-tepid pools – a nice way to relax after a trek in the park. The springs are a 1.3km

walk off the main road, just before the road to the national park.

Climbing Mt Isarog

We highly recommend hiring a guide for the two-day return trek up Mt Isarog. The hike up takes you through the last virgin tropical forest in Luzon; the trek can also be done in one day if you're very fit, but park authorities will still charge you two days' fee. As you get higher, the vegetation turns to mossy forest, which sheds into sparse grassland and stony alpine shelves closer to the summit.

Traditionally, early March to late May has been the best time, weather-wise, to climb. More than one trail snakes its way up the volcano: trekkers typically hike up either the popular trail from Panicuason, or the less-used and more environmentally friendly trail starting at Consocep. Talk to Jojo at Kadlagan Outdoor Shop (p167) in Naga; hiking packages (P5000 for one person, P7000 for two) include both an experienced English-speaking and local guide, camping gear and food, and all transport and permits. Keen climbers should also ask about routes on **Mt Lobo**, in Camarines Norte (Cam Nor), and **Mt Asog**, near Iriga.

To travel to Mt Isarog from Naga, take a jeepney to Panicuason. Note that the last jeepney back to Naga leaves Panicuason around 5pm.

Caramoan Peninsula

Only 50km or so from Naga, the mountainous, thickly jungled Caramoan peninsula may as well be worlds away. Approach it by boat, and you may feel as if you're arriving at the *Jurassic Park* island, with its jagged cliffs, teal sea and pristine strips of sand (minus the dinosaurs and with the addition of bronzed fishermen paddling their bangkas amid the choppy waves). Trundle to Caramoan by bus and you pass through tiny villages, with flaxen natural fibres drying by the roadside and looking like oversized Dolly Parton wigs.

In spite of the fact that Caramoan has been the location for filming of French, Israeli, Norwegian and other countries' versions of *Survivor* and the peninsula has become ever more accessible with the paving of the road, the trickle of travellers is yet to become a torrent, leaving the lucky few with pristine islands and beaches all to themselves.

◉ Sights & Activities

Besides island-hopping ventures, many lodgings organise all manner of activities, from rock climbing and caving to river tubing and river trekking.

Island-Hopping

Floating between the jungle-tufted limestone crags and golden strips of sand that make up the island archipelago off the north coast of Caramoan is one of Caramoan's biggest attractions. You can either go for an island-hopping package, haggle with the fishermen in Bikal or Paniman Beach and commandeer a bangka for a day (around P2000) or rent a sea kayak.

Highlights include pretty little **Matukad** with a hidden lagoon, accessible only by swimming under some rocks; **Lahos**, offshore from Gota Beach and only visible during low tide; plus postcard-perfect **Aguirangan**. The V-shaped **Sabitan Laya** offers long stretches of white sand and a limestone outcrop at the base of the V – there's good snorkelling here. **Tinago** has a secluded pristine cove that's perfect for sunbathing, while **Pitogo** is where the *Survivor* series were shot. The largest of the dozen or so islands is **Lahuy**, with beaches, local gold panners and a fruit bat colony; it's best accessed from barangay Bikal. So is **Tabgon**, set among onshore mangroves, and with a 500-step climb up to an enormous statue of Mary of Peace; it's a popular place of pilgrimage for Filipinos.

Other Activities

Bicol Adventure ATV ADVENTURE TOUR
(☑ 0909 413 1706, 0947 566 4926) This offshoot of Legazpi's Bicol Adventure ATV arranges outings on its fleet of 150cc ATVs (quad bikes), from a staightforward two-hour round trip to Paniman Beach (P999) to the more challenging Culapnit Cave (P2699) multihour rides that take in rougher stretches of the countryside and traverse rivers. Located on the main road in Caramoan.

Caramoan Kayaks KAYAKING
(☑ 0921 987 3157; www.cki-inn.com; 1hr/day P150/1900) The owners of CK Inn offer sea kayaks for rent and can guide paddlers around the islands or else provide camping equipment if you fancy staging a mini-*Survivor* scenario.

🛏 Sleeping & Eating

Caramoan town, a few kilometres from the sea, is a place to stay overnight rather than to linger. Caramoan has no restaurants; food is whatever your guesthouse happens to rustle up. There are a few basic eateries a block from the sea in the coastal barangay of Paniman Beach, 6km away from Caramoan.

If you're intent on living out your *Castaway* fantasy by staying on an uninhabited island, you can rent tents from Kadlagan Outdoor Shop (p167) in Naga, CK Inn near Guijalo and Residencia de Salvacion.

★ Residencia de Salvacion B&B $
(☑ 0939 310 1135; http://residenciasalvacion.weebly.com; r from P800; ❄ 🛜) Surrounded by a bamboo stockade and driftwood sculptures at the north end of Paniman Beach, the new incarnation of Residencia de Salvacion is superb value for money and its vibe encourages lingering for weeks. Multiday packages (two days, one night P1800) include island-hopping and some of the best home-cooked food in Bicol. Staff go out of their way to make you feel welcome.

Crazy Coconut Cottages RESORT $
(☑ 0998 467 2425; www.crazy-coconut.com; r P1000; ❄ 🛜) New beachfront lodgings in the middle of Paniman Beach, run by the delightful Sam and Jenalyn. Besides chilling at the beachfront bar, you can partake in caving, island-hopping and other active pursuits, organised by the ever-helpful hosts.

CK Inn B&B $$
(☑ 0920 474 2637, 0908 203 5082; www.ck-inn.com; d/tr from P1600/1900; ❄ 🛜) A pretty,

family-run guesthouse, the CK is a little out of the way, near Guijalo, but with its helpful staff, spick-and-span rooms, free breakfast and leafy location, it's a lovely option. The family room (P3500) can accommodate you and seven of your nearest and dearest. Run by the folks at Caramoan Kayaks.

Casita Mia Bed & Breakfast B&B $$
(☑ 0917 819 5150; www.casitamia.com.ph; d P2700; ❄🛜) This local take on a Spanish-style hacienda, hiding on a quiet street near the market, is the most upmarket option in Caramoan town. Stylish rooms aside, the attentive proprietress offers all-inclusive bed, board and boat packages that introduce you to the uninhabited islands.

Rex Tourist Inn GUESTHOUSE $$
(☑ 0915 329 5658, 0919 882 1879; www.rextouris-tinn.com; s/d P800/1500; ❄🛜) Long-standing and showing its age, this Caramoan stalwart on the main street has a more appealing off-shoot. Rex Tourist Inn Garden Resort, near the Bikal boat landing, 5km out of town, has a pool, climbing wall and boat trips on offer as well as spacious rooms.

★ Hunangan Cove RESORT $$$
(☑ 0920 967 2942; http://caramoanislands.com; d P5000-7500, ste P10,000; ❄) Managed by the Gota Village Resort at Gota Beach, this is a cluster of luxurious thatched-roof huts with full amenities, hiding in the eponymous, picture-perfect cove that's hemmed in between the jungle and the turquoise sea. Guests are offered a bewildering array of activities, from cliff-diving, island-hopping and kayaking to caving, river tubing and hiking.

❶ Information

Tourist Office (☑ 0928 407 9960; caramoan.tourism@gmail.com; ⊗8am-5pm Mon-Fri) Ultra-helpful Mylene Cordial is knowledgeable about all things Caramoan. The tourist office is inside the Municipal Hall compound on the main street.

---

❶ 'TYPHOON HIGHWAY' SHORTCUT

The quickest way to travel between the Caramoan peninsula and Catanduanes is by hiring a bangka to ferry you across the 'typhoon highway' in Codon (from P1500 per bangka, 1½ hours) or Guijalo port. This is not to be attempted during rough seas (which is much of the time), as the journey can be hair-raisingly dangerous.

---

❶ Getting There & Away

BOAT
If coming from Naga, take an air-con minivan to Sabang (P90, 1½ hours). From Sabang, 'Harry' boats (large bangkas) leave loosely according to schedule, roughly every hour, for Guijalo port (P120, two hours), the last leaving around 1pm.

A scheduled freight and passenger boat between Tabaco and Guijalo port, **MB Gracia Salvacion** (☑ 0919 326 2680), sails daily between Friday and Monday at 7.30am from Tabaco, returning at 2pm. At the time of research, it was temporarily discontinued due to typhoon damage to the Guijalo dock.

On arrival to Guijalo, you have to register and pay a P30 environmental fee. From Guijalo port, it's a 15-minute jeepney or tricycle ride (P60) to Caramoan town.

BUS
The road between Sabang to Guijalo (35km) had been mostly paved at the time of writing, with Raymond bus running daily services to and from Naga (P250, five to 5½ hours). From Caramoan, the bus departs at 7am from next to the market and passes along the main street.

From Legazpi or Tabaco, take a jeepney to Tigaon, switch to another jeepney to Sabang and then either catch the last boat to Guijalo or connect with the daily Rayond bus at around 4pm.

Legazpi
☑ 052 / POP 182,201

This gritty provincial capital is situated right at the foot of active Mt Mayon (2462m), justifiably dubbed the world's most perfect volcano. Its main streets are clogged with traffic, but step even a block away, particularly in Albay, and you find yourself observing quiet houses drowning in greenery, pecking chickens and tricycle drivers napping in the shade.

Legazpi is divided into Albay District and Legazpi City. Most government offices, the airport, and the fancier restaurants and hotels are situated in Albay District. Legazpi City is a noisy, convoluted maze of street stalls, markets, bars and exhaust-stained buildings. The cheaper accommodation is located here, with the bus and jeepney terminal halfway between the two. Hundreds of jeepneys per day connect the two districts, which are 3.5km apart.

◉ Sights

Ligñon Hill HILL
To get a really good glimpse of fiery Mt Mayon (and the city), head up Ligñon Hill

(or drive, or take a trike; expect to pay around P300 for a round trip). It's a steep, but paved, 20-minute walk up the hill; we'd recommend going in the morning before it gets too hot. At the top you'll find an observation post run by the Philippine Institute of Volcanology, and a couple of ziplines and ubiquitous souvenir shops and cafes.

Embarcadero PIER
(http://wowlegazpi.com/embarcadero; Legazpi Blvd) This glitzy waterfront complex just east of Legazpi City, connected by electronic jeepneys to public transport stops, consists of a huge mall, palm-tree-lined seafront walk, a Skywalk for Mt Mayon admirers and a bungee trampoline, a zipline and a go-karting track for more active visitors.

🏃 Activities

Legazpi is a good base for exploring the nearby adventureland of Bicol. Most hotels can set you up with vans and drivers; the going rate for day tours within Albay province is around P3000 to P3500, but inexpensive day tours of Legazpi proper are available through Bicol Adventure ATV.

Bicol Adventure ATV ADVENTURE TOUR, HIKING
(☑0907 290 6409, 052-480 2266; www.bicoladventureatv.com; V&O Bldg, Quezon Ave; ⊙7am-6pm) This enthusiastic, highly professional outfit on the 2nd floor arranges everything from hiking up Mt Mayon to diving and snorkelling trips and ATV outings along old lava trails in the vicinity of the volcano. These guys can also arrange an inexpensive Yellow Bee city tour (P299 plus P500 guide fee).

🛌 Sleeping

There are several good hotels within walking distance of the airport, but they are only really convenient for early flights.

🛏 Legazpi City

Legazpi Tourist Inn INN $
(☑052-820 4880; V&O Bldg, Quezon Ave; s/d with fan P600/700, with air-con P1000/1200; ❋🤶) Festooned with fake flowers, the 3rd-floor Tourist Inn offers modern, well-kept (if not terribly inspiring) rooms with private bathrooms, TVs and lots of mirrors.

Tyche Boutique Hotel HOTEL $$
(☑052-480 5555; www.tycheboutiquehotel.com; cnr Rizal & Governor Forbes Sts; r P2700-3900; ❋🤶) We're not sure this hotel deserves the

SLEEPING LION HILL

Sleeping Lion Hill (Legazpi Blvd) The view that holds everyone's attention in Legazpi is of Mt Mayon, but there's another beautiful panorama many visitors miss: the pretty port of Legazpi itself. Legazpi Blvd leads directly to Sleeping Lion Hill, located near the waterfront and its rump-ish rise does bear a vague resemblance to a snoozing cat. The 30-minute ascent goes up a rough path and culminates with a great view of the waterfront and nearby islands.

'boutique' tag but it's very central, with modern, compact rooms decked out in classic creams and browns, and the staff are sweet and helpful. The restaurant serves a good mix of Filipino and Chinese dishes. ('Tyche' is pronounced 'tay-keh'.)

🛏 Albay District

Mayon Backpackers Hostel HOSTEL $
(☑052-480 0365; http://mayonbackpackers.wordpress.com; Diego Silang St; dm P250-350, d/q P1000/1200; ❋🤶) The only legitimate hostel in Legazpi is the clear top budget choice, with comfy six- and four-bed dorm rooms (albeit with narrow beds), two lovely private rooms, a common kitchen, a computer for guest use and a rooftop with hammocks and views to Mayon.

★ Balai Tinay Guesthouse B&B $$
(☑052-480 8216; 70 Gapo St; r from P1000; ❋🤶) Run by the loveliest, most attentive hosts who are happy to assist with planning your Legazpi adventures, this family-run guesthouse sits on a quiet little street in Albay; head right along the riverside path from Albay Central School. The compact en suite rooms are spick and span and guests can help themselves to fruit and drinks in the common area.

Apple Peach House BOUTIQUE HOTEL $$
(☑052-481 1724, 0977 782 7635; www.applepeachhouse.com.ph; cnr Marquez & Rosario Sts; r P1888-2500; ❋🤶) This shiny glass-and-chrome building houses Albay District's chic new hotel. The vivid contemporary art downstairs balances out the muted, austere charoal-and-white room decor; rooms come with particularly comfortable beds and powerful showers.

Legazpi

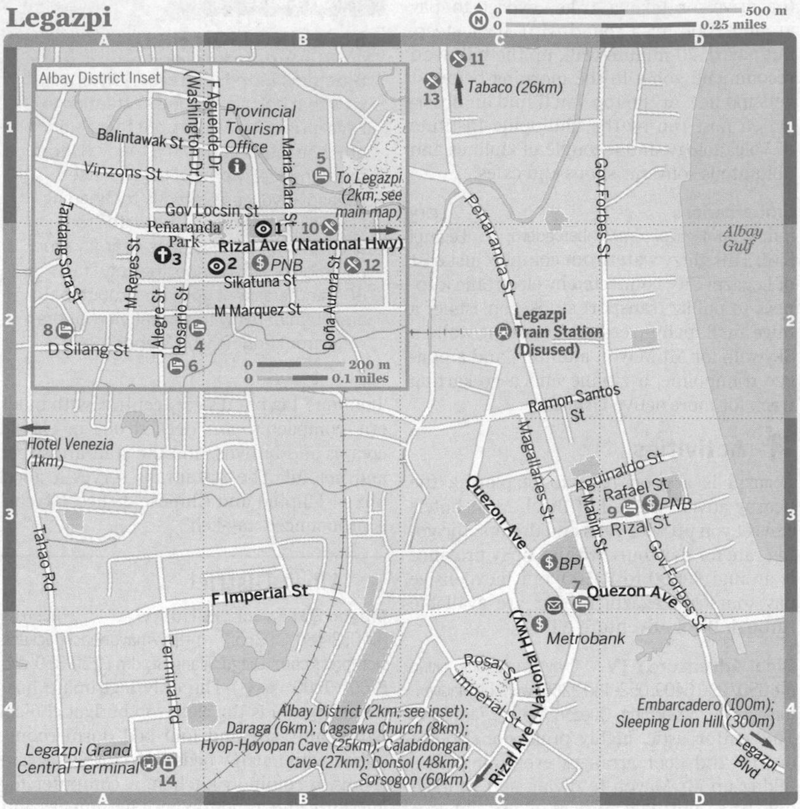

Hotel Villa Angelina HOTEL $$
(☎052-480 6345; www.villaangelinahotel.com; 32 Diego Silang St; r incl breakfast P1800-2500; ❄📶) At the most homey of lodging options in Albay, the rather fussy but well-kept rooms are presided over by a friendly hostess and come with a free breakfast. The downstairs restaurant serves very good Filipino and Western food and the place books up in advance during government conventions in September/October.

Hotel Venezia HOTEL $$$
(☎052-481 0888; Washington Dr; r/ste 2500/4729; ❄📶) One of the classiest hotels in town has ultra-modern rooms decked out in muted greys, beautiful linen and private balconies with views of Mt Mayon. Staff are professional and courteous, and the surrounds are green and pleasant. Skip the restaurant, though.

Eating

Legazpi Centre

★**Waway Restaurant** BICOLANO $$
(Peñaranda St; lunch buffet P249; ⏲noon-10pm Mon-Sat) For authentic Bicol food, head to this local institution for a splendid (though rather meat-heavy) lunchtime buffet of spicy coconut-milk-cooked specialties, *kare-kare* (oxtail and vegetables cooked in peanut sauce), and tempura vegetables as the guest star. It's 1km north of Legazpi City.

Sibid-Sibid SEAFOOD $$
(328 Peñaranda; mains P160-220; ⏲10am-9pm; 📶) A wonderful open-air restaurant 1km north of Legazpi City, Sibid-Sibid specialises in highly original, Bicol-inspired seafood concoctions like fish Bicol *exprés*. Serves some of the best *pinangat* in the region, in our humble opinion.

Legazpi

✖ Albay District

★**Smalltalk Cafe**   BICOLANO $
(Doña Aurora St; mains P60-250; ⊙ 11am-10pm;
✱⊘) This delightful little eatery defines
the notion of Bicol-fusion cooking, and
whether you opt for its Bicol *exprés* pasta, *pinangat*-filled ravioli or Cordon Bleu
chicken, it doesn't matter: it's all glorious!
We are passionate devotees of the moreish
pili nut pie and the appropriately apocalyptic Mayon Hot Lava: a dessert involving
sili (chilli) ice cream.

1st Colonial Grill   BICOLANO $$
(Rizal Ave; mains from P130; ⊙ noon-10pm)
While this place serves up great Bicolano
dishes such as *tinapa* rice (rice with *tinapa* flakes and green mango) and five-spiced
chicken, it's particularly famous for its unusual ice cream flavours, such as *sili* and
pili nut.

🔒 Shopping

Kababayan Handicraft Market   HANDICRAFTS
Next to the bus station, the market is a great
place to stock up on abaca bags and purses,
pili nut products (marzipan, cookies, pastries) and jars of *laing* and Bicol *exprés* for
recreating Bicolano dishes at home.

ⓘ Information

There are plenty of internet cafes all over, and
ATMs both in Legazpi City and Albay District.
Legazpi city's tourism website **Wow! Legazpi**
(http://wowlegazpi.com) is: a) a good portal;
and b) notable for its great, nerdy name. The
website **Musings of the Midnight Writer**
(http://goldimyrr.repolles.com), run by a
Legazpi-based author, is an excellent window
into the cultural calendar of the Bicol region.
Provincial Tourism Office (⊿ 052-820 6314;
Aquende Dr) Inside the Astrodome Complex, the
tourism office offers an excellent free city map.

ⓘ Getting There & Away

AIR
Cebu Pacific and PAL Express each fly at least
once daily to/from Manila (1¼ hours).

BUS
From the **Legazpi Grand Central Terminal**
(Terminal Rd), most air-con and deluxe services to Manila (around P850 to P1100, 11 to
12 hours) depart between 6.30 and 8.30pm,
although 'ordinary' (non air-con) buses depart
throughout the day, both to Manila and local
destinations such as Sorsogon and Tabaco.
Cagsawa (⊿ 052-480 7810) and RSL bus lines
run comfortable night buses to Ermita in Manila.
Isarog (⊿ 052-481 4744) and **Peñafrancia**
(⊿ 052-435 3012) head to Cubao, while **Philtranco** (⊿ 02-851 8078; www.philtranco.com.
ph) serves Pasay.

Across the street from the bus terminal, there
are frequent minivans during daylight hours
to and from Naga (P170, 2½ hours), Sorsogon
(P90, 1½ to two hours), Tabaco (P50, 40 minutes), Donsol (P80, 1¼ hours, 5pm) and Pilar
(P70, one hour).

Around Legazpi

Daraga & Around

In the bustling market town of Daraga, the
baroque-style **Daraga Church**, set on a hill
splendidly overlooking Mt Mayon, was constructed completely from volcanic rock in
1773. From Legazpi take any Daraga-bound
jeepney (P8) along Rizal Ave. Beside the Daraga Church, stop for a cold drink or lunch at
the very stylish **7 Degrees Grill & Restaurant** (dishes from P120; ⊙ noon-10pm), where
several indoor-outdoor terraces offer fantastic views; it serves particularly good *kinilaw*
and and assortment of fiery Bicolano dishes.

A couple of kilometres northwest of Daraga is that most classic of Bicol panoramas:

the forlorn, greenery-topped remains of the sunken Cagsawa Church (admission P30) on a green plain against the backdrop of Mt Mayon. Twelve hundred people took refuge here from Mayon's violent eruption in 1814 and were entombed alive. Come early to avoid the circus of selfie-snappers and souvenir vendors. A few minutes' walk from Cagsawa Church is the local branch of Bicol Adventure ATV (www.bicoladventureatv.com; Cagsawa Trail from P699, Combo Trail from P3000), offering exciting ATV rides in the foothills of Mt Mayon on ATVs ranging from 150cc to powerful 500cc and Terracross vehicles. You'll ride through rivers, across plains and mountainous terrain; at research time, only the 40-minute Cagsawa Trail was accessible due to volcanic activity. From Legazpi or Daraga, take any jeepney (P10) headed to Camalig, Guinobatan or Ligao. Ask the driver to drop you off at the ruins, and walk in about 500m from the road.

Hyop-Hoyopan & Calabidongan Caves

Pottery dating from 200 BC to AD 900 has been found in the easily accessible Hyop-Hoyopan (admission incl lantern P250) limestone cave, set on a quiet hillside above a pretty rural valley. Guides are available at the entrance; experienced Marife Nieva (☑ 0915 286 7221) is one of the better ones. Tips are appreciated.

Hyop-Hoyopan is about 25km from Legazpi. Take any jeepney heading towards Camalig, Polangui, Guinobatan or Ligao and get off in Camalig (P20), then hitch a ride on a motorbike (around P150 one way).

The name of the cave means 'blow-blow', a reference to the cool and somewhat eerie wind that blows through the cave. A tour takes around 30 minutes; ancient pottery aside, you'll see the dance floor where the local equivalents of raves were held in secret during the martial law era under Marcos, and many rock formations, including one that resembles either the Virgin Mary or the Devil, depending on how you squint at it.

Located around 3km from Hyop-Hyopan Cave, the more challenging Calabidongan Cave (literally, Cave of the Bats) is for more adventurous, confident spelunkers as its partially flooded interior requires you to swim a short distance within the cave. It can only be accessed when water levels allow (typically from March to June) and it's a really good idea to bring a waterproof torch. Guides at Hyop-Hyopan can arrange transport; exploration of Calabidongan's subterranean depths takes a couple of hours.

Mt Mayon

The perfect cone of Mt Mayon (2462m) rises dramatically from the flat Albay terrain, and can be seen from as far away as Naga and Catanduanes. The volcano's name derives from the Bicol *daragan magayon,* meaning 'beautiful single lady', and the Philippines' most active volcano is a cantankerous beauty at that, responsible for over 40 deadly eruptions since 1616, the most recent taking place during our research in September 2014.

At the time of writing, warning levels had been raised to 'critical': there was an exclusion zone of 8km around the volcano and the residents of the villages evacuated. The

---

CLIMBING MT MAYON

Though Mt Mayon was erupting when we visited, once activity subsides, it may well be possible to scale its slopes once more. En route, you pass through varied terrain: boulder-strewn desert, grassy plain and forest, and it takes most hikers two days to hike to the top and back. You have to take all gear (tents, warm clothes) and food with you; there are water sources along the way, but purification tablets are a must.

There are three routes up the volcano: one from Legazpi's Buyunan barangay, one via Santo Domingo's Centennial Forest, while the most popular route runs from San Roque barangay, near the PhiVolcs (Philippine Institute of Volcanology & Seismology) research station. The best (and driest) time to hike is traditionally between February and April – though climate change is shifting these parameters. A guide for a Mayon hiking package costs around P7500 for a two-day climb, P5000 for a one-day climb. This fee covers all food, transportation, gear and porters: Bicol Adventure ATV (p173) can arrange a guide for you.

PhiVolcs strongly recommends you don't climb beyond 1800m, although some guides will take you to 2000m. Go much higher than that and you'll be overwhelmed by the sulphurous gases.

last victims of Mt Mayon were four German hikers and a local guide, killed by a minor belch of ash and rocks during their ascent of the peak in 2013. In 2006, after lava flows subsided, a biblically proportioned Typhoon Durian triggered mudslides on Mt Mayon that killed more than 1000 people, while in 1993, 77 people were killed by eruptions, including a team of American vulcanologists. The deadliest eruption to date took place in 1814, destroying the Cagsawa Church and killing over 1200 people.

Mt Mayon is carefully monitored by the **Philippine Institute of Volcanology and Seismology** (PhiVolcs; www.phivolcs.dost.gov.ph), located near Lignon Hill in Legazpi. The institute closes an area of between 6km and 10km around the volcano when there is a danger of eruption.

Tabaco

052 / POP 59,930

Tabaco, in the shadow of Mt Mayon, is the departure point for boats to Catanduanes. The lovely 19th-century facade of the **Church of San Juan Bautista** (Ziga Ave), with greenery growing out of the cracks in the mighty masonry, is a must for colonial architecture buffs. Some of the bricks bear individual masons' marks – a rarity in this country. Otherwise, an early boat departure is the only reason to stay here.

Three blocks from the pier, **Gardenia Hotel** (052-487 8019; Riosa St; r from P1100;) is one of Tabaco's swisher options, with large, clean doubles, volcano views, breakfast thrown in, and a quiet-ish location behind the market. Our favourite, however, is **JJ Midcity Inn** (052-487 4158; www.jjmidcityinn.com; Herrera St; s/d/ste P800/1000/3800;), with spotless rooms with bright splashes of colour, a whirlpool in the suite, and 12-hour rates available. The restaurant at the **Casa Eugenia Hotel** (Ziga Ave; mains from P80;) serves both decent Filipino standards and Chinese dishes.

Cagsawa, Philtranco and Raymond Tours run buses to and from Cubao, Manila (aircon/deluxe from P850/1100, 12 hours). Frequent buses, jeepneys and minivans (P50, 30 minutes) go to and from Legazpi, and minivans run to Naga. Most transport uses the Integrated Terminal on Rizal St.

Daily ferries run to Virac and San Andres (p184; p172), and should soon resume to Guijalo port on the Caramoan peninsula.

Sorsogon

056 / POP 73,375

The eponymous capital of Bicol's southernmost province lies in a beautiful area of beaches, natural springs and rice fields sprawled beneath jungle-clad volcanoes. Sorsogon city itself may not be particularly appealing, but there's good **trekking** on the province's highest volcano, Mt Bulusan, and it provides transport links to the rest of the province. The liveliest time to be here is during the mid-October **Kasanggayahan** festival celebrating the city's history through beauty pageants, music and bangka races.

Sleeping & Eating

There are a couple of fast-food joints on the main street near the jeepney terminal.

Villa Kasanggayahan　　　　GUESTHOUSE $
(056-211 1275; Rizal St; r P800-1150;) The lovely garden, green walls, breezy balconies and outdoor sitting areas make this quiet place a treat to stay in. Rooms are spacious but could use a lick of paint. The guesthouse hides behind a tall gate off the main street.

Fernandos Hotel　　　　　　HOTEL $$
(056-211 1357; www.fernandoshotel.com; N Pareja St; d/tr from P1000/1350;) A block from Rizal park, Fernandos is still the nicest hotel in town. The top-end rooms are spacious and have walls tastefully decorated with abaca and other indigenous fibres; cheaper rooms are functional if small (and are above the music bar). Energetic owner Cecilia Duran and her daughter Angie are the best sources of info on the area.

★**Sirangan Beach Resort**　　　RESORT $$$
(0919 582 2732; www.sirangan.com; r P4500-6500;) Ten kilometres out of Sorsogon at the deliciously named Bacon (pronounced 'Backon') Beach, you'll find this decidedly elegant and upmarket accommodation option. The 12 rooms' private balconies, stylishly crafted local wood furnishings, classic white linen and astonishing bathrooms are popular with local and international visitors.

Fernando 168 Bistro　　　　BICOLANO $$
(N Pareja St; mains from P120; 8am-10pm) In spite of the dark, cafeteria-like decor, this stop next door to Fernandos Hotel serves excellent Bicolano dishes and grilled seafood.

ℹ Information

Several banks in town – PNB, BPI and BDO among them – have ATMs, and there are several internet cafes on Rizal St, the main road.

For tours of the area, camping gear rental, guides for climbing Mt Bulusan, arranging private transport and general info, the owners of Fernandos Hotel are your go-to people.

ℹ Getting There & Away

The jeepney terminal is next to the massive church that resembles the Capitol Building, while buses leave from the stands next to the City Hall.

There are regular buses/minivans to Legazpi (P60/80, 1½ to two hours) and inconveniently timed middle-of-the-night buses to Manila.

Jeepneys run to most Sorsogon province destinations, including Bulan, Barcelona, Bulusan and Matnog. For Donsol, you have to take a jeepney to Putiao (P40, 45 minutes) and get on another jeepney to Donsol (P40, one hour).

Bulusan Volcano National Park & Around

South of Sorsogon is **Bulusan Volcano National Park** (admission P30; ⊙ 7am-5.30pm). Just inside the park, **Bulusan Lake** is a popular picnic spot, and there's a 1.8km **walking trail** around the crater lake. When the mist is low over the surrounding forest and the birds are singing, it's a lovely, peaceful spot and the clear, still water makes for an inviting swim. Climbers must go with a guide; get organised through Fernandos Hotel in Sorsogon, or ask the barangay captain in San Roque for assistance with finding a local guide.

A successful conquest of Mt Bulusan deserves a soak in the **Palogtoc Falls**. This grotto is accessible by a 500m walk from a trailhead off the main road between the park entrance and San Roque (it's also on the Bulusan–Irosin jeepney route). It features a gorgeous cold-water pool fed by falls beside a shady river, with just a few low-key bamboo and nipa huts. Nearby, the **Masacrot Springs** (admission P35) offer the same sort of pool, but with concrete huts and videoke.

ℹ Getting There & Away

The entrance to the park is near San Roque, about 10km west of Bulusan town. A day trip to the lake is feasible if you don't want to take an organised tour; take one of the infrequent jeepneys from Sorsogon to Bulusan (about 1½ hours). In Bulusan, look for the Bulusan–Irosin jeepney; this will drop you at the park entrance track 6km from town, and you can walk the 2km in from there. Alternatively, hire a tricycle from Bulusan directly to the lake (about P260, including waiting time). It's 6km from Bulusan or 8km from Irosin to the park entrance; you can also make this trip from Sorsogon via Irosin.

Donsol

📞 056 / POP 23,470

Until the 'discovery' of whale sharks off the coast here in 1998, Donsol, about 45km southwest of Legazpi, was an obscure, sleepy fishing village in one of Sorsogon's more remote areas. In 1998 a local diver shot a video of the whale sharks and a newspaper carried a story about Donsol's gentle *butanding*. Since then Donsol has become one of the Philippines' most popular tourist locations, though the permanence of its shark population is now in question.

Only one resort accepts credit cards and there are no international ATMs here. Come prepared with plenty of cash. There are a couple of internet cafes in town.

THE ELUSIVE WHALE SHARKS

The mangrove forests that skirt the Donsol River are a rich source of nutrients that feed the microscopic plankton that, in turn, has been bringing whale sharks to Donsol in huge numbers. Over the last several years, however, there had been a drop in whale shark sightings around Donsol. This prompted concern from the WWF that the shark population was being affected by climate change: the rise of the temperature of the water and damage to the mangrove forests was impacting on the sharks' primary source of food, the plankton. Or perhaps the fact that some boat drivers and tourists were disregarding shark interaction rules and touching the animals was distressing the sharks and driving them away. In 2012 the giants of the deep were back in considerable numbers, though earlier than in previous years, appearing in the Donsol waters in October and with scanter sightings between December and April; in 2013 sightings were inconsistent (seven sharks one day, none the next). It remains to be seen whether these patterns will stabilise.

MANTA BOWL

March to May are the peak months to dive the Manta Bowl, a 17m to 22m atoll dive where you hook at the bottom to take a rest from the strong currents. It provides the perfect conditions for a manta ray cleaning station, where mantas positively queue up for cleaner wrasse to remove parasites from their skin. Whale sharks may be seen here too, as well as occasional thresher sharks and hammerheads, while Tuna Alley attracts sheer walls of tuna and barracuda. Manta Bowl is an advanced dive, though operators will take divers with less than 20 dives under their belt as long as they pay for a dive master to go one-to-one with them. Geographically part of Masbate, it's logistically easier to dive from Donsol on mainland Southeast Luzon. To get with good Manta Bowl dive operators, contact Bicol Dive Center. At the time of writing, the cost per person for a two-person, three-dive trip at Manta Bowl (all gear included) was P7500.

🏃 Activities

Whale Shark Spotting

Swimming with these huge, blue-grey, silver-spotted creatures is a truly exhilarating experience – but you do need to be a decent snorkeller to keep up with them!

Whale sharks migrate here between November and June, with the peak months generally being March and April (though avoid super-busy Easter week), but in the last several years sighting haven't always been consistent. Whale shark spotting is also subject to the vagaries of weather – if the sea is rough or a typhoon is on the way, the boats will not go out. Be sure to check the weather conditions to avoid disappointment.

When you get to Donsol, head to the **Donsol Visitors Center** (☑ 0917 868 1626, 0906 504 9287; www.donsolwhalesharkecotour. com; ⊙ 7am-5pm), situated 1.5km north of the river bridge (P35 by tricycle from town).

This is how the process went when we visited. You pay your registration fee (P300), and arrange a space on a boat (P3500, good for six people) for a three-hour tour. The Visitors Center does its best to ensure each boat is full, so if you're a solo traveller, they'll add you to a group. Then off you go! The centre may close earlier (in the day or the season) if weather is bad or if there are no visitors.

Only snorkelling equipment is allowed; scuba diving is prohibited. Snorkelling equipment is available for rent (P300 per session), though it may be limited in peak season. Each boat has a spotter and a *Butanding* Interaction Officer on board – tip them a couple of hundred pesos, especially if you've had a good day. Before you set off, you get a detailed briefing on how to behave around the sharks: namely, no touching them, and avoid their powerful tail.

The experience is quite regimented – given the well-being of the animals, the number of visitors and the need to rotate boat crews fairly – and access to the whale sharks is limited to a maximum of 25 boats per day.

Diving

Divers come in droves to explore the Manta Bowl and other macro dive sites closer to shore. Each resort has a dive centre with a floating population of experienced freelance dive masters.

Bicol Dive Center DIVING
(☑ 0906 801 6852, 0921 929 3811; www.bicoldivecenter.com) Longstanding diving operator offers PADI certification course (P19,500), 5D4N Ticao adventures (P29,000) and day package of two dives in the Donsol area (P7000).

Other Activities

Boats can be hired for day trips to the exquisite San Miguel Island off Ticao, and there's good snorkelling a short boat ride north of the resorts.

An increasingly popular evening experience is to spend a couple of hours on the river after dusk, watching myriad gently floating tiny lights of the fireflies. Boat trips cost P1250 for a maximum of five people, and leave from the 'firefly station' at one end of the river bridge at 5.30pm to 6pm.

🛏 Sleeping & Eating

Most budget lodgings are found in Donsol town proper, whereas the resorts stretch out along several kilometres of coastal road that starts beyond the bridge from Donsol. During off season, from June to mid-November, the resort strip is dead. All resorts have restaurants, and homestays offer meals. The bar at Giddy's is one of the local hotspots.

Donsol

Giddy's Place
RESORT $$

(☑ 0917 848 8881; www.giddysplace.com; 54 Clemente St; d/f from P2800/4480; ❋ 🛜 🖭) Giddy's has significantly upped the game in Donsol lodging: it has a good bar and restaurant, cable TV, modern, clean en suite rooms, an on-site spa and a pool, and arranges kayaking trips (P1500). Giddy's takes credit cards, but bring cash just in case. On-site professional diving instruction available; you can practise blowing bubbles in its pool.

Aguluz Homestay
HOMESTAY $$

(☑ 0920 952 8170, 0918 942 0897; razormarilyn@yahoo.com; San José St; r with fan/air-con P900/1800; ❋ 🛜) Aguluz is the fancy homestay option in Donsol, with excellent home-cooked food and delightful rooms. Besides the wonderfully accommodating family, Marilyn the hostess is a little tornado of energy and she'll do what she can to arrange all your tours and onward transportation. If you're on a shoestring budget, costs really tend to add up.

Coastal Road

★ Victoria's Guest House
B&B $

(☑ 0912 456 8888, 0906 556 0697; www.victorias-guesthouse-donsol.com; Purok 1; r from P500, 2-person cottages P1000) Not only does the lovely Victoria conjure up some of most delicious home-cooked food in Donsol, but it also offers appealing thatched cottages with modern, en suite, fan-cooled rooms on a strip of black-sand beach soon after the bridge, near the police station. Near enough to town to walk there, but far enough away for peace.

Vitton & Woodland Resorts
HOTEL $$

(☑ 0917 544 4089, 0927 912 6313; http://whalesharksphilippines.com; dm P500, r from P1800; ❋ 🖭) These two resorts are managed by the same family: each has a lovely garden, clean accomodation and friendly service. The newer Vitton features a bar and a pool, while the older Woodland's rooms are showing their age, but cater to backpackers as a plus, with fan-cooled basic shared rooms.

Elysia Beach Resort
RESORT $$$

(☑ 0917 547 4466; www.elysia-donsol.com; r from P3150; ⊙ mid-Nov–Jun; ❋ 🖭) Furthest along the coastal road, secluded Elysia is the only dedicated top-end resort in Donsol. It has attractively manicured cabanas with thatched roofs and the air-con rooms arranged around the pool are bright, spacious and come with cable TV. Not the best value for money but top pick if you value your creature comforts.

BARracuda
FILIPINO $$

(mains from P100; ⊙ 5pm-late) Popular waterfront restaurant and bar between Woodland and Vitton Resorts, with an extensive cocktail and beer menu and fresh fish on the grill.

ⓘ Getting There & Away

Jeepneys and buses stop at the terminal on Hernandez St, in the southwest corner of town. There are direct air-con minivans to and from Legazpi (P85, one hour) that leave when full until about 4pm. Jeepneys go via Pilar and take at least twice as long. After 4pm, head to Pilar via jeepney, and connect with more frequent minivans and buses there. A single Philitranco bus leaves for Manila at noon (P850, 12 to 14 hours) but there are more conveniently timed departures from Legazpi.

Pilar

Pilar is a port town where you're unlikely to spend much time, but useful for jeepney connections between Donsol and Legazpi, daily fastcraft boats and ROROs to and from Masbate and connections between Pilar and Ticao Island. Boats are met by air-con vans bound for Legazpi (P70).

MASBATE

🖭 056 / POP 834,650

Shaped like a crooked beckoning finger, Masbate Island is mostly devoted to ranching, which, together with a certain reputation for lawlessness, has earned the island the moniker 'the Wild East'. The island's main visitor draw is the raucous annual rodeo in April in Masbate port; travellers are also drawn by the relative lack of infrastructure, absence of tourist hordes, inland scenery that alternates between pasture land and jungle-shrouded mountains and some offbeat attractions. The main island aside, Masbate Province incorporates the satellite islands of Ticao, with its renowned diving destination of Manta Bowl, and wilder, remoter Burias.

ⓘ Getting There & Away

AIR

PAL Express flies to and from Masbate port to Manila daily.

Masbate

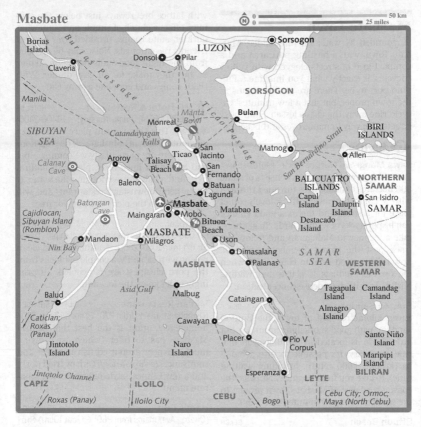

BOAT

Masbate Town is an important shipping port. Roll-on-roll-off (RORO) ferries sail from Masbate to Manila, Pilar and Cebu City, from Mandaon to Mindoro, Sibuyan and Caticlan, from Milagros to Iloilo City, and Cawayan to Bogo. Check out the shipping movements board in the Port Authority office at Masbate pier for full, up-to-date weekly schedules.

Large bangkas go several times a day between Pilar and Monreal or San Jacinto on Ticao Island (P150, two hours) and between Bulan and San Jacinto.

Some of the most popular RORO and fastcraft routes:

2Go Travel (☎056-578 0034; www.2go.com. ph) Ferry departures from Masbate to Manila (Thursdays at 10am, 22 hours) via Romblon (seven hours); Cebu (Tuesdays at 3.30pm, 15½ hours) via Ormoc (nine hours); Coron, Palawan (Sundays at 4.30pm, 46 hours); and Puerto Princesa (Sundays at 1am, 37½ hours).

Return journeys from Manila are on Mondays at 3.30pm, Romblon at 6.30am on Tuesdays, Ormoc at 11.59pm on Wednesdays, Cebu at 5pm on Wednesdays, Coron, Palawan at 4.30pm on Sundays and Puerto Princesa at 1am on Sundays.

Montenegro Lines (☎043 723 6980; www. montenegrolines.com.ph; fastcraft/RORO P396/288) Two daily fastcraft (two to 2½ hours) from Masbate to Pilar run at 5am and noon while RORO ferries (four hours) depart at 8.30am and 2.30pm. Return journeys are at 8am and 4pm for fastcraft and 6am and noon for ROROs. Also runs daily RORO services at noon from Cataingan, Masbate, to Bogo, Cebu (P456); the return journey is at midnight.

Trans Asia (☎032-254 6491; www.tran-sasiashipping.com; 2nd/1st/cabin class P640/875/1505) Trans Asia leaves Cebu for Masbate on Monday, Wednesday and Friday leaving at 6pm and arriving at 7.30am. Return service is at the same time on Tuesday, Thursday and Saturday.

Masbate Town

Surrounded by water on three sides, Masbate Town, with a bustling port area and a compact grid of streets clogged with yellow tricycles, is exactly what you imagine a Filipino port to be. There are no attractions in the town proper, but just a few minutes' tricycle ride away the chaos lessens, and busy streets give way to mangroves and beaches.

◉ Sights

Pawa Mangrove Nature Park   PROTECTED AREA
Pawa Mangrove Nature Park consists of some 300 hectares of mangroves threaded through with a 1.3km boardwalk. It's a lovely, quiet place for a stroll, and there's a good chance you'll spot flocks of wading birds. To get here, take a jeepney to Maingaran and follow the track past the Santos Elementary School. Low tide's a good time to come here, when life on the mudflats is active and wading birdlife is at its most dense concentration.

Buntod Sandbar   BEACH
Seven kilometres east of town, the Buntod sandbar, with good snorkelling around it but little shade, is located in the Bugsayon marine sanctuary. It's possible to hire a bangka (around P600 return, including waiting time), to take you from barangay Nursery, the coastal road east of Masbate Town proper, to the sandbar (20 to 30 minutes each way).

Bituon Beach   BEACH
Fourteen kilomtres south of Matsbate Town, and down a rough dirt road is the attractive crescent Bituon Beach, popular with local families on weekends. If you're not staying at the rather odd-looking **Bituon Beach Resort** (www.bituonbeach.com) – a collection of thatched huts and basic rooms, interspersed with statues of Disney's Goofy and friends – you pay P50 to enjoy the beach and picnic facilities. A tricycle ride to and from Masbate costs around P350, with waiting time.

🛏 Sleeping & Eating

Central accommodation options are, with few exceptions, cheap but rundown. The more upmarket hotels are located along the Punta Nursery seafront strip, a short tricycle ride away from the centre. Dining options are also unlikely to thrill you.

Balay Valencia   HOTEL $
(☑ 056-333 6530; Ibañez St; r from P650; ✹ 🛜) This well-maintained old wooden house,

with lattice breezeways just below the ceilings, offers a clutch of simple and somewhat dark en suite rooms, presided over by very friendly receptionists. Noise may be an issue from the night food stalls below on Ibañez St, but they make for an easy dinner. Wi-fi (P50) comes and goes like a stray cat.

★**MG Hotel & Restaurant**   HOTEL $$
(☑ 056-333 5614; Punta Nursery; r P1400-2400; ✹🛜✹) This German-run place is the most efficient hotel in Masbate. The top-floor rooms here are particularly welcoming – big and airy, with huge beds, plenty of natural light and a balcony overlooking the water. It has a good downstairs restaurant, and will shuttle you to the pier or airport for free.

GV Hotel   HOTEL $$
(☑ 056-333 6844; www.gvhotels.com.ph; Danao St; d/f from 1050/2800; ✹) Anonymous, clean rooms with cable TV, a couple of blocks from the port; cheapest are fan-cooled. Surprisingly quiet given the location.

Minlan Restaurant   FILIPINO, CHINESE $
(Osmeña St; mains from P70; ⊙ noon-10pm) This homey restaurant is the best that central Masbate has to offer (which isn't saying much). Expect deep-fried fish in sweet and sour sauce, *lechón kawali* (crispy fried pork) and a few Chinese-style offerings on a separate menu.

Ham's Cup   FILIPINO $
(Quezon Ave; mains from P60; ⊙ 7am-10pm) Surprisingly good coffee, inexpensive pasta and Filipino dishes are served at this cafe attached to the Caltex petrol station.

ⓘ Information

Tara St – parallel to the pier – and Quezon St above it are the main thoroughfares. Quezon St is where you'll find internet cafes and several banks with ATMs.
Coastal Resource Management Interpretation Center (☑ 0906 212 5684; esperanzadanao@yahoo.com; Capitol Rd; ⊙ 8am-5pm Mon-Fri) Located in the City Hall compound, three blocks north of Quezon Ave. The centre's interpretation officer, Jaja, is helpful about all things marine.

ⓘ Getting There & Around

Tricycle rides around town cost P8. From the integrated terminal off Diversion Rd, just south of the port, there are frequent jeepney and air-con van departures for Aroroy, Mandaon, Cataingan via Palanas, Esperanza and Balud.

Around Masbate Island

Masbate Island's attractions are easily reachable by public transport from Masbate Town. Points of interest include the oldest **lighthouse** in the province in the gold-mining and fishing town of Aroroy and the immense **Kalanay** and **Batongan caves** near the port of Mandaon, complete with underground river (ask about guides at the Mandaon town hall). A jeepney trip to Mandaon is worth it for the views of the mountains and rolling countryside alone. Southeast of Masbate Town, Uson features some surviving **wooden Spanish houses**, while Palanas, further east, has similar **ancestral houses**, but with traditional thatched roofs. Finding these spots requires a bit of DIY spirit and as for finding a place to stay, your best bet is to make a beeline for the town hall.

Ticao Island

Ticao feels on the edge between laissez-faire island time and rapid tourism development. For now: the sweet, rotting scent of copra weaves through the trees and – except in the few small townships – concrete barely interrupts the bamboo and thatch structures. The island's one road bumps and winds and slopes its way through villages such as Batuan, where you can stop and check out the **mangrove boardwalk**.

In **Monreal**, hire a pumpboat for the day (P2500 to P3000) and head along the coast, not missing out on the 30m-tall **Catandayagan Falls** or the lovely **Talisay Beach**, both on the west coast.

🛏 Sleeping & Eating

Ticao Island Resort   RESORT $$$
(☑02-893 8173, 0917 506 3554; www.ticao-island-resort.com; s/d/tr P2000/3400/4800, s/d/tr cabanas P3600/5200/6900; ✳) In Tacdogan, about 8km north of San Jacinto, nine plush cabanas front a perfect and secluded cove, while four fan-only budget rooms huddle off the beach. Divers will enjoy the island's proximity to the famed Manta Bowl dive site, while non-diving guests can go horseriding, kayaking and fishing or learn the secrets of Bicolano cooking. Full board included.

**Altamar Ticao Island
Beach Resort**   RESORT $$$
(☑056-817 7463, 0917 812 8618; www.ticaoaltamar.com; cottages per person P3500; ✳) The Altamar

RIDE 'EM, COWBOY!

Rodeo Masbateño (⊘2nd week of Apr) Masbate hosts a four-day rodeo extravaganza and cowboys and cowgirls from all over the island take part in bull-riding contests, barrel racing (horse and rider slalom) and steer-dogging (leaping from horseback and wrestling steers to the ground by their horns).

Aroroy Wacky Rodeo (⊘May) Taking place in the town of Aroroy, this rodeo pits brave cowboys against a particularly cantankerous creature, the crab. Events include crab races, crab catching, parades, dancing, and the mass consumption of the aforementioned crab. The coveted Miss Crab prize goes to the most bowlegged beauty queen in town. (We're kidding: to the most beautiful).

consists of a series of tastefully decorated beachfront cottages, most built for couples; price includes full board. Staff are attentive and dish up some seriously delicious food, and the friendly owners can arrange diving trips, massages and other fun activities.

ℹ Getting There & Away

Three big pumpboats a day go between Lagundi pier and Masbate Town (P90, one hour), as well as ferries between San Jacinto and Bulan in Bicol, and between Monreal and Pilar (P150, two hours). The last trip is usually around 1pm.

CATANDUANES

🖉 052 / POP 246,300

Catanduanes, aka 'Land of the Howling Winds', is whipped by typhoons. As a result, tourism is yet to make great inroads here, leaving the few travellers who do make it over here to explore the sedate fishing villages, the jagged, beautiful coastline and the caves and waterfalls of the interior at their leisure. Storms roll in from the months of July to November, when heavy rains are eagerly absorbed by lush rainforests that have been mercifully preserved due to both Catanduanes' isolation and sparse population.

Most foreign visitors to Catanduanes are surfers looking to ride the world-famous-if-fickle Majestic surf break. The best waves are during the typhoon season, especially between August and October – but prepare to be patient.

Catanduanes

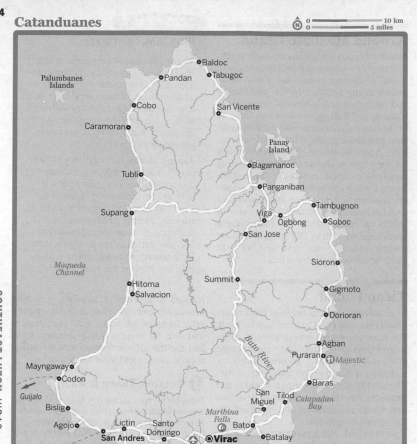

ℹ Getting There & Away

AIR

PAL Express flies daily from Manila to Virac (1¼ hours) and Cebu Pacific flies this route four times weekly. The airport is 3.5km from town; the tricycle trip there will cost about P50.

BOAT

Regina Shipping Lines (☎ 052-811 1707; ordinary/air-con P195/260) has three ferries a day between Tabaco and San Andres, 17km west of Virac (ordinary/air-con P185/240, three hours). The boats leave Tabaco at 5.30am, 8am and 1.30pm, then make the return journey at 9.30, noon and 5.30pm. Virac-bound jeepneys (P25, 45

minutes) and tricycles (P150, 25 minutes) meet the ferry in San Andres. Or, take the MV *Eugenia*, a slower ferry from Tabaco to Virac (ordinary/air-con P216/275, four hours), leaving at 6.30am and returning at 4pm, or else the MV *Star Ferry* at 2pm.

For connections between Codon and Guijalo port in Caramoan, see p172.

Virac

The capital of Catanduanes does not offer much for travellers, but it has a couple of really good restaurants, transport connections to other parts of the island and is a convenient base for day trips to nearby beaches.

There are a few internet cafes in town, and the PNB and BDO on either side of the town plaza have ATMs.

🛏 Sleeping

Marem Pension House GUESTHOUSE $
(☑ 0929 162 0000; www.marem.com.ph; 136 Rizal St; s/d from P550/900; ❄ 🛜) This mazelike building, home to many an aquarium, has an informal atmosphere, a labyrinth of natty rooms and an appealing roof deck. It's very laid-back – a nice thing when it comes to the friendliness of staff. The shoestringer 'ordinary' singles (P250) are fan-cooled shoeboxes.

★Catanduanes Midtown Inn HOTEL $$
(☑ 052-811 0527; http://catmidinn.tripod.com; San José St; s/d/f from P900/1200/2500; ❄) This is still the best hotel located in the middle of town. Its large doubles have classic touches and parquet floors; some have balconies, but what really sets it apart is the friendly and helpful proprietress. Locally popular fast-food joint located next door.

Twin Rock Beach Resort RESORT $$
(☑ 0917 562 9597, 0928 836 8648; www.twinrock.com.ph; d/q from P1000/1800; ❄ 🛜) Ten kilometres south of Virac, Twin Rocks sits in a secluded cove facing a small beach, looking out on a lampshade-like pair of boulders. The location is lovely and the range of activities (diving, kayaking, ATV) is a boon for active travellers, but on weekends there's no escaping videoke, and the cheapest rooms are best avoided.

🍴 Eating & Drinking

Blossoms BICOLANO $
(Salvacion; mains from P60; ⊙ 7am-10pm Mon-Sat) The carved wooden seats, trough water feature and fake sunflowers everywhere lend this split-level restaurant a cheery, rustic ambience, and the dishes – from its signature Blossom Bicol *exprés* to pasta, pizza, *pansit* and more – don't let the side down either. Try the moreish shakes.

★Sea Breeze SEAFOOD $$
(Imelda Blv; mains P180-270; ⊙ 7am-midnight) This excellent restaurant is atmospheric in the evenings, when you can sit under a thatched canopy and feast on sizzling squid, tuna steak and the local take on *kinilaw*.

Café de Au CAFE
(Salvacion St; coffee P60; ⊙ 8am-10pm Mon-Sat) Its interior wouldn't seem out of place in a Western capital, and this friendly coffee shop, run by a knowledgeable guy called Genesis, caters to all your wi-fi and caffeine needs with locally grown and roasted beans.

ℹ Information

Tourist Office (☑ 0929 399 8437; Santa Elena; ⊙ 8am-5pm Mon-Fri) Located in the Old Capitol Building, this little office stocks some info on the island's attractions. The entertaining upstairs museum charts the island's history.

ℹ Getting Around

From the **bus and jeepney terminal** (Rizal Ave), there are several daily departures to Pandan (five hours, P180), Bagamanoc (two hours, P120), Baras (P80, one hour), and other destinations. The road around the island is mostly paved, but given the infrequency of public transport in the north of the island, it helps to have your own wheels. Ask at the tourist office or your lodgings about hiring a van (up to P5000 per day) or a motorcycle with driver.

Northeast of Virac

Puraran

Twenty kilometres northeast of Bato the paved road passes by a turn-off with a serpentine road leading downhill to the stunning wide bay of Puraran, home to Majestic surf break. A P10 fee is payable at the turn-off, used for keeping the beach clean.

It's a wide, idyllic beach, with coconut trees swaying in the breeze, white sand and a coral reef for snorkelling just offshore. All owned by members of the same extended family, the three laid-back surf resorts are where surfers and nonsurfers alike often stay for weeks, basking in the casual ambience of the place, with pro surfers flocking to Puraran for the international surfing competition (8–11 October). Surfing members of the family are happy to give advice, rent longboards (P200 per hour), shortboards (P150 per hour) and boogie boards (P50 per hour), organise surfing lessons (P350 per hour) or arrange a boat to take you around the headland to the north to another good surfing/snorkelling spot.

🏃 Activities

There's good snorkelling to be had at the offshore reef, though beware the occasionally powerful rip tide in the centre of the beach (check conditions with locals before wading in). Resorts rent snorkelling gear for P50.

★ **Majestic** 　　　　　　　　　SURFING
A reef break 200m offshore, powerful Majestic is no beginner's wave. Like most breaks on the country's Pacific coast, Majestic usually only works when there's a typhoon lurking offshore during the *habagat* (southwest monsoon), between July and October. The *amihan* (northeast monsoon) kicks up powerful onshore breezes from October to March, making conditions too choppy for all but pros.

🛏 Sleeping & Eating

It's advisable to book ahead from July to October. All resorts serve set-menu meals for around P130.

Majestic Puraran 　　　　　　　RESORT $
(✆ 0927 357 2665, 0919 558 1460; http://majesticpuraran.com; cottages P650, r P850) This friendly, family-run place is mellow in the extreme. It has simple, comfortable bamboo cottages with private porches, hammocks and ocean views and smarter air-con rooms above the restaurant, as well as board games for rainy days, cable TV in the bar area and a surpassingly family-friendly vibe.

Puraran Surf 　　　　　　　　　RESORT $
(✆ 0915 764 9133, 0921 664 1933; www.puraransurf.com; dm/s/d/f P300/500/600/1000) Puraran Surf offers cute, basic cottages (some showing their age), plus fan rooms with shared bathroom and several air-con rooms in the (less comfortable and less private) main concrete building; the dorm on the top floor has amazing sea views from the terrace but is for serious shoestringers only who don't mind sleeping with 20 other people.

Pacific Surfers' Paradise 　　　RESORT $$
(✆ 0917 804 6648, 0917 738 2941; pacsurfers@yahoo.com.ph; cottages P700, tr P1500) The newcomer on the scene, Pacific Surfers' Paradise looks the part. There are six adorable bamboo-with-thatched-roof cottages (allegedly designed for four people, but we don't see how that's possible) with twin beds, and a much larger one for a group of eight. The air-con triples are less atmospheric.

❶ Getting There & Away

The quickest way to get here is to hire a van (around P1300 one way, one hour); tricycles will do the same trip for around P800 one way.

There is one daily jeepney from Virac to Gigmoto via Puraran (P50, two hours, 32km). It waits for the arrival of the RORO ferry in Virac and leaves around 11am. The trip in the other direction passes through Puraran at an ungodly 4am to 5am; the resorts can arrange tricycle rides (P150) to Baras where it's easy to hop on a bus or jeepney (P50) to Virac.

Around the Island

Catanduanes' attractions are scattered all over the island. Some of the more accessible include the popular **Maribina Falls** (admission P10; ⏱ 8am-5pm), which drain into a series of refreshing pools, 4km northeast of Virac; the vast **Luyang Cave**, near the village of Lictin, en route to San Andres (guides in Lictin ask for around P550 to show you around); the long, pristine stretch of **Toytoy Beach** near Caramoran, its coral formations good for snorkelling; and **Nahulugan Falls**, impressive cascades of water in the jungle, inland from Gigmoto.

MARINDUQUE

✆ 042 / POP 227,828

Soporific Marinduque is a heart-shaped island, appropriately positioned at the heart of the Philippines archipelago. Bound by a scenic 120km paved ring road, it seems the only time this island truly comes to life is during the Moriones Festival at Easter. The rest of the year visitors must content themselves with the laid-back charm of its villages, beautiful scenery, dormant Mt Malindig volcano, a handful of beach resorts, hot springs in the interior and wildlife-filled caves.

❶ Getting There & Away

AIR

The Masbate airport was undergoing renovation at the time of writing but flights to Manila were expected to resume by the end of 2014.

BOAT

The majority of pasenger boats (from Lucena) land at Balanacan, 30 minutes north of Boac. Arrivals are met by tricycles (P150 to Boac) and also jeepneys and air-con vans departing for Boac, Santa Cruz, Torrijos and Buenavista.

Montenegro Shipping Lines (✆ 0917 867 2337; www.montenegrolines.com.ph) Operates two RORO ferries and two 'fastcraft' passenger boats between Lucena and Balanacan daily. Fastcraft leave Lucena at 2am and 10am (P390, 1½ hours), returning at 6am and 2pm, while the RORO ferries (p260, 3¼ hours) depart Lucena at 4am and noon, returning at 8am and 4pm.

Starhorse Shipping Lines (✆ 0921 274 5340) Operates four RORO ferries daily between Lu-

Marinduque

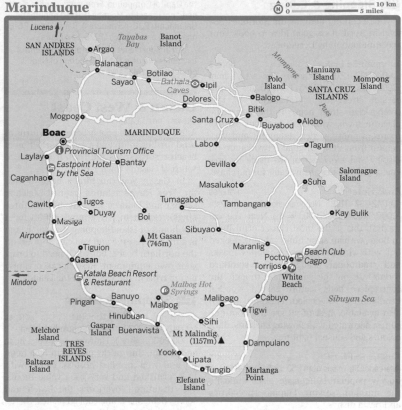

cena and Balanacan. Leaves Lucena for Balanacan at 2.30am, 10.30am, 3.30pm and 11.30pm, returning at 6.30am, 11.30am, 2.30pm and 7.30pm (P260).

ⓘ Getting Around

Exploring the island by public transport is perfectly doable (with the exception of the coastal stretch between Lipata and Tigwi that's not covered by jeepney), but you need to allow several days for it. A much pricier (and more efficient) option is to hire a van to take you around the island for around P3500 per day. Van hire can be organised through the tourist office or hotels.

Boac

📞 042 / POP 52.898

Centred on its mighty cathedral-cum-fortress, Marinduque's capital has considerably more character than most Filipino towns. Its narrow streets are lined with 19th-century ancestral houses in various states of repair, with capiz-shell windows and upstairs verandahs spilling over with flowers.

⊙ Sights

Cathedral CHURCH
(San Miguel St) The focal point of the town, this stone cathedral dates back to the 17th century and its fortified ramparts testify to its role of local refuge during the Moro pirate raids. Above the main doors is a niche containing the 1792 statue of the Blessed Virgin, credited with driving away the pirates with storms and saving the town from natural disasters.

Marinduque Museum MUSEUM
(Mercador St; ⊙ 8am-noon & 1-5pm Mon-Fri) FREE The highlights of this concise museum include its collection of *moriones* masks, Ming-dynasty ceramics retrieved from the sea by Gaspar Island, and *kalutang,* one of the earliest native musical instruments.

Sleeping & Eating

If you're coming here for the Moriones festival in April, it's a good idea to book your accommodation by December.

Tahanan Sa Isok   HOTEL $
(☑ 042-332 1231; 5 Canovas St; s/tw/f from P1000/1200/1800; ❄☺) Located on a quiet side street just off Magsaysay St, this creeper-clad stone house is the best-value place in town, with clean, spacious, simple rooms, a pretty garden restaurant and very helpful front desk. Original artworks are on display and *moriones* masks made by provincial jail inmates are available for purchase.

Boac Hotel   HOTEL $$
(☑ 042-332 1121; Nepomuceno St; s/d/f/ste P1000/1200/2000/2500; ❄☺) Near the cathedral, this is the most characterful hotel in Boac, with an artsy, funky interior, decked out with vintage photos, *moriones* masks and traditional headgear. The standard rooms are on the small side, though the centrepiece beds feature carved wooden headboards. Fan-cooled cheapies (P500) also available. Best of all are the boutique suites, decorated with flowing curtains, dark colours and sensual lighting.

Kusina sa Plaza   FILIPINO $
(Mercador St; mains from P50; ☺5.30am-8pm) A hugely popular buffet-style place opposite the museum serving Filipino specialities and pasta dishes.

Good Chow   FILIPINO $
(Mercader St; mains from P60; ☺7am-7pm) Cheerful snack bar serving *siopao* (steamed buns), pizza and Filipino standards.

Information

The **PNB** (Reyes St) has an ATM but bring extra cash, especially during the Moriones festival. A few **internet cafes** are scattered along the side streets.
Provincial Tourism Office (☑ 042-332 1498; www.marinduque.gov.ph; ☺8am-5pm Mon-Fri) The Provincial Tourism Office is located in the Capitol Building complex, 2km out of town on the main road south. Staff can help you hire a van to take you around the island.

Getting There & Away

There are jeepneys to Boac from the ferry dock in Balanacan (P50, 25 minutes).

From Boac, jeepneys go south to Gasan (P20, 30 minutes) and Buenavista (P40, one hour) via

the Capitol Compound. Frequent jeepneys also head northeast to Mogpog (P10,10 minutes), Balanacan (P30, 45 minutes), Santa Cruz (P60, one hour) and Torrijos (P120, two hours).

All transport leaves from around the central terminal area near the intersection of Nepomuceno and Magsaysay Sts.

Gasan & West Coast
☑ 042 / POP 33,402

A few stretches of pebbly beach that turns to sand further south and a motley selection of beach resorts spans the 17km from Boac to south of Gasan's town proper.

In Gasan you can hire a boat to visit the **Tres Reyes Islands** (named Melchor, Gaspar and Baltazar after the biblical three kings); expect to pay around P2000 for a few hours of island-hopping. Gaspar Island is a marine reserve and you can snorkel off the northern beach, but you'll need to bring your own equipment. Resorts can organise diving trips in the vicinity of the islands.

Sleeping & Eating

Eastpoint Hotel by the Sea   HOTEL $$
(☑ 042-332 2229; www.eastpointhotel.com; r P1000-2000; ❄☺) Halfway between Boac and Gasan, this quirky place, run by a helpful and well-travelled hostess, comes with well-furnished and very good value rooms. The restaurant overlooks the beach and serves delicious home-cooked dishes, there's a van available for island tours, a wellness centre for pampering and a gaggle of friendly dogs named after spices (and Brad Pitt).

Katala Beach Resort & Restaurant   RESORT $$
(☑ 0906 515 8736, 0915 512 4784; www.members. tripod.com/katala.beach.resort; r with fan/air-con P1000/1500; ❄) This German-run establishment, 3km south of Gasan proper, is perched on a wall overlooking a private pier, with a floating pontoon and the Tres Reyes Islands beyond. The rooms are in good shape and you can watch the sunset from your private balcony or in the pretty restaurant – which serves authentic German sausages.

Barbarossa   FILIPINO, INTERNATIONAL $$
(San José St; mains from P90; ☺9am-9pm) German-owned restaurant in Gasan that's popular with a mix of expats and locals due to its tasty takes on Filipino standards and international dishes (mostly pasta).

BEYOND THE MORIONES MADNESS

You know something strange goes on in Marinduque when your first sight is a display of larger-than-life and very colourful plaster statues of Roman centurions – *moriones* – on the roundabout at Balanacan pier. And then there's the island's ring road, fringed with posts on which are mounted *moriones*' heads fashioned into flowerpots – some with wildly overgrown grass hair, some crumbling and sadly neglected.

Marinduque's **Moriones Festival** began in 1807 when Padre Dionsio Santiago, a Mogpog parish priest, organised a play based on the story of Longinus (or Longino), one of the Roman centurions assigned to execute Christ. A drop of Christ's blood miraculously restored sight in Longinus' blind right eye during the crucifixion. Longinus instantly proclaimed his faith, whereupon he was chased around town, captured and summarily beheaded.

These days, a fabulous Easter festival combining folk mysticism with Catholic pageantry turns Marinduque's streets into a colourful re-enactment of those events, drawn out over the seven days of Holy Week. Each municipality in Marinduque holds its own festival, in which hundreds of *moriones* don centurion masks and costumes and arm themselves with wooden swords, spears and shields. The masks take months to prepare and are kept secret from even close friends and family so that the *moriones*' true identity is not known.

Throughout the week *moriones* take to the streets and run amok, engaging in sword fights, dances and sneaky pranks on bystanders, with Longinus hiding behind spectators before undergoing a mock beheading and his 'lifeless' body being paraded around town.

ℹ Getting There & Away

Daily bangkas go from Marinduque to Pinamalayan (P300, three hours) on Mindoro. They tend to leave from Gasan pier early in the morning.

Buenavista & Around

A couple of kilometres inland from Buenavista are the **Malbog Hot Springs** (admission P80), where a series of bathing pools have been constructed to tap the sulphur-scented water and a modest guesthouse welcomes overnight visitors.

A gorgeous coastal road runs between Buenavista and Tigwi, passing thatched fishermen's shacks, bangkas drying on the shore, and winding its way through coconut tree groves. A single jeepney runs between Buenavista and Lipata only, so your only option is to hire a van for a day in Boac or haggle with the Buenavista tricycle drivers.

Elefante Island, offshore from Lipata and once a simple fishing spot, is home to super-upscale **Bellarocca Island Resort** (☑02-403 2418; www.bellaroccaresorts.com; r US$500-960, 2-/6-person villa US$880/2800), which caters to canoodling couples and consists of blindingly white buildings à la Santorini in Greece peeking out of the lush vegetation.

The five-hour hike up and down the perfect cone of **Mt Malindig** (1157m) follows a usually clearly marked trail from Sihi, a barangay of Buenavista. Take a tricycle to Sihi from Buenavista (P400 return), or any jeepney towards Torrijos (P30) and ask in Sihi whether a permit is required, as there's a military post halfway up the volcano.

A morning jeepney makes the pleasant drive over the mountains to Torrijos (P70, one hour); tricycles directly to Poctoy cost around P800 (one hour). There are regular jeepneys from Buenavista to Boac.

Torrijos & East Coast

The whitest and longest beach on Marinduque is well-named **White Beach** (admission P30) – which happens to have a teal oceanfront – in Poctoy, near Torrijos, where there are also views of Mt Malindig's conical snout. You'll find some day-use cottages here, and it gets pretty busy on weekends. Two kilometres north of Poctoy is the appealing **Beach Club Cagpo** (☑0928 559 6005, 0921 993 2537; www.beachclubcagpo.com; dm P350, d with fan P1000-1250, d with air-con P1350-1500) with its own private, pristine beach, a restaurant serving decent pizza and all things grilled, and spacious oceanfront rooms (the rather cramped fan-cooled dorm is for ascetics only). A 125cc motorbike is available for hire – ideal for exploration of the island.

Mindoro

Best Places to Stay

➡ Pandan Island Resort (p207)

➡ Coco Beach Island Resort (p198)

➡ Apo Reef Club (p206)

➡ El Galleon Beach Resort (p196)

➡ Tambaron Green Beach Resort (p203)

Best Hikes

➡ Mt Halcon (p201)

➡ Mt Iglit-Baco (p206)

➡ Siburan Rainforest (p208)

➡ Mt Talipanan (p192)

Why Go?

Bisected by a virtually impassable mountain range – aptly named the High Rolling Mountains – rugged Mindoro is part tropical paradise, part provincial backwater. Forming a dramatic backdrop almost everywhere, the mountains separate the island's two provinces: rough and rugged Mindoro Occidental to the west, and more prosperous Mindoro Oriental to the east.

Most tourists head to the dive resorts around Puerto Galera on the north coast, but there is much more to Mindoro. If you prefer remote to resort, venture into Mindoro Occidental where virtually tourist-free Sablayan, jumping-off point for the pristine dive mecca Apo Reef, awaits. Better roads are making this once hard-to-reach province more accessible.

Mindoro's south coast has unforgettable island-hopping, while in the mountainous interior you can hike to remote villages populated by one of Asia's most primitive tribes, the Mangyan.

When to Go
San José

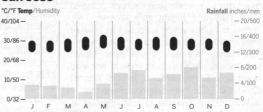

Apr-May The rainy season has yet to begin and the winds are at their calmest for Apo Reef.

Feb-Apr The driest months and the best season for climbing Mt Halcon.

Oct-Nov Another transitional period, windwise, meaning more flat seas for divers.

Mindoro Highlights

1 Submerge among turtles, sharks, wrasses and countless other sea critters at incredible **Apo Reef** (p206).

2 Explore the coves and beaches of **Puerto Galera** (p192) and dive its underwater wonders.

3 Observe the head count of critically endangered *tamaraw* (native buffalo) at **Mt Iglit-Baco National Park** (p206).

4 Discover the unexpected attractions around **Sablayan Prison Farm** (p208).

5 Launch an assault on **Mt Halcon** (p201), the Philippines' ultimate climb.

6 Take in the Philippines' premier open-air music event, Puerto Galera's **Malasimbo Music & Arts Festival** (p195).

ⓘ Getting There & Away

You can fly into San José, but the vast majority of visitors to Mindoro arrive by boat from Batangas in Luzon.

BOAT

Luzon The usual tourist route to Mindoro is by fast bangka (outrigger) from Batangas to Puerto Galera, but there's also a fleet of fast- and slow-craft connecting Batangas with Calapan, while roll-on, roll-off (RORO) car ferries link Batangas with Abra de Ilog.

Marinduque Bangkas leave at 8.30am every morning from Pinamalayan (P250, three hours) on Mindoro's east coast to Gasan.

Panay & Romblon Roxas in southern Mindoro Oriental is linked by frequent car ferries to Caticlan (for Boracay) and almost-daily bangkas to Odiongon, Romblon.

Palawan At the time of research, the only boats to Palawan were bangkas from San José to Coron, and bangkas from San José to the Cuyo Islands.

BUS

If travelling from Manila, it's common to travel by bus straight through to Calapan or Abra de Ilog and points south, with your bus rolling onto a car ferry for the Batangas–Mindoro leg.

ⓘ Getting Around

The road around Mindoro is mostly paved and traversed by a sizeable fleet of buses and jeepneys. However, there is no road link between Puerto Galera and Abra de Ilog in the north of the island; travel between the two is by boat.

Puerto Galera

🖉 043 / POP 32,521

Just a few hours' travel time from Manila, this gorgeous collection of bays and islands is one of the Philippines' top dive destinations. Puerto Galera is Spanish for 'port of the galleons'. Its deep natural harbour, sheltered on all sides, was a favoured anchorage well before the Spanish arrived in 1572, and today it remains a favoured anchorage for long-term yachties and short-term vacationers.

Puerto Galera ('PG', or 'Puerto') typically refers to the town of Puerto Galera and the resort areas surrounding it – namely Sabang, 5km to the east, and White Beach, 7km to the west. Each has its own distinct character, spanning the range from sleaze to sophistication; you'd be well advised to choose carefully.

◉ Sights

Talipanan Falls & Mt Talipanan WATERFALL
Much less touristy than Tamaraw Falls, Talipanan Falls are a short walk from the village of Talipanan. Hire a Mangyan guide (P200) in the Iraya-Mangyan village just off the main road in Talipanan. From here a track behind the school winds for about 30 minutes uphill and through forest to the swimmable, two-tiered falls. Early in the morning you stand a good chance of seeing monkeys.

For a more ambitious hike, the same Mangyan guides can take you up Mt Talipanan (1130m) for P700. It takes about four hours to get up and a few hours to get down, so start early. Nearby Mt Malasimbo (1215m) is another possible full-day hike.

Tamaraw Falls WATERFALL
(admission P30; ⊙ 7am-5pm) From a forested ravine, this waterfall drops into man-made pools off the main Puerto Galera–Calapan road, 13km out of town. It gets busy at weekends, but otherwise you'll be just about the only person here. Jeepneys headed for Calapan will drop you here (P25, 30 minutes).

Excavation Museum MUSEUM
(P Concepcion St, Puerto Galera town; admission by donation; ⊙ 8-11.30am & 1.30-5pm Mon-Sat) The tiny, unattended one-room museum displays some burial jars and ancient Chinese pottery mostly recovered from the area in the 1960s. It's in the grounds of the church.

🏃 Activities

Around Puerto Galera, diving is king (with drinking coming a close second). Campbell's beach resort in Small La Laguna is among several resorts that rent out **paddleboards**. Landlubbers will find plenty to do as well. Renting a motorbike and driving along PG's spectacular coastline is one favourite activity. Every Saturday at 3.30pm, the local branch of the **Hash House Harriers** meets at Capt'n Gregg's Dive Resort for a fun run followed by a drinking session.

Beaches

The best beaches in the area are the western beaches of **Aninuan** and **Talipanan**. They are much quieter and classier than nearby White Beach – for now. Talipanan in particular is developing rapidly. **White Beach** is a decent beach in its own right, but suffers from tasteless development and high-season crowds. During weekdays in the low season it can be quiet and pleasant.

CHUCK'S TOP PUERTO GALERA DIVE SITES

Chuck Driver, who runs Capt'n Gregg's Dive Resort (p196), has seen just about everything there is to see in the waters around Puerto Galera. It was 25 years ago that he arrived in this unexplored dive mecca and started diving with a few other legends of Philippine diving – Capt'n Gregg's founder Brian Homan, now the owner of Magellan's in Subic Bay, and John Bennett.

Driver and Bennett were testing the limits of deep diving back then, descending to 200m at Sinandigan Wall before records were even being kept. What's it like down there? 'Black as black,' says Driver. 'You're doing a night dive after 135m. Otherwise, not that different except it's cold – you need two 6mm wetsuits.'

Bennett eventually made it down to 300m, according to Driver, before dying in a commercial-diving accident, but after 8000 dives or so Driver is still here and still diving. He gave us five dive sites to look out for:

Hole in the Wall to Canyons 'Big fan corals, sweet lips (groupers), tuna and jacks at a max depth of about 27m.' Location: Escarceo Point, 3km east of Sagang.

Sinandigan Wall 'A good multilevel dive with lots of macro life, nudibranches and things like that. Lots of swimthroughs. The light is best in the morning, start at 42m and go multilevel all the way up.' Location: Sinandigan Point, 3km east of Sabang.

Monkey Beach 'Another good multilevel. Start at 30m and gradually go up and up all the way to 4m. Great fish life and lots of different corals.' Location: off Sabang.

Verde Island Dropoff (aka 'Spanish Fort') 'A big wall that goes all the way down to 70m. Lots of jacks and pelagics. Bad-ass currents though. It's a great night dive but nobody does it anymore because it's far away.' Location: Verde Island.

Washing Machine 'You get a big current and man, it's fun. Go with it, then climb your way back through the canyons, pulling yourself by the rocks. A real adventure dive.' Location: Verde Island.

Sabang's filthy little beach is hardly worthy of the name. Head around the point to much better **Small La Laguna** or, further on, pretty **Big La Laguna**.

About 5km south of town on the road to Calapan, **Dulangan Beach** is a locals' favourite, with jetskis and wakeboards for rent. It's easy to combine with a Tamaraw Falls trip.

Diving & Snorkelling

Puerto Galera offers prime underwater real estate. Special critters that live among the coral include frogfish and mandarin fish, pygmy sea horses, ghost pipefish and nudibranches. Some of the best diving is around Verde Island, a few kilometres offshore.

Dive prices vary wildly so shop around (although quality and safety should trump price). Expect to pay between P1000 and P1800 for a dive. An open-water course will set you back P16,000 to P20,000.

Snorkellers shouldn't feel excluded as many of the top dive sites are well-suited for snorkelling. Most dive operators offer a snorkel option. P1200 is the going rate for a three-hour tour.

Asia Divers　　　DIVING
(☎ 043-287 3205; www.asiadivers.com; Small La Laguna) Highly professional, and also manages top technical dive outfit **Asia Tech** (Small La Laguna).

Blue Ribbon Divers　　　DIVING
(☎ 043-287 3561; www.blueribbondivers.com; Small La Laguna) Excellent outfit with good rates as well.

Capt'n Gregg's Dive Shop　　　DIVING
(☎ 043-287 3070; www.captngreggs.com; Sabang) Long-established, reliable operator.

Tina's Reef Divers　　　DIVING
(☎ 0917 532 4555; www.tinasreefdivers.com; Sabang) Good choice for budget travellers, with prices starting at P1000 per dive including equipment.

Badladz　　　DIVING
(☎ 0998 989 8485; www.badladz.com; Muelle Pier) Good choice in Puerto Galera town.

Pacific Divers　　　DIVING
(☎ 0920 613 5140; http://pacificdivers.net; White Beach) The most professional dive outfit on White Beach.

Puerto Galera Beaches

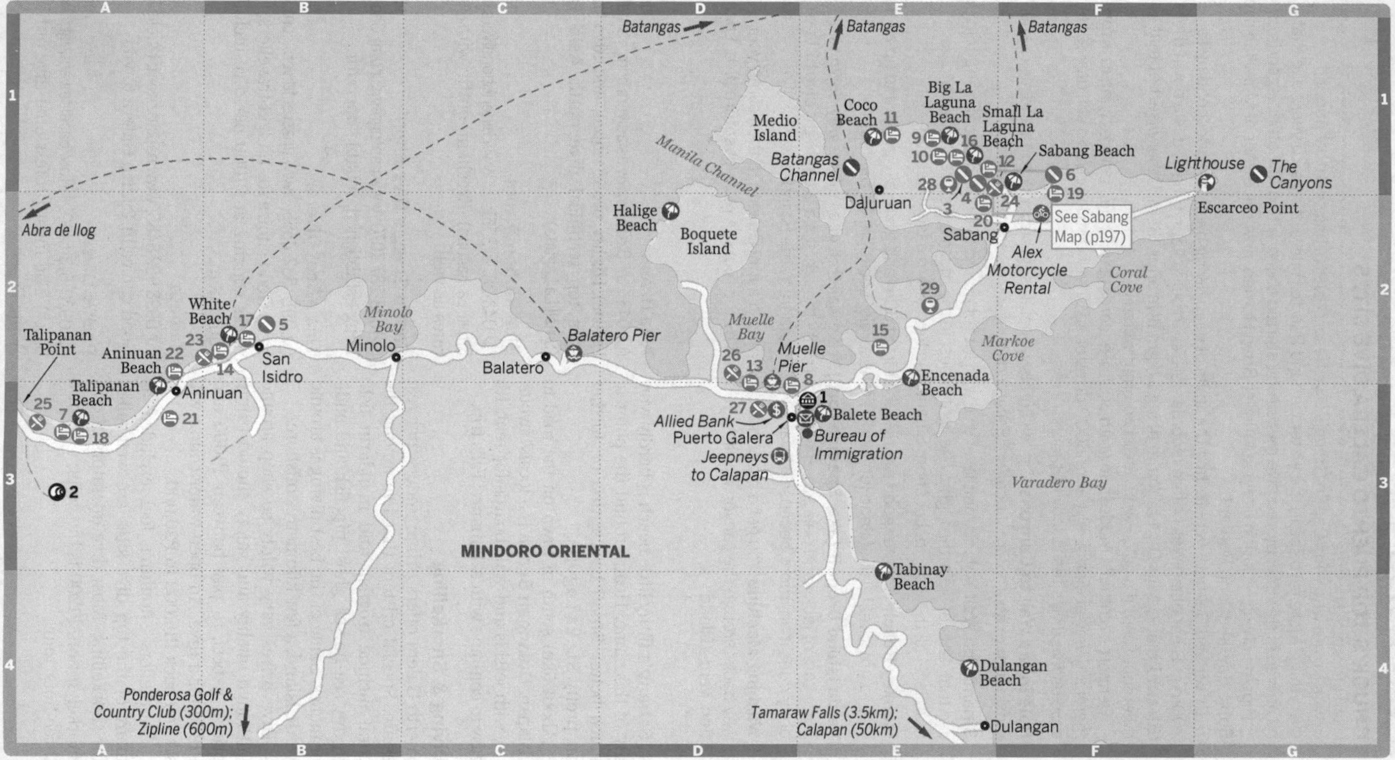

MINDORO

Map legend locations shown:

- The Canyons
- Lighthouse
- Escarceo Point
- Sabang Beach
- Small La Laguna Beach
- Big La Laguna Beach
- Coco Beach
- Batangas Channel
- Medio Island
- Boquete Island
- Halige Beach
- Daluruan
- Sabang
- Alex Motorcycle Rental
- Corral Cove
- Markoe Cove
- Varradero Bay
- Dulangan Beach
- Dulangan
- Tabinay Beach
- Encenada Beach
- Balete Beach
- Bureau of Immigration
- Muelle Pier
- Muelle Bay
- Balatero Pier
- Balatero
- Minolo Bay
- Minolo
- San Isidro
- White Beach
- Aninuan Beach
- Aninuan
- Talipanan Beach
- Talipanan Point
- Abra de Ilog
- Allied Bank Puerto Galera
- Jeepneys to Calapan
- MINDORO ORIENTAL
- Tamaraw Falls (3.5km); Calapan (50km)
- Ponderosa Golf & Country Club (300m); Zipline (600m)
- See Sabang Map (p197)

Map reference numbers: 1–29

Puerto Galera Beaches

Golf

Ponderosa Golf & Country Club GOLF

(☎ 0916 469 3156; www.puertogaleragolf.com; Minolo; 9 holes incl gear & caddy P1350) Golfers can take their hacks at one of the quirkiest courses you'll find anywhere, the diminutive and dramatic Ponderosa Golf & Country Club, cut into a steep mountain 300m above PG town.

Sailing

Puerto Galera Yacht Club SAILING

(☎ 043-287 3401; www.pgyc.org; Puerto Galera town) Keen or novice sailors can head over to the Puerto Galera Yacht Club, which will team you with an experienced sailor for its 'Wet Wednesday' afternoon fun races (P500; 1pm). It rents out Laser sailboats (P1700 for two hours) and Hobie catamarans (P2250 for two hours), and can also help you charter a bigger boat for a half-day cruise (P4000).

Kareem SAILING

(☎ 0927 718 7103; kareem.magill@hotmail.com; half-day P8000) Rents out a luxury catamaran for sunset or longer cruises.

Ziplining

Zipline ZIPLINE

(☎ 0917 506 2280; per ride P500) This dramatic zipline drops 250 vertical metres in the shadow of Mt Malasimbo.

✸ Festivals & Events

Malasimbo Music & Arts Festival MUSIC FESTIVAL

(www.malasimbofestival.com) Launched in 2011, the Malasimbo Festival has quickly blossomed into the Philippines' top open-air music festival, drawing a mix of top Pinoy talent and a few international acts. It takes place every February in a grassy natural amphitheatre up near Ponderosa Golf & Country Club in the foothills of Mt Malasimbo, with incredible views of Puerto Galera's beautiful coastline below.

🛏 Sleeping

Location is everything in PG. As a rule, Sabang is the noisy party zone (adjoining Small La Laguna and Big La Laguna are much quieter). It is also where most divers flock because it's closest to the dive sites. Puerto Galera town is noisy by day, quiet by night. White Beach draws mostly local tourists as well as a smattering of loyal expats and the odd lost backpacker. The western beaches of Aninuan and Talipanan feel the most remote and have the best beaches.

If you're diving, ask about dive/accommodation packages.

MINDORO PUERTO GALERA

🛏 Sabang Proper

Sabang struts its stuff along the eastern shore. By day it's relaxed while divers dive and drinkers sleep; around sunset a metamorphosis takes place as watering holes open, barflies settle in, music cranks up, and all types – and we mean all types – of nightlife emerge. The cheapest lodging is up on the hillside on the eastern end of Sabang beach, where you also might be able to get a homestay in the P500 to P600 range.

★ Capt'n Gregg's Dive Resort   LODGE $
(📞 0917 540 4570, 043-287 3070; www.captngreggs.com; r with fan P800-1200, with air-con P1200-1900; ✳🛜) This Sabang institution has been the best value in town for more than 25 years. The compact but cosy wood-lined 'old' rooms, right over the water, still have the most charm and are also the cheapest. The upstairs rooms are bigger and have private balconies – shoot for the ones in front facing the water.

Reynaldo's Upstairs   GUESTHOUSE $
(📞 0917 489 5609; rey_purie@yahoo.com; Sabang; r P900-1200; ✳🛜) Run by the nicest family you'll ever meet, Reynaldo's has a splendid mix of more-than-passable budget fan rooms and large 'view' rooms with kitchenettes and private balconies on a hillside. Only the bathrooms disappoint. Some rooms even have extras like DVDs and wicker love seats.

Steps Garden Resort   COTTAGES $$
(📞 0915 381 3220, 043-287 3046; www.steps-garden.com; Sabang; d P1600-3000; ✳🛜🏊) A delightful cluster of stand-alone cottages with private balconies in an overflowing and colourful garden, this resort sits high above the beach. It has a lovely pool, breezes, views and is away from the noise. And yes, there are a lot of steps.

Mermaid Dive Resort   RESORT $$
(📞 0916 439 8132; www.mermaiddivers.com; Sabang; d US$63-125; ✳🛜🏊) Reliable Mermaid is off the beach but this shouldn't worry you. It seals off the noise better than most places in Sabang, and the rooms more than make up for the lack of ocean views. Even the cheapest have oodles of space, plush beds, sufficient furniture and all the mod-cons you need.

Oriental Sabang Hill Resort   HOTEL $$
(📞 043-287 3559; www.sabanghhill.com; Sabang; r from P1850; ✳🛜🏊) This Swedish-run hilltop place scores major points for views and for its location on the far end of Sabang's (somewhat) quieter east side. There are services galore, an impressive bar-restaurant, and simple but well-appointed rooms graced with white walls, murals and minibars. Seize that view from your private balcony.

🛏 Small La Laguna

Rounding the headland from Sabang, Small La Laguna offers a better chance of a quiet night's sleep and has a nicer beach to boot.

★ El Galleon Beach Resort   BEACH RESORT $$
(📞 0917 814 5107, 043-287 3205; www.elgalleon.com; Small La Laguna; d incl breakfast US$59-110, villas US$110-315; ✳🛜🏊) Elegant hut-style rooms with wicker furniture and verandahs creep up a beachfront cliff and slink around

---

THE IRAYA-MANGYAN OF TALIPANAN

Shrewd observers will notice two things amiss when they wander into Talipanan's Iraya-Mangyan village. For one, it's in the lowlands (the vast majority of Mangyan live in the mountains). For another it's relatively well-off. The grounds are well-kept, the houses are tidy, and there's even a community centre filled with brand-new computers.

The Mangyan here have come a long way since being driven out of the hills several decades ago amid fighting between the government and communist New People's Army rebels. They settled along the beach just north of Talipanan Beach. But this was land owned by one of the Philippines' richest families, the Ayalas.

Through their Ayala Foundation, the Ayalas instituted a comprehensive sustainable-livelihoods program, including support for health care, education and nutrition within the community. The foundation also helped the village revive the craft of hexagonal *nito* (woody vine) basket weaving.

Tourists visiting the village today will see weavers hard at work and can purchase their beautiful *nito* products. It's a far cry from most Mangyan villages, which are shockingly poor. And, in a country where the divide between rich and poor is stark, it's nice to see one rich family giving back.

Sabang

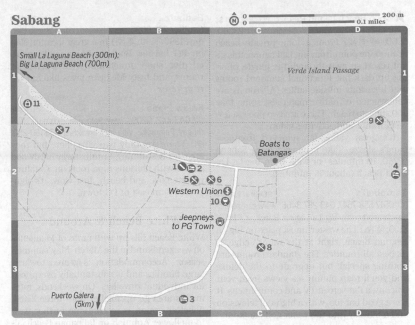

Small La Laguna Beach (300m);
Big La Laguna Beach (700m)

Verde Island Passage

Boats to
Batangas

Western Union

Jeepneys
to PG Town

Puerto Galera
(5km)

a pool. There's a fine restaurant and a top technical dive school on the premises, not to mention the Point Bar, one of the country's best bars. For a modest splurge, ask about the incredible villas.

La Laguna Villas RESORT $$
(☑043-287 3696; www.lalagunavillas.com.ph; Small La Laguna; d villa P2450-5500, apt P12,500-20,000; ❇☏⛱) These luxury hillside villas are a steal, especially when low-season discounts kick in. All have working kitchenettes and most have at least two rooms outfitted with luxurious beds, polished wood floors and flat-screen TVs (although not all rooms have balconies).

Blue Ribbon RESORT $$
(☑0917 893 2791, 043-287 3561; www.blueribbondivers.com; Small La Laguna Beach; d/q P1995/3995; ❇☏⛱) This popular place is doing good things with prices. Not only are the rooms terrific value, but dive rates are fair and divers get a further 20% off accommodation. Extras include a gym (free for guests), a pool, kitchenettes (in pricier rooms) and a beachfront bar with satellite chairs plopped on the sand.

Sha-Che COTTAGES $$
(☑0917 641 0112; r P1000-2500) A collection of good-value, small, self-contained units with

Sabang

⊙ Activities, Courses & Tours
1 Capt'n Gregg's Dive Shop...................B2

⊜ Sleeping
2 Capt'n Gregg's Dive Resort B2
3 Mermaid Dive Resort.........................B3
4 Oriental Sabang Hill Resort...............D2

⊗ Eating
5 Bella Napoli...B2
6 Mira's Bakery & Deli Shop C2
7 Tamarind Restaurant..........................A2
8 Teo's Native Sizzling House...............C3
9 Tina's D1

⊙ Drinking & Nightlife
10 Aquabest...C2

⊕ Shopping
11 Frontier Handicrafts............................A1

patios and kitchens, which lie in concrete rows just off the beach.

⬛ Big La Laguna

One beach east of Small La Laguna, Big La Laguna is even further removed from Sabang's noise and the beach is the best in the Sabang area.

★ Coco Beach Island Resort BEACH RESORT $$
(☏ 043-287 3529; www.cocobeach.com; r P3000-5000; @🖥🛜🏊) From a long private beach around the point from Big La Laguna, this giant resort sprawls through the jungle, offering up dark but functional standard rooms and luxurious hillside suites. All rooms are constructed of native materials; some take 250 steps to reach. There are two pools, a few restaurants, and activities galore.

It's great value, far removed from Sabang's sleaze. Take a bangka from Sabang (P250, 10 minutes) or walk from Big La Laguna Beach (about 15 minutes).

Campbell's BEACH RESORT $$
(☏ 0917 558 7547, 043-287 3466; www.campbellsbeachresort.com; Big La Laguna Beach; r P1550-3100; 🌀🛜) The westernmost place on Big La Laguna Beach, right at the water's edge, is its best all-rounder. The standard rooms are nothing special, but upgrade to the deluxe and you'll reap plump sea views from your balcony, a flat-screen TV and comfy linens. It has a good bar too, with a high-def television and a Sunday into-the-water golf shootout.

Cataquis BUNGALOW $$
(☏ 0916 297 8455; Big La Laguna Beach; r with fan/air-con P1000/1800; 🌀) You get no services here, but the stand-alone concrete cottages, in two separate clusters near where you enter Big La Laguna Beach, have appeal. A couple of them are flush with the beach; the nicer ones are tucked into the trees in back.

🛏 Puerto Galera Town & Around

Some visitors prefer the comparative calm of the waterfront around Muelle Pier in Puerto Galera town to the busy resort areas of the beaches. It's where yachties tend to drop anchor. There are several chic higher-end options on private coves just out of town.

Fisherman's Cove RESORT $$$
(☏ 043-287 3257; www.fishermenscove.com; Barangay Sta Niño; r per person incl full board P3500; 🌀🏊) Located 1km west of PG town, this well-run Italian resort will suit those looking for privacy. The spacious rooms, in a three-storey building overlooking the pool, are tastefully austere and there's a great common library and dive centre. There's no real beach here, but a boat from their pier shuttles guests to nearby beaches free-of-charge.

Badladz RESORT $$
(☏ 0927 268 9095; www.badladz.com; Muelle Pier; d/q P1390/1690; 🌀🛜) In a great location slap on PG harbor, Badladz has a well-regarded dive shop, functional if unspectacular rooms, and tasty Mexican faves like *huevos rancheros*.

Kalaw Place VILLA $$$
(☏ 043-442 0209; www.kalawplace.com.ph; Barangay Palangan; villa incl breakfast US$160-250; 🛜) There are only two villas here but they are simply stunning – multistorey hardwood affairs with glorious nipa roofs on a sublime private cove and beach. Just wow. It's signposted 2km east of PG town.

🛏 White Beach & Around

White Beach fills up with mobs of Manileños on weekends and in the March–May 'summer' season. Accommodation is geared towards large families and is substantially overpriced for individual travellers. On weekends, rates in this area go up further than those listed. A better option is to continue further west to mellower Aninuan or Talipanan Beach, although resorts there are subject to the same neurotic price fluctuations.

★ Amami Beach Resort BEACH RESORT $$
(☏ 0908 206 8534; www.amamibeachresort.com; Talipanan; s/d incl breakfast from P800/1200; 🛜) Run with gusto by a hospitable Italian-Filipino family, this is the best value on Talipanan Beach. The native-style rooms are simple but tasteful affairs with mozzie nets and hot water. Most are off a long shared verandah behind the excellent Amami Ginger Restaurant (mains P180 to P250).

★ IDive DIVE RESORT $$
(☏ 0916 420 5199; www.idivedivingcenter.com; White Beach; d incl breakfast P2200; 🌀🛜) There are only a couple of rooms here but they are by far the nicest on White Beach. With designer soaps and boutique design flourishes, this is one of the few places in this area not geared towards large groups of Filipinos.

Tamaraw Beach Resort RESORT $$
(☏ 0917 504 8679; www.tamarawbeachresort.com; Aninuan; d with fan from P800, with air-con P1300-4000; 🌀🛜) This ever-expanding resort sprawls along sandy Aninuan Beach, with shady gardens and a relaxed vibe. The cosy beachfront cottages are by far the best options, while the rote-basic fan rooms are in a large, concrete edifice.

Mountain Beach Resort BUNGALOW $$
(☑0906 362 5406; www.mountainbeachresort.
com; Talipanan; d with fan/air-con from P1000/2000;
✳@☎) This is the best (and easternmost) of
a cluster of small family-owned resorts on
Talipanan Beach. We prefer the fan rooms,
in a long wooden row house with thatched
walls and a long, lazy verandah.

Luca's RESORT $$
(☑0916 417 5125; www.lucaphilippines.com; Tali-
panan; r from P1800; ✳) Luca's is ideally positioned at the isolated west end of Talipanan
Beach, although service can be wanting. It's
best known for its restaurant, but the rooms
are large and functional, and the setting can't
be beat – this is the nicest strip of beach in the
entire area, although it gets rough at times.

Lenley's Cottages COTTAGES $$
(☑0917 353 8820; White Beach; r with fan/air-con
from P1500/2000; ☎) Set behind a row of
concession stands, this is somewhat of an
oasis in central White Beach. You get your
own private bamboo bungalow with a balco-
ny set around a sandy courtyard.

Sunset at Aninuan BEACH RESORT $$$
(☑0920 931 8924; www.aninuanbeach.com;
Aninuan; old wing P3000-5000, new wing P7000-
14,000; ✳☎✳) There are two sides to the
Sunset story. The old wing consists mainly
of uneventful rooms with TVs, basic beds
and little else. Rooms in the new wing, on
the other hand, are downright luxurious,
with hardwood floors and furniture, tasteful
handicrafts and hangings, and private balconies that stare at the sea. Free kayak use.

✖ Eating & Drinking

Almost everywhere has a happy hour, anytime between 2pm and 7pm.

✖ Sabang & Around

Restaurants in Sabang are, in a word, expensive. But the quality is good compared with
most Philippine resort areas.

Teo's Native Sizzling House FILIPINO $
(mains P150-300; ⊙24hr) Low-key place with
a comprehensive menu of sizzling dishes,
Filipino classics and steaks.

Tina's GERMAN, FILIPINO $$
(Sabang; mains P200-450; ⊙8am-10pm; ☎)
Swiss-tinged Tina's has some of the best
food on the beachfront, and the prices are
good for PG. Do try the schnitzel.

Mira's Bakery & Deli Shop DELI $$
(Sabang; sandwiches P300-350; ⊙6.30am-10pm)
A hole-in-the-wall sandwich shop that also
sells fancy meats, cheeses and other imported picnic supplies.

★**Full Moon** PUB FOOD $$$
(Small La Laguna Beach; mains P200-900;
⊙10am-9pm; ☎) It's worth a walk down to
the end of Small La Laguna just for the chili
con carne – it's the real McCoy. Pastas, steaks
and curries are other specialities. The uber-
filling 'Full Moon breakfast' contains every
breakfast ingredient you could dream of.

Bella Napoli ITALIAN $$$
(Sabang; pizzas P260-450, mains P300-1000;
⊙11am-midnight; ✳) Another Sabang eatery
to file away in the 'damn, that was good but
how did I just drop P1500?' category. A robust wine selection (glass from P140) tempts
oenophiles, while epicureans will relish the
food and relaxed ambience. Unfortunately,
the karaoke joint directly opposite spoils the
atmosphere by night. Try sitting inside.

Tamarind Restaurant INTERNATIONAL $$$
(Sabang; mains P350-1000; ☎) Tamarind lures
you in with the scent of steaks and seafood
being fired up on its open-air BBQ – try the
carabao (water buffalo) steak. Filipino faves,
pasta and schnitzel also grace the menu. It
has a great waterfront location.

Hemingway's INTERNATIONAL $$$
(Sabang; mains P500-2000; ⊙10.30am-10pm;
☎) Has some tasty Caribbean flavours in its
menu to go with more traditional imported
steaks, German sausage and grilled seafood (make sure it's not overcooked). Bonus
points for mellow atmosphere and seafront
locale.

★**Point Bar** BAR
(El Galleon Beach Resort, Small La Laguna) Our
favourite bar. The Point Bar is a mellow
sunset-and-beyond meeting place with great
views and eclectic music. It's one of the few
bars in town where solo women travellers
can feel comfortable. When the weather
is good the action gravitates towards newly opened Barrel Bar on Asia Divers' dock
below. Two-for-one happy hour is 5.30pm to
6.30pm at both places.

View Point BAR
(mains P200-300; ⊙9am-9pm) Atop a ridge on
the winding road between PG town and Sabang, View Point overlooks jaw-droppingly

beautiful Dalaruan Cove, about 2km west of Sabang. Come for the views and stay for English faves like steak and 'shroom pies.

Aquabest WATER STATION
(Sabang; ☺8am-7pm) Water refills: P5 for a 1L bottle.

✕ Puerto Galera Town & Western Beaches

Bars and restaurants front the gorgeous harbour west of Muelle Pier, offering a range of local and Western foods.

★**Puerto Galera Yacht Club** INTERNATIONAL **$$**
(Puerto Galera Town; mains P275-430; ☺noon-9pm, closed Mon in low season) This is a hidden gem, perched in the trees on the west edge of Muelle Bay. A free shuttle boat (three minutes) operates from the Muelle Pier waterfront or you can drive there easily enough. Sunset drinks and a barbecue are the traditional way to celebrate Friday.

★**Luca's Cucina Italiana** ITALIAN **$$**
(Talipanan; mains P200-300, pizzas P260-480; ☺6am-10pm; 🐾) Does great Italian food, usually cooked by the Italian owner. The pizzas, which are cooked in an outdoor brick oven, are especially toothsome and feed three. The restaurant is perched over the beach, with cliffs above and mountains behind. Lovely.

Robby's Cafeteria ITALIAN **$$**
(Main Road, behind Muelle Pier; mains P150-300, pizzas P200-360; ☺8am-9pm) What is it with Italians and Puerto Galera? Straight-out-of-Bologna owner Roberto creates delicious pizzas, deli sandwiches and rich desserts. Eat outside with a view of PG harbour or pop inside for red-tablecloth dining amid walls of wine, available by the glass (from P70).

Ciao Italia ITALIAN **$$$**
(White Beach; mains P300-700, pizzas P240-440; ☺9am-9.30pm) This is one of several authentic Italian restaurants in Puerto Galera. The pizzas are reliable, or opt for the lasagne or gnocchi. Pizzas feed two. It occupies an enviable spot on the much quieter far western end of White Beach.

Hangout Bar PUB FOOD **$$**
(Muelle Pier; mains P180-280; ☺7am-10pm; 🐾) Quality pub grub and internet access (P60 per hour).

Le Bistro FRENCH **$$$**
(Muelle Pier; mains P400-800; ☺7.30am-9.30pm) White tablecloths and authentic French faves like steak tartare and bouillabaisse.

Shopping

Frontier Handicrafts SOUVENIRS
(☺6.30am-9pm) A really good souvenir store tucked in among the restaurants of Sabang. Lots of wooden Ifugao (North Luzon) statuettes plus local handicrafts.

ℹ Information

There are internet cafes along Sabang's covered lane and in PG town (including at Hangout Bar). El Galleon Beach Resort has a retail teller machine ('RTM') that should work for most Western cards (P10,000 limit per transaction).

Allied Bank (National Rd; ☺8am-4pm Mon-Fri) The only reliable ATM in the area; also changes dollars (but not euros or travellers cheques).

Bureau of Immigration (☎043-287 3570; Public Mkt, 2nd fl, Puerto Galera town; ☺9am-noon Mon-Wed) Processes visa renewals within a day.

Post Office (E Brucal St, Puerto Galera town; ☺8am-4.45pm Mon-Fri)

Western Union (Sabang; ☺7.30am-11pm) Changes cash and gives cash advances for a 7% fee.

ℹ Getting There & Away

BOAT
Frequent bangka ferries connect Puerto Galera with Batangas on Luzon. Be aware that the last trip to Batangas from Sabang leaves at 1pm or 2pm (on Sundays and in peak periods there's a later boat). From White Beach the last trip is usually 3pm, and from **Muelle Pier** in Puerto Galera town it's 3.30pm.

From the **Balatero Pier**, 2.2km west of PG town, there's a 10.30am bangka every day to Abra de Ilog (P200, one to 1½ hours).

JEEPNEY & VAN
Jeepneys (P80, 1½ hours, every 45 minutes until 3.45pm) and air-con vans (P100, 1¼ hours, hourly until 5pm) service Calapan, 48km southeast of PG town, along a winding road with spectacular views across Verde Island Passage. Both depart from the **jeepney stop** next to the Petron station in PG town.

To reach Roxas, you must transfer in Calapan.

ℹ Getting Around

Regular jeepneys connect Sabang and PG town during daylight hours (P20, 25 minutes). A tricycle between the two costs P100 (more at night);

from Sabang to Talipanan it's P300. Puerto Galera town to White Beach costs P100. Motorcycle taxis ('singles') are cheaper.

You can rent motorcycles in Puerto Galera at a cluster of shops around **Alex Motorcycle Rental** (Sinandigan Rd) east of the public market. Negotiate, but figure on P400 for a small motorbike and P700 for a trail bike.

Calapan

☑ 043 / POP 124,173

Calapan, the bustling administrative capital of Mindoro Oriental, is a feeder port for Batangas, Luzon and – as far as most tourists are concerned – one of the stops on the bus-boat route between Manila and Boracay. It is also a good base for hiking formidable Mt Halcon and for getting to know a little about Mangyan culture.

◉ Sights & Activities

Mangyan Heritage Center   CULTURAL CENTRE
(☑043-441 3132; www.mangyan.org; St Augustine Bldg, Sto Niño St; ◷8.30am-5pm Mon-Fri, weekends by appointment) ✐ This friendly research centre and library is a treasure trove of books, archival photos and old news clippings about Mangyan culture. Its souvenir shop sells baskets, wild honey, Mangyan Jew's harps (P20), Mangyan-woven shirts and bags, and greeting cards in Mangyan script – all direct-traded at fair prices. Staff will enlighten you about the eight main Mangyan tribes and even teach you how to write in Mangyan script. It's in Calapan centre opposite the old town plaza.

Mt Halcon   TREKKING
Mt Halcon (2582m), which looms over Calapan to the west, is considered by many to be the most challenging big peak in the Philippines. The hiking season is mid-January until the end of May; the mountain is closed at other times. If you're keen, drop by **Apâk Outdoor Shop** (☑0916 241 1780; richard. alcanices@yahoo.com; Quezon Blvd). The owner, Richard, is a member of the Mt Halcon Mountaineering Association, which arranges trips up the mountain. The standard trip is two days up, two days down.

You'll first need to secure various permits (P350) from the municipal office in Baco, the next town north from Calapan. The association can handle this for you, as well as provide you with transport to the trailhead, a Mangyan porter (per day P500), and a guide (P2000 per day for up to five people). Full equipment costs a flat P1000.

Richard and the association can also arrange a host of alternative outdoor pursuits around Calapan and Puerto Galera – day

MINDORO CALAPAN

THE MANGYAN

The Mangyan were the first settlers of Mindoro, arriving around 800 years ago. They are a proto-Malay people, derived from the same ethnic stock as the majority Malay. The Mangyan comprise eight linguistically similar tribes spread along the length of the island's mountainous interior. They are estimated to make up about 10% of Mindoro's population.

The Mangyan have preserved their culture to a much greater extent than many of the other Philippine indigenous groups. Many tribespeople still wear traditional costumes, such as the trademark loincloth (ba-ag), that is worn by males. Animism – belief in the spirits that inhabit nature – remains a potent force in Mangyan cosmology, though often now with some Christian influence.

Most Mangyan are swidden farmers. During the dry season they burn scrub and forest to clear the ground and fertilise the soil; they then plant a succession of crops, including tubers, maize, pulses and 'mountain' rice (a dry rice variety). In the wet season, if there is enough game, they will hunt pigs, monkeys, birds and other small animals. The Mangyan descend to the lowlands on market days to trade crops and handicrafts with non-Mangyans.

The Mangyan have a long history of being persecuted by newcomers to the island or otherwise being involuntarily caught up in their wars. The Spanish punished the Mangyan for their close relations with the Moros, and the Americans put the Mangyan to work on sugar estates or forced them into reservations. In more recent times, Mangyans have been caught in the crossfire in conflicts between the Philippine Army and the New People's Army (NPA).

That they are still able to hold on to their culture despite centuries of incursions from outsiders is a testimony to their vitality and tenacity. If you are interested in finding out more, visit the Mangyan Heritage Center in Calapan.

hikes, birdwatching, caving in San Teodoro, and tubing on the Baco River out of barangay (village) Sta Rosa (elevation 1200m) are just some of the options.

Apâk is directly opposite the Land Transportation Office (LTO), about 1.5km east of the centre on the road to the pier.

🛏 Sleeping & Eating

★ Don Amando's Inn   LODGE $
(☎ 0918 552 5629; donamandosinn@yahoo.com; cnr San Agustin & G Paras Sts; d P350-650, tr P850; 🖥) More like a cosy hostel than an inn, super-friendly Don Amando's is the perfect choice for a group of climbers. It has a lovely communal kitchen and common area, nine no-frills but clean and meticulously painted rooms, and a relatively quiet location near the old town plaza.

Filipiniana Hotel   HOTEL $$
(☎ 043-286 2624; www.filipinianacalapan.com; M Roxas St; r P1750-3500; 🅿🖥🏊) Helpful staff, comfortable, well-kept rooms, a large pool in lush grounds, and a location opposite Robinson's Mall make this the top choice for business travellers to Calapan. Be sure to ask for the 'promo rate'.

Calapan Bay Hotel   HOTEL $$
(☎ 043-288 1309; calapanbayhotel@ymail. com; Quezon Blvd; r P1100-1200; 🅿@) Just a five-minute walk west of the pier, this waterfront hotel has large, cheerful rooms and a terrace where you can dine while admiring the offshore islands. Pick a room as far from the road as possible.

Cargo Grill   FILIPINO $
(JP Rizal St; burgers from P110; ⊙10am-midnight) The speciality at this bar-and-grill is carabao (water buffalo) meat, served in many forms, most popularly burgers. It's 2km south of the city centre in the Tawiran district.

Dutch Cafe   CAFE $
(JP Rizal St; snacks P50-70; ⊙10am-9pm; 🅿🖥) A peaceful little cafe tucked incongruously into the middle of Calapan's chaotic centre, with coffee drinks, a few snacks, wi-fi and even air-con! It's just north of the town's central traffic light. A larger second branch is next to the Filipiniana Hotel.

ℹ Information

BDO, BPI and Metrobank have functional ATMs along the main drag in the centre, JP Rizal St, and internet cafes are plentiful too.

ℹ Getting There & Away

BOAT

The pier is 4km from the town centre (P20 to P30 by tricycle). The only destination from Calapan is Batangas, Luzon. Tickets can be purchased on-the-spot at the pier. The impressive **FastCat** (☎ 043-288 8121; www.fastcat.com. ph) boats are the most reliable (P190 to P250, 1¼ hours, eight day trips); **SuperCat** (www. supercat.com.ph) also runs a fastcraft (P280 to P360, one hour, seven daily). Slower RORO (roll-on, roll-off, or car) ferries run at least every hour around the clock (P200, 2½ hours).

BUS & JEEPNEY

Jeepneys to Puerto Galera (P80, 1½ hours, every 45 minutes) mainly leave from the jeepney terminal next to the Flying V petrol station on JP Rizal St, 1.5km south of central Calapan. You can also just wait for a passing jeepney in Tawiran (south of the centre) at the Puerto Galera road junction. Vans to PG depart from the Calapan City Market on Juan Luna St (P100, 1¼ hours, every 45 minutes). Trips dry up after 5pm.

Also from the Calapan City Market, vans leave to Pinamalayan (P100, 1½ hours), Roxas (P200, three hours) and San José (P500, 5½ hours), departing regularly from 7am to 6pm.

Roxas

☎ 043 / POP 49,854

Roxas is a dusty little spot with ferry connections to Caticlan. Few travellers stay here intentionally, but some get stuck when the notoriously flaky ferries cancel trips. If you have time, stroll into the centre and check out the **market** (best Wednesday and Sunday mornings, when Mangyan people and other villagers sell their wares). There's a functional Allied Bank ATM in the centre of town.

🛏 Sleeping & Eating

Tulip Residence Inn   HOTEL $$
(☎ 043-289 3150; Dangay Pier; r 6hr/24hr P1000/1500; 🅿@🖥) Easily the best of the pier options, with sturdy wood doors opening to tidy rooms with bright bedsheets and even flat-screen TVs.

Lyf Hotel & Restaurant   HOTEL $
(☎ 043-289 2819; Magsaysay Ave; r with fan P300, with air-con P650-850; 🅿) Right on the National Hwy, the roomy top-whack air-con rooms are as good as it gets in the centre. The windowless fan and standard air-con rooms are dingy, however, and the hotel exterior beyond grim. The restaurant (mains P60 to P150) does about the only cook-to-order food in town.

ℹ Getting There & Away

BOAT

Roxas' **Dangay Pier** is about 3km from the centre (P10 by public tricycle or P50 for a special trip). Vans arriving from points north do drop-offs at the pier before heading into the centre.

If you are heading to Caticlan (P400, four hours), call the **Ports Authority** (☑043-289 2813) at the pier, about 3km from the centre, to check the car-ferry schedule, as it changes often and departures are infrequent during the day. In the high season (November to May), **Montenegro Shipping** (☑0932 461 9096) usually has three daytime departures, but times vary – 10am, noon, 2pm and 4pm are possible times. In the low season there is usually only one departure, at 2pm. Montenegro and other companies run several night trips year-round.

Besides Caticlan, Roxas has services to Odiongan, Romblon, by bangka (P350, three hours) every morning except Tuesday. Times vary, so call the Ports Authority.

BUS & VAN

Vans to Calapan (P180, three hours) via Pinamalayan (P100, 1½ hours) meet the ferries at the pier. More vans depart from several points in the town centre throughout the day. Going the other way, vans leave roughly hourly from the centre to Bulalacao (P80, one hour) and San José (P250, 2½ hours) until 4pm or so.

From the highway, a few passing Dimple Star buses per day head south to San José and north to Calapan and Manila (P640, eight hours – with a little help from a ferry). Ceres Liner has comfortable direct buses to Manila from Roxas at 7am and 7pm.

Around Roxas

Bait

The Friday Market (*tiangge* – Mangyan for 'market day') in Bait, a barangay of Mansalay, is fantastic. Mangyan tribespeople trek down from the hills for up to five hours to trade tubers, maize, rice and other vegetables for lowland products. Many of the men wear *ba-ag* (loincloths), while women don colourful woven garments. Always ask before taking photos of individuals. The market starts at the crack of dawn and runs until noon or so. To get here, turn right (west) off the National Hwy about 6km south of Mansalay and follow the rough road 2.7km (you'll need to ford a couple of streams in the rainy season).

Buktot Beach

About 30km south of Roxas you'll encounter a gorgeous sweep of white sand and clean, calm water at Buktot Beach. Visit during the week and you'll have it to yourself. Weekends occasionally draw crowds. From a well-marked turnoff 10km south of Mansalay, it's 1.7km to the beach. You can sleep on the beach if you're so inclined, or head to nearby **RC Farm & Resort** (☑0915 251 2164; rcfarmresort@yahoo.com.ph; Barangay Manaul; r with fan/air-con P700/1100; ❋☞☎), with a few cute concrete cottages set around a tidy courtyard and a small pool. It's 1km south of the Buktot Beach turnoff.

Bulalacao

POP 33,754

This unassuming coastal town is surrounded by lost coves and practically uninhabited islands ripe for exploring. Larry at South Drive Restobar organises island-hopping trips, rents out motorbikes (per day P500) and has a car for hire. Many Mangyans come to town on market days (Tuesdays and Saturdays). There is no ATM in Bulalacao.

🛏 Sleeping & Eating

Tambaron Green Beach Resort   BEACH RESORT $
(☑0919 993 4987; www.tambaron.com; dm/d P350/1500) This resort on Tambaron Island is almost too good value to be true. The island has four private white-sand beaches that you can walk to and snorkelling at your doorstep. Rooms are simple thatched concrete affairs, and buffet meals (P200 to P250) are all-you-can-eat. Hire a bangka from Bulalacao (P700, 30 minutes).

J Felipa Lodge II   LODGE $
(☑0947 868 5277; d with fan/air-con P500/800; ❋☞) This exceptional deal is nestled amid well-manicured gardens on the water 2km west of town near the new roll-on, roll-off ferry (RORO) terminal. Fan rooms can sleep four in two queen beds, but lack sinks. Request a mosquito net.

South Drive Restobar & Homestay   GUESTHOUSE $$
(☑0917 541 2761; tr P1000; ❋@☞) Not only is the sea-facing restobar the best place to eat in town, it also rents out three comfortable and welcoming air-con rooms.

ℹ Getting There & Away

A few vans leave to San José but you're better off flagging down a more comfortable Dimple Star bus on the main road (P140, 1½ hours, six daily). Vans are more frequent in the other direction to Roxas (P80, one hours), or flag down a Manila-bound Dimple Star to Roxas or beyond.

San José

☑ 043 / POP 131,188

The southernmost town in Mindoro Occidental, San José has a cluster of three pretty islands – White, Ambulong and Ilin – just off-shore. It's notable for having an airport, and its position as a transport hub is what brings most travellers through. It's also the place to restock on cash from the only ATMs in Mindoro Occidental.

Attractions around San José include Mangyan markets and waterfalls, and Michelle at the tourist office can help arrange visits to the islands. Ilin is the largest and most developed, with a new ring road and, on the back side, powdery white-sand Inakasang Beach.

🛏 Sleeping

We recommend staying on Aroma Beach, just a 1.5km tricycle ride (P10) north of town, instead of in the noisy, fumy centre. It's clean and good for walking, with decent swimming at high tide.

Sikatuna Beach Hotel   HOTEL $
(☑043-491 2182; www.sikatunabeachhotel.com; off Airport Rd; d P1250-1350; ❄@🛜) This big place on Aroma Beach is a huge step up on anything in the centre. Shoot for the light, bright newer rooms (request one with a seafront balcony). Its restaurant (mains P175 to P400) qualifies as an oasis in San José and specialises in seafood.

Jazmine Royal Hotel   HOTEL $$
(☑043-491 4269; Sikatuna St; s/d from P900/1200; ❄) Easily the pick of the centre options, with spiffy beds, relatively good soundproofing and a cheery orange motif. The singles are windowless but upgrade to a double and you are in business.

Mindoro Plaza Hotel   HOTEL $
(☑043-491 4661; P Zamora St; s P300-850, d P400-950; ❄) The fan rooms will appeal to budget travellers; otherwise this place is unspectacular, with maintenance issues even in the pricier rooms.

White House Beach Resort   HOTEL $$
(☑043-491 1656; edithpark@yahoo.com; off Airport Rd; r P2500-3500; ❄🛜) This Aroma Beach option is more like a well-to-do and classy relative's mansion than a hotel. It's the most luxurious place in town, with balconies and huge marble bathrooms (and bidets!), but is somewhat sleepy and overpriced.

🍴 Eating & Drinking

★ Kusina ni Lea   FILIPINO $
(Sikatuna St; mains P80-150; ⏲8am-10pm; ❄) Kusina has friendly service and a good seafood selection, including sweet-and-sour *lapu-lapu* (grouper) and grilled squid. It also might be the only restaurant in Mindoro Occidental – except for Jollibee – with air-con.

Chowder   RESTOBAR
(Rizal St; mains P50-150; ⏲24hr) This centrally located restobar draws raucous live-music acts by night and serves decent Filipino food around-the-clock.

Grandiya   RESTOBAR
(Airport Rd; ⏲6pm-late) Grandiya has a big stage for nightly live-music acts and serves the usual range of Filipino bar food. It's opposite Aroma Beach next to the gigantic Aroma Family Hotel.

ℹ BORACAY TO PALAWAN VIA MINDORO?

Plans were still being formulated at the time of research, but all signs pointed to a Mindoro–Coron (Palawan) RORO (roll-on, roll-off) route opening by 2015 or 2016. If this happens, it would enable relatively easy travel by sea and land between the country's two trendiest locales, Boracay and Palawan – a Holy Grail of sorts in Philippine tourism circles.

San José and Bulalacao are both in the mix for this new route. Bulalacao has a new RORO terminal and was negotiating with up-and-coming FastCat to launch direct daily trips to Coron Town. San José, for its part, was set to open a new RORO terminal at its Caminawit Port and hopes are that Coron will be one of the first routes served when it opens. The race is on.

San José

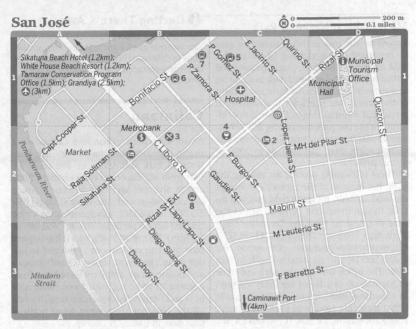

Sikatuna Beach Hotel (1.2km);
White House Beach Resort (1.2km);
Tamaraw Conservation Program
Office (1.5km); Grandiya (2.5km);
(3km)

Pandururan River

Mindoro
Strait

Caminawit Port
(4km)

ℹ Information

There are several internet cafes along Rizal and C Liboro Sts.

Geox (per hr P20; ☺8am-7pm) Internet cafe.

Metrobank (C Liboro St)

Municipal Tourism Office (☎043-491 1301; Municipal Compound, Rizal St; ☺8am-5pm Mon-Fri) Provides good ideas on things to do around San José.

ℹ Getting There & Away

AIR

San José's airport, 3km northwest of the centre, was closed for an upgrade at the time of research. When it's open, expect at least a few weekly flights to Manila.

BOAT

Weather permitting, bangkas to Coron Town in northern Palawan (P800 including lunch, eight hours) leave on Tuesdays, Wednesdays, Thursdays and Saturdays at 8am from San José's main Caminawit Pier, 4km south of town.

From the 'Fish Port' near Caminawit Pier, there's a boat to Manamok in the Cuyo Islands on Tuesday and Friday mornings (P800, eight hours).

For updated schedule information, call the **Ports Authority** (☎043-491 2707; Caminawit Port).

San José

🛏 Sleeping
1 Jazmine Royal Hotel..........................B2
2 Mindoro Plaza Hotel..........................C2

🍴 Eating
3 Kusina ni Lea B2

🍸 Drinking & Nightlife
4 Chowder..C2

ℹ Transport
5 Dimple Star..C1
6 Jeepneys to Manoot...........................B1
7 Vans to Roxas and Calapan................B1
8 Vans to Roxas and Calapan................B2

BUS & JEEPNEY

Air-con **Dimple Star** (☎0908 700 7769; Bonifacio St) buses to Manila (P850, 12 hours) go via Abra de Ilog (six trips daily) or Calapan (five daily). Northbound buses get you to Calintaan (P60, one hour) and Sablayan (P140, 2½ hours). Eastbound Dimple Star buses transit Bulalacao (P170, 1½ hours) and Roxas (P250, 2½ hours).

Similarly priced vans, with several departure points, are another option to Abra de Ilog and Calapan. These leave when full – morning departures are much more reliable. Cheaper jeepneys and rickety ordinary buses are slower options to Calintaan and Sablayan.

Mt Iglit-Baco National Park

Travellers who trek to this remote area may be rewarded with a sighting of the elusive wild *tamaraw,* the Philippines' endangered native buffalo. The national park is made up of sweeps of grassland (the favoured habitat of the *tamaraw*), Mangyan slash-and-burn areas, and forested ridges. Conservation efforts within the park are paying off: *Tamaraw* counts have risen steadily over the last several years, from 253 animals in 2002 to 382 in 2014.

There is a simple process for visiting the park, but because of the protected status of the wild animals, it's quite rigid and you do need to sign in and get permits (free at the time of research) from the Tamaraw Conservation Program Office (043-491 1236; tcp.denroccmin04@gmail.com; Off Airport Rd; 8am-5pm Mon-Fri) on Aroma Beach in San José. The office will call the park entrance in Mantancob (a *sitio* of barangay Poypoy) in Calintaan municipality, so that a guide (P350 including food) and porter (optional, P500) are waiting for you. If you can't make it to the park office or want to arrange a permit outside of office hours, call project head Rodel Boyles (0918 511 1323, 0917 715 4489; rmboyles@yahoo.com), who will tell you everything you need to know about visiting the national park.

From Mantancob it's a three-hour-ish hike to the Iglit Station (station 1) bunkhouse, where you can stay overnight. Or you can continue on two hours to the Magawang Station (station 3), where there's a newer bunkhouse and a viewing platform where you will hopefully observe *tamaraw* gambolling on the plains below. You will need your own gear for these hikes. December to April are the best climbing months, and in April you may coincide with and observe the annual *tamaraw* count. Access is difficult to impossible during the rainy July-to-September period.

The Tamaraw Conservation Program runs a breeding station known as the Gene Pool inside the park. Here captive-bred *tamaraw* are raised. It's in barangay Manoot, Rizal municipality, about one hour by 'single' (P500) or 1½ hours by occasional jeepney (P50) from San José. You can hike from the Gene Pool station in Manoot to the Mt Magawang viewing platform (about four hours).

❶ Getting There & Away

There are a few direct jeepneys to Poypoy from San José that go straight to Mantancob, or take a bus to Calintaan (P60, one hour) and a tricycle to the park entrance in Mantancob (P75, 35 minutes).

Calintaan

POP 28,148

About 40km north of San José, Calintaan is a potential launch point for both Mt Iglit-Baco National Park and Apo Reef. You could depart from Manila on an early-morning flight and be diving at Apo Reef the same morning out of Swiss-owned Apo Reef Club (0917 815 2499, 02-506 1801; www.aporeefclub.com; r incl breakfast & dinner per person with fan P1450, with aircon from P2650; ❉ @ 🐾 🛎), which has a speed boat that can get you out to the reef in just one hour. The resort serves big buffet meals and boasts smart, shiny concrete beachfront cottages to go along with more rustic nipa huts and simpler 'backpacker rooms'. It's 1km off the National Hwy, about 10km north of Calintaan in barangay Concepcion.

Sablayan

043 / POP 76,153

A welcome sight after the long journey from either the north or the south, rural and friendly Sablayan sits astride the Bagong Sabang River. It has a lively market and makes a good base for several worthwhile terrestrial excursions. However, the main attraction here is Apo Reef, the country's best dive site besides Tubbataha, less than two hours offshore.

◉ Sights & Activities

Apo Reef Natural Park   DIVING

At the time of research, four operators were doing dive and snorkelling trips to Apo Reef: North Pandan Island Resort, Gustav's Place and the Ecotourism Office in Sablayan; and Apo Reef Club in Calintaan. Small groups looking to split costs with other divers are advised to contact the Ecotourism Office, which can sometimes set you up with a group (its own group or another dive operator's group).

The costs for a day or overnight trip through the Ecotourism Office are P8500 per group for the boat (up to 15 people, two hours each way); an entrance fee of P650/2450 per person for snorkellers/divers (much less for

Filipinos); P800 per day for a divemaster; and P150/2000 for snorkel/dive equipment (including one tank; additional tanks P300). Bring your own lunch, water and snacks. You'll pay more with the other two dive operators in Sablayan, but you'll benefit from better equipment and dive masters. Overnight trips involve sleeping in hammocks or on the floor of the open-air park ranger station on Apo Island (or on boats).

☞ Tours

Ecotourism Office TOURS, TOURIST INFORMATION
(☑ 0915 995 3895, 043-458 0028; www.sablayan. net; Town Plaza, P Urieta St; ⊙ 8am-5pm) This office is unique in that it actually runs tours as opposed to just dishing out pamphlets and advice. Apo Reef dive trips are the big one, but staff can arrange excursions to Sablayan Prison Farm, Mt Iglit-Baco National Park and a two-day forest trek taking in several Mangyan villages.

🍴 Sleeping & Eating

★ **Pandan Island Resort** BEACH RESORT $
(☑ 0919 305 7821; www.pandan.com; budget r P800, bungalows P1600, q cottage from P2400; ☎) This postcard-perfect, privately owned resort island is a low-key tropical paradise. Several prime dive spots surround the island, and you'd be unlucky not to see a green turtle as you snorkel. Early mornings are prime bird-watching times; rare resident species include black-naped orioles, tabon scrub fowl and emerald doves. The resort itself is on a long, curving, white-sand beach.

Rooms are a combination of rudimentary budget rooms with shared bathroom, and comfortable bungalows. There's limited, solar-powered electricity, which means no fans in the budget rooms (hope for a breeze). Tasty buffet meals cost P470 and guests are required to take at least one; full board is P1000. To get here take the clearly marked shuttle bangka on the Sabang River just southwest of the Emily Hotel (P200 for one person, P50 for each additional passenger, 20 minutes). Entrance is P150 for day-trippers.

Along D' Beach HOTEL $
(☑ 0947 964 6238; National Hwy; r with fan/air-con P350/700; ❄) On the water just south of the centre, this place is dishevelled but has great views, and the fan rooms are good value.

Emily Hotel HOTEL $
(☑ 0916 737 4710; Gozar St; r with/without bathroom from P400/200; ❄) Downright awful, but cheap and well located opposite the boats to North Pandan Island. Recently added some *slightly* snazzier air-con rooms.

Gustav's Place BEACH RESORT $$
(☑ 0939 432 6131; www.grabler.at; r with fan P800-1400, with air-con P2200) Located out on Sablayan's wide gray-sand beach, Gustav's has a real remote quality. Rooms are simple thatched concrete affairs, some stand-alone, others in a central house. Pricier digs have air-con and hot water. Activities offered include forest walks, kayaking and of course diving. From the public market, cross the footbridge and walk 1.5km north along the beach.

MINDORO SABLAYAN

APO REEF

At 35 sq km, Apo Reef Natural Park (not to be confused with Apo Island off the south coast of Negros) is the largest atoll-type reef in the Philippines. The crystal-clear waters abound with life, including 285 species of fish and 197 species of coral. It's the only readily accessible dive site in the Philippines where snorkellers and divers alike are practically guaranteed heavy pelagic (large fish) action – mostly white tip and black tip sharks, reef sharks, wrasses, jacks and tuna. On a day trip from Sablayan we saw so many sharks we lost count. You also stand a chance of seeing trophy creatures such as hammerhead sharks, whale sharks and manta rays out here. The three islands off the reef play host to a variety of turtle and bird species, including the endangered, large-chicken-sized Nicobar pigeon.

Your average bangka does the trip out to Apo Reef in about two hours from Sablayan in flat seas (a bit less from North Pandan Island). Apo Reef Club in Calintaan has a fast boat that does it in one hour. Live-aboard trips from Anilao and especially Coron also make it out here.

The best time to make the trip to Apo Reef is when the seas are flattest – April to May and October to November. The journey is very rough during the windy December to March period. During the height of the southwest monsoon (July–September) it's often impossible to get out to the reef and some operators shut down – be sure to call ahead.

WORTH A TRIP

SABLAYAN PRISON FARM

A wonderfully quirky experience, the Sablayan Prison Farm (admission free) offers much more than a chance to meet-and-greet prisoners in their element. There are also a host of prisoner-guided excursions on offer in the lush forests around the farm, and you can even sleep out here within earshot of snoring prisoners in the prison guesthouse.

You must secure a permit (P50) from the Ecotourism Office in Sablayan to enter the prison grounds. A half-day of activities might combine an hour or so guided hike in Siburan Rainforest (admission P50) with a visit to Libuao Lake (admission P50), some time talking to prisoners at the central subprison and a visit to Pasugi subprison, where you can buy prisoner-made handicrafts.

Siburan rainforest and Libuao Lake are prime birdwatching spots, and one of the prisoner-guides knows birds and can point out endemic black-hooded coucals, critically endangered Mindoro bleeding-heart pigeons and white-billed and serpent eagles if you're lucky. The lake is famed for its lotuses, and is a popular spot for fishing and boating (P150). Take a picnic and relax. Secure a guide (P150) at the Siburan subprison barracks, 5km northeast of the central subprison.

Prisoners throughout the compound greet visitors cheerfully, wearing uniform T-shirts that say 'minimum' or 'medium inmate'. Maximum-security inmates are kept away from tourists, but the orange 'maximum' shirts sold discreetly by some inmates make great souvenirs.

The prison farm makes a perfect half-day excursion from Sablayan by single (about P800) or self-drive motorbike. Turn off the National Hwy 17km south of Sablayan and proceed east 7km to the central subprison. Going straight to the Siburan subprison makes for a smoother ride; follow the National Hwy north out of Sablayan for 19km, then turn right in barangay Yapang at the 341km mark. Proceed about 2km to the Siburan subprison.

Camalig
FILIPINO $

(mains P130-350, snacks P50-100) Easily the best restaurant in town, Camalig serves freshly prepared curries and other Filipino food under a soaring nipa canopy. It's just off the National Hwy opposite the town plaza, behind a Card Bank.

GVD Kubo
FILIPINO $

(Town Plaza, P Urieta St; meals P75-100; ☺7am-9pm) Offers a mix of pre-made and cooked-to-order dishes. You can cobble together a takeaway lunch of cold chicken legs and other snacks for your Apo Reef trip the next day.

❶ Getting There & Away

Air-con Dimple Star buses rumble through town every three hours or so on their way to Cubao in Manila (P800, nine hours, about eight daily) via Abra de Ilog (P220, 3½ hours), and in the other direction to San José (P140, 2½ hours). Air-con vans are somewhat more frequent in both directions.

You can rent motorbikes (P400 per day) at the *habal-habal* (motorcycle taxi) stop just north of the public market, which fronts the Sabang River near the Emily Hotel.

Abra de Ilog
☑043 / POP 28,255

The dusty town of Abra de Ilog is the northern gateway to Mindoro's west coast. If you arrive by water you'll see why there's no usable road west of Puerto Galera: a cloud-scraping wall of jagged mountains runs right to the shore.

You likely won't linger long in Abra. If you're not aboard one already, try to hop on a San José–bound Dimple Star bus that's rolling off the ferry, which will take you via Sablayan (P220, 3½ hours). Otherwise, take one of the cramped air-con vans that await arriving passengers at the pier and head south to San José (P350, six hours) via Mamburao (P80, one hour) and Sablayan (P220, three hours). There are a few (grim) accommodation options in both Abra de Ilog and Mamburao, Mindoro Occidental's sleepy capital.

Montenegro (☑0919 878 8055) ROROs depart six times daily to Batangas (P260, 2½ hours); the 10am, 2pm and 5pm are most convenient. There's also a daily 9am bangka to Puerto Galera's Balatero Pier (P200, one to 1½ hours).

Boracay & Western Visayas

Why Go?

In general, the western Visayas attracts three types of visitors. The most common is the vacationer drawn by Boracay's gorgeous White Beach, and the commercial hubbub that surrounds it: a collection of resorts, restaurants, bars, and tour promoters all lined up along one great stretch of sand. As the latest tour group from Asia will attest, it's the perfect place for that selfie in the waves. Next comes the diver drawn to world-class undersea destinations, from Romblon Island in the north to Apo Island in the south. Finally, there's the off-the-beaten-track traveller braving endless miles of roadside shacks to discover the region's discrete rewards, including mountain trekking and cave exploration, pockets of vibrant nightlife, some fascinating architectural history, alluring beach resorts, and oases of fine food. Thus the key question: have you packed your compass, your snorkel, or your selfie stick?

Best Nightlife

➡ Area 51 Secret Party Facility (p223)

➡ KGBar (p245)

➡ Red Paprika (p236)

➡ Bar 360 (p232)

Best Beach Resorts

➡ Discovery Shores (p218)

➡ Cabugan Adventure Resort (p239)

➡ Kookoo's Nest (p252)

➡ Aglicay Beach Resort (p269)

When to Go

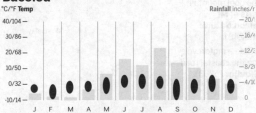

Bacolod

Dec–Apr Best diving conditions.

Jun–Oct Risky. Tropical storms and occasional typhoons makes this the off-season for a reason.

Oct–Jun High tourist season. Bring wallet to Boracay.

Boracay & Western Visayas Highlights

1 Stroll the famous White Beach Path in **Boracay**.

2 Snorkel the colourful reef at **Apo Island** (p253).

3 Trace the aquamarine **Malumpati River** (p230) back to its mysterious source in the jungle of Panay.

4 Kayak around **Danjugan Island** (p250), an ecotourist's dream.

5 Crash the **expat happy hour** in charming Romblon Town (p270).

6 Sample fruit at the organic **Spring Bloom Farm** (p237) on Guimaras.

7 Tour the historic sugar mansions of **Silay** (p246).

8 Explore unspoiled **Sipaway Island** (p250) by motorcycle.

9 Beam down to the **Area 51 Secret Party Facility** (p223), a Boracay classic.

10 Refresh yourself in the cool mountain resorts of **Mt Kanlaon Natural Park** (246).

11 Ride a motorcycle along the coastal road of **Siquijor** (p263).

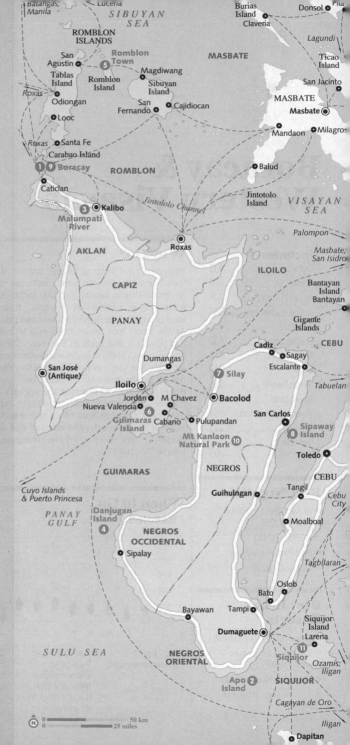

BORACAY

036 / POP 30,000

While only 7km tall and at its bikini line 500m wide, tiny Boracay has rapidly become the Philippines' top tourist draw, fuelled by explosive growth and a tsunami of hype; in 2013 the readers of *Travel & Leisure* voted it the second-best island destination in the world after Palawan. The centre of the action is dreamy White Beach, a 4km, postcard-perfect stretch of sand lined from one end to the other with hotels, restaurants, bars, and dive shops now several blocks deep. The beach path is typically awash with visitors, including large groups of package tourists drawn from all over Asia – most commonly Korea, Taiwan and China. The ocean is full of romantic *paraws* (an outrigger sailboat) giving rides; colourful parasails fill the air. After perfect sunsets, live music breaks out, and firedancers twirl their batons. The party goes on all night. All of this can be great fun, à la Waikiki, and can easily occupy your entire visit. Just don't expect the Boracay of 30 years ago, when visitors revelled in the fact that their dirt-cheap nipa hut had no electricity.

Beyond White Beach the island continues to undergo unchecked growth. New multimillion-dollar properties rub shoulders with tin shacks. Construction continues on the massive Newcoast development, a planned community aping Santorini, Ibiza and other brand locations, which has swallowed 14% of the island. If you're looking for authenticity, however, you can still find it. Head north to peaceful Diniwid Beach for a break in the action, or east to Bulabog Beach, home to the local watersports crowd, with its welcoming community vibe. All things considered, Boracay is a place where you can find whatever you want if you know where to look. Otherwise, grab that *weng weng* cocktail, sink into your waterfront beanbag chair and just marvel at the spectacle of it all.

◉ Sights

Believe it or not, Boracay has other beaches that are almost as pretty as White Beach, if not quite so endless. A scenic walk around the headland at the island's north end brings you to lovely and secluded Diniwid Beach, where there are excellent accommodations and dining. On the north tip of the island, pretty Puka Beach is popular in the off-season, and has a few eateries. Some of the best *puka* jewellery (popular necklaces,

anklets and bracelets made from the tiny shells of the cone snail) is found in the handicraft stalls here. Other northern beaches are well off the package-tourist radar and nearly deserted. Try to find hard-to-reach Ilig-Iligan Beach, in the northeast, which looks onto a couple of scenic limestone islets that are snorkelling distance from shore. A scenic *paraw* fleet beaches here in the off-season.

★ White Beach   BEACH
(Map p214) With its glorious, powdered-sugar sand, White Beach is the centre of the action in Boracay and the only sight most visitors ever see. Beach locations are defined relative to three former boat stations, where bangkas (outriggers) from Caticlan used to arrive. The area south of Station 3, known as Angol, contains most of the budget accommodation, including a few remnants of Old Boracay.

White Beach North & Around

0   200 m
0   0.1 miles

Punta Rosa (300m);
Nami Boracay (600m);
Spider House (600m)

8

28

40

17

13

Balabag
Plaza

35

10

BALABAG

6

1

27

Mt Luho
View Deck
(1km)

Carabao
Island

Station 1

3

Pond

5

Bulabog Rd

Bulabog
Beach Boat
Station

4

23

31

30

Tablas
Strait

2

16

9

Boracay Lying-
In & Diagnostic
Center

11

12

Road 1A

34

20

7

14

38   33

22

Metrobank

24

21

D'Mall

18

32   29

26

36

15

37

25

BPI

Department
of Tourism

39

42

19

41

43

See White Beach South
& Around Map (p214)

White Beach North & Around

BORACAY & WESTERN VISAYAS BORACAY

The stretch between Station 1 and Station 3 is busy and commercial. Most top-end accommodations are on an incredible stretch of beach north of Station 1. The entire beach is paralleled by a sandy pedestrian highway – the White Beach Path – where motorised vehicles are officially banned.

Mt Luho View Deck VIEWPOINT
(Map p211; Lapus-Lapus Rd; admission P120) Looming high above the east coast, this viewpoint has stunning views across the island, though the steps up were designed for giants. The lush cross-country road linking it with the main road is quite a contrast to the coast.

🏃 Activities

You can try your hand at a broad range of outdoor activities. Daily games of football, volleyball and ultimate Frisbee kick off in late afternoon on White Beach. Yoga is offered at Mandala Spa (p220) from 9.30am to 10.45am and True Food Indian restaurant at Station 2 from 9am to 10.30am for P400. For more far-flung adventures, consider heading down to Antique Province (see Tours), or take a bangka to Romblon Province.

Sailing
Sunset *paraw* trips are a quintessential Boracay experience. Trips start at P700 per hour for up to five or six passengers, and you can usually haggle for lower. Boats depart Station 1 and 3 in season (Oct to Jun), and from Bulabog Beach in the offseason (Jun to Oct).

Red Pirates BOAT TOUR
(☑ 0921 782 1494, 288 5767; red-pirates.blogspot.co.uk; per boat P800) Red Pirates has a super-sized *paraw* (12-person capacity) and does the standard cruises off White Beach, plus longer trips to secret spots around northern Panay and Carabao Island.

D'Boracay Sailing BOAT TOUR
(☑ 0906 308 8614; www.boracay-sailing.com) For an upscale sail, this company organises two-hour sunset cruises, including wine, beer and canapés on a 42ft luxury catamaran (per person P3500). Reserve online.

Parasailing
Several providers compete for business, but if you're going to hang from a parachute over the water, don't skimp. Go at sunset!

White Beach South & Around

See White Beach North & Around Map (p212)

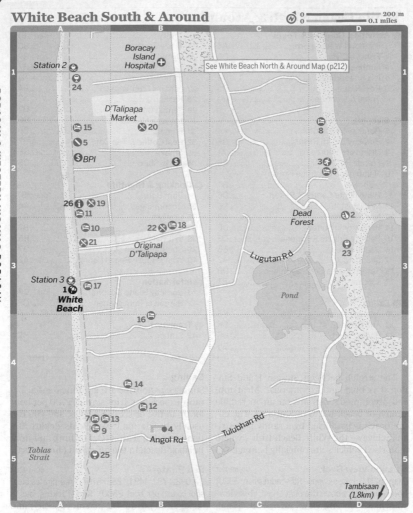

See White Beach North & Around Map (p212)

Diamond Watersports PARASAILING
(Map p212; ☎288 6621; flight P2500) Perhaps the best known in the business. Prices cut in half during low season.

Diving & Snorkelling

Diving around Boracay pales in comparison with more renowned hot spots like Puerto Galera, but there are some OK spots around. Yapak (Map p211), off the northern tip, is a sheer soft-coral-covered wall running from 30m to 65m. Big-fish lovers adore this spot, though depth, currents and surface chop restrict it to advanced divers. There are also drift dives and cave dives. Crocodile Island, off the small beach at Tambisaan, is a popular snorkelling destination in good weather.

There are many dive centres on Boracay, but prices are set by the Boracay Association of Scuba Diving Schools. Walk-in prices are P1800 per dive with full gear, and P22,500 for an open-water diving certificate. The high prices generally means the quality of equipment and instruction is high, and fly-by-night operations fail. Nevertheless, always exercise caution with rental dive equipment. Dive resorts on White Beach offer diving vacations.

White Beach South & Around

Calypso Diving   DIVING
(Map p214; ☎288 3206; www.calypso-boracay.com; Station 3) PADI five-star development centre for instructors, part of the upscale Calypso Resort.

Victory Divers   DIVING
(Map p214; ☎288 3209; www.victorydivers.com; btwn Stations 2 & 3) Five-star PADI centre and local marine conservation pioneer, part of Victory Beach Resort.

Fisheye Divers   DIVING
(Map p212; ☎288 6090; www.fisheyedivers.com; Station 1) PADI dive centre. Operates three dive boats, including one live-aboard.

Kitesurfing

During the height of the *amihan* (northeast monsoon; December to March), excellent conditions and decent prices (about P19,000 for a 12-hour certification course) make Bulabog Beach on the east side of the island the perfect place to learn kitesurfing. The action shifts to White Beach during the *habagat* (southwest monsoon; May to October), when heavy onshore chop makes it more of an expert's sport. Water-sports businesses rotate location accordingly.

Isla Kitesurfing   KITESURFING
(Map p212; ☎288 5352; www.islakitesurfing.com; Bulabog Beach) Lessons, equipment, trips and bungalow accommodations from a 12-year veteran.

Freestyle Academy   KITESURFING
(☎0915 559 3080; www.freestyle-boracay.com) Located north of Station 1 during low season.

Habagat   KITESURFING
(Map p214; ☎036-288 5787; www.kiteboracay.com) Located at White Beach from May to October; get information from Steakhouse Boracay, near Boracay Beach Club.

Windsurfing

Boracay was an Asian windsurfing mecca long before kitesurfing was even invented, but now windsurfers are in the minority on Bulabog Beach. The season is the same for both. Per hour board-rental prices are P700 to P1300, and per hour lesson prices are about P1300. It's not hard to find a good-quality short or long board to rent in the high season.

Funboard Center Boracay   WINDSURFING
(Map p212; ☎288 3876; www.windsurfasia.com; Bulabog Beach) Equipment and multi-lingual courses in both windsurfing and kitesurfing.

Reef Riders   WINDSURFING
(Map p212; ☎0908 820 2267; www.reefriders-watersports.com; Bulabog Beach) Equipment and lessons. Also offers stand-up paddleboarding.

Adventure Windsurfing   WINDSURFING
(Map p214; ☎288 3182; www.adventure-windsurfing-boracay.com; Bulabog Beach) Instruction and equipment for both windsurfing and kitesurfing.

Tours

Tribal Adventures
ADVENTURE TOURS

(Map p212; 0920 558 7188, 288 3207; www.tri-baladventures.com; Sandcastles Resort, Station 2) Offers a host of adventures on mountainous mainland Panay, including kayaking trips in Tibiao, as well as more far-flung journeys to Palawan. Pricey, but well-organised.

Sleeping

Boracay has every form of accommodation under the sun, including dive hotels (White Beach) and kitesurfer hotels (Bulabog Beach), which combine accommodations with instruction and rentals.

Angol (South of Station 3)

You can still find good-value rooms in Angol, where some say the spirit of the 'Old Bora-cay' survives. There are really no drawbacks to staying down here; it's an easy, pleasant walk to central White Beach.

White Beach Divers Hostel
HOSTEL $

(Map p214; 036-288 3809; www.whitebeach-divers.com; dm P300, d/tr without bathroom P650/1000;) A stellar deal, especially if you get the spacious bamboo loft at the back, which sleeps three. Other rooms are more basic. Most have shared bathrooms. The owner has set up a small information booth out front and is a fountain of knowledge about tours in Romblon and other nearby areas.

FRIENDS OF THE FLYING FOX

One of Boracay's iconic scenes is the nightly migration of hundreds of enormous flying foxes (fruit bats) across the sky. This includes the large flying fox, the common island flying fox, and the endangered golden crowned flying fox, the world's heaviest bat. These amazing creatures also perform a vital function, as the seeds they extrude plant trees as they go, accounting for 95% of forest re-growth on cleared land. With the local bat population plunging in the face of development, The Friends of the Flying Foxes Boracay (288 1239; www.fb.com/friendsoftheflyingfoxesboracay) is attempting to create a reserve in the north of the island. Part of their efforts includes regular bat counts, which anyone is welcome to join.

Hey! Jude South Beach
HOTEL $$

(Map p214; 0917 861 6618, 288 2401; www.heyjude-boracay.com; r incl breakfast P2800-4750;) Local legend Jude has taken all the lessons learned from his sister property near D'Mall and constructed Boracay's perfect midrange beach hotel. The minimalist style with large, open rooms, all of which face the sea, is just right, while the low-key breakfast by the White Beach Path is the ideal start to the day. Add helpful staff and a very attractive price and you simply can't beat this for value.

Boracay Pito Huts
BUNGALOWS $$

(Map p214; 0922 820 9765, 288 2457; www.bo-racaypitohuts.com; bungalow P3500;) You're forgiven for scratching your head when you see the stockade fence off the beach, looking like an Old West fort. Yet inside the white sand enclosure lies one of the island's great gems. With an A+ for originality, these seven ('pito') huts have a winning, modern design, with angled walls and twilight interiors, an alluring complement to the bright beach beyond. Each sleeps three with P500 for an extra bed. The coolest bungalows are on the beach.

Dave's Straw Hat Inn
COTTAGES $$

(Map p214; 288 5465; www.davesstrawhatinn.com; r with fan/air-con P1300/2490;) The air-con rooms here are comfy modern cottages with nipa roofs and private verandahs, set in a leafy and secluded garden. The fan rooms are less charming but still excellent value. Dave scores points for the breakfasts, especially the discus-sized pancakes, but doesn't take credit cards.

Ocean Breeze Inn
HOTEL $$

(Map p214; 288 1680; www.oceanbreezeinn.info; r P1100-1900;) The best rooms here are also the cheapest: the rattan-swathed standalone cottages in the garden. These complement the simple, well-appointed air-con concrete rooms. No restaurant, but guests share a kitchen.

Angol Point Beach Resort
BEACH RESORT $$

(Map p214; 288 3107; cottage P3000;) A loyal cadre swears by this clutch of nipa huts in a beachfront coconut field, whose massive porches offer classic hammocks. For others, it's a bit too spartan.

Sulu-Plaza
HOTEL $$

(Map p214; 288 3400; www.sulu-plaza.com; r P2300;) For a very reasonable price you get a stylish room filled with two bamboo chairs, comfy thick beds and attractive art, plus a beachfront location right at Station 3. Or opt for the spacious corner apartments for two on the upper floor (P3600).

Melinda's Garden BUNGALOW **$$**
(Map p214; ☑288 3021; www.melindasgarden. com; r with fan P1500, with air-con P2500-3500; ❄☎) If you're looking for old Boracay, this 25-year-old institution offers nipa huts in a private courtyard, although they're a bit dark. The upper-storey rooms (P1500) are also very atmospheric, with rattan hammocks on large balconies where you can easily blow an entire afternoon.

Blue Mango Inn HOTEL **$$**
(Map p214; ☑288 5170; www.bluemangoinn. com; r incl breakfast P2800-4900; ❄@☎) The stylish cottages with small patios in the leafy back courtyard are probably your best bet here, although some rooms are musty. The dive centre has closed.

🛏 Central White Beach (Stations 1–3)

If you stay here you are committed to being in the thick of things. The trappings of Boracay's success are everywhere: resorts, restaurants, bars, beach vendors, touts, masseuses, souvenir shops, transvestites and petty thieves. That said, most resorts are set well back from the beach, so you can still get a decent night's sleep.

You'll pay a slight premium for staying on this stretch, but there's a complex of budget resorts around Tans Guesthouse, roughly behind Summer Place, that pack in local tourists. Overseas visitors usually prefer Angol.

Trafalgar Garden Cottages BUNGALOW **$**
(Map p214; ☑288 3711; trafalgarboracay@hotmail.com; r with fan/air-con P650/1500; ❄☎) A backpacker's delight, this leafy little village of budget rooms is close to the main road yet not as noisy as you might think. The P650 stand-alone cottages are as cheap as it gets on Boracay, and have small porches with hammocks. It's just a short walk to the beach.

★**Frendz Resort** RESORT **$$**
(Map p212; ☑288 3803; www.frendzresortboracay.com; dm P600, r with fan/air-con P1600/1800; ❄@☎) Dedicated management, improved prices, cosy rooms and a community atmosphere have turned this hostel into backpacker heaven. Live music (Wednesday and Sunday), pub food and cheap cocktails

enliven the bar, while dedicated beach beds (a two-minute walk) complement your nipa hut. Single-sex dorms; 11pm curfew.

Boracay Beach Resort BEACH RESORT **$$**
(Map p212; ☑288 3208; www.boracaybeachresort.com; cottages P2750-4356, ste P7385-11,420; ❄☎) The standard cottages have seen better days here, but the deluxe models have fully tiled marble bathrooms, curved surfaces, inviting linens, and large and well-furnished verandahs. Try asking for a free transfer from Caticlan.

Taj Guesthouse HOTEL **$$**
(Map p212; ☑288 4628; tajboracay@gmail.com; d/q P2000/2500; ❄☎) One of several nondescript hotels in this area. Check out the flashier annex.

★**Calypso Resort** BEACH RESORT **$$$**
(Map p214; ☑288 2038; www.calypso-boracay. com; r P5650-9830; ❄@☎) Superbly appointed deluxe rooms (oh, the beds!) with an inviting contemporary-meets-local design and great views define this dive-centric hotel, which also offers walk-in discounts. There are also some budget digs for long-term divers out back (P2000).

Nigi Nigi Nu Noos BEACH RESORT **$$$**
(Map p214; ☑288 3101, 0923 701 2163; www. niginigi.com; walk-in r from P5000; ❄☎) The polygonal two-storey cottages, set in a lush garden, have huge rooms, balconies, and loads of Balinese atmosphere; they're easily the most elegant choice on this stretch of beach if you're into tropical style.

ⓘ BORACAY BOOKING TIPS

➡ Some hotels give discounts to walk-in guests – ask before reserving.

➡ About half of Boracay hotels charge credit-card users a 3% to 5% surcharge.

➡ Always ask for a 'promo rate', especially in the low season (even if rooms are already discounted).

➡ Bargain hard always, but especially in the low season. Rates drop 20% to 50% from June to October.

Sandcastles
APARTMENTS $$$

(Map p212; ☎ 288 3207, 0920 558 7188; www.boracaysandcastles.com; 1-bedroom P9890-12,765; ❄@🛜) The large one- to two-bedroom apartments are truly stylish, with luxurious sofas and beds, and nicely appointed kitchens. The costlier beachfront rooms are just steps from the beach path, and maximise views. Built to survive beach-goers, they're comfy nonetheless. Heavily discounted (up to 50%) in low season; rather pricey otherwise.

🛏 North of Station 1

Any promotional photo of Boracay you've seen was probably taken at this heavenly stretch of White Beach. At low tide the expanse of white sand seems infinite, and the sunset *paraw* action – a Boracay trademark – is particularly intense. As are the prices.

★Discovery Shores
BEACH RESORT $$$

(Map p212; ☎288 4500; www.discovery-shoresboracay.com; 1-bedroom/2-bedroom P19,000/30,000; ❄🛜☷) This is without a doubt the greatest resort on White Beach. The fantastic modern design, like a small white city, is everywhere open and spacious, especially in the multi-level rooms, which are more like chic lofts. Elegant touches, like closets that illuminate upon opening, reflect great attention to detail.

From the private beach one flows into the bar, past the stylish pool and into the lobby as if borne on a wave. The staff is so smooth that they appear to have landed from Planet Hospitality. Add all the usual trimmings – spa, restaurants etc – and you have the recipe for a perfect stay. Honeymooners, get the relatives to pay up for this!

★Hampstead Boutique Hotel Boracay
BOUTIQUE HOTEL $$$

(Map p212; ☎288 2469; www.hampsteadboracay.com; r P5500; ❄🛜) If you want to be near White Beach, but prefer peace and quiet, this artsy new boutique hotel just a short walk from Station 1 is an ideal choice. Well-appointed rooms, including robes and espresso machines, a rooftop bar, spacious public spaces with lots of light, and some outstanding art make for a stylish getaway.

The in-house bistro specialises in crab and vintage luggage tags, a charming collection of which adorn the walls.

Nigi Nigi Too
BEACH RESORT $$$

(Map p212; ☎288 3150; www.niginigitoo.com; r incl breakfast P6195-7560; @🛜) This appealing pink-and-white hotel has two storeys of well-furnished rooms overlooking a central courtyard, with attractive balconies. The Asian decor melds well with an otherwise Mediterranean style to form a funky yet tasteful beachfront retreat.

Punta Rosa
BOUTIQUE HOTEL $$$

(☎0917 500 7878, 288 6740; www.puntarosa.com; d incl breakfast P4800-9000; ❄🛜) Stylish Punta Rosa is located just off the beach at the nearly deserted far northern end of White Beach. In-the-know Manila expats head here and reap rewards like peace, quiet, cosy platform beds, flat-screen TVs, DVD players and lots of throw pillows.

Boracay Beach Club
BEACH RESORT $$$

(Map p212; ☎288 4853, 0910 777 8888; www.boracaybeachclub.com; r incl breakfast US$110; ❄🛜) The 'BBC' is across the road from White Beach, but don't let that deter you. It has a lovely pool area with plenty of shade less than a minute's walk from the beach. Standard rooms are compact but uber-comfortable with not a thing out of place. The sizeable Admiral Suite (US$120), with views to both pool and sea, is excellent value.

Sea Wind
BEACH RESORT $$$

(Map p212; ☎288 3091; www.seawindboracay.ph; r P9250-10,350; ❄@🛜☷) This hotel is an odd mix, as it has expanded in waves from an old beach hotel. The original courtyard reception area is a jumble, but the adjoining rooms have an attractive vintage feel, though disadvantaged by road noise. The villas across the street are real gems, however; pay up a small amount for the super deluxe rooms, which really are. In any case you get an exquisite patch of sand.

Diniwid Beach

Continue north from White Beach along the narrow concrete path that hugs the point and you get to peaceful and quiet Diniwid Beach. It's a beautiful spot, highlighted by a strip of the softest white sand you'll find anywhere and an extraordinary collection of hillside bungalows perched over the sea.

Beach House   BEACH RESORT $$
(0928 931 1075, 288 3934; cja1025@yahoo.com; d incl breakfast P2500-3500; ❋@❋) The best midranger here, Beach House's rooms are clean and have style, but what really makes it is the front-and-centre location on Diniwid Beach. Shoot for a beachfront room.

★Spider House   BEACH RESORT $$$
(0949 501 1099; www.spiderhouseresort.com; r from P3150; ❋) This iconic hotel is a bamboo warren of rooms and decks suspended over the sea in a gravity-defying act. The magic begins at the entrance, where a narrow beachside path leads through a cave, and ends with ladders to the highest rooms. If you don't mind thin walls, this is an utterly unique getaway, as much an experience as it is an accommodation. No air-con; some shared bathrooms.

★Diniview   BUNGALOWS $$$
(0917 799 2029; www.diniviewboracay.com; villas P10,000-12,000; ❋❋❋) High up the green valley behind Diniwid Beach, these five private hillside villas look ready for an architectural magazine photo shoot. The owner has lavished attention on every detail of their design and decoration; think 'high-end tropical'. Each sleeps four to six, and comes with everything you can imagine, including all mod cons and a fully stocked kitchen.

A pool is shared. You are quite a walk from the beach, but an electric shuttle is coming soon. Minimum three-night stay.

★Nami Boracay   BEACH RESORT $$$
(288 6753; www.namiresorts.com; r incl breakfast P10,675-13,725; ❋❋) Perched above a fantastic beach like a deluxe tree house, Nami offers privacy, breathtaking views, and a bamboo elevator to save your legs. The 12 luxury rooms have their own outdoor jacuzzis above the ocean, while the restaurant serves a champagne brunch (P650 to P875, 10am to 2pm) with an eclectic menu offering everything from Filipino and Asian fusion to burgers and goat's cheese filet mignon. A honeymooner favourite.

Banyugan Beach

Shangri-La Boracay Resort & Spa   BEACH RESORT $$$
(288 4988; www.shangri-la.com; r P13,900-15,900, 1br villa P32,000-40,000; ❋❋❋) There's no doubt about it: this is Boracay's most impressive resort. Occupying the northwest tip of the island, it offers everything you might wish for: two private beaches (including beautiful Banyugan Beach), huge pool, tropical lodge, beach bar, massive gym, impressive spa etc. But here's the rub: this self-contained world could be absolutely anywhere in the tropics.

In an effort to be exclusive, the resort has built a mighty high wall between itself and the rest of the island, to the point where its own boats will whisk you directly from Caticlan to its own private dock, thereby avoiding any contact with the rest of Boracay. So if you are looking for Shangri-la, you have definitely found it, but if you are looking for Boracay – keep looking.

Bulabog Beach

Across Boracay's narrow middle from White Beach – just 10 minutes' walk from D'Mall, the pedestrian arcade at White Beach's midpoint – is watersports haven Bulabog Beach, with its laid-back community vibe. The water here isn't as clean, since much of Boracay's sewage empties on this side of the island, although upgrades are underway. Investors must be confident in the future, as a large number of outstanding new accommodations have opened here in recent years. Rates rise during the December-to-March kitesurfing season. During the low season a charming bangka fleet beaches itself.

★MNL Hostel   HOSTEL $
(Map p212; 0917 702 2160; www.mnlhostels.com; Rd 1a; incl breakfast dm P650-700, s P1000; ❋❋) This high-rise hostel has quickly become the backpacker's choice on Bulabog. Super-clean, intelligently designed (eg private outlets at your dorm bed) and lots of fun, with a rooftop lounge and karaoke once a week. No curfew, hot rain showers and free breakfast don't hurt either. Double rooms are twice the single rate, making them somewhat less attractive.

Banana Saging   BEACH RESORT $
(Map p214; 288 6121; www.boracayguest-house.com; r with fan/air-con from P1000/1500;

❄ 📶) Super deal steps from Bulabog Beach; rooms are clean and have design flourishes like funky lights and sculptures.

★Palassa Private
Residences   BOUTIQUE HOTEL $$$
(Map p212; ☑288 2703; www.palassapriva-teresidencesboracay.com; studio P4900, 1br apt 6600-6900; 📶❄) When super-talented local artist Antonio Gelito San Jose Jr allowed this classy new hotel to be constructed on his land, he did so with the proviso that his beachfront art studio be incorporated into it. The owners went one step further and incorporated his art into every room. The result works extremely well.

San Jose's colourful portraits fit the minimalist rooms just right. Some are even playfully hung on easels. It feels like you're living in a gallery, as opposed to an apartment building, striking just the right note on beautiful Bulabog Beach.

★Pahuwayan Suites   BEACH RESORT $$$
(Map p212; ☑288 1449, 0917 807 5810; www.pa-huwayan.com; r incl breakfast P3750-4250; ❄📶) Kitesurfers with an eye for style and some

extra money to blow might consider this nicely outfitted place. All the rooms have flat-screen TVs, awesome beds, fancy fixtures and semi-private patios done right. Top-floor rooms have prime ocean views that include a vast *paraw* fleet in the off-season.

★Aissatou Beach Resort   BOUTIQUE HOTEL $$$
(Map p214; ☑288 5787, 0917 492 1537; www.kiteboracay.com; r from P3500; 📶) The nine rooms here are impeccably maintained and generously fitted out with handcrafted furniture, imported toilets and locally commissioned art. Number 12, a fantastic upper-floor water-view one-bedroom, is one of the best deals around. Private chaise lounges line the beach out front.

Seven Stones Boracay Suites   APARTMENTS $$$
(Map p212; ☑288 1601; www.7stonesboracay. com; r P11,025, ste 15,345-26,460; ❄📶❄) This beautifully designed if pricey apartment complex has its own private swimming area on Bulabog Beach, and a nice pool to match. The 30 rentals are of the highest quality, with all the mod cons, including entertainment centres and lots of glass for admiring

TOP THREE BORACAY SPAS

You've come to the land of the spa treatment. It pays not to skimp in this department, so here are the three top spas on the island. If you're new to all this, try the signature massage.

Mandala Spa (Map p214; ☑288 5857; www.mandalaspa.com; Angol; 90min signature massage P2995, yoga P400; ☉10am-10pm) Located on a lush hilltop on the edge of Angol, yet worlds away from White Beach, this spa immerses you in nature, providing a wonderfully tranquil ambience. You can come for a treatment, or a more extended retreat that includes an entire detox program. Uniquely, a tree is planted in your name for every night's stay.

There are a dozen beautiful, light-filled tropical villas for rent ($270 includes breakfast, yoga and a 15-minute massage) with all the right touches, including large baths, and also a popular pool villa ($420). Treatments run from around P2600 for a facial to around P9500 for the 'Princess Treatment'. Perfect for either a romantic or therapeutic stay.

Tirta Spa (☑260-2488; www.tirtaspa.com; Sitio Malabunot, Manoc-Manoc; 90min signature massage P3355; ☉9am-9pm) The most exotic spa on Boracay, Tirta feels like you are entering Angkor Wat. The owner is a serious collector of Asian art, and has impeccable taste. The grounds are a beautiful fusion of doors, sculptures, fountains and more drawn from India, Thailand, the Philippines and beyond.

A long list of treatments take place in three royal suites and three outdoor pavilions fit for a pasha, making for a fantasy visit. Uniquely, the owner also rents two rooms (P4400 to P6050) in her own attractive on-site house.

Chi (☑288 4988; www.shangri-la.com/; Shangri-La Resort; 75min signature massage P5800; ☉10am-10pm) Located within the enormous Shangri-La Resort, Chi is a sanctuary within a sanctuary. And a beautiful one at that. There are four different treatment villas, each named after a Tibetan village, with all the right Asian design flourishes. Forget the massage, you'll want to move in! Treatment options are more limited than the competition, but more than enough to wash all cares away; their focus is removing blockages from your 'chi', or living energy.

the views. The attractive use of light stone and tiles gives it a Mediterranean feel. A classy new addition to the beach.

Hangin Kite Center & Resort · BEACH RESORT $$$
(Map p212; ☎288 3766; www.kite-asia.com; Rd 1a; r P3000-3500; ❃🛜) The ground-floor garden and upper-floor sea-view rooms here are good, but are as minimal as board, kite and wind, with tile floors, flat screens and nice baths. And when the day is done, you can relax at the Hang Out bar, a popular watering hole.

✖ Eating

White Beach Path is one long fantastic food court – half the fun of dining is taking a walk at sunset and checking it out. You'll also find an impressive variety of ethnic restaurants clustered around D'Mall, the busy pedestrian arcade at White Beach's midpoint.

✖ Angol & Station 3

★ Sunny Side Cafe · CAFE $$
(Map p214; ☎288 2874; www.thesunnysideboracay.com; meals P225-395; ⏰7am-9.30pm; 🛜) If you're looking for breakfast outside your hotel, come here first. You'll be amazed by the depth of the cuisine at this contemporary beachfront cafe, where even standard entries get a fresh spin. It's known for its all-day breakfast, but you may find yourself stopping by anytime for the bacon and mango grilled cheese sandwiches or the chorizo baked mac-n-cheese. Beware the huge portions!

★ Cowboy Cucina · INTERNATIONAL $$
(Map p214; mains P180-600; ⏰7am-11pm; 🛜) True to its name, the menu is ranch-perfect: burgers, steaks, chilli, a splash of Mexican, and the island's best ribs, all of it eaten with your toes in the sand. A welcome anomaly: veggie options! There's also a kids' menu and a Sunday roast buffet. Chow down!

✖ Central White Beach

Budget Mart · SUPERMARKET $
(Map p212; D'Mall; ⏰7.30am-11.30pm) Best selection of groceries.

Crazy Crepes · CREPERIE $
(Map p212; crepe P95-150; ⏰10am-11.30pm) This bubblegum-coloured box on the beach in front of D'Mall offers a great variety of sinful dessert crepes, the perfect ending to a meal.

Smoke · FILIPINO $$
(Map p212; meals P120-180; ⏰24hr; 🍴) Smoke is excellent value, with freshly cooked Filipino food, appetising coconut-milk curries and breakfast. The branch closest to the main road is open from 7am to 10pm.

Jammers · MEXICAN $$
(Map p212; sandwiches P100-300; ⏰24hr) Delicious, quick and affordable fish sandwiches, tacos and burgers on a prime patch of real estate.

★ Plato D'Boracay · SEAFOOD $$
(Map p214; D'Talipapa Market; cook to order P150-250; ⏰8am-9pm) Choose lobster, prawns and other shellfish from the D'Talipapa market, and this family-style grill will cook them for P150 to P250. The result is prices that substantially undercut the seafood barbecues on the beach.

Cyma · GREEK $$
(Map p212; D'Mall; mains P170-350; ⏰10am-11pm; 🍴) This popular and well-run Greek restaurant is known for grilled meat, appetisers such as flaming *saganaki* (fried salty cheese) and outstanding salads. Affordable gyros are available for thriftier diners. Service is slick and professional, and the Mediterranean-blue dining room makes you forget you're in D'Mall.

Real Coffee & Tea Cafe · CAFE $$
(Map p212; ☎288 5340; Station 1; breakfasts P200-350; ⏰7am-7pm; 🍴) This old favourite has a great new upper-storey location facing Station 2, but the winning recipe remains the same: creative teas and coffees, exotic drinks, and homestyle American cooking. The name harkens back to a time, not so long ago, when you could only get Nescafé on Boracay.

Zest Boracay · FILIPINO $$
(Map p214; Original D'Talipapa; meals P100-250; ⏰8am-8pm) A bright oasis near the original D'Talipapa Market, this clean budget eatery offers Filipino staples and the full complement of breakfasts.

Heidiland · DELI $$
(Map p212; D'Mall; ⏰7am-7pm) Amazingly well-stocked deli offers beach-picnic supplies, along with sandwiches, bread and gourmet imports. After another rice breakfast, you'll be caressing that jar of Nutella.

THE ENVIRONMENTAL CHALLENGE

Boracay's small size and rapid development has put it under particularly intense environmental pressure. Problems include an inadequate sewage system, frequent electricity brownouts, waste-management problems and a lack of regulatory enforcement. One highly visible result has been green algae blooms along White Beach from February to May.

Now local government is fighting back. A Beach Management Program has been put in place, led by an anti-smoking policy backed up by fines. All structures within 30m of the sea have been removed. The company that handles the sewage system in Manila has been brought in to install a new central system by 2017. A windfarm is going up near Caticlan to improve the power situation. Most ambitiously, all gas tricycles on the island are slated to be replaced by electric models in the next few years. For those who identify the Philippines with the tricycle, the silent E-Trike is a cheerful reminder that progress can occur in the most unexpected places.

★ Aplaya   MEDITERRANEAN $$$

(Map p212; ☑ 288 2841; www.fb.com/aplayaboracay; mains P350-600; ⊙ 8am-1am) This open-air Mediterranean restaurant and mellow beach bar is Boracay at its best. Design furniture inside, beanbag chairs on the sand, a massive tropical drink menu, ambient grooves, uber-cool sheesha pipes and endlessly creative cuisine can capture you here for hours. Just make sure you include a sunset.

★ Cozina   SPANISH $$$

(Map p212; ☑ 288 4477; www.fb.com/cozinaauthenticspanish; mains P380-680; ⊙ 7am-11pm) Barcelona on the beach: this classy Spanish restaurant wins with its warm interior design, fine wine selection, beautifully presented food, progressive menu and great location.

Dos Mestizos   SPANISH $$$

(Map p214; ☑ 288 5786; tapas from P300; ⊙ 10am-11pm) Outstanding traditional Spanish cuisine infused with local flavours – including sophisticated tapas, authentic paella, bean soups and hearty stews – makes this an island treat favoured by other restaurateurs, not to mention St James himself, whose statue graces one wall. The amiable owner is steeped in Boracay's fascinating modern history. See the wall of photos depicting the 'founders of modern Boracay'; each one has quite a story behind it.

Lemon Cafe   INTERNATIONAL $$$

(Map p212; ☑ 288 6781; D'Mall; mains P300-550; ⊙ 7am-11pm) Fresh and healthy define this colourful D'Mall cafe, which serves big salads, creative sandwiches, classic eggs Benedict brunches, tropical juices and tasty quiches. At P450, the lunch-box special – soup of the day, green salad, choice of sandwich or rice dish and dessert – is a wise pit stop.

Pamana   FILIPINO $$$

(Map p212; ☑ 288 2674; www.pamanarestaurant.com; Station 1; mains P250-700; ⊙ 10am-11pm) Boracay offers surprisingly little high-end Filipino cuisine, but this is a noteworthy exception. With branches in Manila and Tagaytay, Pamana has managed to make its name by elevating tastebuds with vintage dishes. The smallish restaurant with family memorabilia matches the home recipes. Alfresco dining available.

Aria Restaurant   ITALIAN $$$

(Map p212; ☑ 036 288 5573; mains P288-573; ⊙ 11am-11.30pm) Aria has a prime people-watching location on the beach path at D'Mall's entrance. The stylish and modern dining room serves fabulous Italian food, like wonderful *tagliatelle con tartufu* (white truffle). All the pasta is homemade.

Mañana Mexican   MEXICAN $$$

(Map p212; mains P275-550; ⊙ 11am-10pm; ☑) Boracay's top Mexican restaurant serves classic burritos and tortillas, and mixes a mean mango margarita.

Crafty's   INDIAN, THAI $$$

(Map p212; Main Rd; dishes P250-350; ⊙ 11am-late) Never mind what's on White Beach, truly the best Indian food on Boracay emerges from the kitchen of this rooftop bar looming over D'Mall. And yes, it's actually spicy. It's also known for burgers and ribs.

✕ North of Station 1

Jonah's Fruit Shakes   FILIPINO $$

(Map p212; shakes around P110; ⊙ 7am-11pm) Amid plenty of competition, Jonah's proudly boasts the best shakes on the island – the avocado and banana mix is sensational. Also has an extensive menu of Filipino faves.

Kasbah
MOROCCAN $$$

(Map p212; mains P200-900; ⏰9am-9pm Mon-Fri, to 11pm Sat & Sun) This posh resort strip is the last place you'd expect to find an unpretentious Moroccan restaurant like Kasbah. We're not complaining. The delectable *kemias* (appetisers) like hummus and *mechoum* (roasted peppers with spices) are worthy of Marrakech. Postmeal, kick back with some watermelon sheesha.

✗ Bulabog Beach

Sushi Shiro
JAPANESE $$$

(Map p212; ✆288 2587; Road 1a; nigiri lunch P650; ⏰noon-10pm) The real art of sushi is found here. Everything is either hand-selected at the local market or homemade on site – even staples like miso and soy sauce. Interesting menu options go above and beyond the normal fare.

🍷 Drinking & Nightlife

Evenings on White Beach kick off with one long happy hour, mostly starting around 4pm or 5pm and finishing somewhere between 7pm and 9pm. Many bars don't usually close down until between 1am and 3am or when the last customer stumbles home.

Follow thumping beats to find the discos; five of them carry momentum into the wee hours, even in the low season. Live music is practically everywhere between about 6pm and 11pm.

If you like your parties mobile, there's also a popular pub crawl (✆917 808 8433; www. pubcrawl.ph/boracay; female/male P690/790; ⏰7.30-11.30pm Mon, Wed, Fri & Sat) four times per week, run by a company of the same name. Ten free shots included in the cover.

★ Area 51 Secret Party Facility
CLUB

(Map p214; ✆288 2343; Lugutan Beach; cover P100-200) Apart from having one of the greatest club names ever, Area 51 is (low voice) the only underground party spot on the island. Its schedule is appropriately linked to the phases of the moon, ie there are full-moon and black-moon parties each month, as well as others in the high season.

Here you'll meet the locals, of course, and experience the unique island vibe that is all Boracay. Expect food stalls, music, tribal drumming, fire dancing and the usual refreshments, uniting one and all. These are some of the biggest parties around, 400 to 500 strong, particularly on special holidays like Halloween and New Year's Eve, and last from midnight to sunrise. Look for the sign on the fence in front of the Dead Forest, on the road by Lugutan Beach. Aliens welcome.

★ Epic
CLUB

(Map p212; www.epicboracay.com; admission Fri & Sat P300; ⏰10pm-3am) This flashy club with its world-class DJs remains the most popular of the beach discos, and is also known for its Wednesday night table-football matches. During the day, it's a bar and grill; happy hour lasts from noon to 10pm – far longer than you will.

★ Cocomangas
BAR, DISCO

(Map p212; ⏰11am-3am) Attempting Cocomangas' 'Drink for Your Country' shooters challenge is a Boracay tradition, but is just the beginning of the antics that animate this packed-to-the-rafters all-night high-energy bar and disco. The recipe includes Asian package tourists, hard-drinking expats, local disco freaks, backpackers and the usual working girls. Mix well and watch what happens.

Red Pirates
PUB

(Map p214; Angol; ⏰10am-2pm) Way down at the south end of White Beach, this supremely mellow bar throws funky driftwood furniture onto the sand and best captures the spirit of the 'Old Boracay'.

White House Beach Lounge
BEACH BAR

(Map p212; www.whitehouseboracay.com; north of Station 1; ⏰7am-10pm) A shot of Ibiza, this tasteful all-white beach bar, the first north of Station 1, is also the venue for big rave parties in season.

Nigi Nigi Nu Noos
BAR

(Map p214; ⏰10am-midnight) The legendary mason jars of Long Island iced tea (they're two-for-one during happy hour: 5pm to 7pm) more than capably kick-start any evening. And you may just stay for the revamped menu, featuring juicy steaks.

Exit Bar
BEACH BAR

(Map p212; Station 2; ⏰5pm-2am) This chilled-out watering hole could be renamed Expat Bar. And as Boracay's expats are a colourful lot, that's not a bad thing.

Bom Bom
BAR

(Map p212; Station 2; ⏰8am-midnight) With nightly bongo-infused live music, laid-back Bom Bom practically defines cool and is the best spot to kill time between dinner and late-night dancing.

Crafty's
BAR

(Map p212; Main Rd; ⊙restaurant 9am-10pm, bar 11am-close) This breezy expat hideaway atop Craft's Supermarket is great for views and Indian food; the forthcoming elevator will make it irresistible. Best during happy hour (4pm to 7pm), which is full of local colour.

Juice
CLUB

(Map p214; btwn Stations 2 & 3; ⊙4pm-3am) The smallest, most down-to-earth and gay-friendly of the central beach discos, with equal numbers of people dancing and just hanging out by the bar.

Summer Place
CLUB

(Map p212; www.summerplaceboracay.com; Station 2; ⊙11am-close) This seething disco is known for staying open the latest, making it White Beach's last call; at times it's a little less savoury for it.

Information

INTERNET ACCESS
Internet (per hour P30 to P70) and wi-fi (usually free) access are everywhere.

MEDICAL SERVICES
For serious ailments, diving boats can provide fast transport to the mainland and then patients are taken to Kalibo or flown to Manila.
Boracay Lying-In & Diagnostic Center (Map p212; ☑288 4448; D'Mall; ⊙24hr) The expats' private clinic of choice.

MONEY
BPI (Map p212; D'Mall) and **Metrobank** (Map p212; D'Mall) have user-friendly ATMs, and there are a few others along the main road and the beach path. Many resorts and the tourist centre also handle foreign exchange.

POST
Avoid the postal counter at the tourist centre, which charges a whopping 50% service fee, and use the **post office** (Map p212; Main Rd; ⊙9am 5pm Mon Sat) at the northern end of the Main Rd.

TOURIST INFORMATION
Boracay Tourist Center (Map p214; Station 3; ⊙9am-10pm) Everything you need: postal and telephone services, general Boracay information, money changing (including Amex travellers cheques) and a fast internet connection (P70 per hour).
Filipino Travel Center (Map p214; ☑036-288 3704, 036 288 3705; www.filipinotravel.com. ph; Station 3; ⊙9am-6pm) In the Boracay Tourist Center; helpful and professional, and offers ticketing services.

VISAS
Bureau of Immigration (Map p212; ☑036-288 5267; Main Rd; ⊙8am-5pm Mon-Wed, to noon Thu) Easy visa renewals.

❶ Getting There & Away

AIR
Boracay has no commercial airport. Travellers arrive via one of two airports on nearby Panay, Caticlan or Kalibo. The swiftest route is via Caticlan, which is also the closest seaport. However, flights fill up during the high season. A cheaper alternative is the airport in Kalibo, from where it's an easy 1½ to two hours by road to Caticlan.

BOAT
A fleet of bangkas shuttles people back and forth between Caticlan and Boracay (P200, 15 minutes) every 15 minutes between 5am and 7pm, and then as the need arises between 7pm and 10pm (sometimes later if a ferry is late). The fare is a combination of terminal, environmental and boat fees. All boats arrive at Boracay's **Cagban Pier** (Map p211), where a queue of tricycles awaits to take you to your hotel. They cost P25 per person or P150 per tricycle (more if you are going north of Station 1).

From June to November, brisk southwesterly winds mean you'll often be shuttled round the northern tip of Caticlan to Tabon, where the same fleet of boats will take you to Boracay's alternative pier at **Tambisaan** (Map p211).

If you arrive after the last regular bangka has departed, you will have to charter a private bangka or sleep at one of the basic pension houses in town.

VAN
All-inclusive round-trip transfer from Caticlan Airport to your hotel, via a combination of van and boat, ranges from P800 to P1500 per person, depending on location. Call **Southwest** (☑288 2026), **Island Star Express** (☑288 3888), or **BLTMPC** (☑288 3271). Many hotels outsource these services, or have their own, sometimes complimentary service; enquire for a better deal.

❶ Getting Around

To get from one end of White Beach to the other, either walk, take a pedicab (nonmotorised push tricycle) along the walking strip (P10 to P100) or flag down a tricycle along the main road. Tricycles cost only P10 provided you steer clear of the 'special trips' offered by stationary tricycles (P100). Try a silent new E-Trike, whose roominess feels luxurious.

PANAY

POP 4,030,000

For most visitors to the Philippines, Panay is the island they land on in order to get to Boracay. Think of Panay as distinct provinces, as the locals do, all of which can be circumnavigated on Panay's excellent road network.

In the northwest, Aklan Province (which includes Boracay) is known for hosting the amazing Ati-Atihan Festival, the country's largest fiesta, in its capital, Kalibo, every January. Capiz Province, to the northeast, has long been known for the fishponds dotting its capital, Roxas, and increasingly for the massive religious statues being erected in

Panay

Map of Panay showing towns including Kalibo, Roxas, Iloilo City, San José (Antique), Boracay, Caticlan, and the provinces of Aklan, Capiz, Antique, Iloilo, and Guimaras, with neighboring islands Romblon, Masbate, and Negros. See Boracay Map (p211). See Guimaras Map (p238).

the surrounding hills. Antique, on the west coast, is the least developed province, making exploration doubly interesting; ecotourism is increasingly taking hold among its attractive mountains and rivers. Iloilo Province, to the east, contains the most sophisticated city on Panay and numerous coastal islands begging for exploration.

ⓘ Getting There & Away

The main airports are in Iloilo in the south, and Caticlan and Kalibo in the north. Kalibo has a few international connections, including new service from AirAsia direct from Kuala Lumpur, and is a budget alternative for people heading to Boracay.

On the seas, car ferries to Caticlan from Roxas (Mindoro), and fastcraft to Iloilo from Bacolod, Negros, are the most popular boat connections. But you can reach a host of additional islands from the main ports of Caticlan, Kalibo, Roxas, Iloilo and Dumangas.

Caticlan

🕿 036 / TRANSPORT HUB

Caticlan is little more than a springboard to Boracay. People either fly in to its tiny airport or take a bus from Kalibo Airport. Visitors can walk from the airport to the pier in five minutes or take a tricycle (P50). Buses unload at the pier, as do roll-on, roll-off (RORO) vessels. Guides lead all arrivals through the terminal and onto outrigger boats for the short journey to Boracay.

ⓘ Getting There & Away

Caticlan is expanding its airport to become an international hub for the western Visayas by 2016. Meanwhile, the existing airport continues service. Currently planes cannot land in Caticlan after dark, so delays past 6.30pm result in planes being rerouted to Kalibo.

Caticlan Airport is served by AirPhil Express and Cebu Pacific for flights to Manila (hourly) and Cebu (two to three daily). Seair serves Clark and Puerto Princesa several times per week.

Kalibo

🕿 036 / POP 70,000

The capital of Aklan Province, Kalibo is, for travellers, primarily an alternative port of entry to Boracay and the site of the granddaddy of all Philippine festivals, the raucous Ati-Atihan Festival in January. At other times of the year it's a fairly typical loud and congested Philippine provincial city draped in spaghetti-like electrical lines.

BOATS & BUSES FROM CATICLAN

Boats

DEPARTS	DESTINATION	FARE (P)	DURATION (HR)	DAILY FREQUENCY
Caticlan Port	Boracay	200	¼	frequent*
Caticlan Port	Carabao (Lanas)	85	1	1
Caticlan Port	Carabao (San José)	75	¾	1
Caticlan Port	Roxas (Mindoro)	430-460	4	5-6
Caticlan Port	Batangas	950	10	1, except Tue
Caticlan Port	Tablas (Odiongan)	300	2	Thu & Sun
Caticlan Port	Tablas (Looc)	300	2½	1

Bangkas depart for Boracay every 15min from 5am-7pm, then as necessary until 10pm (sometimes later if a ferry is late). Private bangkas can be hired 24hr.

Buses

DEPARTS	DESTINATION	COMPANY	TYPE	FARE (P)	DURATION (HR)	DAILY FREQUENCY
Caticlan Port	Iloilo	Ceres	bus	350	6	hourly
Caticlan Port	Iloilo	various	van	400	4	morning
Caticlan Port	Kalibo	Ceres	bus	107	2	hourly
Caticlan Port	Kalibo	various	van	100-200	1½	hourly
Caticlan Port	Kalibo	various	jeepney	80	2½	intermittent
Caticlan Port	Antique	Ceres	bus	250	3½	every 2hr

Aklan was settled in 1213 by Malay settlers from Borneo. The local dialect is Aklanon. It's one of the Philippine's youngest provinces, having broken away from neighbouring Capiz in 1956.

◉ Sights & Activities

Kalibo can get *very* hot. Enjoy the extremely large pool at the Marzon Hotel for only P80.

Museo It Akean   MUSEUM

(☑268 9260; Martelino St; admission P15; ☺8am-noon Mon-Sat, 1-5pm Sun) This little downtown museum, in a nicely restored school building between the market and Pastrana Park, offers a rare look at Aklan history, culture and traditions. It is worth the visit as it only takes 30 minutes and there is nothing else like it.

⚡ Festivals & Events

Ati-Atihan Festival   CULTURAL

(☺Jan) This fantastic festival is the nation's biggest and best mardi gras. It most likely dates back to the days of the Borneo settlers. Described by its promoters as a mix of 'Catholic ritual, social activity, indigenous drama and tourist attraction', it's a week-long street party raging from sunrise to sundown, peaking on the third Sunday of January.

🛏 Sleeping

For Ati-Atihan you should book a hotel months in advance and expect to pay two to five times the normal price.

Ati-Atihan County Inn   HOSTEL $

(☑268 6116; atiatihancounty@yahoo.com; D Maagma St; dm/d/tr/q P150/840/960/1400; ❄🛜) Just a few blocks south of the city centre, this government-run hotel offers good value, particularly during the Ati-Atihan Festival, when its rates don't change. The basic rooms are clean and air-conditioned, while the 16-bed fan dorm is spotless. Wi-fi costs P100.

Garcia Legaspi Mansion   HOTEL $

(☑262 5588; garcialegaspimansion@yahoo.com; 1016 Roxas Ave; r with fan/air-con from P800/P880; ❄🛜) The best thing about this place is the eccentric and in-the-know owner, Gerwin. Rooms are well furnished and well maintained, but overlook the noisy main street. One block east of the market.

★Marzon Hotel   HOTEL $$

(☑268 2188; www.marzonhotelkalibo.com; Quezon Ave Ext; d/tr/q incl breakfast P1800/2352/3136;

❄🛜❄) Kalibo's top hotel, this extremely well-appointed place only five minutes from the airport would be P6000 in Boracay, but then again you don't have the beach. You do, however, have a 25m pool. It's 2.5km from the city centre.

Kalibo Hotel   HOTEL $$

(☑268 4765; www.kalibo-hotel.com; 467 N Roldan St; r P1232-1960; ❄🛜) This friendly, clean and professionally run midranger is just two blocks from City Hall, yet manages some quiet. The best rooms are street-facing suites.

✕ Eating

Kitty's Kitchen   INTERNATIONAL $

(☑268 9444; Rizal St; dishes P75-400; ☺10am-9pm; ❄) An air-conditioned oasis in the centre, Kitty's has Mexican food and other Western surprises like Kansas City ribs.

★Roz and Angelique's Cafe   FILIPINO $$

(☑268 3512; www.rozandangeliques.com; Quezon Ave; mains P200-325; ☺9am-10pm) This metal-roofed plantation hut has a surprising burst of style and dishes up some tasty fare in large portions. It's known for *patatim* (pig leg) and Peking duck. This place is moving to an undetermined location in the near future, but it's very popular, so any tricycle will find it.

Latte Cafe & Internet Station   CAFE $$

(Jaime Cardinal Sin Ave; mains P150-300; ☺7am-7pm Mon-Sat; ❄🛜) Hip and modern Latte is a delightful refuge from Kalibo's urban mayhem. There's a broad range of coffees, and internet is available (per hour P30).

★Primavera   ITALIAN $$$

(☑268 3533; 19 Martyrs St; mains P225-995; ☺10am-10pm) With big portions, a long specials menu, outdoor seating and a wine list, this new restaurant a few blocks east of Pastrana Park has raised the bar in Kalibo. The air-con doesn't hurt either. Think classic pastas, steaks and sandwiches. For dessert, head next door to Peil (same hours).

🍷 Drinking & Nightlife

★Lorraine's Tapsi   CAFE

(Mabini St; ☺10am-11pm Sun-Thu, to 1am Fri & Sat) This roadside cafe, with its tiki-hut feel, serves decent Filipino food, but really shines for its laid-back island vibe, ice-cold beers and weekend DJs. Popular with foreigners. Two blocks north of Roxas Ave/Mabini St intersection.

Abregana RESTOBAR
(☑262 1482; Martelino St; ☉3pm-1am) Kalibo's party spot, with nightly live music. It's 100m from the eastern end of Roxas Ave.

ℹ Information

Bureau of Immigration (BOI; ☑500 7601; Municipal Hall, United Veterans Ave; ☉8am-5pm Wed-Fri) Handles visa renewals. Staff divide working hours between here and a separate office in the airport.

Kalibo Tourism Office (☑262 1020; 2nd fl, Municipal Hall, United Veterans Ave; ☉8am-5pm Mon-Fri) Helpful staff can arrange local tours and help find you a room if everything is booked out for Ati-Atihan.

ℹ Getting There & Around

Travellers bound for Boracay can now fly straight to Kalibo from various Asian cities with discount carrier AirAsia. Service is seasonal, however, and highly dynamic.

There are no rental cars at the airport. Tricycles charge a flat P150 to take you to the centre of Kalibo. Alternatively, you can walk 500m out to the highway and flag down a tricycle or jeepney for P10. Buses leave from the **Ceres Bus Terminal** (☑0917 771 1230; Osmeña Ave). Vans depart from several points in the centre, the main cluster being near La Esperanza Hotel at the corner of Toting Reyes and Quezon Ave.

Kalibo Airport is served by AirPhil Express, AirAsia, Seair and Cebu Pacific for flights to Manila (hourly). Cebu Pacific also flies to Cebu (daily). AirAsia offers seasonal services from East Asian destinations.

Ferries depart from Dumaguit, about 20km southeast of the city.

Roxas (Capiz)
☑036 / POP 160,000

Welcome to the self-described 'seafood capital of the Philippines'. The busy capital of Capiz Province and commercial capital of northern Panay, Roxas ships out tonnes of seafood daily, much of it from a huge network of local fishponds. A large new development, Pueblo de Panay, has greatly expanded the city's footprint to include a new transportation terminal. There's a few beach resorts to choose from, some very cheap lobster and a handful of sights, including a growing network of huge religious statues.

◉ Sights & Activities

Ang Panublion Museum MUSEUM
(☑522 8857; Hughes St; ☉9am-5pm Mon-Sat) **FREE** Originally built as a water-storage tank, this quirky museum on the plaza will give you a quick (30 minute) introduction to the city. A Heritage Walk booklet will lead you around the nearby area.

Baybay Beach BEACH
About 3km north of downtown Roxas is this 7km gray-sand beach lined with eateries and picnic shelters. It varies greatly in width depending on the location and tide. Watch fishermen unloading their catch at dawn and again at dusk.

Cadimahan PARK
(admission P10) Mangrove park with bamboo walkway. Offers two-hour tours on bamboo paddle boats (P150 per person), with the unique addition of a foot massage as you go.

BOATS & BUSES FROM KALIBO

Boats

DEPARTS	DESTINATION	FARE (P)	DURATION (HR)	DAILY FREQUENCY
Dumaguit	Manila	1000	18	Tue & Fri

Buses

DEPARTS	DESTINATION	FARE (P)	DURATION (HR)	DAILY FREQUENCY
Ceres Bus Terminal	Caticlan	87-105	1¾	frequent
Ceres Bus Terminal	Iloilo	186-240	5	frequent
Ceres Bus Terminal	San Jose, Antique	195	6	4 Fri-Mon
various, city centre	Caticlan	100	1½	frequent
various, city centre	Iloilo	200	3½	frequent
various, city centre	Roxas	120	2	frequent

🎊 Festivals & Events

Sinadya sa Halaran Festival CULTURAL
(☉early Dec) A colourful four-day event that celebrates the Immaculate Conception. It includes a solemn, candlelit parade on the Roxas River.

Capiztahan FESTIVAL
(☉Apr) Three-day festival celebrating the founding of Capiz, culminating in a parade of lights and fireworks.

🛏 Sleeping

Halaran Plaza Hotel LODGE $
(☑621 0649; Gov Abalo St; d with fan P550, with air-con P750-850; ❄⊛) An old-school wooden lodge in the centre, it's amazingly noisy but has character, fresh paint and huge rooms.

Hotel Veronica HOTEL $$
(☑621 0919; hotelveronicaroxascitycapiz@gmail.com; Sacred Heart of Mary Ave; r P1600; ❄⊛) This new business hotel in Pueblo de Panay is the place to stay if you want to be near the terminal. A restaurant with live music and a pool will give you something to do.

Roxas President's Inn HOTEL $$
(☑621 0208; www.roxaspresidentsinn.com; cnr Rizal & Lopez Jaena Sts; s/d from P1180/1800; ⊖⊛☎) A mix of old-world charm and modern amenities, this is the best place to stay in the centre. The rooms are stylishly furnished. There are only two economy singles.

San Antonio Resort BEACH RESORT $$
(☑621 6638; www.thesanantonioresort.com; Baybay Beach; d P1000-2840; ⊛☎⊠) This big, bustling resort, popular with Filipino families, is not actually on the beach (it's across the road), but does have a huge pool and lagoon. Rooms are fairly spartan unless you upgrade; the best rooms are on the lagoon.

🍴 Eating

Baybay Beach is lined with around a dozen seafood restaurants, about half in the concrete Seafood Court and the rest to the left looking seaward. The best strategy is simply to walk this stretch until you see something that strikes your fancy. Prices are amazingly inexpensive.

BORACAY & WESTERN VISAYAS ROXAS (CAPIZ)

BOATS & BUSES FROM ROXAS

Boats

DEPARTS	DESTINATION	COMPANY	TYPE	FARE (P)	DURATION (HR)	FREQUENCY
Culasi Seaport	Odiongan	Super Shuttle	RORO	650	7	Mon, Wed & Fri
Culasi Seaport	Batangas	Super Shuttle	RORO	800	15	Mon, Wed & Fri
Culasi Seaport	Manila	Moreta	ferry	1000	21	every 5 days
Culasi Seaport	Romblon City	2GO	RORO	1990	5	3pm Sat
Culasi Seaport	Batangas	2GO	RORO	958	14	3pm Sat
Culasi Seaport	Odiongan	various	bangka	350	4	varies; call port
Culasi Seaport	Sibuyan (San Fernando et al)	various	bangka	350	5	9am daily
Banica	Masbate (various ports)	various	bangka	250-500	2-7	daily

Buses & Vans

DEPARTS	DESTINATION	COMPANY	TYPE	FARE (P)	DURATION (HR)	FREQUENCY
Roxas City Terminal	Iloilo City	Ceres Liner	bus	150	3	hourly
Roxas City Terminal	Kalibo	GM's Tours	van	120	1½	hourly
Roxas City Terminal	Caticlan	GM's Tours	van	220	3	hourly

DON'T MISS

SACRED HEART OF JESUS STATUE

In addition to its seafood, Roxas is becoming known for its religious statues. The wealthy Catholic landowners behind the Pueblo de Panay development are populating the surrounding hills with enormous ones. About 1.5km from the terminal is the newly constructed Sacred Heart of Jesus Shrine (Pueblo de Panay), one of the largest Jesus statues this side of Rio (the builders claim 132ft, but this is highly debatable!) Originally the hands were supposed to be outstretched in welcome, but the sculptor made them vertical for structural reasons, creating an 'I surrender' look. You can climb inside to the top. Occupying a hilltop location, the site offers great views of the region, including the many fishponds that go unseen at sea level. A complementary statue of Mary is visible when approaching Roxas from the east. Other statues are due to follow on surrounding hills until the Trinity is complete.

Cebrew   CAFE $
(Gaisano Arcade, opposite Gaisano Mall; drinks & snacks P50-125; ⏱11.30am-2am Mon-Thu, to 3am Fri & Sat, to midnight Sun; 🛜) A nice air-conditioned and trendy escape from the city. Come here for coffee drinks, frappes, brownies, ice cream and, of course, free wi-fi.

 Drinking & Nightlife

Grand Ville at Gaisano Arcade   CLUB
(Arnaldo Blvd) Nightlife in Roxas is centred on the Grand Ville at Gaisano Arcade, where you'll find karaoke, two dance clubs, and a live street band on weekends. Busy to 3am Thursday to Saturday.

ℹ️ **Information**

The widely distributed EZ Map Panay includes a Roxas city map that's much better than the one handed out for free by the tourist offices.

City Tourism Office (📱621 5316; ⏱8am-5pm Mon-Fri) On the northern bank of the river by the bridge. Stop here to get a guide to the new downtown tourist trail currently under development.

Provincial Tourism Office (📱621 0042; Capitol Bldg; ⏱8am-5pm Mon-Fri) Good source of ideas for things to do around Capiz Province.

ℹ️ **Getting There & Away**

Airline offices are at the airport, a five-minute tricycle ride (P15) north of central Roxas. **Culasi Port** (📱522 3270) is about 3km west of Baybay Beach. The small Banica pier is to the east of town. All land connections are through the new integrated terminal in Pueblo de Panay.

Antique Province

For years this province of rugged peaks and jungle rivers hugging Panay's west coast – pronounced an-TEE-kay – was somewhat forgotten, cut off from the rest of the island by poor infrastructure and a soaring mountain range. Now there is an excellent road from one end to the other, and Tibiao in particular has become an adventure getaway from Boracay. There are certainly other attractions, most notably in Pandan, but you do have to cover a great deal of ground between them, so if you wish to explore this region it helps to have your own vehicle, or base yourself out of a resort that provides tours. Otherwise there is regular bus service along the national road.

Pandan

 036 / POP 33,000
While not as well-known as Tibiao, Pandan is an excellent base for ecotourists interested in pursuing off-the-beaten-track adventures.

👁️ **Sights & Activities**

⭐ **Malumpati River**   RIVER
(Pandan) One of the most striking natural features in the western Visayas, the astonishing Malumpati River emerges from nowhere in the midst of the jungle, a perfectly clear and beautiful turquoise, before flowing to the sea. It's considered a spring, but given the volume of water and the number of caves in the region an underground river might also be at work.

The river is signed off the national road. You come first to Malumpati Health Spring Resort (P10 entrance), which consists of some basic pensions (rooms P1000), two ziplines (P200) of 200m and 300m, and a diving board. The source of the river is a 30-minute walk upstream. Guides (required) are P200. Wear water shoes. From here you can also take a bamboo raft downstream (P450 per person for five people), which is a lot of fun.

🛏 Sleeping & Eating

★Phaidon Beach Resort   BEACH RESORT **$$**
(📞0929 599 2308, 278 9901; www.island-dreams.
com; Pandan; r incl breakfast P2500; ❄️🛜) This
is both a great place to stay and adven-
ture-travel HQ. This very private resort has
its own white sand beach, a small indoor
pool, a seaview restaurant, some smallish
bungalows, and a great lineup of adven-
tures including trekking, birdwatching, riv-
er boating, island-hopping, and especially
diving. Tours range from P800 to P3500.
Credit cards accepted.

Rose Point Beach Resort   BEACH RESORT **$$**
(📞0946 242 4524; rosepointbeach.webs.com;
Pandan; bungalow P2500-2800; ❄️🛜) Dramatically sited at the mouth of the Bugang River,
this resort offers a restaurant/bar and simple bungalows, but you're really here for the
lovely views across Pandan Bay to the mountains, and the chance to kayak upriver.

Tibiao

📞036 / POP 25,000

Tibiao is the most well-known ecotourism
site in Antique, thanks mainly to visitors
from Boracay; you're only about 1½ hours
(85km) from Caticlan here. The town has
branded all the activities around the Tibiao
River the **Tibiao EcoAdventure Park** (TEA
Park; www.tibiaoantique.info; Km 172, National Rd),
signed near Km 172 on the national road.

Regular buses between San José and Caticlan stop at Tibiao in front of Town Hall.
Travel to Caticlan is via Buruanga or Nabas.

⦿ Sights & Activities

Bugtong Bato Falls   WATERFALL
(TEA Park) This series of seven scenic cascades at the end of the TEA Park road can
be ascended one by one, offering some fine
swimming holes. The first fall (around 60ft)
is reached after a pleasant 30-minute hike;
get your guide at the barangay booth (P100
for five people).

Tibiao Zip Trip   ZIP LINING
(TEA Park; per zip P300; ⊙9am-5pm) Two impressive 500m zips across the Tibiao River
valley.

☞ Tours

Katahum Tours & Fish Spa   TOURS
(📞0917 631 5777; www.katahum.com; 1-day TEA
Park tour P1600) Well-run trips to Seco and
Malalison islands, the Malumpati River,

TEA Park (includes beginner kayaking)
and caves. A unique offering, *lambaklad*
fishing, involves going out with local fishermen at daybreak and hauling up nets full
of migratory fish, particularly tuna. Uniquely, the downtown office is located in a fish
spa where swarms of fish nibble your feet
clean – beware the big ones!

Tribal Adventures   ADVENTURE TOURS
(📞Edwin 0921 570 1947, Sheila 0928 779 0776; TEA
Park; 🖮) Walk-ins can take advantage of the
TEA Park operation of this Boracay-based
tour provider. Kayaks are P200 for an hour,
with downstream pick-up. Various treks are
P250 to P500, plus P500 for the guide. Also
has basic accommodation (P250 per person).

🛏 Sleeping & Eating

University of Antique Hometel   HOTEL **$**
(📞0920 476 2670; Tibiao; d without bathroom
P450-1000; ❄️) Clean, simple and cheap
rooms close to highway. Suite 6 is good value.

Bugtong Bato Falls Inn   BUNGALOWS **$$**
(📞0998 980 4726; Bugtong Bato Falls; bungalow
P2500) These three two-floor nipas face the
last cascade of the falls and sleep six. An
atmospheric spot. Bring your food and defi-
nitely bargain beforehand.

Rosh Al Cafe   FILIPINO **$$**
(mains P100-300; ⊙7am-10pm) This outdoor
cafe behind the Petron station is the only
game in town. Wi-fi!

Patnongon

📞036 / POP 35,000

This municipality north of San Jose is unre-
markable with the exception of **Parola Or-
chids** (📞0915 586 0997; parolaorchids.com; r incl
breakfast P2500; ❄️🛜). A real surprise, this is a
beautifully done and very comfortable European hotel, with a lighthouse on the roof. It
offers large and nicely furnished rooms, a big
restaurant with an international menu, and
a private beach. Rare high-quality stone, tile
and woodwork throughout makes you wonder how the owners pulled it off. It's signed
near Km 123 on the national road; overlook
the garish murals at the entrance.

San José de Buenavista

📞036 / POP 54,800

'San José Antique', as it's often called, is
the provincial capital, but offers little to
the traveller apart from the province's only

ISLAS DE GIGANTES

Comprising eight islets and two large islands, Gigantes Norte (North Gigantes) and Gigantes Sur (South Gigantes), this little archipelago off the northeastern tip of Panay makes for a great bout of island exploration. The islands are all very different, and equally alluring, offering attractive beaches, caves, a turquoise lagoon and more scallops than you've ever seen in your life. The only economical way to get here is from Estancia harbour (one hour from Roxas, three hours from Iloilo, four hours from Bantayan), where four bankgas serve various villages (P80). These depart at 1.30pm and return at 9am.

Gigantes Sur is the only island with accommodation. The western side has several similar beach resorts, with basic huts running P1000 to P1800 for four people. A better choice is Gigantes Hideaway (☑0918 468 5006, 0999 325 4050; Gigantes Sur; dm P200, cottage P1000, bungalow P1500), in the main fishing village. While it has no beach, this well-run resort has nice nipas and a good restaurant. Its package deal is also your best approach to these islands. Transportation from Estancia, a full day of island-hopping, two nights' accommodation and all meals is P2300 per person for three people. Otherwise the price of island-hopping alone is P1500 to P2000 for a boat.

ATM machines, a few internet cafes on the main drag (TA Fornier St) and two dynamic nightspots. If you need to stay over, the central new Eagles Inn (☑540 7265; TA Fornier St; r 1100-1300; ❄🛜) is the best bet, followed by the adjacent Centillion House 2000 (☑540 9853; www.centillionhouse.com; TA Fornier St; s/d incl breakfast P900/1300, wi-fi P50; ❄🛜). For eating, Boondoc's (mains P90-180; ⏱11am-11pm), on a hill behind the main mall, has seafood and terrific views over the entire town. For fun, downtown Parillahan (TA Fornier St; ⏱8.30am-1.30am Sun-Thu, to 3am Fri & Sat) is a popular restobar with live music on an open-air courtyard. But the real party lies across the street at Bar 360 (TA Fornier St; ⏱5pm-3am), a rooftop club owned by a trio of local women with a great live stage that jams until 3am.

Frequent Ceres buses go east to Iloilo (P105, 2½ hours) and to all points north.

Tobias Fornier & Anini-y

This area on the southwestern tip of Panay feels like a well-tended hideaway; you'll notice the difference right away. Tourism is focused on a handful of beach resorts that offer great value. South of Tobias Fornier, Dala-ag Campsite & Resort (☑0926 448 1063; www.fb.com/dalaag; Poblacion Norte, Tobias Fornier; r P1200) is a sprawling complex, with a huge pool and water slide, aimed at everyone from backpackers to local families. Charming Punta Hagdan (☑0917 950 1094, 0916 795 0264; puntahagdan@yahoo.com; Paciencia, Tobias Fornier; r P500-1250) has some excellent budget rooms, a cook-to-order kitchen,

and rental kayaks in a park-like setting by the sea – the perfect spot at which to refresh if you've been travelling awhile. Hacienda Feliza (☑0917 363 0631; Paciencia, Tobias Fornier; r 1500-2300; ❄) is a lovely 13-hectare hilltop estate that gets little traffic. Take the cottage, Casa Isabel, for only P1500, and have the vast grounds to yourself; you'll need your own transport. This is also a good hike from Punta Hagdan.

In Anini-y, Dive House (☑0920 952 8869; all meals, lodging & 2-3 dives per day P6500) offers a charming lodge built from reused materials, dive packages and trips to Nogas Island; a walk-in room is P1500. The very local Sira-an Hot Spring (☑0929 295 0879) combines a thermal bath with fine views and grilled fish at the Kanza Grill.

Iloilo

☑033 / POP 425,000

Once second only to Manila in prominence, Iloilo City is finally starting to emerge from half a century of hard times. Badly fading grandeur defines the congested old city, which is basically everything south of the Iloilo River and east of its tributary, the Dungon River. The future is being cast to the north and west, in the Mandurriao district, from the new riverside Esplanade to the vibrant Smallville entertainment complex and on to the upscale Plazuela arcade, near SM City mall. The opening of the impressive new Iloilo Conference Center in 2015 is viewed as a threshhold moment by Ilonggo, the people of Iloilo.

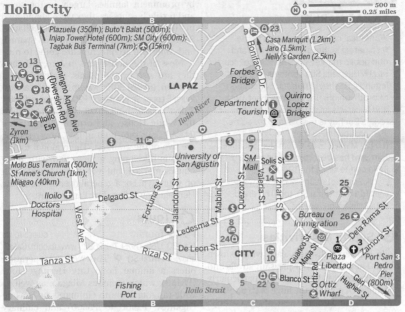

Iloilo City

History

The last capital of the Spanish Empire in Asia, Iloilo City was surrendered in Plaza Libertad to the Filipino Revolutionary Army in 1898 after Manila had already fallen to invading American forces. The seat of government was temporarily transferred here,

as the city's deep-water port had already made it an important centre of trade and commerce with Europe. Only a week later a 3000-strong American force shelled and took the city, thus marking the official beginning of the war of independence against the USA.

LOCAL KNOWLEDGE

LA PAZ MARKET

Want local colour? In addition to the fascinating sights and smells of a cha-otic public market, **La Paz Market** (cnr Rizal & Huervana Sts) contains two local legends. Bachoy, a popular concoction of broth, onion, rice noodles, beef, pork and liver, was invented here, and Ne-tong's Bachoy is the place to try some. Just around the corner, **Madge Cafe** (La Paz Market; ⊙5am-6pm Mon-Sat, to 1pm Sun) has been serving up roasted Iloilo coffee since the 1940s.

Like markets? Check out the **Central Market** (Rizal St), too. The dried-fish stalls go on forever.

◉ Sights & Activities

Iloilo has seven districts, each with its own plaza. These plazas offer pleasant strolls and some impressive historic sites, particularly churches. Of note are the huge **Metropolitan Cathedral** in Jaro, the seat of the Catholic diocese in the western Visayas, and the adjacent **Jaro Belfry**; lovely **St Anne's Church** (Molo Plaza) on Molo Plaza, 1km west of the centre; and downtown **San Jose Church**.

City Hall VIEWPOINT
(Plaza Libertad; ⊙8am-6pm Mon-Fri) FREE For the best view of the old city, climb to the roof above the 7th floor. You'll be surprised how different it appears. Nice views to Guimaras.

Museo Iloilo MUSEUM
(Bonifacio Dr; admission P50; ⊙9am-5pm Mon-Sat) Offers a worthwhile display on the indigenous Ati (Negrito) people and a collection of old *pinya* (pineapple fibre) weavings, for which the area is famous. It also has treasure plucked from sunken ships, and jewellery unearthed from Spanish burial sites.

★**Iloilo Esplanade** WALKING
This new riverside walkway is beautifully done, and a credit to the city, which had to move mountains to build it. It's 1.3km long, paved with brick, and for pedestrians only. A major long-term extension is being undertaken, all the way to the old Muelle Loney Pier.

Historic Mansions HISTORIC BUILDINGS
Iloilo has an impressive number of historic mansions from the 19th and early-20th centuries, the legacy of a far more prosperous era, when the city had the highest concentration of millionaires outside Manila. Owned by prominent families largely in the sugar and textile businesses, they were abandoned in the face of war and economic collapse. Sadly, these beautiful examples of Spanish and American architecture are going to rot.

Most of the houses are in Jaro, although they are also by the plazas. Stately **Nelly's Garden** (☑320 3075; www.fb.com/nellygardens-tours; E Lopez St; per person P200, minimum P1000, 3 days' notice), built 1928, which resembles the White House, and ornate **Villa Lizares** (MacArthur Dr, Jaro), built in 1937, now a school, are two of the grandest. The regional tourist office is developing a new map with these houses marked, but you won't learn much on your own. For a general overview, take the Heritage Tour offered by Panay Tours.

☞ Tours

Panay Tours GUIDED TOURS
(☑330 1769, 0929 751 2692; www.fb.com/CafeP-anay; 45 Rizal St) ✐ This well-run operation offers a unique Iloilo City Heritage Tour (P3450), which includes Miagao, as well as wide-ranging tours to Guimaras or Islas de Gigantes (P2900 to P3500) and culinary tours too. Uses accredited guides. Co-located with sister-business Cafe Panay, where you can not only grab a cuppa, but purchase various products from around the island.

✸ Festivals & Events

★**Dinagyang Festival** CULTURAL
Celebrating the Santo Niño with outrageous costumes and dances, this three-day mardi gras–style party takes place in the fourth week of January. If you miss it, see the colourful exhibition at City Hall (8am to 5pm Monday to Thursday).

Paraw Regatta REGATTA
A race from Iloilo over to Guimaras in traditional sailing outriggers (*paraw*), held the third weekend in February.

⌇ Sleeping

There's a surfeit of good-value accommodation in Iloilo; much of it is conveniently located along the river on General Luna St, and in nearby Smallville.

Riverside Inn HOTEL $
(☑508 3488, 0922 838 0191; www.riverside-inn.net; General Luna St; s/d from P510/670; ❇@🛜) Great-looking hotel for the price, but with street noise. The rooms at the back address the issue; take riverview #241. Wi-fi extra.

Iloilo Grand Hotel HOTEL $

(☑335 1801; www.iloilograndhotel.com; Iznart St; s/d incl breakfast P995/1600; ✹🛜) The best of several faded downtown relics, the 110-room Grand brings to the table large suites with desks and clean beds, but little else. Singles are good value. Ask for the promo rates and request a quiet room at the back. Wi-fi costs extra.

Eros Travellers Pensionne PENSION $

(☑337 1359; General Luna St; s/d from P490/570; ✹) Motel-style cheapie with basic rooms set back from the street.

★**Injap Tower Hotel** HOTEL $$

(☑330 7111; www.injaptowerhotel.com.ph; Aquino Rd; r incl breakfast P2850; ✹🛜🏊) This new high-rise hotel has thought of everything, outshining the competition in many respects. In addition to rooms with amenities like robes and 46in flat-screen TVs, it has a super rooftop complex containing a chic pool with swim-in bar; the Horizon Cafe, with a Western-Asian menu (mains P250 to P380, open 6am-10pm); and a spa (one-hour treatment P300 to P500). Best of all, prices are reasonable. If you do get antsy, you're just a walk away from Smallville's nightlife.

★**Smallville 21** HOTEL $$

(☑501 6821; www.ann2.net/hotels/smallville21; Smallville; r P1800-3300; ✹🛜) Great value, the Smallville 21 has a super-stylish design, all the mod cons you need and fluffy beds that invite entry via flying leap. If the festive location doesn't bother you, this is a top choice.

Circle Inn HOTEL $$

(☑508 0000; www.circleinn-iloilo.com; Iznart Street; r 1800-3100; ✹🛜🏊) While not in a prime location, this new upscale business hotel offers huge rooms and large balconies. Get the deluxe rooms facing the wading pool or, better yet, a premium room facing the sea (P3100).

GO Hotel HOTEL $$

(☑335 0375; www.gohotels.ph; Robinsons Mall; r P1200; ✹🛜) This new chain is cloning a decent hostel and attaching them to every Robinsons Mall. The hook: advance online booking can yield discounts over 50%.

Skinetics Wellness Center BOUTIQUE HOTEL $$$

(☑320 8726; www.skinetics.com.ph; Boardwalk Ave, Smallville; r incl breakfast P3500-6509; ✹🛜) This strange hybrid high-rise – part therapeutic spa, part cosmetic clinic and part boutique hotel (all on separate floors) – is aimed at the medical-tourism industry, but can be taken piecemeal. The hotel offers the city's finest suite (P12,000), which sleeps six on two levels, comes with full kitchen and has a wall of glass with a grand view. Standard rooms are high-end business, with comfy beds and wood panelling. The reasonably priced spa is equally professional.

Grand Dame Hotel HOTEL $$$

(☑320 5252; cnr Rizal & Huervana Sts; r incl breakfast P5335; ✹🛜) This establishment with the feel of Old Europe, near La Paz market, delivers with quality. Enquire about promo rates.

✗ Eating

One approach to eating out in Iloilo is simply to wander around Smallville, the nearby Boardwalk, and the upscale Plazuela outdoor arcade, where there is a plethora of restaurants. Coffee Break (open 8am to 10pm) is the city's pleasant Starbuck's clone, with numerous outlets, particularly in malls.

Seafood lovers should head 10km west out of town to the village of Arevalo, where several seafood buffets await with picnic-table seaside dining. Try the popular Breakthrough (dishes P100-150; ⏱7.30am-9pm) for good atmosphere and so-so service. Most 'Arevalo' jeepneys get you here.

★**DoVa** INTERNATIONAL $$

(Javellana Street; mains P150-350; ⏱9am-9pm) Known for its all-day brunch, this atmospheric modern cafe across from La Paz market is a real green shoot, featuring music, views and nicely-presented Western meals with Filipino twists. Way above the competition.

★**Wawa Heritage Restaurant** INTERNATIONAL $$

(☑321 0315; E Lopez St; meals P135-150; ⏱11am-2pm & 5pm-midnight; 🛜) Now here's what this city needs more of. Situated amid the historic homes of Jaro, this charming locavore's delight feels like a 19th-century living room, and serves a tasty mix of Filipino, Chinese and Spanish 'heritage dishes'. The homey ambience is a welcome alternative to the mall-like feel of the 'new Iloilo'. Amazingly inexpensive, too.

ⓘ **NO SMOKING**

As of 2014 Iloilo is a smoke-free city. Smoking is not allowed in any public places, including restaurants and bars.

Bluejay Coffee & Delicatessen CAFE $$
(Ayala Technohub, Smallville; sandwiches/mains from P85/150; ⊘7am-11pm; 🛜🖊) Starbucks meets German deli. Get your meaty sandwich here, or for a brain freeze, try the cinnamon cappuccino frappe.

Buto't Balat FILIPINO $$
(Solis St; mains P120-175; ⊘10.30am-10.30pm) Sit in a thatched dining pavilion and munch on Ilonggo specialities such as *tinuom* (chicken in banana leaves) at this ever-popular, well-manicured garden restaurant. Most dishes serve two to three diners. Branches in Jaro Plaza and south of Plazuela on Pison Ave.

Freska FILIPINO $$
(✒321 3885; Ayala Technohub, Smallville; mains P100-200; ⊘11am-3pm & 5pm-1am) The theme here is traditional Ilonggo seafood, with snapper and shellfish taking pride of place on the menu. Best of all, it has broken the San Miguel monopoly, offering a broad selection of foreign beers.

 Drinking & Nightlife

Smallville has a block of clubs (just listen) that is the city's dance hub. **Flow** (Smallville; P200 Fri & Sat; ⊘8pm-4am Wed-Sat), **G-Lounge** (Smallville; ⊘9pm-4am Wed-Sat), **MO2 Ice** (Smallville) and **Aura** (⊘9pm-4am Wed-Sat) all cater to Iloilo's sizeable student population; bring your earplugs and leave your flip-flops behind. Admission is free on weekdays and up to P200 on weekends, when closing time is 2am to 4am; some clubs only open Wednesday to Saturday.

★**Red Paprika** RESTOBAR
(Riverside Boardwalk; ⊘10am-2pm & 4pm-1am) This open-air Asian restobar and stage is a real pleasure to hang out in. It's known for its house cover band, Binhi, which plays 'oldies

BOATS & BUSES FROM ILOILO

Boats

DEPARTS	DESTINATION	COMPANY	TYPE	FARE (P)	DURATION	SCHEDULE
Iloilo River Wharf	Bacolod	Weesam Express, 2GO, Ocean Jet	fastcraft	560-600	1hr	hourly
Port San Pedro	Manila	2GO	ferry	1243	27hr	Sun, Wed & Thu
Port San Pedro	Cagayan de Oro	2GO	ferry	1113	14hr	Sat
Port San Pedro	Bacolod	2GO	ferry	595	4hr	Sun
Port San Pedro	Cebu	Trans-Asia, Cokaliong	ferry	760-800	13hr	Tue-Sun
Ortiz Wharf	Jordan, Guimaras	various	bangka	28	20min	every 30min
Parola Wharf	Buenavista, Guimaras	various	bangka	29	20min	every 30min
Lapuz Terminal	Jordan, Guimaras	FF Cruz	RORO	70 + vehicle	1hr	every 2hr
Lapuz Terminal	Cuyo/Puerto Princesa	Milagrosa, Montenegro	RORO	950-1220	12hr/24hr	Thu & Sat

Buses

DEPARTS	DESTINATION	FARE (P)	DURATION (HR)	FREQUENCY
Tagbak Terminal	Kalibo	238	3	hourly
Tagbak Terminal	Caticlan	291	4½	hourly
Tagbak Terminal	Roxas City	145	2¾	every 30min
Tagbak Terminal	Antique (via Miagao)	275	5	every 30min
Tagbak Terminal	Northern Iloilo	45-170	up to 4½	every 30min
Tagbak Terminal	Central Iloilo	8-60	up to 1¾	1
Molo Terminal	San Jose, Antique	110 (to San Jose)	3 (to San Jose)	1

but goldies' Monday to Wednesday and Friday. Located on the Boardwalk, the strip mall on the southern boundary of Smallville.

★ **JLK Music Lounge & Bar** LOUNGE
(Red Square Building; ⊙ 7pm-2am) Head splitting from the clubs? For a truly chilled-out experience, submerge into the cool blue lighting and retro tunes of this new Smallville lounge.

Zyron CLUB
(R Mapa St; ⊙ 9pm-2am Tue-Sun) If you like wild evenings, or at least the occasional pajama party, Zyron, at the western end of the Esplanade, is your place. You can't miss it: the entrance is an enormous wolf's mouth.

🛍 Shopping

Robinsons is the big downtown mall, while **SM City** (Diversion Rd; ⊙ 9am-8pm) beyond Smallville on Benigno Aquino Ave is where uptown mall rats hang. Both have the usual complement of movies, restaurants etc.

★ **Camiña Balay nga Bato** HANDICRAFTS
(Lola Rufina Heritage Curio Shop; ☑ 396 4700, 336 3858; 20 Osmeña St) This beautifully restored Spanish home (1865) offers private tours of the upstairs living area (P150, minimum five people) and a downstairs shop where the ancient art of weaving *hablon* cloth is practised. The shop sells *hablon* skirts *(patadyong)* and a rare, if limited, selection of other local handicrafts and food.

ℹ Information

ATMs are all over town, but especially in malls and along central Iznart St.
Bureau of Immigration (BOI; ☑ 509 9651; 2nd fl, Customs House Bldg, Aduana St)
Department of Tourism (DOT; ☑ 337 5411; deptour6@mozcom.com; Capitol Grounds, Bonifacio Dr; ⊙ 8am-5pm Mon-Fri)
Iloilo Doctors' Hospital (☑ 337 7702; West Ave) The most modern hospital in town.

ℹ Getting There & Away

In September 2014 fastcraft operations to Bacolod shifted from longstanding Muelle Loney Pier, which closed to accommodate a future extension of the Esplanade, to the new **Iloilo River Wharf** directly across the river. The RORO to Guimaras and Puerto Princesa will also move here when facilities are complete. Until then they will continue to use the nearby **Lapuz Terminal**. The frequent RORO to Bacolod continues to operate from Dumangas, 20km north of Iloilo City (P90, two hours).

The big malls have ticketing offices open from 9am to 8pm daily. Boat tickets can be bought pierside.

Iloilo Airport serves Manila (hourly), Davao (daily) and has several flights a week to Cagayan de Oro, General Santos, Puerto Princesa, Singapore and Hong Kong.

ℹ Getting Around

TO/FROM THE AIRPORT
The airport is 15km north of town in Santa Barbara. Airport shuttle buses (P70, 20 minutes) depart from the Travellers Lounge at SM City from 4am to 6pm. The schedule is a bit sporadic; get there at least two hours before your flight. A taxi from Iloilo City centre will cost about P300.

CAR
Hire cars, either self- or driver-driven, are readily available through your hotel. Figure on P2500 per day for an air-con van to cruise around the countryside, excluding petrol.

GUIMARAS

☑ 033 / POP 163,000
Just a short boat ride from Iloilo City, rural Guimaras is a world away. Known for its sweet mangoes, this is an island of winding roads (perfect for motorbikes), green plantations, coral islets and, most of all, resorts. For its size, Guimaras harbours an extraordinary number of outstanding beach, island and nature resorts, most of them moderately priced. If you want to play castaway for a few days, Guimaras makes an ideal getaway.

🔭 Sights & Activities

Navales VILLAGE
The only heritage church on the island, the quaint Spanish-era **Navales Church** (1880) is made of coral blocks blackened by the years. The much-photographed summer retreat of the wealthy López family, **Roca Encantada** (Enchanted Rock), lies nearby, just off Navales Beach. Navales is a P400 tricycle ride from Jordan.

★ **Spring Bloom Farm** TOUR
(☑ 336 3858, 0908 821 1269; btwn Km 100 & 101; tour P150) This peaceful organic farm offers very personal and highly recommended tours with a day's notice. You'll see 24 hectares of bananas, papayas, cashew, pineapple and more, but the real treat is sitting in the farm's charming white cottage sipping fresh calamansi juice.

Guimaras

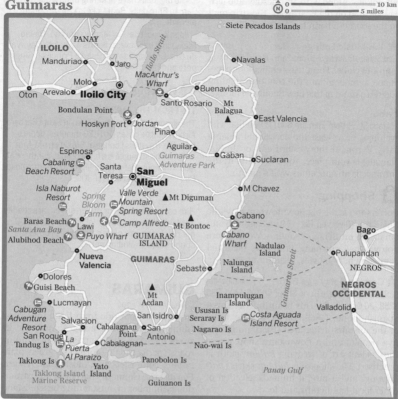

★✦ Festivals & Events

Manggahan Sa Guimaras Fiesta FOOD
The island's main festival honours the admired mango, just after harvest time (April or May). A parade and carnival are held in San Miguel, and a mango eating contest that sent the last winner (13kg!) to the hospital.

Ang Pagtaltal Sa Guimaras RELIGIOUS
Jordan's Easter ceremony draws crowds to Guimaras every Good Friday.

🛏 Sleeping & Eating

🛏 San Miguel & Around

**Valle Verde Mountain
Spring Resort** RESORT $
(📱0918 730 3446; www.valleverdemtnresort.com; d with fan P500-800, with air-con P1500; ✴🌊) This budget hilltop retreat is a refreshing change from the beach. Accom-

modations are very basic, and the pool a bit green, but there are wonderful views of a jungle-covered valley with Lawi Bay in the distance. Turn off the highway 6km south of San Miguel and proceed 1km down a rough road (P100 by tricycle from San Miguel).

★ Camp Alfredo RESORT $$
(📱0908 123 2977; Ring Rd, after Km 101; cottage P2000; ✴🌊) Midway between San Miguel and Nueva Valencia, this new nature resort is superbly done. Set in an attractive forest with concrete pathways and a running stream, it offers a beautiful open-air dining pavilion, and an even more beautiful horizon pool that can easily capture your entire day. If not, there's always the 325m zipline course (P425 for visitors).

The modular cottages aren't luxurious, but are inexpensive and do fit the site. Only 30 minutes from Jordan Wharf, this is the perfect green escape from Iloilo.

Cabaling Beach Resort BEACH RESORT $$
(www.cabalingbeachresorts.com; Cabaling; r with fan/air-con P2000/3000) This resort on its own peninsula south of Espinosa has beautiful facilities, but you don't want to walk the beach to reach it – call ahead for a bangka pick up (P2000 for the boat from Iloilo). Once there you'll find huge rooms with big balconies on an attractive cove with a narrow beach, a beautiful horizon pool and untrained staff.

Watch add-ons, like food, as you'll be eating there your entire stay.

★**Pitstop** PIZZA, BURGERS $
(☑0927 894 9395; thepitstoprestaurant.com.ph; San Miguel; mains P35-140; ☺8am-8pm) This little gem on main street San Miguel wins points for both its signature mango pizza (a must), plate-sized hamburgers and general enthusiasm. Other outlets have opened in Nueva Valencia and Buenavista.

Sa Payaw Seafood Grill SEAFOOD $
(☑0916 263 5286; meals P95-145; ☺7am-10.30pm Mon-Thu, to 2am Fri & Sat) This inexpensive outdoor restaurant near the electric company in San Miguel serves excellent grilled seafood and more beneath its thatched roof. Videoke will drive you out late.

🛏 South Coast

★**Cabugan Adventure Resort** BEACH RESORT $
(☑0917 321 0603, 0939 921 5908; www.fb.com/cabuganadventureresort; near Lucmayan; r with fan P900-1200, air-con P2200) Our favourite budget resort in the western Visayas, Cabugan is a particular kind of earthy tropical paradise. The resort hides on a spit of white sand between a headland and a huge coral rock; think of Scaramanga's lair in *The Man with the Golden Gun*. On one side a sea of islets, on another a private bay.

Nipa huts sleeping four or more cling to the cliffs, with views in all directions; the Sunrise rooms (P1200) are to die for. Lunch and dinner (P250 each) are too. Crabs, lobsters, and big barracuda are caught nearby. A central beach volleyball court brings guests together. Canoes are available for wider exploration. The secret recipe: it's not really a resort, it's a new way of life.

★**Magic Island Resort** BEACH RESORT $
(www.fb.com/magicislandresortguimaras; near Lucmayan; cottage incl 3 meals, boat transfer & 90min island-hopping for 2 P3500; ✸🛜) This tiny resort island – you can walk around it in 10 minutes – sits in an alluring sea of coral islets. Very well-managed, it offers superb food and accommodations of various kinds, including two-floor 'Vietnamese houses' (P300!) and comfy waterfront cottages. Rooms surprise with their light, cleanliness and Western baths. Canoes available, too.

★**Jannah-Glycel Beach House** INN $$
(☑0929 281 6498, 582 1003; www.jannahglycelbeachhouse.com; Nueva Valencia; r P1450 1800; ✸🛜) Serving primarily European and American clients, this private and classy waterfront villa sits at the very quiet end of Alubihod Beach. Guests stay in separate quarters below, next to an attractive seaside garden. Rooms are high quality. Bangkas take you island-hopping directly from the beach. Tired of the noisy resorts at the other end of Alubihod? This is the perfect antidote.

Costa Aguada Island Resort BEACH RESORT $$
(☑752 3688, in Manila 02-896 5422; www.costaaguadaislandresort.com; r with fan/air-con from

BOATS FROM GUIMARAS

DEPARTS	DESTINATION	COMPANY	TYPE	FARE	DURATION (HR)	FREQUENCY
Hoskyn Port	Lapuz Terminal, Iloilo*	FF Cruz	RORO	P25	½	4 Mon-Sat, 2 Sun
Sebaste Port	Pulupandan, Negros	Montenegro	RORO	P80	1	9am & noon
Hoskyn Port	Ortiz Wharf, Iloilo	various	bangka	P14	¼	every 20min
MacArthur's Wharf	Parola Wharf, Iloilo	various	bangka	P15	¼	every 20min
Cabalagnan Port	Valladolid, Negros	various	bangka	P150	2	1
Tumanda Wharf	Pulupandan, Negros	various	bangka	P60	¾	10am & 3pm

*RORO vessels will use the new Iloilo River Wharf as soon as facilities are ready.

P1500/2250; 🏊) This resort on Inampulugan, a large island 30 minutes off the southeast coast, is a good place to play Robinson Crusoe in style. The 68 bamboo and nipa cottages are spacious, the open-air restaurant serves fresh seafood and there are four nearby islands to explore. Or you can just sit by the pool.

La Puerta Al Paraizo   BEACH RESORT $$
(📞 0927 507 9024; www.fb.com/lapuerta.alparaizo; r with fan P1800, with air-con P2800-3800; 🌀 🛜 🏊) Well-kept La Puerta occupies an enviable location on a limestone bluff overlooking two private white beaches. We'd prefer more balconies, but you can't argue with the spectacular views of mushroom-like islands from the hilltop rooms, or just the pretty pool. Turn off the main highway about 6km south of Alubihod; the resort is 5km further on.

Isla Naburot Resort   BEACH RESORT $$$
(📞 0918 909 8500, 321 1654; www.fb.com/Isla-Naburot; cottages P5990) Occupying its own island, this absolutely private resort is one of the best offshore options. Those who fantasise about being a castaway will enjoy the eight cottages made from natural materials, including pebbles, shells, tree trunks and the discarded parts of other houses. Each rustic structure is well designed and comfortable. For reservations/access contact the resort.

🛏 North Coast

Kelapa Gading Beach Resort BEACH RESORT $$
(📞 0917 921 0277; r with fan/air-con from P1000/1500; 🌀) There are a couple of resorts on a narrow beach in the township of East Valencia (Buenavista). None are great value, but this one has a few affordable fan nipa huts to go with some very basic air-con rooms.

❶ Information

The helpful **tourist office** (www.guimaras.gov.ph; ⏰ 7.30am-5pm) at Hoskyn Port, Jordan is worth a stop. Transport rates for all island destinations are posted here.

❶ Getting There & Away

There's no airport in Guimaras. Visitors arrive by sea from Iloilo City and Negros (Pulupandan and Valladolid), each with RORO service.

❶ Getting Around

The tourist office at Hoskyn Port can help you hire a tricycle or multicab to any resort. Public jeepneys link Jordan with San Miguel (P15), but aren't convenient for most resorts, which often lie several kilometres off the highway.

NEGROS

POP 3.6 MILLION

With its rugged mountain interior, unspoilt beaches, underwater coral gardens and urban grooves, Negros has the most to offer in the western Visayas after Boracay. This is particularly true of its southern coast, stretching from Danjugan Island around the tip to Bais, where diving has become big business. Here the natural base is Dumaguete, a funky college town and expat hangout with a good-time vibe. In the north, Bacolod has largely culinary treats, nearby Silay is a living museum of historic homes from a bygone age, and the cool mountain resorts of Mt Kanlaon offer a refreshing alternative to the beach.

Politically, Negros is divided into two provinces lying either side of a central mountain range. To the west lies Negros Occidental, whose capital is Bacolod, and whose language is Ilonggo; while to the east lies Negros Oriental, whose capital is Dumaguete, and whose people speak Cebuano. To the traveller, however, it makes more sense to think of Negros in north-south terms, as the mid-section of the island offers little of interest.

❶ Getting There & Around

Bacolod and Dumaguete airports are serviced by flights from Manila and Cebu City. Bacolod and Dumaguete are also the island's major ports, although a number of smaller towns are also accessible by boat. Ferries connect Negros to Cebu, Bohol, Mindanao, Panay and Siquijor. Getting around the island is easy: there are good roads and virtually nonstop bus services around the coast.

Bacolod

📞 034 / POP 512,000

Once the hub of a booming sugar industry, Bacolod has an unfair reputation as being little more than a transport hub today. In reality it is one of those cities whose attractions are diluted by sprawl, so if you know where to go you can have a great time. The city feels more plugged into the rest of the world, with more sophisticated cuisine than elsewhere, and green shoots of environmental consciousness. For nightlife, the Art District can't compare with Iloilo's Smallville, but in compensation you can easily reach Mt Kanlaon Natural Park or the historic district of Silay, which should not be missed.

Negros

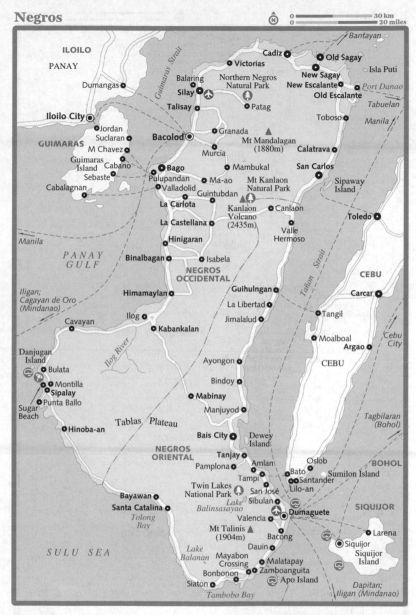

Sights

★ Negros Forests & Ecological Foundation

ZOO

(www.negrosforests.org; South Capitol Rd; admission by donation; ⊙9am-noon & 1-4pm Mon-Sat) A zoo with a difference, the Negros Forests & Ecological Foundation seeks to preserve endangered animals endemic to Negros. It houses mostly birds, including an extraordinary collection of rare and colourful hornbills that alone justifies a visit. There are also flying foxes, Visayan leopards and local deer.

Bacolod

0 500 m
0 0.25 miles

Fresh Start (700m); Delicioso (900m);
Ceres Bus Liner North Terminal (1.5km);
Art District (3km); Banago Wharf (4km);
(15km); Silay (15km)

BS Aquino Dr

San Juan St

Gatuslao St

Aguinaldo St

Lacson St

La Salle Ave

17
18
11 21st St
13

18th St

17th St

Guimaras
Strait

BS Aquino Dr

12

14th St
13th St
12th St

8

9 16

5
10th St

9th St
19
8th St
7th St
6th St
5th St
4th St
3rd St
2nd St

15

North Capitol Rd
Negros
Occidental
Tourism Center
Lake
2

South Capitol Rd
1 Negros
Forests &
4 Ecological
Foundation

UPTOWN

22

Bredco Port
(1km)

1st St

Burgos St

3

Galo St

San Juan St

San
Sebastian
Cathedral

10
Nueva St
20

Cuadra St

14

City
Plaza

@

7

6

City
Hall

Bacolod
Central
Market

Rizal St

DOWNTOWN

Gonzaga St

Luzuriaga St

23

21

Lopez Jaena St

Mabini St

Locsin St

Araneta St

San Sebastian St

Office of the Park
Superintendent (800m)

Rosario St

Bacolod

Capitol Park & Lagoon   PARK
(cnr Lacson & 6th Sts) The city's central gathering place is worth a stroll, particularly on weekends, when it's a popular picnic spot. Bring some food for the resident tilapia.

Dizon Ramos Museum   MUSEUM
(☑434 8512; Burgos St; admission P40; ☉10am-5pm Tue-Sun) At first you might think it is a moving sale, but this unpretentious and oddly affecting museum will win you over with its hysterically curated collection of family hobbies. Holy land trinkets? Ceramic horses? Crystal? Keychains? They each have their own room. And where else does the guide stop to play a 1950s Guy Lombardo record on an old turntable?

Negros Museum   MUSEUM
(☑433 4764; www.thenegrosmuseum.org.ph; Gatuslao St; adult/child P50/25; ☉9am-6pm Mon-Sat, cafe 10am-10pm Tue-Sun) Houses an eclectic collection, from a room dedicated to the sugar industry to one containing toys from around the world. Don't miss the fake cannons used to scare the Spanish, including coconut cannonballs. It also has a small art gallery, a gift shop and a popular outdoor cafe.

🏃 Activities

Permits for trekking in nearby Mt Kanlaon Natural Park are obtained in Bacolod, at the **Office of the Park Superintendent** (☑441 3329, 435 7411; www.fb.com/mountkanlaon; cnr Porras & Abad-Santos Sts, behind Plaza Hotel; ☉8am-5pm Mon-Fri); your best contact is Angelo Bibar (0917 301 1410, angelobibar@gmail.com). To get here, take a Bata–Libertad jeepney to Lupit Church and then a tricycle to the office.

🎊 Festivals & Events

MassKara Festival   CULTURAL
On the weekend nearest to 19 October each year, the city goes joyfully crazy with the MassKara Festival, with participants wearing elaborate smiley masks (*máscara* is Spanish for mask) and dancing in the streets.

🛏 Sleeping

★ Hotel Sea Breeze   HOTEL $
(☑433 7370; San Juan St; r from P785; ✳🛜) An attractive throwback, Sea Breeze provides an inexpensive glimpse into the grandeur of the sugar-plantation glory days. A grand wooden staircase leads past an old ballroom up to worn but functional rooms. There's a nice garden courtyard out back. Choose the artful standard doubles over the budget rooms.

11th Street Bed & Breakfast Inn   GUESTHOUSE $
(☑433 9191; www.bb11st.webeden.co.uk; 11th St; s/d/tr incl breakfast with fan P400/550/650, with air-con P650/850/1060; ✳🛜) Enjoying a calm sidestreet location, yet still within walking distance of all the action on Lacson St, this leafy pension feels like you're staying in a well-heeled family home. Rooms are no-frills, but are immaculately clean and very inexpensive.

Pension Bacolod GUESTHOUSE $
(🖉 433 3377; 27 11th St; s/d with fan P150/250, with air-con P470/560; ✳🛜) This warren of connected courtyards is well run but definitely budget. So if you want a cheapie, you've got 76 reasonably sized rooms to choose from.

Check Inn HOTEL $
(🖉 432 3755; www.checkinn.com.ph; Luzuriaga St; s/d from P650/850; ✳@🛜) With midrange comforts such as hot water and cable TV at budget prices, this slick downtown chain hotel is great value and runs like clockwork. There is free use of a gym.

★**Suites at Calle Nueva** BOUTIQUE HOTEL $$
(🖉 708 8000; www.thesuitesatcallenueva.com; 15 Nueva St; s/d incl breakfast from P1000/1500; ✳🛜) The best value for money in town, this centrally located boutique hotel has tasteful rooms every bit as comfortable as a mini high-end hotel. Beds are new and comfy, couches are embellished with pillows, and rooms have plasma TV and sparkling bathrooms. Generous buffet breakfast included.

★**Nature's Village Resort** RESORT $$
(🖉 495 0808; www.naturesvillageresort.net; Talisay City; r P1800-2400, ste P4200; ✳🛜🐾) This 3-hectare ecoresort is at the forefront of sustainable hospitality. Accommodations are in the Village Hotel, a rustic yet high-quality hacienda decorated with textile art and furniture beautifully made out of railroad ties. The adjoining Village Restaurant is first rate, and partly supplied by an on-site organic farm. The popular pool is open to the public. Located in Talisay City, midway between Bacolod and Silay, you can reach either city in 10 to 15 minutes, or remain immersed in nature.

L'Fisher Hotel Complex HOTEL $$
(🖉 433 3731; www.lfisherhotelbacolod.com; cnr 14th & Lacson Sts; r P989-5000; ✳@🛜) Three hotels in one mall-like complex. Budget Ecotel (r P989) is a loss. The midrange Chalet (r from P1500) and high-end L'Fisher (r 3500) both have very nice rooms, although it pays to opt for the former as facilities are shared, including spa, gym and a rooftop infinity pool with bar. Management seems oddly disengaged.

🍴 Eating

Manokan Country FILIPINO $
(Rizal St; chicken P70) This strip of open-air restaurants is known for serving the city's famous chicken *inasal* (marinated in lemon and soy, and barbecued on charcoal). Cheap beer and oysters (P35 per plate) don't hurt either.

★**Fresh Start** VEGETARIAN $$
(www.freshstartorganic.com; Robinsons Mall; mains P175-195; ⏱ 10am-9pm; 🖉) This wonderfully health-conscious restaurant, with its own organic farm behind it, is a vegetarian delight. Combine a veggie wrap with a bottle of Bog's Brew, a rare example of local craft beer. There's another outlet in Ayala Mall.

★**365 Modern Cafe** PIZZA $$
(🖉 435 2351; cnr BS Aquino Dr & Kamagong St; mains P185-275; ⏱ 9am-10.30pm Sun-Thu, to midnight Sat) Don't dismiss this green cafe because it is located in a Fuelstar gas station – it harbours a skilled chef who dishes out superb pizza, along with beautiful pasta and fall-off-the-bone ribs. Great value!

C's CAFE $$
(🖉 433 3731; cnr Lacson & 14th Sts; mains P210-380; ⏱ 7am-10pm) An authentic patisserie run by a French chef, with an ever-changing selection of gourmet treats.

Pala Pala SEAFOOD $$
(North Capitol Rd; ⏱ 10am-late) This huge market-like shed is a local favourite. Head first to the adjoining fish market to choose your seafood dinner before picking any of the small hole-in-the-wall eateries that'll charcoal barbecue your fish, prawns or lobster. Cooking fees start from P120 per kilogram.

21 Restaurant FILIPINO $$
(www.21restaurant.com; Lacson St; mains P175-360; ⏱ 10am-11pm) Crisp white tablecloths, professional waiters and an appetising menu set the tone for this classy and reasonably priced restaurant. It's known for its bachoy and seafood, like the grilled squid stuffed with lemongrass.

★**Tyrol** AUSTRIAN $$$
(🖉 703 1878; 12th St; mains P225-395; ⏱ 5-11pm Mon, 11am-11pm Tue-Sun) This authentic Austrian restaurant is what you'd expect – wooden benches, the odd deer antler, and great schnitzel. The spectacular King Ludwig mixed platter (P1295, good for six to eight people) samples the best of the menu. The owner also runs a cooking school: the Bacolod Academy for Culinary Arts (www.culinary-bacolod.com).

Inaka JAPANESE $$$
(Lacson St; meals P100-750; ⏱ 10am-4pm & 6-10pm Tue-Sun) Tastefully decorated with modern art, Inaka has an authentic Japanese menu with a good sushi and sashimi selection and a teppanyaki chef. Vegetarians

will want to try tofu steak with mushroom rice (P250). If it's full, try nearby L'Kaisei, which has an identical menu.

Drinking & Nightlife

The open-air Art District complex of bars and restaurants on Lacson St in Mandalagan is more a party spot than an art venue, and is frequented by a young crowd. With its scarily cheap drinks menu, **Gypsy Tea Room** (Art District; ⊙2pm-2am) gets particularly raucous; a sign warns of the P250 fine for vomiting. The more chilled-out **Café Joint** (⊙4pm-late) is an outdoor hang-out for creative types.

★**KGBar**   BAR
(cnr Lacson & 23rd Sts; ⊙6pm-1am) Well hidden behind a nondescript wall, this mellow, candle-lit jungle bar is hip, funky and uber-relaxed. Pillowed chairs, ambient grooves, and avant-garde art invite long conversation, attracting a mix of artists, expats and worldly locals. The Asian fusion menu (mains P135 to P185) is a perfect fit.

Mushu   BAR
(cnr Lacson & 20th Sts) At groovy, ever-popular Mushu you can enjoy sickly sweet house cocktails and watch local bands while eating excellent Chinese counter meals.

Shopping

Bacolod has three major malls: **SM City** (Rizal St), **Robinsons** (Lacson St) and **Ayala North** (Lacson St north of Robinsons). The first two have cinemas.

★**Negros Showroom**   HANDICRAFTS
(☑433 3728; www.anp-philippines.com; cnr 9th & Lacson Sts; ⊙10am-8pm) ⬦ A one-stop shop for local handicrafts and organic products, including native jewellery, MassKara masks and *piaya* (sugary flat cakes). Also at Robinsons mall.

Information

All tourism-related queries should be taken to the **Negros Occidental Tourism Center** (☑433 2515; tourism.negros-occ.gov.ph; Provincial Capitol Bldg, Gatuslao St), which is passionate about its work.

Getting There & Away

Bacolod-Silay Airport is 15km northeast of Bacolod City; a taxi to the city centre is around P500. Bacolod-Silay Airport services Manila hourly on Cebu Pacific, PAL, and Seair. Cebu Pacific also flies to Cebu two to three times per day, and to Davao and Cagayan de Oro several times per week.

Bredco Port is about 1km west of the centre (P15 by tricycle), Banago Wharf is 7km north,

BOATS & BUSES FROM BACOLOD

Boats

DEPARTS	DESTINATION	FARE (P)	DURATION (HR)	DAILY FREQUENCY
Bredco	Iloilo	300	1	every 30min
	Dumangas	120	2	hourly
Banago Wharf	Manila	1130	20	Wed, Thu & Sun
	Cagayan de Oro	1360	21	Fri
Pulupandan	Guimaras	80	1	3–4

Buses

DEPARTS	DESTINATION	FARE (P)	DURATION (HR)	DAILY FREQUENCY
Ceres South Terminal	Dumaguete	260-315	6	hourly
Ceres South Terminal	Sipalay	185	5	every 30min
Ceres North Terminal	Silay	15	½	frequent
Ceres North Terminal	San Carlos (inland route)	165	3	2
Ceres North Terminal	San Carlos (coastal route)	165	4	frequent
Ceres North Terminal	Sagay	90	2½	frequent
Ceres North Terminal	Cebu (via Escalante-Tabuelan)	380-420	8	4
Ceres North Terminal	Cebu (via San Carlos-Toledo)	320-420	8	6

and Pulupandan is 25km southwest (by jeepney P15, 25 minutes) and Valladolid is 5km further on. All ferries have pierside ticketing offices; **2GO Travel** (☏ 441 0652) also has an office in Robinsons mall.

Ceres has two bus terminals. The new **north terminal** (☏ 433 4993, 0917 771 1213; Lacson St) serves destinations north of Bacolod (including San Carlos), while the **south terminal** (☏ 434 2387; cnr Lopez Jaena & San Sebastian Sts) serves southern destinations. If you're stuck, try the nearby north and south bus stations, which service smaller bus lines.

Jeepneys for Ma-ao (P25, 30 minutes) and Mambukal (P25, 45 minutes) – and hence the mountain resorts – are stationed behind the market between Libertad St and Lizares Ave.

❶ Getting Around

Lacson St is the spine of downtown Bacolod. The north bus terminal is on it; to reach it from the south terminal take a 'Shopping' jeepney. Both 'Bata' and 'Mandalagan' jeepneys run north–south along it.

A car with driver is about P1800 per day; you can organise this through the Tourism Center (p245) and many hotels.

Mt Kanlaon Natural Park

Mt Kanlaon Natural Park is 24,388 hectares of cool, dense forest surrounding a towering active volcano with a deep crater. The park is home to diverse wildlife, including wild boar, civet cat, leopard cat, spotted deer, hornbill, hawk eagle and bleeding-heart pigeon. However, most of these are rare, endangered or nocturnal, making spotting them difficult, even with a guide. For fit hikers, there are established trails to the summit, making for a challenging trek. Most visitors will focus on the mountain resorts, which offer diverse activities, making this area an ever-popular, and refreshing, escape from Bacolod, even if just for a day.

🏃 Activities

Most activities in this region are organised through the mountain resorts. This includes on-site activities as well as guided tours of the surrounding area.

🛏 Sleeping & Eating

The cool, refreshing forest and streams on the western foothills of Mt Kanlaon have long been a popular escape from Bacolod. There are several inexpensive mountain resorts here, owned by local municipalities, that are a wonderful complement to the beach. These offer various activities for overnighters and day-trippers alike.

⭐ Mambukal   RESORT $

(☏ 473 0601; mambukal.negros-occ.gov.ph; barangay Minoyan; dm P100, r P600, villa P4000; ✳ ☷) Negros' best and most popular mountain resort is set in the forest beside a stream and large pond. Hot springs feed a very nicely done Japanese bath. Accommodation includes dorm beds, rooms and attractive two-bedroom, two-bathroom family villas that sleep six to ten. There is lots to see and do, including a nifty canopy walk (P50), various waterfalls, a climbing wall (P25) and a spa. There's a jeepney service from Bacolod.

Buenos Aires Mountain Resort   RESORT $

(☏ 034-461 0540; tourismbago@yahoo.com; dm P200, cottages from P800, r with air-con from P1250; ✳ ☷) This 1930s resort is famous for having hidden President Quezon from the Japanese during WWII. The large (5 hectare) hacienda-style property is nicely situated by a river in Ma-ao, with a restaurant and classic spring-fed pool. Accommodation varies in quality. Pay up for the hostel rooms, which are a walk up the hill, but have nice balconies with attractive views.

The nearby Kipot Twin falls make a nice side trip. From Bacolod, catch a jeepney (p246) to Ma-ao (P40, 1½ hours) and a tricycle to the resort (P200, 30 minute).

Guintubdan Visitors Center   GUESTHOUSE $

(☏ 460 0286; www.lacarlotacity.net; Guintubdan; d & tr P1000) This beautiful building with fine views offers only basic and somewhat overpriced accommodations. There's a guest kitchen, but the availability of food is iffy. Guides can take you on excellent day trips (P100) to any of seven nearby waterfalls. The adjacent **Rafael Salas Park** (☏ 461 0540; www.bagocity.gov.ph/travel-tourism/resort-beaches/), under renovation during research, promises a more upscale experience by December 2015. Jeepneys reach Guintubdan from Bacolod via La Carlota.

Silay

☏ 034 / POP 121,000

Just 14km north of Bacolod, Silay was once the jewel in the crown of the Negros sugar boom, when plantations connected the island to the world. During its Golden Age

CLIMBING MT KANLAON

The challenging climb to the summit of Mt Kanlaon (2435m) competes with G2 on Sibuyan and Madjaas on Panay for the best in the western Visayas.

Route There are four trailheads to the summit: Wasay, Mananawin, Maput and Guintubdan. Most routes take two days, with the exception of Guintubdan, which can be done by fit hikers in one. Whichever one you choose, the best place to camp on the first night is Margaha Valley, the spectacular flat basin of the old (extinct) crater. The most rewarding part of the climb is the home stretch from Pagatpat Ridge to the summit, where, on a clear day, you can see Margaha Valley below, the smoking crater above and Bacolod in the distance. The hardest part of the climb is the long, steep incline leading up to Pagatpat Ridge itself.

Risk For keen hikers, Mt Kanlaon is not a tricky or demanding climb, but there is some risk involved. Every few years sees some volcanic activity, or 'sneezing' as locals call it. There is daily monitoring for any threat of eruption, with no permits issued in such cases. The park superintendent will sometimes evacuate the mountain and enforce a clearance zone of 8km around its base. The last eruption occurred in August 1996, killing three hikers.

Equipment The weather can be unpredictable, and the terrain challenging, so bring a light waterproof jacket and climbing shoes. Prepare for a chilly night: thermals and a woolen hat are recommended.

Permits & Fees Anyone trekking within a 4km radius of the summit (ie climbers) must obtain a permit (P700) from the Bacolod-based Office of the Park Superintendent (p243). This requires a scanned copy of your passport clearly showing your age.

Guides & Porters A mandatory guide (P700 per day, maximum 10 trekkers, five per guide) can be arranged either through the Park Superintendent or the **Department of Environment & Natural Resources** (DENR; ⊙8am-5pm Mon-Fri) office in Guintubdan. Porters cost an additional P500 per day.

When to Go The primary climbing season is March to May and October to December. In the off-season the park imposes a 30 person per day limit, so walk-ins run the risk of the mountain being full.

Tours Volcano-climbing tours are available, but cost significantly more than going it alone. In Bacolod, **Billy Torres** (☑0917 887 6476; billytorres369@yahoo.com; ML Inc, Goodyear Servitek, Capitol Shopping Ctr, BS Aquino Dr) arranges trips for P7000 per person, with group discounts and no accommodations; P500 is donated to the Negros Forest Foundation. Advance notice of two months or more is ideal. In Maolboal, Cebu, **Planet Action** (☑0916 624 8253, 032-474 3016; www.action-philippines.com) offers all-inclusive three-day trips for P10,000. In Dumaguete Harold's Mansion (p255) arranges occasional two-day trips for P8000 all-inclusive. It will also help you book the various elements of your own trip, which reduces the cost to around P2500 plus food, and is perhaps the best of both worlds.

(1880–1935) 29 surviving 'ancestral homes' were built here, of which three are now museums. These sugar mansions were bastions of refinement and privilege, forming a culture reminiscent of *Gone with the Wind* (as in Iloilo). But it wasn't to last. World War II and the collapse of the sugar industry left the town in mothballs, making this a fascinating stop for any history or architecture buff.

◉ Sights

The tourist office has a useful free map of the historic district.

★**Hofileña**
Heritage House　　　HISTORIC BUILDING
(☑495 4561; Cinco de Noviembre St; adult/child P50/30; ⊙10am-5pm Tue-Sun, otherwise on request) This stately house contains an astonishing private art collection, as well as antiques belonging to one of Silay's principal families. The house is owned by the charismatic and loquacious Ramon Hofileña, a tireless preserver of the region's cultural heritage. If you book ahead, Ramon will proudly show you around his priceless collection of local artworks.

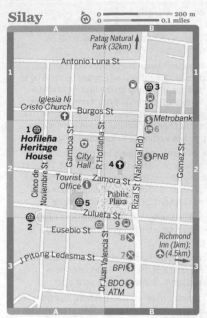

Silay

Silay Museum   MUSEUM
(Civic Centre, cnr Zamoa & Gamboa Sts; ⏱8am-noon & 1-5pm Mon-Fri) Start your tour with this well-done, succinct overview of the town's history, using models, gowns from the Sugar Era, and vintage photos of historic homes.

Bernardino Jalandoni
Ancestral House   MUSEUM
(📞495 5093; Rizal St; adult/child incl tour P60/30; ⏱9am-5pm Tue-Sun) Known as the 'Pink House' (1908), this museum looks like the owner left yesterday. In the back room are old photos of beauty pageant winners from the 1940s and '50s, and a glass case filled with dozens of Ken and Barbie dolls in traditional Filipino costume, including General MacArthur Ken re-enacting the (staged) Leyte landing, and Imelda Marcos Barbie surrounded by dozens of shoes.

Balay Negrense Museum   MUSEUM
(📞714 7676; Cinco de Noviembre St; adult/child P60/30; ⏱10am-6pm Tue-Sun) Also known as the Victor Gaston Ancestral Home (1898), this hardwood home has the most photogenic exterior of any house in Silay. The house has been painstakingly restored and furnished with period pieces donated by locals. The bevelled-glass windows and Chinese carved lattice work are all original.

Church of San Diego   CHURCH
(Rizal St) On the main road through town, the silver-domed, Romanesque Church of San Diego (1927) is topped by a crucifix that, when lit at night, is visible far out to sea. Don't miss the garden set in the adjacent ruins of the previous church, which houses an attractive prayer room screened with capiz windows.

🍴 Sleeping & Eating

There are several seafood restaurants by the mangroves in Balaring, providing atmospheric dining. Take Rizal St to the north edge of town, turn left on Balaring Rd and follow to the end.

Winbelle Pension Hauz   PENSION $
(📞495 5898; www.winbelle.weebly.com; Rizal St; r P700, ste P1500; ❄) This second-storey family-run hotel in downtown Silay could use a coat of paint, but manages to feel a bit homey and offers good value.

Richmond Inn   HOTEL $$
(📞0923 521 8618; www.richmondinnsilay.com; J Pitong Ledesma St; r incl breakfast P1500-1800; ❄🛜) The best choice in Silay, the mission-style Richmond has decent rooms. For light, choose the ones facing the street. On the edge of town, towards the airport.

El Ideal Bakery   BAKERY $
(Rizal St; pies & cakes P45-50; ⏱6.30am-6.30pm) Just south of the public plaza, this well-known bakery was set up in 1920, during

Silay's heyday, to provide snacks for gamblers who couldn't drag themselves away from the table. Its dark wooden interior retains this atmosphere.

Some of its famous creations include *lumpia ubod* (spring rolls filled with pork, shrimp and the juicy tip of the coconut palm) and *piaya* (flatbread sprinkled with brown sugar and sesame seeds).

★ **Café 1925**   ITALIAN $$
(J Pitong Ledesma St; mains P135-180; ⊙ 9.30am-9.30pm; 🔊) Foodies will delight in this little Italian bistro with a serious chef offering weekly menu specials and generous servings of homemade everything. Try the crabmeat pasta (P180) and some wonderful mango cheese ice cream (P60) for dessert.

ℹ Information

Silay's **tourist office** (🖂 495 5553; silaycity_tourism@yahoo.com; cnr Zamora & Gamboa Sts; ⊙ 8am-noon & 1-5pm Mon-Fri) is located inside the civic centre, and can organise tours to nearby sugar plantations and permits to Patag Natural Park.

There are several ATMs, with **Metrobank** (cnr Burgos & Rizal Sts) having the largest withdrawal limit.

ℹ Getting There & Away

Silay airport is approximately 10 minutes away from the city proper. A van will cost P50.

Both buses and jeepneys travel between Silay and **Bacolod** (P14, 30 minutes). In Silay, all buses and jeepneys heading north and south stop along Rizal St.

From Silay, there are buses all day stopping at the coastal towns towards **San Carlos** (P130, three hours).

Sagay

🖂 034 / POP 19,323

Near the northern tip of Negros is Sagay City, which is actually two cities: New Sagay on the National Hwy, and Old Sagay on the coast, 5.5km away (P9 by tricycle). The city is best known as the guardian of the 32,000-hectare **Sagay Marine Reserve**, established in 1999. For visitors, highlights are the 200-hectare **Carbin Reef** (P100 entry), about 15km northeast of Old Sagay (20 minutes by bangka), and **Suyac Island** (P20 entry), where you can walk an elevated 400m bamboo boardwalk and kayak through the mangroves (P300).

To organise a boat, ask at the **tourist office** (🖂 488 0649; sagaycityinfo@yahoo.com; City Hall, New Sagay). Failing that, ask at the pier. A small boat will cost P1200 (maximum 10 people). Snorkelling equipment (P300) can be arranged at the tourist office (it's too shallow to dive). You'll see different species of giant clam, but fish are scarce indeed. Not so at **Museo Sang Bata Sa Negros** (🖂 457 8003; www.fb.com/museosangbatasanegros; Old Sagay Port; admission adult/child P40/20; ⊙ 8am-5pm), an interactive marine museum near the Old Sagay port, where on certain weekends children dressed up as reef animals narrate the exhibits. This is utterly heartwarming and not to be missed.

The tourist office can also help organise accommodation in town. Avoid the government-run Balay Kauswagan, a characterless convention centre with dirty rooms and no restaurant.

Ceres buses run regularly to Cadiz (P16, 30 minutes) and Escalante (P9, 15 minutes). From Cadiz there is a ferry service to Bantayan Island (P200, four hours) every other day or so, normally at 10am, but check at the port. For a safer and smoother ride choose a ferry over a bangka.

Escalante

🖂 034 / POP 14,569

Like neighbouring Sagay, Escalante is a city of two parts – with Old Escalante on the coast and New Escalante on the highway. City Hall, the town plaza, the bus terminal and BDO bank are all in New Escalante; the port of Danao, from where the boats to Cebu leave, is in Old Escalante. It's 7km between the two, and a tricycle will cost around P10 (15 minutes).

The helpful **tourist office** (🖂 454 0696; www.escalantecity.gov.ph; City Hall, New Escalante)

LOCAL KNOWLEDGE

HERITAGE TOURS

For 41 years, Ramon Hofileña has run the **Annual Cultural Tour of Negros Occidental** (tours P1000). The three one-day tours are scheduled in December, and take in attractions from the nearby region. With a few days' notice, Ramon can arrange architectural tours of Silay as well. Enquire at the Hofileña Heritage House (p247).

can assist with accommodation and activities. It can also arrange guides (P1000 per day) for the nearby caves, some used by the Japanese as hideouts in WWII, or for birdwatching at Kalanggaman.

Tiny Isla Puti (aka Enchanted Isle), a 20-minute bangka ride from Old Escalante (also approachable from Vito Port, Sagay), is a sandbar island connected to Jomabo Island at low tide. Boats (good for 10 people; P900, 20 minutes) can be organised at Barcelona pier or (far more cheaply) through the tourist office. You can stay at Jomabo Island Paradise Beach Resort (☑0920 438 8963, 0922 864 5706; jestermontalbo@yahoo.com; Jomabo Island; cottage P2820-3380).

In town, the best sleeping option is Rodeway Inn (☑454 0185; www.facebook.com/rodewayinnescalanteph; National Hwy, New Escalante; r from P850; ✸☏), a friendly and efficient family-run operation with comfortable and secure accommodation. It's located opposite the pretty town plaza.

The RORO ferry for Tabuelan, Cebu (P180, two hours) departs four times daily from Old Escalante's Port Danao; times fluctuate. There are direct buses from Escalante to Bacolod (P145, two hours), and to Dumaguete via San Carlos (P250, five hours).

San Carlos & Sipaway Island

☑034 / POP 40,000

San Carlos is the main port city connecting Negros to Cebu, with daily ferries heading to Toledo, on Cebu's west coast. It's not overflowing with charm, but is fine for an overnight stay, particularly during the wild Pintaflores Festival (☺5 Nov), a parade of people dressed in amazing flower costumes. Skyland Hotel & Restaurant (☑312 5589; cnr Endrina & Broce Sts; r with fan/air-con P475/625; ✸☏), halfway between the pier and the bus terminal, has hot water in spotless rooms. The restaurant food (mains P150) is well prepared.

In contrast to San Carlos, nearby Sipaway Island is a wonderful place to spend a few days, and is only 15 minutes by bangka from San Carlos port (P15). This beautiful, well-kept island is made even better by a perfect concrete path that leads through palms and villages from one end to the other, with great views back to Negros. Rent a *habal-habal* (motorcycle taxi; P60) at the pier and slowly explore. The island is long and thin, so you

can't get lost, and the residents are a happy lot; it feels as if you have gone back to a simpler time. The place to stay is the German-run Whispering Palms Island Resort (☑0929 873 1146; www.whispering-palms.com; Sipaway Island; r P1500-2300; ✸☏☒), which has spacious, spic-and-span rooms, its own mini-zoo, and a dive centre on 4 hectares of beachfront (high-tide swimming only). Book ahead for the private shuttle.

There are also falls, caves and rice terraces in the San Carlos area. Contact the City Tourism Office (☑312 6558; www.sancarloscityinteractive.com; City Hall; ☺9am-5pm) for more information.

✆ Getting There & Away

M/V Lite Ferry (☑729 8040; www.liteferries.com; San Carlos Port) has daily boats to Toledo (P110, 1¾ hours) at 5am, 7am, 10am, 1pm and 3.30pm. **EB Aznar** (☑467 9447; San Carlos Port) has several fastcraft that do the same run in under an hour (P225) at 7.30am, 9.30am, 11.30am and 3.30pm. The schedule changes frequently.

There are regular all-day buses from San Carlos' bus station (1km from the pier; P8 by tricycle) to Dumaguete (P145, four hours) and Bacolod (P155, four hours).

Bulata & Danjugan Island

The little town of Bulata is the doorway to southern Negros. Turn off here and a 3km track will lead you to the swish Punta Bulata Resort & Spa (☑473 0235; www.puntabulata.com; r P4500-5500, cabana P5700; ✸☏☒), which occupies its own kilometre of golden sand facing a set of islets. Designed by its architect-owner, the main complex is an attractive modern-Asian style with local touches. Wide-ranging accommodations include enormous rooms in a semi-courtyard around an attractive swimming pool, and beach cabanas with huge beds and indoor-outdoor baths. It has an elegant waterfront restaurant with an impressive seafood menu, and a dive centre. The resort blurs the distinction between hotel and spa, producing a very relaxing stop.

Doubling the value of a stay at Punta Bulata Resort is its exclusive proximity to Danjugan Island Marine Reserve & Sanctuary, which lies just offshore. Managed by the Philippine Reef & Rainforest Conservation Foundation (PRRCF; ☑0918 600 1589, in Bacolod 034-441 6010; www.prrcf.org) in

Bacolod, this 42-hectare island is a model of intelligent ecotourism. Well-maintained paths provide access through thick forest to idyllic deserted beaches, sea eagle nests and a screeching bat cave where pythons feed at the entrance, striking bats during their evening exodus. There are also kayaks available and a dive centre (P1300 per person, minimum four people). Offshore there are three no-take zones, making for improved fish-watching. Lodging is simple open cabanas with mosquito nets. Day trips can be arranged through PRRCF or Punta Bulata Resort for P1750 per person, including boat trip, lunch, kayaking, trekking, snorkelling and all necessary gear. Overnights (P2750) add lodging and meals, and are arranged through PRRCF. Three-day advance notice recommended.

Sugar Beach

With just a handful of eclectic, home-spun resorts, a gorgeous stretch of beach and psychedelic sunsets, Sugar Beach remains one of Negros' best-kept secrets, helped along by a tidal river that cuts it off from the road network. The atmosphere is low key, so if you're looking for a beach party, you're better off heading to Boracay.

🛏 Sleeping & Eating

Most resorts are strung along the beach.

★Big Bam Boo Beach Resort BEACH RESORT $
(☑0999 671 6666; www.bigbamboobeachresort. com; dm P300, r with fan P600-1200, air-con P1600; ❄🛜) This well-managed newcomer is making some of the old-timers on the beach look bad. The varnished cottages are all high-quality and tidy, the restaurant dishes out popular Filipino food, there's a new dive centre, and pricing is excellent.

★Sulu Sunset BEACH RESORT $
(☑0919 716 7182; www.sulusunset.com; Sugar Beach; r P550-1200) The right recipe: nice nipa huts with tile floors, ensuite bathrooms, and verandahs with hammocks facing the sea, at very attractive prices. The A-frames are the best deals on the beach, particularly the twin (P550).

Driftwood Village BEACH RESORT $
(☑0920 900 3663; www.driftwood-village.com; Sugar Beach; dm P250-300, d from P450; 🛜) Offers a classic mellow beach vibe with hammocks and nipa huts of variable quality

scattered about its leafy grounds. The kitchen specialises in Thai food, but European classics are also available (dishes around P200).

★Takatuka Lodge & Dive Resort BEACH RESORT $$
(☑0920 679 2349; www.takatuka-lodge.com; r P1700-2400; ❄🛜) The amount of love and energy that has gone into this wacky German-owned hotel is in evidence *everywhere*, particularly its nine themed rooms. The Mad Mix room features quirky touches like an upside-down toilet as a showerhead, while the Rockadelic room comes complete with Marshall amps, electric guitars and a gold record mounted on the wall.

Accommodation prices are discounted 15% to 25% if you opt for fan and/or cold water. Light switches are creatively hidden, sometimes in naughty spots. The zany restaurant has the best food around, with a huge varied menu. The two dive boats are the only serious equipment.

Bermuda Beach Resort BEACH RESORT $$
(☑0920 529 2582; www.bermuda-beach-resort. com; r with fan P1050-1950, air-con P1450-1550; ❄@🛜) While the simple rooms here are nothing special, the atmospheric restaurant is a pleasure to spend time in, and has an excellent kitchen serving European cuisine.

🍷 Drinking & Nightlife

Sugar Rocks Music Bar BAR
(☉11am-late) Looking for something to do? This new bar atop the hill at the end of the beach, with its narrow but sweet view, makes for a noble destination. Occasional music.

❶ Getting There & Away

Sugar Beach is isolated by a tidal river, which makes getting there problematic. If the weather is good, the quickest and easiest way is to take a bangka (P300 to P350, 10 minutes) from Poblacion Beach in Sipalay, 3km to the south. Many resorts pick up clients here.

Otherwise, from barangay Montilla, 3km north of Sipalay, catch a tricycle (P110) to barangay Nauhang, where paddle boats row you across the river (P15 per person; agree on price beforehand). Sugar Beach is a short walk around the point. During high tide, particularly in the rainy season, you may need to get a motorised boat (P200) from the bridge in Nauhang, or otherwise call your resort to fetch you.

Sipalay

📞 034 / POP 67,400 / TRANSPORT HUB

The only reason to visit this sprawling coastal town midway between Bacolod and Dumaguete is to catch a bus. There's regular service to Bacolod (regular/air-con P189/289, six hours). To get to Dumaguete involves three separate Ceres buses, all with regular services; firstly head to Hinoba-an (P25, 30 minutes), transfer to Bayawan (P80, two hours) and then on to Dumaguete (P100, 2½ hours).

If for some reason you get stuck, **Sipalay Suites** (📞 473 0350; www.sipalaysuites.com.ph; Mercedes Blvd; r with fan/air-con from P700/1500; ❋ 🛋) has comfortable rooms, a nice large pool, and seaside dining on Poblacion Beach (mains P90 to P150, open 6am to 8pm), a popular place to view the sunset. The tiny **Sipalay Tourist Information Centre** (www.sipalaycity.gov.ph; Poblacion Beach; ⏰ 8am-5pm daily Oct-May, Mon-Fri Jun-Sep) can assist with boat hire and accommodation.

There's only one ATM in Sipalay, at Landbank; the next closest is in Kabankalan, 2½ hours away. So if you're heading to nearby Punta Ballo or Sugar Beach, it makes sense to arrive with money in your pocket, just in case.

Punta Ballo

Punta Ballo is a promontory with a divine white beach of fine shell sand (high-tide swimming only) and a backdrop of wooded hills. But it's best known for what lies underwater: some of the best diving in Negros. At last count there were four PADI diving schools, at least 10 marine sanctuaries, and 42 dive sites, including three wrecks. Prices are fairly standard: P1500 per dive, P750 more for equipment and P18,000 for an open-water certificate. The entrance fee for marine sanctuaries is P50 for snorkelers, P150 for divers.

🛏 Sleeping & Eating

There are several other local/seasonal resorts in addition to these listings.

⭐**Nataasan Beach Resort & Dive Center**   BEACH RESORT **$$**
(📞 0915 670 5027, 453 8936; www.nataasan.com; r P1600-1800, bungalows P2200-2900; ❋ 🛜 🛋) Located on a bluff overlooking Punta Ballo Beach, this bamboo-style, family-friendly resort sports a large lodge with impressive views, good local food and large rooms located around a central pool with swim-up bar. The restaurant's cliffside perch is a great place for morning breakfast.

Artistic Diving Beach Resort   BEACH RESORT **$$**
(📞 453 2710, 0919 409 5594; www.artisticdiving.com; r without bathroom P500, with fan/air-con P1350/1770; ❋ @ 🛜 🛋) Named after its owner (Arturo), Artistic has large and comfortable sea-facing cottages with private balconies, cable TV and hot-water bathrooms set in a well-tended garden by the beach. It serves tasty Swiss food with homebaked bread, and good veggie curries. Dive-accommodation packages available.

Easy Diving Beach Resort   BEACH RESORT **$$**
(📞 0917 300 0381; www.sipalay.com; r with fan/air-con from P1600/1950; ❋) Easy Diving has pleasant and spotless Mediterranean-style rooms, a nice beach and a well-set-up dive centre, with far-ranging multiday trips. Pass on the super-deluxe rooms in favour of the deluxe, as the difference is P1150 for a TV.

ℹ Getting There & Away

The turn-off for Punta Ballo is at the Sipalay town plaza, on the left as you come into town. A 7km *habal-habal* (motorcycle taxi; P50) or tricycle trip leads you to the resorts, which all face the sea.

Tambobo Bay

📞 035

At the southernmost point of Negros, gorgeous Tambobo Bay has the hideaway ambience of a pirate's cove. Popular with yachties who anchor in the safe waters at the mouth of two small rivers, the entrance to the bay has a few stretches of white beach with an evening view of spectacular sunsets. There's also some real buried treasure here, too. The **Kookoo's Nest** (📞 0919 695 8085; www.kookoosnest.com.ph; Tambobo Bay; cottage for 3/4 P1000/1500) is a 1700-step descent from the main road, but you won't mind when you get there. Situated on a lovely white-sand cove, with soothing breezes and breaking waves, this idyllic mini-resort of six bamboo cottages could also be called the Love Nest. It has a dive centre and a surprisingly sophisticated restaurant. For variety you can also take a boat to several impromptu eateries on the cove serving local live-aboards. To get here arrange a pick-up service with the hotel.

Malatapay & Zamboanguita

☑ 035

Malatapay is best known by tourists for its huge and lively **market**, where every Wednesday morning villagers, fishers and Bukidnon tribespeople can be found loudly bartering their goods and feasting on *lechón* (spit-roasted whole pig).

Malatapay is also known for being the departure point for Apo Island, with boats leaving from the beach in front of the market.

If you want to stay here to access Apo Island dive sites, **Thalatta Resort** (☑ 0920 668 7393, 0917 314 1748; www.thalattaresort.com; Zamboanguita; r P3300; ❀ 🛜 ≋) in nearby Zamboanguita delivers fine food and excellent lodging in bungalows set around a lovely infinity pool with ocean views. The park-like grounds are a bit faux, but the French owner runs a tight ship, including a dive centre. Most clients are European, roughly half divers.

Apo Island

☑ 035 / POP 920

This tiny 12-hectare volcanic island, with its one beachfront village, is known for having some of the best diving and snorkelling in the Philippines. You'll also find gorgeous white coral-sand beaches, some fine short walks, a friendly island community, and excellent views back to Negros, crowned by Mt Talinis. Word is out, however, so if you want more nature and less company consider Danjugan Island. Electricity in the village is only available in the evenings.

🏃 Activities

During high tide in the mornings, just out front on the main beach, you're almost guaranteed to encounter massive green sea turtles feeding in the shallows, providing a memorable snorkel.

Apo Island Marine Reserve & Fish Sanctuary   DIVING

(admission P100, additional snorkelling/diving fee P50/300) This 15,000-sq-metre protected area is one of the most successful marine reserves in the Philippines. The reserve contains a vital marine breeding ground and is a favourite site among divers and snorkellers for its superior visibility. Due to reopen by 2015 after recovering from typhoon damage.

BAYAWAN SURFING

Surfers take note: there's a burgeoning surf scene in Bayawan, midway between Sipalay and Dumaguete, mainly from June to October. The action takes place along the town's 2km seafront boulevard, and is both safe and friendly. Boardmaker **Rex Lamis** (☑ 0916 665 2477, 0947 270 3613; www.facebook.com/negroshapers) is the local expert, and can provide both advice and rental equipment.

🛏 Sleeping & Eating

There's limited lodging on Apo, so reservations are recommended (well in advance for the December to January peak season). In addition to the few resorts, a smattering of homestays offer basic rooms for around P500.

Mario Scuba   GUESTHOUSE $

(☑ 0906 361 7254; www.marioscubadiving-homestay.com; dm P300, d P500-1000; 🛜) This small and somewhat messy dive centre has sunny rooms, with the pricier ones (P1000) being top value: super-spacious with polished floorboards and balcony. Breakfast is P100, lunch and dinner P180.

★ Liberty's Lodge & Dive   RESORT $$

(☑ 0920 238 5704; www.apoisland.com; dm/s/d incl full board from P900/1500/1950; @🛜) Perched high above the beach, this is the place that most divers head for. Top instruction is one attraction, but the friendly, laid-back atmosphere and wide range of well-designed rooms with balconies and excellent views are equally memorable. Room prices include three hearty meals, providing fantastic value. A boat dive including equipment is P400.

Apo Island Beach Resort   RESORT $$

(☑ 0917 701 7150; www.apoislandresort.com; dm P800, d from P2700) Tucked away in an ultra-secluded cove, this refined dive resort claims the best white-sand beach and most peaceful atmosphere. The Spanish Mission rooms and cottages have fan and cold-water bathrooms. The simple menu has good Filipino food (dishes P175 to P210). During high tide, it's accessed via steps leading up past the nearby Liberty's resort – or better yet, through the surf and a rocky gorge.

❶ Getting There & Away

Apo Island is about 25km south of Dumaguete. The departure point is from Malatapay Beach, where boats (P300, 30 minutes) depart three to four times per day from 7am to 4pm. Otherwise you can try to organise a ride with one of the resorts, share a trip with others or hitch a ride with a dive company. Chartering your own boat costs P2000 for four people, P3000 for eight. Waterproof your valuables.

Dauin

☑ 035 / POP 25,000

Dauin (dow-*in*) is a haven for dive resorts. It's known for its macro diving in the marine reserve of Masaplod Norte, as well as good snorkelling over the drop-off about 20m from shore. The beach is not very attractive, so you'll probably be sticking to the pool otherwise. Most of the resorts offer local excursions, with Twin Lakes and Lake Balanan being popular. There's also the sulphur **Baslay hot springs** (admission by donation), along a bumpy road 10km off the main highway, best accessed by motorcycle or *habal-habal* (motorcycle taxi).

🛏 Sleeping & Eating

Puerto Citas Beach Resort   BEACH RESORT **$**
(☑ 0919 656 2244; www.puertocitas.com; r from P950; ❄ ☒) There's no restaurant or dive centre in this polyglot compound, but the relaxed and pleasant garden bungalows are among the cheapest you'll find in Dauin.

Pura Vida Beach &
Dive Resort   BEACH RESORT **$$**
(☑ 0928 507 7167, 400 6959; www.sea-explorers. com; r with fan/air-con incl breakfast P2900/3900; ❄ ☒) An outpost of the Philippines-wide dive company Sea Explorers, this is a top-quality and very friendly dive resort and spa, with beautifully varnished accommodations. You're near the neighbours, though.

★ Atmosphere   BEACH RESORT **$$$**
(☑ 400 6940, 0917 700 2048; www.atmosphereresorts.com; r P9600, apartment P11,500; ❄ 🛜 ☒) Atmosphere has raised the bar for hospitality on Negros. The staff is outstanding; the spacious suites and apartments are all tastefully designed, with nice wicker furniture; the landscaping is perfect; the huge thatched restaurant is a pleasure to dine in; and the spa is the very best in the region, with four treatment cabanas (one hour P2650) in their own serene water garden.

★ Atlantis Dive Resort   BEACH RESORT **$$$**
(☑ 424 2327, 0917 562 0294; www.atlantishotel.com; r incl breakfast US$150; ❄ 🛜 ☒) Atlantis combines beautiful accommodation with many years of Philippines diving experience to offer an unbeatable package for high-end divers. It offers a thorough focus on safety, five scheduled dives per day and a far-ranging liveaboard boat that does up to 10-night trips. Non-divers will also appreciate the charming Spanish-style buildings, expert masseuses, lovely pool and relaxing tropical atmosphere.

Azure Dive & Yoga Resort   BEACH RESORT **$$$**
(☑ 422 6715; www.azuredive.com; Masaplod Norte, Dauin; r P4250; ❄ 🛜 ☒) The only Filipino-owned resort in Dauin, brand-new Azure has been thought through nicely. Tasteful minimalist rooms have attractive local decorations and wooden touches, while on-site yoga makes a nice complement to the diving focus. The main market is Asian divers, so the food is Filipino-Chinese.

Dumaguete

☑ 035 / POP 130,000

A favourite among travellers, Dumaguete is far more hip and urbane than your average provincial capital, partly because it is a university town, and partly because 4000 expatriates live here (as opposed to 400 in Bacolod). It's a confident place that really knows how to be a town, with a cosmopolitan harbourfront promenade lined with upmarket bars, restaurants and food stalls. It's also an ideal base for nearby dive sites, forays into the wilds of Negros Oriental or exploring the nearby islands of Siquijor and Cebu.

◉ Sights

Two landmarks in town are the coral-stone **Bell Tower** (cnr Perdices & Teves Sts) near the public square (1754–76), and the large and lively **public market** on Real St.

Rizal Boulevard   STREET
While Filipino cities aren't generally known for their beauty or charm, Dumaguete's waterfront promenade along Rizal Blvd is an exception to the rule. Constructed in 1916, this scenic quarter-mile lined with old-fashioned streetlamps is a peaceful spot to stroll, attracting families on picnics, power-walkers and those content to sit on benches gazing out to the sea. Nearby are a good selection of restaurants, bars and food stalls.

Silliman University Anthropology Museum
MUSEUM

(admission P60; ⊗8.30-11.30am & 2-4.30pm Mon-Fri) Set in an unmissable American stick building salvaged from a New York theatre, this very nice anthropology/ethnobotany collection on the university campus includes artefacts from the indigenous Negritos and the Islamic period, including a massive ceremonial *kris* (sword) 10ft long.

Centrop
ZOO

(Center for Tropical Conservation Studies; ☑422 6002; Ipil St; adult/child P10/5; ⊗9am-5pm Mon-Sat) Opposite the hospital is this small zoo and research centre housing 16 species of indigenous mammals, reptiles and birds, including the critically endangered Negros bleeding-heart pigeon, Philippine spotted deer and the Visayan warty pig. Donations are appreciated, and needed.

Sidlakang Negros Village
CULTURAL VILLAGE

(☑226 3105; Blanco Dr) On the same site as the provincial tourism office, this cultural centre promotes products and crafts from Negros Oriental. The best time to visit is during a festival, as otherwise many of the pavilions are often closed. To find it, take the National Hwy towards the airport and turn right at the side street opposite the Mercury Drugstore.

🏃 Activities

Dumaguete is primarily a base of exploration, so travellers should learn what is available in the surrounding area. Most dive centres are in the resorts south of town.

Scuba Ventures
DIVING

(☑035-225 7716; www.dumaguetedive.com; Hibbard Ave; ⊗9am-noon & 1-6pm Mon-Sat) A good Filipino-run outfit offering diver training and trips to Apo Island, Siquijor and Cebu.

👉 Tours

★Provincial Tourism Office
TOUR

(☑225 1825; negrostourism.com; EJ Blanco Dr; ⊗7am-7pm Mon-Fri) Unlike many tourism offices, this one acts more like a travel agency, taking an active role in planning trips for visitors, including the provision of exceptional guides (like Jac Señagan, a birdwatching expert: tourguidejac@yahoo.com). Local tours include waterfalls in Valencia, dolphin and whale watching in Bais, swimming with whale sharks in Oslob (Cebu), forest hikes in Twin Lakes National Park, caving in Mabinay, and birdwatching around Lake Balanan.

Harold's Mansion
TOUR

(☑225 8000; www.haroldsmansion.com; 205 Hibbard Ave) The Harold's empire includes an inexpensive tour operation that ranges far and wide, including trekking to Mt Talinis and Mt Kanlaon, swimming with whale sharks in Oslob (Cebu), visiting Malatapay market, and a special focus on diving (it operates a live-aboard boat in Dauin).

🛏 Sleeping

★Harold's Mansion
HOSTEL $

(☑035-225 8000; www.haroldsmansion.com; 205 Hibbard Ave; dm/s/d from P250/350/500; ❅@🛜) Local boy Harold knows what makes backpackers tick, and this high-rise hostel reflects it. While the rooms are concrete-simple, they are clean and well priced, with wi-fi, breakfast and transport pick-up included. Best of all is the sociable rooftop bar/restaurant, a great place to meet fellow travellers. Harold also runs a variety of tours around Negros.

Vintage Inn
INN $

(☑225 1076; Surban St; s/d from P300/400; ❅🛜) A safe, clean and central budget option, opposite the market.

GO Hotel
HOTEL $

(☑0922 464 6835; www.gohotels.ph; Real St, behind Robinsons Mall; r P888; ❅🛜) Excellent budget choice for transiting travellers.

Florentina Homes
APARTMENTS $$

(☑422 0827; www.florentinahomes.com; Rovira Rd; r P1500-2500, apartments P3000-5000; ❅🛜❅) Perfect for young families, this complex offers playfully decorated rooms, huge apartments in European themes, an eclectic bistro full of travel bric-a-brac (mains P175 to P395), an ice-cream parlour and a superb pool.

Island's Leisure
BOUTIQUE HOTEL $$

(☑035-994 9291; www.islandsleisurehotel.com; Hibbard Ave; d incl breakfast P1000-1400; ❅🛜❅) This offbeat property doesn't work well as a spa due to street noise, but it has some very attractive common areas, particularly the central courtyard with its small bar, lounge seating and contemporary Asian artworks. The midrange rooms are a bit bare, but the backpacker rooms – rare in a boutique hotel – are an absolute steal at P450.

C&L Bayview Inn
HOTEL $$

(☑421 0696; www.clhotel.com.ph; Teves St; r incl breakfast P1150-1700; ❅🛜) This hotel is known for its psychedelic colour pattern,

Dumaguete

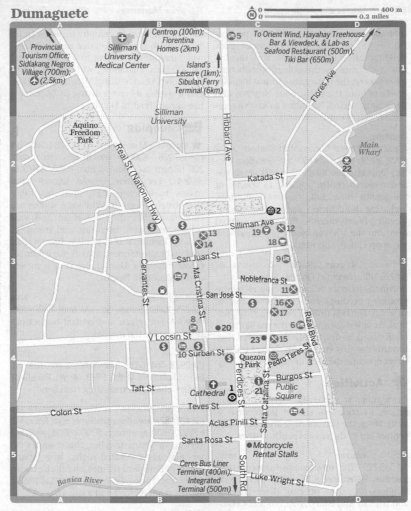

which ranges from bright yellow to flaming orange to lime green, but otherwise the rooms are nice and spacious, and come with balconies in case you can't take it anymore.

Bethel Guest House
HOTEL **$$**

(☎ 225 2000; www.bethelguesthouse.com; Rizal Blvd; s P900-1500, d P1100-2200; ❈ @ ☎) Tired of your sinful ways? This Christian hotel will help straighten you out. Even if it fails, you'll still appreciate the exterior rooms, especially the corner family suites with their great views of the city, or the Villa Suite (P4500), one of the city's finest digs.

Hotel Palwa
HOTEL **$$**

(☎ 422 8995; www.hotelpalwa.com; Locsin St; r from P979; ❈ @ ☎) In the middle of the action, bright and cheerful Palwa has neat pastel-coloured rooms and an in-house travel agency for arranging tours. The light-filled and spacious triples (P1499) are good value, but stay above the 3rd floor or you'll be staring at a wall.

Hotel Essencia
HOTEL **$$**

(☎ 422 1136; www.hotel-essencia.com; 39 Real St; r incl breakfast P1500-1800; ❈ ☎) This high-rise offers solid value rooms, with flat screens

Dumaguete

and very nice linen, but choose the deluxe over the standard for light.

Honeycomb Tourist Inn   HOTEL $$
(☑ 225 1181; www.honeycombtouristinn.com; cnr Locsin St & Rizal Blvd; s/d incl breakfast from P800/1000; 🅱 🛜) The rooms are a bit beaten up here, but history lends this hotel some charm, and it's great value for Rizal Blvd. Staff are helpful, and the seafood restaurant is good. Book well ahead for sea-facing rooms (P2300).

La Residencia Al Mar   HOTEL $$
(☑ 225 7100; www.laresidenciaalmar.com; Rizal Blvd; r P2000-2900; 🅱 🛜) A faux Spanish hacienda, replete with oil paintings, a wide wooden staircase and pots overflowing with ferns. The rooms have solid wooden floors and colonial-style decor. Unless you go for the pricier, sea-facing rooms, you're probably better off trying elsewhere. Has a good Japanese restaurant.

✖ Eating

For a cheap and tasty option, there's a half-mile of food stalls set up along Rizal Blvd in the evening. Try a *balut* (duck embryo) if you dare; don't mind the feathers.

★ Two Story Kitchen   KOREAN $
(☑ 522 0126; Santa Catalina St; Korean meals P189-250; 🕙 10am-11pm Sun-Thu, to midnight Fri & Sat) What, never been to a two-storey Korean cafe? The upstairs teahouse is the draw, with elevated floor seating in semi-private

stalls cushioned by cosy floor pillows. The menu is double-sided: standard cafe fare (sandwiches, pasta, pizza etc) on one side and Korean meals on the other. A fun and popular hang-out.

Sans Rival Cakes & Pastries   BAKERY $
(☑ 225 4440; 3 San José St; 🕙 9am-7pm) Don't leave town without trying the addictive silvanas (cookies filled with buttercream) or a slice of cake from this long-term bakery (1977). Unfortunately, the nearby Sans Rival Bistro, with its picture menu, doesn't measure up (beautiful building, lame food). So if you want lunch, better to have your pasta and sandwiches here.

Panda Ice Cream   ICE CREAM $
(☑ 225 9644; www.yumchacatering.net; Ma Cristina St; 🕙 9am-8pm) Known far and wide for its fried ice cream (P55).

★ Kri   INTERNATIONAL $$
(☑ 421 2392; 53 Silliman Ave; mains P200; 🕙 10.30am-9.30pm Fri-Wed; 🛜) This chic contemporary restaurant, where the chef works in a glass cube, offers sophisticated dining at affordable prices. The highly international fusion menu defies easy synopsis, but don't worry, there's something creative for all tastes. The inner dining room is more upscale than the adjacent cafe, but the latter is a great stop for a dragonfruit shake.

★ Lab-as Seafood Restaurant   SEAFOOD $$
(☑ 035-225 3536; Flores Ave; meals around P250; 🕙 10am-2pm) Loud and lively, this

Dumaguete institution has expanded from a small seafood restaurant in 1988 to a diverse culinary, drinking and entertainment complex. Tanks of fresh seafood are on hand, as well as a steakhouse and sushi bar. It's a one-stop evening, and it's all well done.

★**Casablanca** EUROPEAN $$
(cnr Rizal Blvd & Noblefranca St; mains P185-575; ✷ 🕿) One of Dumaguete's most popular restaurants, Casablanca tries its hand at most cuisines, but is known primarily for its hearty Austrian dishes. In a lovely spot on the waterfront, it serves up crispy and succulent roast pork and schnitzel, with a delicious eggplant variation for vegetarians. Sesame-seared tuna with salsa makes a fine appetiser, and there's a good sandwich selection for lunch.

Coco Amigos MEXICAN $$
(🖉 226 1207; Rizal Blvd; meals from P180; ⊘ 7am-midnight Mon, Thu & Sun, 7am-1am Fri & Sat; 🖉) A colourful Mexican restaurant on the boulevard, offering everything under the sun, including 200+ drinks.

Pasta King ITALIAN $$
(🖉 421 0865; www.pastakingasia.com; 5 Locsin St; mains P100-300; ⊘ 11am-9pm Mon-Sat, 4pm-9pm Sun) Classic Italian menu, no frills but tasty.

🍸 Drinking & Nightlife

★**Hayahay Treehouse Bar & Viewdeck** BAR
(🖉 226 3677; 201 Flores Ave; ⊘ 4pm-late) From its streetside tables to its upstairs treehouse, this is a great place to go out for a drink or meal (it shares a kitchen with Lab-as Seafood Restaurant next door). There is a different style of music every night; on Friday and Saturday the bands keep crooning until 4am. And the pizza is superb!

Tiki Bar BAR
(tiki.ph; Escaño Beach; ⊘ 5pm-2am Sun-Thu, to 4am Fri & Sat) This hopping late-night beach bar offers riotous DJs and live party music from its concert stage. Expect a young crowd and weekend tailgates. At Escaño Beach, about 1km north of the Main Wharf.

El Amigo LIVE MUSIC
(Silliman Ave; ⊘ 9am-1pm) Open-air live music makes this a fun and lively bar. Mexican food helps wash down the San Miguel.

Zanzibar BAR
(www.zanzibardumaguete.com; 2 San José St; ⊘ 5pm-late) Popular with a young student crowd, intimate Zanzibar has dance music that pumps over two small levels.

Bo's Coffee CAFE
(🖉 422 2119; cnr Rizal Blvd & San Juan St; ⊘ 7am-midnight; 🕿) The Starbucks of Dumaguete.

ℹ️ Information

The **Bureau of Immigration** (BOI; 🖉 225 4401; 38 Locsin St; ⊘ 8am-5pm Mon-Fri) is a good place to extend your visa minus the crowds, and it's usually issued on the same day. It's next to the Lu Pega Building.

The **Provincial Tourism Office** (🖉 225 1825; www.negrostourism.com; Blanco Dr; ⊘ 7am-7pm Mon-Fri) has exceptionally helpful staff with great info on all of Negros Oriental. It shares a site with the Sidlakang Negros Village. The smaller but more central **Dumaguete Tourism Office** (🖉 422 3561; www.dumagueteunitown.com; Quezon Park; ⊘ 8am-5pm Mon-Fri) focuses on the city proper. The Department of Tourism has also accredited two travel agencies, **Maganda Travel & Tours** (🖉 225 8256; cnr Santa Catalina & Locsin Sts; ⊘ 9am-5pm) and **Orient Wind** (🖉 225 3536; Flores St; ⊘ 9am-5pm).

An excellent resource for anyone planning to hang around Dumaguete for awhile is www.dumagueteinfo.com, which includes an active forum.

There are several banks in town with ATMs, including branches of BPI, Chinabank, Metrobank and PNB. The main **post office** (cnr Santa Catalina & Pedro Teres Sts) is near Quezon Park. The best medical facilities are at **Silliman University Medical Center** (🖉 225 0841; V Aldecoa Rd; ⊘ 24hr).

ℹ️ Getting There & Away

The airport is on the northern edge of town (by tricycle P12). From Dumaguete Airport, Cebu Pacific and AirPhil serve Manila four times per day. Cebu Pacific also serves Cebu every morning.

The Main Wharf is downtown. The Sibulan Ferry Terminal is 4km beyond the airport. The Tampi port is 22km north of the city; Ceres buses leave for Tampi hourly from 2am to 2.15pm.

The **Ceres Bus Liner Station** (🖉 225 9030; Calindagan Rd) is just south of town. The new **Integrated Terminal** (Robinsons Mall) lies 100m further south (behind Robinsons Mall) and handles all north and south jeepneys.

After Cebu City, Dumaguete is the best connected port in the Visayas. A number of companies have offices at the pier.

ℹ️ Getting Around

Abundant tricycles charge P10 to P15 for trips around town.

There are several **motorcycle rental stalls** on the corner of Santa Rosa and Perdices Sts. Expect to pay around P300 per day or P1750 per week. It pays to compare prices and check brakes and headlights.

Valencia & Around

035 / POP 31,477

Valencia is a clean and leafy town with state-ly tree-lined avenues and a large, grassed central square. It sits at the foot of **Mt Talinis** (1904m), whose twin peaks are known as Los Cuernos de Negros (The Horns of Negros). There are four trails to the summit. Guides can be arranged by the Provincial Tourism Office (p255) in Dumaguete and Harold's Mansion (p255).

Housed in a private residence on the out-skirts of town, the **Cata-al War Memorabilia Museum** (035-423 8078; entry by donation; 8am-5pm) contains a collection of war relics from World War II – bombs, helmets, bullets etc. Most were uncovered by the owner, Felix Cata-al, in the jungle around Mt Talinis, where some estimate up to 10,000 Japanese soldiers died during a month of bombing.

West of town 2km (P15 by tricycle), **Forest Camp** (422 7027; entry P80, r P1000-2500; 8am-6pm) and **Tejero Highland Resort & Adventure Park** (400 3977; www.tejerohighlandresort.com; entrance adult/child P60/40; 9am-6pm) are adjacent ecoparks that make a superb day trip, a very popular choice with local families. Forest Camp is an attractive complex of streams, pavilions,

BOATS & BUSES FROM DUMAGUETE

Boats

DEPARTS	DESTINATION	COMPANY	TYPE	FARE (P)	DURATION	DAILY FREQUENCY
Main Wharf	Tagbilaran	Ocean Jet	fastcraft	680	2½hr	1
Main Wharf	Cebu	Ocean Jet	fastcraft	950	4½hr	1
Main Wharf	Dapitan	Ocean Jet	fastcraft	680	1hr 40min	1
Main Wharf	Dapitan	Montenegro, Aleson, Cokaliong, George & Peter	RORO	295-360	4-6hr	4-5
Main Wharf	Siquijor	GL Shipping	fastcraft	120	1½hr	5 Mon-Fri
Main Wharf	Siquijor	Ocean Jet	fastcraft	200	40min	1
Main Wharf	Siquijor	Aleson	RORO	100	2hr	2
Main Wharf	Larena, Siquijor	Montenegro	RORO	136	2hr	2
Main Wharf	Zamboanga City	George & Peter, 2GO	RORO	942-1489	10-11hr	Tue & Sun
Main Wharf	Cebu City	George & Peter, Cokaliong	RORO	320-430	6hr	1-2
Main Wharf	Manila	2GO	RORO	2500	15hr	Tue
Sibulan	Lilo an	various	fastcraft	62	20min	10
Sibulan	Lilo-an	various	bangka	47	20min	every 45min
Tampi	Bato, Cebu	Maayo	RORO	70	30min	every 90min

Buses

Jeepneys service all points from the integrated terminal.

DEPARTS	DESTINATION	FARE (P)	DURATION (HR)	DAILY FREQUENCY
Ceres Bus Station	Bacolod	241-284	5	every 30min
Ceres Bus Station	San Carlos	171	4	hourly
Ceres Bus Station	Bayawan	100	2	every 45min
Ceres Bus Station	Sipalay (via Hinobaan)	285	4½	every 45min
Ceres Bus Station	Cebu City (via ferry)	270	5	hourly

ziplines and natural pools integrated into the jungle. The sprawling Tejero adds ATVs, segways, a restaurant, a longer zipline and more pools. Tejero also operates an impressive 600m trans-valley zipline (P250, closed Monday) at Tierra Alta, a hilltop resort 4km away.

4km from town are the glorious, 30m Casaroro Falls (admission P15) – most refreshing after the required 335-step descent. A *habal-habal* (motorcycle taxi) from the market (P150) will drop you at the top. En route is Harold's Ecolodge (☏0999 816 8055; www.haroldsmansion.com; dm/r P200/500), of Harold's Mansion fame, which offers dorm rooms (P250) and bare-bones cabins (P500) at the Apolong trailhead to Mt Talinis (P1000, two days). The nearby videoke is a blight, but thankfully finishes up before dark.

Along the Valencia-Bacong Rd, around 2km from the coast, the peaceful and well-loved Bambulo Resort (☏0999 797 33 18; www.bambulo.com; Valencia-Bacong Rd; r P690, bungalow s/d P1610/1840; ☏☀) has great pizza in wood-fired ovens, an atmospheric outdoor restaurant, a lovely shaded pool on two levels, light and airy bungalows with nice bamboo touches (P1850 to P2070), and inexpensive rooms with shared baths and a nice common area (P690). A great spot to recharge your batteries.

Jeepneys run all day between Dumaguete and Valencia (P12, 30 minutes). A *habal-habal* costs around P150.

Twin Lakes National Park

About 20km northwest of Dumaguete, the twin crater lakes of Balinsasayao and Danao offer some wonderfully scenic hiking. The area is virgin forest and full of wildlife, including monkeys and birds; if you're lucky you might spy a rare Philippine spotted deer or Visayan warty pig.

Entry to the park is P100, payable at the checkpoint office – where guides (P300) are available, but it's better to arrange a guide from the Provincial Tourism Office (p255) in Dumaguete. Keep going 900m beyond the gate to reach the first lake, where there are kayaks (per hour P100) and paddle boats (per hour P250) available. There's also a pleasant restaurant overlooking shimmering Lake Balinsasayao. Hiking trails include a short trail connecting the lakes; a popular 30-minute trail to some waterfalls; and

a longer three-hour trail to the twin falls in Red River Valley. Pack good shoes as this trail can get very slippery.

Arriving from Dumaguete, the entry point for the 13.5km scenic track to Twin Lakes is just before San José on the coastal road at Km 12.4 (you'll see the sign pointing inland). A *habal-habal* from here to the lake is a P400 round trip. To get to the turn-off from Dumaguete, catch one of several daily buses from the north bus terminal (P25) or a jeepney from Real St.

Bais City & Around

☏035 / POP 80,700

About 45km north of Dumaguete (P50, one hour by Ceres bus), Bais City is one of the country's top spots for dolphin and whale watching. More species of cetaceans (including killer whales) have been seen in the squid-filled, 3000ft deep Tañon Strait between Negros and Cebu than anywhere else in the Visayas. Various species of dolphin are common, and swim in large pods; Spinner dolphins perform acrobatic leaps. Whale sightings are quite rare, especially outside of their March to October migration season.

The Bais City Tourist Office (☏0998 344 0588, 402 8338; City Plaza; ⊙8am-5pm Mon-Fri) organises excellent outings combining whale watching with a snorkelling stop at the Manjuyod sandbar and birdwatching at the 250-hectare Talabong Mangrove Forest and Bird Sanctuary, where there's a network of raised walkways. A 20-seat boat is P4020, so the cost to the individual depends on the size of the party. Boats depart from Capiñahan Wharf, 4km from town (P25 by tricycle from the plaza), where you can also arrange boats for a similar price. Trips last from 7am to 2pm, and are very scenic, with beautiful island backdrops.

The best place to stay in Bais is the historic La Planta Hotel (☏402 8321; www.laplanta.com.ph; Mabini St; r from P1450; ☀☏☀), which has pleasant shady surrounds, large and bright doubles, and an atmospheric if overpriced restaurant.

Heading a further 8km north you'll reach Manjuyod, where you can arrange a visit to its exquisite white sandbar, a narrow 7km stretch at low tide, from Canibo port (P2500 all day). Basic accommodation is available in four stilt cottages (cottage P3000-4000); at high tide the water rises just above the foundations, making the houses appear marooned in the middle of the ocean. Lighting is solar-powered; bring your own supplies. The rate includes return boat transfer and can be arranged through the Manjuyod tourist office (☏ 0917 622 4678, 404 1136; manjuyod-tourismoffice@yahoo.com.ph; ⊙ 8am-5pm Mon-Fri). This is a great opportunity to spot banded sea snakes by day, and unlimited stars by night.

At the junction on the road to Manjuyod, head left (inland) a further 20km to get to Mabinay, 87km from Dumaguete, home to a complex of over 400 caves. Guides and information are available from the very helpful Bulwang Caves Information Centre (☏ 0917 789 2445; entry per beginner/advanced cave P15/30), which can arrange guides (from P400 for seven people) to the eight caves that are open to the public, ranging from beginner to extreme. The most popular and accessible (with lighting and a walkway) is Crystal Cave, an underground fantasy-land of sparkling crystal and milky white stalactites. Spelunking is also possible in the 8.7km-long Odloman Cave, the second largest in the Philippines. This involves a vertical entrance rappel and is only accessible during December to May; a subterranean river rages through it at other times. Serious cavers are advised to bring their own equipment, as only limited helmets and flashlights are available.

The information centre can also arrange trips to visit a nearby Aeta village, the Ne-grito ethnic group who are indigenous to Negros. In the village there's thought to be fewer than 20 pure-blooded Aeta left.

If you're wanting to stay the night, Econotel Guest Inn (☏ 0918 510 3997; r from P500; ❄) has a range of rooms (some featuring Jacuzzis and waterbeds!), 3km before the caves.

There are regular buses to Dumaguete (2½ hours, P110).

SIQUIJOR

☏ 035 / POP 91,000

For most Filipinos, Siquijor is a mysterious other-world of witchcraft and the unknown. True, this tiny island province is famous for its mountain-dwelling *mangkukulam* (healers) who brew traditional ointments for modern ailments. But these days Siquijor's most popular healing practice involves a cocktail and a deckchair at any number of its laid-back and wonderfully affordable beach resorts. Attractions include great diving, waterfalls, caves and forest walks in the hilly interior. Just about everywhere on Siquijor is great for snorkelling – find the nearest beach and dive in. Like many beaches in the Visayas, swimming is only possible during high tide, and wearing flip-flops is recommended as protection against sea urchins.

THE SHAMANS OF SIQUIJOR

Long associated with tales of shamans, witchcraft and black magic, Siquijor is often tagged with the moniker 'the Mystique Island'. Local authorities and indeed most locals are quick to downplay the existence of black magic or evil spirits on the island, instead promoting Siquijor as a place for 'white magic', in reference to the island's many 'folk healers'. They come in three types: herbal healers, faith healers and *bolo-bolo* (water-and-stone) healers.

Herbal healers, most of whom reside in the mountains around San Antonio, work their magic with potions derived from herbs found in Siquijor's allegedly enchanted forests. Faith healers, who are found throughout the Philippines, use incantation and prayer to perform their magic. Unique to Siquijor, *bolo-bolo* involves a glass of water containing a black stone being blown through a straw, and hovering the glass over the patient's body until it becomes a browny colour, which identifies the ailments.

It takes a bit of pluck to find Siquijor's *mangkukulam* (healers). Villa Marmarine can point you in the direction of lowland *bolo-bolo* healers around Tulapos and Bitaug. San Antonio and Cantabon are where most herbal healers reside, and both towns also have resident faith healers and *bolo-bolo* healers. Annelyn, the tour guide secretary in Cantabon's Barangay Hall, can point you in the right direction.

The best time to visit herbal healers is during Holy Week, which sees a congregation of folk healers and shamans from all over the Philippines come for the Lenten Festival of Herbal Preparation (⊙ Black Saturday; day before Easter) in Bandila-an Mountain View Park.

BORACAY & WESTERN VISAYAS SIQUIJOR

Siquijor

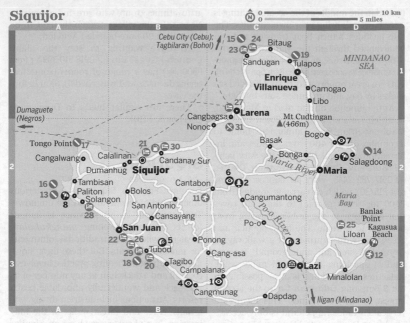

Siquijor

ℹ Getting There & Away

The vast majority of travellers arrive in Siquijor by boat from Dumaguete. Less frequent ferries from Cebu, Bohol and Mindanao are also an option. The island's two main ports are Siquijor town and Larena.

Note that the last trip to the island from Dumaguete is the 6pm Montenegro RORO to Larena;

the first trip off the island is GL Shipping's 6am fastcraft from Siquijor town; the last trip off the island is Aleson's 5.30pm RORO from Siquijor town.

Services from Siquijor town:

Fastcraft to Dumaguete are run by **Oceanjet** (☑ 0923 725 3732; Siquijor town pier) (P210, one hour, 1.50pm) and **GL Shipping** (☑ 035-480 5534; ⊘ 4.30am-5pm) (P140, 1¼ hours, five daily). In heavy seas, opt for the more stable, twice-daily RORO run by **Aleson Lines** (☑ 035-422 8762; ⊘ 6am-4am) (P100, two hours).

Note that Seventh-day Adventist GL Shipping does not run trips on Saturdays, while Oceanjet sometimes adds a second trip in the high season.

Oceanjet boats continue on to Tagbilaran (P910, three hours) and Cebu (P1410, six hours).

From Larena, Montenegro Lines has two RORO trips daily to Dumaguete (P136, two hours) in Negros. **Lite Shipping** (☑ 0926 160 4932; Larena Pier) services Cebu (P350, eight hours) via Tagbilaran, Bohol (from P220, 3½ hours), on Tuesdays, Thursdays and Sundays at 7pm. Lite Shipping services Plaridel, Mindanao, three times a week (from P345).

ⓘ Getting Around

A great way to explore the island is by motorcycle. The 75km coastal ring road is practically devoid of traffic and distances from Siquijor town are clearly marked with yellow kilometre signposts. With leisurely stops along the way you can easily circumnavigate the island in a day. The hilly interior is also well-covered by sealed roads and ripe for exploring by motorcycle.

Motorcycle hire is available everywhere; the going rate is P300. A good strategy is to hire a bike right when you arrive at the pier in Larena or Siquijor so you can ride to your resort yourself.

Air-con vans, multicabs and three-passenger jeeps are also available for hire through most resorts. Expect to pay P1500 to P2000 for a guided trip around the island by jeep or van, or about P1000 for a multicab.

Public tricycles cost P25 for a 10km trip between major towns; a special trip will set you back about P250. Public multicabs meet the ferries and circle the island, but are sporadic and stop running around 3pm.

Siquijor Town

☑ 035 / POP 25,500

Other than a lively market selling fresh fish and the usual selection of small shops, there's not much going on in Siquijor town. There's a picturesque coral-stone **church** built in 1783 that you can climb up for a bird's-eye glimpse of the town.

Internet access is available at **Das Traum Cafe** (per hr P15; ⊘ 7am-7.30pm) at the pier.

🛏 Sleeping

Das Traum Guesthouse   GUESTHOUSE $
(☑ 0917 366 2704; Siquijor town; d with fan P250-350, with air-con P700; ✱) If you want to save money and don't mind being off the beach, this place has big, bright, slightly run-down rooms on the east edge of Siquijor town.

★ **Villa Marmarine**   GUESTHOUSE $$
(☑ 0919 465 9370, 035-480 9167; www.marmarine. jp/en; Km 2.5; s/d bungalow with fan P500/700, d with air-con P3500-4500; ✱@☎) Run by an irrepressibly cheerful Japanese couple, Villa Marmarine features a Japanese-inspired design that makes it all hang together so well. *Furo* baths, wooden ceiling fans and Japanese super-toilets feature in some rooms, no two of which are alike. Many cottages have two levels; the newest have sprawling sea-facing balconies.

It's on a great white-sand beach, complete with deckchairs, and also has an on-site dive centre. Other pluses: wheelchair accessibility, free use of kayaks, free snorkelling gear and a tennis court with open late-afternoon sessions run by owner Daman.

Larena & Around

☑ 035 / POP 12,931

Larena has a laid-back provincial feel, a couple of decent restaurants and a slew of resorts on enticing Sandugan Beach, 6km north of the town centre. Unlike increasingly popular San Juan, Sandugan still feels pretty remote – it's the place for those who want little more than to stare at the sea for hours. There's a post office and a PNB bank with an unreliable ATM in Larena proper.

🛏 Sleeping

Kiwi Dive Resort   RESORT $
(☑ 0908 889 2283; www.kiwidiveresort.com; Km 16.9, Sandugan; r with fan P450-690, with air-con P990-1190; ✱@☎) It's a lovely walk down a trellis-covered pathway from the simple and clean hillside rooms to the beach, sitting area and small bar. There's a dive centre, and motorcycles, mountain bikes and kayaks are available for hire.

Islander's Paradise Beach Resort   BEACH RESORT $
(☑ 035-377 2412; www.islandersparadisebeach. com; Km 16.9, Sandugan; cottages with fan/air-con

P850/1150; ✳ @) One of Siquijor's oldest resorts, Islander's has eight faux nipa cottages with little concrete verandahs right on the water, perfect for incredible sunsets.

Sea Breeze
GUESTHOUSE $

(☑ 0998 182 4304; Larena; s/d without bathroom P200/300) Simple place at the sometimes noisy pier in Larena, convenient for late arrivals or early departures on the Montenegro ferry. Extreme penny-pinchers should ask about staying in their son's student dorm on the road to Basak (P100 per head).

✗ Eating

Larena Triad
FILIPINO $

(Km 8.5; mains P100-150; ⊘ 7am-9pm) The weird and wonderful Triad is perched on a hill above Larena like a giant Jesus-themed UFO. The food is nothing special, but you'll hardly notice with such an impressive view. From the highway it's 1km straight up on a rough road; a tricycle one-way will cost P30. Admission is P20 if you're not eating here.

Break Point
RESTOBAR $

(mains P80-120; ⊘ 8am-midnight) A good spot to hang out with the locals, this outdoor restobar in Larena is nice for a cold beer on a balmy evening and does a decent chilli squid.

San Juan & Around

☑ 035 / POP 13,525

Boasting Siquijor's best dive sites, some of its best beaches and an excellent range of accommodation, San Juan is where most visitors to Siquijor flock these days. The town itself is a typical small Visayan municipality, centred around a plaza and a landscaped enclosure known as Calipay's Spring Park.

Northeast of San Juan is the stunning white-sand Paliton Beach (Km 66.6). The water is as clear as glass and there are wonderful views of Apo Island. Take the turn-off at the little church in Paliton village, near the island's westernmost point, and head along a sealed track for about 1km to get to the beach. Keep walking west to discover yet more empty white-sand beaches.

The best diving in Siquijor is along a wall that runs from Paliton Beach southeast to Tubod Beach. There are several marine sanctuaries along this stretch, a Japanese shipwreck and a 'sunken island'. This part of the island is also the best jumping-off point for dive trips to Apo Island. Divers not staying at a dive resort should head to Last Frontier

Divers (☑ 0917 553 0454; per dive without/with equipment P1100/1400), located on the National Hwy in the centre of San Juan.

From barangay Tubod, 2.5km southeast of San Juan, a paved road leads 3km up to lovely Lugnason Falls, which cascade into a crisp and clean teal-green swimming hole.

Further ahead, just before the village of Campalanas, is a tremendous balete tree (banyan tree; Km 51.3) FREE, estimated to be 400 years old and believed by some to be enchanted. In front of the tree is a spring-fed pool filled with flesh-nibbling fish – dangle your feet in for a free fish spa.

🛏 Sleeping & Eating

A backpacker strip of sorts is emerging a couple of kilometres northwest of San Juan in barangay Solangon. Hostels, cheap cafes and even a bar or two have opened up. Just don't expect Boracay quite yet. Most resorts here offer free kayak use and slash prices by at least 20% in the low season.

★ JJ's Backpackers Village & Cafe
HOSTEL $

(☑ 0918 670 0310; jiesa26@yahoo.com; Km 64.6, Solangon; tent/dm P250/350, d P500-600; @ 🛜)
Laid-back JJ's is a throwback to the carefree days when you could camp on a beach, cook your own food and enjoy yourself without any worries. Located on a well-maintained patch of beach, there are only a few rooms here; if those are booked you're free to pitch a tent.

Its cafe serves cheap and very tasty food on the beachfront, with the burgers and fruit shakes highly recommended. It also bakes its own bread and uses fresh milk. Each morning a fisherman stops by selling fish, which you can cook for dinner.

Tori's Backpacker's Paradise
HOSTEL $

(☑ 0907 132 6666; torisbackpackersparadise@gmail.com; Km 60.8, Tubod; dm/d from P350/400; 🛜) Run by an exceedingly nice couple, this small backpacker crash pad has a handful of basic rooms near the water and a delicious (if slow) restaurant up by the road. It's on a rocky strip of shoreline, but within walking distance of the white-sand beach around Coco Grove Beach Resort.

Hambilica Ecolodge
RESORT $

(☑ 0917 700 0467; www.hambilicasiquijor.com; Km 62.4, Maite; d incl breakfast P900-1700; 🛜) 🍃 For something a bit different, consider this genuinely green resort just southeast of San Juan. The stand-alone cottages are sort of no-frills but are spacious and clean, and some have kitchenettes. There's no real beach here, but there are view decks over the rocks and the mangrove location is conducive to their evening firefly-watching tours (P100 admission for outsiders).

★ Coco Grove Beach Resort BEACH RESORT $$
(☑ 0939 915 5123, 0917 325 1292; www.cocogrovebeachresort.com; Km 60.5, Tubod; d P2950-5800, ste P6900-8700; ❋ 🛜 🏊) Coco Grove has a well-deserved reputation for excellent service and comfortable accommodation by the beach. It has two large swimming pools, several bars and restaurants, a spa and activities galore, not to mention a highly regarded dive centre and access to the wonderful Tubod marine sanctuary straight out front. This just might be the best-value upmarket resort in the Philippines.

Royal Cliff Resort BEACH RESORT $$
(☑ 0999 751 7944; www.royal-cliff-resort.de.tf; Km 61.3, Maite; r P980-1600; 🛜) A low-key resort with concrete duplex cottages; the more expensive rooms are large, homey and well decorated. Its restaurant has unbeatable sea views, and abundant hammocks up on the rocks over the beach provide good sunset vantage points.

Coral Cay Resort BEACH RESORT $$
(☑ 019 269 1269; www.coralcayresort.com; Km 65.2, Solangon; d with fan/air-con P1000/2000; ❋ 🛜 🏊) The original Solangon resort and still its best – largely because of its enviable beach. The charming wood-floored beachfront duplexes are what you want here. Well-appointed garden cottages and functional fan rooms are at the back. The great beach bar has sunset views over Apo Island.

The Bruce BEACH RESORT $$
(☑ 0928 601 1856; thebrucesiquijor@yahoo.com; Km 65.3, Solangon; d P750-1200, q P1800; 🛜 🏊) The huge wooden beachfront cottages, with furnished sunset-facing balconies, are front and centre at the Irish-run Bruce, which sprawls along a prime stretch of Solangon Beach. Cheaper rooms are in a row at the back and there's a quirky fan-cooled treehouse and a small pool as well. Nice value.

Ceasar's Place RESTOBAR
(☑ 0916 310 4810; Km 62.5, Maite; 🛜) Known for its raucous Friday nights, Ceasar's has live bands on its stage out back, and also has rooms (d P500 to P800).

Lazi & Around
☑ 035 / POP 20,024

The quiet southeastern town of Lazi is bisected by the island's only major river, the Po-o (po-oh). The town is home to the impressive and stylishly time-worn, pink-coral-stone and timber San Isidro Labrador Church, built in 1884. Over the road, flanked by centuries-old acacia trees, is the oldest Catholic convent in the Philippines, a magnificent timber and stone villa, creaky with age and eerily serene. Upstairs is the small Siquijor Heritage Museum (admission P20; ⊙10am-4pm Tue-Sun). Downstairs is a working Catholic grade school.

From Lazi, a sealed road leads 2km north to several refreshing swimming holes at Cambugahay Falls on the Po-o River. Access from the road is via a long set of steps. Never leave valuables unattended, as theft is a regular occurrence.

Between the towns of Lazi and Maria, Kagusua Beach is reached via the pretty village of Minalolan – look for the turn-off to the barangay of Nabutay and travel past the old limestone mine. A good road leads from the village down to Kagusua, where steep concrete steps take you down to a string of beautiful secluded coves that you're guaranteed to have all to yourself.

Between Kagusua and Salagdoong is the large horseshoe-shaped Maria Bay, where Princesa Bulakna Resort (☑ 0917 202 6720; www.princesabulakna.com; Km 37.2; r P1200-2500; ❋ 🛜 🏊) abuts a stunning beach. The seven sterile rooms are poor value for Siquijor, but it's worth stopping in for lunch and to snorkel in the marine sanctuary just offshore. It's 1km off the highway.

A few kilometres past the town of Maria, Salagdoong Beach (Km 29.5; admission P15) is popular with day-trippers. There's a half-open water park that has seen much better days, and you can jump into the ocean from 5m to 10m platforms built into the rocks. There's accommodation and a noisy restaurant here, but we wouldn't recommend either.

About 200m beyond the turnoff to Salagdoong Beach is the sleepy Olang Arts Park (☑ 0915 186 5618; annacornelia@yahoo.com; Km 29.3). There's usually a resident artist or two hanging about, plus a performing arts stage, a modest collection of modern art, a gallery of antiques and memorabilia, and a wall of nude photos by the late American lensman Marlon Despues.

Cantabon & Around

The small mountain village of Cantabon is the site of Siquijor's most thrilling adventure: the 800m spelunk through **Cantabon Cave** (admission P20). Tours of the cave are arranged through the well-run Barangay Hall in Cantabon and cost P500 for up to three people, inclusive of guide (mandatory), helmet and flashlight. There's no swimming or ropes involved, but expect to get dirty and wet navigating through narrow vertical climbs, waist-deep water and high humidity. Flip-flops are OK but river sandals or sneakers are better. There are several other caves in the area but they were off-limits at the time of writing.

Cantabon is also near Siquijor's highest peak, **Mt Bandila-an** (557m). Concrete steps lead 10 minutes up to the peak from two clearly marked points on the road between **Bandila-an Nature Centre** and **Bandila-an Mountain View Park**. There's a viewing platform at the peak from where the whole of Siquijor is visible. The nature centre has been largely neglected but does have walking trails and some impressive trees and other floral life. Bandila-an Mountain View Park is more like a public garden, with lots of flowers, walking paths and little pavilions for picnics. Both places are great for bird- and butterfly-watching. The nature centre is 2km east of Cantabon, and Mountain View Park another kilometre along.

Cantabon is easily accesed via steep and windy roads from Siquijor town (10km), San Juan (12km) or Lazi (15km). All roads leading up here are sealed. A tricycle from the lowlands will cost about P500 with wait time.

ROMBLON PROVINCE

☏ 042 / POP 284,000

Romblon Province consists of three major islands – Sibuyan, Romblon and Tablas. These are difficult to reach, partly because their rewards are so uneven. Large Sibuyan has Mt Guiting-Guiting to climb, but little else. Tablas has some nice beach resorts, but has taken corruption to a new level. Little Romblon is the hidden pearl, with a sleepy tropical-port charm, some good food and accommodation, two dive centres – the only ones in the province – and a hilarious group of local expats, making it worth the journey.

In the off-season, resorts throughout the province are often completely deserted. Getting cash can be a problem anytime.

There are few ATMs, they are finicky with the cards they accept, some are closed weekends, and all are closed when the power goes down. Don't be caught without money.

Romblon Province is politically part of the administrative district that includes Mindoro and Palawan.

ⓘ Getting There & Away

AIR

The only functioning airport in Romblon Province is a landing strip near Tugdan on the east coast of Tablas. At time of research it was only being used intermittently by **Seair** (☏ Manila 02-849 0101; www.flyseair.com), with flights back and forth to Manila on Monday, Wednesday and Friday (P2725, 40 minutes). These flights do not show up on online booking engines. Other carriers could begin service at any time.

BOAT

The most popular ferry connections are from Caticlan (to Looc on Tablas island) and Batangas (to Odiongan on Tablas and to Romblon town). Looc and Odiongan also have regular connections with Roxas, Mindoro. Sibuyan Island is connected to Roxas (Panay) and Mandaon (Masbate). Keep in mind that tropical storms often halt ferry service during typhoon season (June to November), when it helps to stay flexible.

Anchor Bay Watersports (p270) on Romblon Island has speedboats that can take you straight to/from Boracay in 20 minutes to one hour (P12,000 to P22,500 per boat):

Tablas Island

☏ 042 / POP 160,000

Tablas has loads of tourist potential. It has some excellent beaches, it's the main entry point to the province, and it's the closest of the three main islands to Boracay. However, it continues to self-destruct from corruption and mismanagement. During research the power had not been on for five days as the backup diesel supply had been sold off for someone's personal profit. One major resort had shut down after an armed stand-off with local police. With officials on the run, yet still running the show, the future remains in a holding pattern.

ⓘ Getting There & Around

The airport in Tugdan is little used; only Seair was offering sporadic flights to Manila during research. Most visitors arrive by sea, through one of four ports around the island; the Poctoy port serves nearby Odiongan.

Romblon

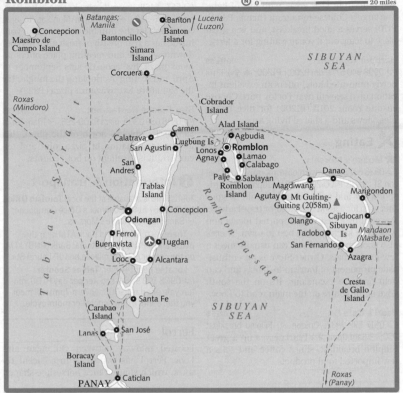

Jeepneys connect the main towns throughout the day but run fairly infrequently, the exception being the more popular Looc–Odiongan route (P50, one hour). There are more trips in the morning. Jeepneys between Looc and Odiongan dry up around 3.30pm. The last trips from San Agustin to Looc (P100, two hours) and Odiongan (P100, two hours) are around 2pm, when the last ferries from Romblon arrive. Morning trips in the other direction should get you to the ferries on time.

By far the quickest way around the island is a motorcycle taxi, known as a 'single' here. Looc to Odiongan (35 minutes) is around P120; Looc to San Agustin (1¼ hours) is around P400. Tricycle and single prices double after dark.

Odiongan

Almost halfway up the west coast of Tablas, Odiongan has accommodation and ATMs.

The tiny **Provincial Tree Park & Wildlife Sanctuary** in barangay Rizal (P250, 30 minutes by motorcycle taxi) makes for a pleasant morning walk. For beaches head south

to Ferrol. For a longer excursion, take the rugged and scenic road north to San Andres, where there are waterfalls to explore.

🛏 Sleeping

Kamella Lodge HOTEL **$**
(📞0907 442 8593; r with fan/air-con P300/600; ❄) Only 2km from Poctoy port, this sparkling new budget hotel offers six-hour rates if your ferry arrives after midnight. Across from Wavefront Resort.

Sato-Dizon Arcade HOTEL **$**
(📞567 6070; www.facebook.com/SatoDizonArcade; 039 Quezon St; r with fan P300, air-con P400-1200; ❄📶) On the beach side of town, this bright new hotel and restaurant offers clean rooms and small balconies 50m from the sea.

★ Wavefront Resort BEACH RESORT **$$**
(📞567 5376; doodsendaya@yahoo.com; r P1200-1800; ❄) This local gray-sand beach resort 2km from Poctoy port has a lot of charm. Only

some rooms have hot water, but all are clean and waterfront #1 is great, with lots of light. The largely Chinese restaurant (mains P80 to P170) serves a good breakfast, and is a great place to hang out if you're waiting for a ferry.

Harbour Chateau HOTEL $$
(☑ 0908 940 6771; dm P200, r P1200; ❉ ☎) This newly renovated hotel offers an excellent location on a seawall near Poctoy port. Choose ensuite room 201B (P1200) for nice balconies, views and a shared living area.

✗ Eating

★ **Mouse's Morsels** INTERNATIONAL $
(☑ 0926 637 3048; www.mousesmorsels.com; Quezon St; meals P100-200; ☺ 9am-10pm; ☎) This sports bar and sidewalk cafe should be your first stop for a good meal and/or travel advice. Powered by a deli with imported meats and wines, the kitchen is the best in town. There's also good music and you can usually meet a few local expats. Owner Steve is an enthusiastic proponent of tourism in Tablas and can help organise excursions. It's on the south edge of the centre on the main road to Looc.

Pearl's Cafe CAFE $
(☑ 0917 592 7932; Quezon St; Filipino breakfast P50; ☺ 6am-9pm; ❉) Pearl serves up a great Filipino breakfast, slings coffee and sells a few imported food products.

★ **Ghetto Plates** PIZZA $$
(☑ 567 6169; www.facebook.com/ghettoplates; pizza P175-350; ☺ 9am-10pm Mon-Sat, to 8pm Sun) Don't let the humble entrance fool you: inside lies a real breath of fresh air. This cool downtown cafe and meeting place offers famous pizza, live acoustic acts September to April and seating overlooking the jungle. Try the signature Extravaganza pizza (P325).

Star Palace Restaurant PIZZA $$
(☑ 0918 639 0309; pizza P200-295; ☺ 10am-10pm Sun-Fri) Two blocks north of the plaza, this unique combination of pizza joint and tea emporium is excellent on both counts.

❶ Information & Transport

Tourist info is available at the local **Tourism Office** (☑ 042 567 5145; Governor's Office Compound; ☺ 8am-5pm) or Mouse's Morsels.

There's a reliable Land Bank ATM near the plaza, and a Philippine National Bank (PNB) ATM on the corner of M Formilleza and JP Laurel Sts.

Located near the pier, **Tablas Scooter** (☑ 0908 199 9684; scooter per day P700, motorcycle per day P1000; ☺ 7am-7pm) will meet you there with a new scooter or motorcycle.

Ferrol

Located midway between Odiongan and Looc, Ferrol has two well-run adjacent resorts, which share a nice horseshoe-shaped

BOATS FROM TABLAS

DEPARTS	DESTINATION	COMPANY	TYPE	FARE (P)	DURATION (HR)	DAILY NUMBER
Santa Fe	Caticlan	various	bangka	200	1	1
Santa Fe	Carabao	various	bangka	200	1	1
Looc	Caticlan	various	bangka	200	1½	1
Odiongan (Poctoy)	Culasi, Roxas	Super Shuttle	RORO	650	6	Sun & Wed
Odiongan (Poctoy)	Romblon Town	Montenegro	RORO	320	3	Sun, Tue & Fri
Odiongan (Poctoy)	Dangay, Roxas (Mindoro)	various	bangka, ferry	350	3½	1, except Tue
Odiongan (Poctoy)	Batangas	2GO, Super Shuttle, Montenegro	RORO	760-850	7-10	2
Odiongan (Poctoy)	Caticlan	2GO	RORO	300	3	Tue-Thu, Sat, Sun
San Agustin	Romblon Town/ Sibuyan (Magdiwang)	Montenegro	RORO	175/375	1/3½	1
San Agustin	Romblon Town/ Sibuyan (Magdiwang)	various	bangka	150/350	1/3½	2

beach between two headlands. The **Binucot Sunset Cove Resort** (☑0918 214 0545; www. binucotsunsetcove.com; bungalow P1800-2800; 🕾) offers two interesting types of bungalows, charming Bali-style bamboo huts (P1800) and larger, airy octagonal models (P2800) with nice design features. Dorm beds for P300 are available. It offers excellent seaside dining and flexible meal plans. The **Binucot Beach Resort** (☑0918 633 1643; www.facebook.com/Binucot.Beach; r P1800-2000; 🕸🕸) is more motel-like, but has nicely appointed rooms and a small pool. Ask for pierside pick-up.

Buenavista

South of Ferrol, in the small fishing village of Buenavista, are the superb **Buenavista Cottages** (☑0921 271 9637; cottage P1500), which come with kitchens, fridge and nice loft balconies facing the sea. There's only simple meals nearby (bring food), and only one jeepney passes by per day, but there's long-term discounts, making this a perfect place to unplug and dig in for awhile. For fun, you can snorkel the **Buenavista Marine Sanctuary**, which surrounds a tiny islet about 7km north of Looc, in search of giant clams, lobsters and baby sharks. A bangka will take you there from the village.

Looc

Looc (law-awk) is the first stop on a journey from Boracay to Romblon Province. The local fruit and produce market, an interesting sight, is near the pier. Everything else is on the town plaza, a short walk away. The **KOICA** (☑0918 500 9136; ⏰8am-5pm) office at the pier has visitor information, and arranges visits to the **Looc Bay Marine Refuge & Sanctuary** (☑0919 787 6693; admission P100), a 48-hectare protected coral reef 10 minutes away by bangka. The boat ride is included in the price of admission for groups of four or more; for smaller groups it's P300. Snorkelling equipment (P50) is available. Boats take you to the sanctuary's moored bamboo raft, from where you can see giant clams.

There are few places to eat in town – try **Ashley Bakeshop** (Rizal St; mains P90-130; ⏰7am-6pm), with a big picture menu of Filipino food and breakfasts (avoid the pizzas, however). If you're staying overnight, the atmospheric, family-owned **Angelique Inn** (☑0927 315 3638; r with fan/air-con P400/800; 🕸) offers breezy upstairs rooms with shared

bathrooms and cold water, and a homey downstairs restaurant. Otherwise **Caesar's Lodging Inn** (☑0919 657 3906; joyglori06@ yahoo.com; Grimares St; r P850-1200; 🕸) offers standard concrete boxes in a compound one block from the plaza.

Alcantara

Alcantara is a small town with a decent beach, but the main reason to come here is to stay at the **Aglicay Beach Resort** (☑0915 425 6898; www.aglicaybeachresort.com; s/d from P900/1200; 🕸), some 4km off the highway. With the finest location on the island, the 20-hectare resort sits on a long and private white-sand beach framed by two headlands, with the closest offering spectacular views down a coastline carved with numerous scalloped bays. It offers a nice outdoor cafe/ restaurant; island hopping, snorkelling and kitesurfing; and pleasant if conventional rooms. If you're on the lam from the feds, this is the place to hole up. Transfer from Looc by tricycle (P400).

San Agustin

San Agustin is a picturesque stop on the way to or from the island of Romblon. Although you would never plan on staying the night, you won't have a choice if you miss the last ferry at 1pm. If you get stuck here, there are several streetside barbecues and food stalls around the market.

Accommodation options are clustered on a street running perpendicular to the main road, a one-minute walk from the pier. **Kamilla Lodge** (☑0921 375 2288; r with fan/ aircon P400/600) is the pick of the bunch, a cosy, friendly place in a striking modernist structure. **August Inn** (☑0919 592 2495; s/d without bathroom P200/400, tr with bathroom P800; 🕸) offers a few small tiled rooms on the 2nd floor of a bright pink building; shared bathrooms have scoop showers.

Calatrava

Remote Calatrava lies about 20 minutes by motorcycle taxi (P30) from San Agustin. Here you'll find **Paksi Cove Resort** (☑0946 145 6356; www.paksicoveresort.com; cottages P750-1000), which has a handful of cottages set on a secluded cove with its own beach. It's a great place to get away from it all, with a lush jungle backdrop adding to its romance. Call ahead.

Romblon Island

♪ 042 / POP 40,000

Utterly authentic and only lightly touristed, Romblon Island is the charming gem at the heart of its self-named province. A small island, it's even smaller for the visitor, as nearly everything you want to see is within a few kilometres of its main port and only significant settlement, Romblon town. This includes a handful of excellent resorts, eateries and activities; more than enough for a few relaxing days.

Surrounded by green hills, Romblon town is like the setting for a Hemingway novel, a languid, somewhat raffish tropical port town filled with bustling tricycles, bangka traffic and a colourful collection of local expats. For those without access to cable, a night walk through the market east of the plaza is better than TV.

◉ Sights

For the best views of Romblon town, walk up the stairs to the ruins of **Fort San Andres**, a crumbling 17th-century fort overlooking the centre.

Head west on the coastal road from Romblon town and you'll first reach **Bon Bon Beach** (a 20-minute walk from the road) then **Tiamban Beach** (tricycle P100, jeepney P12), both good for swimming. **San Pedro** also has a lovely beach, and decent snorkelling.

Romblon is best known for its grey marble, which graces the floors of churches and resorts all over the province and neighbouring Boracay. Quarries and workshops are most common along the road about 5km east of town, near Lamao. Finished pieces can be purchased on site or in the alley of souvenir shops facing the plaza.

🏃 Activities

Water Sports

Anchor Bay Watersports   WATER SPORTS
(☑0918 247 9941; www.anchorbaywatersports. com; ⊙8am-9pm) This jack-of-all-trades on the water 5km west of town primarily rents out watersports equipment – paddleboards, kayaks, hobie cats, windsurfers. However, it also rents rooms (P1500) with excellent views and shared bathrooms, and serves popular sunset meals, including steak and seafood (P200 to P500), along with drinks from the Marlin sports bar. Short on cash? It does cash advances from credit cards (10% commission).

Diving

Romblon Island has the only two dive centres in the province, one at the Three P Holiday & Dive Resort; known as Ducks Diving) and the other at Cabanbanan Dive Resort, a well-run operation with its own marine reserve. Dive sites include a **WWII Japanese wreck** north of Romblon Island, and the **Blue Hole** – the inside of an old volcano – off Tablas, favoured by advanced divers.

Snorkelers: don't miss taking a boat from Romblon town to Cabanbanan to see the marine reserve; the resort rents equipment and can arrange transport. For a wonderful day trip combine with Lugbung Island sightseeing (P650).

🛏 Sleeping

Fiesta time in Romblon town runs for a week in mid-January; book accommodation well in advance at this time.

🛏 In Town

Romblon Plaza Hotel   HOTEL **$**
(☑507 2269; rphreservation@yahoo.com; Roxas St; r with fan/air-con from P650/1100; ✾@) This high-rise opposite the town basketball court has clean rooms and helpful staff. The pricier rooms have views, but the location adjacent to the plaza means it gets *very* noisy if there's a public event. No hot water.

D'Maeastro Inn   LODGE **$**
(☑0949 930 277; d with fan/air-con P400/700; ✾) This simple family-run wooden lodge looks over the harbour. It's on the bend in the road 300m south of Romblon Deli.

★**Punta Corazon Resort**   BEACH RESORT **$$**
(☑0909 674 2606; puntacorazonresort@yahoo. com; r from P1200; ✾) Magnificently sited at the entrance to Romblon harbour, with panoramic views encompassing the nearby islands, this well-tended resort offers a variety of rooms and a large saltwater pool. The ensuite cabanas (P1200) and hilltop apartment with its great balcony (P3000) are best. There's also cheap dorm rooms (P250). Views and price make this resort the clear winner for Romblon town. Access is by sea only, but don't be put off: a shuttle to town is only P25.

★**Casa Joebelle**   HOTEL **$$**
(☑0929 721 0309; otik_riano@yahoo.com; Manuel Roxas St; r P1000-1700) Clean, modern rooms with 3rd-floor balconies and lots of light make this new hotel a winning choice. Inland half a block from the plaza.

Stone Creek House
GUESTHOUSE $$

(☑0906 212 8143; r with fan/air-con from P2000/3000, ste P4000, whole house P8500; ✳@⊛) This sophisticated stone town-house is the most fully stocked rental you can imagine, and sleeps six. The design is smart and guests get the run of the common room, which has a big flat-screen TV and Playstation. The owner prefers to book out the whole house, which is perfect for families, but may take individual bookings if you email in advance.

Blue Ridge Hotel
HOTEL $$

(☑0919 991 8132; Fetal Vero St; d P1200) A few minutes' walk from the town plaza, the Blue Ridge is a standard concrete box with tidy rooms, a few haphazard pieces of furniture and no hot water.

Outside Town

★San Pedro Beach Resort
BEACH RESORT $

(☑0928 273 0515; minamingoa@yahoo.com; Ginablan; cottages P700) This well-managed resort refuge is set on a little white-sand beach in Ginablan, about 10km south of Romblon town. From the spotless bamboo cottages you can peer through the jungle canopy to the beach below, where there is good snor-kelling at high tide.

It has an affordable restaurant serving breakfast and lunch (order dinner in advance), as well as a library of discarded books to help you while away your days. From town, a tricycle to the resort costs around P150. If you're arriving from Rom-blon town under your own steam, you'll need good directions – signage is virtually nonexistent.

★Cabanbanan Dive Resort
BEACH RESORT $

(☑0910 283 7612, 0920 711 5451; www.romblon-isl. com; cottages P800-1000) This superb getaway dive resort is located on a beach 20 to 30 min-utes by boat from Romblon town. The Swiss owner runs a spic-and-span PADI dive centre, with a magical marine reserve out front. Accommodation is simple but well-kept and with luxurious hammocks. Call in advance for free boat transfers if you're staying over-night. March to June is prime season.

Snorkellers can catch a boat from Moro Pier just north of the bridge in town, and see Lugbung Island afterwards (P600). Full snorkel equipment is P120. Single dive with equipment is P1400.

Dream Paradise Mountain Resort & Spa
HOTEL $$

(☑0908 748 2272; www.facebook.com/DPM-Resort; dm P350, r P1500-1800; ✳⊛) Is it a tropical version of the Potala Palace? This sprawling, gaily coloured hillside complex soars over the rice paddies below, bursting with balconies, stairways, flags, balustrades, a central pool, and various nice rooms, no two of which are alike. Dreamy? Gaudy? You choose. Located in Mapula, 9km south of Romblon town.

Three P Holiday & Dive Resort
NIPA HUTS $$

(☑0929 440 7135; www.the-three-p.com; cottag-es P1000; ✳) This dive operation has a few well-appointed nipa huts in a leafy com-pound on the beach about 7.5km southwest of Romblon town.

✖ Eating

★Romblon Deli & Coffee Shop
INTERNATIONAL $$

(☑0929 304 0920; mains P100-250; ⊘6.30am-10pm) Front and centre on the waterfront near the ferry docks, this unassuming ven-ture is the beating heart of Romblon's expat scene: part bar, part bistro, part tourist info centre. If you've been eating elsewhere in the province, you'll delight at the fluffy banana pancakes, fantastic omelettes, creative burg-ers and packed sandwiches. And after its Fri-day night happy hour, you may crawl back for the notorious 'Feeling Shitty Breakfast': two smokes, a Coke and a coffee for P70.

Republika Bar & Restaurant
INTERNATIONAL $$

(☑0921 284 3175; meals P150-220; ⊘6am-9pm) On the waterfront is this excellent eatery featuring huge sandwiches and a creative menu. Sit outside for great people-watching.

JD&G Italian Food
ITALIAN $$

(mains P120-350; ⊘7am-8pm) This new hole-in-the-wall – think bar seating in a thatched box – does justice to pizza and pasta.

ℹ Information

The post office and police station are in their usual place near the plaza.

INTERNET

There's no public wi-fi on the island; there's an **internet cafe** near the plaza, and the Plaza Hotel has some terminals.

MONEY

A PNB bank with a Visa-only ATM is located opposite and up the street from Republika.

TOURIST INFORMATION

There's a **tourism office** (romblongov@gmail.com; Capitol Bldg; ⊘ 8am-5pm) in the capitol building, but the best source of local information are David and Tess Kershaw, the owners of Romblon Deli (p271), who are happy to provide it.

❶ Getting There & Around

A circuit of the island by tricycle is very difficult because of road condtions on the western side. You're better off hiring a motorcycle (with driver P700 not including petrol, without driver P300 to P500 per day) at the park near the pier. You should be OK driving solo, but be careful in rainy conditions. Jeepneys go around most of the island, but are irregular and thin out the further you go from Romblon town.

Sibuyan Island

📞 042 / POP 35,249

At first glance, Sibuyan looks like ecotourism heaven. The island has an impressive peak, an exceptional amount of intact primary forest, loads of waterfalls and a high percentage of endemic species, leading local resorts to cleverly promote it as 'the Galapagos of Asia'. But the reality is this: there is only one quality resort, hardly any beaches, very little snorkelling (the island is surrounded by a coral plate), no towns of note and no poster animals. The only endemism that a visitor is likely to see is tropical plants, most of which are unlikely to move you unless you are a botanist. Add to this a feuding group of local German expats and one concludes that Sibuyan's obscurity is actually quite well deserved. The one exception is the spectacular Mt Guiting-Guiting (2058m), one of the Philippines' best climbs.

❶ Getting There & Around

Magdiwang's Ambulong port, 2km from town, is the most common port of entry, but the most adventurous route is the five-hour bangka ride from Roxas, Panay, to San Fernando. Boats to San Fernando divert to nearby Azagra if weather demands it.

There are around two jeepneys daily between Magdiwang and Cajidiocan (P70, 1½ hours), and between Magdiwang and San Fernando (P100, two hours). Some of these are timed to meet ferries at the pier. San Fernando and Cajidiocan are also linked by jeepneys (P55, one hour, three daily). Most trips are morning trips.

A ring road makes the island easy to navigate, although it is only intermittently paved. You can hire singles and tricycles to take you between the three main towns. A tricycle from Magdiwang to San Fernando runs P500. Resorts hire out motorbikes (around P600 per day) and mountain bikes.

Magdiwang

The entry point to Sibuyan Island for most visitors and gateway to Mt Guiting-Guiting Natural Park, riverside Magdiwang has a few cute houses but little else; there is hardly anywhere to eat in town.

◉ Sights

Mt Guiting-Guiting Natural Park　　　PARK
This 15,200-hectare natural park (pronounced gee-TING gee-TING) is a biological treasure, with an estimated 700 plant species, 130 bird species and a few rare mammals, including the small, nocturnal tube-nosed fruit bat; many of these are endemic. However, there is little infrastructure. The park is known mainly for its striking peak, G2, which attracts about 100 climbers per year.

Apart from the difficult trail to the summit, there is a moderate cross-country trail (about 18km) from Magdiwang (Jao-asan) to Olango (Espana), which crosses some rivers. This only attains a maximum 300m elevation, and can be done in two hours. Enquire at the Protected Area Office (p274).

Cataja Falls　　　WATERFALL
This three-tiered waterfall cascading into a refreshing swimming hole makes for a great half-day excursion. Walk (or ride) east out of Magdiwang past the basketball court

BOATS FROM ROMBLON

DEPARTS	DESTINATION	COMPANY	TYPE	FARE (P)	DURATION (HR)	DAILY FREQUENCY
Romblon Town	Tablas (Odiongan)	Montenegro	RORO	320	3	Tue, Fri & Sun
Romblon Town	Batangas	Montenegro	RORO	954	13	Tue, Fri & Sun
Romblon Town	Tablas (San Agustin)	Montenegro	RORO	96	1	1
Romblon Town	Batangas	Navios	RORO	900	11	Wed & Sat
Romblon Town	Cajidiocan	Navios	RORO	300	3½	Wed & Sat

(leaving it on your right). Continue about 1km to a fork in the road. Take the right fork, then another quick right up a hill, and continue for another 2km or so to the first sign of civilisation – a cluster of nipa huts. Ask around for a guide to take you through farms and forest to the falls (P100, 30 minutes).

Lambingan Falls WATERFALL
This beautiful waterfall and swimming hole is about 12km from Magdiwang (4km past the turn-off for the natural park). Tricycles can take you here (P130, 25 minutes).

🛏 Sleeping & Eating

⭐**Magdiwang Nature's View Lodge** HOTEL $
(☑ 0921 463 9422; Rizal St; dm P200, r with fan/aircon from P600/850) This bright and friendly new downtown entry offers spotless rooms at an excellent riverfront location, with a limited menu. Definitely get the corner triple (P1200) for views.

Bagumbayan Beach House & Tapsihan Restaurant BEACH RESORT $
(☑ 0919 976 5596; r with fan/air-con from P200/700; ❄) This is a quiet 14-room place with almost nonexistent service on a brown-sand beach outside town. It operates a small marine sanctuary, a 15-minute boat ride to sea with advance notice. Their basic roadside restaurant, **Tapsihan** (mains P20-50; ⏲ 5am-midnight), is a rare resource hereabouts, with a Filipino menu and beer.

Rancher's GUESTHOUSE $
(☑ 0908 786 4006; José Rizal St; s P250, d with fan/air-con from P500/800; ❄) The only place with a hint of style in town, Rancher's offers basic rooms and a rooftop where you can have a drink and wonder how you ever ended up in Magdiwang. Arranges one-hour bangka trips upriver (P200).

⭐**Sanctuary Garden** RESORT $$
(☑ 0920 217 4127; www.sanctuarygardenresort.com; camping/dm P100/250, r P1100-1800; ❄) Easily the best resort on the island, Sanctuary Garden does absolutely everything well, thanks to its talented owner, Edgar. The 30-hectare property is nestled in the jungle, offering fine views, short walks and a running stream. Accommodation ranges from a nice campsite to a superb dorm to elegant eco-bungalows with marble baths.

The outdoor restaurant offers great food. This is THE base camp for climbing G2, with a location near the trailhead and, most importantly, all the local knowledge, guides and equipment you need. Kayaking also available (per hour P160). Located across the river, 1.5km east of town.

Olango

In the middle of the southern coast, Olango offers several vacation rentals. The **Boathouse** (www.isledreams.com; dm P350, s/d P650/1300) has two floors and sleeps six; one bed is shaped like a boat. Rooms are priced per person. A rocky beach is nearby and the owner, who lives next door, dishes up good meals. Other properties nearby can be viewed on his website, www.isledreams.com. This includes the **Sa Agoha Beach Resort** (www.isledreams.com; enquire for prices; 🔊), a collection of four excellent cottages that would be attractive except that the resort is normally deserted.

BOATS FROM SIBUYAN ISLAND

DEPARTS	DESTINATION	COMPANY	TYPE	FARE (P)	DURATION (HR)	DAILY FREQUENCY
Magdiwang (Ambulong)	Romblon	Montenegro	RORO	228	2	1
Magdiwang (Ambulong)	Tablas (San Agustin)	Montenegro	RORO	324	3½	1
Azagra	Batangas	Navios	RORO	1000	16	Fri & Sun
Cajidiocan	Romblon	various	bangka	300	2½	Fri
Cajidiocan	Romblon	Navios	RORO	900	4	Wed & Sat
Cajidiocan	Batangas	Navios	RORO	1000	16	Wed & Sat
Cajidiocan	Mandaon, Masbate	various	bangka	450	4	Tue & Fri
Cajidiocan	Culasi, Roxas City	various	bangka	350	5	Tue
San Fernando	Culasi, Roxas City	various	bangka	350	5	Sun-Fri
San Fernando	Romblon	various	bangka	250	3	Thu & Sat

CLIMBING G2

G2, also known as Mt Guiting-Guiting (2058m), is one of the best climbs in the Philippines; some in-the-know climbers call it *the* best. The peak is remarkable for its long and dramatic knife edge, which must be walked like a tightrope to reach the summit. Getting there is often a hand-over-hand rock scramble. You don't need rappelling equipment, but you do need a guide, and to be very careful. A dry ascent is one thing, but in wet weather the summit becomes treacherous and is often closed for days.

The traditional route begins near Magdiwang and takes you up and back in two to three days. You reach the first camp on day one, spend the night and reach the summit before noon the next day. At that point you either try to make it all the way back to Magdiwang or overnight en route. There is also a trail from the summit that continues on to Olango, on the other side of the island. This is more for experienced jungle trekkers, particularly near the end, which is a tough slog. However, in all cases it is recommended that the journey begin in Magdiwang, as there is no established, trustworthy guide service from the Olango side of the island – a critical factor in this climb.

You need a permit (P300) to climb the mountain. These are available from the **Protected Area Office** (☑ 0928 490 1038, 0949 651 6340; mt_guiting2@yahoo.com; ⊙ 8am-5pm Mon-Fri, but staff generally present on weekends) at the park entrance, about 8km east of Magdiwang (P100 by tricycle). If you want to arrange the trek yourself, you can hire a guide (P800 per day, one guide per five climbers) and porters (P600 per day, optional) here, ideally at least one day prior to setting out. Rain gear, cold-weather gear, and good rock-climbing shoes are essential. If you want an established firm to arrange the trek for you, Sanctuary Garden (p273) is the only one with the experience necessary to organise a safe and successful journey, and to include all necessary equipment. This is the recommended option.

San Fernando

This town is the home of the rocky Cantingas River. While overstated as an 'Eco-adventure Zone', the public access point to the river does offer a dive tower, a rusty zipline (P200), and some basic rooms (P300) with cooking facilities in a lovely if isolated spot – all that remains of a resort destroyed by Typhoon Frank in 2008.

For a more remote getaway, private bangkas from the port can take you to **Cresta de Gallo**, a small white-coral sand island off the southern tip of Sibuyan. You can walk around the island in about half an hour and see little but your own footsteps. There is some OK snorkelling, but bring your own gear. Prices start at P2500 for six people, and vary depending on the length of stay.

On the coastal side of town, the **Sea Breeze Inn** (☑ 0921 211 6814; chuchiandres@yahoo.com; r P800-1500) occupies a nice seafront location in the middle of a fishing village; bamboo huts with verandahs face out to sea. There is a common kitchen and an attached cafe. R-Hub, a hostel under construction on Don Carlos St during research, could well have better rooms when complete.

The market area has three inexpensive eateries with irregular opening hours.

Cajidiocan & Around

Cajidiocan is perhaps most famous for having Sibuyan's only ATM – with its P200 withdrawal fee. It's located on the orderly town's main street, across from the aptly named **Marble House** (☑ 0926 887 0037; s P250, d with aircon P700-800; ❄). There's no signposting, but you can't miss this B&B. Inside, the rooms are well furnished and very cosy, with shared bathrooms. The owner, Miguel Rivas, also rents out **Alaheg Farm** (☑ 0926 887 0037; enquire for pricing), an impressive fruit farm with a two-storey, well-furnished, thatched-roof lodge that sleeps six and is the perfect jungle retreat. It's located in Danao, midway between Cajidiocan and Magdiwang.

For food you're in luck, as **Duane's Store & Burger House** (pizza P200-600) does the trick, especially the pizza. From San Fernando turn right at the public plaza, then left at the pharmacy, and it's on the left.

A few kilometres south, in Cambiang, is **Laura's Shop** (☑ 0916 958 9765; cottage P600), which offers bargain duplex cottages with exposed beams and marble floors; ask in the village.

Cebu & Eastern Visayas

Why Go?

Battered but not broken by duelling natural disasters in 2013, this region showed that it's more than just a glorious island playground. It's also incredibly resilient. Less than a month after an earthquake levelled Bohol's historic Spanish churches and denuded its iconic Chocolate Hills, super-Typhoon Yolanda (international name Typhoon Haiyan), flattened large parts of Samar, Leyte and Cebu. The heaviest-hit areas are still very much in recovery mode. Yet the message from the people was one of optimism: We're open for business, visit us, hear our story, help us heal. Meanwhile *most* of this region's prime attractions – the coral reefs and white-sand beaches of Bohol and Cebu, the waterfalls of Camotes and Biliran, the waves and caves of Samar and Leyte – were unaffected by the disasters. They remain as wonderful as ever, and ripe to be explored.

Best Beaches

➜ Malapascua (p292)

➜ Bantayan (p295)

➜ Alona Beach (p308)

➜ Anda (p315)

Best Places to Stay

➜ Nuts Huts (p314)

➜ The Henry (p285)

➜ Mike & Diose's Aabana Beach Resort (p293)

➜ Abacá Boutique Resort & Restaurant (p291)

When to Go
Cebu

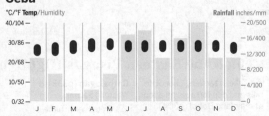

Jul–Sep Barring a typhoon, Samar and Leyte are dry while most of country is sopping.

Apr–May Flat waters for divers in Bohol, Cebu and Southern Leyte.

Jan The coolest month, plus the Sinulog festival in Cebu.

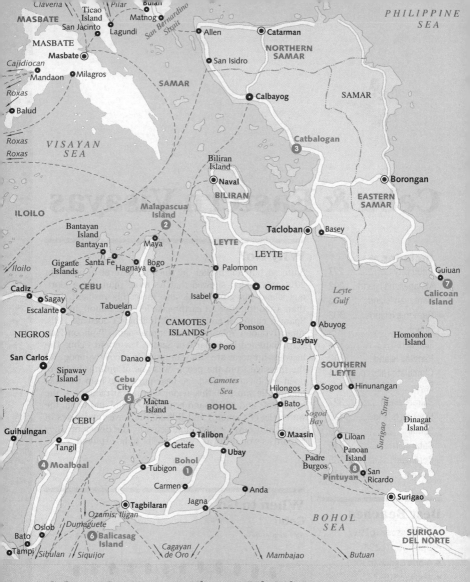

Cebu & the Eastern Visayas Highlights

1 Take in tarsiers, chocolate hills and rice terraces on a tour of mainland **Bohol** (p304).

2 Experience close encounters of the thresher-shark kind on chilled-out **Malapascua** (p292).

3 Swim, scramble and slog through the caves around

Catbalogan (p333) in Western Samar.

4 Freedive with the swirling vortex of sardines off **Moalboal** (p297).

5 Experience the fine museums, pulsating nightlife and emerging restaurants of **Cebu City** (p277).

6 Go scuba-diving amid the coral reefs of **Balicasag Island** (p311) off Bohol.

7 Drop in at **Calicoan Island** (p337), Samar, the country's best surf spot after Siargao.

8 Snorkel with the gentle *tiki-tiki* (whale sharks) of **Pintuyan** (p326), Southern Leyte.

CEBU

POP 2.6 MILLION

Simply being from Cebu carries a certain cultural heft, and it's not hard to see why. Cebu is the hub around which the Visayas revolve. It is the most densely populated island in the Philippines and is second only to Luzon in its strategic and economic importance to the country. The main attractions are its white-sand beaches and spectacular diving, namely off the northern tip of Cebu at Bantayan and Malapascua islands, as well as on the southwest coast at Moalboal. And don't ignore much-maligned Cebu City, which has lively bars, emerging eateries and great island-hopping opportunities.

❶ Getting There & Away

Cebu City is the gateway to the Visayas. It has the nation's busiest port and its second-busiest airport. If you happen to be travelling from Asia, it's an attractive alternative to entering the country at Manila, with several direct international flights to Cebu City.

From the busy port, a veritable armada of fast and slow craft head off to points north, east and south. Alternatives to Cebu City for accessing neighbouring islands include Argao for Bohol,

Danao for Camotes and Bogo for Leyte. Negros can be accessed from no less than five ports on the west of Cebu island.

Cebu City

⬀ 032 / POP 866,171

Cebu City is like an entrée-sized Manila; it's energetic, exciting and fast-paced, or loud, dirty and ruthless, depending on your perspective. On the surface, it does its worst to attract tourists, with its honking jeepneys spluttering exhaust fumes, shopping-mall culture and lack of world-class sights. Yet give it a chance and you'll find plenty to do here. Cebu has a rich history that's well documented in several good little museums. The upscale Lahug district comes alive by night with bars and clubs to suite every taste. And just over the bridge is Mactan Island, one of the few places in the world where you can experience world-class diving within minutes of a major international airport.

History

When Ferdinand Magellan sailed into the Port of Cebu on 7 April 1521, an eyewitness account relates that he was already a

LEGACY OF A SUPER TYPHOON

On 8 November 2013, Typhoon Yolanda (internationally known as Typhoon Haiyan), one of the most powerful recorded storms in history, made landfall near Guiuan in southeastern Samar. The storm plotted a course due west through the heart of the Visayas, crossing directly over five major islands: Samar, Leyte, Cebu, Panay, and Coron in Palawan. Worst hit was the Eastern Visayas' capital, Tacloban. A 5m storm surge swept over this city of 250,000 and the nearby towns of Palo, Tanuan, Tolosa, and Basey in Samar. The official death toll according to the National Disaster Risk Reduction and Management Council is around 6400, with casualties still being validated a year on. Some locals and relief workers have questioned the official figure, believing the true number to be in the tens of thousands.

One year on, most Yolanda-affected areas were looking in reasonably good shape, all things considered. Many hotels in the worst-hit areas reopened quickly post disaster to service the influx of relief workers. A few reefs were destroyed, but most of the area's many attractions – the shipwrecks of Coron, the beaches of Bantayan, the thresher sharks of Malapascua – were unaffected. Even central Tacloban, dominated by sturdy concrete structures that survived the deluge, was relatively restored, and its bar and restaurant district was beginning to regain its buzz.

The coastal outskirts of Tacloban told a different story. Near the airport in barangay San Jose, where thousands died, surviving residents were still residing in a vast 'tent city'. Further south, Palo, Tanuan and Tolosa looked every bit like places that have suffered a major catastrophe. Guiuan was spared Tacloban's horrific death toll, but Yolanda's 350 km/h winds ripped apart all but the most solid concrete structures and left its 16th-century church in ruins. These areas are well off the main tourist trail, but if you want to visit, the locals will be happy to tell you their story – it's all part of the healing process.

For the latest on the recovery efforts, check the website of the United Nations Office for the Coordination of Humanitarian Affairs (OCHA; www.unocha.org/philippines). The Philippine Red Cross (www.redcross.org.ph) is also a good source of information.

Cebu

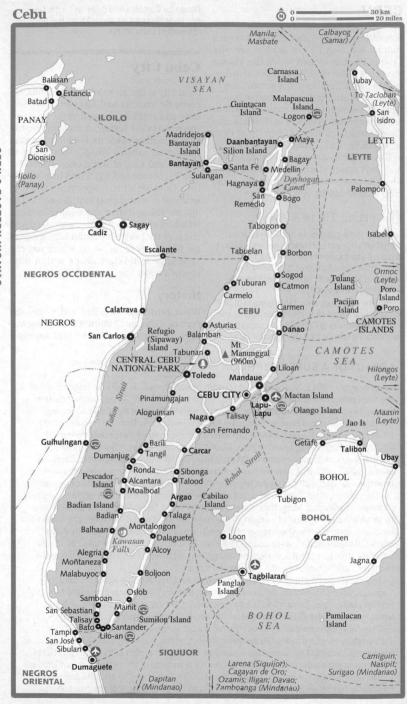

N
0 ——— 30 km
0 ——— 20 miles

Manila;
Masbate

Calbayog
(Samar)

VISAYAN
SEA

Carnassa
Island

Jubay

To Tacloban
(Leyte)

San
Isidro

Balasan

Batad
Estancia

PANAY

ILOILO

Guintacan
Island

Malapascua
Island

Logon

Maya

LEYTE

LEYTE

San
Dionisio

Madridejos

Daanbantayan

Bagay

Iloilo
(Panay)

Bantayan
Island

Silion Island

Medellin

Bantayan

Santa Fe

Dayhogan
Canal

Sulangan

Hagnaya

Palompon

San
Remedio

Bogo

Sagay

Cadiz

Tabogon

Isabel

Escalante

Tabuelan

Borbon

NEGROS OCCIDENTAL

Sogod

Tulang
Island

Ormoc
(Leyte)

Poro
Island

Tuburan

Catmon

Pacijan
Island

Poro

Calatrava

Carmelo

CEBU

Carmen

CAMOTES
ISLANDS

NEGROS

San Carlos

Asturias

Balamban

Danao

Refugio
(Sipaway)
Island

Tabunan

Mt
Manunggal
(960m)

CAMOTES
SEA

CENTRAL CEBU
NATIONAL PARK

Liloan

Hilongos
(Leyte)

Toledo

Mandaue

Talon Strait

Pinamungajan

CEBU CITY

Mactan Island

Aloguinsan

Naga

Talisay

Lapu-
Lapu

Olango Island

Maasin
(Leyte)

San Fernando

Jao Is

Guihulngan

Barili

Getafe

Talibon

Dumanjug

Tangil

Carcar

Ubay

Ronda

Sibonga

Bohol Strait

Pescador
Island

Alcantara

Talood

BOHOL

Moalboal

Argao

Badian Island

Cabilao
Island

Tubigon

Badian

Talaga

BOHOL

Balhaan

Montalongon

Kawasan
Falls

Dalaguete

Loon

Carmen

Alegria

Alcoy

Montaneza

Jagna

Malabuyoc

Boljoon

Oslob

Tagbilaran

Samboan

Mainit

San Sebastian

Panglao
Island

Talisay

Bato

Sumilon Island

BOHOL
SEA

Pamilacan
Island

Tampi

Santander

San José

Lilo-an

Sibulan

SIQUIJOR

Camiguin;
Nasipit;
Surigao (Mindanao)

Dumaguete

NEGROS
ORIENTAL

Dapitan
(Mindanao)

Larena (Siquijor);
Cagayan de Oro;
Ozamis; Iligan; Davao;
Zamboanga (Mindanao)

latecomer: 'Many sailing vessels from Siam, China and Arabia were docked in the port. The people ate from porcelain wares and used a lot of gold and jewellery...'

He may not have been the first outsider to visit Cebu, but Magellan brought with him something that nobody else had: missionary zeal. Even his death at the hands of warrior chief Lapu-Lapu on Mactan Island, a few weeks later, would only afford the natives temporary respite from the incursions of the conquistadors. The arrival of avenging Spaniard Miguel López de Legazpi in 1565 delivered Cebu – and eventually the whole of the Philippines – to Spain and Catholicism. The founding in 1575 of Villa del Santísimo Nombre de Jesús (Village of the Most Holy Name of Jesus) marked Cebu City as the first Spanish settlement in the Philippines, pre-dating Manila by seven years.

Orientation

The city is divided roughly into uptown and downtown; the latter has more impoverished, vice-strewn streets, but most of the sights are here. Just a short drive up Pres Osmeña Blvd brings you to the central Fuente Osmeña roundabout and, further north, the Capitol Compound. A bit further northeast is the Lahug district, where most of the best restaurants, bars and nightclubs are.

⊙ Sights

★ **Basilica Minore del Santo Niño**   CHURCH
(Pres Osmeña Blvd) This holiest of churches is a real survivor. Established in 1565 (the oldest church in the Philippines) and burnt down three times, it was rebuilt in its present form in 1737. Its bell tower came crumbling down in the 2013 earthquake, but the church proper suffered only minor damage.

Perhaps the church owes its incendiary past to the perennial bonfire of candles in its courtyard, stoked by an endless procession of pilgrims and other worshippers. The object of their veneration is a Flemish image of the infant Jesus, sequestered in a chapel to the left of the altar. It dates back to Magellan's time and is said to be miraculous (which it probably had to be to survive all those fires). Every year, the image is the centrepiece of Cebu's largest annual event, the Sinulog festival.

On Sundays and Fridays, the street outside the church is closed off to vehicular traffic, all-day outdoor masses are held and the basilica turns into a sea of pilgrims, water sellers and replica Santo Niño salespeople.

Magellan's Cross   HISTORIC SITE
Ferdinand's Catholic legacy, a large wooden cross, is housed in a stone rotunda (built in 1841) across from Cebu City Hall. The crucifix on show here apparently contains remnants from a cross Magellan planted on the shores of Cebu in 1521. A painting on the ceiling of the rotunda shows Magellan erecting the cross (actually, the locals are doing all the work – Magellan's just standing around with his mates). After the Santo Niño, this is the most venerated religious relic in Cebu.

Fort San Pedro   FORT
(S Osmeña Blvd; student/adult P20/30; ⊙8am-8pm) Built in 1565 under the command of Miguel López de Legazpi, conqueror of the Philippines, Fort San Pedro has served as an army garrison, a rebel stronghold, prison camp and the city zoo. These days it's retired as a peaceful, walled garden and handsomely crumbling ruin. It's a perfect retreat from the chaos and madness of downtown Cebu, especially at sunset.

Museo Sugbo   MUSEUM
(MJ Cuenco Ave; adult/child P75/50; ⊙9am-6pm Mon-Sat) This terrific museum comprises several galleries in an sturdy old coral-stone building that was Cebu's provincial jail from 1870 to 2004. Most interesting are the Spanish-era and American-era galleries. The latter contains an interesting collection of letters and memorabilia from Thomas Sharpe, one of 1065 teachers known as Thomasites who arrived in the early days of the American period to fulfil President McKinley's pledge to 'educate the Filipinos'.

Upstairs a WWII gallery has an American bomb that was dropped in Cebu, Japanese propaganda newspapers and a Purple Heart and Bronze Star earned by Uldrico Cabahug, a native Cebuano who is still alive and drops by from time to time. The museum's newest gallery is a collection of rare Spanish-era architectural blueprints, maps and charts, on loan from the National Archives.

Casa Gorordo Museum   MUSEUM
(35 L Jaena St; admission P70; ⊙9am-5pm Tue-Sun) Downtown, in a quieter residential area, Casa Gorordo Museum was originally a private home built in the 1850s and purchased by the Gorordos, one of Cebu's leading families. The lower part of the house has walls of Mactan coral stone and the stunning upper-storey living quarters are pure Philippine hardwood, held together not with nails but with wooden pegs. The museum

Cebu City

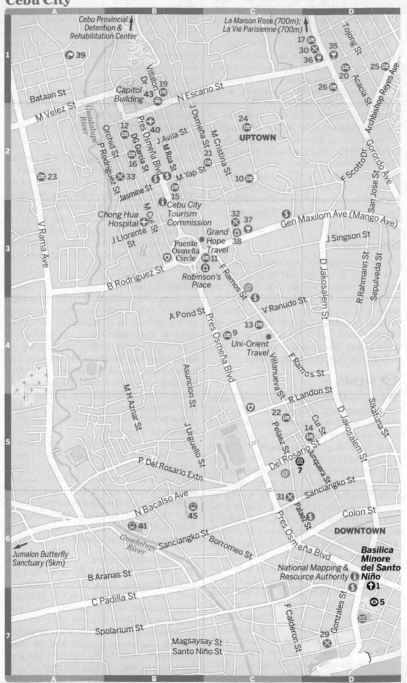

Cebu Provincial Detention & Rehabilitation Center

La Maison Rose (700m); La Vie Parisienne (700m)

Tojong St

Archbishop Reyes Ave

Acacia St

San Jose Dr

Gorordo Ave

F Scotto Dr

Villalon Dr

Capitol Building

Bataan St

M Velez St

Guadalupe River

N Escario St

J Osmeña St

M Cristina St

UPTOWN

Pres Osmeña Blvd

Orchid St

P Rodriguez St

J Avila St

J M Roa St

M Yap St

DG Garcia St

Jasmine St

M Cui St

J Llorente St

Chong Hua Hospital

Cebu City Tourism Commission

Fuente Osmeña Circle

Grand Hope Travel

Gen Maxilom Ave (Mango Ave)

J Singson St

D Jakosalem St

R Rahmann St

Sepulveda St

V Rama Ave

B Rodriguez St

Robinson's Place

F Ramos St

A Pond St

Pres Osmeña Blvd

Uni-Orient Travel

V Ranudo St

F Ramos St

R Landon St

Villanueva St

Asuncion St

M.H Aznar St

J Urguello St

P Del Rosario Extn

Del Rosario St

Pelaez St

Cui St

Junquera St

Sanciangko St

D Jakosalem St

Sikatuna St

N Bacalso Ave

Guadalupe River

Sanciangko St

Borromeo St

Palaez St

Colon St

DOWNTOWN

Jumalon Butterfly Sanctuary (5km)

B Aranas St

C Padilla St

Pres Osmeña Blvd

National Mapping & Resource Authority

Basilica Minore del Santo Niño

Gonzales St

F Calderon St

Spolarium St

Magsaysay St
Santo Niño St

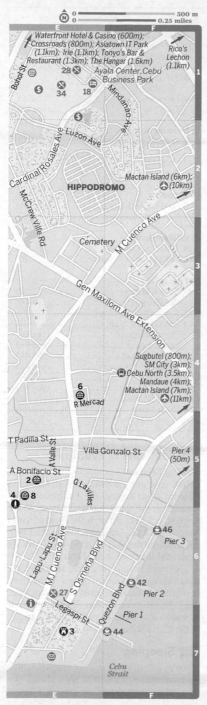

was closed for extensive renovations when we dropped by.

While you're in the area check out the 18th-century **Yap-Sandiego ancestral house** (Mabini St), among the country's oldest wooden houses, and the brash **Heritage of Cebu Monument** (Mabini St), depicting 500 years of city history. *Tartanilla* (horse-drawn carriages) sometimes hang out near Casa Gorordo and can be hired for short jaunts.

University of San Carlos Museum MUSEUM

(Del Rosarios St; admission P30; 🕘8am-noon & 1.30-5pm Mon-Fri, 8am-noon Sat) This well-put-together museum is best known for its anthropological and archaeological exhibits, including displays depicting the 16th-century practise of artifical skull deformation on infants for aesthetic reasons. We'll let you be the judge of that. There are ancient boat coffins dug up in Anda, Bohol, in the 1970s, and some fascinating limestone burial jars dating from about the 6th century. Note the covers – carved phalluses for men, roofs for women, faces for *datu* (chiefs).

Tops Lookout VIEWPOINT

(admission P100) Make your way to JY Square Mall in Lahug, where *habal-habal* (motorcyle taxis) depart for the thrilling 20-minute ride (round trip P200) up a winding road to the Tops lookout point, 600m above Cebu. To get to JY Square take any jeepney labelled 'JY Mall' heading north on Pres Osmeña Blvd or east on N Escario St. A taxi to Tops from the centre will cost around P1000; negotiate a fixed price before you head off.

Adrenaline junkies might want to make a stop at the **Doce Pares zipline park** en route.

Cebu Provincial Detention & Rehabilitation Center PRISON

(CPDRC; ☏032-253 5642; Villaron Dr) This is where you can catch the inmate dance performances that became an internet sensation on YouTube several years back with a performance to Michael Jackson's 'Thriller'. The performance was the brainchild of chief warden Byron Garcia, whose love of '80s pop inspired him to groove up the regular prison exercise drill. There are free performances on the last Saturday of each month at 3pm. Registration starts at noon. Limited spots are on a first-come, first-serve basis so show up early.

The prison is about 4km north of the provincial capital compound. Take a taxi or a *habal-habal* (P150 round-trip including wait time) from the **stop** on the corner of N Escario St and Villaron Dr.

Cebu City

🏃 Activities

Bugoy Bikers   MOUNTAIN BIKING
(☑ 032-321 6348; www.bugoybikers.com) Has a range of exciting half-day to multiday mountain-bike tours, including tours to neighbouring islands like Bohol and Leyte. Also has some budget rooms available (including breakfast P1200). It's tucked away in a residential area in Lahug, roughly behind Outpost (p286) bar.

Island Buzz Philippines   KAYAKING
(☑ 0927 568 3799; www.islandbuzzphilippines. com; tours per person P4000) Island Buzz's tours take you over to Kon-Tiki Resort on Mactan Island, where a fleet of kayaks and stand-up paddleboards await for guided trips through the sublime mangroves of Olango Island, among other spots.

🎊 Festivals & Events

Sinulog Festival   CULTURAL
Cebu's epic annual Sinulog Festival draws pilgrims from around the Philippines. Celebrated on the third Sunday of January, the Sinulog, or Fiesta Señor, is the Feast of Santo Niño (the Christ Child) and is marked by a colourful procession bearing the basilica's venerated image of Santo Niño.

The word *sinulog* is a Visayan term for a dance that imitates the rhythm of the river. It originated as an animist ritual, but after the Cebuanos' conversion to Christianity it morphed into a dance to honour the image of the Santo Niño.

🛏 Sleeping

If you're planning on staying uptown, which we recommend, it's best to book ahead. Hotel choices downtown are generally just a notch up from a night in the gutter. Most of the acceptable downtown places are on Junquera St in the youthful University of San Carlos (USC) area.

Downtown

★ Elicon House
HOTEL $

(☑ 032-255 0300; www.elicon-house.com; crn Del Rosario & Junquera Sts; s/d/tr/q P550/800/1050/1300; ❋@☂) ✎ The downtown version of its sister Mayflower and West Gorordo hotels. Same idea here – clean and no-nonsense rooms, delightful common spaces loaded with games, great vego-friendly cafe and slogans on permaculture philosophy plastered on the brightly painted walls.

Sugbutel
HOTEL $

(☑ 032-232 8888; www.sugbutel.com; Osmeña Blvd nr Rd East; dm P250-450, d from P1200; ❋☂) Sort of a new concept in Cebu lodging, the Sugbutel is a full-service hotel with compact, highly functional rooms and three GIANT air-con dorms (we're talking about 75 to 85 beds). Bunk beds are equipped with small safes under the pillows and curtains for privacy. It's near SM City Mall.

Teo-Fel Pension House
PENSION $

(☑ 032-253 2482; 4 Junquera St; s P500-600, d P750-950; ❋☂) Doubles have hot water and all rooms have air-con and windows at this tall, slim hotel. For those who value a quiet and central location, this is good value.

Diplomat Hotel
HOTEL $$

(☑ 032-253 0099; www.diplomathotelcebu.com; 90 F Ramos St; r P1360-2400; ❋☂) With efficient reception staff and smart leather couches, the 150-room Diplomat has an air of international confidence. The rooms are a little dated but huge and practical, with ample desk space and good lighting. It's fantastic value and well-placed between uptown and downtown.

Uptown

★ Pensionne La Florentina
GUESTHOUSE $

(☑ 032-231 3318; 18 Acacia St; r from P950; ❋) On a quiet street, this elegant and time-worn classic is a good uptown budget option and a charming alternative to a stuffy hotel. No on-site restaurant but it hardly matters when you're only a five-minute walk from the Ayala Center. Downstairs rooms are dark; head up for the nicer rooms; 3A is the pick of the bunch.

Travelbee Guesthouse
GUESTHOUSE $

(www.travelbee.ph; 225 Elizabeth Pond St; r from P600; ❋@☂) Cebu's top value choice in the budget range. The core rooms are essentially four- and six-bed dorms, but beds cannot be booked individually so it works best for small groups. There are nifty doubles as well, and all rooms are clean, bright and en suite. It's central but hidden on a quiet side street; have them call a cab.

Tr3ats
HOSTEL $

(☑ 032-422 8881; www.tr3ats.com; 785 V Rama Ave; dm/d/q P375/900/1600; ❋☂) Has a claim to being Cebu's only true hostel, with three eight-bed air-con dorms and a few tidy en-suite private rooms. However the location isn't perfect and the dorms are cramped. There's not much of a common area; chill in the rooftop bar.

Arbel's Pension House
GUESTHOUSE $

(☑ 032-253 5303; 57 Pres Osmeña Blvd; d with fan P45, with air-con from P750; ❋☂) This is about as cheap as it gets in Cebu without venturing into 'disgusting' territory. Rooms are predictably basic but at least they have windows and the location is relatively quiet. It's behind a 7-11.

★ Mayflower Inn
HOTEL $$

(☑ 032-255 2800; www.mayflower-inn.com; Villalon Dr; s/d/tr/q P850/1150/1400/1750; ❋☂) ✎ The Mayflower bills itself as a 'permaculture' hotel – don't laugh, the green credentials are legit. Besides tidy, meticulously painted rooms you get a feng-shui-friendly garden cafe and a hangout lounge/library with ping pong, foosball, stacks of National Geographic mags and board games. An automatic choice if you're travelling with kids.

West Gorordo Hotel
HOTEL $$

(☑ 032-231 4347/8; http://westgorordo.com; 110 Gorordo Ave; s/d/tr incl breakfast from P1380/1980/2580; ❋☂) ✎ A sister of the equally delightful and eco-friendly Mayflower and Elicon hotels, this place has a strict no-guests policy and touts its zero-carbon philosophy. They have an edible garden out front, don't use plastic and encourage guests to use the stairs. The tidy rooms have comfy beds and motivational art. The travel-themed Journeys Cafe is downstairs.

WORTH A TRIP

JUMALON BUTTERFLY SANCTUARY

Julian Jumalon (1909–2000), a renowned Cebuano artist and avid butterfly collector, set up this **sanctuary** (☎ 032-261 6884; admission P50; ⊙ 9am-5pm) at his home west of downtown. His knowledge was all acquired through his observations during expeditions into the forests to study butterflies, rather than any formal scientific training (he is credited for discovering new Philippine butterfly species and won countless awards in the field of biology).

The most interesting reason to visit the sanctuary is for the attached small art gallery displaying Jumalon's lepido-mosaic works – artworks made entirely from damaged butterfly wings that he collected from lepidopterists around the world. Jumalon's original watercolour paintings are shown side-by-side with the lepido-mosaic versions, which are superb. At the outbreak of WWII, Jumalon was commissioned by the Philippine government to design emergency currency notes; these notes are now considered collectors' items and can be seen on display at Museo Sugbo.

The sanctuary itself is a must for butterfly lovers. The best time of day for viewing is the morning, particularly during breeding season from August to January. The sanctuary is now run by Jumalon's equally passionate son and daughter, who provide an informative tour of the garden, including the living display of the life cycle of the butterfly and Jumalon's exhaustive collection of butterflies and moths in the main room.

To get to the sanctuary, catch a jeepney (number 9 or 10) from N Bacalso Ave, which turns into Cebu South Rd, and hop off at a the barangay hall in barangay Basak Pardo. The sanctuary is behind the Basak Pardo elementary school. A taxi will get you there from downtown for around P80.

Gran Tierra Suites HOTEL **$$**
(☎ 032-253 3575; www.grantierrasuites.com; 207 M Cui St; s/d P789/989; ❄ 🛜) Cebu has some terrific value at the midrange, and this is a prime example. Bordering on boutique, rooms are equipped with canvas prints, small flat-screen TVs and ample desk space.

Cebu R Hotel HOTEL **$$**
(☎ 032-505 7188; www.ceburhotel.com; 101 M Cui St; s/d incl breakfast from P950/1250; ❄ @ 🛜) Everything is tasteful here, from the smartly uniformed staff to the lime-and-dark-wood colour scheme. Rooms are kitted out with desks and flat-screens. Deluxe rooms are a jump up in size.

Fuente Oro Business Suites HOTEL **$$**
(☎ 032-268 7912; www.fuenteoro.com; 173 M Roa St; d P1295-2950; ❄ @ 🛜) It's not really a business hotel, considering that wi-fi doesn't reach the rooms. But it is good value nonetheless, with spacious rooms that have most of what you need: desks, night-stands, good lighting and soft beds for lazing on after one too many treats from the downstairs Cupcake Society cafe.

Premiere Citi Suites HOTEL **$$**
(☎ 032-266 0442; www.premierecitisuites.com; M Yap St; r P1500-2400; ❄ 🛜) This smart, centrally located hotel has bright rooms with crisp white linen, flat-screen TVs and paper lampshades. There's complimentary filtered water on each floor or head up to the rooftop bar and take in the mountain views. Some of the cheaper rooms are windowless.

Casa Rosario PENSION **$$**
(☎ 032-253 5134; www.casarosario.multiply.com; 101 R Aboitiz St; d P1000-1400; ❄ @ 🛜) This long-running and reliable establishment has friendly service and brightly painted rooms that vary in quality – ask for a renovated room on the 3rd or 4th floor.

Tune Hotel HOTEL **$$**
(☎ 032-232 0888; www.tunehotels.com; 36 Archbishop Reyes St; d from about P800; ❄ @ 🛜) The rates here fluctuate wildly according to demand. Get in at the low end and the small but extremely functional and identical rooms are a great deal. More often, you're looking at P1500 to P2000; you can do better in Cebu for that price.

Marriott Hotel LUXURY HOTEL **$$$**
(☎ 032-411 5800; www.marriottcebu.com; Cardinal Rosales Ave; d from P5700; ❄ 🛜 🏊) Brushing up against the Ayala Center is the ultraplush Marriott. No piped muzak or cheesy white-suited pianist will intrude on your thoughts here. The comfortable rooms are tastefully decorated and bathrooms are

fitted out with rainfall showerheads. Rates drop a bit on weekends.

Harold's Hotel
HOTEL $$$

(✆032-505 7777; www.haroldshotel.com.ph; Gorordo Ave; r from P3200; ✳️🛜) The best thing about staying here is being so close to its rooftop bar; with a 360-degree view of the city, it serves as an after-work meeting place for Cebu's fabulous set. The next best thing are the splendid beds.

Cebu Midtown Hotel
HOTEL $$$

(✆032-239 3000; www.cebumidtownhotel. net; Fuente Osmeña Circle; r/ste incl breakfast P3400/7000; ✳️🛜🏊) The business-standard rooms in this tightly managed place are so well insulated from the traffic noise you'll forget where you are – right in the middle of the action on Fuente Osmeña. Cool off at the end of the day in the rooftop pool. Showing a Cebu Pacific boarding pass might net you a P1000 discount.

🛏️ Lahug & Banilad

★ The Henry
BOUTIQUE HOTEL $$$

(✆032-520 8877; www.thehenryhotel.com; M Cuenco Ave, Banilad; d incl breakfast P3600-7900; ✳️🛜🏊) There's a high 'wow' factor here, from the industrial-style lobby to the ginormous, individually designed rooms to the sumptuous cafe. There are murals and pop art, contemporary furniture and king-sized beds that invite entry via flying leap. The *smallest* rooms are a whopping 36 sq metres. Yes, it's in Banilad, but that's just 10 minutes by taxi to Ayala Mall, and puts you in range of Lahug's many great restaurants and bars.

Waterfront Hotel & Casino
LUXURY HOTEL $$$

(✆032-559 0888; www.waterfronthotels.com.ph; 1 Salinas Dr, Lahug; d from US$100; ✳️🛜🏊) Misleadingly named, as it is more than 2km from the water, the Waterfront appeals to those taken by the thought of 24-hour gambling and countless food and beverage outlets, discos, gyms, piano bars etc. The deluxe and superior rooms boast the finest views in Cebu.

🍴 Eating

Long a laggard in the food department, Cebu is finally seeing some decent restaurants open. Lahug is foodie central – in particular Asiatown IT Park and the Crossroads strip mall. For shoestringers there's a generous serving of budget food stalls in Carbon Market (MC Briones St).

🍴 Downtown

AA BBQ
BARBECUE $

(Manalili St; dishes P70-125; ⏱️9am-10pm) Vegetarians have nowhere to hide at this popular outdoor chain restaurant where diners choose their own raw meat or seafood and have it charcoal-grilled on the spot. This is a top spot for a chilled beer after an evening stroll along Fort San Pedro.

Our Place
INTERNATIONAL $$

(cnr Pelaez & Sanciangko Sts; meals P150-275; ⏱️7am-11pm; ✳️🛜) In a character-laden house with a long bar and beautiful wood floors, this is a blokey spot but nonetheless has the best Western food in the downtown area. The emphasis is firmly on meat, with sausages a specialty.

🍴 Uptown

Rico's Lechon
FILIPINO $

(www.ricos-lechon; F Cabahug St, Mabolo; portions from P135; ✳️🛜) Cebu is the place to eat that signature Filipino delicacy, *lechón* (spit-roasted suckling pig), and Rico's has the best in town. It's cooked every morning at its uptown headquarters and shipped off to *lechón* addicts in Manila and abroad, or served at this unassuming eatery east of Ayala Mall. Opt for the spicy version.

★ STK ta Bay! Sa Paolito's Seafood House
SEAFOOD $$

(✆032-256 2700; 6 Orchid St; meals P95-300; ⏱️10am-2.30pm & 5-10pm; ✳️🛜) Ask a Cebuano where to dine in Cebu City and those in the know will often point you to this large ancestral-home-turned-restaurant chock full of family heirlooms. Jerry's crab curry is a favourite but the not-to-miss dish is hot 'n' spicy *calamares* – tender calamari fried in a spice coating and topped with green chillies.

Aranos
SPANISH $$

(✆032-256-1934; 31 Fairlane Village, Gaudalupe; meals P100-300; ⏱️6-10pm Mon-Sat) Upon entry at this authentic Basque restaurant you'll be greeted by the elderly and impressively moustached Spanish owner, Señor Arano himself. The cosy front room is all gingham tablecloths and Spanish memorabilia, and leads out to an intimate fairy-lit garden dining area where you can feast on home-cooked paella and *caldereta* (beef stew).

Cab drivers should know Fairlane Village; look for the wooden door hiding among the leaves.

Handuraw Pizza FILIPINO $$
(☑032-505 2121; Gorordo Ave; pizzas P300-400; ◷11am-1am; ✱ 🛜) This Cebu institution adds native twists to its famous thin-crust pizzas. Try the mildly spicy Pizza Cebuana topped with the local chorizo. Sit inside with air-con or outdoors.

Terraces INTERNATIONAL $$
(Ayala Center, Cebu Business Park) There's an array of quality restaurants at the Ayala Center malls' dining precinct. Standouts include **Canvas Bistro Bar** (☑032-417 1978; mains P300-1000; ◷7am-11pm) for steaks, meat pies and famous Jambalaya; **Tsim Sha Tsui** (mains P100-200; ◷11am-11pm), a hot-pink-and-lime dim sum and a tea bar that's perfect for a yum cha fix; and **Red Kimono** (mains P120-500; ◷11am-11pm; ✱ 🛜) for contemporary Japanese. All are on the second level.

Persian Palate MIDDLE EASTERN $$
(Mango Sq Mall, J Osmeña St; dishes P75-300; ◷10am-9pm; ✱ 🛜 ✍) The flagship restaurant of this popular franchise is tucked away behind National Bookstore in Mango Sq. Middle Eastern mains like spinach hummus are complemented by too-mild South Asian and Thai fare. Its menu includes a rarity in Cebu City – a large vegetarian selection.

✗ Lahug

★Maya MEXICAN $$$
(☑032-238 9552; Crossroads, Gov M Cuenco Ave; mains P300-600; ◷5-11pm Sun-Thu, to 2am Fri & Sat; ✱ 🛜) Enter through heavy carved wooden doors to this classy, candlelit restaurant with arguably the best Mexican food in the country. Authentic hits like lime and coriander grilled-fish soft tacos and a range of 100% agave tequila earn it kudos. Also offers tequila tasting tours.

La Maison Rose FRENCH $$$
(☑032-268 5411; 371 Gorordo Ave; mains P250-1200; ◷noon-2pm & 6-10pm; ✱ 🛜) A little slice of France in the middle of Cebu, La Maison offers fine dining in the main building, done up like a French Indochine villa, and light bites on a large outdoor patio next door at **La Vie Parisienne** (371 Gorordo Ave; sandwiches P150-220; ◷7am-2am; 🛜) bakery and deli.

The former features sumptuous *prix fixe* meals and French classics. The latter gets a little hot by day but is lovely in the evening when groovy tunes play and you can order chilled wine by the bottle.

☗ Drinking & Nightlife

Cebu has a deserved reputation as a party town and there's no shortage of pumping nightspots scattered about the place.

★Outpost BAR
(976 Veterans Dr, Lahug; ◷6pm-2am Tue-Sun) Live music in a rambling old wooden house? Works for us. Try to catch Cuarenta, an adrenalin-fuelled blues-rock band. Pub grub and good cocktails to boot. For sleaze-free good times look no further.

Asiatown IT Park CLUBS
(Salinas Dr, Lahug) The long, orderly streets in this upscale business enclave are lined with all manner of eating and drinking establishments. Cebu's best clubs are generally found here – brand-new **Den** (India St; cover P200; ◷Wed-Sat) was the it place when we visited, but stroll around and see what looks hot. Also here you'll find **Irie** (Geonzon St; ◷11am-2am; 🛜), the first sign that Manila's craft-beer surge may be heading south to Cebu. They pour a range of home brews (pints P255 to P300) to complement a menu of pub grub.

Koa BAR
(157 Gorordo Ave; ◷9.30am-2.30am Sun-Thu, 24hr Fri & Sat; 🛜) Named after a Hawaiian tree, Koa has a great outdoor space and live tunes indoors from hump night on. While the beer is cheap and the food is decent, it's the pizzas from on-site La Bella Pizza Bistro that really shine.

Tonyo's Bar & Restaurant BAR
(The Hangar, Salinas Dr, Lahug; ◷24hr) A quintessential Cebu experience, Tonyo's is a huge, always-packed open-air restobar roughly opposite Asiatown IT Park. Fill up on a 3L tube of beer delivered to your table (P225) while watching live cover bands croon.

Kukuk's Nest BAR
(124 Gorordo Ave; ◷24hr) This bohemian 24-hour restobar has an interesting mix of local arty types and expats. If you've had one too many, ask about the budget accommodation on offer (room P700).

The Social BAR
(Ayala Center; ◷11am-midnight, to 2am Fri & Sat; 🛜) Up on the 3rd floor of the Ayala Center near the Terraces, this buzzing outdoor/indoor bar is a great place to warm up before continuing the night further uptown. Abundant big screens are conducive to sports viewing.

The Distillery LOUNGE
(Crossroads, M Cuenco Ave; ☺6pm-3am) This place fills up every night with young and beautiful faces who come to socialise, drink single malts and – in the wee hours – dance to some of Cebu's grooviest tunes.

Mango Square BAR, CLUB
(Gen Maxilom Ave; admission per club P50-100) A clubber's heaven attracting a fun, lively crowd, although certain places can get a little sleazy. It gets going around 10pm and the more popular places stay open until sunrise. The club names change often so just walk around and pick the most happening spot.

🛍 Shopping

Fully Booked (Terraces, Ayala Center; 10am-11pm) and **National Bookstore** (cnr J Osmeña St & Gen Maxilom Ave; ☺9am-8pm) are good places to stock up on maps, while Fully Booked also has a terrific literature selection. Additional National Bookstore outlets are in most malls.

ⓘ Information

EMERGENCY
Emergency Hotlines (☑032-166, 032-161)
Report Child Sex Tourism National Hotline (☑in Manila 02-524 1660)
Tourist Police (☑0939 519 4321, 032-412 1838)

INTERNET ACCESS
Most of the malls have an internet cafe or two.
1Waretech (F Ramos St; per hr P15; ☺24hr)
Cebu Central Internet Cafe (Palaez St; per hr P15; ☺9am-11pm)

MAPS
Decent enough tourist maps can be picked up free from tourism offices and some hotels. The widely sold E-Z Map Cebu City (P100) thoroughly covers Cebu City, Mandaue and Mactan Island.

For nautical and topographical maps and charts, set a course for the **National Mapping & Resource Authority** (NAMRIA; Room 301, 3rd fl, Osmeña Bldg, cnr Pres Osmeña Blvd & D Jakosalem St; ☺8am-noon & 1-5pm Mon-Fri).

MEDICAL SERVICES
Cebu Doctors Hospital (☑032-255 5555; Pres Osmeña Blvd; ☺24hr)
Chong Hua Hospital (☑032-255 8000; M Cui St) The most recommended medical facility in Cebu City.

MONEY
You'll find plenty of ATMs around Fuente Osmeña and in the Ayala Center and other malls.
Citibank (Cebu Business Park, Mindanao Ave) Near Ayala Center. Changes cash and travellers cheques; P15,000 withdrawal limit at the 24-hour ATM.
HSBC (Cardinal Rosales Ave; ☺9am-4pm Mon-Fri) Allows P40,000 ATM withdrawals; opposite Ayala Center.

POST
Outside the main entrance to the Ayala Center are the branch offices of international couriers.
Central Post Office (Quezon Blvd; ☺8am-5pm Mon-Sat) A landmark downtown opposite Fort San Pedro.

TOURIST INFORMATION
Airport Tourist Information Desk (Mactan-Cebu International Airport; ☺5am-9pm) At the arrivals terminal; staff are eager to help.
Bureau of Immigration (☑032-340 1473; P Burgos St, Mandaue) The BOI has two offices in Mandaue, a satellite suburb of Cebu – this main one behind the Mandaue Fire Station, which was closed for renovations at the time of writing; and a new office at the J Centre Mall (☑032-340 1473; AS Fortuna St). Also has an office in Lapu-Lapu City at Mactan Gaisano Mall.
Cebu City Tourism Commission (☑032-412 4355; www.cebucitytourism.com; Pres Osmeña Blvd; ☺8am-5pm Mon-Fri) Will answer most of your questions about the city and can arrange tours of the main sights with accredited guides. For a self-guided walking tour of the downtown area, ask for a 'Cebu Heritage Walk' booklet.
Department of Tourism Region VII Office (☑032-254 2811; LDM Bldg, Legazpi St; ☺8am-5pm Mon-Fri) Has information on the entire Central Visayas region, including some maps and useful pamphlets.
Travellers Lounge (☑032-232 0293; ☺6am-8.30pm) Located just outside SM City Mall, this handy lounge has a bag-drop (P30, same-day pickup only) and showers (P50), and sells certain ferry tickets.

TRAVEL AGENCIES
You'll find agencies selling plane and certain boat tickets in most of the shopping malls as well.
Grand Hope Travel (☑032-255 4091; grand-hope_travel@yahoo.com; Rajah Park Hotel, Fuente Osmeña Circle; ☺8am-6pm) Sells fastcraft tickets to Ormoc and Tagbilaran.
Uni-Orient Travel (☑032-253 1866; www.uniorient.com; Diplomat Hotel, 90 F Ramos St; ☺8.30am-5.30pm) Among a host of travel agents in the foyer of the Diplomat Hotel.

ⓘ Getting There & Away

With its vast seaport, Cebu is the best-connected hub in the region and as such it is something of a vortex, sucking in travellers and spitting them out again at destinations throughout the Visayas.

AIR

Cebu's user-friendly Mactan-Cebu International Airport (p449) is on Mactan Island, 15km east of Cebu City. There's a terminal fee of P550 for international flights, payable in cash.

Within the Philippines, the major domestic airlines service Manila and an ever-growing list of provincial cities, including Bacolod, Cagayan de Oro, Caticlan, Davao, Iloilo, Legazpi, Puerto Princesa, Siargao and Tacloban.

BOAT SERVICES FROM CEBU CITY

DESTINATION	TYPE	COMPANY	PRICE (P)	DURATION (HR)	FREQUENCY
Biliran					
Naval	RORO	Roble Shipping	P450	9	M, W, F, Sa 8.30pm
Bohol					
Getafe	Fastcraft	MV Star Crafts	200	1	4 daily
Tagbilaran	Fastcraft	Oceanjet, Weesam, Supercat 2GO	500-650	2	frequent
Tagbilaran	RORO	Lite Shipping	210	4	2 daily
Talibon	RORO	VG Shipping	240	4	noon & 10pm
Tubigon	Fastcraft	MV Star Crafts	220	1	8 daily
Tubigon	RORO	Lite Shipping, Island Shipping	100	3	several daily
Leyte					
Bato	RORO	Medallion	280	5½	8.30pm
Hilongos	Fastcraft	Gabisan	280	3	2.30pm
Hilongos	RORO	Gabisan, Roble	240	5	daily
Ormoc	Fastcraft	Oceanjet, Supercat 2GO, Weesam	625	2½	several daily
Ormoc	RORO	Lite Shipping	400	5	daily
Luzon					
Manila	Passenger	2GO, Philippine Span Asia	1200	23	Tu, W, F, Su
Masbate					
Masbate	Passenger	2GO, Trans-Asia	700	10	M, W, Su
Mindanao					
Cagayan de Oro	Passenger & RORO	2GO, Super Shuttle Ferry & Trans-Asia	650-980	8-12	1 or 2 daily
Camiguin	RORO	Super Shuttle Ferry	880	11	Fri 8pm
Surigao	RORO	Cokaliong	825	7	6 weekly
Zamboanga	RORO	George & Peter	1000	29	Mon 10pm
Negros					
Dumaguete	RORO	Cokaliong & George & Peter	300	6	daily
Dumaguete	Fastcraft	Oceanjet	950	4½	daily 8am
Panay					
Iloilo	Passenger	Trans-Asia	600	12	4 weekly
Samar					
Calbayog	RORO	Cokaliong	690	11	M, W, F
Catbalogan	RORO	Roble	650	12	M, Th
Siquijor					
Larena	RORO	Lite Shipping	350	8	3 weekly
Siquijor Town	Fastcraft	Oceanjet	1410	6	daily

Several airlines have offices at MCIA.

AirAsia Zest (www.airasia.com)

Cebu Pacific (☎ 032-230 8888; www.cebu-pacificair.com)

Philippine Airlines (PAL; ☎ 032-340 9780; www.philippineairlines.com)

Tiger Airways (☎ in Manila 02-798 4499; www.tigerair.com)

BOAT

Cebu's vast, multipiered port is linked with the rest of the country by scores of speedy so-called 'fastcraft' passenger ferries, slower 'roll-on, roll-off' (RORO) car ferries, and large multidecked passenger vessels.

All shipping information is vulnerable to change. The *Cebu Daily News* publishes a schedule that is generally reliable, but it is always good to double-check your schedules directly with the shipping companies. Also confirm the pier from which your boat is departing.

In most cases the shipping company's booking office is at the pier from which its boats depart. You can purchase tickets for 2GO, Supercat 2GO, Oceanjet and Trans-Asia at SM City Mall's Travellers Lounge (p287). Some travel agents sell various ferry tickets, and there are 2GO offices in all of the malls.

Cebu City ferry companies:

2GO Travel (☎ 032-233 7000; http://travel.2go.com.ph; Pier 4)

Cokaliong Shipping (☎ 032-232 7211-18; Pier 1)

Gabisan Shipping Lines (☎ 0917 791 6618; Pier 3)

George & Peter Lines (☎ 032-254 5154; Pier 2)

Island Shipping (☎ 032-416 6592; Pier 3)

Lite Shipping (☎ 032-416 6462; Pier 1)

Medallion Transport (☎ 032-412 1121; Pier 3)

Oceanjet (☎ 032-255 7560; www.oceanjet.net; Pier 1) Oceanjet has fastcraft to Tagbilaran (P520, two hours, five daily) and Dumaguete (P970, four hours, two daily).

Philippine Span Asia (☎ 032-232 5361-79; Sulpicio Go St, Reclamation Area) Philippine Span Asia has Sunday (9am) and Wednesday (8pm) trips to Manila.

Roble Shipping Lines (☎ 032-419 1190-95; Pier 3)

M/V Star Crafts (☎ 032-520 5212; Pier 1)

Supercat 2GO (☎ 032-233 7000; www.2go.com.ph; Pier 4) 2GO's fastcraft arm.

Super Shuttle Ferry (☎ 032-345 5581; Pier 8)

Trans-Asia Shipping Lines (☎ 032-254 6491; www.transasiashipping.com; Pier 5)

VG Shipping (☎ 032-238 7635; Pier 3)

Weesam Express (☎ 032 231 7737; www.weesam.ph; Pier 4)

BUS

There are two bus stations in Cebu: the **South Bus Station** (Bacalso Ave) and the **North Bus Station** (☎ 032-345 8650/59; M Logarta Ave) beyond SM City Mall. Ceres Bus Liner is the main company operating out of both stations.

From the South Bus Station, buses leave every 15 minutes or so to Bato (P170, four hours) via Moalboal (P115, 3½ hours) or via Argao (P83, two hours) and Oslob (P155, 3½ hours). Quicker air-con vans ('V-hires') leave for Moalboal (P100, two hours) from the **Citilink Station** (Bacalso Ave), near the South Bus Station, where you'll also find frequent vans to Toledo (P100, two hours).

From the North Station, Ceres buses leave every 30 minutes or so to Hagnaya (ordinary/air-con P132/160, 3½ hours) for Bantayan Island, and to Maya (P180, 4½ hours) for Malapascua Island.

ⓘ Getting Around

Taxis are the best way to get around Cebu. They are cheap, plentiful, easy to catch and will almost always turn their meter on. Flagfall is P40 and then P3.50 for each additional 300m (or two minutes waiting time). Jeepneys are great for short hops (P8) along major boulevards and to get to major landmarks like Ayala Mall, SM City Mall or Carbon Market (just read the placard).

TO/FROM THE AIRPORT

As you leave the terminal, walk right and look for the rank of yellow airport metered taxis, which have a P70 flagfall and cost P300 to P350 to get into the city. There's a rank of regular metered taxis upstairs at departures, although lines here can be serpentine; these cost about P200 to P250. To avoid the lines you can always opt for a coupon taxi, which cost a flat P475/350 to get to most destinations in Cebu City/Mactan. Taking public transport into the centre involves three jeepney changes; if you insist, ask directions from the helpful tourist information desk at arrivals.

TO/FROM THE PIER

To get uptown from the ports, catch one of the jeepneys that pass by the piers to Pres Osmeña Blvd, then transfer to a jeepney going uptown. Taxis are plentiful at all of the piers and cost about P70 to Fuente Osmeña.

Around Cebu City

Mactan Island

☎ 032 / POP 325,000

If you're flying into Cebu City, nearby Mactan (sometimes referred to as Lapu-Lapu) is where you'll actually land. Connected to Cebu City by two bridges, this busy island has some great diving off its southeast coast, and its all-inclusive resorts are popular for in-and-out trips from Manila, Hong Kong and Korea. For independent travellers, the main draw is island-hopping trips in the Bohol Strait between Cebu and Bohol.

◉ Sights

Mactan Shrine
HISTORIC SITE

Mactan is the improbable site of one of the defining moments in the Philippines' history. It was here, on 27 April 1521, that Ferdinand Magellan was fatally wounded at the hands of Chief Lapu-Lapu. The event is commemorated at the Mactan Shrine on a stone plinth bearing the date that Magellan was felled. Next to it is a statue of a ripped and pumped Lapu-Lapu, looking like a He-Man action figure.

In the months leading up to this fateful moment, Magellan had managed to curry the favour of all the most powerful chiefs of the region, with the single exception of Lapu-Lapu. So with 60 of his best soldiers, Magellan sailed to the island to teach him a lesson in gunboat diplomacy. But Lapu-Lapu and his men defended their island with unimagined ferocity, and Magellan was soon back on his boat – fatally wounded by a spear to his head and a poisoned arrow to his leg.

Alegre Guitar Factory
HANDICRAFTS

(Old Maribago Rd; ⊙ 7.30am-6.30pm Mon-Sat, 8am-6pm Sun) Mactan is famous for guitar-making, and this factory in Abuno, a short jeepney or tricycle ride from the popular Maribago resort area, is the best place to observe how they are made – and buy them if you wish. Prices range from the P2500 decoration 'cheapie' to the P70,000 'export quality'. The most expensive model is made from exquisite black ebony imported from Madagascar. Some beautiful hand-crafted native mandolins are here as well.

🏃 Activities

The coral reefs around heavily populated Mactan have taken a toll from destructive fishing methods over the years. Still, there's surprisingly good diving in the turtle-infested waters off Mactan and nearby Nalusuan and Hilutungan islands, where marine reserves have been established. Finding diving this good so close to an international airport is rare indeed, and divers from Korea and Hong Kong fly into Mactan just for the weekend.

Dive rates in Mactan are quite expensive by Philippine standards, averaging

P2500 per dive including equipment. **Free Crew Dive Center** (✆ 032-495 4210; www. freecrew-diving.com; Maribago Wharf) bucks the trend, charging just P1000 for a shore dive. It costs more to go to the islands. Other reputable companies include **Kon-Tiki Divers** (✆ 032-495 2471; www.kontikidivers.com; Club Kon Tiki, Maribago Beach) and **Freediving HQ** (✆ 0917 718 5508; http://freedivinghq.com; Mar Beach, Marigondon), which offers freediving courses and also has accommodation.

🛏 Sleeping & Eating

Independent travellers should target the Maribago area near the midpoint of the long southeast coastline, which is otherwise populated with exclusive high-rise resorts that target families. Ask about free airport transfers.

🛏 Airport Area

Hotel Cesario
HOTEL $$

(✆ 032-340 0211; ML Quezon Hwy; d incl breakfast from P1400; ❄ 🛜 ⊛) The rooms are starting to show wear but it's the only airport hotel that won't break the budget and it does come with some perks, such as free airport transfers and free use of the pool at its sister hotel next door, the Bellavista.

Waterfront Airport Hotel & Casino
HOTEL $$$

(✆ 032-340 4888; www.waterfronthotels.com.ph; Airport Rd; d from P3200) For those who like a little splash of ritzy fun in their airport stopovers, this is the younger, less flamboyant sister of the Waterfront Hotel in Lahug. Prices and facilities are comparable but the airport branch is more low-key.

🛏 Southeast Coast

La Place
GUESTHOUSE $

(✆ 0922 851 5422; Quezon National Hwy; d without/ with bathroom P800/1000, q per bed P500; ❄ 🛜) This is akin to a boutique hostel, with smart rooms, even smarter shared bathrooms and a popular restobar in an oasis-like garden roughly opposite Maribago Grill.

Club Kon-Tiki
BEACH RESORT $$

(✆ 032-495 2434; www.kontikidivers.com; Maribago Beach; s P1125-2025, d P1350-2250; ❄ 🛜) Mactan's best midrange option. It's a peaceful, isolated spot right on the water with coconut palms and a breezy open-air restaurant. There's no real beach but the deluxe rooms net you ocean views.

★ Abacá Boutique Resort & Restaurant BEACH RESORT $$$
(☎ 032-495 3461; www.abacaresort.com; Punta Engano Rd; ste & villas incl breakfast P15,900-28,900; ❄📶🏊) The ultimate in boutique luxury, Abacá has it all. With its secluded oceanfront position, infinity pool and butler service, you might expect to see James Bond sipping a martini at the poolside bar. Rooms showcase the work of local designers in dark woods, warm tones and cooling slate and stone.

And the exquisite Abacá restaurant (mains P750 to P1500) simply has no equal in Cebu. This could well be the reason to visit Mactan Island, despite it not having much of a beach.

Inday Pina's Sutukil SEAFOOD $
(Mactan Shrine; ⏲7.30am-10pm) The best of the rustic seafood restaurants hidden behind the market area near the entrance to Mactan Shrine. Pick up your seafood, sniff it and hand it to the chef. Squid, grouper, lobster and crab are available daily at market prices (P180 per kilo for squid to P750 per kilo for crabs and grouper).

Maribago Grill & Restaurant SEAFOOD $$
(Quezon National Hwy, Maribago; mains P100-450; ⏲10am-10pm) Individual nipa hut tables set amongst lush fairy-lit gardens attract a mix of locals and tourists to this dining oasis. Opt for the seafood and get your hands dirty ripping into meaty garlic crabs or decadent lobster.

ℹ Getting There & Around

Jeepneys run all day to Cebu City from Lapu-Lapu (P15). A taxi from Cebu to the southeastern beaches will cost a good P300. Within the island, jeepneys and tricycles work well for short hops, but be sure to set a price beforehand with any tricycle driver – P50 should do it for short trips. Taxis are easy to flag down anywhere.

Olango Island & Around

☎ 032 / POP 30,000

Just 20 minutes from Mactan by public bangka, Olango Island is home to the **Olango Island Wildlife Sanctuary** (☎ 0915 386 2314; www.olangowildlifesanctuary.org; admission P100; ⏲9am-5pm, closed major public holidays). Taking in 1030 hectares of sand flats and mangroves on Olango's southern shores, the sanctuary supports the largest concentration of migratory birds found in the Philippines – 48 species, including the rare Chinese egret, the Asiatic dowitcher and several types of sandpiper and plover.

Timing is everything here. The peak months are October to November for the southward East-Asian–Australasian migration, and February to March for the northward leg. Be sure to visit at low tide, when the birds take to the sand flats en masse to fill up on worms, snails and small fish. There aren't many birds here from May to August, but the sanctuary remains an austerely beautiful spot in its own right. You can kayak through the mangroves around here with Island Buzz Philippines (p282).The sanctuary is 15 minutes from Olango's Santa Rosa pier by tricycle (P250 round-trip with wait time).

Olango is also known for its **floating restaurants** on the back side of the island in barangay Caw-oy. These are most definitely tourist traps that charge double what you would pay elsewhere for grilled shellfish, squid and crabs. If you go, negotiate a price up front, as prices aren't displayed (for a reason). Most island-hopping trips will gladly take you here – the boatmen get a commission, after all – or take a tricycle (P50, 10 minutes) from the Santa Rosa pier.

South of Olango is a vast area of shallow water known as the **Olongo Reef Flat**, and three more islands that are frequently visited by island-hopping trips and have accommodation: Nalusuan Island, Hilutangan Island and Caohagen Island.

Of these, **Nalusuan Island** has the most appeal because of its excellent marine sanctuary, managed privately by **Nalusuan Island Resort & Marine Sanctuary** (☎ 032-516 6432; www.nalusuanislandresort.com; r P3500; ❄📶). The snorkelling on the house reef is simply wonderful, and the over-water cottages with private balconies are great value, especially considering how close to Cebu you are. The place does fill up with groups of day-trippers from mid-morning to mid-afternoon, but once they've cleared out you have the island practically to yourself. Electricity and air-con work from 6pm to 8am. For day-trippers there's a P200 fee to snorkel or dive on the reef and use the resort facilities. Round-trip boat transfers for guests of the resort cost P2000.

Just northwest of Nalusuan is larger, populated **Hilutangan Island**. It's also surrounded by a **marine sanctuary** (entrance P200), albeit the snorkelling isn't as good here as at Nalusuan, the reefs having been damaged years ago by destructive fishing methods and chlorine bleaching. The island's one resort has been mothballed, but you can arrange homestays (☏ 0916 231 3391; P500) near its shell on the southeast side of the island – look for Wilson, who also has a basic over-water nipa hut available that would make for an interesting night. There are busy restaurants geared toward day-trippers on the northwest side of the island.

Those after a more Robinson Crusoe experience might want to make a stop on their island-hopping trip at the lesser-known Caohagan Island (entrance P200), which has a nice beach backed by seafood shacks and a single Japanese-owned, electricity-free resort (☏ 0917 623 3158; r without/with bathroom P2000/3400). Beachfront accommodation is basic and overpriced.

❶ Getting There & Away

Maribago Wharf in Mactan is the best place to organise island-hopping trips taking in up to four islands. P2500 is the standard price including snorkelling equipment. The Punta Engaño Port near the Hilton and Marigondon Wharf near Plantation Bay Resort are also good places to find boats. Resorts can organise these trips but of course will charge a premium.

Public bangkas serve Santa Rosa, Olango Island (P15, 20 minutes, every 40 minutes) from the Punta Engaño Port until 6pm in either direction. There are also public bangkas every afternoon to Hilutangan (from the Cordova pier) and Caohagan (from Marigondon Wharf), returning to Mactan the next morning.

Danao

☏ 032 / POP 119,252

With a scenic mountainous backdrop, the coastal town of Danao, 25km north of Cebu, is where you catch the ferry to the Camotes islands. Near the pier is gracious, coral-stone St Tomas de Villanueva Church, built in 1755 and restored from near ruin in 1981.

The schedule changes often but you can usually rely on at least five departures per day to Consuelo, Pacijan Island, with Jomalia Shipping (☏ 032-346 0421; P180, two hours). The last trip is at 5.30pm, with a 9pm ferry added on Fridays, Saturdays and Sundays.

Malapascua Island

☏ 032 / POP 4500

While it's the world-class diving that attracts most visitors to the tiny and idyllic island of Malapascua, its lovely beaches and air of *joie de vivre* are what confirms its reputation as one of Cebu's most popular destinations.

Diving with the thresher sharks is the main highlight. Nowhere in the world do these distinctive-tailed sharks congregate in shallower waters than at Mondad Shoal.

Malapascua took a direct hit from Typhoon Yolanda, which tore off every roof on the island and snapped most coconut trees. Miraculously there were no fatalities. Most resorts quickly rebuilt and reopened, although more remote parts of the island still looked a bit devastated when we visited.

If you are heading to Malapascua from Maya and miss the last boat, you can overnight there at Abba Family Lodge (☏ 0926 984 9333; s/d from P200/300; ❋), 100m from the pier.

❊ Activities

Besides diving, you can relax on signature white-sand Bounty Beach, where a string of resorts offers seating in the sand. A good three-hour walk will take you all around the coast of the island, with plenty of photo opportunities and attractions such as the waterside cemetery, with its sun-bleached graves; a lighthouse in Guimbitayan; and a 12m-high lookout at the typhoon-destroyed Los Bambos resort on the island's northwest tip, which some brave souls treat as a cliff jump. Bring water. You can also tour much of the island by motorcycle, widely available for rent for P200 per hour.

Diving

Divers head out at 5am to Monad Shoal, where they park on the seabed at 25m hoping to glimpse thresher sharks, who congregate here early morning to get their beauty scrub courtesy of the wrasses (cleaner fish) that await them. The chances of spotting them are pretty good – about 75%. For more on thresher sharks contact the Thresher Shark Research & Conservation Project (www.threshersharkproject.org), which is studying the behaviour of these animals at Monad Shoal. By day Monad Shoal attracts manta rays.

Macrophotographers will love the area around Gato Island, a marine sanctuary and sea snake breeding ground (from February to September). The Dona Marilyn ferry, a passenger ferry that sank during a typhoon in 1988 killing 250 people, is now a site of soft corals and abundant marine life. Lapus Lapus Island is a good site just off the northwest tip of the island; bring a picnic to enjoy on the beaches and caves that appear here at low tide.

Malapascua Island

0 ——————— 500 m
0 ——————— 0.25 miles

There are numerous dive centres on the island, most offering standard rates – one dive for US$25, equipment rental US$8 and an open-water diving certificate for US$350. There's a P50 marine fee to dive Monad Shoal, a P150 marine fee per day to dive the other sites, and a P500 marine fee to dive Calangaman Island. The fees pay for guards to patrol the shoals and reefs.

Recommended diving companies on Malapascua include **Evolution Diving** (☎0917 628 7333; www.evolution.com.ph), **Exotic Divers** (☎032-516 2990; www.malapascua.net) and **Thresher Shark Divers** (☎0927 612 3359; www.threshersharkdivers.com), plus the more budget-friendly **Fish Buddies** (☎0917 576 8632; www.fishbuddies.net), which charges P1400 per dive including equipment.

Island Hopping & Snorkelling
Good snorkelling spots include **Dakit Dakit Island**, a short boat ride off Bounty Beach,

and the **Coral Garden** off the east side of the island. A short snorkelling tour by boat costs a very negotiable P1200 for a small group. Further out, the islands of **Carnassa** (one hour) and **Calangaman** (two hours) both have stunning beaches as well as excellent snorkelling, with prices around P3000 for full-day hire.

🛏 Sleeping
Ask about low-season discounts and dive/accommodation packages.

★ **Mike & Diose's Aabana
Beach Resort**   BEACH RESORT $
(☎0905 263 2914; www.aabana.de; d incl breakfast P500-2200; 🌀🅿) Lavish deluxe suites, smart budget rooms, big duplex air-con rooms with kitchens – no matter what you choose, you're in for a treat. Easily Malapascua's best value. And management is as friendly as can be. Bounty Beach feels almost private down here at the extreme east end.

White Sand Bungalows   BUNGALOW $
(☎0927 318 7471; www.whitesand.dk; bungalow P900-1200; 🅿) Near the boat landing on

quiet Poblacion (Logon) Beach, the Danish-owned White Sand has four comfortable and reasonably priced nipa huts equipped with lofts and roomy balconies. Its service approach is minimalist but that will probably suit you just fine.

Villa Sandra   HOSTEL $
(☏ 0917 820 9041; jonjonmalapascua@gmail.com; dm P300; @☎) Very much a backpacker pad next to the elementary school in Logan village, with simple shared doubles and quads, a kitchen, a hangout patio and dudes in dreads hanging about. Jonjon is your informative host.

Mr Kwiz   GUESTHOUSE $
(☏ 0906 620 5475; r with fan/air-con P500/1500) Great bargain in the village, looking in fine form after post-typhoon repairs. Even the fan rooms have private bathrooms, balconies and some furnishings. Super-budget meals available here as well. It is accessed via a small path running beside Evolution, 100m from the beach.

★ Tepanee Beach Resort   BEACH RESORT $$
(☏ 032-317 0124; www.tepanee.com; d P2200-2700; ✳☎) There's a lot to like about this Italian-run hillside resort on Logon (Poblacion) Beach, starting with the sturdy concrete cottages, which feature soaring Balinese-style thatched roofs, solid wood floors and excellent beds draped in mosquito nets. All rooms have private balconies and great views, but the ocean-view rooms, perched over a private white-sand beach, are the best Malapascua has to offer.

Evolution Resort   BEACH RESORT $$
(☏ 0917 628 7333; www.evolution.com.ph; r incl breakfast with fan/air-con from P2000/3500; ✳☎) On the southeast edge of the beach, this laid-back English/Irish-run dive resort is doing great things. Staff are personable, rooms are simple and comfy, while the Craic House restobar serves up quality food – the spicy tuna burger gets rave reviews. The duplex fan rooms, with balconies and partial sea views, might be preferred here.

Exotic Island Dive Resort   RESORT $$
(☏ 032-516 2990; www.malapascua.net; s/d with fan from P500/600, s/d with air-con incl breakfast from P3100/3600; ✳☎) Located on the quiet east end of Bounty Beach, Exotic is a tale of two resorts. The main complex is a self-contained dive resort with some of Malapascua's smartest rooms; request one with

a view. Set apart from the main resort, the 'backpacker' complex has fan doubles that are perfect for penny-pinching couples. Big low-season discounts here.

Ocean Vida   BEACH RESORT $$
(☏ 0917 303 8064; www.ocean-vida.com; s/d incl breakfast with fan P2400/2900, with air-con from P3400/3900; ✳☎) This full-service resort smack in the middle of Bounty Beach has some of the nicest rooms on Malapascua behind its popular beachfront restaurant. Plush beds, cosy private balconies, classy prints and a nice array of dark-stained wooden furniture are highlights. Splurge for a beachfront dwelling.

✗ Eating & Drinking

Most bars have happy hour between 5pm and 6pm.

Ging-Ging's Garden Restaurant   FILIPINO $
(mains P60-100; ⊘ 7am-10pm; ⊘) Inland from the beach, Ging-Ging's serves tasty, cheap and filling vegetarian food and curries.

Kiwi Bakhaw   FILIPINO $$
(meals P130-180; ⊘ 7am-10pm) This place is well worth sniffing out for its gorgeous cordon bleu and curries. Quality food takes time to prepare: expect to wait up to an hour. Bring bug spray. From the path next to Mike & Diose's Resort, walk to Malapascua Starlight hotel, turn right and keep going.

★ Angelina   ITALIAN $$$
(mains P255-595; ⊘ 8am-10pm) The eponymous chef at this *ristorante* on Poblacion Beach cooks up heavenly creations that will have you craving Italian food for weeks. The homemade *tagliatelle asparagi* is al dente bliss, or try the risotto with crab, shrimp and squid cooked in wine sauce. Many ingredients are imported from Italy and there's an extensive wine list.

Amihan   MEDITERRANEAN $$$
(mains P350-500; ⊘ 5-10pm; ☎⊘) Up on a hill overlooking Poblacion Beach, dinner-only Amihan infuses Euro fare with Filipino elements. You'll find toothsome *kinilaw* and *lumpia* alongside pasta and a sumptuous mixed-meat grill. There's an extensive vegetarian selection and sensational desserts.

Cocoy's Maldito   BAR
(⊘ 24hr) On Poblacion Beach, Cocoy's is the most raucous and popular bar on Malapascua, with the action extending into the night.

Bar games like table football and pool lure punters in; strong cocktails keep them there.

Other Place BAR
We love this place – and not just because it's Liechtenstein-owned. Great burgers and a cool crowd. Where the locals hang out.

ℹ Information

There's no ATM on Malapascua, so cash up before you arrive; the closest ATM is at Bogo.

ℹ Getting There & Away

Bangkas from Maya (P80, 30 minutes) to Malapascua leave when full, roughly every hour until 5.30pm or so (until 2pm from Malapascua). The usual drop-off point on Malapascua is Poblacion Beach, but during the *habagat* (southwest monsoon, June to October) you may be dropped off on Bounty Beach or even beyond Bounty Beach in Pasil.

Especially late in the day, boatmen in Maya are notorious for trying to get tourists to pay extra for a special trip, claiming they don't have any passengers. Relax – there's always a last trip that leaves at 5.30pm or so.

From Maya there is also a bangka to San Isidro, Leyte, every morning at 10am (P300, 1¾ hours). And from the Polambato Pier near Bogo, an hour south of Maya, **Super Shuttle Ferry** (☑ 0906 291 2573) has a noon RORO every day to Palompon, Leyte (P250, three hours). Departure from Palompon is at 7.30am. There's also a midnight boat from Polambato to Cataingan and Cawayan on Masbate.

Ceres buses depart Maya pier for Cebu (ordinary/air-con P163/180, 4½ hours) every 30 minutes until mid-evening.

Bantayan Island

☑ 032 / POP 137,000

Those looking for a place where there's nothing to do other than laze on a beach will love Bantayan Island. There's no diving, no canyoning or volcanoes to scale, just a blinding white-sand beach, fantastic food and lively drinking spots. The relaxed, bucolic town of Santa Fe on the island's southern coast is where you'll find the nicest stretch of beach and low-key resorts. About 10km west of Santa Fe is Bantayan town (P15 by jeepney), the island's beautifully preserved administrative heart.

Holy Week sees Bantayan turn into an epic fiesta. People sleep on the beaches, locals rent out their houses, and hotel prices double, triple and even quadruple.

⚹ Activities

Island-hopping trips are possible to nearby **Hilantagaan Island** and **Virgin Island**, which have coral outcrops. It costs P800 for a half-day tour for up to three people, not including snorkel gear.

In addition to sleeping and reading, a popular activity is exploring the island on two wheels. Most resorts can organise a bicycle for P150 per day, while motorcycle can be hired at the pier or through any resort from P300.

About 5km southeast of Santa Fe, then another 4km off the highway, the village of Maricabon has a **mangrove garden** (admission P50; ⊙ 8am-5pm) accessible via a stilted bamboo boardwalk. You can rent kayaks here for P150 per hour, or tour the mangroves by bangka (P350).

🛏 Sleeping

The resorts of Santa Fe are strung along the beach, north and south of the pier (which is a little north of the town proper). Many resorts offer free pick-up from the pier.

Sunday Flower Beach Hotel & Resort BEACH RESORT $
(☑ 032-438 9556; www.bantayan-resort.com; d with fan/air-con P800/1100; ❋ 🛜) On glorious Sugar Beach on the south edge of Santa Fe, this Australian-run resort is the best value on Bantayan. Air-con rooms have roomy balconies, plasma TVs, ample wood furniture and plenty of pizazz, while the fan nipa huts are much simpler affairs.

Bantayan Cottages COTTAGE $
(☑ 032-438 9538; www.bantayancottages.com; d with shared bathroom and fan P400, d/q with air-con P650/1600; ❋ 🛜) On the main road a little south of the pier, this shoestringer delight makes up for its lack of beachfront with friendly services and rustic, verandah-equipped cottages set around a lush garden. 'Backpacker' rooms are basic affairs in the main house.

St Bernard Beach Resort BEACH RESORT $$
(☑ 0917 963 6162; www.bantayan.dk; cottages with fan/air-con from P950/1400; ❋ 🛜) About 1km north of Santa Fe pier, St Bernard fronts a wide white beach. It has a wonderfully relaxed island vibe with rows of thatched-roofed cottages set amid palm trees and aviaries of parrots. No two cottages are exactly alike, but all feature polished wood, throw rugs and lace curtains.

Marlin Beach Resort
BEACH RESORT $$

(📱032-438 9093; www.marlin-bantayan.com; d P1950-4900; ❄️📶) Close to the restaurant and bar action in 'downtown' Santa Fe, Marlin's large motel-style rooms may not inspire, but its attractive beachside location, complete with bar and restaurant, is very much its saving grace.

Yooneek Beach Resort
BEACH RESORT $$

(📱032-438 9124; www.yooneekbeachresort.com; s P1000-1590, d P1290-1890; ❄️📶) An old reliable on Sugar Beach just south of Santa Fe's centre, Yooneek took a year to rebuild after Typhoon Yolanda but come back it did, and it again offers spacious rooms near the water and one of the most laid-back beach bars on the island.

White Beach Bungalows
BEACH RESORT $$

(www.white-beach-bungalows.com; r P1990-2990; ❄️📶) If Santa Fe just isn't sleepy enough for you, head 5km south of town to Maricabon Beach. Typhoon Yolanda ravaged this resort along with most of Bantayan's south coast, but it rebuilt and again offers some seclusion and well-appointed, spacious rooms. Unfortunately food must be ordered, or you can hire a motorcycle (P350) and ride to town.

Coral Blue Oriental
BEACH RESORT $$$

(📱032-316 8054; www.coralblueoriental.com; r/villa incl breakfast P3500/9950; ❄️📶) Sophisticated polished bamboo-and-wood bungalows right on the beach are the closest you'll find to luxurious accommodation on the island. The villas are huge and well suited to families.

🍴 Eating & Drinking

For such a small island, Santa Fe has an impressive strip of lively restaurants just off the main road in the centre of town.

Bantayan Island Artisan Foods
DELI $

(mains P75-200; ⊙7am-8pm) Run by a couple from Seattle, Artisan Foods is one half deli, one half bakery. It serves up fresh bread, naturally cured ham, gourmet meats and coffee. 20% of proceeds go to a charity for street kids. It's on the main road a bit south of the pier.

Cou Cou's
INTERNATIONAL $$

(📱032-438 9055; www.hotelbantayan.com; mains P150-200; ⊙7am-11pm; 📶) This popular Belgian-owned restaurant covers a range of Filipino fare (*adobo*, Bicol *exprés*), Western fare like burgers and even some Thai tastes. The thin-crust pizzas are tasty and there is a good wine list. Also has some smart rooms out back (P1350 to P1600).

Blue Ice
SCANDINAVIAN $$

(mains P200-275; ⊙8am-10pm Sun-Thu, to 3am Fri & Sat; 📶) Known both for its food – a mixture of Asian cuisine and Scandinavian specialties like *gravlax* (marinated salmon on toast) – and its bar, which features live music on weekends.

★ Caffe del Mar
ITALIAN $$$

(mains P280-500, pizzas P340-400; ⊙10am-midnight; 📶) Homemade pasta, pumpkin gnocchi, grilled steaks and pizza: Caffe del Mar does it all well and has a great bar to boot (happy hour 1pm to 6pm). Friday is live reggae night.

ℹ️ Information

There is a PNB ATM just off the main plaza in Bantayan town, but it's highly advisable to cash up before you arrive.

For regularly updated island info, have a look at www.wowbantayan.com.

ℹ️ Getting There & Away

Hagnaya is the jumping-off port to Santa Fe, with RORO companies **Super Shuttle Ferry** (📱0939 850 6438) and **Island Shipping** (📱0929 678 7930) alternating trips every hour until 5.30pm (P170, one hour). Returning back to the mainland, the last boat from Santa Fe to Hagnaya departs at 4.30pm.

Ceres buses depart Hagnaya for Cebu City (ordinary/air-con P132/160, 3½ hours) every 30 minutes until evening.

GETTING TO NEGROS FROM NORTHWEST CEBU

PORT	DESTINATION	TYPE	COMPANY	PRICE (P)	DURATION (HR)	FREQUENCY
Toledo	San Carlos	RORO	Lite Shipping	110	1¾hr	5 daily
Toledo	San Carlos	Fastcraft	EB Aznar	225	1	7.30am, 9.30am, 11.30am, 3.30pm
Tabuelan	Escalante	RORO	Various	180	2	4 daily

WOLFGANG DAFERT: FREEDIVER INSTRUCTOR

A self-described 'merman' of 16 years, the 40-year-old Austrian Wolfgang Dafert is one of the foremost freedivers in the Philippines. He offers freediving instruction through Freediving Philippines (p299) and also runs Cyan Adventures (p299). We talked to him about the growing phenomenon of freediving.

What exactly is freediving? Freediving is diving without the use of heavy scuba equipment, just on a single breath of air. The silence is like a kind of meditation, and an added bonus is that without the annoying bubbles you're able to get closer to the fish while freely enjoying being part of the ocean.

How do you do learn to do it? After two days of training, students will learn the right breathing and relaxation techniques while knowing how to deal with the urge to breathe. Everybody can learn to dive deeper and longer than you'd think is possible. For beginners, the urge to breathe is the first hurdle you have to overcome. In the course, you will learn the right relaxation techniques (similar to yoga) and how to 'transfer' this first breathing reflex into a relaxed sensation so you can still stay underwater longer. It's mind over matter, in that you learn and experience that you *can* hold your breath longer than your body is actually telling you.

What is your record depth and time spent underwater? Freediving down to 70m depth (as deep as a 23-storey building), while holding my breath for seven minutes and 10 seconds.

What's the best thing about diving in Moalboal? For fun freediving, it's the massive resident school of millions of sardines – a one-of-a-kind natural spectacle in itself. Uh... and let's not forget another air-breathing underwater creature – there are plenty of turtles in Moalboal!

From Bantayan town, a bangka ferry bound for Cadiz, Negros (P300, three hours) departs daily at 9am. On alternate mornings, a bangka sails for Estancia (P350, four hours) on Panay.

Toledo

032 / POP 152,960

You can catch boats to Negros from Toledo on Cebu's west coast, as well as from Tabuelan, 65km north of Toledo. Toledo is served by frequent Ceres buses (P70, 2½ hours) and V-hire vans (P100, 1½ hours) from Cebu's south station. Tabuelan is served by less frequent V-hires and local buses from Cebu's north station.

Those headed to Bantayan or Malapascua from Toledo will likely have to make several transfers. Head to Tuburan by slow ordinary bus, then transfer to a jeepney north to Tabuelan, then another jeepney north to Hagnaya for Bantayan, or to Bogo for Malapascua. Those heading to Moalboal from Toledo will need to catch a bus inland to Naga (P50, one hour) and then another bus to Moalboal.

EB Aznar (032-467 9447) and **Lite Shipping** (032-467 9604) are ferry companies in Toledo.

Moalboal

032 / POP 27,676

Diving, drinking and dining (in that order) top the list of activities in Moalboal (hard to pronounce – try mo-ahl-bo-ahl). About 90km from Cebu City, Moalboal proper is on the main road; the part that tourists mean when they say 'Moalboal' is actually **Panagsama Beach**, a cramped and rowdy resort village a short tricycle (P100) or *habal-habal* (P30) ride west of town. In recent years Panagsama has become internationally renowned for the incredible **sardine run** that delights divers and snorkellers just metres offshore.

While diving is Moalboal's raison d'être, a dizzying array of terrestrial activities in the area make this a prime destination for the adventurous traveller. And for beach bums there's nearby **White Beach**, which unlike Panagsama has a decent beach. Popular with locals, it's subject to the usual flux of domestic tourist spots: relatively quiet during the week, it's overflowing on weekends and holidays. White Beach is a 20-minute tricycle (P150) ride from Panagsama, or a 15-minute tricycle (P100) or *habal-habal* (P50) ride from Moalboal.

Panagsama Beach

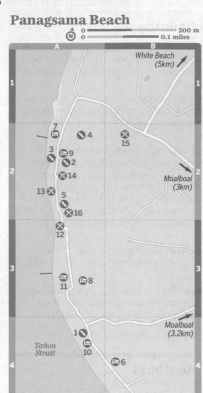

Panagsama Beach

🏃 Activities, Courses & Tours
1	Blue Abyss Dive Shop	A4
	Cyan Adventures	(see 2)
2	Freediving Philippines	A2
3	Freediving Planet	A2
4	Nelson's Dive Shop	A2
5	Neptune Diving	A2
	Planet Action	(see 11)

🛏 Sleeping
6	Blue Abyss	B4
7	Cora's Palm Resort	A2
8	Mayas Native Garden	A3
9	Moalboal Backpacker Lodge	A2
10	Quo Vadis Beach Resort	A4
11	Tipolo Beach Resort	A3

🍴 Eating
12	BB's Seaview	A3
13	Chilli Bar	A2
14	French Coffee Shop	A2
15	Lago di Garda	B2
16	Lantaw	A2
	Last Filling Station	(see 11)

Falls. The hottest spring tops out at 42.9°C and, according to the signage, 'cures skin disease and sickness of the body'. Clamber up the pretty canyon behind the springs to a series of 3m to 8m falls dropping into peacock-green swimming holes.

🏃 Activities

Diving & Freediving

The big draw in Moalboal these days is the **sardine run**, a dense column of schooling fish that shimmy around en masse to form incredible geometric shapes 5m to 10m under the surface. Traditionally Pescador Island has been the place to observe this mesmerising display, but in 2013 the sardines relocated to the wall just 30m off Panagsama Beach. It's a routine shore dive for scuba divers, or just throw on a mask and snorkel and swim out on your own. Thresher sharks occasionally make cameos in pursuit of the sardines, although you have to be lucky to see this.

Moalboal also has some of the Visayas' best reef-diving thanks to a long wall that runs the length of town just offshore and, further out, tiny **Pescador Island**, which is accessed via an often-choppy 3km boat ride from Moalboal's Tongo Point diving spot. **White Beach** also has spectacular shore diving and snorkelling.

Dive prices run from P1200 to P1600 per dive, including equipment. An open-water

👁 Sights

Kawasan Falls
WATERFALL

(admission P10) Located 17km south of Moalboal, Kawasan Falls comprise a series of three waterfalls; the largest cascades 20m into a massive, milky-blue swimming hole. Unfortunately this main pool has been a little spoilt by weekend crowds and over-development. The second and third waterfalls are more peaceful, and you can even scramble beyond these to more secluded spots, or otherwise arrange canyoning trips in Panagsama.

The turnoff to the falls 8km south of Badian, from where it's an easy 20-minute walk to the falls. Any southbound bus from Moalboal can drop you at the turnoff. Motorcyclists must pay P50 to park at the turnoff.

Mainit Springs
SPRING, WATERFALL

(admission P20) These natural springs in Montañeza, 32km south of Moalboal, are much less touristy than nearby Kawasan

certificate will cost P16,000 to P19,000. There is a reef conservation fee of P100 to dive at Savedra Reef and Pescador. Recommended dive operators include **Blue Abyss Dive Shop** (032-474 3036; www.blueabyssdiving.com), **Nelson's Dive Shop** (Ocean Safari Philippines; 032-474 3023; www.ibara.ne.jp/~bitoon) and **Neptune Diving** (032-495 0643; www.neptunediving.com).

Helped by the sardines and that righteous wall just offshore, Moalboal has emerged as the Philippines' top spot for **freediving**. A host of talented freedivers have moved here, and instruction is available through **Freediving Planet** (0908 608 7864; www.freediving-planet.com) and **Freediving Philippines** (0938 263 4646; www.freediving-philippines.com), which both offer level 1 to level 4 freediving courses.

Other Activities

There is a decent **golf course** in Badian.

Planet Action ADVENTURE TOUR
(032-474 3016; www.action-philippines.com) Run by the wry and affable Jochen, Planet Action offers some of the most exhilarating adventure tours in the Visayas (from P2200). Tops on the list are the mountain-biking, canyoning and river-climbing tours, which take place in several area rivers. Other options include horse riding and trekking tours on Negros or up Osmeña Peak (1013m), Cebu's higest peak. Multiday tour packages available. Planet Action is reason alone to come to Moalboal. Also rents high-quality mountain bikes (from P500 per day).

Cyan Adventures ADVENTURE TOUR
(0927 426 6886; www.cyan.ph) This is a newish adventure-tour company with a small range of tours, including canyoning at Kawasan Falls and climbing Osmeña Peak.

🛏 Sleeping

🛏 Panagsama Beach

Ask the dive resorts about cheap package deals combining diving and accommodation.

Cora's Palm Resort GUESTHOUSE $
(0998 364 0880; cora_abarquez@yahoo.com; r with fan P500, with air-con P1000-1500; ✻🤙) Cora's is perched right on the waterfront smack dab in the centre. Shoot for the cosy and cheap fan rooms. Pricier rooms have kitchenettes and small fridges.

Moalboal Backpacker Lodge HOSTEL $
(0917 751 8902; www.moalboal-backpacker-lodge.com; dm/s/d/cottage P275/350/550/750; 🤙) This hostel has airy mixed and women's dorms and a couple of semiprivate rooms over a coffee shop, plus two fabulous two-floor cottages that are a steal.

Mayas Native Garden BEACH RESORT $
(0915 480 9610; www.mayasnativegarden.com; cottage with fan/air-con P800/1500, house P2500; ✻🤙) Has wonderfully simple thatched-roof cottages in a lush garden setting. The double-storey house is incredible value with all mod cons.

★**Tipolo Beach Resort** BEACH RESORT $$
(0917 583 0062; www.tipoloresort.com; d P1500-2000; ✻@) Run by the folk from Planet Action, this small seaside resort is Panagsama's best all-rounder. It boasts pleasant rooms with clean tiled floors and sturdy bamboo furniture, along with mod cons like hot water, fridge and a safe. But the balconies are what win us over, amply furnished and with partial sea views.

Quo Vadis Beach Resort BEACH RESORT $$
(032-474 3068; www.quovadisresort.com; d with fan P1340, with air-con P1625-3775; ✻🤙🏊) Has solid nipa huts positioned amid lovely gardens, while the more expensive cottages open right up to the beach, with stylish decor, polished floorboards and big bathrooms that make them among the nicest in town.

Il Sogno B&B $$
(0915 696 5124; www.bedandbreakfastcebu.it; d P2500; ✻🤙) This homey three-room bed and breakfast is a welcome addition to the bland Moalboal resort scene. Two rooms face the ocean and have king-sized beds and huge bathrooms. The third room, with an outside bathroom and twin beds, is smaller but still cosy. It lacks open air but does have a nice public verandah out front.

Love's Beach & Dive Resort BEACH RESORT $$
(0917 618 5458; www.lovesbeachresort.com; d P1600-3000; ✻🤙🏊) Love's Beach is the furthest south of the Panagsama resorts, which means peace and quiet to go along with a cosy bar/pool area, a restaurant with excellent views of Pescador Island, a small private beach and well-furnished if slightly dark rooms, each with a balcony. We'll forgive the liberal use of woodcrete on the grounds. Super value.

Blue Abyss   RESORT $$

(☏032-474 3012; www.blueabyssdiving.com; r P1500; ❄🛜) Located a short walk south of the Blue Abyss dive shop, the concrete rooms here are spartan but clean, functional and practical for divers on a budget.

🏖 White Beach

Prices shift up a notch at White Beach; the extra dosh affords you a *real* beach.

★Blue Orchid Resort   BEACH RESORT $$

(☏0929 273 1128; www.blueorchidresort.com; d with fan P3000, with air-con from P3500; ❄🛜🏊) Blue Orchid has a wonderful secluded location on the rocky coastline just north of White Beach. The snorkelling offshore is the area's best, or just relax by the pool or in one of the polished-wood gazebos that look over sparkling turquoise waters to Negros. The large rooms are austere but have wooden poster beds, spacious blue-tiled showers and private balconies. Also has an excellent restaurant and a dive shop.

Delgado's   HOTEL $$

(☏0908 532 8162; r with fan P1000, with air-con P1500-2000) Right next to – and sharing a prime stretch of beach with – fancy Club Serena Resort, no-frills Delgado's is the closest thing to backpacker accommodation here.

Asian Belgian Resort   BEACH RESORT $$

(☏032-358 5428; www.asian-belgian-resort.com; d P2000-4000; ❄) A friendly midranger just south of White Beach, it lacks a sandy coastline but has a good lookout over the house reef, a dive company, free kayak use and – most importantly – Belgian fries! Pricier rooms are oceanfront.

Club Serena Resort   BEACH RESORT $$$

(☏032-516 8118; www.clubserenaresort.com; r P3000-6000; ❄🛜🏊) Luxurious and quirky in equal measure, Serena is a little gem right on the beach. Every structure, from the spacious octagonal bar-restaurant to the sprawling tree-house room, is designed with personal flair and fitted for maximum indulgence. It has the Aquaholics dive shop on-site.

🏖 Badian

Terre Manna Beach Resort & Camping   RESORT $$$

(☏032-475 0296; www.terramannaresort.ph; tent incl breakfast per person P600, d incl breakfast P3500-3800) This sprawling property 10km south of Moalboal plops down tents for tourists on a grassy field in view of the water. Or opt for tastefully austere stand-alone cottages. There's no real beach, but a lovely seaside lounging platform allows easy access to snorkelling just offshore. Take the Badian Island turnoff, 2km south of Badian town.

★Badian Island Resort & Spa   BEACH RESORT $$$

(☏032-401 3303-05; www.badianhotel.com; r from P11,000; ❄@🛜🏊) This luxurious resort on Badian Island, 10km south of Moalboal, boasts some of the most sumptuous rooms in the Philippines. The pool villas, which feature their own private salt-water infinity pools, are the ultimate in opulence. Look out for attractive low-season promo rates. A day trip here costs P500 plus P400 for the boat transfer (you can walk at low tide).

🍴 Eating & Drinking

There are plenty of good eats and a drinking spot to suit most tastes at Panagsama Beach, so bar hop till you find something you like. Nightlife is nonexistent on White Beach.

Chilli Bar   RESTOBAR $

(mains P150-210; ⏰9.30am-last customer) A Panagsama institution known for big pizzas, chilli con carne, Swedish meatballs and a lethal cocktail menu. 'The liver is evil and it must be punished', proclaims a big board by the pool table, where billiard comps take place every Wednesday.

★Lago di Garda   ITALIAN $$

(mains P150-250, pizzas P180-250; ⏰11am-2pm & 6-10.30pm) Mauro, a doctor from the lake area for which the restaurant is named, has raised the bar for eating out in Panagsama with this rambling open-air eatery. The pizzas and bread are particularly toothsome.

French Coffee Shop   CAFE $$

(salads P220-280, crêpes P100-220; ⏰7am-10pm) Surely the healthiest restaurant in town, it does what it says on the label – French coffee – plus crêpes, fresh bread, breakfasts and salads. It's off the water but you can dig your feet in the imported sand.

Lantaw   ASIAN $$

(mains P150-250; ⏰7.30am-10pm) Lantaw features Indian and Indonesian tastes on its menu but is best known for Thai dishes such as green chicken curry. There are superb views of Pescador Island and Negros beyond from its perch above the waterfront.

Last Filling Station INTERNATIONAL $$
(meals from P180; ☺ 7am-10pm; 🔊 📶) Famous for energy-boosting breakfasts, with yoghurt, muesli, baguettes and protein shakes. It also does a decent strong brewed coffee.

BB's Seaview FILIPINO $$
(mains P60-360; ☺ 7am-10pm) BB's is right in the centre of Panagsama but relatively sealed off from the noise so you can really enjoy that sea view. Opt for the fresh seafood.

❶ Information

There's a Metrobank ATM in the 360 Pharmacy on the highway in the centre of Moalboal, but it's often out of order so bring cash. Otherwise the closest ATM is in Barili. There are internet cafes 200m east of Panagsama on the road to Moalboal, and in central Moalboal.

❶ Getting There & Away

Buses from Moalboal to Cebu City depart hourly until 8.30pm or so (ordinary/air-con P107/130, 3½ hours). Squashy air-con vans (P100, 2½ hours) depart every 30 minutes until 5pm. A taxi will cost P2000 – or as little as P1200 if you find a driver heading back after a drop-off (ask around).

Frequent southbound buses terminate a few kilometres beyond the RORO pier in Bato (air-con P73, 1½ hours). Ferries from Bato depart every 1½ hours or so to Tampi, Negros (P70, 30 minutes), where you can pick up transport to Dumaguete.

Santander & Around

📞 032 / POP 16,105

The gorgeous coastline around Santander is home to several worthwhile attractions, namely diving in the Tañon Strait around barangay Lilo-an or off **Sumilon Island**. Lilo-an is also where many tourists arrive to catch boats to Sibulan near Dumaguete in Negros Oriental. In recent years this area has risen to prominence as the site of a controversial whale-shark interaction program 8km north of Santander in the village of Tan-awan, a barangay of Oslob.

The marine sanctuary off Sumilon Island is one of the success stories of conservation in the Philippines. The resorts in Lilo-an run dive trips over there, or you can base yourself in luxurious **Sumilon Bluewater Island Resort** (📞 032-318 3129; www.bluewatersumilon. com.ph; r from P9000; 🅿 🔊 🏊). Nonguests can use the resort's facilities for P600 and avail of their free boat transfer from a pier in Banlogan, 1km south of Tan-awan. Visitors to the sanctuary are charged a P10 entrance fee and there is a further fee of P150 for diving.

🛏 Sleeping & Eating

Kingdom Resort BEACH RESORT $$
(📞 032-480 9017; r from P1500; 🅿 🔊) A South Korean dive resort at the bottom of the hill on the beach at Lilo-an, with spacious but time-worn upstairs rooms looking out to Negros.

CEBU & EASTERN VISAYAS SANTANDER & AROUND

THE WHALE SHARKS OF OSLOB

In recent years the village of Tan-awan, a barangay of Oslob, has risen to prominence as a site where tourists can interact with whale sharks. It all started in 2011 when internet videos surfaced that showed an Oslob fisherman luring a whale-shark away from his catch with small fish.

While the program has been a huge financial boon to Tan-awan, many conservationists worry about possible adverse affects that the hand-feeding might have on a highly migratory endangered species that is just recovering from centuries of exploitation. Scientists studying the program report that about a dozen juvenile whale sharks have stopped migrating and remain in Tan-awan, where they rely at least partially on these 'hand-outs' for sustenance. The Reef-World Foundation (www.reef-world.org), Save Philippine Seas (www.savephilippineseas.com) and Green Fins (www.greenfins.net) are among several organisations that have come out against the tourism activities in Oslob, noting that the practice of feeding wildlife is unsustainable. Proponents of the hand-feeding respond that the project protects the whale sharks by keeping them safely around Oslob and away from the hazards of the open ocean, where they risk being poached.

Regardless of how you feel about the ethics of feeding wild animals, you may or may not be impressed with the Oslob whale-shark interactions. There are scores of people in the water at any one time, most of them not swimming but just pressing their masks to the water to watch up to a half-dozen or so whale sharks hover near the surface begging for food. It feels a bit like swimming in an aquarium. The whale-shark interaction programs in Donsol and Pintuyan (Southern Leyte) offer a more natural experience.

★ **Eden Resort** BEACH RESORT $$$
(☏ 032-480 9321; www.eden.ph; r incl breakfast P3800; ❈ 🛜 ❈) The luxurious cabanas at this Mediterranean-style resort are dramatically perched on a cliff overlooking the Tañon Strait. It has a tennis court, an infinity pool, good pizza and great snorkelling in the current-heavy waters offshore. Worth staying here whether you're a diver or not.

ℹ Getting There & Away

From Lilo-an, frequent fastcraft (P62) and bangkas (P37) alternate trips from neighbouring piers to Sibulan near Dumaguete (25 minutes). The last trip is the 7.30pm fastcraft.

Ceres buses run all day from Lilo-an to Cebu City (P169, three hours). For Moalboal, you must change buses in nearby Bato.

Argao
☏ 032 / POP 69,503

With a lovely town plaza set around an old Spanish church, Argao makes for a good lunch stop if you're heading down to Santander or Negros from Cebu City. Otherwise, it's mainly a place to catch obscure boats to Bohol. Lite Shipping sends ROROs to Tagbilaran from the pier in barangay Taloot daily at 4am and noon (P200, 2½ hours). There are also bangkas to Cabilao Island from barangay Looc on Tuesdays and Saturdays at 1pm (P120, one hour).

CAMOTES ISLANDS
☏ 032 / POP 92,000

Just two hours from mainland Cebu, the Camotes offer an authentic slice of island life. The group's two main islands, Poro and Pacijan, are connected by a mangrove-fringed land bridge that enables visitors to explore the two by motorcycle, the main mode of transport here. The best beaches and most accommodation is on Pacijan. Visitors rarely make it to the third island, Ponson, which looks to Leyte rather than Cebu as its main link to the world. Bring cash because there are no ATMs in the Camotes.

ℹ Getting There & Away

RORO ferries to Danao, Cebu, leave from the village of Consuelo on Pacijan Island. Jomalia Shipping (p292) runs this route five times daily, with the last trip at 5pm (P180, two hours). One Wednesday trip continues on to Kawit on Ponson Island.

Super Shuttle Ferry (☏ 0915 646 6857) has twice daily trips scheduled to Danao from Poro on Poro island, but these are often cancelled.

The eastern port of Pilar on Ponson Island is well-connected by public bangka to Ormoc, Leyte, with two early-morning and one early afternoon departure (P150, 1½ hours). At least one of these originates in Kawit.

ℹ Getting Around

The best way to get around Pacijan and Poro Islands is to charter a *habal-habal* or rent a motorcycle, as jeepneys are sporadic. Most resorts on Pacijan hire out motorcycles for P400 to P500. *Habal-habal* drivers should accept P800 for an all-day trip.

To get from Poro Island to Ponson Island, charter a bangka from Puertobello to Kawit (P250, 20 minutes). On Ponson, *habal-habal* charge P150 for the 25-minute drive from Kawit to Pilar. If arriving in Puertobello from Kawit, there is a *habal-habal* stand at the pier with prices posted to San Francisco (P200) and other towns and tourist destinations.

Pacijan Island
☏ 032 / POP 47,357

Pacijan's main attractions are the white-sand beaches around Santiago Bay, which is where the majority of Camotes' resorts are located. The main town is **San Francisco** ('San Fran').

◉ Sights & Activities

Near Esperanza on Pacijan's northwest tip is touristy **Timubo Cave** (admission P20), where a set of stairs leads down to a refreshing cave pool. Just north of the cave is the village of Tulang Daku, where you can ask a fisher to take you out to the pretty beach on **Tulang Island** (P500 return). Off the main road south of Esperanza is stunning **Borromeo Beach**, a blinding expanse of white powder with a couple of sleepy, often empty resorts.

Ocean Deep DIVING
(☏ 0908 457 9355; www.oceandeep.biz; dive incl equipment P1500) The Camotes' only dive shop is a low-key operation based at Mangodlong Paradise Beach Resort. There is good wall diving around Tulang Island and along the northwest coast of Ponson Island, including at Rubber Tire Reef on Ponson's northern tip. Marine sanctuaries have been established off Poro Island near Esperanza and Tudela, but unfortunately they were heavily damaged by Typhoon Yolanda.

Camotes Islands

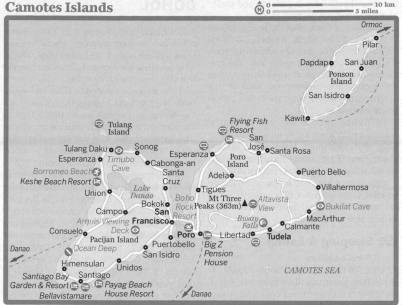

🛏 Sleeping & Eating

On Santiago Beach, neighbouring **Pito's Sukotil** (mains P75-100) and **Nena's Grill** (mains P75-100) both do excellent seafood and sell the native cookies, which are made with – what else – *camote* (sweet potatoes). Ask Pito's Sukotil about their budget rooms.

Payag Beach House Resort BEACH RESORT $
(☑ 032-233 1158; Santiago; r with fan P800, with air-con P1500-1800; ❄🛜) Plonked directly on a private white-sand beach, chilled-out Payag is the sort of place that suits Camotes to a tee. It's a tiny place with only a handful of basic rooms, which adds to its low-key appeal.

Bellavistamare BEACH RESORT
(☑ 0917 792 5583; Santiago Beach; d with fan/air-con P950/1450; ❄) This no-frills Italian-run place right on the beach should suit budget travellers just fine. Rooms are brightly painted and have sea views from a public balcony, but could use some more furniture.

Santiago Bay
Garden & Resort BEACH RESORT $$
(☑ 032-345 8599; www.camotesislandph.com; Santiago Beach; r with fan P1000, with air-con P1500-3000; ❄) Overlooking a crescent-shaped Santiago Bay, this resort boasts one of the island's finest plots of real estate. It sprawls all over the place and overdoes it with the woodcrete and tacky art, but the views are terrific. Most rooms lack hot water.

Keshe Beach Resort BEACH RESORT $$
(☑ 0929 892 5792; Borromeo Beach; r P1000-1500) A simple resort with a couple of beachfront cottages on the Camotes' most stunning beach. Food is problematic here as there's no restaurant; rent your own two-wheeler if staying here.

ℹ Information

In San Francisco you'll find the informative **City Tourism Office** (☑ 0921 471 1434; www.travelcamotes.com; ⏰ 8am-5pm Mon-Fri), in a little shack opposite the church. It sells a brochure and map outlining Pacijan Island's main sights for P50.

Poro Island

☑ 032 / POP 21,529

Poro is the lesser of the two main islands of the Camotes. It lacks the beaches of Pacijan but its mountainous roads are better for bike touring, especially on an off-road bike.

Poro is the main town on the island, an unassuming coastal settlement with a hint of the Spanish Mediterranean to it. There's really not much reason to stay here unless the Poro-Danao ferry is running and you're planning an early morning escape.

Just west of Poro, near the bridge to San Francisco, Boho Rock Resort (admission P20) is an absolute gem of a swimming spot, with a platform for jumping into the turquoise ocean and good snorkelling among the rocks. Unfortunately the whiz of the neighbouring power plant spoils the atmosphere somewhat.

In Tudela, next to the Tudela Central School, a path leads for 10 minutes to Busay Falls, with swimming holes and a natural water slide. Easy access means it can get crowded but it's a pleasant spot nonetheless.

Just east of MacArthur, the well-marked Bukilat Cave (admission P10) is worth a stop to swim in the tidal brackish-water pool within, best at high tide.

🛏 Sleeping & Eating

Big Z Pension House PENSION $
(📞0932 724 9837; r with fan/air-con P350/1000; ❄) In Poro town, this place in a rustic wooden house is a shoestringer option with simple fan rooms and cold-water bathrooms.

Flying Fish Resort BEACH RESORT $$
(📞0908 876 5427; www.camotesflyingfishresort. com; r with fan P1000, with air-con P1600-2600; ❄🛜) Isolated on the north end of the island 5km east of Esperanza, Flying Fish is perched above a rocky beach with comfortable cottages, some facing the sea. Unfortunately the marine sanctuary out front was wrecked by Typhoon Yolanda, but it remains a place to truly get away from it all. Free kayak rental and a cave pool on-site.

Ponson Island

📞 032 / POP 11,564
The charm in visiting a place as remote as Ponson is the attention you'll get, which varies from warmly effusive to wryly amused. Very, very few travellers make it this far, despite it being relatively easy to get here from Ormoc. There are two main towns on Ponson: Pilar and Kawit. Kawit is the more picturesque of the two, with a lovely long, white-sand beach in the town proper. Fronting this beach is delightfully friendly, if basic, Halikana Resort (📞0918 349 8349; d with fan P600-1000, with air-con P1500). This is a great place to interact with locals in a small-island community. There's also accommodation in Pilar in the form of the rustic LPM Lodge.

BOHOL

📞 038 / POP 1.26 MILLION
Just a quick ferry journey from Cebu, Bohol offers independent travellers a wealth of options both on and off the beaten track. The island province is promoted almost exclusively through images of cute bug-eyed tarsiers and the majestic Chocolate Hills, and while both are fantastic highlights, in reality it's the diving on Panglao Island that brings in the crowds. Add a jungle interior, an adventure sport paradise, rice terraces and pristine white beaches, and you get a more rounded picture of what Bohol really is about.

Boholanos still affectionately call their province the 'Republic of Bohol', in reference to the island's short-lived independence at the turn of the 19th century. It's an appropriate appellation – today's successors of the republic are fierce protectors of Bohol's distinctive cultural heritage. The 7.2 magnitude 2013 earthquake killed more than 200 people and destroyed several of the island's Spanish-era churches. One year on, the churches remained down, but few additional outward effects of the catastrophe were visible.

ℹ Getting There & Away

There are plenty of flights to Tagbilaran from Manila, and Tagbilaran is also the main port. By boat, Bohol is connected to Cebu, Manila, Leyte, Mindanao, Siquijor and Negros. Other ports include Tubigon, Jagna, Ubay and Talibon.

Tagbilaran

📞 038 / POP 96,792
Derived from two Visayan words meaning 'hidden shelter' (tago bilaan), the name Tagbilaran is a reference either to its positioning on a calm, protected strait or its historical role as a sanctuary from Moro invaders. Today the town is overrun by legions of noisy tricycle taxis and there's nothing calming about it. If your interests are divided between the watery and land-based kind, this commercial city is a practical place to base yourself.

◉ Sights & Activities

Blood Compact Monument MONUMENT
(National Hwy) This great monument 1km east of Tagbilaran celebrates the March 1565 blood compact, where Spanish conquistador Miguel López de Legazpi and Boholano chieftain Rajah Sikatuna shared a cup of each other's blood as a peace treaty.

Bohol

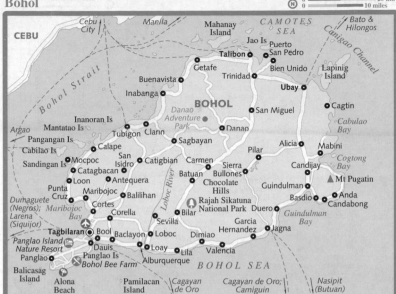

National Museum   MUSEUM
(admission P20; ⊘ 8am-5pm Mon-Fri) This small miuseum has a few anthropologically interesting items discovered around Bohol, including five artificially deformed skulls, a 500-year-old Boholana and a display on the cave paintings of Anda.

★ Kayakasia   KAYAKING
(☑ 0933 358 0081, 0932 855 2928; kayakbohol@gmail.com; trips from per person P1950) Departing from nearby Cortes at sunset, Kayakasia's memorable evening kayak trips set out to see the fireflies, which pulsate in the trees like Christmas lights. Grab a few beers for the leisurely paddle along the nipa-palm-lined Abatan River. In harvesting season you'll stop en route to watch villagers weaving the walls and ceilings for nipa huts. The trip climaxes as night descends, revealing the sight of trees full of shimmering fireflies.

★彡 Festivals & Events

Sandugo Festival   CULTURAL
The Sandugo Festival celebrates the March 1565 blood compact, and is followed by a string of arts and other festivals that have turned the whole of July into one big party month.

🛏 Sleeping

For a slice of Boholano life, consider a homestay outside of Tagbilaran (p308).

Nisa Travellers Hotel   GUESTHOUSE $
(☑ 038-411 3731; www.nisatravellershotel.com; CPG Ave; s/d incl breakfast from P500/600; ❈@☚) You won't find cheaper or more central accommodation in Tagbilaran. It's a hotel with a hostel vibe – welcoming and traveller-friendly, with clean rooms and 24-hour checkout. They can also arrange tours.

Sun Avenue   HOTEL $
(☑ 038-412 5601; www.sunavenueinn.com; C Gallares St; s/d from P800/950; ❈☚) Clean, modern and welcoming hotel well-located between the pier and the centre of town. Only upstairs rooms have windows. The attached Sun Cafe has some of the best food in town.

Ocean Suites   BOUTIQUE HOTEL $$
(☑ 038-411 1031; www.oceansuites.ph; National Hwy; r incl breakfast P2500-5500; ❈☚⊠) Next to the Blood Compact monument, Ocean Suites raises the bar, with contemporary rooms, a bright cafe and an infinity pool overlooking the Tagbilaran Strait and Panglao Island beyond. Splurge for deluxe ocean-front rooms, which have balconies and are much bigger than road-facing 'superior' rooms.

Tagbilaran

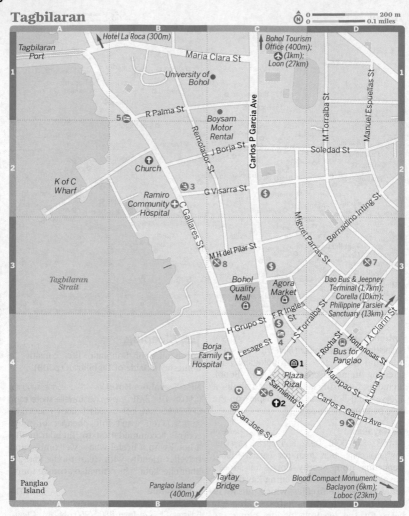

✕ Eating & Drinking

Gerarda's
FILIPINO **$$**

(JS Torralba St; meals P120-250; ☺8am-2pm & 5-10pm; ❋) In a historic family house with antiques, scuffed-wood floors and sparkling cutlery, sophisticated Gerarda's does fabulous Filipino food. The seafood *kare kare* (fish and crab in peanut sauce) is a winner.

Garden Cafe
AMERICAN **$$**

(JS Torralba St; meals P130-210; ☺6.30am-9.30pm; ❋☎) A fun cowboy-themed restaurant that employs deaf waiters and chefs. The menu, which includes a beginner's guide to sign language, is chock-full of good ol' Yankee and Tex Mex fare. Upstairs, dial your order through to the kitchen from tableside phones.

Payag
FILIPINO **$$**

(CPG Ave; mains P100-150; ☺10am-10pm) In a lovingly renovated Spanish-era home with a few quirky additions; everything on the menu is excellent (we checked), but the sizzling *gambas* (prawns) are to die for.

Martin's Music Restobar
RESTOBAR **$$**

(cnr C Gallares & MH del Pilar Sts; meals P70-150; ☺6pm-late) An upstairs bar that's popular with students for its regular live music.

Tagbilaran

⦿ Sights
1 National Museum.................................. C4
2 St Joseph the Worker
   Cathedral C4

◉ Activities, Courses & Tours
3 Kayakasia...B2

⛁ Sleeping
4 Nisa Travellers Hotel C4
5 Sun Avenue... B1

⊗ Eating
6 Garden Cafe... C4
7 Gerarda's D3
8 Martin's Music Restobar.....................C3
9 Payag...D5

ℹ Information

INTERNET ACCESS
There are several internet cafes in the streets surrounding the University of Bohol.

MEDICAL SERVICES
Ramiro Community Hospital (☎ 038-411 3515; 63 C Gallares St)

MONEY
Most major banks have branches with ATMs along central CPG Ave, including **Metrobank**, **BDO** and **BPI**.

TOURIST INFORMATION
Bohol Tourism Office (☎ 032-412 3666; www. tourism.bohol.gov.ph; Governor's Mansion Complex, CPG North Ave; ⊘ 8am-6pm Mon-Fri) Wonderfully helpful and professional staff here can provide maps, assist with travel information and book tours and transport. It also has small branches at the airport and pier.

ℹ Getting There & Around

AIR
PAL, Cebu Pacific, and AirAsia Zest each have a couple of daily flights between Manila and Tagbilaran. The airport is a 10-minute tricycle ride north of the centre (P50).

BOAT
Ferry ticket offices are at the pier.
Lite Shipping (☎ 038-531 8074)
Oceanjet (☎ 0932 873 4885)
SuperCat 2GO (☎ 0925 582 4824)
Trans-Asia Shipping Lines (☎ 038-411 3234)
Weesam Express (☎ 0917 301 5749)

BUS
Buses with 'Tawala Alona' signboards head to Alona Beach at least hourly until 5pm from the corner of Hontanosas and F Rocha Sts.

Most other public transport departs from the **Dao Bus & Jeepney Terminal**, which is next to Island City Mall, 3km north of the centre. Here you'll find frequent buses to Carmen for the Chocolate Hills (P60, 2½ hours), via Loboc (P25, one hour). Buses also serve Ubay (P120, 3½ hours) via Jagna and Guindulman; transfer in Guindulman for Anda. Buses to Talibon (P100, 3½ hours) go via Tubigon (P50, 1½ hours) and Getafe; buses to Danao go via Sagbayan All routes are serviced frequently until about 6pm.

V-hire vans also depart from Dao terminal, providing a much quicker option to Jagna (P100, 1½ hours, hourly), Ubay and Tubigon.

ℹ Getting Around
To avoid expensive van hires and slow public transport, consider hiring your own motorcycle in Tagbilaran (P500 per day) to explore the rest of Bohol. This can be done in town at **Boysam Motor Rental** (☎ 0908 936 2866; R Palma St), or at the pier through **Mario** (☎ 0929 855

FERRIES FROM TAGBILARAN

DESTINATION	TYPE	COMPANY	PRICE (P)	DURATION (HR)	FREQUENCY
Argao	RORO	Lite Shipping	200	2½	7.30am, 4pm
Cagayan de Oro	RORO	Trans-Asia	680	10	M, W, F 7pm
Cebu City	Fastcraft	Oceanjet, Weesam, Supercat 2GO	500-650	2	frequent
Cebu City	RORO	Lite Shipping	210	4	noon, 10.30pm
Dumaguete	Fastcraft	Oceanjet	700	2	daily
Larena, Siquijor	RORO	Lite Shipping	220	3½	M, W, Sa 8pm
Manila	Passenger	2GO	from 600	29	W
Siquijor town	Fastcraft	Oceanjet	910	3	daily

6357) – call him in advance and he'll have a bike waiting for you when you walk off the boat.

Both of the above can also find you a car or a van for day trips, or you can use one of the numerous car-hire services at the pier. The going rate is P2000 per day for a car, or P3000 for a van.

Panglao Island

📶 038 / POP 62,083

Panglao Island is generally associated with **Alona Beach**, a congested strip of resorts and dive centres on the southern side of the island. With a few exceptions, lodging and especially food is overpriced on Alona. That said, the underwater scene around Alona is indeed exceptional, and divers can score nifty package deals by combining dives with accommodation. Alona also has some decent nightlife. Just 15km from Tagbilaran, it works just fine as a base for exploring the rest of Bohol – especially when you can return home at the end of the day to two-for-one cocktails in the sand.

Just as you cross over the bridge to Panglao Island from Tagbilaran, take a moment to look around the scenic village of **Dauis** and admire the magnificent exterior and interior of the 19th-century Lady of Assumption Cathedral, which was damaged in the 2013 quake but remained open. It's adjacent rectory houses the **Dauis Pilgrim & Heritage Center** (dishes P125-185; ⊙9am-9pm; 📶), which has a healthy cafe and a gift shop selling fine, locally crafted jewellery and an array of coffee-table books on local culture.

🏃 Activities

Most people head to Bohol proper for any activities that aren't dive-related. On Panglao Island, the Bohol Bee Farm makes a

---

BOHOL HOMESTAYS

For an authentic slice of Boholano life, contact **Process-Bohol** (📶038-416 0067; www.boholhomestay.com; fan/air-con incl breakfast P600/700, additional meals P200; ❄) 📶, a nonprofit community-run organisation that arranges cheap homestays with families across Bohol. The fee helps struggling communities maintain a sustainable livelihood. At the time of writing homestays were available in Maribojoc, Cabilao Island, Anda, Balilihan and Ubay. Book at least 24 hours in advance.

---

worthwhile stop, or you might check out **Hinagdanan Cave** (admission P25; ⊙7.30am-6pm), which has a pool for swimming. It's near Panglao Nature Resort on the island's north coast.

Diving

Diving is what draws tourists to Panglao, in particular the underwater paradise of Balicasag Island. Pamilacan Island is also very nice, but less visited as its corals are left to recover from dynamite fishing.

You can probably score the best deal by combining accommodation with diving. The average prices are one dive for US$25, equipment rental US$8 and open-water diving certificates for US$350. Those looking for a more budget-friendly dive can try a cut-rate local operator like Baywatch (📶038-502-9028), which charges just P2200 per person for a two-dive trip to Balicasag including equipment and lunch.

Snorkellers can swim 75m straight out to enjoy the soft corals of Alona's house reef.

There are several recommended operators based on Alona Beach.

Genesis Divers   DIVING
(📶032-502 9056; www.genesisdivers.com; Peter's House) Long-running, reliable operator.

Sea Explorers   DIVING
(📶in Cebu 032-234 0248; www.sea-explorers.com; Alona Vida Beach Resort) Does dive-safaris across the Visayas as well.

Philippine Fun Divers   DIVING
(📶038-416 2336; www.boholfundivers.com; Lost Horizon Beach Resort) With a fun team, it lives up to its name.

SeaQuest Divers   DIVING
(📶038-502 9069; www.seaquestdivecenter.net; Oasis Resort) Reliable operator on central Alona Beach.

Tropical Divers   DIVING
(📶038-502 9031; www.tropicaldivers-alona.com; Alona Tropical) Reliable Filipino operator.

Dolphin Watching & Island Hopping

You can arrange to go on early-morning dolphin-watching tours near Pamilacan Island through most resorts and dive centres, though there have been negative reports that this more resembles 'dolphin chasing' – so you might be better to organise this through Pamilacan Island Dolphin & Whale Watching Tours (p312) out of Baclayon, 6km from Tagbilaran. Figure on paying P1500 for a

Alona Beach

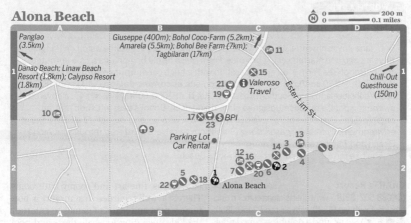

four-person boat out of Alona – more if you want to extend that into an **island-hopping** trip taking in Pamilacan, Virgin and Balicasag islands.

🛏 Sleeping

🛏 Alona Beach

You'll pay a huge premium to stay on the beach. Prices drop as you walk up the Alona Beach access road towards the highway.

Peter's House BEACH RESORT **$**
(☏032-502 9056; www.genesisdivers.com; r nondivers P1200-1400, divers P900-1100; 🛜) A nipa-hut complex with a friendly and laid-back communal vibe, Peter's House is a dive resort for those on a budget. There are only a few rooms, all sharing cold-water bathrooms. Unless it's low season it's exclusively for divers.

Alona Grove Tourist Inn NIPA HUTS **$**
(☏032-502 4200; alongagrove@yahoo.com; hut with fan/air-con P700/1200; ❄🛜) A chilled-out budget option just up from the beach with nipa huts scattered among its pleasant garden with manicured grass.

Casa-Nova Garden GUESTHOUSE **$**
(☏038-502 9101; s with shared bathroom P300, d P500-1000; ❄🛜) True shoestring accommodation survives in Alona thanks to this cosy oasis. It's a bit out of the way, however. The turn-off is 700m beyond (west of) T2 Lounge.

★ Chill-Out Guesthouse GUESTHOUSE **$$**
(☏038-502 4480, 0912 926 5557; www.chill-out-panglao.com; r with fan/air-con P1000/1500; ❄🛜) Spacious, boutique-quality rooms

Alona Beach

with hardwood floors and roomy private balconies; leafy walkways link the rooms with a delightful open-air common area/restaurant. For this price? Sign us up. It's a 10-minute walk to the beach, or rent a motorcycle for P300 per day.

THE BOHOL BEE FARM

Boholana environmentalist Vicky Wallace dug a small-scale vegetable patch on Panglao 15 years ago and started selling produce. From these fertile beginnings a cafe sprouted. Today, Bohol Bee Farm is an epic operation with a huge oceanfront **restaurant** (mains P200-800; ☺ 5.30am-10pm; 🖥 🚗) 🥾, lovely on-site **accommodation** (☑ 038-510 1822; http://boholbeefarm.com; Southern Coastal Rd, Km 11; r P3000-6000; ❄ 🛜 🏊) 🥾, a covered swimming pool, a purpose-designed sunbathing deck, Bohol's best gift shop and an organic farm. Branches of its heralded **Buzz Cafe**, with organic munchies and a range of environmentally friendly *pasalubong* (small souvenirs), are scattered throughout Alona Beach and Tagbilaran.

The bee farm is located 7km east of Alona Beach..

ChARTs Resort　　BOUTIQUE HOTEL **$$**
(☑ 038-502 8918; www.charts-alona.com; d incl breakfast with fan P1500, with air-con P2450-3850; ❄ @ 🛜 🏊) Set around a dolphin-shaped pool, the gorgeous rooms here evoke a Dalíesque Mediterranean-Asian atmosphere; there are no sharp edges and the stucco-textured walls highlight the fine varnished furniture. There's also a suitably arty upstairs cafe.

Oasis Resort　　RESORT **$$$**
(☑ in Cebu 032-418 1550; www.oasisresortbohol. com; r incl breakfast P3000-6600; ❄ 🛜 🏊) The name is not a misnomer at this mellow resort, with well-appointed duplex and triplex cottages set around a pleasant garden and pool behind the busy beating heart of Alona beach. Standard rooms are twin configuration; upgrade to a deluxe for a queen bed.

🏖 Danao Beach

The next beach over from Alona to the west is a bit isolated but offers pretty good value. From the Alona beach access road junction (near T2 Lounge), it's 700m to the Danao Beach turnoff. It helps to rent a motorcycle if staying here.

Calypso Resort　　RESORT **$**
(☑ 038-502 8184; www.philippins.info; r P800-1200; ❄ 🛜 🏊) Set well back from Danao Beach, this place would be a good deal even without a free motorcycle. Throw in that motorcycle (one per room) and it's a fantastic deal. If you don't ride, hang out at the pool all day and order cocktails from the cosy bar, equipped with billiards and other games.

Linaw Beach Resort　　BEACH RESORT **$$$**
(☑ 038-502 9345; www.linawbeachresort.com; r P4950-7450; ❄ 🛜 🏊) Rooms at this rambling mansion-on-the-beach are exceedingly comfortable and well-appointed, with huge flat-screens, fine art and roomy bathrooms. There's a well-regarded restaurant, a boutique-y pool and loads of games to entertain the kids, including foosball, darts and pool. It's smack dab on Danao Beach.

🏖 Around the Island

⭐ **Bohol Coco-Farm**　　HOSTEL **$**
(☑ 0917 304 9801; boholcocofarm@yahoo.com; Southern Coastal Rd, Km 13; dm/d incl breakfast P300/600; 🛜) 🥾 If you prefer the sound of crickets to the sound of the ocean, this organic farm 5km east of Alona Beach is for you. The basic nipa huts are entirely appropriate for the rustic setting. The organic cafe (mains P100 to P190, beer P40) is fantastic, and they even have a 30-minute 'sky walk' (P30).

They do not supply mosquito nets, but do sell home-made citronella insect repellent.

⭐ **Amarela**　　BEACH RESORT **$$$**
(☑ 038-502 9497; www.amarelaresort.com; Southern Coastal Rd, Km 12.5; d P6000-9900, ste P12,000-23,000; ❄ 🛜 🏊) A beach getaway with elegance and class, Amarela is so boutique it has its own art gallery. Rooms with polished floorboards get plenty of sun, and most have balconies. Hammocks and deck-chairs await you at its lovely private beach, or relax at the superb pool surrounded by lush gardens. It's 5.5km east of Alona Beach.

Panglao Island Nature Resort　　BEACH RESORT **$$$**
(☑ 038-411 5878; www.panglaoisland.com; r incl breakfast & dinner P7610-13,560; ❄ @ 🛜 🏊) The best rooms at this sprawling, beautifully integrated property on Panglao's north coast have showers that look out onto private gardens, terraces inlaid with jacuzzis and sweeping ocean views. The cheaper 'superior' rooms are a let-down by comparison. Nonguests can pay the P450 fee to use its stunning white-

sand beach, two infinity pools and private artificial island just offshore.

Eating

Alona Beach is awash with beach barbecues specialising in seafood, but you'll pay a premium.

Trudi's Place
FILIPINO $$
(mains P140-240; ⏰6.30am-11pm; 🛜) Trudi's qualifies as budget eating on Alona Beach proper. Bonus: P40 San Miguel.

Hayahay
PIZZA $$
(pizzas from P200; ⏰7am-midnight) On the beach, Hayahay serves up pizzas, Thai, and meat pies for homesick Aussies.

★Giuseppe
ITALIAN $$$
(☑038-502 4255; mains P300-800; ⏰11am-11pm; ❄🛜) There's a crazy amount of good Italian restaurants in the Visayas, and Giuseppe is right up there with the very best of them. The pizza is divine, the pasta mouthwatering and the specials board might include such surprises as tiger prawns or ostrich fillet. It's cool and classy and has an extensive wine cellar (house wine P120).

L'Elephant Bleu
FRENCH $$$
(www.lelephantbleu.com; mains P260-500; ⏰10am-10pm; 🛜) This casual restaurant serves exceptional flambéed garlic prawns, escargot, crème brûlée and other French faves, not to mention wine, cheese and great coffee.

CU Biergarten
GERMAN $$$
(mains P160-600; ⏰6am-midnight; 🛜) Serves all kinds of schnitzel and sausage, plus its famous fried meatloaf topped with a fried egg. Great big breakfasts as well.

🍸 Drinking & Nightlife

The best strategy is to just stroll Alona Beach and see what's happening. After midnight or so, the action moves to two adjoining discos up on the highway, **Linarella** and **Aimz Bar.**

T2 Lounge
LOUNGE
(⏰24hr; 🛜) Definitely the most happening bar when we were there, it draws a healthy mix of peeps and is less blokey than some of the bars up on the hill. Also has good food and a pub quiz on Mondays.

Panglao Birdwatchers
BAR
(☑0912 710 8328; www.panglaobirdwatchers.com; 🛜) This Aussie-run beach bar is a great place for happy hour, drawing a fun crowd that often lingers at least long enough to ingest a few delicious California-style tacos from adjoining Woody's On The Beach barbecue shack. Has rooms too.

Coco Vida Bar
BAR
(⏰8am-late) The most buzzing bar on the beach when we visited.

❶ Information

There's a **BPI** ATM machine on the Alona Beach access road.

❶ Getting There & Around

Buses head from Alona to Tagbilaran roughly hourly until about 3pm (P25, 45 minutes). The quicker and easier option is to hire a *habal-habal* (P150), tricycle (P200) or taxi (P350).

For day tours, cars and vans can be hired from a **parking lot** on the Alona Beach access road, or from **Valeroso Travel** (☑0916 543 1702; www.boholtourguide.com; ⏰6.30am-9pm), for about P500 more than you'd pay in Tagbilaran. Motorcycle rental is also available here, and from most resorts, for P500 per day.

Balicasag Island

One of the premier diving spots in the Philippines, Balicasag, about 6km southwest of Panglao, is ringed by a pristine reef that has been declared a **marine sanctuary** (entrance fee snorkellers/divers P150/200). It drops away to impressive submarine cliffs as deep as 50m. Soft and hard corals can be found around the cliffs, as can trevally, barracuda and wrasse.

Balicasag Island Dive Resort (☑0928 217 6810, 0917 309 1417; ptabidr@bohol-online.com; dm P500, d incl breakfast P3200-3700; ❄🏊) has air-con duplex nipa cottages with private bathrooms and verandahs. It has friendly staff, a good restaurant and a coral-sand island all to itself. The dormitories here can sleep up to eight people, though smaller groups may be required to pay for the empty beds.

Balicasag is a 45-minute boat ride from Alona Beach, and is visited mainly by dive companies, but otherwise ring ahead for the resort to arrange your pick-up.

Pamilacan Island

☑038 / POP 1189

The tiny island of Pamilacan, about 23km east of Balicasag, is cetacean central, home to whales and dolphins. Since the 1992 ban

CEBU & EASTERN VISAYAS BALICASAG ISLAND

on capturing these creatures, Pamilacanons, descendants of three generations of whalers, have had to find other ways to earn a living.

No fewer than three community-based outfits organise expeditions and employ former whalers. All use converted whaling boats and local crews. The trip includes a full day on the water and transfers from Baclayon (on Bohol) or Panglao; boats hold four to six people. Whale sightings are relatively rare, but the best time for spotting them is February to July; dolphins are common year-round. **Pamilacan Island Dolphin & Whale Watching Tours** (PIDWWT; ☑ 0919 730 6108, 038-540 9279; http://whales.bohol.ph; group of 1-4 P3300, lunch per person P300) is one good operator. Rates are higher than what you would pay in Alona Beach, but keep in mind that these are more eco-friendly tours, and that rates include a lengthy stop to picnic, snorkel and swim on Pamilacan Island, which cheaper tours out of Alona do not include.

There are several accommodation options on Pamilacan, all providing basic meals. Electricity functions only from 5pm to midnight. **Nita's Nipa Huts** (☑ 0921 320 6497; r without bathroom per person incl full board P750) is the cheapest and most well-established option; the double rooms with views on the water's edge are the best positioned. Nita can organise snorkelling or a night-time squid-fishing trip for visitors, and arranges a pick-up from Baclayan/Panglao for P1000/1500. PIDWWT runs the simple **Pamilacan Island Tourist Inn** (☑ 0919 730 6108; d incl full board P1500).

You can arrange a boat between Pamilacan and Baclayon (one way/return P1500/2000, 45 minutes). Boats from Alona Beach will take you to Pamilacan for a bit more.

Cabilao Island

☑ 038 / POP 3,200

Legend has it that idyllic Cabilao is inhabited by the dreaded dog-shaped Balikaka monster that sporadically attacks livestock. In reality Cabilao is so chilled out, the only sounds to break the perfect calm are church bells and the odd rooster. There are limited beaches here, so Cabilao is a destination that attracts primarily divers, but otherwise it can make a great spot if you want to slow down.

Like Balicasag and Pamilacan Islands to the south, the waters off Cabilao contain an impressively rich dive site, with two community-run **marine sanctuaries**. You might spot the odd shark and the area is also full of microlife, including the difficult-to-spot pygmy seahorse *(Hippocampus bargibanti)*, which tops out at 8mm and camouflages itself among the surrounding red coral.

The island's top reef is off the northwestern point, near the lighthouse. Highly regarded **Sea Explorers** (☑ 0917 727 8248; www.sea-explorers.com) is based at Pura Vida Cabilao resort. On top of dive fees, there's a one-off entrance fee of P100 for diving or snorkelling in the marine sanctuary, plus the municipality of Loon levies a P150 per day scuba-diving fee.

🛏 Sleeping

Sleeping options on Cabilao are mostly on the northwestern side of the island, a short *habal-habal* ride from the pier in Talisay or a slightly longer ride from the Cambaquiz pier.

★ **Pura Vida Cabilao** BEACH RESORT $$
(☑ 0918 943 6057; www.cabilao.com; r P2900-4000; ❄ ☎) Often still referred to by its old name, Cabilao Beach Club, Pura Vida sits alone on the northeastern tip of the island. Its sophisticated and spotless thatched cottages have modern tiled bathrooms. The restaurant has therapeutic ocean views and Sea Explorers is on-site. Big discounts in the low season. It's a five-minute walk from the pier in Cambaquiz.

Polaris Resort BEACH RESORT $$
(☑ 0918 903 7187; www.polaris-dive.com; r with aircon P3500-4100, fan tree-house P1860; ❄ @ ☎ ☎) Has decent large rooms in concrete cottages as well as two 'tree-houses' up on stilts. It's a good family option; kids will love the Disneyland-esque artificial rock pools and hillocks. Extra ticks for partially using solar energy. There is an attached PADI dive centre. Nearby is a sandbar that at low tide is good for swimming and snorkelling.

❶ Getting There & Away

To get to Cabilao Island you must head several kilometres north of Loon to Mocpoc (a good 20 minutes on a bumpy road by *habal-habal* (P60). Loon is 27km from Tagbilaran (bus or jeepney P30, 45 minutes). From Mocpoc, public bangkas (P20) leave when full to Cambaquiz pier (for Pura Vida Cabilao) and Talisay (for the northwestern resorts), or pay for a special trip (P250 to P300). Weather often disrupts trips to Talisay, in which case head to Cambaquiz.

There is also a twice-weekly boat from Cabilao to Argao, Cebu, (P120, 1½ hours) on Monday and Saturday at 8am.

Antequera

038 / POP 14,481

Just out of Antequera, about 20km from Tagbilaran (bus or jeepney P30), are **Mag-aso Falls** – the largest falls on the island – and **Inambacan Spring & Caves**. Cave guides can be found at the trailhead to Mag-aso Falls, or text **Antolin** (☎ 0919 808 6079) if you want to book a guide in advance.

Tarsier Sanctuary

In Canapnapan, a barangay of Corella, you can see saucer-eyed tarsiers in the wild at the **Philippine Tarsier Sanctuary** (☎ 0927 541 2290; www.tarsierfoundation.org; admission P50; ⊙ 9am-4pm). About 10 of these territorial primates hang out in the immediate vicinity of the centre – the guides will bring you right to them. This is a much more humane, ecofriendly and rewarding way to appreciate the tarsier than at the tour-group-packed Loboc Tarsier Sanctuary.

The simultaneously crazy and cuddly looking tarsier can fit in the palm of your hand yet leap 5m, rotate its head almost 360 degrees and move its ears in the direction of sound. It has huge imploring eyes, 150 times bigger than a human's in relation to its body size.

The tarsier is not only one of the world's smallest primates and the oldest surviving member of the primate group at 45 million years old, it is also an endangered species. The main threats to its survival are habitat destruction, introduced species, hunting and the pet trade. While also found in Samar, Leyte and parts of Mindanao, Bohol is the province that is doing the most to promote awareness of the tarsier and attempting to ensure its survival.

The visitors centre includes information boards, a captive breeding area (off-limits to visitors) and photographs – check out the framed photograph of former First Lady Amelita Ramos presenting a tarsier to Prince Charles in 1997.

Keen hikers can arrange longer guided walks in the surrounding wildlife sanctuary, although you are unlikely to spot tarsiers outside of the immediate vicinity of the visitors centre. For a chance to spot these creatures in their nocturnal element, sign up for a night tour with Habitat Bohol (p315) in Bilar.

To get here from Tagbilaran, catch a bus to Sikatuna (P20, one hour) from the Dao terminal and ask to be dropped off at the sanctuary. From Nuts Huts or Loboc, the sanctuary is a 30- to 45-minute motorcycle ride, or you can take a jeepney from Loboc (P25, 45 minutes).

CAGED CRITTERS FREED?

Tour operators in Loboc used to exploit tarsiers for financial gain by catching them and stuffing them into small cages for the admiration of tourists, or as curios to liven up shop corners. Many of these animals would die prematurely of disease or, worse, commit suicide. Tarsiers, it turns out, are particularly ill-suited to a life in captivity, according to the Philippine Tarsier Foundation, Inc (PTFI).

Finally, in 2011, the governor of Bohol, in liaison with the Department of Environment & Natural Resources (DENR), largely put an end to this practice by confiscating the caged tarsiers and moving them to the **Loboc Tarsier Sanctuary** near the border of Loboc and Bilar, where they would be free to roam in the surrounding jungle.

That was the idea, at any rate. Unfortunately, the Loboc sanctuary has come under criticism for leaving its tarsiers vulnerable to many of the same threats they faced when stuck in cages. Rules that are strictly enforced at the PTFI's Philippine Tarsier Sanctuary (p313) in Corella, such as restrictions on visitor numbers and a ban on flash photography, are not in place in Loboc. And caretakers at the Loboc sanctuary feed the tarsiers and move them around by hand for easier viewing.

While life at the Loboc sanctuary surely beats life in a cage for these fragile and endangered critters, NGOs like the PTFI are not satisfied. They have criticised the treatment of tarsiers in Loboc, and have raised questions about the DENR's role in establishing the Loboc sanctuary, which was set up as a for profit venture and given a 'wildlife farm' permit that allows tarsiers to be displayed for commercial purposes.

Located just minutes from the Chocolate Hills, the Loboc sanctuary gets hundreds of visitors each day, but it's a better – and more ethical – experience at the Philippine Tarsier Sanctuary in Corella, which comes closest to replicating the tarsiers' natural habitat.

Chocolate Hills Loop

The well-travelled path to the Chocolate Hills can be done as a day trip out of Tagbilaran or Alona Beach. If you have time, it's highly recommended to spend a night or three in Loboc and loop back to Tagbilaran via the scenic road to Sierra Bullones and Jagna, with a short detour to Pilar, which has a scenic lake and rice terraces. It's also easy enough to work the Tarsier Sanctuary in Corella into this loop.

With little traffic and smooth roads, the Chocolate Hills route is tailor-made for a motorcycle. Otherwise, you're looking at P2000/2500 for a day tour in a car out of Tagbilaran/Alona Beach, or P3000/3500 for a 10-passenger van.

Baclayon

📞 038 / POP 18,630

About 6km from Tagbilaran, Baclayon is home to coral-stone Baclayon Church (1727), which was severely damaged in the 2013 earthquake. Local authorities say that the church will be rebuilt but it remains closed indefinitely. The adjacent museum (admission P50; ☺8am-5pm), with a collection of religious artefacts was open, however.

Baclayon is the best spot to arrange trips to Pamilacan Island for whale- and dolphin-watching tours.

It also has wonderful heritage houses, saved from demolition by the Baclayon Ancestral Homes Association (BAHANDI; 📞 0917 620 1211; 🖉), which can arrange walking tours to its 67 Spanish colonial houses, dating back to 1853. It also offers homestays in the ancestral houses.

The tourist office (📞 0946 296 4297; www.baclayontourism.com) at the port can prebook boats and has information on additional accommodation options in the area.

Loboc

📞 038 / POP 16,312

Floating restaurants blasting the tunes of Frank Sinatra and other oldies cruise a stretch of the Loboc River north of the town of the same name. Even this incongruous soundtrack doesn't diminish the appeal of Loboc, poking out from the jungle underbrush. The San Pedro Church (c 1602), the oldest on Bohol, was lying in ruins at the time of writing, brought down by the 2013 earthquake.

Just upriver from the town proper is the legendary backpacker Shangri-La Nuts Huts. It's well worth a lunch stop if you're passing by on the Chocolate Hills loop. Beyond Nuts Huts is Tontonan Falls and the Visayas' oldest hydroelectric plant. Loboc Eco Adventure Park (📞 038-537 9292; zipline P350) has a thrilling 500m zipline running 120m over the falls. A tamer chairlift (P250) plies the same route. Guided paddleboarding on the Loboc River is possible through Suptours (📞 0947 893 3022; www.suptoursphilippines.com; Paddles Up Guesthouse; 1hr/½-day tour per person P950/1450); the night-time firefly tour is highly recommended.

Loboc is about 24km from Tagbilaran, accessed by bus (P30, one hour).

🛏 Sleeping & Eating

★Nuts Huts   HOSTEL $

(📞 0920 846 1559; www.nutshuts.org; dm P300-400, nipa huts P900-1200) Ensconced in the jungle on the Loboc River, 2km north of Loboc town, Nuts Huts is the perfect place to base yourself for explorations of interior Bohol. The stilted nipa huts are hidden at the bottom of the steep hill along the river. All have balconies for hangin' though they're very basic, for roughing it in the jungle.

Meals are served in the wonderful dining room/lounge area, where a wall of jungle on the opposite bank of the river completely fills the view. Guided treks head to nearby caves and Rajah Sikatuna National Park. It also has kayaks for rent and a wood-heated herbal sauna.

To get to Nuts Huts from Tagbilaran catch a Carmen-bound bus and get off at the Nuts Huts sign about 3km beyond Loboc. From there, it's around a 15-minute walk along a rutted dirt path. You can also take a *habal-habal* (P50) straight to Nuts Huts from Loboc. A more atmospheric way to arrive is by shuttle boat up the Loboc River from the Sarimanok landing north of Loboc centre (P200/300/450 for one/two/three people).

Paddles Up Guesthouse   HOSTEL $

(📞 038-537 9011; rooms@suptoursphilippines.com; dm/cottage P450/1200; 🖥) With the opening of this small, supremely chill riverside guesthouse, Loboc has itself another backpacker gem. Lodgings are basic but chances are you'll be spending more time paddleboarding on the Loboc with Suptours (p314), or exploring the area by motorcycle (per day P500). It's a little southwest of Loboc's centre.

Loboc River Resort   RESORT $$
(☑038-510 4565; www.lobocriverresort.com; cottage incl breakfast P2800-5000; ❀🛜🏊) For something a little more upscale in Loboc, this fine river resort about 1km south of town has comfortable native-style concrete cottages with polished-wood floors and balconies – pay just P200 extra to be on the river, or splurge for a humongous suite villa.

Bilar

☑038 / POP 17,098

A popular stopover for day trippers 1km south of Bilar, **Habitat Bohol** (☑038-535 9400; http://boholconservation.com; admission P40, night safari P900, s P550, d P850-1000; ⊙7.30am-5pm) houses a popular butterfly garden, but the main attraction are its **night safaris** (5.30pm to 7.30pm), which offer a decent (about 40%) chance of spotting tarsiers in the wild close to Rajah Sikatuna National Park. Even if you don't spot one, it's a nice experience to walk through their natural habitat, also home to owls, frogmouths, bats, civet cats and fireflies. Book these tours a day ahead. Habitat Bohol has accommodation available in the form of comfortable cottages nestled in the forest, and there's also a restaurant. Bilar is about 22km northeast of Loboc.

Chocolate Hills

One of Bohol's premier tourist attractions, and certainly its most hyped, are the Chocolate Hills, a series of majestic grassy hillocks that span far into the horizon. The hills get their name from the lawnlike vegetation that roasts to chocolate brown in the driest months (February to July). They were supposedly formed over time by the uplift of coral deposits and the effects of rainwater and erosion. Since this explanation cannot be confirmed, the local belief that they are the tears of a heartbroken giant may one day prove to be correct.

Straddling three municipalities, the largest and most visited concentration is 4km south of Carmen, site of the **Chocolate Hills Main Viewpoint** (admission P50). From the base of the viewpoint, motorcycles can whisk you up the hill (P40 one way for two passengers), where the views are compromised by kiosks selling kitschy souvenirs. Of course, you can also walk up the hill (20 to 30 minutes).

The same *habal-habal* drivers will take you on a thrilling motorcycle tour (half-/one hour P250/350) along winding roads to the main viewing sites, as well as to lesser-known spots, such as the **Eight Sisters Hillocks**. Fun ATV and buggy tours are also available near the base of the viewpoint.

If you want to sleep somewhere around here, **Banlasan Lodge** (☑038-525 9145; d with fan/air-con & shared bathroom from P400/600; ❀🛜🏊) is on the highway between the viewpoint and Carmen.

For less touristy Chocolate Hills, your best bet is northeast of Sagbayan on the road to Danao.

🛈 Getting There & Away

From Tagbilaran there are regular buses from the Dao terminal to Carmen (P60, two hours). From Loboc, the Chocolate Hills are a 45-minute motorcycle ride, or you can flag down a Carmen-bound bus. From Carmen there are also buses to and from Talibon (P62, two hours) and Tubigon (P50, 1½ hours).

Jagna

☑038 / POP 32,566

Jagna is where you catch the useful ferry to Camiguin, Mindanao. **Oceanjet** (☑0932 873 4885) has a daily 1.30pm fastcraft from Jagna to Benoni, Camiguin (P600, two hours), that continues to Cagayan de Oro (P900, five hours). **Super Shuttle Ferry** (☑in Camiguin 0909 236 1790) has a RORO to Balbagon, Camiguin, on Mondays, Wednesdays and Fridays at 1pm (P400, 3½ hours). In addition, **Lite Shipping** sends a RORO to Cagayan de Oro on Tuesdays, Thursdays, Saturdays and Sundays at 10pm (from P600, seven hours). These do sometimes get cancelled, so be sure to confirm departures with the ferry companies or with the Bohol Tourism Office (p307) in Tagbilaran.

V-hire vans connect Tagbilaran and Jagna (P100, 1½ hours, hourly).

Anda

☑038 / POP 1412

Dubbed the 'cradle of Boholano civilisation' for its significant prehistoric sites, the Anda peninsula on the southeast corner of Bohol still seems to belong to a forgotten time. From Anda town, resorts are strung along almost 3km of empty white-sand beach stretching west along the coastline. Peace and privacy are the order of the day; if you like to be surrounded by activity, you might find Anda a little *too* chilled. There's no ATM in Anda; the closest one is in Ubay.

◉ Sights & Activities

In Anda proper, the **town beach** is wide and wonderful but can fill up with day-trippers. Quieter beaches can be found at most resorts.

There's some good diving on **Basdio Reef**, which can be arranged through **Anda Divers** (☑ 0929 454 1635; www.anda-divers-enjoy.com; dive incl equipment €25) in the town proper. A couple of the resorts also have dive centres.

The karst-laden Anda peninsula is home to scores of **caves** and there are several **cave pools** in the immediate vicinity of the town. The helpful **tourist office** (☑ 0912 758 0360, 0908 793 6643; ◷ 8am-5pm) in Anda has details on how to explore them.

Lamanok Island   CAVE
(tour per person P300) This island 7km north of Anda proper has several anthropologically important cave paintings – made with bare hands – that date back tens of thousands of years. Travel 15 minutes by *habal-habal* or tricycle to the jumping-off point, where small boats bring you out to the island. On the island a small information centre will arrange your tour, which involves walking and canoeing through caves to see these ancient rock paintings as well as old dugout coffins and fossilised giant clams.

⌇ Sleeping & Eating

For a budget sleeping option consider a homestay through Process-Bohol (p308). On the town beach, **Quinale Beach Bar** (meals P100-150; ◷ 9am-9pm) has Filipino faves and San Miguel for P40.

Anda Global Beach Resort   BEACH RESORT $
(☑ 0948 355 2542; r with fan/air-con P700/1500; ❋ ☎) Just off the busy town beach, this simple place is a nice alternative to the pricier resorts west of town, which might feel too isolated for some.

Dapdap   BEACH RESORT $
(☑ 0921 833 2315; www.boholdapdaresort.com; r with fan P900, with air-con incl breakfast P1500-3200; ❋ ☎) Filipino-owned Dapdap is really the only budget option of the western resorts. The beach here is nice, and there's a high-tide cliff jump, but it's a bit samey as far as beach resorts go.

Vitamin Sea Beach Resort   BEACH RESORT $$$
(☑ 0918 310 9683; armie.calugay@gmail.com; r P3500; ❋ ☎ ☎) Anda's best all-arounder does just about everything right. It has a lap-sized pool, a great little bar, a bright and breezy restaurant with a view and a stupendous white beach. The great-looking rooms, lined up under the restaunt, have two tiers: one for sleeping and one for hanging.

Anda White Beach Resort   BEACH RESORT $$$
(☑ 0920 946 8127; www.andabeachresort.com; r incl breakfast P4300-6380; ❋ ☎ ☎) The highlight here is the fantastic beach. Rooms are stylish enough and well-appointed, but a bit overpriced. Shell out for the balcony-equipped beachfront rooms. Nonguests can use the beach and infinity pool for a consumable P600 (ie usable for food and drinks).

❶ Getting There & Away

From Tagbilaran or Ubay, catch a bus to the market in Guindulman, then a public *motorilla* (10-passenger tricycle) to Anda (P30, 30 minutes), passing the turnoffs to the western resorts along the way.

Ubay
☑ 038 / POP 3698

At the opposite end of Bohol to Tagbilaran, the remote town of Ubay has a lively market near the pier. It has boats to Leyte and offers uncharted tourism territory around nearby **Lapinig Island**. If you're marooned, **JRC Pension** (☑ 038-518 8888; d P500-550; ❋ ☎) is near the pier.

For Leyte, **Medallion Transport** (☑ 0923 242 9827) sends a daily RORO to Bato at 1pm (P270, three hours). Additionally, there are two morning bangkas to Bato (P280, 2½ hours), and twice-daily bangkas to Hilongos, Leyte (P250, 2½ hours). Buses run between Ubay and Tagbilaran (P120, 3½ hours).

Talibon
☑ 038 / POP 61,373

Talibon, on the north coast, is an alternative entry point from Cebu for those heading straight to Anda, Carmen or Danao.

The neighbouring town of Bien Unido is the unlikely site of a dive centre out of **Bien Unido Double Dive Camp** (☑ 0905 428 1452, 0935 476 9108; d P1200; ❋ ☎), which has flash little rooms and a swimming pool. It's based at Bien Unido's Puerto San Pedro pier, 5km northwest of the town proper, opposite Jao (pronounced 'how') Island. Diving is off the island on **Danajon Double Barrier Reef**, where 5m religious statues of the Santa Maria and Santo Niño have been sunk to liven things up.

Talibon Pension House (☎0939 241 0377; d P250-1000; ✴🕯) on the main road out of town offers budget accommodation, and there are a couple of slightly flashier options at the pier.

VG Shipping (☎038-515 5168) has regular RORO ferries to Cebu City (from P240, 3½ hours) departing at 10am and 10pm daily.

Buses depart to Tagbilaran (P110, 3½ hours) via Tubigon, and to Carmen (P50, 2½ hours) for the Chocolate Hills. For Guindulman/Anda, take a multicab to Ubay (P30, 45 minutes) and transfer to a southbound bus. V-hires at the pier can be hired for special trips around Bohol.

Buenavista

☎038 / POP 27,031

Buenavista has a friendly, picturesque **market** on a mangrove inlet. Here, or at the river crossing 3km south on the main road, you can buy the local delicacy – urchin gonads.

For something even more special, you can go on a **Cambuhat Village Ecotour**, a cruise up the mangrove-lined Daet River from Buenavista to the village of Cambuhat, where you'll see an oyster farm and raffia weaving. Call the Buenavista **tourist office** (☎038-513 9188) for more information.

Tubigon

☎038 / POP 44,902

The ramshackle fishing town of Tubigon is served by frequent fastcraft from Cebu, but there's little advantage in arriving here unless you are heading straight to Danao, or perhaps to Carmen.

Buses and vans south to Tagbilaran are plentiful from the pier, while buses inland pass by every hour or so to Danao (P70, two hours) and Carmen (P50, 1½ hours).

Danao

☎038 / POP 17,952

Set among mountainous jungle with spectacular gorges, caves and raging rivers, **Danao Adventure Park** (☎0917 302 1700; www.eatdanao.com; Suislide P350) is a giant playground for adrenaline junkies. Rappelling, caving, rock climbing, kayaking and tubing are all highly recommended, but it's the thrill-seeking activities that it's best known for. The 'Suislide' zipline will have you soaring across a 500m gorge like Superman, or you can take the 'Plunge' with a breathtaking 75m free fall into the valley, supposedly the largest in the world.

Unfortunately the park took a hit from the 2013 quake, which was centred in nearby Sagbayan. A year after the quake, a few activities, including the Plunge, remained closed. The rooms (camping including tent P300, rooms with fan/air-con P600/1000) are pretty good value considering the sublime jungle setting. It's cool at night so you probably won't need that air-con.

Buses from Tagbilaran to Danao (P85, three hours) travel via Sagbayan. Bits of the new road from Sagbayan to Danao remain unsealed, but there are great views of rice terraces and solitary chocolate hills along this stretch. From Danao proper, the park is another 8km further on (P40, 15 minutes by *habal-habal*).

LEYTE

For students and historians of the Pacific and WWII, the word 'Leyte' conjures up images of bloody naval battles and the site of MacArthur's famous return. For Filipinos it's equally associated with the rags-to-riches rise of Imelda Marcos and the nostalgic, romanticised portrait she painted of her birthplace after she made good in the capital. For travellers, Southern Leyte, wrapped around the deep-water Sogod Bay, is one of the Philippines' many diving hot spots. The Cebuano-speaking Leyteños live in the south, and their Waray-speaking neighbours live in the cattle-ranching country of northern Leyte. Leyte's north endured the worst of Typhoon Yolanda's tyranny in 2013.

ⓘ Getting There & Away

The most common way into Leyte is by boat, or overland from Samar. The key ports are Ormoc in the northwest, with myriad connections to Cebu City; and San Ricardo in the far south, linked by frequent ferries to Surigao on Mindanao. Several lesser ports on the west coast have services to Cebu City as well as to northern Bohol.

Tacloban

☎053 / POP 221,174

Once the pearl of Leyte, Tacloban became forever associated with natural disaster on 8 November 2013. This was Typhoon Yolanda's

Leyte

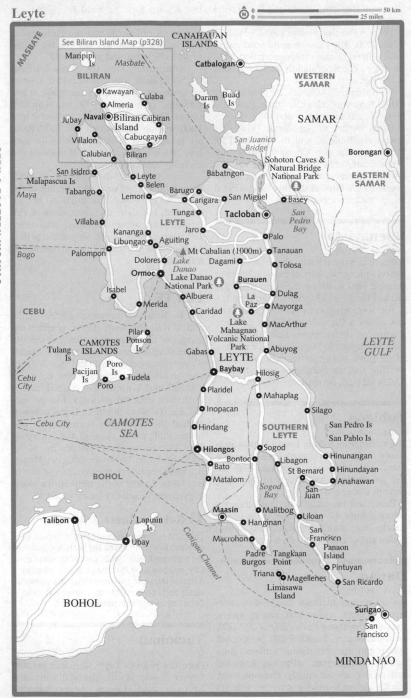

'ground zero'. Walking through the centre of Tacloban today, it's impossible to imagine the post-apocalyptic tableau that greeted its citizens on that fateful morning. Since then, the city centre has been largely fixed up, physically at least. Hotels have been repaired and are open. The bars are finally starting to fill up with locals instead of relief workers. Tacloban has resumed is role as the commercial heart of both Leyte and Samar.

The psychological wounds will take longer to heal. The images of destruction, the memories of loved ones lost, the scent of death that permeated the city for weeks after the typhoon...none of this will be forgotten anytime soon. Perhaps to some degree the elephant in the room that is Yolanda will always be present in Tacloban.

One thing that everybody can agree on: the people of Tacloban want their tourists back. While relief workers were a major boon to the city's economy during the recovery period, Tacloban needs tourists to fill the void now that most relief works have moved on. The city was never a huge tourist draw, but it's a useful jumping-off point to pretty much everywhere else in Samar and Leyte, and is worth a day or two in its own right.

For the foreseeable future, among its sights will be a pair of huge **ships** that were cast inland during the storm and remain as they landed, surrounded by passing traffic and rebuilt shanties. The ships, located a bit west of the centre in Barangay 68, seem certain to become a lasting memorial and symbol of a storm that took the lives of so many.

◎ Sights & Activities

Be sure to drop by the Hotel Alejandro (p319), which has a brilliant permanent collection of photos on the walls tracing Tacloban's domestic and war history.

Santo Niño Shrine & Heritage Center   HISTORIC SITE
(admission for up to 3 people P200; ⊙8am-5pm) Tacloban's most famous daughter is Imelda Romualdez Marcos, whose family home is in Tolosa, one of the coastal towns most devastated by Typhoon Yolanda. The family's influence in Tacloban is evident in street names and in this prominent old mansion built with the Marcos' millions, yet oddly never slept in. Today it houses a varied display of antiques and objets d'art, with each room dedicated to a Filipino province, as well as a bizarre diorama of Imelda doing good deeds.

Bukid Outdoor Shop   ADVENTURE SPORTS
(☑053-523 7625; 206 Burgos St; ⊙9am-7pm Mon-Sat, climbing wall 1-7pm Mon-Sat) Here you'll find a group of outdoor enthusiasts with information and local contacts for kayaking, mountain biking and hiking. There's a rock-climbing wall on-site (P50).

★☆ Festivals & Events

Late June is all about festivals in Tacloban, and makes for a great time to visit with various fiestas; you'll need to book accommodation well ahead.

Pintados-Kasadyaan   CULTURAL
The 'painted' festival, held on 27 June, celebrates the traditional tattooing practised here before the Spanish arrived; nowadays water-based paints are used for the festival's body decoration.

Sangyaw   CULTURAL
Mardi gras Leyte-style, with colourful floats and dancing troupes through the streets of Tacloban on 29 June.

⊨ Sleeping

It's highly advisable to stay 'uptown' in the restaurant and bar zone around Burgos St rather than in the gritty downtown area.

★ Yellow Doors Hostel   HOSTEL $
(☑0906 389 1131, 0917 934 9499; jakepalami@ yahoo.com; cnr Burgos & Juan Luna Sts; dm P450-550, d P1100; ❄@🖱) A great new addition to the Tacloban accommodation scene, Yellow Doors has super beds with privacy-protecting curtains and two common areas – one being its roomy balcony. Owner Jacques dispenses travel advice, organises walking tours and can help out with ideas for volunteering as well – 'travel to change' is the hostel's mantra.

Welcome Home Pension   GUESTHOUSE $
(☑053-321 2739; 161 Santo Niño St; s P400-800, d P600-1200; ❄@🖱) Set around a quiet garden courtyard, these budget rooms are time-worn but clean; the cheapest share bathrooms.

Hotel Alejandro   HOTEL $$
(☑053-321 7033; Patermo St; d P1800-3000; ❄🖱▨) This three-storey hotel built around the classic 1930s home of Alejandro Montejo looks like a regal colonial villa. The rooms are nothing special but the common areas of the old building, which are festooned with classic photos and memorabilia, make up

Tacloban

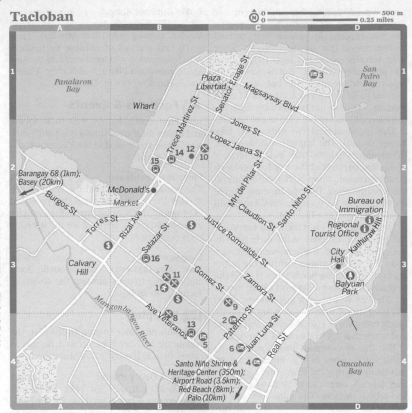

CEBU & EASTERN VISAYAS TACLOBAN

for this. A newer wing houses a small roof-top pool and terrace, plus 15 deluxe rooms.

Rosvenil Pensione GUESTHOUSE **$$**
(☎053-321 2676; 302 Burgos St; r P1280-2880; ❋ 🛜) A solid midrange choice, built around a rambling 1940s wooden house. In the old building are clean basic rooms; the newer, more sizeable and comfortable rooms are in a beautiful three-storey building with wrought-iron railings and a balcony.

Leyte Park Hotel HOTEL **$$**
(☎053-325 6000; leyteparkhotel@yahoo.com; r P1680-5000; ❋🛜🏊) This crumbling behemoth, once Tacloban's premier resort, housed the Red Cross in the early days after Typhoon Yolanda. Atop a hill, it was spared the storm surge that inundated much of the city. It continues to have maintenance issues but it's worth staying here for the views and the pool (nonguests P150). Rooms vary wildly; shoot for something renovated.

✗ Eating & Drinking

Tacloban's once-buzzing restaurant and bar scene was just starting to come back to life when we visited. **Barbecue stands** can be found along Magsaysay Blvd.

Libro CAFE **$**
(cnr Santo Niño & Gomez Sts; sandwiches from P50; ⊙noon-8pm Mon-Sat) A fantastic secondhand bookstore that serves real coffee (P38), sandwiches on ciabatta bread (from P50) and a great selection of cakes.

Ochó Seafood & Grill SEAFOOD **$$**
(Senator Enage St; meals P200-500; ⊙10am-10pm; ❋🛜) A unanimous favourite with locals, Ochó is a rowdy affair with a glimpse of suave. Select your fish, squid or shellfish from the display and get them to cook it as you like it. Vegos are also catered for, and can choose the cooking style for tofu and green veggies.

Tacloban

Canto Fresco CAFE $$
(Burgos St; mains P100-220; ⊘noon-midnight;
✷🛜) This great little hole-in-the-wall punch-
es above its weight with tasty 10-inch pizzas,
sandwiches, original salads and Asian tastes.

Sunzibar VEGETARIAN $$
(Burgos St; mains P100-200; ⊘11am-8pm Tue-Sat;
🛜🍴) Stylish, minimalist eatery with a most-
ly vegetarian menu, including Mexican and
Middle Eastern flavours.

Giuseppe's ITALIAN $$
(☑053-321 4910; 173 Ave Veteranos; mains P150-
500; ⊘10.30am-10.30pm; ✷🛜) A long-stand-
ing Tacloban eatery, brick-walled Giuseppe's
is decorated like an Italian bistro and serves
pastas and pizzas.

Socsargen Grill GRILL $$
(meals P100-150; ⊘7am-2pm & 5.30-10pm) Part
of the Rosvenil Pensione, this casual and
popular open-air restaurant does raw fish
(sashimi), barbecued *lapu-lapu* (grouper)
and sizzling *gambas*.

ⓘ Information

Metrobank (Burgos St) and **BDO** (Rizal Ave) are
among the many ATMs.

Bureau of Immigration (☑053-325 6004;
Kanhuraw Hill; ⊘8am-5pm Mon-Fri) Next to
the Regional Tourist Office.

Regional Tourist Office (☑053-321 2048;
dotreg8@yahoo.com; Kanhuraw Hill; ⊘8am-
5pm) Exceptionally helpful, it can provide you
with an abundance of information for both
Leyte and Samar.

Welcome Home Internet Cafe (161 Santo Niño
St; per hr P40; ⊘8am-8pm) Internet access.

ⓘ Getting There & Away

AIR

Tacloban is well connected to Manila, with **Cebu
Pacific** (Senator Enage St), PAL, and AirAsia
Zest all flying several times daily. Cebu Pacific
adds flights to Cebu. The airport is about 8km
south of the centre of town. A jeepney will cost
P20, or it's P100 for a tricycle.

BUS, VAN & JEEPNEY

Throughout Samar and Leyte, 13-passenger
air-con vans take precedence over buses. They
are quicker, more frequent and cost negligibly
more than the bus. Tacloban is the headquarters
for the main companies, including **Duptours**
(☑0939 937 7002) and **Van Vans** (☑053-523
1274; Salazar St), which have vans servicing the
following destinations every 30 minutes or so
until 5pm or 6pm:

Borongan (P230, 4½ hours)
Catbalogan (P130, two hours)
Guiuan (P180, 3½ hours)
Maasin (P220, four hours)
Naval (P150, 2¾ hours)
Ormoc (P130, 2½ hours)

Grand Tours (☑053-325 4640; cnr Trece Mar-
tirez & A Mabini Sts) does trips to Ormoc and
Catbalogan, as well as to Basey until 6pm (P50,
45 minutes). Duptours has the only direct trips
to Calbayog (P220, four hours, last trip 4pm);
with the other companies you must change vans
in Catbalogan. Getting to Allen usually requires a
change in Catbalogan or Calbayog.

You'll find slow local buses and additional vans
to all of the above destinations at the **New Bus
Terminal** at Abucay, about 2km west of the city
centre. Additional destinations served by bus or
van include Sogod (P150, 2½ hours, every two
hours until 4.10pm), Hinunangan (P150, three
hours, last trip 2pm) and Allen (P300, six hours,
last trip 4pm). To get to Padre Burgos, transfer
in Sogod or Maasin. Also at the bus station are
frequent jeepneys to Basey (P30, one hour).

Long-distance buses from the bus station to
Manila do not typically provide passage to points
south of Manila unless you pay the full fare.

Around Tacloban

Palo

Palo is where General MacArthur 'returned' with US liberating forces on 20 October 1944. More recently, Palo and the next three towns south – Tanuan, Tolosa and Dulag – were destroyed by Typhoon Yolanda as a 5m storm surge swept over the beach. Large parts of these towns still lay in ruins at the time of writing. The once-luxurious Oriental Resort next to Red Beach lay in ruins, and Palo's convention centre remained a twisted heap of metal – a testament to the storm's power.

War buffs might still want to come here to visit the Leyte Landing Memorial and Guinhangdan Hill, known in WWII as Hill 522, the scene of fierce fighting.

To get to Palo take any southbound jeepney marked 'Palo' or 'Tanuan' from Real St in Tacloban, and tell the driiver to let you off at the Red Beach roundabout about 2km before you reach Palo proper. Pedicabs (P10) can take you the final 1km to Red Beach.

Sohoton Caves & Natural Bridge National Park

Although this national park (entrance P200) is on Samar, it is easiest to access it from Tacloban. The journey upriver to the park from Basey, the access town, is half its charm, with the wide swath of water flanked by palms and higgledy-piggledy villages of bamboo houses on stilts. Upstream the river narrows and limestone outcrops appear and extend upwards until the boat is travelling through a small gorge into the park itself. Another 10 minutes further upstream and a 300m walk through the forest, there's a wide swimming hole under the arch of the limestone natural bridge that gives the park its name. Surrounded by forest, it's a quiet, steamy green outpost where local villagers are actively engaged in managing the park and guiding visitors to caves with enormous, sparkling stalactites and stalagmites. Kayaking trips are available.

Heavy rain can cause flash floods and the park is often closed during the wettest months of December to February.

Trips and guides should be arranged through the Basey Municipal Tourism Information Office (☑0928 335 8783; ABC Hall, Municipal Complex; ⊘8am-5pm), where staff will organise the round trip, which takes between four and five hours – an hour each way by boat, and then a couple of hours in the park. Boats do not leave Basey after 1pm.

Costs are complicated but go something like this: a pumpboat from the pier in Basey costs P1500 per group. A guide, who joins either in Basey or at Sohoton, costs P350 to P550 per group. On top of that, each person in your group will need a hurricane lamp (P300). Lastly there's the individual entrance fee and a mayor's permit fee of P50. You might save a bit of cash by making your own way by road to barangays Guiran or Inutan near the park entrance, where chartered boats cost just P500. But then you'll miss out on a good chunk of that great river trip up to the park entrance.

From the natural bridge inside the park an optional side trip takes you to Balantak waterfalls. You'll need to secure a separate guide (P300) for this 30-minute walk.

Basey itself is worth a stop to buy the fine woven *banig* mats for which it is famous. The town could use your tourist dollars: Basey endured the full brunt of Typhoon Yolanda's storm surge, suffering hundreds of casualties.

To get to Basey, take an air-con van (P50, 30 minutes) or a much slower jeepney from the bus station in Tacloban. Take a packed lunch – there's no food or water available beyond Basey. The last van back to Tacloban is Grand Tours' 6pm trip.

Ormoc

☑053 / POP 191,200

The hillsides surrounding Ormoc Bay make a scenic backdrop for those arriving by boat from Cebu, but otherwise it's a typical busy port city. Its saving grace is its breezy waterfront promenade with some decent restaurants and bars. Some of the bloodiest WWII battles in the Philippines took place in Ormoc Bay in 1944. The bay is literally littered with shipwrecks, but you'll need your own gear and some serious technical diving experience to explore them.

🛏 Sleeping

★ David's Inn   HOTEL $

(☑053-255 7618; www.davidsinn.com; Carlos Tan St; d P800-900; ❖🗟) It's rare indeed to find a budget hotel that puts this much TLC into everything they do. From the well-appointed rooms with designer vanities and attractive art, to the exceptional service and the suave cafe, this quiet little gem is a godsend in chaotic Ormoc.

Ormoc

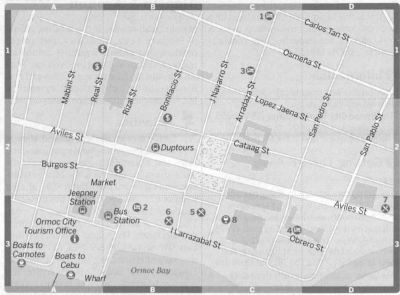

OCCCI Hostel & Training Center　HOSTEL $
(☑ 053-255 4612; OCCCI Bldg, Arradaza St; dm/d P350/1200; ▣ 🖙) A surprisingly decent upstairs hostel that even has functioning wi-fi in the air-con dorm rooms.

Hotel Don Felipe　HOTEL $
(☑ 053-255 2460; hdfelipe@yahoo.com; I Larrazabal St; s P440-1600, d P530-3650; ▣ 🖙) The elephantine Don Felipe has a startling mix of well-kept new rooms and grungy fan-cooled old rooms. The main reason to stay here is the central location, right by the pier and bus station.

Ormoc Villa Hotel　HOTEL $$
(☑ 053-255 5006; www.ormocvillahotel.com; Obrero St; s/d P2300/2700, ste P3600-6750 ; ▣🖙▣) A palatial oasis in the middle of the city with large and comfortable rooms set around a prettily landscaped garden. The restaurant serves a good selection of food and the pool (P100 for nonguests) has a swim-up bar.

✖ Eating & Drinking

Just west of the Superdome is a cluster of **barbecue stalls** (Burgos St) that come to life from sunset onwards. Try the fresh, juicy pineapple sold by vendors, which the region is known for.

Ormoc

🛏 **Sleeping**
1 David's Inn C1
2 Hotel Don Felipe B3
3 OCCCI Hostel & Training
　Center C1
4 Ormoc Villa Hotel C3

🍴 **Eating**
5 Barbecue Stalls B3
6 Lorenzo Cafe B3
7 Roma Cafe D3

🍷 **Drinking & Nightlife**
8 Bebidas Coffee Bar C3

Roma Cafe　CAFE $$
(Aviles St; mains P150-250; ⊙ 9am-midnight; ▣🖙) American-owned Roma Cafe has healthy salads, Thai, and Mexican tastes to accompany the specialty noodle dishes. It's next to Ormoc Doctors Hospital.

Lorenzo Cafe　CAFE $$
(I Lazzarabal St; mains P100-150; ⊙ 7am-midnight; ▣) This large, popular cafe with wraparound windows looking out at the promenade has surprises like lamb chops and a tuna melt on its diverse menu, plus coffee ordered from the counter.

★ **Bebidas Coffee Bar** BAR
(Superdome; ⊘9am-2am Mon-Sat, from 4pm Sun;
🔊) At this this funky little cafe-bar built into
the Superdome, local trendies drop in for a
good coffee or dangerously cheap cocktails
mixed by experts behind the bar.

ℹ Information

Ormoc bristles with internet cafes and the major
banks are well-represented.

The **Ormoc City Tourism Office** (🖉053-255
8356; www.ormoc.gov.ph/tourism; Ebony St;
⊘8am-5pm) is right next to the port.

ℹ Getting There & Away

BOAT
Oceanjet (🖉053-834 5066), **SuperCat 2GO**
(🖉053-561 9818) and **Weesam Express**
(🖉053-561 0080) each have three daily fastcraft that ply the Ormoc–Cebu City route (P625,
2½ hours). Slower boats to Cebu (P420, four
hours) include Lite Shipping at 10pm daily and
Roble Shipping (🖉053-255 7613) at 10am daily.

For Camotes, there are usually three daily
bangka to Pilar on Ponson Island (P150, 1½
hours), departing between 9am and noon. One
of those continues on to Kawit. There are sometimes boats to Poro Island, but not daily.

The City Tourism Office has updated schedules.

BUS & VAN
Duptours has air-con vans to Tacloban every
30 minutes until 7pm, with plenty more vans
and slower buses leaving from the bus station.
Also at the bus station you'll find regular vans to
Naval (P130, two hours) until 4pm, and to Pal-
ompan (P80, 1¼ hours) and Maasin (for Padre
Burgos, P170, three hours). Buses are a slower
and less frequent (and not much cheaper) option
to all of these places.

If heading to Sogod (P360, 2½ hours) or San
Ricardo (P420, 3½ hours) in Southern Leyte, hop
on an air-con Bachelor Tours bus bound for Davao
or Mati in Mindanao, departing roughly hourly.

Around Ormoc

A good day trip from Ormoc is to Lake
Danao Natural Park (permit P45), a beautiful
body of fresh water in the hills 18km from
town. There's some great hiking around the
lake and on and around the undermain-
tained Leyte Mountain Trail. Keen hikers
should get in touch with Kim of the Eastern
Visayas Adventure Team (🖉0923 744 9954;
k.lumogdang@yahoo.com), who can organise
treks and ascents throughout Leyte and Biliran Island.

Maasin & Around
🖉053 / POP 81,250

Maasin (mah-*ah*-sin) is the bustling capital
of Southern Leyte, a laid-back, picturesque
province that offers a wealth of natural attractions and great diving in Sogod Bay. Maasin is a suitable base for some hikes and also
has a beautiful early 18th-century church,
but for travellers it's mainly a transport hub.

🏃 Activities

Few people explore the area around Maasin,
even though there are several good hikes, and
caves and waterfalls to explore. Among the
more accessible options is the hike to Guin-
sohoton Cave and Cagnituan Falls, an easy
jaunt out of Maasin; look for the turnoff in
barangay Maria Clara 4.5km east of town.
The cave has a neat subterranean river where
you can swim. The helpful Provincial Tourism Office (🖉0915 879 4923, 053-570 8300;
www.toursouthernleyte.net), in the provincial
compound 1km east of Maasin centre, has
a glossy brochure outlining Southern Leyte
province's attractions, and can point you in
the direction of more strenuous treks and
canyoning opportunities; talk to Nedgar.

🛏 Sleeping & Eating

Ampil Pensionne PENSION $
(🖉053-570 8084; T Oppus St; d P400-800; ❄🔊)
This passable budget option has rooms set
off the street around a small courtyard, so
it's relatively quiet.

Villa Romana Hotel HOTEL $$
(🖉053-381 2228; villaromanahotel@ymail.com;
s/d incl breakfast from P950/1350; ❄@🔊) Slap
bang on the water and overlooking the pier,
this smart hotel is the best sleeping and
eating option in town. Rooms are elegant
and well furnished, and the downstairs wa-
terfront restaurant, Kinamot (meals P60 to
P150), serves excellent seafood.

ℹ Getting There & Away

BOAT
Most ferries call in a bit further north in either
Bato or Hilongos. From Maasin, Cokaliong has
four ferries a week to Cebu City (P350, six
hours) and services Surigao (P325, four hours)
on Thursdays and Saturdays at 3am.

From Bato, Medallion Transport sails daily to
Cebu (P280, 5½ hours) at 9pm. Medallion also has
a daily 9am RORO to Ubay (P270, three hours) on
Bohol, and there are two daily bangkas to Ubay.

From Hilongos, **Gabisan Shipping Lines** has a daily fastcraft to Cebu (P300, three hours) at 8.30am, and a slow craft (P240, five hours) at 9pm daily except Saturday, while Roble Shipping has twice-daily ROROs to Cebu and **Leopard Shipping** (☑ 0917 702 9299) has twice-daily bangka ferries to Ubay, Bohol (P250, 2½ hours).

BUS

Jeepneys head east to Padre Burgos every 15 minutes until 5pm or so (P30, 45 minutes).

Duptours and Van Vans send vans to Tacloban every hour until 4pm (P220, four hours). You can find vans to Ormoc at the bus station (P170, three hours) and occasional vans to Sogod, but buses are more common to Sogod; some Sogod-bound buses continue on to San Ricardo for Mindanao (last trip 2pm), or to Hinunangan.

Padre Burgos & Around

☑ 053 / POP 10,525

Laid-back Padre Burgos (just 'Burgos' to locals) straggles for about 3km in a lazy green line along the edge of the lovely **Sogod Bay**. It's considered to be one of the premier diving spots in the Philippines for its pristine hard and soft coral reefs, deep wall, cave and current dives.

There's an internet cafe near the pier but the closest ATMs are in Maasin and Sogod.

⊙ Sights & Activities

Diving is the reason most people come here, and can be arranged through the resorts. They can organise dive trips to Limasawa Island and across Sogod Bay to several marine sanctuaries off Panaon Island. They also arrange trips to snorkel with the **whale sharks** (if they're around) around Pintuyan.

Tangkaan Point, the narrow peninsula extending 3km south from town, offers good offshore **snorkelling**.

Limasawa Island   ISLAND

(rems_0418@yahoo.com) If you have time to spare, head to sleepy Limasawa Island, a place of historical and religious significance in the Philippines. It's where the Spanish first celebrated mass on 31 March 1521, thereby starting the Christianisation of the country. A five-minute walk to the left from the pier leads to the original **mass site**. Next to it, a set of 450 steps leads up to the commemorative **Magellan's cross**.

From here you can gaze at gorgeous views across the ocean to Mindanao, Bohol and mainland Leyte. The island also has small coves ideal for swimming and snorkelling.

You can sleep on the island at a homestay or at a **guesthouse** (☑ 0917 633 8215; r P450; ❄) run by the local government unit near the municipal hall in the island's main barangay, Cabulihan. The two rooms have aircon, but only from 6pm to 1am, after which the island's power cuts off. The Limasawa tourism officer, Remigilda, is the contact.

Three or four big bangkas make the journey to and from Burgos each day (P50, 45 minutes). The last trip from Burgos is at 3.30pm, while the last trip off the island is at 12.30pm. Chartering a bangka will cost between P1000 and P1500 return.

San Roque Falls   WATERFALL

These pleasant, easy-to-reach falls make for a refreshing dip. The path to the falls begins just west of the turnoff to Southern Leyte Dive Resort. From the highway it's about a seven-minute walk.

Cambaro Caves   CAVING

The turnoff to these spectacular caves is 10km west of Burgos in Molopolo, a barangay of Macrohon. From here a partially paved road leads 7km to Cambaro, where you can secure guides and flashlights at the barangay hall.

🛏 Sleeping & Eating

Most of the accommodation is 2km north of the town centre in barangay Lungsodaan. All of the resorts listed have good restaurants.

Peter's Dive Resort   RESORT $

(☑ 0917 791 0993; www.whaleofadive.com; Lungsodaan; dm P400, r with shared bathroom P880-980, r with private bathroom P1300-2750; ❄ 🛜 🛇) Peter's is just off the road on a pebble beach with a great variety of rooms catering to all budgets. The dorms and budget rooms are in the main building over the restaurant, while the larger, more comfortable private cottages are right on the water. Try to get a room with a balcony. Rooms are slightly more expensive for nondivers.

JD Beachfront Hotel   GUESTHOUSE $

(☑ 0921 576 1155; Pook Beach; d with fan/air-con P800/1000) A bit cheaper than the dive resorts, albeit with fewer mod-cons and services. It has five spacious, spiffy rooms and a great beachfront location on Tangkaan Peninsula, 500m south of Burgos centre.

Southern Leyte Dive Resort   BEACH RESORT $$

(☑ 053-572 4011; www.leyte-divers.com; San Roque; d P1500-2200, tr P2100-3700; ❄) The

HINUNANGAN

The town of Hinunangan on the eastern frontier of Southern Leyte province is a place to escape civilisation entirely. It's home to sublime, honey-brown **Tahusan Beach**, one of the finest in the Visayas, with great swimming and occasional surf. Lounge here, or walk or horseback ride to nearby caves and waterfalls – get advice from the helpful **municipal tourist office** (☑ 0909 354 6023) at the municipal hall. Or hire a bangka (P1200 return) and head out to the nearby offshore islands of San Pedro and San Pablo, both with white coral sand, snorkelling and swimming. You can sleep on San Pedro at simple **Vista Resort** (☑ 0919 241 0637, 0915 548 2335; r P350-500); it's electricity-free unless you pay to use their generator. **Doña Marta Boutique Hotel** (☑ 0915 670 5900; Tahusan Beach; r incl breakfast P2000-2200; ❋ ☎) is the best place to stay in Hinunangan, and there are plenty more budget-friendly places to stay both on and off the beach. Be sure to pop in for a seafood meal at the splendid **Captain's Place** (☑ 0917 501 0131; mains from P80; ☎) restaurant. Occasional buses make the long slog to Hinunangan from Tacloban, Maasin and Sogod.

oldest and prettiest of the dive resorts, the nine cottages here – bamboo with fans, or comfortable modern air-con – are off the main road and front a sandy beach. There is a sundowner platform and hammocks and potted plants are everywhere. Excellent food in the garden restaurant includes sashimi, pasta, salad and German sausages.

Leyte Dive Resort RESORT $$
(☑ 0927 533 5724; www.leytedive.com; Malitbog; r P1000-1600; ❋ ☎) Located 1km south of Malitbog, the next municipality north from Burgos, this is a peaceful alternative to the resorts in Burgos. The extra-large top-whack rooms, with great big beds, are the best value around.

Sogod Bay Scuba Resort RESORT $$
(☑ 0915 520 7274; www.sogodbayscubaresort.com; Lungsodaan; r/beachfront cottage P1100/1500; ❋ @ ☎) The rooms are nothing special here but the prime waterfront location is. Hang out on your balcony or in the restaurant and stare at the sea. The cheaper rooms are in a concrete building 200m up the road, away from the water. Unfortunately the nicer beachfront rooms are all twin configuration.

❶ Getting There & Away

Regular jeepneys to Maasin leave from the pier (P30, 45 minutes). Connect in Maasin for Ormoc and Tacloban.

Jeepneys heading toward Malitbog and Sogod pass every 30 minutes or so. You can connect to Tacloban in Sogod, but you may have to wait awhile (morning is best). There are also connections in Sogod for San Ricardo and Hinunangan.

Panaon Island
☑ 053

This beautiful island, connected to mainland Leyte by a bridge at Liloan, is home to a highly seasonal whale-shark interaction program out of the town of Pintuyan.

This is also where you go to catch the ferry to Lipata, near Surigao City on Mindanao. The port is in Benit, San Ricardo, on the island's southern tip, with RORO ferries departing for Lipata (P140, 1¼ hours) every four hours or so around the clock. Occasional ferries to Lipata still leave from the old port in Liloan, although the sinking of a ferry on this route in 2014 may have been the final nail in the coffin for Liloan's port.

Liloan has basic accommodation in the form of **Ofelia's Lodge** (☑ 0912 497 8460; d P250-350) near the market. From here you can find *habal-habal* to points south on Panaon Island. Local buses from Sogod serve Liloan, Pintuyan and San Ricardo. From Benit, a *habal-habal* (P100) is the best way to get to Pintuyan.

◉ Sights & Activities

Whale-shark watching is the big draw, but there is also great diving all along the west coast of Panaon Island. **Napantao Reef**, off the Coral Cay Conservation group's base in San Francisco, is a highly regarded and popular site. Dive trips originate out of Padre Burgos across the bay, or out of Pintuyan Beach Resort.

Whale Sharks ECOTOUR
(☑ 0917 301 4047) Few tourists make the scenic journey down to Pintuyan,

where the local tourist office organises community-based snorkelling trips to see whale sharks (locally known as *tiki-tiki*) in three-passenger bangkas owned by the local fishermen's association. Tours are run out of barangay Son-ok, about 3km north of Pintuyan, and cost P1600/1850/2100 for one/two/three people, including boat, guide and spotters. Snorkelling equipment costs P150.

Dive shops in the Sogod Bay area also run trips here, but guests are not allowed to dive at the main site in Son ok. You may get lucky and spot *tiki-tiki* while diving elsewhere, however. This is a much more ethical way to see whale sharks than in Oslob, Cebu, where they are hand-fed. And the visibility is much better here than in the Philippines' most famous whale-shark site, Donsol. The season for whale-shark spotting is roughly November to May.

Keep in mind that Pintuyan's *tiki-tiki* are fickle – some years they show up only briefly, or not at all. Other years offer a bounty of sightings. 2012 and 2013 were banner years; in 2014 there were hardly any sightings. Before setting out, contact Moncher Bardos of the local **Ecotourism Office** (☑ 0917 301 4047; moncher64bardos@yahoo.com) to see if they are around.

Coral Cay Conservation VOLUNTEERING
(www.coralcay.org) Check out the website of this international organisation to see why a program of working with local communities in this area to preserve and conserve the reefs is so important. It accepts only volunteers arranged well in advance.

🛏 Sleeping & Eating

La Guerta Lodge LODGE $
(☑ 0926 142 6986; s P200-350, d P300-450; ❋) Simple motel-style rooms in a row off the water near the centre of Pintuyan.

Pintuyan Beach Resort RESORT $$
(☑ 0921 736 8860; www.pintuyan.com; r incl full board €45; ❋ 🗢) This is the best place to stay on Panaon Island and a fine place to base yourself for diving excursions in Sogod Bay.

BILIRAN ISLAND

☑ 053 / POP 150,000

Tourism is slowly taking off on this quiet island province, which has the potential to be an adventure wonderland. It has a long and beautiful coastline and a mountainous interior, plus several sandy white beaches on offshore islands. A mostly sealed ring road runs around the island, offering up stunning vistas of volcanoes and vivid green rice terraces. It's a great spot to escape the crowds for a few days and do some DIY exploring.

Biliran became a province separate from Leyte in 1992; a short bridge connects the two. The island is lush and it can rain any time, with the most rainfall in December and the least in April. Most people are subsistence farmers or fishers who generally speak Cebuano on the west coast and Waray-Waray on the east.

Joni from Trexplore (p334) in Catbalogan, Samar, has started running canyoning, caving and trekking tours on Biliran Island. Get in touch with him for details.

ℹ Getting There & Away

Biliran is essentially an extension of Leyte, and as such the vast majority of travellers arrive by land from Leyte. Handiest are the air-con vans run by Duptours and **Van Vans** (☑ 0927 270 2975). These run every 30 minutes until 4.30pm to Tacloban (P150, 2¾ hours) and Ormoc (P130, two hours). A few local-yokel buses make trips to both places in double the time for about the same price.

From Naval's *embarcadero* (waterway landing), Roble Shipping sends a RORO ferry to Cebu City at 8.30pm four days a week.

ℹ Getting Around

Public transport is sporadic so you're best off exploring the island by motorcycle. *Habal-habal* ask P800 to P1000 for an all-day trip around the island. The only motorcycle rental we found was at **Norkis** (Vicentillo St, Naval; per day P400).

The bus and jeepney terminal in Naval is at the public market next to the pier. Buses and jeepneys make regular daily trips from Naval north to Kawayan (P25, 40 minutes) via Almeria until 5pm. Rickety buses head across the island to Caibiran hourly until 3pm (P50, one hour), and there are a few morning trips to Bunga via Cabucgayan along the southern route (P40, 1½ hours).

Pedicabs are the way around the towns. The flat fee for short local trips is P5.

Naval

☑ 053 / POP 48,799

Naval (nah-*vahl*), the provincial capital, is stretched along a road from a handful of government buildings to the low rise harbour area. There's little to do here but it makes a handy base for day trips around the island. The **Provincial Tourism Information Office** (http://tourism.biliranisland.com;

Biliran Island

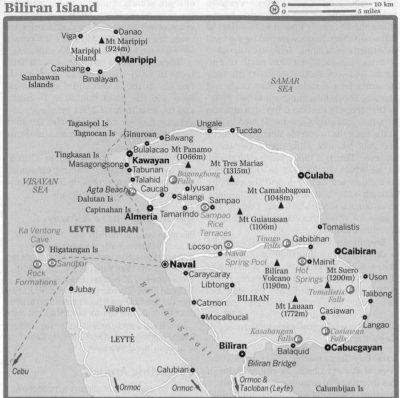

⊙8am-5pm Mon-Fri) can help with ideas. The office is on on the 2nd floor of the Provincial Capitol building. Naval has an ATM at Metrobank.

🍴 Sleeping & Eating

Food-wise, very little stands out in Naval proper. Your best bet is to head 1km out of town to Marvin's, or to **D'Adaone** (213 P Inocentes St; meals P170-200; ⊙6am-midnight; ✳🛜) in D'Mei Residence Inn's main branch, one of the few cook-to-order places in town.

La Concepcion Lodge PENSION $
(✆0946 533 7413; P Inocentes St; d with fan/aircon P400/600; ✳) This basic place is noisy but cheap and welcoming, with a decent cook-to-order restaurant downstairs.

Marvin's Seaside Inn HOTEL $
(✆053-500 9171; marvinsseasideinn@yahoo.com; s P1000, d P1200-1700; ✳🛜🌊) Marvin's is a mustard-yellow, three-storey modern build-

ing 1km north of town. It's on the water but lacks any sort of beach. It does have a nice pool, however (nonguests P30), plus well-kept rooms, an attractive common area and the best food in Naval.

D'Mei Residence Inn Naval HOTEL $$
(✆053-500 9796; dmei.residence.inn@gmail.com; 213 P Inocentes St; s P750, d P950-1300; ✳🛜) Easily the smartest hotel in Naval, this is the preferred of its two branches – the other **branch** (✆053-500 9796; P Inocentes St; d P1280-1840; ✳🛜) is above WAD Mall, with even smarter but mostly windowless rooms. Some rooms at this main branch have outstanding mountain views.

Chamorita Resort RESORT $$
(✆0918 608 3499; www.chamoritarp.com; Km 1018; r P1300-1500; ✳🛜) This waterfront resort in Catmon, 7km south of Naval, has the most comfortable rooms on Biliran, not to mention a great bar loaded with booze

and bar games. Rooms have great big beds, kitchenettes and flat-screens. There's no real beach but several hangout pavilions provide prime sea views. American owner Leo is a fountain of information on Biliran.

North of Naval

The pretty stretch of coast from Naval to Kawayan is the only part of the island that is easy to explore by public transport. Beyond Kawayan, the road is now mostly sealed all the way around the northeastern part of the island to Caibirian, but public transport along this stretch is rare.

About 4km north of Naval is the turnoff to the **Sampao rice terraces**. While they can't compare in scale to the Banaue terraces, they're very photogenic with the peaks of Biliran as a backdrop. The villages of Iyusan and Salangi also have rice terraces; each are about 5km off the main road.

From barangay Upper Looc, 500m north of Almeria, a road takes you up to Caucab, where a sealed track gets you most of the way to pretty **Bagongbong Falls**.

About 4km north of Almeria is **Agta Beach**, where Biliran's largest concentration of resorts is, although it's a fairly mediocre beach compared with most in the Visayas and it can fill up with karaoke-loving locals on weekends. However, Agta beach is a good base for visiting **Dalutan**, an island with white sand and good snorkelling just offshore, and, closer to shore, **Capinahan Island**. The resorts offer island-hopping trips by bangka for P700/1000 return for one/both islands. You can kayak to Capinahan; Agta Beach Resort rents out kayaks (per hour P150) and snorkelling gear.

Continuing north, **Masagongsong**, 2km south of Kawayan, is known for its natural springs.

🛏 Sleeping

Estreller's Sunset View

Spring Pool RESORT **$**
(☑ 0916 360 0467; estrellersunsetviewspringpool@yahoo.com; Km 1041, Masagongsong; d P800; ❄ ❄) This place has its own natural spring-fed pool overlooking the ocean. The rooms are some of the cosiest on the island but have shared bathrooms.

Agta Beach Resort RESORT **$$**
(☑ 0927 150 0335; shaunshine83@yahoo.com; Km 1038; d P1200-3000; ❄ 🛜) Rooms here aren't

flash, but they do have marble floors, nice TVs and raised sleeping areas that make them stand out amid the generally mediocre offerings on Agta Beach. We would like to see balconies, however. Has decent food and Biliran's only dive centre.

Maripipi Island

Off the northwest tip of Biliran, this dramatic island is dominated by dormant Maripipi Volcano (924m). A *habal-habal* (P250) can take you around the 23km island in an hour or so. On the back side of the island is delightful **Napo Beach Resort** (☑ 0921 212 5164; http://tourism.biliranisland.com/napobeachresort.php; r P1000-2500; ❄ ❄), with a range of rooms, the cheapest of which share bathrooms. Power cuts out at midnight but they supply battery-operated fans. From Maripipi pier it's a 20-minute *habal-habal* ride to the resort.

One or two daily passenger boats leave from Naval to Maripipi (P70, 1½ hours) midmorning, returning the following day. Or hire a bangka (one-way P1000, 30 minutes) at the pier in Kawayan, 17km north of Naval. From Kawayan you can also arrange an all-day island-hopping trip (P2500) taking in Maripipi and uninhabited neighbouring **Sambawan Island**, which has white-sand beaches and is good for snorkelling. The resorts on Agta Beach also offer these trips but they cost more.

East & South of Naval

Situated off the cross-country road, **Tinago Falls** (admission P10) is the most accessible of Biliran's many waterfalls, with a paved access road and concrete bleachers that spoil the atmosphere only somewhat. If the water's not flowing too fast, there are two big swimming holes at the base of the falls. Also off the cross-country road you'll find several hot springs; talk to the provincial tourism office in Naval about which ones are accessible.

To the south of the cross-country road you'll see several peaks, including **Biliran Volcano**, which last erupted in 1939; it can be climbed in a steady 1½ hours. Check with the provincial tourism office in Naval for directions. You'll need a guide, which can be arranged in Caibiran at barangay Pulang Yuta.

On the east coast, and reputed to have exceptionally sweet water, the **Tomalistis Falls** pour from a cliff face and are accessible only at low tide (or otherwise by boat).

North of Cabucgayan, Casiawan Falls can put on a good show depending on the amount of recent rainfall, and remain appealingly undeveloped. They're a 20-minute drive on a track off the south coast road at Cabucgayan, and then another 10 minutes by foot.

A few kilometres west of Cabucgayan is multitiered Kasabangan Falls (admission P10), which have been fitted out with concrete bleachers and draw crowds of locals on weekends. Access is via a rickety suspension footbridge not far from the highway.

Higatangan Island

West of Naval is Higatangan Island, where a shifting white sandbar is good for swimming and snorkelling. On the western side of the island, accessible by boat only, is a series of interesting rock formations with small sandy bays between them. Former President Marcos, along with fellow resistance members, reportedly took refuge on the island in WWII, and Marcos Hill is named in his memory.

There's accommodation on the island in the form of the simple and welcoming Higatangan Island Beach Resort (☑0910 573 5963; www.higatanganislandresort.com; r P800-1200; ❄). There's a 10am daily bangka from Naval (P60, 45 minutes), and the boats leave in the other direction at 7am, so overnighting is a must if you're using public transport. A one-way charter costs around P1500.

SAMAR

The word most often associated with Samar is 'rugged'. It has a heavily forested, virtually impenetrable interior, around which runs a beautiful coastline of turquoise bays, secret surf breaks, towering cliffs and sandy beaches. Not surprisingly, Samar tends to draw a more adventurous tourist – the spelunker; the canyoner; the diehard surfer looking for an undiscovered break. Southern Samar was on the front line of defence when Typhoon Yolanda swept ashore in 2013. One year on, the region was still rebuilding. The main language of Samar is Waray-Waray.

History

Magellan first set foot in the Philippines here in 1521, on the island of Homonhon in the south. During the Philippine-American war, Samar was the scene of some of the bloodiest battles. Tales of brutal combat wove their way into US Marine Corps folklore, and for years after the war American veterans of the campaign were toasted in mess halls by their fellow marines with, 'Stand, gentlemen, he served on Samar'.

ℹ Getting There & Around

The main way into Samar is by regular RORO ferry from Matnog, Sorsogon, in Luzon, or by van or bus from Tacloban, Leyte. There are a few weekly flights from Manila to Calbayog and a few weekly flights from Manila from Catarman.

The road that runs most of the way around Samar is sealed, but not always in very good shape. Be ready to be jarred by a few potholes.

Catarman

☑055 / POP 81,000

Catarman, the administrative capital of the untouristed Northern Samar region, has an airport and some pretty beaches nearby that occasionally get surf. The airport makes Catarman a good starting point for forays around Samar and into Leyte.

The eastern bits of Northern Samar have long been a refuge for small groups of the New People's Army (NPA). The conflict has died down in recent years, and any action tends to occur in the remote hinterlands and does not affect tourists.

Catarman is the only town in Northern Samar with reliable ATM machines, including Metrobank and BDO.

⍾ Sleeping & Eating

North Hill Pension HOTEL $
(Marcos St; s P450-550, d P650-850; ❄❅) This is the cleanest and most attractively designed of the budget hotels in the centre. The air-con singles in particular are good bang-for-the-buck.

UEP White Beach Resort BEACH RESORT $
(☑0909 513 6517; d P800; ❄❅) Located 6km east of Catarman, this place has six standard concrete rooms and a large pool on a lovely stretch of beach. It's owned by the University of Eastern Philippines and gets occasional surf from October to December.

Café Eusebio Bed & Breakfasat B&B $$
(cnr Annunciacion & Marcos Sts; d incl breakfast P1500-3000; ❄❅) Chalk this up as surprise: a legitimate boutique in downtown Catarman. The magnificent dark-wood floors are the eye-opener; designer sinks, lush beds and huge flat-screens fill out the resume. It's attached to the back of a BDO bank.

Samar

Miko Miko Resort BEACH RESORT **$$$**
(cottage incl breakfast P5000; ❄️🛜🏊) The first higher-end accommodation to open on Northern Samar's stunning coastline. Miko Miko features five exquisitely designed private cottages and an infinity pool set above a wind-swept beach. It's remote feeling and makes for a great romantic getaway. Now the question: will the romancers travel this far? It's 10km east of Catarman, in Mondragon.

Isla Cafe CAFE **$**
(GH del Pilar St; meals P100-250; ⏰8am-7.30pm; ❄️🛜) This homey cafe with air-con, functional wi-fi, various coffee drinks and grilled seafood is an oasis in busy downtown Catarman.

ℹ️ Getting There & Away

PAL Express services Catarman from Manila with four early-morning flights at week. The airport is 3km from town (P100 to P150 for a private tricycle, P20 for a public one).

Jeepneys to Allen depart from the bus terminal every 30 minutes until 5.30pm (P60, 1¼ hours), while **Grand Tours** (JP Rizal St) vans take the cross-country road to Calbayog (P100, two hours) and on to Tacloban (P330, five hours), departing hourly until 2pm. Mostly morning RORO buses serve Manila (ordinary/air-con P850/1150, 16 hours).

Around Catarman

Bobon Beach is a stunning long swath of powdery white sand with occasional surf between September and March. Along with neighbouring **San José**, both are just starting to offer some facilities for visitors. Tidy **Binang & Cadio Resort** (📞0906 574 9367; d P1850; ❄️🛜) occupies an enticing sweep of Bobon Beach, with four spacious rooms done up in attractive 'Euro' or 'native' styles. They are amply furnished and have concrete verandahs facing a small pool. Further along, **Playa del Carmen** (📞0947 593 2088;

bukopie@hotmail.fr; d with fan P950-1950, with air-con P2450-2850; ✱ ☎) is a cluster of somewhat overpriced huts in various styles on a bluff overlooking the beach.

The road along the north coast is open as far as Rawis, 30km east of Catarman. Getting around the point to Palapag requires two separate boat rides: a short hop from Rawis to Laoang Island, and a longer river motorboat ride from Laoang Island to Palapag. **Laoang Island** has empty beaches and unexplored surf breaks, plus a picturesque US-built **lighthouse** near the boat landing, which has been withstanding typhoons since 1907.

Biri Island

At the centre of the marine-protected Biri group of islands, Biri Island is known for its marvellously bizarre rock formations, tidal pools and seawaterfalls. Head to the northeast edge of the island, where two boardwalks take you halfway out to the formations. Continue to the rocks via a vast tidal area where some prime swimming holes have formed; a few are deep enough to snorkel in. The cliff-like **Magasang** and **Magsapad** formations are our favourites. If the tide allows, walk behind them and observe the incredible power of the open ocean as it meets the land here. If it's calm you can jump in and snorkel off the west side of Magasang.

The rock formations are 2km to 3km from Biri proper. *Habal-habal* charge P300 for an excursion with wait time. There are more rock formations at nearby Talisay Island, accessible by boat (or on foot at low tide) from barangay Kauswagan on Biri Island. Both islands get great **surf** on occasion near the rock formations, especially from October to January. The best waves are at **sitio Cogon** on Talisay Island.

You can go **diving** through **Biri Resort & Dive Centre** (☎0915 509 0604; http://biri-resort.com; ✱), which is working to restore the island's damaged coral reefs through the **BIRI Initiative** (http://biri-initiative.org).

Biri Island can be done as a day trip or you can sleep here; just be aware that the electricity cuts off at midnight. You may be asked to pay extra for generator use to keep the fans running. Or hope for a breeze.

Homey **Glenda's B&B** (☎0926 743 5479; johnryan55599@yahoo.com; r P1100-1300; ✱ ☎) is our favourite among the three hotels on the island. It has attractive, spacious rooms, good food, a nice waterfront location, and –

importantly – battery-operated fans. It's near the boat landing in barangay Sto Niño, 2km south of Biri town proper.

Food on Biri is problematic. Get your hotel to make you something, or head to the *turu-turò* joints in Biri town.

Boats from Lavezares (P50, one hour), 8km from Allen, leave to Biri when full until 5.30pm or so, or you can take a special trip for P500. Most mornings there is a cargo/passenger bangka to Matnog (P150, 1½ hours).

Allen
☎055 / POP 22,330

This small port town services the ferry route between northern Samar and southern Luzon. A word of advice: if it's getting late, stay the night in Allen and catch a morning boat. You do not want to be benighted in Matnog where the ferries arrive – trust us on this one.

Kinabranan Lodge (☎0917 324 6328; d P850; ✱ ☎) offers the best accommodation in town. Attached to a meat shop on the water next to the Dup Dup pier, it's about the last place you'd expect to find modern, well-designed rooms with plush beds and plasma TVs. Bonus: the meat shop sells cold beer. Short-stay discounts available if you're arriving late and leaving early.

There are el cheapo lodgings at the main pier and 5km south of town on pretty **Buenos Aires Beach**.

RORO ferries from Allen to Matnog (P120, one to 1½ hours) are serviced by several companies at the main **Balwharteco Pier** (☎055-300 2041; terminal fee P20). There are no set schedules, but expect a departure at least every few hours round the clock. Call the pier for weather and schedule updates. Some Matnog-bound ferries use the much mellower Dup Dup pier, 2km south of town.

There's a bus to Tacloban (P350, eight hours) at 9am. Otherwise, hop by van to Calbayog (P100, 1¾ hours), then Catbalogan, then Tacloban through **Grand Tours** (☎0917 700 8071). Jeepneys run to Catarman (P60, 1¼ hours) up until 5pm.

Dalupiri Island & Around

More commonly called San Antonio after its only municipality, Dalupiri has good beaches and clear water, and is close to the mainland. Such is its appeal, it's the kind of place where it's easy to get stranded longer than you planned.

There is a growing range of chilled-out accommodation options on the beachfront. Electricity is off from 6am to noon each day, so rooms can be hot if there is no breeze.

The Swedish-owned **Crystal Sand Beach Resort** (☑0917 336 9740; www.crystalsandbeachresort.weebly.com; d with fan P1000-1500, with air-con P1800; ❋⊜) is up from the village centre with a great location 500m off a marine sanctuary. There's a dive centre and snorkelling equipment for hire. The main rooms are in a very pink concrete structure, but simple bungalows are better suited to its beach location. It can arrange trips to the nearby but rarely visited **Seven Islands** (Naranjo Islands), where plans are in the works for a new backpacker resort on **Sila Island** (San Vicente), known for its pink beach.

Other options include the prettily landscaped and well-established **Haven of Fun** (☑0917 303 1656; www.havenoffunbeachresort.com; r with fan P700-1000, with air-con P1400-2000; ❋), just a walk from the pier, and, next door, the laid-back **Puro Beach Resort** (☑0917 790 0243; purobeachresort@yahoo.com; r with fan P600-800, with air-con P1200-1400; ❋).

Public boats to San Antonio (P30, 20 minutes) leave when full from Victoria, 8km southeast of Allen. To avoid waiting, spill out P390 for a special trip. Additionally there are three daily bangkas to San Antonio from the Dup Dup pier in Allen (P40, 45 minutes).

The forested island of **Capul**, to the west, has an even slower pace of life. It was a galleon staging post during Spanish days – the name probably comes from Acapulco, where the ships were headed – and has a lighthouse and ruined fort, which you can just glimpse upon arrival, where sentries once combed the horizon for Moro pirates. Chilled out **Capul Island Beach Resort** (☑0921 672 6524; www.perfectplaces.com/vacation-rentals/33125.htm; r with fan/air-con P500/1000; ❋) has decent rooms on a lovely beach. There's only electricity from 4pm till midnight.

Public bangkas leave Capul in the early morning bound for Allen's Balwharteco Pier and Matnog, Sorsogon (both P100, about one hour); return trips are around 11.30am from Allen, and around 10am from Matnog.

south or north. As with Catarman and Catbalogan, a ban on motorised tricycles on most central streets allows the quieter pedicabs to take over, creating a sleepy vibe. The **tourist office** (National Rd; ⊙8am-5pm Mon-Fri) next to City Hall hands out a city map and a list of sights in the area. The Ciriaco Hotel runs tours to natural attractions in the area.

For accommodation, **Eduardo's Hotel** (☑055-553 9996; Pajarito St; d with fan/air-con from P400/500; ❋⊜) is a cheap, central option, with a wide variety of rooms, all fairly time-worn. It's just around the corner from **Carlos & Carmelo's** (Nijaga St; meals P150-200; ⊙10am-9pm, to 2am Fri & Sat), which has burgers and the best ribs in the eastern Visayas, plus live music on Fridays and Saturdays.

Much better, but poorly located 2.5km northwest of town, is **S&R Bed & Breakfast** (National Hwy; d P1300-1650; ❋⊜), which has immaculate rooms in a single-storey row. Another rung up the ladder is **Ciriaco Hotel** (☑055-533 9300; www.ciriacohotel.com; National Rd, Km 735; d incl breakfast P2500-4000, ste P7500; ❋⊜), 2km southeast of the centre. It's often booked out for conventions, however.

ⓘ Getting There & Away

PAL Express flies between Calbayog and Manila five times a week. The airport is 10km north of town in Biri.

Grand Tours (055-209 6177; National Rd) has vans every 30 minutes to Catbalogan (P100, 1½ hours), and at least hourly to Allen (P100, 1¾ hours) and Catarman (P100, two hours). Change in Catbalogan for points further south. Vans stop running at 5pm. Reserving a few hours ahead is not a bad idea.

Local buses and jeepneys can take double the time of the vans and don't save you much money. They depart from the new **bus terminal** (Magsaysay Ext) 2km southeast of town, or flag them down on the highway. Buses to Tacloban stop at noon. The last trip to Allen is the 4pm jeepney.

Cokaliong Shipping has ferries to Cebu City (from P690, 11 hours) on Tuesday, Thursday and Saturday at 7pm, departing from the new pier in Maguino-o, 15km north of Calbayog. Tickets can be bought in Calbayog at the Fredlar Hotel. From the city pier, there is a bangka to Masbate (P600, six hours) departing Fridays and Sundays at 8am.

Calbayog

☑055 / POP 147,200

Calbayog, the largest city in Western Samar Province, has an airport and is a pleasant enough place for a stopover if you're heading

Catbalogan

☑055 / POP 84,180

Catbalogan, the capital of Western Samar Province, is the preferred base for exploring the interior of Samar, with spelunking, climbing, birdwatching and canyoning opportunities. It's a pretty spot; from the pier you can spot about 30 islands offshore, plus some giant peaks on Biliran Island off Leyte. In **Pita Park**, near the church, there is a memorial to the terrible 1987 Doña Paz ferry disaster; most of the 5000 or so victims were from Catbalogan and elsewhere on Samar.

Activities

Trexplore
CAVING

(☑055-251 2301, 0919 294 3865; www.trexplore.weebly.com) Run by Joni Bonifacio, Trexplore is the one-stop shop for adventure tours in Samar. Caving is Joni's first love, but canyoning and trekking tours are also on offer.

His tour of the **Jiabong caves**, near Catbalogan, is one of the Visayas' top one-day adventures. One-third of the six-hour tour, which ends with a pleasant 45-minute paddle in a dugout canoe, is spent swimming underground in full spelunking kit.

Tours of the huge **Langun-Gobingob cave** near Calbiga, 50km south of Catbalogan, include a night camping underground. It is thought to be the Philippines' largest karst system. The main cave, Langun-Gobingob, has a chamber the size of three football fields. Joni often discovers new caves and adds tours accordingly. Tours of the newly discovered **Central cave** involve five hours of walking (round-trip), an 18m rappel and four hours inside the cave, all on a gruelling day trip out of Catbalogan.

Joni also offers half-day canyoning tours to multi-tiered **Bangon Falls** near Catbalogan. **Pinipisakan Falls** are a long day trip involving a four-hour round-trip trek. Beyond Pinipisakan you can explore the **Sulpan cave** on an overnight trip.

Give Joni at least a few days' notice before showing up. Costs start from P2500 per person for canyoning and from P3000 for caving, with discounts for larger groups. Rates include food, transport, equipment and a CD of photos taken by Joni during the day. Trexplore also has a shop which sells a range of quality outdoor clothing and equipment.

Sleeping & Eating

Trexplore rents out a couple of backpacker rooms for P200 per head.

Rolet Hotel
HOTEL $

(☑055 251 5512; Mabini Ave; d P950; ❉ 🛜) The well-kept rooms here (some windowless) are somewhat small, but you could bounce a 25 centavo coin on the expertly made beds.

Fortune Hotel
HOTEL $

(☑251 2147; 555 Del Rosario St; d without/with bathroom from P390/490, d/tr with air-con P880/1200; ❉ 🛜) Even the budget rooms here are fastidiously cared for, and it has a bustling, air-conditioned Chinese restaurant on the ground floor (meals P100 to P150).

Summers Garden Pension House
GUESTHOUSE $

(☑055-251 5135; Del Rosario St; s from P750, d incl breakfast P1000-1200; ❉ 🛜) This old house with creaky wood floors and a sunny patio and garden out front will suit those looking for more homey accommodation. The rooms are clean and well-kept, and the elderly owners charming. Breakfast is a big cook-up of bacon and eggs.

★ San Francisco Hotel
HOTEL $$

(☑055-543 8384; San Francisco St; d incl breakfast P1350-1550, tr P2400-2800; ❉ 🛜) A flash new hotel with a contemporary design and modern art hanging about. The rooms aren't as snazzy as the lobby and are on the small side, but easily surpass anything else in town in terms of amenities, flair and soundproofing.

Flaming Hat
FILIPINO $

(City Plaza; meals P60-210; ⊙10am-midnight; ❉ 🛜) This smart restaurant has a good selection of Filipino dishes and pizzas, but the garlic pepper shrimp and grilled pork belly are standouts.

103 Bar & Grill
RESTOBAR $

(cnr Callejon St & Allen Ave; meals P50-200; ⊙4pm-1am) This the place for sizzling Filipino fare washed down with San Miguel (P32). Live music at weekends.

ℹ Information

BDO and Metrobank have ATMs, while air-conditioned **Gizmo** (Mabini Ave; per hr P15; ⊙8am-9.30pm) is the best of the internet cafes.

ℹ Getting There & Away

Duptours (☑0907 276 4342; cnr Allen Ave & San Francisco St) and **Grand Tours** (☑055-251 5243; San Bartolomew St) vans head to Tacloban (P130, two hours) and Calbayog (P100, 1½ hours) until 6pm or so. For Allen or Catarman, you must transfer in Calbayog. Duptours has a 6.30am and sometimes a 1pm trip to Borongan (P200, four hours).

Much slower buses serve Calbayog (P80, 2½ hours) until 4.30pm, with a few continuing on to Allen (P180, six hours) or Catarman (P180, six hours). There are two daily buses to Guiuan

(P200, 5½ hours, last trip noon) and three daily services to Borongan (P140, five hours, last trip 1pm). Buray, a 30-minute jeepney ride south of Catbalogan, has additional services to Taft and Borongan on the east coast. The bus station is next to the wharf in the centre of town.

Buses to Manila (ordinary/air-con P1100/1300, 18 hours) leave fairly regularly around the clock. These buses do not accept passengers for local trips. You'll have pay the full fare if heading to, say, Allen or anywhere in Bicol.

Roble Shipping Lines runs to and from Cebu City (P650, 12 hours) on Tuesdays and Fridays from Catbalogan wharf.

Borongan

053 / POP 59,350

Much like Baler in North Luzon, Borongan is a genuine beach town. The spiritual centre is honey-brown Baybay Beach, where BBQ shacks and vendors of all stripes line a long boulevard. Head here to catch the sunrise, jog, body surf or, in the late afternoon, imbibe cheap beer with the locals. Baybay Beach has five 'stations' – Baybay 1 is to the south, Baybay 5 to the north.

The capital of Eastern Samar Province, Borongan is a good base for DIY travellers or surfers who want to explore Samar's largely untouched Pacific coastline. While the southern bits of the province took a direct hit from Typhoon Yolanda in 2013, Borongan and points north were spared heavy damage

Sights & Activities

Borongan is also a surf town. When the waves are up (October to January is best), the local surfing cabal emerges to take advantage on Baybay or on the next beach south, Bato Beach. There's no organised board rental in Borongan, but resident surfers can scare up a board if you ask, or head south of Borongan to Maydolong, where Surf Omawas (p335) rents boards.

The dense jungle around Borongan has waterfalls and caves to explore, including the nearby Talobnagan Cave in barangay Bato. The barangay office can set you up with a guide (P300 to P500 depending on how far you go). Huplag Speleo (0928 995 0449; http://huplagspeleo.weebly.com) is a local group of spelunkers who run caving and other adventure tours in the area.

Divinubo Island
ISLAND

Just offshore from Borongan, pretty little Divinubo is ringed by white-sand beaches

and has a few secret surf breaks. There's a lighthouse built by the Americans in 1906. It's a good spot to take a picnic. To get here, take a tricycle to barangay Lalawigan south of town (P60, 15 minutes), where you can wait for a boat to fill up (P20) or charter a special trip (P300, 15 minutes). Alternatively, at low tide you can just walk across from Lalawigan.

Therapeutic Massage
MASSAGE

(Baybay 2; per hr P200; ⊗8am-6pm) No-nonsense full-body massages by blind masseurs, next to the tourist office.

Sleeping & Eating

The barbecue stands at Baybay Beach are a fine option in the evening.

Villa Maria Brozas
HOTEL $

(0906 595 3421; r from P800) This hulking concrete structure right on Bato Beach looks decades older than its 10 years, and the pool was out of action when we visited. But the location and views are unbeatable. If they actually renovate the place and reinvigorate the pool, as planned, this will be the place to be.

GV Hotel
HOTEL $

(055-560 9791; d with fan/air-con P450/650; ✳️🛜) Part of a cookie-cutter budget hotel chain, GV won't excite but is nonetheless Borongan's best budget option.

Surf Omawas
B&B $

(0932 934 3164; www.surfomawas.com; Maydolong; r incl surfboard rental P700) Finally there's organised surfing in the Borongan area. This surf camp is on the beach in Omawas, a barangay of Maydolong, the next town south from Borongan.

Boro Bay Hotel
HOTEL $$

(0936 604 2336; Baybay 5; d incl breakfast P1200-3500; ✳️🛜) Enjoying a quiet location at the far north end of Baybay Beach, this is Borongan's fanciest hotel. Rooms are clean and nicely designed, with flat-screen TVs, although wi-fi coverage is poor. It's behind beach-facing Starpoint Cafe.

Hotel Dona Vicenta
HOTEL $$

(055-261 3586; hoteldonavicenta@yahoo.com; r P980-3070; ✳️🛜🛜) Billing itself as Borongan's business hotel (it even has a lift!), Dona Vicenta suffers from small standard rooms and hospital-like corridors. Upgrade to the roomy deluxe rooms up above Uptown Mall, with mountain views. The adjoining Poolsite Restobar is a good place to eat and its pool is a welcome facility.

Domsowir Restaurant
FILIPINO $

(☑ 055-560 9093; meals P100-150, snacks P25-75; ☺ 7am-9pm; ✻ 🛜) The ageing but character-laden Domsowir has a great location on the riverbank, a good range of Filipino food, and ice cream. Also has some grubby rooms downstairs (rooms P385 to P755).

Phenpoint Grill
FILIPINO $

(meals P100-150; ☺ 7am-10pm) Pleasant open-air eatery up the road from Baybay Beach, serving cheap and tasty Filipino dishes. Try the *lapu-lapu* (red grouper) with garlic sauce (P95).

ℹ Information

There are internet cafes on Abenis St just east of Mercury Drug, and you'll find Chinabank, PNB and Metrobank ATMs in town. The **tourist office** (☑ 0917 426 9167; muntour@yahoo.com; Baybay Beach 2; ☺ 8am-5pm Mon-Fri) has a city map and brochures and can help you get to the nearby islands.

ℹ Getting There & Away

Vans are your best bet to Tacloban, with Van Vans (hourly until 4pm) and Duptours (hourly until 5pm) doing trips (P230, 4½ hours) via Basey. Duptours has an early-morning trip to Catbalogan (P100, four hours).

From the bus terminal, hourly jeepneys serve Guiuan until 2pm (P120, 3½ hours), and local buses serve Catbalogan daily at 4.30am and 1pm (P140, five hours). A better way to get to Catbalogan is on a morning Manila-bound bus. These depart from several bus company offices in town.

Guiuan

☑ 053 / POP 43,460

The literal and metaphorical end of the bumpy road to the southeastern tip of Samar, Guiuan (ghee-won) is slowly coming back after being flattened by Typhoon Yolanda, which made its first landfall here. Protected by Calicoan Island, Guiuan was fortunately spared the type of storm surge that killed so many people around Tacloban – miraculously less than 200 people died here as record 400km/h winds pummelled the town. But the storm nonetheless destroyed or heavily damaged most buildings, tore off every roof and snapped most coconut trees in this heavy coconut-farming area. Relief was slow

to arrive and the mayor skipped town, leaving a leadership gap that led to mass looting. Distant Guiuan never did get quite the attention that Tacloban received, and a year after the storm in many ways it looked worse than Tacloban.

That said, Guiuan's hotels rebuilt quickly and it was very much open to tourism when we visited. Its main attraction, the prime surf breaks of Calicoan Island, were unaffected by the typhoon. The many nearby islands remain ripe for exploring. And the friendly people of Guiuan will be happy to see you.

⦿ Sights & Activities

The town's impressive 16th-century **church** and watchtower were casualties of Typhoon Yolanda; it's unclear whether they will be rebuilt.

Weather Station
VIEWPOINT

During WWII, the US military transformed the area into a launching pad for attacks on Japan, and it was once the largest PT (patrol boat) base in the world, with as many as 300 boats and 150,000 troops stationed here, including a young future-President Kennedy. You can walk up to the pale-blue weather station for wide sweeping views across the Pacific Ocean and Leyte Gulf. The 2km US-built **runway** below was instrumental in getting relief supplies to the town post-Yolanda.

🛏 Sleeping & Eating

The best options by far look out on a sparkling bay in barangay Luboc, 1km to 2km northwest of town.

Marcelo's Hotel
HOTEL $

(0905 372 3637; Luboc; r P900; ✻) One of the first hotels to reopen after Typhoon Yolanda, teal-green Marcelo's has no-nonsense air-con rooms that are fine value for Samar. Most rooms sleep three.

Tanghay View Lodge
RESORT $$

(☑ 0936 531 9495; susan_guiuan@yahoo.com.ph; Luboc; d P1000-1400; ✻ 🛜) Managed for many years by gregarious Susan Tan, three-storey Tanghay has tidy rooms and a waterfront restaurant opposite Tubabao Island. Try its speciality, conch in a gingery stir-fry (P110). Susan is a great source of information on Southern Samar and can arrange tours to the islands and elsewhere in the area.

Misty Blue Boathouse
BEACH RESORT $$

(☑ 0906 251 9663; mistyblueboathouse@hotmail. com; Luboc; r P1000; ✻ 🛜 ✻) Run by a burly, ultrafriendly Australian, this laid-back resort has all the fundamentals covered with its gorgeous seaside location, inviting pool and superb open-bar and restaurant serving wood-fired pizzas and burgers. Only two rooms here had reopened at the time of writing but more will follow. Check out the beast of a jet ski, which can be used to zip guests to nearby islands with great swimming.

Amy's BBQ   BARBECUE $$
(Luboc; mains P100-270; ☺6am-midnight; ☜) Norwegians Klaus and and Amy run this friendly place opposite Marcelo's Hotel. They serve giant pork chops and can concoct a mean salad if you want some greens. There's live acoustic on weekends and a convivial crowd most nights.

❶ Information

The **tourist office** (TIPC; ☑0927 458 1175; City Plaza; ☺9am-noon & 1-7pm) can provide information on the region, and doubles as a souvenir store. There are PNB and Metrobank ATMs in town, but bring cash in case they are down.

❶ Getting There & Away

Vans are the best way to Tacloban; Duptours and Van Vans leave hourly until 5pm (P180, 3½ hours). From the bus station behind the market, slow local buses serve Tacloban until 3.30pm (P140, six hours), and jeepneys serve Borongan until 12.40pm (P200, 3¾ hours).

Calicoan Island

Easily accessible by bridge from Guiuan, sparsely populated Calicoan Island took a direct hit from Typhoon Yolanda. Its main resort, the upscale Calicoan Surf Camp, was obliterated. Calicoan's beaches remain beautiful, however, and its famous waves still delight surfers.

The best surfing is two-thirds of the way down the island at **ABCD Beach**, named after the four reef breaks along this coast, and also after 'Advance Base Construction Depot', which is one for the WWII buffs. It has great left- and right-handed reef breaks between June and October. The **ABCD Surf Community**, led by local surf guru Jun Jun, is based in a nipa hut opposite Calicoan Villa. Here you can rent surfboards (per hour P250) or try a lesson (per hour P250). If you get stuck for accommodation Jun Jun can organise a place to stay. He's also a great contact for other surf spots along Samar's southeast coast.

Calicoan Villa (☑0917 206 9602; www.calicoanvilla.com; d with fan/air-con P1200/1500; ❄☜❄) has now reopened on ABCD Beach. The new pool and restaurant stare right at the surf break. The six smart rooms are across the road, with more to be opened beachfront next to the main building.

Continuing south, the fishing village of **Sulangan** on neighbouring Sulangan Island is linked by bridge to Calicoan's southeastern tip. You'll find some amazing white-sand beaches and swimming around here, as well as the fantastic Italian restaurant/resort **La Luna Beach Resort** (☑0917 324 3129; www.resortlaluna.com; d with fan/air-con incl breakfast P2200/2500; ❄☜). It's best known for owner Giampo's home-cooked three-course meals (P650 to P700). Even if you're not staying here, it's well worth dropping in for lunch or dinner. The rooms, with high ceilings, lofts and wood furniture, are also great.

Infrequent multicabs and jeepneys run between Guiuan and Sulangan via ABCD Beach (P30), or you can hire a tricycle (P300 round-trip). The last jeepney back to Guiuan is around 2pm.

Homonhon & Suluan

The island of **Homonhon**, where Magellan first landed in the Philippines on 16 March 1521, and the island of **Suluan** beyond were terribly exposed to Typhoon Yolanda and have yet to recover. The islands are known for their caves and beaches, and a derelict lighthouse on Suluan. If you want to have a look around, public bangkas depart both islands for Guiuan early in the morning and return in the afternoon, weather permitting. Ask the tourist office in Guiuan for details.

Marabut Islands

This pretty cluster of tiny jagged limestone islands adds interest to the already scenic stretch of coastline between Basey and Marabut; the views here are vaguely reminiscent of Vietnam's Halong Bay, but in miniature. Unfortunately, the area was completely annihilated by Typhoon Yolanda and accommodation and services have yet to reopen. **Caluwayan Palm Island** (www.caluwayanresort.com; ❄) was fixing up and should reopen at some point; it traditionally hires out paddle boats to explore the islands.

Mindanao

Best Off the Beaten Track

➡ Sugba Lagoon (p361)
➡ Kapatagan (p372)
➡ Tinago Falls (p347)
➡ School for Indigenous Knowledge & Traditions (p374)

Best Places to Stay

➡ Camiguin Action Geckos Resort (p352)
➡ Sagana Beach Resort (p360)
➡ Ponce Suites (p363)
➡ Chema's by the Sea Resort (p370)

Why Go?

Despite jaw-dropping beaches, killer surf, rugged mountain ranges and indigenous cultures living very much as they have for centuries, Mindanao remains off tourism's radar. Of course, the conflict that has ebbed and flowed now for several generations bears much of the responsibility. That's not to say there isn't urbanisation – much of the northern coastline has been paved over, and the southern city of Davao is cosmopolitan and sophisticated – but much of what has been lost elsewhere in the Philippines is alive in Mindanao.

Though the area is big, because of its varied ethnographic make-up, competing land claims and highly prized abundant natural resources, Mindanao can seem undersized. Since the 1950s Muslims have been the minority and are the majority in only four of the 21 provinces, where 14,000 sq km given over to the pending Bangsamoro, an autonomous region previously known as the ARMM that includes islands stretching towards Malaysia and Indonesia.

When to Go
Cagayan De Oro

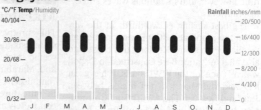

Jun-Sep The driest season on the eastern seaboard; big swells.

Nov-Mar The wettest season on the eastern seaboard.

Nov-Apr The driest season for most of the island; Helobung Festival in Lake Sebu held in November.

History

Mindanao's history diverged early on from that of the rest of the Philippines simply because of geography, and more specifically its proximity to centres of Arab influence. Islam was introduced in the Sulu archipelago in the early 1300s, and was soon after brought to Cotabato and the Lanao area. Afterwards, the region was united by the sultanate under a supreme council and most of the population converted to Islam. When the Spaniards arrived in 1527, their dominance was stymied by an already entrenched and semi-organised power, and they were only able to establish outposts in northern Mindanao and Zamboanga.

It was only in the middle of the 19th century that the Spaniards, with the advantages of superior firearms and steam power, were able to make substantial inroads in Mindanao and assert their sovereignty. The US became the next colonial power in 1898, but its presence in Mindanao wasn't felt for years and it wasn't until a decade or so later that the province was formally incorporated as an administrative region under the suzerainty of the government in Manila.

From the beginning the rights of tribal minority groups and traditional property rights were violated. The peoples of Mindanao were economically and demographically threatened by the influx of Christian Filipinos from the north, who were encouraged by the government to settle in less-populated Mindanao. Some argue that the policy simply opened up a sparsely populated region to immigration and created a more diverse ethnic mix. Others claimed it was the occupation and annexation of their homeland and armed resistance developed in the late 1960s.

Soon after, large multinational agricultural companies entered the region en masse, invariably impacting small-scale farming and traditional ways of life regardless of ethnicity or religion. Less militant groups (as well as the communist NPA which is active in Mindanao) argue that the crux of the conflict is not simply the inevitable result of Muslim and Christian populations living as neighbours, but the result of the exploitation of the island's resources without ensuring that the people see the benefits of development.

In the late '60s presidents Macapagal and Marcos both hoped to add a large chunk of territory to the archipelago by taking advantage of its historical independence, which

was causing so much conflict. They made a bid to annex Sabah, a part of North Borneo recently incorporated into Malaysia. After an unrealistic proposal to include the region in a superconfederacy called Maphilindo fell flat, Marcos initiated a program to train Muslim commandos from Mindanao with vague plans to promote unrest in Sabah, but the secret was exposed and ended with most of the guerrilla recruits being killed in mysterious circumstances.

In 1976 an agreement was struck with one of the rebel groups, the Moro Islamic National Liberation Front (MNLF), establishing the Autonomous Region of Muslim Mindanao (ARMM); in 1996 the MNLF was legitimised as a political group by Manila. Other groups didn't agree that limited autonomy within a federalised system was adequate (of course, some objected because they weren't considered when divvying up the spoils); as a result a breakaway group, the Moro Islamic Liberation Front (MILF), was established in 1978. The most radical of the groups is the Abu Sayyaf, a small group of former MILF members (estimated 300 members) affiliated with Al Qaeda. The government also claims that Jemaah Islamiyah, an Indonesia-based organisation, and other separatist groups are using remote parts of Mindanao to train recruits.

Successive government regimes have tried to assert their control through different means; Marcos tried through a combination of military action and amnesty offers, but it was talks between Cory Aquino and Nur Misuari, the founder of the MNLF, that finally led to a reduction in violence in the late 1980s. Unfortunately, most of the outstanding issues were never resolved, and in the late 1990s and early 2000s the violence resumed.

In August of 2005 Zaldy Ampatuan was elected the new governor of the ARMM, which made him the first leader not to be a member of a rebel group. However, in early August 2008, before the Memorandum of Agreement on Ancestral Domain (MoA-AD) was signed by the Arroyo administration, the Philippines Supreme Court ruled it unconstitutional. One of the primary sticking points was the MILF's desire for an independent court system. The agreement called for a separate Muslim homeland and would have recognised the 11,000-strong Moro Islamic Liberation Front (MILF) as a juridical entity.

MINDANAO

PALAWAN

NEGROS
OCCIDENTAL

NEGROS

Cebu
City

CEBU

NEGROS
ORIENTAL

CEBU

Tagbilaran

● Basey

● Dumaguete

Siquijor
Island

● Lazi

SIQUIJOR

0 —————————— 100 km
0 —————————— 50 miles

Baliangao
Wetland
Park

SULU
SEA

Dapitan
Dipolog ●

● Manukan

Baliangao ●

Calamba ●

● Plaride

Oroquieta ●

MISAMIS
OCC.

● Burgos
● Jiminez
● Clarin

Ozamis ●

Tangub ●

● Sindangan

Liloy ●

ZAMBOANGA
DEL NORTE

Molave ●

Tubod ●

Baroy ●

Pagadian ●

● Kapatagan

Kabasalan ●

Dapusilan
Bay

● Ipil

ZAMBOANGA
DEL SUR

Lapuyan ●

Alicia ●

● Margosatubig

Olutanga
Island

Moro
Gulf

● Curuan

Bolong ●

Zamboanga ● 6

Sacol Island

Basilan Strait

Santa Cruz
Island

● Isabela

BASILAN

Basilan
Island

Sandakan
(Malaysia)

Jolo ●

Jolo Island

SULU

MINDANAO SEA

Mindanao Highlights

1 Hop from natural springs to waterfalls around lush **Camiguin** (p347).

2 Catch a wave at **Cloud Nine** (p360), the surf break on Siargao.

3 Roll through white water on the **Cagayan de Oro River** (p346).

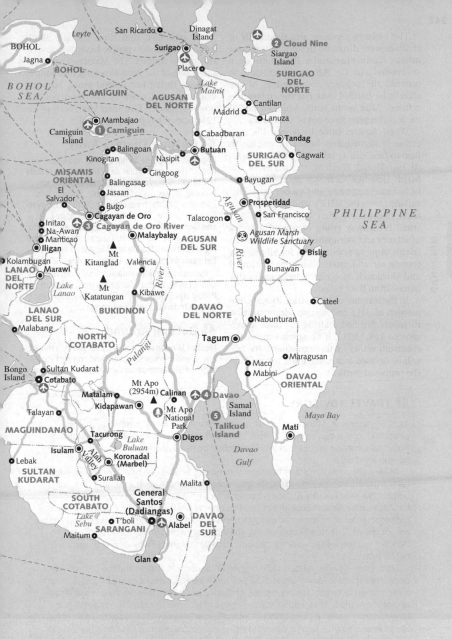

Leyte

San Ricardo

Dinagat Island

BOHOL

Jagna

BOHOL

Surigao

Placer

Lake Mainit

2 Cloud Nine

Siargao Island

SURIGAO DEL NORTE

CAMIGUIN

AGUSAN DEL NORTE

Cantilan

Madrid

Lanuza

BOHOL SEA

Mambajao

1 Camiguin

Camiguin Island

Balingoan

Kinogitan

Nasipit

Gingoog

Butuan

Cabadbaran

Tandag

SURIGAO DEL SUR

Cagwait

MISAMIS ORIENTAL

El Salvador

Balingasag

Jasaan

Bugo

Cagayan de Oro

3 Cagayan de Oro River

Malaybalay

Bayugan

Prosperidad

San Francisco

PHILIPPINE SEA

Initao

Na-awan

Manticao

Iligan

▲ Mt Kitanglad

Valencia

Talacogon

Agusan River

3 Agusan Marsh Wildlife Sanctuary

Bislig

LANAO DEL NORTE

Kolambugan

Marawi

Lake Lanao

▲ Mt Katatungan

Kibawe

AGUSAN DEL SUR

Bunawan

LANAO DEL SUR

BUKIDNON

DAVAO DEL NORTE

Cateel

Malabang

NORTH COTABATO

Pulangi River

Nabunturan

Tagum

Maco

Mabini

Maragusan

DAVAO ORIENTAL

Bongo Island

Sultan Kudarat

Cotabato

Talayan

Matalam

Kidapawan

Mt Apo (2954m) ▲

Calinan

Mt Apo National Park

4 **Davao**

Samal Island

5 Talikud Island

Mayo Bay

Mati

MAGUINDANAO

Tacurong

Isulam

Lebak

SULTAN KUDARAT

Alah Valley

Koronadal (Marbel)

Surallah

Lake Buluan

Digos

Davao Gulf

DAVAO DEL SUR

Malita

SOUTH COTABATO

Lake Sebu

T'boli

General Santos (Dadiangas)

SARANGANI

Alabel

Malita

Maitum

Glan

4 Bar-hop from one buzzing compound to the next in cosmopolitan **Davao** (p362).

5 Escape from the city to a nearby white-sand beach on **Talikud Island** (p370).

6 Take in the island's history and ethnic diversity in **Zamboanga** (p375).

The violence resumed and thousands of civilians were displaced in some of the most intense fighting in decades. Peace talks were suspended and the Arroyo administration ordered the primary commanders of the attacks be handed over but the opposition refused. After seven years, Malaysia pulled its peacekeeping force out of Mindanao.

When Aquino came to power, his government immediately began to engage in face-to-face peace talks in Malaysia with Al Haj Murad Ebrahim, the leader of the MILF. However, there was another upsurge in violence beginning in October 2011. Dissatisfied with the MILF's willingness to continue negotiations after 14 years of talks, a small breakaway group organised a series of attacks and skirmished with government troops. Aquino resisted calls for all-out war though air and ground assaults continued and thousands of civilians were again displaced from their homes.

In the summer of 2014 a transitional commission of MILF and Aquino administration members finished drafting the Basic Bangsamoro Law (BBL). If Congress ratifies the constitutionality of the agreement, its fate will be decided in a referendum by voters in the proposed territory.

It's estimated that since the late 1960s more than 160,000 people have died as a result of the conflict. The Maguindanao massacre, one of the most shocking incidents of violence in the last several years, however, was motivated more by clan and political power struggles. Five years later, none of the 194 accused has been convicted.

ⓘ Getting There & Away

Between Philippine Airlines (PAL) and Cebu Pacific there are regular daily flights from Manila to Butuan, Cagayan de Oro, Cotabato, Davao, Dipolog, General Santos, Ozamiz, Surigao and Zamboanga City; from Cebu to Camiguin, Davao, General Santos, Siargao and Zamboanga City; and Cebu Pacific has a daily flight between Iloilo City on Panay and Davao. Tigerair also has some flights between Manila and Mindanao and flies between Singapore and Davao, as does Silk Air.

You can get to Mindanao by boat from Bohol, Cebu, Leyte, Luzon, Manila, Negros, Palawan, Panay and Siquijor in the Philippines, and directly from Indonesia (to Zamboanga City).

ⓘ Getting Around

Most of Mindanao is easily traversed by a mix of buses and minivans. Quality and comfort varies widely within companies and routes. Less-com-

---

ⓘ TRAVEL ADVISORY

As of September 2014 the political situation in Mindanao was at a turning point, yet again. With corruption so deeply entrenched and the spoils so rich, it's not entirely unlikely that whatever groups that aren't enriched by the new Bangsamoro agreement will take up arms again.

Aside from periodic clashes between the military and rebels (primarily confined to certain provinces in or around the Bangsamoro), there have been a number of deadly bombings elsewhere (the Khilafah Islamiyah Movement is said to be responsible for the 2013 Limketkai Complex and 2012 Maxandrea Hotel bombings in Cagayan de Oro). Kidnappings for ransom carried out by rogue elements of rebel groups and armed gangs are of concern. The New People's Army (NPA) is very active in Mindanao and there are frequent clashes with government troops; however, ordinary Filipinos and tourists are not targeted.

Embassies of many nations, including Australia, Britain, France and the US, actively discourage travel to Mindanao and the Sulu archipelago. Attacks against transportation and commercial targets (buses, ferries, shopping malls etc) have resulted in significant loss of life. At the time of writing, the provinces of Miasmis Occidental, Lanao del Sur, Maguindanao, Sultan Kudarat, North Cotabato, the Sulu Islands – really any part of the Bangsamoro region – were considered risky; you should exercise caution if planning to travel to Marawi in Lanao del Norte. Check with Filipinos who know specific parts of Mindanao well, before venturing into any potentially dangerous areas.

All these caveats aside, as long as you rely on local knowledge, stay away from specific hot spots and err on the side of caution when choosing where and how to travel, you should be fine. The northern Mindanao islands of Siargao and Camiguin have been excluded from the troubles elsewhere. Davao, the business and commercial capital of Mindanao, and the surrounding communities are also considered safe.

fortable jeepneys might be required for out-of-the-way locations. The two-lane highway linking Davao to the northern cities of Cagayan de Oro and Butuan was undergoing extensive work at the time of research – it's narrow and snakes through some mountainous regions. These days it's possible to fly between Camiguin and Siargao, two of the most popular northern Mindanao destinations, with a stop in Cebu. Most people choose not to travel overland on the Zamboanga Peninsula and fly (or less commonly take a boat) to Zamboanga City from Davao.

NORTHERN MINDANAO

The coastline from Cagayan de Oro to Surigao and the offshore islands off the far northeastern tip is a region apart from the rest of Mindanao. Though largely spared from the violence elsewhere, it's often inaccurately stigmatised simply by dint of association. The university town of Cagayan is both a gateway to the region and a base for adventures in the surrounding Bukidnon Province. Volcanic Camiguin Island is seventh heaven for outdoor-lovers and Siargao is one of the best places in the Philippines to hang ten or simply to hang.

Cagayan de Oro

📞 088 / POP 602,000

Like university towns the world over, the energy and promise of youth endows otherwise ordinary places with a jolt of *joie de vivre*. Anyone over the age of 18 can feel like a fuddy-duddy walking the crowded, student-laden downtown streets of Cagayan de Oro (the 'Oro' refers to the gold discovered by the Spanish in the river here).

Much of Cagayan's economy centres on the Del Monte pineapple-processing plant north of town. Nestlé and Pepsi also make their corporate homes in the Philippines here. Popular with Korean tourists who come for English lessons, the relatively cool climate and golf, the city is also the base for outdoor adventures including rafting, hiking, rock climbing and caving.

◎ Sights & Activities

Museum of Three Cultures MUSEUM
(Corrales St; admission P100; ⊙9am-noon & 2-6pm Mon-Fri, 9am-noon Sat) The three galleries here have an interesting mix of photos, ceramics, art and artifacts, including several huge ceremonial M'ranao swords and a full-scale *pangao*, a four-poster bed meant to accommodate the sultan's entire family. It's housed in a building of classrooms on the grounds of Capitol University, a short walk from Gaisano Mall north of the city centre.

Viajero Outdoor Centre OUTDOOR ADVENTURES
(📞0917 708 1568, 088-857 1799; www.viajerocdo. com; 137 Hayes St, Cagayan de Oro) One of the hubs of Cagayan de Oro's outdoor adventuring community is the husband and wife who run this one-stop shop. Eric and Reina Bontuyan can arrange, teach and guide mountain treks, rock climbing and spelunking trips.

🛏 Sleeping

Nature's Pensionne HOTEL $
(📞088-857 2274; T Chavez St; r P750-1250; ❄) Ideally located only a few blocks from Divisoria, it's a professionally run operation and the all blonde-wood rooms in the 'business class' wing come with good-quality flat-screen TVs and modern bathrooms; the older building's rooms have flimsy wooden walls. Wi-fi is available in the lobby of the attached **Grand City Hotel** (📞082-857 2272; Apolinar Velez St; r P1000-1280; ❄🖥).

While this sister hotel has a fancier lobby and elevator, other than faux-wood floors and large queen-sized beds, Grand City rooms don't reflect the step up in price.

Victoria Suites HOTEL $
(📞088-309 2222; www.victoriasuitesonline.com; Tirso Neri St; s/d incl breakfast P650/850; ❄🖥) The two four-storey Romanesque pillars and awnings on this centrally located hotel's facade make it easy to spot. Inside, it's less grand and certainly not Victorian, the minimal furnishings echoing private rooms in a hospital. That said, there's security, a coffee shop, an in-house masseuse and shiny tile floors.

New Dawn Pensionne HOTEL $$
(📞088-857 1776; www.grandcityhotelscdo.com; cnr Apolinar Velez & Macahambus Sts; r P1500; ❄🖥) The seven-storey New Dawn has compact and efficiently designed rooms – green and white is the prevailing colour scheme. Only a short walk to Ayala Centro and Gaisano Malls.

Mallberry Suites HOTEL $$
(📞088-854 1999; www.mallberrysuites.com; Florentino St; r P2000-2900; ❄🖥) A short stroll to the Limketkai Complex, the aptly named Mallberry is a seven-storey business hotel. Several restaurants and a bar add some edge

Cagayan de Oro

Cagayan de Oro

to the corporate sensibility; however, there's no warmth in the plain and ordinary rooms.

VIP Hotel HOTEL **$$**
(☎ 088-856 2505; www.theviphotel.com.ph; cnr Apolinar Velez & JR Borja Sts; r incl breakfast P1950-2800; ❋🛜) Somewhat barren rooms and mismatched furniture in need of an

upgrade; however, the centrally located six-storey VIP does have professional staff and a welcoming lobby and restaurant.

Maxandrea Hotel HOTEL **$$**
(☎ 088-857 2244; www.maxandrea.com; cnr JR Borja & Aguinaldo Sts; r P2100; ❋🛜) An eight-storey business-class hotel halfway between Divisoria and Limketkai. Service can be spotty; make sure you get a room with windows and natural light.

Limketkai Luxe Hotel HOTEL **$$$**
(☎ 088-880 0000; www.limketkailuxe.com; Limketkai Ave, Limketkai Centre; r P5000-6500; ❋🛜🏊) Something of a fish out of water, this towering building looks like a Trump casino with flashy gold-coloured windows. International business-class-quality rooms with some boutique-hotel-style touches and an attractive outdoor swimming pool. Relatively newly opened, service was not yet up to par.

✕ Eating

The **Rosario Arcade** in front of the Limketkai Complex, a few kilometres northeast of Divisoria (Golden Friendship Park), is one of Cagayan's culinary and entertainment centres (the other primary one is the new **Ayala Centro Mall** (Claro M Recto Ave) across from the older Gaisano Mall; Ayala is loaded with restaurants and cafes and the high-end Seda Hotel is attached. A variety of international cuisines are represented, including Thai (Siam Thai Cuisine), Japanese (Ramen Tei) and Mediterranean (La Vetta). To reach Limketkai, you pass pedestrian-unfriendly Sergio Osmena St which is lined with auto repair shops.

The once-popular weekend Night Cafe, basically an open-air dinner market on Divisoria, was shut down by the new mayor because of traffic flow concerns. You can find a miniaturised version on Apolinar Velez St just south of Divisoria any night of the week. Street vendors hawk *isaw* (chicken intestines) for P5 a skewer and the questionably appetising *proven* (or proben, a fried mix of parts from the chicken's digestive system). Also look out for the region's specialty *kinilaw,* which is spiced with *tabon tabon,* a fruit native to northern Mindanao. Cagayan foodies claim their city's *lechon baboy* (roasted pig), stuffed with lemongrass and other herbs and spices, is the tastiest in Mindanao.

The freshest seafood is served at **Panagatan** (Opol; mains P200) and **Seablings** (Opol; mains P200; ⏰6:30am-10:30pm), two restaurants perched on stilts over the water around 10km west of the city on the highway to Iligan.

Marcky's Grill   FILIPINO $
(Apolinar Velez St; mains P120; ⏰24hr) Not the most logical spot for alfresco dining since the air is thick with jeepney exhaust fumes. Nevertheless, one of the wobbly stools perched over the street makes for good people-watching. The menu features barbecue meats, including baby back ribs (P240), as well as the usual varieties of *pansit.*

Lokal Grill   FILIPINO, SEAFOOD $$
(Corrales Ave; mains P120-300; ⏰noon-2am) In addition to standard Filipino meat and noodle dishes, Lokal does its own version of *pinakbet* (an Ilocano dish of mixed vegetables steamed in fish sauce) which is mixed with deep-fried squid. Other specialties are grilled tuna belly, crocodile *sisig* and seafood by weight cooked to your preference.

Thai Me Up   THAI $$
(⏰088-310 8424; Capistrano St, btwn Mabini & Montalban Sts; mains P150-P280; ⏰11am-10pm) One of the few standalone restaurants within walking distance of downtown hotels, Thai Me Up's overgrown garden setting and open-air dining room are at least as much of a draw as its Filipino-style Thai dishes. Every Wednesday and Friday is an all-you-can-eat buffet (P300). Another generic looking location in Ayala Centro mall.

ℹ Information

All the major banks are here and have ATMs. Several are located along Divisoria and Apolinar Velez St. There's a Citibank in the Limketkai Complex.

There are more than a dozen internet cafes in the blocks south of Divisoria; a handful are on Hayes St between Apolinar Velez St and Corrales Ave.

Bureau of Immigration (BOI; ⏰088-272 6517; Room 205, BPI Bldg, Sergio Osmeña St; ⏰8am-5pm Mon-Fri) Provides visa extensions.

City Tourism Office (⏰088-857 3165; Divisoria Park & Apolinar Velez St; ⏰8am-5pm Mon-Fri) Flyers for hotels and transportation; not much English spoken.

Department of Tourism (DOT; ⏰088-856 4048; dotr10_nmy@ahoo.com; Gregorio Pelaez Sports Center, Apolinar Velez St; ⏰8.30am-5.30pm Mon-Fri) A large office with enthusiastic, if somewhat ill-informed staff; can make calls to verify transportation schedules.

ℹ Getting There & Away

AIR
There are several daily flights from Manila (1½ hours) with **Cebu Pacific** (⏰088-856 3936; cnr Rizal & Hayes Sts) and **Philippine Airlines** (⏰088-857 2295; Tirso Neri St); **Tigerair** (⏰in Manila 02-798 4499; www.tigerair.com/ph) has one flight daily. Cebu Pacific also flies daily to Cebu (45 minutes) and Davao (one hour). All flights now operate out of Laguindingan International Airport, 30km west of the city and 55km east of Iligan.

BOAT
You can get to Macabalan pier by jeepney; a taxi will cost about P70.

2GO (⏰088-854 7000; www.travel.2go.com.ph) services the following destinations: six weekly trips to Manila (P2100 to P3400, 35 hours); Cebu City (P925, 10 hours, Tuesday, Wednesday and Friday); Iloilo on Panay (P1800, 14 hours, 11pm Saturday); and Dumaguete on Negros (P1000, midnight Sat). Trans Asia services Tagbilaran on Bohol (P750, 10 hours, 7pm Tuesday,

Thursday and Saturday). Lite Shipping has four weekly trips between Cagayan de Oro and Jagna on Bohol (from P600, seven hours).

BUS

Eastbound and southbound buses leave from the Integrated Bus Terminal at the Agora fruit and vegetable wholesale market. Air-con buses stop running in the early evening. To catch a boat to Camiguin, take any eastbound bus to Balingoan. For Surigao (departure point for boats to Siargao), you must transfer to another bus in Butuan. Westbound buses depart from the terminal a few kilometres northwest of the city centre in barangay Bulua. In general, buses leave every 30 minutes to an hour.

DESTINATION	FARE (P)	DURATION (HR)
Balingoan	148	1¾
Butuan	350	4¼
Davao	600	6
Iligan	145	2

TAXI

A taxi to Balingoan (P2500) or Iligan (P200) isn't such an extravagance for groups of three or four.

❶ Getting Around

A taxi between the airport and town is around P500 (30 to 45 minutes). Another convenient option is **LAX Shuttle** (☑ 0917 710 1529; from town/from airport P199/P150), which runs hourly minivans from the Ayala Centro Mall (head to the Capt V Roa St entrance).

Jeepneys to many points, including the pier, Cugman (for Malasag Eco-Tourism Village) and the Limketkai Complex, pass by in front of Nature's Pensionne.

Renting a car is a convenient and economical option for groups of two or more. **Avis** (☑ 088-857 1492; www.avis.com.ph; RT DeLeon Plaza, cnr Yacapin & Apolinar Velez Sts) has an office in town and it's possible to return the car in Davao. Rates average around P2700 per day (petrol not included); chauffeur-driven cars and vans are also available.

Around Cagayan de Oro

Cagayan is the gateway to outdoor adventures including rafting only an hour's drive south of the city in Bukidnon Province.

◉ Sights & Activities

Malasag Eco-Tourism Village   VILLAGE
(☑ 088-855 6183; admission P30) Set in acres of botanical gardens with a small wildlife collection of butterflies, birds and deer, the Malasag Eco-Tourism Village is a theme park of sorts, featuring tribal houses, a museum and an education centre. There are camping, cottages (from P500), a swimming pool (P50) and a pleasant restaurant. Take a jeepney to Cugman and get off at Malasag, then take a motorcycle (P25) up the hill to the village. A taxi will cost about P150 one way.

Whitewater Rafting   RAFTING
The standard three-hour rafting trip (P700 to P900) takes you through 14 Class II to III rapids; several Class IV rapids are part of an alternative longer trip (P1000 to P1500, six hours); plus P200 for a grilled lunch. Much of the trip is spent floating past bucolic scenery, and enthusiastic guides and excited first-timers add to the fun. Six companies are officially registered, including the recommended **1st Rafting Adventure** (☑ 88-856-3514; www.raftingadventurephilippines. com; 86 Jongko Bldg, Tiano Hayes St) and **CDO Bugsay River Rafting** (☑ 88-850 1580; cdo-bugsayrafting@yahoo.com; cnr Apolinar Velez & San Agustin Sts).

Rafting is good year-round – during the dry season, from January to May, the water is clearer and the runs more technical, while in June and July the water is faster if brown and murky.

Makahambus Adventure Park   ADVENTURE PARK
(☑ 0916 234 6776; sky bridge, zipline & rappelling P500; ☺ 8am-5pm) This is a common stop for rafters (and often offered as a package), since it's on the way to the river. There's a 120ft-long sky bridge tethered over 40m above the jungle, a zipline and rappelling on offer.

Just a few metres before the park is **Makahambus cave** where Filipino soldiers and their families sought refuge during the Philippines-American war. There's a viewing deck over the river and steps to the bottom of the gorge.

Mapawa Adventure Park   ADVENTURE PARK
(www.mapawa.com; admission P50; ☺ 9am-5pm Tue-Fri, from 7.30am Sat & Sun) Located a few kilometres from Malasag, this nature park has a zipline and natural water slide and pools – a canyoning package is P1000.

Del Monte   PLANTATION
(☑ 088-855 5976; ☺ 8am-1pm Sat) Whatever your level of fruity passion, the sight of pineapples as far as the eye can see is fairly sur-

real. The pineapple plantations, all 95 sq km of them, are about 35km north and east of Cagayan, on the Bukidnon plateau at Camp Phillips (where General Douglas MacArthur fled after the battle of Corregidor Island in 1942). Jeepneys run to Camp Phillips but the plantations lie behind the complex, a clubhouse and golf course and are no longer open to the general public.

Del Monte does offer free tours of its pineapple processing factory at Bugo, approximately 15km east of Cagayan. You need to contact Ronald Badayos (badayosre@del-monte-phil.com) in advance to book.

Iligan

063 / POP 322,800

Although it's promoted as the 'City of Magnificent Waterfalls', the inevitable first impression you have of Iligan is of a sprawling industrial park with countless cement and food-processing factories. Hydroelectric power (supplying 95% of Mindanao's needs) harnessed from the water of Lake Lanao in the hills above the city has meant Iligan has outstripped its neighbours in terms of development, though it still lags in terms of charm. The best time to visit is the end of September during the city's fiesta.

Sights & Activities

Pat Noel from the **Iligan Tourism Office** (0919 320 9944; www.iligancitytourism.com) can act as a guide or simply provide travel advice.

Tinago Falls WATERFALL
(admission P10) Hidden deep in a mountain, Tinago Falls is the most spectacular of Iligan's waterfalls; you can drive to the start of the very steep stairway (365 steps) down. During the wet season, it's a loud violent cascade, but no matter what time of year, you can swim in the pool at the base (life vests are provided). There's even a jerry-rigged bamboo version of Niagara Falls' Maid of the Mist to take you into the spray.

President Gloria Macapagal-Arroyo's Childhood Summer Home NOTABLE BUILDING
Directly in front of Timoga Springs, along the main highway, this is only really interesting to political buffs. Perhaps most curious are the family photos of Macapagal-Arroyo from child to sultry adult (she's lying down on her side wearing a slinky gown in one large painting).

Maria Cristina Falls WATERFALL
(admission P30) Even though the twin Maria Cristina Falls are being harnessed for their hydroelectric power, you can climb to the top of an observation tower for excellent views (there's a small zipline, an eatery and a crocodile park at the base).

Timoga Springs SPRING
The super-cold Timoga Springs are refreshing on a hot day; plenty of food stalls surround these developed pools complete with slides.

Sleeping & Eating

Pinakurat, a chopped wild-boar dish, is an Iligan specialty (hunting boar is banned except in Muslim areas).

Rene's Diner & Pension House HOTEL $
(063-223 8441; Roxas Ave Extension; r with fan/air-con P350/480;) The most convenient option if you want to spend the night is Rene's, directly on the main road, a few minutes west of the centre. Rooms are spacious if poorly maintained.

Corporate Inn Boutique Hotel HOTEL $
(063-221 4456; corpor8inn@yahoo.com; 5 Sparrow St, Isabel Village; s/d incl breakfast from P750/1050;) Quieter but more out of the way, this is a more personable place than the unfortunate name implies, especially the outdoor sitting area. A handful of restaurants are within walking distance.

Cheradel Suites HOTEL $$
(mobile 0917 459 6773; Jeffery Rd; r incl breakfast from P1290;) The somewhat kitschy top-end choice in Iligan is about five minutes east of town near the post office and Landbank.

Gloria's Ihaw Ihaw FILIPINO $
(mains P100) Across the street from Timoga Springs and along the waterfront is Gloria's Ihaw Ihaw, serving delicious *kinilaw,* grilled fish and chicken.

Camiguin

088 / POP 83,800

Relatively unspoiled and of an ideal size for exploration, Camiguin (cah-mee-*geen*) can be singled out for its imposing silhouette – drop it down next to Hawaii or Maui and it wouldn't look out of place. With over 20 cinder cones 100m-plus high, Camiguin has more volcanoes per square kilometre than

Camiguin

Camiguin

◎ Sights
1 Binangawan Falls	C3
2 Cantaan Kabila White Beach Giant Clam Sanctuary	D4
3 Katibawasan Falls	C2
4 Philippine Institute of Volcanology & Seismology (Philvolcs) Station	B2
5 Spanish Watchtower	D4
6 Stations of the Cross	A2
7 Tuwasan Falls	B3

⊕ Activities, Courses & Tours
8 Ardent Hot Springs	B2
Camiguin Action Geckos	(see 17)
9 Dive Special	D3
10 Johnny's Dive N' Fun	B1
11 Saii Springs	B2
12 Santo Niño Cold Spring	B3
13 Taguines Lagoon	D3
14 Tangub Hot Spring	A2

⊜ Sleeping
15 Agohay Villa Forte Beach Resort	A1
16 Bahay-Bakasyunan sa Camiguin	C1
17 Camiguin Action Geckos Resort	B1
18 Casa Roca Inn	A1
19 Enigmata Treehouse Ecolodge	C2
20 Nypa Style Resort	B1
21 Puesta del Sol	A2
22 Sector 9 Hotel & Bar	B1
23 SomeWhere Else Boutique Resort	B1
24 Volcan Beach Eco Retreat & Dive Resort	A1

⊗ Eating
25 Checkpoint	A1
26 J&A Fishpen	D3
27 La Dolce Vita	B1
Luna Ristorante	(see 25)
Vjandeap Bakery	(see 22)

MINDANAO CAMIGUIN

any other island on earth. And because it's uncorrupted by large-scale tourism and one of the more tranquil islands around – the 10km waters of Gingoog Bay separating the island from the mainland are partly responsible – those who do come here tend to feel proprietorial about this little jewel and guard news of its treasures like a secret. Besides the usual diving, snorkelling, sandy beaches (except for offshore ones, beaches have brown sand), waterfalls and hot and cold springs, Camiguin offers the chance for jungle trekking, volcano climbing, rappelling and anything else the masochistic endurance athlete can dream up.

Mambajao (mah-bow-ha), the capital of Camiguin, is about half an hour's ride from the port at Benoni. There are shops, a market, government buildings and a few places to overnight, but most visitors stay closer to the northern beaches. With environmental concerns in mind, Mambajao has made the fairly progressive move of banning the use of plastic bags in stores.

◉ Sights & Activities

The waters surrounding Camiguin are good for diving, especially for beginners who can see interesting rock formations in shallow waters, a result of the lava flow from Hibok-Hibok's previous eruptions. There are over 10 sites of note; the best diving is probably off White Island and Mantigue Island; Black Forest and Sunken Cemetery are other favourites. Expect to pay about P3000 for two boat dives including equipment (the municipal government is now charging an additional P150 per diver per dive in marine-protected areas). Snorkelling equipment is rented out for P200 (mask and snorkel), plus another P200 for fins and booties.

Customised climbing, trekking, mountain biking, fishing and any other action adventure can be arranged through Camiguin Action Geckos or Johnny's Dive N Fun, or through your accommodation.

◉ Benoni to Mambajao

Katibawasan Falls WATERFALL
(admission P35) A beautiful clear stream of water dropping more than 70m to a plunge pool where you can swim and picnic. The few souvenir kiosks and concrete walkway means it doesn't feel like a natural refuge. A special trip by jeepney or multicab from Mambajao will cost about P300 return; from the resorts around Agoho it's about P350 return.

Camiguin Action Geckos OUTDOORS
(☑088-387 9146; www.camiguinaction.com; Agoho) Full-service highly recommended operation at the resort of the same name. Open-water PADI courses are P19,000.

Johnny's Dive N' Fun OUTDOORS
(☑088-387 9588; www.johnnysdive.com) This outfit has offices at Caves Dive Resort in Agoho and Paras Beach Resort in Yumbing; canyoning trips are an option.

Dive Special DIVING
(☑0905 858 9992; www.dive-special.com; Mahinog) A newly opened shop part of an operation based in Cagayan de Oro.

Free Diving DIVING
(www.freediving-philippines.com; Agoho) Wolfgang Dafert, an accomplished freediver and instructor, is based at Camiguin Action Geckos for several weeks every May when calm water can be guaranteed. Groups might be able to arrange customised courses at other times.

Mantigue Island DIVING, SNORKELLING
Between Benoni and Mambajao you'll see Mantigue Island – sometimes called Magsaysay – offshore. A few fishing families live here and a marine sanctuary means there's still some good coral in the cordoned area and stretches of a pretty white-sand beach. A return trip to the island from the village of San Roque will cost P550. It's also a popular dive site; the island usage fees – entrance P20, plus P120 for divers (P75 for snorkellers) – are usually included in dive packages.

Reconnect Discover MEDITATION, YOGA
(☑0908 430 8444; www.reconnectdiscover.com; Agoho; per person 3 days €160-220, 1 week €800-1200) Kaisa and Arno, a warm and friendly Sweedish-Dutch couple based at Action Geckos, organise and run three-day to weeklong retreats combining yoga, meditation, life coaching and diving.

Hibok-Hibok Volcano HIKING
Hibok-Hibok volcano (1320m), which last erupted in 1951 (when nearly 600 people were killed as a result), provides a dramatic spark – no pun intended – to the island's interior. Housed in a building about 525m off the main road is the **Philippine Institute of Volcanology & Seismology (Philvolcs) Station**, which monitors the volcano's activity. A hired motorcycle or multicab will take you there to see the lacklustre equipment

MINDANAO CAMIGUIN

and memorabilia of past eruptions. Just past here is a small shop-cum-cafe.

It's possible to climb the volcano, but it's a demanding three- to four-hour steep, rocky climb (nearly the same time for the descent) and you should be reasonably fit (only possible in dry weather). From the peak it's possible to see Bohol, Cebu and Negros on a clear day. Most resorts can provide guides (per person P1500, plus admission P500 and P200 environmental fee); aim to leave around daybreak. Action Geckos offers a package for P2400 that includes guide, transportation, lunch, water and admission; its hike starts from Ardent Hot Springs.

Ardent Hot Springs   SPRING
(admission P30; ⊙ 6am-10pm) Head out late in the afternoon when the air temperature has cooled down for the lukewarm to hot waters. The big pool is emptied for cleaning on Wednesday and takes the best part of the day to refill. The springs are in a lush but developed setting and get very busy on weekends.

Saii Springs   SPRING
FREE Around 4km-plus (the final 1km is walked) inland from the church in Mambajao is this concrete pool fed with cold spring water.

Taguines Lagoon   LAGOON
Just south of Benoni is the artificial Taguines Lagoon, used primarily as a fish-breeding area. If you're interested in the **zipline** (☑ mobile 0915 896 6585; P400; ⊙ 6am-8pm) that crosses over the lagoon, stop in at the J&A Fishpen Restaurant.

⦿ North Coast to Guinsiliban

Kuguita, Bug-ong, Agoho and **Yumbing** are the most developed of the northern beaches, and where much of the accommodation is located. However, because of erosion, a great deal of the actual beach between Agoho and Yumbing continues to disappear into the sea. In fact, a number of sea walls have been erected to protect seafront properties. Where the beach does still exist, it's of the dark and coarse variety, a result of the island's volcanic activity.

Cantaan Kabila White Beach
Giant Clam Sanctuary   BEACH
Some of the best-preserved coral around Camiguin, as well as giant clams, can be found in the waters just off this small white-

sand beach halfway between Benoni and Guinsiliban in barangay Cantaan. However, typhoons Sendong (2011) and Pablo (2012) did cause significant damage and the giant clam population has yet to rebound. The family that owns the property charges for a guide (P150), entrance (P50) and environmental fee (P25), and rents masks and snorkels for P250 (they actually enforce a 'corkage' fee if you bring your own gear so might as well rent theirs).

White Island   BEACH
(admission P20) Uninhabited White Island (Medano Island), a pure, white-sand bar a few hundred metres offshore, is accessible by boats (P500, up to six people) that now only leave from a spot next to Paras Beach Resort in Yumbing. At any time but the early morning, the sun can be brutally intense. The shape of the island is constantly evolving, fighting a constant battle against the tide, erosion and occasional sand theft.

Binangawan Falls   WATERFALL
This, the shortest of the falls on Camiguin at 15m or so, is one of the most difficult to reach and only advisable with a guide arranged through your accommodation or the tourism office (P1500). The turn-off is just past the village of Sagay; from here it's another 7km or so up until the road deteriorates and then another few kilometres at a steep pitch along a rough rocky path. Actually reaching the falls involves plenty of walking and bushwhacking with a machete because there's no proper trail.

Tuwasan Falls   WATERFALL
This previously unspoiled and beautiful spot has been disfigured by the construction of a paved road up and over the falls (part of a future all-asphalt cross-island road), which once thundered below into a canyon of boulders. There's a cold-water pool in **Bura** on the way here.

Stations of the Cross   VIEWPOINT
Just before Bonbon you'll pass the Old Camiguin Volcano, whose slopes have been turned into a steep and beautiful Stations of the Cross. There are great views from the top and a few souvenir stalls clustered at the bottom of the steps.

Sunken Cemetery   LANDMARK
Between the hillside and Bonbon you'll see an enormous white cross floating on a pontoon in the bay, marking the spot of the

Sunken Cemetery, which slipped into the sea following the earthquake of 1871; it's a popular snorkelling and diving spot.

The same earthquake destroyed the 17th-century Spanish church in Bonbon; its quiet ruins still stand, with grazing cattle nearby and a makeshift altar inside.

Spanish Watchtower   HISTORIC SITE
In Guinsiliban, behind the elementary school by the pier, are the remains of this centuries-old sight which used to guard against possible Moro attacks from the mainland. A pretty shrine is maintained here.

Tangub Hot Spring   SPRING
Water temperatures here fluctuate with the tides, from cold to warm to hot, depending on the source; a volcanic spring below the sea bed provides the hot water at this completely undeveloped site around 12km west of Mambajao.

Santo Niño Cold Spring   SPRING
(admission P20; ⊙24hr) Close to Catarman and several kilometres off the highway along a paved road.

🎉 Festivals & Events

Lanzones Festival   CULTURAL
The annual paean to this delicacy, a small yellow fruit that tastes like a mix of lemons and lychees, is celebrated around the third week of October. Gluttony is encouraged during a week of parades, pageants and dancing.

Panaad   RELIGIOUS
During Holy Week, the Panaad involves a 64km walk around the island, an expression of devotees' penitence and commitment. Stations of the Cross are placed on the route, ending with 'Tabo' on Easter Sunday in Mambajao.

🛏 Sleeping & Eating

Reservations are recommended during Camiguin's high season from March through May. Of course it's hot, but reliable weather means boat and flight cancellations are rare and visibility excellent for diving. January and February, though they are rainy months, are also busy with Europeans escaping their winter. Locals celebrate family homecomings during Christmas and the semester break from late October to early November.

Because Camiguin fishermen are mostly after anchovies, sardines and varieties of flying fish, seafood isn't as emphasised on menus as it is elsewhere. However, fresh tuna is available from around the end of April to late October.

🛏 Mambajao & Around

Mambajao has several simple eateries, groceries and market stalls.

★ Enigmata Treehouse Ecolodge   HOSTEL $
(☑088-387 0273; www.camiguinecolodge.org; Balhagon; dm/ste P300/1050; 🛜) ✈ Alternative eco meets alternative art at this whimsically designed treehouse-cum-lodge. There are branches, bottles and fabrics everywhere – unsurprisingly, privacy isn't a priority, but communal living is (especially if a student group is in residence). Located up a hill off the main road (look for the large tribal Tarzan statue) about 2km southeast of Mambajao; phone before turning up.

Sector 9 Hotel & Bar   HOTEL $
(formerly Rooftop; ☑0918 589 8915; cnr Neriz & Rizal Sts, Mambajao; r P500-1500; ❄🛜) Each of the seven light-filled, wood-floor rooms on the 3rd floor has high ceilings and homey touches. The cavernous all-concrete ground-floor restaurant (6am to 11pm) qualifies as the finest dining in Mambajao, serving up pizzas (P250), burgers, sandwiches and Filipino standards (P150). There's a billiards table and the 2nd floor is turned into a disco weekend nights.

Bahay-Bakasyunan
sa Camiguin   RESORT $$$
(☑088-387 1057; www.bahaybakasyunan.com; r incl breakfast P3400-P4900; ❄🛜🏊) The most upscale of Camiguin's resorts, this property stretches from the highway to the water, shaded by a towering grove of coconuts. Stylish and modern A-frame cottages face older bamboo bungalows across a manicured lawn that runs down to a seaside pool and restaurant. Especially good for those wishing to be close to town.

Vjandeap Bakery   BAKERY $
Stop by Vjandeap Bakery for the island's specialty pastries.

La Dolce Vita   ITALIAN $$
(National Hwy; mains P250; ⊙5am-11pm, closed Mon low season; 🛜) Allesandro, the Italian owner-chef at this open-air place across from the airport, fires up delicious thin-crust brick-oven pies using only high-quality

imported ingredients. Pastas and cappuccinos (P110) are also standouts.

J&A Fishpen
SEAFOOD $$

(mains P95-400) Seafood (such as bangus P55 per 100g) comes straight from the pens on the Benoni lagoon which this restaurant overlooks; popular with large groups on weekends.

Northern Beaches

★ Camiguin Action
Geckos Resort
RESORT $$

(☑088-387 9146; www.camiguin.ph; Agoho; s/d without bathroom P700/900, cottages P2000-2900; ❋☎) Every island in the Philippines should have a place just like this. 'Rustic sophistication' says it all – you'll find perfectly constructed, spacious, hard-wood cottages with verandahs combined with touches of class and taste. For more value, try one of the small but appealing 'travellers' rooms' upstairs from the open-air restaurant. There's a full-service dive shop on the premises.

Besides diving, every type of outdoor activity can be organised here and, to top it all off, it sits on one of the widest stretches of beach around.

Casa Roca Inn
INN $$

(☑088-387 9500; www.casarocacamiguin.com; Naasag; r with shared bathroom P1000-1500; ☎) Gnarly tree branches serve as pillars holding up this two-storey home perched on a rocky headland with waves breaking below. Sunset views from the mahogany balcony in the sea-facing room alone justify a stay. For guests in the two other rooms with polished wood floors and plenty of natural light, the recommended **restaurant** (mains P200) and waterfront garden make great lounging areas.

Volcan Beach Eco Retreat & Dive Resort
COTTAGES $$

(☑088-387 9551; www.camiguinvolcanbeach.com; Naasag; r with fan/air-con P1500/2500; ❋☎) A line of well-constructed thatch-roofed cottages face one another across a palm-tree-filled garden (with several hammocks) that ends on a rocky shore batterd by waves. Each has its own small private balcony, high ceilings and mosquito nets. German-owned Volcan, just opened at the time of research, will have a full-service dive shop.

Nypa Style Resort
COTTAGES $$

(☑0921 638 3709; www.nypastyleresort.jimdo. com; Bug-ong; r incl breakfast P1300-1900; ☎) If sea views aren't a priority, the tranquil garden ones at this meticulously maintained property 500m inland from the highway are a recommended alternative. Each of the four bamboo cottages are uniqely designed. The Italian owners brew some of the best espresso and change up their set menu daily (nonguests can make reservations).

Also has a small spring-fed stonge plunge pool and a separate cottage for massages.

Agohay Villa Forte Beach Resort
HOTEL $$

(☑0927 805 1050; www.agohayvillaforte.com; Agoho; r with fan/air-con P900/1700; ❋☎≋) Besides two large rooms that can sleep six, there's one smaller, overdecorated room worth a stay for the outdoor shower area landscaped with rocks and plants. Well managed only when owners on property.

Puesta del Sol
HOTEL $$

(☑0906 606 6172; www.puestadelsolcamiguin. com; Yumbing; r P2000; ❋☎≋) A quiet little compound with a postage-stamp-sized plunge pool and equally small beach surrounded by large concrete walls. Only three modern cottages with nice bathrooms and a small restaurant. Construction was ongoing on a six-room annex.

★ SomeWhere Else Boutique Resort
VILLA $$$

(☑088-387 9550; www.somewherecamiguin.com; Agoho; r P3800-4500; ❋☎) European modernism with a tropical twist describes these two large villas set back from the beach in a lush lawn. Each is stylishly furnished with whimsical flourishes and open-floor plans. Both have outdoor showers and one has a small plunge pool and roof deck. Not clearly signposted from the highway.

Balai sa Baibai
VILLA $$$

(☑0918 962 2800; elcoventures@gmail.com; Agoho) This high-end Balinese-style villa located on the Agoho beach was scheduled to open by December 2014.

★ Luna Ristorante
ITALIAN $$

(National Hwy, Yumbing; mains P200; ☺7am-11pm; ☎) Located on the main road in Yumbing, right after the turn-off for the Paras Beach Resort. It does excellent thin-crust brick-oven pizza, as well as pasta and calzones; the outdoor concrete gazebo is a nice place to spend an afternoon.

Checkpoint FILIPINO, STEAKHOUSE **$$**
(National Hwy, Yunbing; mains P150-450; ☺7am-11pm; 🛜) Two restaurants, **Rocky's** and **Filete Isla Resto**, with their own kitchens and menus, share the open-air 2nd-floor space of the Checkpoint mini-mall at the 'major' intersection in Yunbing. Somewhat confusingly, you can order off both menus at once. Choices run the gamut from simple sandwiches to porterhouse steaks made with imported Australian beef. It's a pleasant spot with mountain views.

The Filete Isla Resto chef won the 'best main course' (for a fish dish) at the Camiguin lanzones festival in 2013.

ℹ Information

Philippine National Bank (PNB) and Landbank in Mambajao have unreliable ATMs; the PNB accepts Mastercard. PNB changes US dollars but only accepts extremely crisp bills US$5 and above (Swiss francs accepted but travellers report difficulty changing euros). A better option is **All in One Island**, a store on the road between the Sector 9 Hotel & Bar and church, which changes US dollars and euros at good rates.

Drachir's Internet (Rizal St, Mambajao; ☺8am-11pm) By the Shell station in town; unreliable opening time but purportedly the fastest internet on the island (per hr P35).

Tourist Office (📋088-387 1097; www.camiguin.gov.ph; Provincial Capitol Bldg; ☺8am-5pm Mon-Fri) Part of a complex of government buildings up a hill just southwest of Mambajao.

ℹ Getting There & Away

AIR
Cebu Pacific (📋88-387 0593; National Hwy, Mambajao; ☺8am-5pm Mon-Sat, 8am-noon Sun) flies a 60-plus passenger single-prop daily between Mambajao and Cebu (from P700 to P3500, 30 minutes, 7.20am). The ticketing office is across the street from the old Landbank near the PNB. There's a 15kg limit on checked-in baggage and weather delays aren't uncommon.

BOAT
Camiguin has two functioning ports relevant to travellers: **Benoni**, 18km south of Mambajao, where ferries connect to Balingoan on the mainland, and **Balbagon**, only a few kilometres south of town, with connections to Cebu and Jagna on Bohol.

Boats ply the channel between Benoni and Balingoan roughly hourly from 4am until 5pm (P170, 1¼ hours). If whitecaps are visible the crossing can be unpleasant in the smaller and less-seaworthy-looking ferry. Before leaving, local kids climb up the outside of the boats and leap into the water soliciting for tips.

There's an on-again, much more often off-again Oceanjet fastcraft service between Cagayan de Oro and Benoni and then from Benoni to Jagna on Bohol. Both legs cost P600 and take two hours. Check with resorts (via email, not websites which often contain outdated information) for the latest but do not depend on this.

From the Balbagon pier, Lite Shipping has a daily roll-on, roll-off (RORO) ferry to Cebu (P880, 11 hours, 7pm); unfortunately, its ferry (P425, 3½ hours, 8am) to Jagna is unreliable, especially during the low season.

ℹ Getting Around

The road around the island is 64km long and paved, so it's possible to make the circuit in a few hours. For ease of travel and access to places that jeepneys and *motorellas* (the local term for a version of a motorised tricycle) don't go, the best option is to rent a motorcycle (P300 to P500); be sure to wear a helmet and carry your license. Less thrilling but convenient is to hire a multicab that can comfortably seat six (P1500).

Air-con minivans, jeepneys, *motorellas* and multicabs meet arriving boats in Benoni to transport passengers to Mambajao (P30, 30 minutes). A special ride to Mambajao costs P100 to P150; to the resorts north of Mambajao you'll pay P250 to P500. Then from Mambajao, it's easy to hop on a 'westbound' *motorella* (these are red; 'eastbound' *motorellas* are green) for the majority of resorts. Getting around on these is simple, convenient and cheap (P9).

Butuan
📋085 / POP 309,700
Historical and archaeological interest aside, this city sprawled along the banks of the Agusan River, 9km south of the coast, is a typical provincial city in every way – traffic-clogged, exhaust-fume-filled and growing. It is, however, a logical stop, even for a night, if you're travelling by boat and bus between the islands of Camiguin and Siargao. A major port to some degree since at least the 4th century, Butuan is widely recognised as the earliest-known place of settlement and sea trade in the Philippines. And like Limasawa in Leyte, Butuan claims the honour of the

first Mass (8 April 1521) held by Magellan on Philippine soil at nearby **Magallanes**, north of the city at the mouth of the Agusan River; a memorial marks the spot.

◉ Sights

Balangay Shrine Museum
MUSEUM

(⊙ 8.30am-4.30pm Mon-Sat) FREE Towards the airport, at barangay Libertad, is the Balangay Shrine Museum, home to the remains of a *balangay* (seagoing outrigger boat) dating from 321, one of the oldest-known artifacts in the Philippines. (The word 'barangay' in fact derives from *balangay,* as the boats were big enough to move whole communities of settlers in one journey.) Unearthed a few metres away are several coffins dating to the 13th and 14th centuries. A tricycle (P50) will take you to the site.

⊨ Sleeping

VCDU Prince Hotel
HOTEL $

(☑ 085-342 7587; www.vcduprincehotel.com.ph; Montilla Blvd; s/d P800/P1000; ❋ ❈) Centrally located, this high-rise offers good value even if rooms are minuscule.

Hensonly Plaza Lodge
LODGE $

(☑ 085-342 5866; San Francisco St; r with share/private bath P180/450; ❋) No frills budget option.

Almont Inland Resort
RESORT $$$

(☑ 085-342 7414; www.almont.com.ph; JC Aquino Ave; r incl breakfast P3000; ❋ ❈ ⊷) For those looking from some comfort and outdoor space.

✖ Eating

There are a handful of fast-food joints in the Rizal Park area, as well as in **Gaisano Mall**, a few kilometres west of the centre on JC Aquino Ave and in the new and flashy **Robinsons Place** mall a few kilometres further west from there.

Weegols Grill Haus
FILIPINO $$

(Montilla Blvd; mains P160) A Butuan institution.

Rosarios
CHINESE, FILIPINO $$

(JC Aquino St; mains from P170) A good choice for Chinese, Filipino and seafood dishes.

❶ Getting There & Away

AIR

The airport, 10km west of the city centre, is reachable by taxi (P200) or tricycle (P150).

Cebu Pacific and PAL have several flights a day from Manila and Cebu Pacific has direct flights to Cebu.

BOAT

Butuan's main port area is at Nasipit, about 24km west of town. Jeepneys run between Nasipit and Butuan (30 minutes). 2GO has boats running every Friday to Manila (from P940, 22 hours) and every Sunday to Cebu (from P470, 10 hours).

BUS

The bus terminal is 3.5km north of the city centre; plenty of tricycles wait to ferry you into town. The last air-con bus for Davao leaves around 2.30pm; however, ordinary buses leave periodically 24 hours. The following table refers to air-con buses.

DESTINATION	FARE (P)	DURATION (HR)
Balingoan	201	3
Cagayan de Oro	325	4½
Davao	500	7¼
Surigao	205	3

Surigao

☑ 086 / POP 140,500

For those heading to Siargao Island, this fairly nondescript, gridlocked city, the capital of Surigao del Norte Province, is usually a necessary overnight stop (unless flying directly). The town plaza is the centre of activity, hosting everything from impromptu chess matches to first dates, while a portion of the long waterfront boulevard is lined with makeshift alfresco KTV bars and nighttime second-hand clothing stalls. Attractions in the area include **Silop Cave**, 7km away, with its 12 entrances leading to a big central chamber; **Day-asin**, a floating village, 5km from the city; and **Mati**, to the south, where the Mamanwas people have created a 'village' to showcase their culture. There are also several beaches nearby, including **Mabua Pebble Beach**, where you can spend a few hours waiting for your outbound flight.

Filipino and international environmental organisations as well as local communities have protested nickel mining in the province of Surigao del Sur to the south of the city.

⊨ Sleeping

E.Y. Miner Suites
HOTEL $

(☑ 086-826 5440; Navarro St; s P795, d P895-1450; ❋ ❈) The mirrored glass facade shouts Chi-

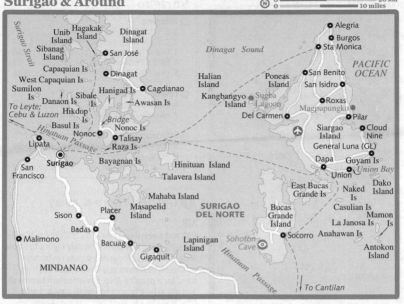

nese office building and the lobby's plastic ambience screams massage parlour. However, this place and its newer **sister hotel** ([☎]086-826 6480; Borromeo St; r P1100) (it has a shiny, slightly kitschy lobby and dining area) of the same name on Borromeo St offer the best-value accommodation within walking distance of the port.

Bathrooms in the Navarro location are cramped, the sort where you could practically shower on the toilet seat.

Metro Pension Plaza   HOTEL **$**
([☎]086-231 9899; Navarro St; s/d P500/800; [✱][☎]) The neatly dressed security guard and painted facade are promising. However, most rooms are poorly lit and gloomy. The showers are cold and the toilets seat-free, but the cable TVs are top-notch. Wi-fi only in the outdoor 'lobby' area.

Hotel Tavern   HOTEL **$$**
([☎]0918 963 6184, 086-826 8566; www.hoteltavern.com; Borromeo St; r incl breakfast P1900-3600; [✱][@][☎]) The most upscale place in Surigao and the only hotel to take advantage of the city's waterfront location. More sophisticated sea-view rooms in the annex are worth the price. In addition there's a outdoor bar (open 5pm to 1am) with live music most nights of the week, and a coffee shop (open

6am to 1am). Free airport transfers are a bonus.

One Hive Hotel & Suites   HOTEL **$$**
([☎]086-232 0065; www.onehivehotel.com; Rizal St; s/d incl breakfast P1200/1500; [✱][☎]) Newly opened and boasting an elevator (a big amenity in these parts), rooms in the sterile and efficient five-storey Hive are small and simply furnished. The menu of the 2nd-floor **restaurant** (7am to 9pm) has Filipino, Japanese and Korean dishes (mains P150).

✕ Eating

The restaurant at the Hotel Tavern is comfortable but ordinary. Fast-food restaurants are clustered on the southwest side of the plaza on Rizal St and a few are in the **Gaisano Mall** (Figaro Cafe is a good place to relax while waiting for a bus) next to the bus terminal; an appetising row of **fruit stalls** lines the east side of the plaza (Magallanes St). **Barbecue stalls** (open at night) can be found on Borromeo St around the pier.

★ **Calda's Pizzeria**   PIZZA **$$**
(Borromeo St; pizza P180; ⊙9am-midnight) Excellent and massive thin-crust pizzas with a few tables and waterfront boulevard seating. 'Extra super-size' pies are a ridiculous 36 inches with 50 slices.

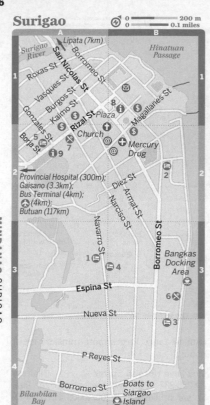

Surigao

Getting There & Away

AIR

PAL and Cebu Pacific have daily flights to Manila; the latter also has several weekly flights to Cebu. A caveat: PAL's stringent luggage restrictions on this flight means you should have cash on hand for a penalty. Also, pay attention to arrival and departure times in order to connect with boat transfers to and from Siargao. Airline announcements are piped in to **Basti's** (Airport; mains P75-200), a coffee shop with pastries and an extensive food menu just inside the airport entrance. Catch a tricycle (P30) or jeepney (P10) to the airport, 5km west of the town centre.

BOAT

The most important boat connection for travellers is Siargao. And the most recommended boat for relative comfort (if you opt for air-con have a sweater handy and ear plugs for the high-volume action movie) and a reasonable departure time is the 11.45am *Fortune Angel* (P240, 2½ hours) leaving from the **main pier** (aka Eva Macapagal Terminal, Borromeo St), 2km south of the plaza. In bad weather, opt for the daily roll-on, roll-off (RORO) ferry (P250, four hours, 6am), which also uses the main pier. Other options are the 5.30am and 6am bangkas leaving from the **boulevard area** in front of the Hotel Tavern.

If your destination on Siargao is Burgos in the north, an option is to take the noon bangka (P200) to Santa Monica from **Punta Bilang Bilang**, a short walk southwest from the main pier.

Cebu Cokaliong Shipping has trips daily except Monday at 7pm (from P825).

Dinagat Bangkas (P100) for San José on the island of Dinagat leave at approximately 7am, 9am and noon from the boulevard area in front of the Hotel Tavern.

Leyte ROROs serving the Southern Leyte towns of San Ricardo (P140, 1¼ hours, 12.30am, 3am and 2pm) and Liloan (P300, four hours,

Island's Seafood Restaurant
SEAFOOD, FILIPINO **$$**

(Rizal St; mains P160; 🖥) A small, bustling, modern place serving up seafood by weight (*lapu-lapu;* grouper; P80 per 100g) and standard meat and chicken dishes.

Information

There are several banks with ATMs (get cash before heading to Siargao) around the plaza (the main port terminal also has a Metrobank ATM) and internet cafes are scattered around town.

Surigao City Tourism Office (☏086-Luneta 826 8064; www.surigaocity.gov.ph; Luneta Park; ◷8am-5pm) Conveniently located in the central plaza, but don't expect more than maps and brochures here.

Surigao del Norte Provincial Tourism Office (☏086-231 9271; www.surigaodelsur.gov.ph; Rizal St) For information about travel elsewhere in the region; located by the city grandstand (basketball courts and soccer fields).

6.30am, 11am, 1pm, 6pm and midnight) leave from the pier in Lipata, 8km west of Surigao.

BUS

The bus terminal is next to the new Gaisano Mall about 4½km west of town and around 50m before the airport; a jeepney to or from the pier costs P10 and a tricycle around P30. For Cagayan de Oro or Balingoan (for boats to Camiguin), you must change buses in Butuan. Minivans also service the destinations listed here.

DESTINATION	FARE (P)	DURATION (HR)	FREQUENCY
Butuan	205	3	every half-hour or so
Davao	500	8	hourly
Tagum	580	8½	9pm
Tandag	315	5	when full

Siargao

Initially drawn to Siargao (shar-*gow*) by good year-round waves and a tranquillity and beauty lost in other Philippine islands, a small group of passionate Aussie, American and European surfers are still living the good life. There's been an uptick of recent development in the form of several mid-sized condos and hotels; however, laid-back resorts happily making do with the tourists who find them are still the norm. Besides surfers looking for the next challenge on their international *wanderjahr,* low-key do-it-yourself types do well here. There are rock pools, mangrove swamps, offshore islands with strange rock formations and wildlife, waterfalls, forests and hammock sitting, usually the coda to any day.

The port is in the main township of Dapa. On arrival you'll probably want to head straight over towards one of the resorts located along the newly paved (and unnecessarily wide) road between General Luna (known locally as GL) and 'Cloud Nine'.

🏃 Activities

Surfing is year-round, but generally considered best from August to November when there are big swells as a result of typhoon winds. The period from December to April has some strong crosswinds, while from May to July the surf tends to be lighter. Surfboard rental can be arranged at resorts around the island. Booties are highly recommended to protect your feet, since the break is along a reef, albeit a 'soft' one. **Stand-up paddle-boarding** is becoming more popular and many resorts rent boards and offer lessons.

Deep caves, such as the Blue Cathedral, mean that some of the more interesting dives in the area are for the experienced only. However, in general there's excellent visibility and a large number of sites making it a good place to learn. **Palaka Siargao Dive Center** (📞 0918 626 2303; www.palakadivecenter. com; General Luna), owned and operated by an enthusiastic and professional Frenchman, is located on the beachfront just behind the public market in Dapa (it has a cool little cafe). Palaka also runs free diving clinics, and an increasingly popular course for surfers.

Siargao is also one of the few places in the country with organised **deep-sea fishing** (day trip for up to three people P5000); by all accounts it's top-notch. Reeling in a 130kg sailfish isn't uncommon – mahi-mahi and Spanish mackerel are also on the menu. The fishing's generally good year-round, although seas can be rough December through February. Contact **Junior Gonzalez** (📞 0920 772 8875), who also offers accommodation at his home in Pilar.

Golfers should head to the **golf course** (18-holes per person incl clubs, balls & tees P650) beneath the Villa Maya Resort (p361). This narrow slice of property has been transformed into a par-three course with nine distinct holes (the longest is 145m). It's open year-round and is the only course open to the public in Siargao. Only one group can play at a time and most choose to play a full 18, which means there's usually only a morning and afternoon tee time.

🎉 Festivals & Events

Siargao Cup SPORT

This surfing competition, one of the largest international sporting events in the country (over 8000 people attended in 2014), is held at Cloud Nine in late September or early October. The **Filipino National Cup**, another competitive surfing event, is usually the week before.

> ### ℹ SIARGAO WEATHER
>
> Unlike other parts of Mindanao, and Manila for that matter, the wet season on Siargao coincides with the northeast *amihan,* roughly from December to March. The dry season, when the *habagat* winds blow from the southwest, is from June to September.

ⓘ Information

Wherever you are on the island, room rates increase during surfing tournaments and Holy Week. The two banks in Dapa – Green Bank and Cantilan Bank – should not be relied upon for cash withdrawals (some report Green Bank accepting foreign Visa cards). Both Dapa and General Luna each have at least one internet cafe; most resorts have wi-fi and some have a stand-alone computer with internet access.

ⓘ Getting There & Away

AIR
Cebu Pacific has daily (50 minutes, 12.45pm) direct flights between Cebu and Siargao's **Sayak airport** near Del Carmen. Another option is to fly from Manila to Surigao and connect by boat from there. A few *habal-habal* (motorcycle taxis) wait outside the airport's gates for arrivals; however, it might be more convenient to arrange transport in advance with your accommodation.

BOAT
Three early-morning boats leave from Dapa to Surigao (all departure times are approximate): 5.30am is a small, local-style bangka; the 5.45am *Fortune Angel* (2½ hours) with an indoor air-con cabin is most recommended; the 6am Montenegro lines boat is a roll-on, roll-off (RORO) ferry. The 10.30am boat is the slowest. You can purchase tickets (P270) the morning of departure. The early-morning boats allow you to connect to flights in Surigao or travel by bus to Cagayan de Oro and Davao in a single day (these would be long, tiring days); however, it means leaving Cloud Nine extremely early. Arrange a motorcycle to Dapa through your accommodation.

Bangkas to Socorro on Bucas Grande leave from the municipal wharf next to the main one.

ⓘ Getting Around

Jeepneys run from Dapa to GL (one hour); a better option is to hop on a *habal-habal* (motorcycles large enough to seat more than one passenger with bags and usually jerry-rigged with a canopy to guard against the elements) to GL or the nearby resorts (P100 to P200, 20 minutes) or Cloud Nine (P150 to P300, 30 minutes). Price depends on your negotiating skills and time of day (early morning trips always P300). Tricycles cost nearly the same but are much slower. A great way to spend the day is to tour the island on your own (the majority of the 'circumferential road' is now paved); the going rate for motorcycle hire is around P300 for half a day to P500 for the day.

General Luna & Around
POP 15,000

Several blocks of dirt roads, dilapidated buildings and a few eateries ending in a public beach lined with a row of *sari-sari* (neighbourhood) stores and barbecue shacks: that's General Luna, and to the visitor who stays at one of the resorts on Cloud Nine, it might as well be the big city. At the time of research, a surfing museum was being built next to the new police station near the sandy waterfront. There are several surfing breaks south of GL reached by bangka, including a few around offshore islands. A river perfect for swimming during high tide is near the village of Union, between GL and Cloud Nine.

🛏 Sleeping

Some of the places between GL and Cloud Nine are on a narrow sandy beach, unfortunately not suited for swimming. The area is experiencing something of a mini construction boom, including a few large condo and hotel developments. The ultra-luxurious Dedon Island Resort is around 8km southwest of GL.

Kermit Surf Resort HOTEL $
(☑0915 606 4227; www.kermitsiargao.com; dm P350, d with fan/air-con P900/1250; ❋🛜) Located down a quiet road just northeast and inland from the centre of GL, Swiss-Italian owned Kermit is a deservedly popular choice for budget-minded surfers closed out of Cloud Nine. In addition to the well-maintained dorm there are several large stand-alone thatch-roofed cottages with tile floors and large, modern bathrooms. Pizza and pasta are the restaurant's specialties.

Paglaom Hostel HOSTEL $
(☑0947 768 5312; dm P250; 🛜) Rock-bottom prices for rock-hard beds (well, very thin mattresses). Two semi-enclosed areas with 10 bunks each with mosquito nets; only one ceiling fan! Cold showers, seatless toilets; separate kitchen area for guests use. But creature comforts of course aren't the draw; get to know your bunkmates in the open-air hang-out area.

★ Buddha's Surf Resort HOTEL $$
(☑0919 945 6789; www.siargaosurf.com; r incl breakfast P2200-2600; ❋🛜) This spacious property on the inland-side of the road has a sophisticated, contemporary island vibe.

The five rooms are sparsely furnished with flat-screen TVs and nice bathrooms and the large open-air pavilion restaurant has a Thai-influenced menu (a traditional pig roast can be prepared upon request). Towering palm trees provide shade over the manicured lawn.

Turtle Surf Camp
HOTEL $$

(☑ 0939 569 2498; www.surfcampsiargao.com; s/d with fan P1600/1800, with air-con P1800/1950; ❄️ 🛜 🏊) Intimate and cool, this small spot with only three rooms is especially good for groups of surfing friends. Minimally designed concrete rooms have modern features and you can cool off in the small pool or watch videos in the little lounge. A family room (with fan/air-con P3900/4200) with its own lounge sleeps four.

One of the few places on Siargao to offer kite-surfing lessons.

Siargao Inn Beach Resort
BUNGALOW $$

(☑ 0999 889 9988; www.siargao-inn.com; r P1800-3900; ❄️ 🛜) Owned and operated by a young friendly couple, one of whom is a top surfer who can school you on the basics, this laid-back place has a number of simple cottages with nipa roofs and mahogany floors and walls; the bathrooms are especially nice, and there's a pleasant beachside restaurant-bar.

Chill Out Siargao
COTTAGES $$

(☑ 0947 229 5128; www.chilloutsiargao.com; r with fan/air-con P1500/2500; 🛜) Newly opened beachfront spot with four nipa-roofed cottages with high-end furnishings. The young Swedish owners have plans for a total of 10 to 12 rooms. A wooden shack with room for two stools serves as a charming makeshift bar.

Villa Solaria
COTTAGES $$

(☑ 0921 725 3331; www.villa-solaria.com; r P1200; 🛜) New owners were taking over this property at the time of our research. Worth checking in, however, since Solaria has tastefully designed compact thatch-roofed cottages lining a nicely landscaped garden. Off the road with no direct beachfront access.

★ Kalinaw Resort
BEACH RESORT $$$

(☑ 0921 320 0442; www.kalinawresort.com; villas for 2 incl breakfast from P9900; ❄️ 🛜 🏊) The five villas of this French-owned resort could make the centrefold of any contemporary design magazine. Massive and whimsical bathrooms are the highlight, but minimal-

ism reigns throughout. A refreshing breeze often blows through the sophisticated open-air restaurant (mains P440 to P600), which does the best pizza (only after 7pm) on the island.

Isla Cabana
RESORT $$$

(☑ 0928 559 5244; www.islacabanaresort.com; r incl breakfast P4800-6400; ❄️ 🛜 🏊) High marks go to the design of the large cabanas at this new upscale development. Only two face the water, the rest open inward onto a narrow, landscaped sandy path that ends at the pool (no shade) and beach (exists at low tide). Less personal intimacy than elsewhere; occasionally hosts weddings and banquets.

Palm Paradise Island Resort
RESORT $$$

(formerly Island Dream; ☑ 0939 891 4538; www.islandreamsiargao.com; cottages P4000; ❄️ 🛜 🏊) The bathrooms in these villas are equal in size to the bedrooms, with stone floors, windows to the ceiling and tubs a honeymoon couple would love. Each has its own large porch and surrounds a well-manicured lawn and pool with an open-air restaurant-lounge fronting the road.

The downsides are no shade in the pool area, daytime nonguests might diminsh the feeling of privacy, and while the staff are well-meaning, service can be slow.

🍴 Eating & Drinking

All of the resorts have restaurants and most welcome nonguests; Kalinaw is the best. Barbecue shacks line the town beachfront and there are a few basic eateries, really just informal places with an array of dishes lined up buffet-style on the street.

Ronaldo's
FILIPINO $

(mains P75-125; ⏱ 7am-10pm; 🛜) Cheap juices, shakes and noodles, including more than a dozen varieties of *pansit*, are the specialty at this fan-cooled open-air place.

Lulay Grill
BARBECUE $

(skewer P15; ⏱ 9am-10pm) Indistinguishable from the other barbecue shacks lining the town beach, for whatever reason this is the one where expats congregate in the early evening.

Nine Bar
BAR

A handsomely built expat favourite on the road between GL and Cloud Nine with a large-screen TV showing British Commonwealth sports. Excllent burgers as well.

Jungle Disco NIGHTCLUB

(Tattoo; ⏰8pm-late Thu-Sat) A motley mix of locals, expats and travellers get down and dirty on, appropriately enough, a dirt dance floor.

Cloud Nine

Solidly ensconced in the international surfing circuit (if it's April it's Fiji, December, Costa Rica etc), the surf break at Cloud Nine is unmistakably marked by the raised walkway and three-storey wood pavilion with front-row seats to the action. It's a friendly and open surfing community, with plenty of up-and-coming local Filipinos welcoming foreigners and beginners alike. There are several other breaks for the experienced, accessible by bangka, including **Rock Island**, visible from the Cloud Nine beach, and at least a dozen good beaches are within an hour by boat or road.

All the resorts here can help organise day tours and boat trips as well as arrange surf lessons (P500 per hour, including equipment) and board rental (P300 per half-day). Or stop by **Hippie's Surf Shop** (www.surfshopsiargao.com; ⏰6am-6pm) just before the Ocean 101 Beach Resort; Hippie also teaches yoga classes (P200) on many mornings.

🛏 Sleeping & Eating

Ocean 101 Beach Resort HOTEL $

(☑0910 848 0893; www.ocean101cloud9. com; r with fan P500-1300, with air-con P1400-2500, villa for 2/4 P6000/9000; ❄@🛜) Budget-conscious surfers end up at this compound built on a seawall a short walk north of the Cloud Nine break. Two main buildings and a simple eatery front a well-trimmed lawn, and a low-slung building with basic, concrete rooms leads out towards the road; nicely furnished rooms with high ceilings, big bathrooms and sea-view balconies are in front.

It's a high-volume operation which means you're more likely to find others to share the cost of a boat trip here. A couple of hammocks and a two-storey waterfront pavilion provide extra lounging space. The food at the **restaurant** (mains P100 to P300) is ordinary (though the waitstaff friendly) and you might have to pony up for the cost of hand soap.

Wayfarer's HOTEL $

(www.wayfarerscloud9.com; r with fan/air-con P650/P950; ❄🛜) Sure, it has zero atmos-phere and the 'office' looks like a storage closet, but rooms in this low-slung building are perfectly acceptable with hot water and fairly modern furnishings. Lack of an inviting common space means you'll have to find elsewhere to spend your non-sleeping hours.

Siargao Island Emerald House COTTAGES $$

(☑0949 161 9265; www.emeraldhousevillage.com; r P1000, cottage P1400-2500; 🛜) A large and leafy property on the inland side of the road (still under construction during our visit), with a mix of attractively designed and stylishly furnished cottages, is excellent value. From a small loft apartment to a large house with full kitchen, a variety of layouts are available. Discounts for weekly and monthly stays.

Boardwalk at Cloud 9 HOTEL $$

(☑0909 682 1875; reaganboardwalk@yahoo.com; r with fan/air-con P1500/2500; ❄🛜) Under new management, this once popular place with absolutely prime real estate directly in front of the Cloud Nine pavilion is struggling. The spacious if generic rooms are standard hotel-type. A few cheaper basic rooms are in a small native-style building in back.

★**Sagana Beach Resort** RESORT $$$

(☑0919 809 5769; www.cloud9surf.com; per person incl 3 meals P3300; ❄🛜❄) 🚭 This low-key, high-end resort occupies prime beachfront real estate steps away from the Cloud Nine pavilion. Each of the Balinese-inspired cottages features dark-wood floors, porches with hammocks and large bathrooms. Owners Jerry and Susan Deegan are warm and knowledgeable about virtually everything happening on the island. Meals, dinners especially, are worth the price alone; in our opinion it has the best food on the island.

There's a small saltwater pool to cool off in. Generally closed December through February. Dinner reservations for nonguests should be made in advance (mains P440).

Kawayan Resort COTTAGE $$$

(☑0920 364 0663; www.kawayansiargaoresort. com; r incl breakfast P6500; ❄🛜) Just behind the highly recommended restaurant of the same name are a few beautifully crafted, sophisticated wood cottages, with stone-lined outdoor showers and toilets with palm fronds and trees poking through. It's on the opposite side of the road as the beach in a leafy garden.

Kawayan's **restaurant** (P350-650; ⏰7am-2pm & 6-9.30pm) does French-, Basque-,

MINDANAO SIARGAO

Moroccan- and Filipino-inspired cuisine (Moroccan tagine is the specialty) served in a sumptuously furnished all-wood dining area; the **bar** area with billiard table stays open late.

Villa Maya Resort & Golf Course　　　　GUESTHOUSE $$$
(☑ 0908 875 3292; www.siargaovilla.com; r incl breakfast from P3500; ❋ ☎) Perched on a hill overlooking the golf course (p357) is this large villa which resembles a suburban Mc-Mansion. The three large rooms, more like apartments, are very tastefully furnished and feel quite homey. Nonguests can eat and drink here – the Israeli owner is known for his shwarma.

To find it, carry on past the last resort at Cloud Nine and hang a left at the end of the road; it's less than a kilometre away.

Northern Siargao

On the road north from Dapa you pass through barangay **Pilar**, which is largely built on stilts over mangrove flats; **Blue Cathedral** is a dive site off the coast. Not far north of Pilar is **Magpupungko**, a beach with a number of crystal-clear swimming holes at low tide; it's only a half-hour boat ride (per boat P800) from Cloud Nine, and is crowded with locals on weekends.

When you approach the lovely little town of **Burgos** from the south, it's worth stopping at the top of the rise in the road, taking in the view of the crescent-shaped beach and light-blue waters below. It's quite an inspiring sight. The waves are excellent, involving long paddles out and reef breaks (six within 1km), good for experienced surfers year-round. Locals might be willing to let you tag along on fishing trips.

Bohemian Bungalows (☑ 0947 551 4528; www.bohemianbungalows.com; r P750) has a room on the 2nd floor of a small charming house and a separate rondavel guesthouse two doors down. It's a self-described 'getaway for hippies and surfers' and caters to long-term guests. The handy and talented caretaker prepares meals including homemade bread. A few kilometres south of Burgos in barangay Pacifico is **Jafe Surf & Sail Camp Resort** (☑ 0919 991 2685; www.jaferesort.com; s/d with fan P300/550, r with air-con P900; ❋), a large octagonal-shaped house with a restaurant, beachfront property and nearby surf breaks.

Vans (P2000) or *habal-habals* (P550) can transfer you to any place in the area from Dapa; the trip is over an hour. In theory, a 5am bangka (P250, three hours) leaves from nearby Santa Monica for Surigao on the mainland; however, this is unreliable.

On the western side of Siargao, around 10km from the airport, **Del Carmen** is the gateway for highly recommended boat trips through the **mangrove swamps** of Caob and to picturesque **Sugba lagoon** (an even better choice these days than the more high-profile Sohoton Cave and Lagoon trip, which involves a long boat transfer and potentially boatloads of other tourists). Mornings during high tide is the best time to visit. Get in touch with **Gill Cariaga** (☑ 0921 339 7694; gill.cariaga@gmail.com) at **Krokodelios** (mains P75-340; ◷ 9am-9pm), his waterfront restaurant in Del Carmen (open late Wednesday and Friday nights for dancing and a 'night cafe' in the parking lot). Del Carmen is known for its enormous farmed crabs, which you can order here. Motorised boat trips through the mangroves to the lagoon cost P1600 plus an additional P100 per person environmental fee; bring your own snorkel equipment. Or you can take a paddleboat (per person P250) or motorboat (for up to six people P600) to the mangroves only. Alternatively, many resorts in GL and Cloud Nine can arrange trips (including transfer by van for around P2000). Gill can also arrange **homestays** in Del Carmen for P1500 for a double room. Two daily bangkas (P225, 2½ hours, 6am and 10am) travel from Del Carmen to Surigao.

MINDANAO SIARGAO

Islands Near Siargao

Just off the southern coast of Siargao is the tiny white-sand-and-palm-fringed islet of Guyam (Gilligan's Island); the bigger Dako with its beautiful beach, snorkelling and diving; and Naked Island, a white sand spit with zero shade. A round-trip bangka to one or two runs between P1000 and P1500 and to all three between P2000 and P3000.

There are surf breaks (and excellent snorkelling) around La Janosa and Mamon Islands, and it's possible to paddle a surfboard between the two. You can spend the night in one of the very primitive cottages on La Janosa. To get here, hire a bangka from the pier at GL. Prices depend on distance and time, but expect to pay around P1500 per person.

South of Siargao, Bucas Grande is worth visiting for the Sohoton Cave and Lagoon, not to be confused with the park of the same name in southern Samar. This inland lake with all kinds of weird marine creatures and nonstinging jellyfish has Chocolate Hills–like mounds rising like the humps of an underwater monster and is accessible only during low tide. Surprisingly, for such a relatively remote location it can get crowded with boatloads of Filipino tourists. An all-day trip from GL or Cloud Nine, arranged through one of the resorts, costs around P2000 per person. Those prone to sea-sickness might want to consider conditions for the crossing.

Though it's much larger than Siargao and closer to the mainland, the island of Dinagat (nah-gat) sees few visitors, primarily because accommodation is limited. The island is home to several fishing communities and the northwest coast is especially picturesque, featuring jungle-clad karst formations jutting out of turquoise waters. During Holy Week, pilgrims visit the twin lakes of Bababu on an islet near Basilia, believing the waters have curative powers. Three daily bangkas (P100, four hours) leave at 8am, 10am and noon from in front of the Hotel Tavern (p355) in Surigao for San José on Dinagat.

SOUTHERN MINDANAO

The area around Davao is ripe for adventures, from climbing Mt Apo and hiking opportunities in the Compostela Valley to exploring the long coastline, both north and south of the city, not to mention several offshore islands. It sees few foreign travellers, but does get more than its fair share of weekending Davaoeños. Lake Sebu is an out-of-the-way spot to experience tribal cultures, not to mention the beauty of the countryside. Wherever you travel in the region, roadside stands are piled high with distinctive fruits such as marang, mangosteen, rhambutan, lanzones, doco (a variety of the former) and of course durian (there are more than eight varieties available), not to mention more ordinary fruits (bananas, pineapples and papayas are farmed on an industrial scale).

Davao

☏ 082 / POP 1,444,300

This sprawling city, the culinary, cultural, economic and commercial capital of the south is, for better or worse, becoming more like Manila. More traffic, more malls, more multinationals, more subdivisions hidden behind security gates. However, Mt Apo looms majestically in the distance symbolising the typical Davaoeños dual citizenship as both an urbanite and someone deeply rooted to the land outside the city. Locals know Davao (dah-*bow*, and sometimes spelt 'Dabaw') has more than enough action to keep them satisfied, and yet it's only a short drive or boat ride to forested slopes and white-sand beaches.

Able to hold out against the invading Spaniards until the mid-19th century, the city is an interesting mix of Muslim, Chinese, tribal and even Japanese influences – the latter because of early abaca-processing warehouses in the area and less happily because of WWII. Predominantly Christian, the city has seen its share of hard times, especially in the 1980s when there was guerrilla fighting in the streets. These days there's also a significant number of South Indians, many studying at Davao Doctor's Hospital; but there are few Korean expats, it's said because of the city's strict anti-smoking laws.

While Davao continues to expand, especially south towards Toril, much of the land outside the city has been turned over to massive plantations growing export quantities of pineapples, bananas and citrus.

◉ Sights & Activities

Some key streets are confusingly referred to by both old and new names. The city sprawls along the Davao Gulf to the south and the older city centre is bounded by the Davao River to the west.

For information on outdoor activities, especially hiking and climbing Mt Apo, stop by **Edge Outdoor Shop** (☑082-300 0384; Wheels N More Compound, JP Laurel Ave; ◷5-9pm), owned by Erwin 'Pastor' Emata, who made one of the fastest ascents of Everest in 2007.

Museo Dabawenyo   MUSEUM
(cnr A Pichon & CM Recto Sts; ◷9am-5.45pm Mon-Fri) **FREE** An excellent museum with two floors of well-designed galleries exploring the complex patchwork of indigenous tribal groups, religions and ethnicities of Davao and Mindanao as a whole. Especially interesting are the photographic exhibitions documenting both the Japanese and American occupations of the city.

Davao Crocodile Park   ZOO
(☑082-286 1054; www.adventurephilippines.ph; admission P300; ◷8am-6pm Mon-Thu, to 7pm Fri-Sun) Around 5km north of the city centre is this large complex of facilities spread out along the Davao River. A combination conservation centre and zoo, there are croc 'shows', including feeding sessions, tightrope walking, a cultural show and excellent riverfront restaurant serving up crocodile four ways – sizzling, pasta, omelette and plain old steak – as well as other meats (including ostrich) and seafood. Also runs a zipline (P300) in the hills nearby with panoramic views.

Kublai's Gallery   ART GALLERY
(Yahu Plaza, cnr Magsaysay Ave & Bangoy St; ◷9am-6pm) An unconventional setting for a fine-art gallery, paintings by artist Kublai Millan fill the walls of this large space. Take an elevator to the 4th or 5th floor of this ordinary Chinatown shopping plaza. See p372 for more information on Millan.

People's Park   PARK
(◷5.30-10am & 3-11pm) **FREE** A family-friendly expanse of more concrete than green space with larger-than-life-sized sculptures of native peoples of Mindanao, all designed by artist Kublai Millan.

Dabaw Museum   MUSEUM
(admission P20; ◷9am-5pm Mon-Sat) This museum, next to the Waterfront Insular Hotel northeast of downtown, has a good collection of tribal weavings and artifacts from most of the Mindanao tribes.

Bankerohan Public Market   MARKET
(cnr A Pichon St & E Quirino Ave; ◷7am-noon & 4-6pm) Vibrant, chaotic, claustrophobic, smelly and resembling a sprawling shanty town, Bankerohan provides a taste of local flavour. Everything that appears in Filipino kitchens is sold here. Mornings are the best time to visit.

Davao Wildwater Adventures   RAFTING
(☑0920 954 6898, 082-221 7823; www.riverraftingphilippines.ph; per person P2000) If you're planning on rafting the Davao River west of the city, expect to spend some time in the water, especially in rapids that resemble washing machines after heavy rains. The best time to go for thrills is June or anytime in the wet season. This highly recommended professional outfit can be found on the same premises as the Crocodile Park.

✦ Festivals & Events

Kadayawan sa Dabaw Festival   CULTURAL
Much more than a simple harvest celebration, this festival held in the third week of August showcases tribal cultures, agriculture and crafts with street parades, performances and fantastic displays of fruit and flowers.

🛏 Sleeping

★**Ponce Suites**   HOTEL $
(☑082-227 9070; www.poncesuiteshotel.com; cnr 3 & 4 Rds, Doña Vicente Village, Bajada; s/d from P595/700; ❊🖥) Practically every inch of this mother-and-son-run hotel, inside and out, is covered with art – sculptures, poetry, photographs and paintings – all of it by the incredibly prolific Kublai Millan, who has transformed an otherwise ordinary building into a funky vision of hospitality. Rooms are ordinary motel quality, but the Gaudí-esque rooftop is the whimsical highlight of the Ponce Suites.

The lobby and bathrooms have been renovated and a half-day 'Kublai Art Tour' is offered. It's on a quiet block next door to a tennis club.

Green Windows Dormitel   HOTEL $
(☑082-300 3893; www.greenwindowsdormitel. com; 5th fl, FTC Tower, 1034 Mt Apo St; dm/d P188/1450; ❊🖥) A centrally located large high-risc with a wide range of accommodation options including good-value dorm rooms – many with flat-screen TVs, and all have lockers.

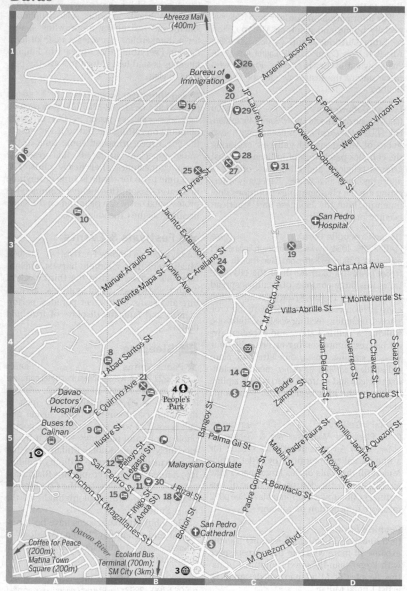

Las Casitas   HOTEL $
(☎082-222 3001; www.casitashotels.com; 185 J
Rizal St; s/d from P870/950; ☀☎) Sporting a
small comfortable lobby, downstairs coffee
shop and elevator, this downtown hotel is not
a bad base if space isn't a priority (look at sev-

eral rooms to avoid claustrophobia-inducing
ones) and you don't mind peeling paint.

Manor Hotel   HOTEL $
(☎082-221 2511; www.manorhoteldavao.com; A
Pichon St; s/d P750/850; ☀☎) The pleasant

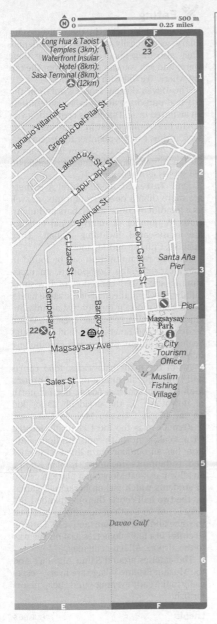

Davao

◎ Sights
1 Bankerohan Public Market A5
2 Kublai's Gallery E4
3 Museo Dabawenyo B6
4 People's Park.......................................B4

☉ Activities, Courses & Tours
5 Carabao Divers....................................F3
Edge Outdoor Shop ....(see 31)
6 South Shore Divers A2

⌂ Sleeping
7 Casa Leticia Boutique Hotel...............B5
8 Green Windows Dormitel....................B4
9 Hotel Galleria A5
10 L.A. Interline Hotel A3
11 Las Casitas B5
12 Legaspi Suites B5
13 Manor Hotel A5
14 Marco Polo Hotel C4
15 My Hotel B6
16 Ponce Suites.......................................B2
17 Royal Mandaya Hotel C5

⊗ Eating
18 Claude's Le Cafe De Ville B6
19 Gaisano Mall C3
20 Gomone C1
21 Hanoi Restaurant................................B4
22 Kong-Ai Vegetarian Centrum..............E4
Lachis ....(see 6)
23 Malagos Farmhouse............................F1
24 Tadakuna..C3
25 Tiny Kitchen...B2
26 Victoria Plaza Compound C1
27 Yellow Fin C2

☕ Drinking & Nightlife
28 Green Coffee C2
29 Pryce Tower...C2
30 Rizal Promenade..................................B5
31 Starr Club & Bar..................................C2

⌂ Shopping
32 Aldevinco Shopping Centre................C4
Got Heart Community
Shop ....(see 19)

ⓘ Information
Department of Tourism ....(see 29)

ground-floor coffee shop is a bonus at this small, professionally run downtown place. Some of the cosy – read, small – and efficient rooms with modern bathrooms and TVs have more light than others.

My Hotel ⠀⠀⠀⠀⠀⠀⠀⠀⠀⠀⠀HOTEL $
(☏ 082-222 2021; www.myhoteldavao.com; San Pedro St; s/d P800/1000; ❄️📶) A colourfully painted high-rise with sparkling-clean floors and large modern rooms; street-facing ones get good light.

Legaspi Suites ⠀⠀⠀⠀⠀⠀⠀⠀⠀HOTEL $$
(www.legaspisuites.com; 115 Pelayo St; s/d incl breakfast P1500/1700; ❄️📶) One of

downtown's best midrange options and one of the few anywhere in the city to be housed in a building with colonial-era architectural features. The red-tile Spanish-style roof and white clapboard exterior are a nice counterpoint to comfortable, modern rooms. A coffee shop, a spa and a travel agency are part of the same complex.

Casa Leticia Boutique Hotel HOTEL $$
(☎082-224 0501; www.casaleticia.com; J Camus St; s/d incl breakfast P2800/3000; ❄@📶) It's all business at this convenient choice opposite People's Park, which isn't necessarily a bad thing. Decorated with wicker furniture and outdated patterns, the rooms, especially the extra-narrow studios, aren't for everyone.

Hotel Galleria HOTEL $$
(☎082-221 2480; hotelgalleriadvo@yahoo.com; General Duterte St; r P1100-2100; ❄📶🏊) Something of a refuge in the crowded city centre, this professionally managed hotel's rooms surround an inner courtyard with a small pool; there's also a lobby cafe to hang out in. The rooms are modern and clean, though they're not especially spacious and could use some updating. No elevator so avoid a 3rd- or 4th-floor room.

L.A. Interline Hotel HOTEL $$
(☎082-222 5389; lainterline.hotel@yahoo.com.ph; cnr Mabini & Voyager Sts; r incl breakfast from P1800; ❄📶) This new and gleaming multistory hotel has a large lobby and nice cafe. F Torres St restaurants are within walking distance.

Marco Polo Hotel HOTEL $$$
(☎221 0888; www.davao.marcopolohotels.com; CM Recto Ave; r from P4800; ❄@📶🏊) The city's most luxurious hotel couldn't be more centrally located. Has several recommended restaurants.

Waterfront Insular Hotel HOTEL $$$
(☎082-233 2881; www.waterfronthotels.com.ph; r incl breakfast from P3500; ❄@📶🏊) If you want some breathing room, try this sprawling complex with gardens and a small private beach, 8km northeast of the city centre.

Royal Mandaya Hotel HOTEL $$$
(☎082-225 8888; www.theroyalmandayahotel.com; Palma Gil St; r incl breakfast from P3000; ❄@📶🏊) Large convention-style hotel in the centre of old downtown, with a nice restaurant.

Eating

Davaoeños take pride in their diverse culinary scene, easily the best in Mindanao. They also brag about the quality of their water and say you can drink it from the tap anywhere. We did with no worries.

The Davao durian, iconic symbol of the city and purported aphrodisiac, is definitely an acquired taste. During its acquisition you might lose your interest in acquiring it. The season runs from September to December – the rest of the year, try durian ice cream or durian cappuccino (available at several coffee shops) as a substitute.

On **F Torres St**, off JP Laurel Ave, there are more than a dozen restaurants, as well as a handful of coffee shops, bars and nightclubs. A number of international cuisines are represented including Italian, Thai, Spanish, Chinese and Japanese.

Another restaurant hub can be found in the **Victoria Plaza Compound**, an unassuming sun-baked collection of low-slung buildings behind the mall of the same name. More than a dozen quality restaurants, including several large seafood (Sen Ton Whan Seafood, Grand Emerald Seafood and Ahfat Seafood), Chinese, Korean and Filipino, are here.

All of the malls have cafes, food courts and more upscale dining options. **Abreeza Mall** (⏲10am-9pm store hours), not far north of downtown, is the decidedly fancy kid on the block; **Gaisano Mall** (JP Laurel Ave; ⏲10am-10pm) is the most centrally located ('The Peak', a new 5th- and 6th-floor addition, has an outdoor plaza lined with cafes and restaurants, including Kublai Khan's, an all-you-can-eat Mongolian place. A crowd of students watch pickup basketball games on the two half-courts there); expanded **SM City** is not far south of downtown just past the Ecoland Subdivsion; and **SM Lanang Premier** is a few kilometres east on the way to the airport. All have cinemas.

The eateries around Santa Aña Pier and the Muslim Fishing Village are lively – especially in the early evening – and cheap places for fish.

Lachis FILIPINO $
(☎82-224 5552; Ruby St, Marfori Heights; mains P90-150; ⏲11am-8pm Mon-Sat) Especially busy at lunch, this brightly coloured and casual restaurant is best known for its homestyle cooking, barbecue pork ribs, pies, cakes and a wide variety of pastries.

ROAD TRIPPING FROM DAVAO

White Water Inner tubing (P200) down the Sibulan River outside Santa Cruz, between Davao and Digos, is a do-it-yourself affair. Get on any Digos- or General Santos–bound bus and ask to be dropped at the Sibulan Crossing. Water flow depends on the new hydroelectric plant upriver. If driving, stop for lunch in Santa Cruz at **Tabing Dagat**, a waterfront 'point and cook' seafood restaurant. And a little further south in Digos is **Mer's Kitchenette**, a bustling restaurant and shop famous for its wide variety of snacks and desserts like *bibinga* (rice cakes with coconut) and *bokayo* (small coconut balls). This whole area is known for the Japanese soldiers who stayed in the area after WWII; many of their descendants became permanent residents in Japan.

Mati & Around Around a three-hour drive east and then south from Davao is Mati, in Davao Oriental, and nearby **Dahican Beach**, especially good for kayaking, windsurfing, surfing and snorkelling. The waters around Mati are also blessed with several white-sand islands and vibrant marine life including manta rays, sharks, turtles, dolphins and dugongs. Further south of here, at the very tip of a peninsula jutting into the Davao Gulf, is remote **Cape St Augustine** with kilometres of white-sand beaches. The closest town with accommodations is in **Governor Generoso**.

Cateel A long drive north from Mati along a road reminiscent of Hwy 101 in California brings you to Cateel, one of the oldest Spanish settlements in the Philippines. The 4km **Long Beach** is entirely undeveloped and good for surfing and skimboarding. East of Cateel is stunning **Aliwag Falls** and to the south an impressively bio-diverse **mangrove reserve**.

Mainit Hot Springs These sulphuric springs near Maco on the eastern side of the Davao Gulf can soothe tired bones (open 24 hours). Further north from here, the **Toyozu Inland Resort** (☑0917 753 8615; cottages P750) in Nabunturan, the capital of Compostela Valley, has spas filled with water from a nearby spring. A small 1.5m-high mini volcano provides the heat – it's still growing.

Waterfalls There are over two dozen waterfalls near Maragusan (640m), 83km southeast of Nabunturan. The two most worth visiting are Marangig Falls and Tagbibinta, though the water is very cold. A nice place to stay is **Haven's Peak Highland Resort** (☑0926 719 7558; www.thehavenspeak.com; dm/cottages P4000/2800), with absolutely stunning views of the surrounding countryside.

Kong-Ai Vegetarian Centrum   VEGETARIAN $
(☑082-225 5894; Gempesaw St; mains P60; ◷10am-7pm; ☑) A basic Chinatown eatery serving cafeteria-style vegie meals popular with local shop workers.

★**Balik Bukid**   FILIPINO $$
(☑0917 972 8540; Quimpo Blvd, Sandawa Park; mains P200; ◷11am-10pm Mon-Sat, 5-10pm Sun) 🌿 Three siblings – a chef, a decorator and a farmer – have opened up this 'barn to table' restaurant in which they've vowed to get back to the basics. Most everything – primarily, except the fresh fish – on the plate comes from their chemical-free organic farm. The airy dining room has a high ceiling and handicrafts decorating the bamboo walls.

Tadakuna   JAPANESE $$
(☑0927 960 5507; Jacinto Extension, near Arellano; mains P220-400; ◷9am-9pm Mon-Sat, to 9pm Sun) Tadakuna doesn't look like much: a handful of tables in a modest dining room. However, the owner, a passionate fisherman, knows how to turn out some of the best sushi and sashimi in town.

Tiny Kitchen   SPANISH $$
(☑82-305 9232; F Torres St; mains P210-375; ◷10am-8.30pm Mon-Sat) Paellas and other Iberian-style meat dishes dominate most of the chalkboard menu at this bustling and homey place where the owner roves the tables greeting regulars. Also known for its artisanal bread, cakes, pastries and other desserts displayed up front.

Gomone   KOREAN $$
(Surveyor St; mains P200) A modest place serving authentic Korean dishes across the street from Victoria Plaza Mall. More leafy greens than others so a good choice for vegetarians.

Yellow Fin   SEAFOOD $$
(F Torres St; mains P200; ⊙10am-2pm & 5.30-
10pm) One of three locations in the city, this
informal and popular eatery specialises in
seafood by the kilo (eg lapu lapu P80 and
tuna P75 per 100kg). When busy, most dish-
es take close to half an hour to arrive.

Hanoi Restaurant   VIETNAMESE $$
(✉082 225 4501; J Camus St; mains P200) Styl-
ish Hanoi serves tasty Vietnamese cuisine;
some dishes are dumbed-down versions to
appeal to standard tastes, like Chinese restaurants in America.

★**Claude's Le
Cafe De Ville**   EUROPEAN, FRENCH $$$
(✉082-222 4287; www.claudescafedavao.com; 143
J Rizal St; mains from P700; ⊙10.30am-10.30pm
Mon-Sat, 5.30-10.30pm Sun) The polished
wood floors, carved trellis work and white
clapboard exterior make this beautifully
restored colonial-era home one of Davao's
treasures. Easily the most elegant and ro-
mantic restaurant in the city, Claude's cui-
sine rivals its atmosphere. Steaks by weight
are the specialty – from T-bones to wild boar
and deer – but fish and pasta dishes are
equally good choices.
   Has an extensive wine selection; reserva-
tions are recommended.

🍷 Drinking & Nightlife

A nightlife focal point great for bar-hopping
is **Brick Lane Square** near the corner of
Palma Gil and Guzman Sts. A half-dozen
bars of various persuasions attracting young
students as well as older business types sur-
round a small courtyard. **Rizal Promenade**
(Rizal St), an enclosed arcade with several
bars and KTV spots, is a focus of nightlife in
the older centre of the city. A few bars and
restaurants in the various compounds on **F
Torres St** including K1 are good for a late-
night drink.
   A handful of places serve 'frozen beer', a
Davao speciality – it's cooled to five degrees
below zero (holding the frosted bottle can
be painful). Most of the top-end hotels here
offer live music and dancing on weekends.
Everything shuts down at 2am – the city-
wide curfew.
   Coffee houses are big business in Davao.
You'll find several at MTS, on F Torres St and
in the **Pryce Tower** (off JP Laurel Ave) complex
(Cafe France and Blugre Coffee) off JP Lau-
rel Ave just south of Victoria Plaza Mall.

★**Matina Town Square**   BAR, NIGHTCLUB
(MTS; Gen Douglas MacArthur Hwy) A collection
of outdoor bars and food joints, as well as
a handful of more upscale restaurants and
clubs, MTS is a lively and fun spot. Every
Tuesday night there's a free outdoor show
of indigenous music and dance, and other
live music, usually of the pop variety, every
night; the stage fronts dozens of tables and
more than a half-dozen barbecue restaurant
stalls which compete for your order. The vol-
ume is loud, making conversation difficult.
Also in MTS is **Kanto Jazz Blues**, a nice bar
with singer-songwriter-type performers.

Starr Club & Bar   NIGHTCLUB
(Palma Gil St; ⊙8pm-2am) The soundtrack is
usually techno and house music at this fake-
smoke-filled club popular with university
students and well-to-do postgrads.

Coffee for Peace   CAFE
(www.coffeeforpeace.com; G/F Frederic Bldg,
MacArthur Hwy, Matina; ⊙8am-11pm, closed Sun;
☎) 🍴 This small cafe is the retail outpost
of a fair-trade community-oriented organi-
sation, one of the first in the Philippines to
export arabica coffee. A quarter of the net
profits go towards projects with its partner
Peace Builders, an NGO working with indig-
enous communities in the Philippines.

Malagos Farmhouse   CAFE $$
(✉082-221 1395; www.malagosfarmhouse.com;
Bolcan St) 🍴 The base for Olive Puentespina
and her husband's (Dr Bo, a veterinarian)
growing artisanal cheese-making business.
Tastings accompanied by wine and Olive
available in the afternoons.

Green Coffee   CAFE
(F Torres St; ⊙24hr; ☎) A large Starbucks
equivalent with better cakes and pastries, as
well as comfy indoor and outdoor seating.

🛍 Shopping

Aldevinco Shopping Centre   HANDICRAFTS
(CM Recto Ave; ⊙7.30am-8pm) If you're looking
for handicrafts, shop around this rabbit warren of stalls with textiles, batik, weavings,
carvings and jewellery. Take your time and
bargain – almost every day is a slow day. The
stallholders are also keen to change euros
and US dollars.

Got Heart Community Shop   ART GALLERY
(✉0906 496 2153; Gaisano Mall; ⊙1-9pm) 🍴
Head up to the 5th floor, part of an outdoor
plaza called The Peak, for this shop selling

locally produced products such as organic cacao, coconut oil and ginger candy as well as the work of local artists.

ℹ️ Information

All of the major banks have branches here, all with ATMs.

Internet cafes are clustered in the streets south of People's Park and on CM Recto Ave near the Marco Polo Hotel. Of course, there's at least one internet cafe in each mall.

Bureau of Immigration (BOI; ☑ 082-228 6477; JP Laurel Ave; ⊙8am-5pm Mon-Fri) Directly across the street from Victoria Plaza Mall.

City Tourism Office (☑ 082-222 1958; www.davaotourism.com; Magsaysay Park Complex; ⊙8am-5pm Mon-Fri) General information and contact details for people and agencies handling hiking, diving and other activities.

Davao Doctors' Hospital (☑ 082-222 8000; www.ddh.com.ph; cnr E Quirino Ave & Gen Malvar St)

Department of Tourism (☑ 082-221 6955; www.discoverdavao.com; Room 512, LANDCO Corporate Center, JP Laurel Ave)

ℹ️ Getting There & Away

AIR

The Francisco Bangoy International Airport is 12km north of the city centre; a metered taxi is around P150. From the city, jeepneys heading for Sasa go towards the airport; you'll then need to take a tricycle to the airport terminal.

Silk Air (☑ 082-227 5301; www.silkair.com; Suite 056, 5th Floor Pryce Tower, JP Laurel Avenue, Bajada) and Tiger Airways (p450) fly to Singapore several days a week.

PAL and Cebu Pacific fly to Manila, Cebu, Zamboanga City and Iloilo City.

BOAT

Big interisland boats use the terminal at Sasa, by the Caltex tanks 8km north of town. This is also where boats to Paradise Island Beach Resort on Samal Island leave from. Jeepneys run here, or take a taxi for about P85.

Other boats to Samal and Talikud Islands go from Santa Aña Pier in town.

BUS

All long-distance bus transport is based at the Ecoland terminal, 2km south of the city centre. Buses generally leave every 30 minutes to an hour. Minivans service many of the same destinations including General Santos and Mati; there's a northbound terminal near the Victoria Plaza entrance and another outside the Gaisano Mall (vans for Kidapawan leave from here).

DESTINATION	FARE (P)	DURATION (HR)
Butuan	500	7¼
Cagayan de Oro	500	6
General Santos	275	3½
Surigao	500	7

ℹ️ Getting Around

Jeepneys and tricycles clog the streets, sometimes making walking a more efficient option. A taxi to the Ecoland bus terminal will cost about P75, a jeepney about P12.

If you want to rent a car to explore the area on your own, Avis has offices at the airport and Airport View Hotel.

Samal Island

☑082 / POPULATION 95,900

Ignore the official name, the Island Garden City of Samal (Igacos): this island just across the bay from Davao is simply referred to as Samal. Much like New Yorkers heading to the Hamptons or the Jersey Shore on weekends, Davaoeños flock to this island's 116km of beaches. Of course, not all of this beachfront is picture perfect – in fact, the majority of the resorts on the west coast face unsightly refineries and shipping terminals just across the busy channel. The east side of the island is quieter and more unspoiled.

⊙ Sights & Activities

If you just want to escape the city for a day, all of the resorts charge day fees (P50 to P400) for use of their beach and pools if they've got one – even if you eat at their restaurants. There are **snorkelling** and dozens of **diving** opportunities around the island, including two Japanese wrecks just off Pearl Farm beach, Big and Little Liguid islands off the northeast coast and several good wall dives with healthy coral. Try **Carabao Divers** (☑ 082-300 1092; www.divedavao.com; Monteverde St, St Ana Pier) or **South Shore Divers** (☑ 082-300 2574; www.southshoredivers-davao.com; Ruby St, Marfori Heights); two-/three-tank dives with equipment run to around P1950/2350.

The road around the island is now almost entirely paved; a day on a motorbike can be had for around P600.

Hagimit Falls WATERFALL
(admission P50; ⊙6am-6pm) Near San Jose in barangay Cawag, Hagimit Falls has a seemingly endless number of small cascades and

pools you can navigate in your own private slip 'n' slide tour. This is a very developed site with concrete paths and picnic huts, not a place to commune with nature.

Monfort Bat Cave
CAVE

(admission P100; ☺8am-5pm) In barangay Tambo, around 11km north of Babak, is the largest colony of Geoffroy's Rousette fruit bats in the world. A knowledgeable guide will walk you around the five openings where an estimated 2.5 million of these nocturnal and smelly creatures flutter and hang (no smoking since the guano is like gunpowder). Visit at dusk just before they wake in search of food, mostly overripe bananas and mangoes.

🛏 Sleeping

Much of the western coastline from the Babak pier south to Peñaplata is chock-a-block with resorts (and a condo complex or two), many of which are crowded and noisy, especially on weekends. Some beaches are pleasantly wide, some extremely narrow, especially during high tide. Some of the resorts will let you sleep outdoors in picnic huts for a few hundred pesos.

Bluewaters Resort
RESORT $$

(☎0919 337 6987; www.ebluwaters.com; r with fan/air-con P1200/1500; ❋≋) This resort has a handful of cottages and nondescript 'apartment' rooms, plus a nice infinity pool (day guests pay P100).

★Chema's by the Sea Resort
RESORT $$$

(☎0917 814 0814, 082-303 0235; www.chemasbythesea.com; d/q cottage P4700/5600; ❋≋) The relatively intimate Chema's has large, beautifully furnished upscale native-style cottages with Balinese influences. The property is on a leafy hillside leading down to an infinity pool and beach with a wonderful patio and lounge area.

Pearl Farm Beach Resort
RESORT $$$

(☎082-221 9970; www.pearlfarmresort.com; r incl breakfast P6200-12,000; ❋@☎≋) For true world-class luxury, head to Pearl Farm, where you'll find five-star versions of stilt houses; if these or the hilltop villas aren't exclusive enough, more bungalows are located on the resort's own small offshore island.

Paradise Island Park & Beach Resort
RESORT $$$

(☎082-233 0251; www.paradiseislanddavao.com; cottages from P3200; ❋@☎) This long-lasting

Samal stalwart is its own mini Boracay. It's a huge immaculately landscaped complex with its own zoo and a sandy beachfront strip lined with shops, eating and activity areas; every water sport is available, only a pool is missing. Most of the 76 rooms are nicely furnished cottages with porches and their very own private fenced-in garden.

ℹ Getting There & Away

Bangkas go regularly to Samal (P10, 10 minutes, frequent from 5am to 11pm) from the big Caltex tanks near Davao's Sasa pier; walk through the village market to reach the departure point. Most of the resorts organise transfers for their guests from different piers around Davao. The Island City Express (P40, every 15 minutes) runs from the Ecoland terminal in Davao to the Sasa pier and then continues dropping passengers off on Samal.

A motorbike from the pier on Samal to your resort will run anywhere from P20 to P150 depending on the distance and your negotiating skills.

Talikud Island
☑082

This little island to the southwest of Samal offers a real refuge for those looking to escape. Developers are eyeing its beaches; however, for now, there's not much here other than a few low-key resorts. A handful of good dive sites are off the west coast and there's a chance of spotting dugongs. Some beaches get crowded with day-trippers on weekends.

🛏 Sleeping

The enterprising can camp out on a beach with the permission of the property's caretaker.

Isla Reta
COTTAGES $

(☎0928 214 1487; cottages P400-800) On a beautiful beach on the eastern side of Talikud Island facing Samal, Isla Reta has basic bamboo cottages (and tents for campers). Simple meals (P180) can be provided and it's the closest accommodation to the pier in Santa Cruz; some boats will drop you here. Book in advance. It can feel overcrowded at times.

Babu Santa
COTTAGES $

(☎0918 726 1466; camping P75, r P400) For off-the-grid, do-it-yourself accommodations in basic cottages on a beautiful white-sand beach, head to this place on Talikud's north-western tip. Worth bringing your own food supplies.

★**Leticia's by the Sea**   COTTAGES **$$$**
(📞0917 702 5427; www.leticiabytheSearesort.com; r with 3 meals P5000-11,000; ❀🛜) This exquisite property on the eastern side of the island (the same owners as Casa Leticia in Davao) combines rustic, native-style touches with contemporary features. Cottages are set in meticulously landscaped gardens with hardwood balconies – less expensive are the charming 'Bali Houses', essentially luxury versions of sleeping outdoors in a picnic hut.

Pacific Little Secret   COTTAGES **$$$**
(📞0920 909 3181; r incl 3 meals P6000) On the southern coast of the Talikud Island, this relatively upscale place comprises two beautiful breezy houses with plenty of patio space fronting the water and beautiful views. Primarily for big groups.

ⓘ **Getting There & Away**

Boats run to the tiny township and jetty at Santa Cruz on Talikud (P80, one hour) hourly from 6am to early afternoon from Santa Aña Pier in Davao.

Philippine Eagle Research & Nature Center

To view the largest eagles in the world (in terms of their 7ft wing span), head to the **Philippine Eagle Center** (PEC; 📞082-224 3021; www.philippineeagle.org; adult/child P100/50; ⏰8am-5pm), which is dedicated to conserving this endangered species. Also known as monkey-eating eagles, these birds, with an average lifespan of 20 years in the wild (longer at the centre), are threatened by deforestation and hunting. About 500 remain in the wild in the Philippines and around 20 of the 35 here were bred through artificial insemination. The complex is set in a lush pocket of native forest near Malagos, 36km north of Davao. There are other wild birds flitting around and other animals, including the Philippine brown deer and Philippine warty pig. Volunteer guides are around to answer questions.

To stay overnight in the area, try the collection of cottages at **Malagos Garden Resort** (📞0917 625 2467, 082-221 1545; www.malagos.com; dm per person P350, q from P2400; ❀), set in a large landscaped property with gardens, walking paths, a bird park and a butterfly sanctuary. Dr Bo, a veterinarian who owns Malagos with his wife Olive, and known as 'the bird whisperer', runs his own eagle (mostly serpent and fishing eagles) rehabilitation center and puts on a 'bird show' (P125) every Sunday at 10.30am (in good weather). Tents for large groups are provided for those interested in camping (P350) and nonguests can visit for P100. Popular with corporate retreats and weddings and the like. Easy to find, around 300m before the Eagle Center.

ⓘ **Getting There & Away**

From Davao, catch a bus to Calinan (P45, one hour) from the Annil Terminal across the street from Bankerohan Public Market. Though decreipt, the bus is still a more comfortable option than a jeepney (P45). The latter leave from in front of Ateneo University across from the Marco Polo Hotel. In Calinan, grab a motorcycle or tricycle uphill to the research center or Malagos (P20, 10 minutes). A taxi from Davao runs around P400 one way.

Mt Apo & Around
📞082

Literally the 'grandfather' of all mountains, Mt Apo is a volcano that has never blown its top and, at 2954m, is the highest peak in the Philippines. Most mornings it is clearly visible towering above Davao. However, by 8am a mass of clouds resembling a fluffy snake usually conceal the peak. Local tribes believe deities reside near the summit and worship it as a sacred mountain, but it's the environmental stress caused by too much human traffic that makes permission sometimes difficult to obtain. The situation is fluid and should be sussed out at the tourist office in Davao (which can provide a list of reputable guides), Crocodile Park or in Kidapawan, 110km from Davao and the closest municipality to the starting point for hikes to the summit (the office of the **Kidapawan Tourism Council** (📞064-278 7053) is in the City Hall). Coffee is grown on the mountain's slopes, at the same latitude as Ethiopia.

The **climb** takes in primeval forests, rushing waterfalls and the possibility of spotting endangered plant and animal species, such as the carnivorous pitcher plants and the Philippine eagle. *Vanda Sandariana*, more commonly known as waling-waling, considered the mother of all commercial orchid plants, is endemic. Since the ascent is strenuous (extremely steep in parts) and the path almost impossible to follow on your own, you'll have to visit one of the tourist offices anyway to hire a guide. Experienced climbers recommend allowing a minimum of four days, and you'll need warm clothes and sleeping gear, since temperatures drop at night near the peak. Hiking permits cost P500, guides and porters around P400 and P300 per day respectively; food and equipment aren't included. A so-called 'VIP trail' spirals to the peak through property of the Philippine National Oil Company (PNOC; exploring geothermal projects in the area) and takes only four to five hours one way. Few take this route since both the mayor and governor need to grant permission. The best time to go is from March to August when there's less chance of rain.

Most people actually begin their climb after a jeepney ride to **Ilomavis** and Lake Agko (1193m), where they stay overnight and arrange porters before heading for Lake Venado (2182m) and the summit.

For the longest **zipline** (P300) in Southeast Asia, stop at Camp Sabros near Kapatagan, on the southern slopes of Mt Apo – it's long enough to feel like you are flying over pine trees below. **Tudaya Falls**, one of the highest in the Philippines at 300ft, is nearby.

🛏 Sleeping

Mt Apo Highland Resort   RESORT **$$**
(☑ 0918 959 1641; www.davaocrocodilepark.com; Kapatagan; tent per person P300, cottage P2000; ☒) Nearby are **Lake Mirror** and **Hillside**, both part of Mt Apo Highland Resort. Camping is a good option at both, and air mattresses and tents are available for rent. Otherwise, there are a handful of small cot-

tages on concrete stilts. The restaurant at Hillside has a great view of Mt Apo.

Eden Nature Park Resort   RESORT **$$**
(☑ 0918 930 7590; www.edennaturepark.com.ph; d P1400-4000; ☒☒) This once denuded slope, a victim of overzealous logging, at the foot of Mt Talomo has been transformed into a lush forest with hiking trails, sports fields, playgrounds and a 20-second-long zipline. A wide variety of cottages are scattered throughout the property. Shuttle service available from the park's main office in Matina Town Sq in Davao.

🛈 Getting There & Away

From Davao, take a bus from the Ecoland bus terminal to Kidapawan (P80, two hours, every 30 minutes). To jump-off points for the trek, take a jeepney from Kidapawan to Ilomavis (P55, one hour), 17km away.

General Santos (Dadiangas)

☑ 083 / POP 538,000

Known to locals as 'Gensan', to fishmongers as the 'Tuna Capital of the Philippines' and to sports fans as the hometown of Manny Pacquiao (aka Pacman), General Santos is the southernmost city in the Philippines. Formerly Dadiangas, the city was renamed in 1965 in honour of General Paulino Santos who, with accompanying Christian Visayans and Tagalogs, established a settlement here in 1939. These days it's a typically congested city, notable mostly for the huge ships that dock at the port here on Sarangani Bay, loading up freshly caught tuna for the journey to dinner tables all over Asia (more than 80% of

---

KUBLAI MILLAN'S SCULPTURES OF PEACE

The southern slopes of Mt Apo end in a lush and beautiful valley near the town of Kapatagan (literally, 'the valley'). On a hill with commanding views of both Apo and the valley is the **Agung House**, a sculptural park built by prolific Davao-based artist Kublai Millan. Agung, translated as 'river of clouds', refers to the daily pattern that obscures the summits of Apo and the Middle Earth, Hobbit-like structure Kublai originally built as a place for friends to sleep and star gaze. Over the years the number of sculptures has grown, most larger than life and with inspirational poetry accompanying scenes of rural life and indigenous peoples. Kublai hopes locals as well as foreign travelers visit the property to meditate, play, picnic, relax and above all 'get away' from their daily concerns. Feel free to turn up anytime during daylight hours. Mt Apo Highland Resort is nearby or if you don't have your own vehicle a motorbike from Digos should run to around P175. If Kapatagan is not on your itinerary, not to worry, Kublai's sculptures, envisioned as monuments to peace and Mindanao culture, are everywhere on the island.

the country's commercial tuna catch, including smaller skipjack and frigate tuna as well as large yellowfin, is shipped through here). The best time to see the action is around 5am (a taxi one way is P300 and rubber wading boots and guides are provided free).

Prior to the city's establishment, the area was inhabited mostly by Maguindanao Muslims and B'laan tribespeople, and this history is showcased at the **Museum of Muslim & Tribal Culture** at the MSU campus, near the airport (open during school hours).

Gensan is really only worth a detour during the **Tuna Festival**, held in the first week of September, and the **Kalilangan Festival**, celebrated in the last week of February and commemorating the founding of Gensan in 1939 with traditional dance, cooking and handicrafts.

In Sarangani Province, around 56km south of General Santos, **Glan** has a white-sand beach bordering a bay. Unfortunately, its beauty is marred by the proliferation of concrete waterfront resorts. White-sand **Gumasa beach** is another 6km south of here.

Sleeping

Nearly a dozen midrange options line the National Highway between Jose Catolico Sr Ave and Aparente St.

Driggs Pension House HOTEL $
(☑ 083-553 0088; Eve St, Paradise Subdivision; d incl breakfast P800-1000; ❀ ⏶) Located in the City Heights neighbourhood a few kilometres north of the centre is this well-cared-for two-storey building with clean rooms and professional service.

Hotel San Marco HOTEL $$
(☑ 0947 893 2237, 083-301 1818; www.hotelsanmarco.com.ph; Laurel East Ave; s/d incl breakfast P1680/1980; ❀ ⏶) The faux Italianate facade and Three Tenors lobby soundtrack signal San Marco's striving for sophistication. Many rooms lack natural light but all are modern, comfortable and have coffee makers and large flat-screen TVs. Front-desk staff can help with transportation plans and it's within walking distance of several restaurants and Gaisano mall.

The low-rise attached budget annex called the **Morocco Rooms** (s/d incl breakfast P880/1280; ❀ ⏶) offers less luxury.

Dolores Tropicana Resort Hotel RESORT $$
(☑ 083-553 9350; www.doloreshotels.rdgropu.com.ph; Tambler; r incl breakfast P1300; ❀ ⏶ ⏶)

A better choice than staying in the city, the beachside cottages at this large complex, though nothing spectacular, have views of Sarangani Bay right out their front doors. It has a pleasant open-air restaurant.

Eating

Try tuna and opah, also known as moonfish, the specialties of Gensan at one of Grab-A-Crab's locations. Interestingly, restaurants throughout Mindanao are more likely to offer the tail and head of the tuna because the body of the fish is generally reserved for export. **SM** and **Verranza** are the two largest malls with loads of cafes and restaurants; the latter is newer and more upscale.

Kambingan sa Depot FILIPINO $
(KSD; Acharon Blvd; mains from P50) Directly across the street from several large oil depots, this spot serves goat meat in a variety of ways, including goat balls soup – which some consider to be the Filipino Viagra. Many of the dishes sell out before early afternoon.

Tiongson Arcade SEAFOOD $$
(Tiongson St; mains P150; ⏱ 6-10pm) An outdoor night market and culinary adventure where pointing at your choice of freshly caught seafood results in a delicious meal minutes later.

Getting There & Away

AIR
Tambler airport is 12km west of the city centre; a taxi costs around P125. Cebu Pacific and PAL fly daily from Manila (two hours). Cebu Pacific has flights to Cebu (1½ hours).

BOAT
Makar Pier is 2km west of town. 2GO has boats bound for Manila (54 hours) via Zamboanga and Iloilo (30 hours), on Panay, several days a week; it also runs weekly trips to Zamboanga City (12 hours).

BUS
Yellow Bus, Rural Bus, Husky and Holiday run regular buses between General Santos and Davao (P265, 3½ hours); executive-class buses with wi-fi and air-con leave a quarter after every hour till 7pm. For Cagayan de Oro, only two Rural buses go direct (P800, 10 hours, 3am and 10am).

For the first leg of the the trip to Lake Sebu, hop on a bus or van to Marbel (Koronadal City; P107, one hour, every 20 minutes).

The integrated bus and jeepney terminal is at Bula-ong on the western edge of town, about 1km from the town centre (tricylce P15).

SCHOOL FOR INDIGENOUS KNOWLEDGE & TRADITIONS

School for Indigenous Knowledge & Traditions (School for Living Traditions; SIKAT; ☑0912 976 4041; oyog-todi@hotmail.com) has a mission is to educate, advocate, lobby and promote cultural tourism. Maria Todi, an accomplished chanter, dancer and musician (hegalong, the two string lute of the T'boli), founded and runs SIKAT. Because there's no official titling in T'boli culture, one of the unresolved issues involves land rights. Besides T'boli, other tribes in the area are Ubo, Tasaday and Manobos. You're introduced to artists and elders and have the chance to learn about T'boli customs, history and stories. Music and dance classes for area children are held every Saturday. You can sleep on a mattress (P250) in the *gono bong* (longhouse) on the main road that leads through town; SIKAT also offers homestays. Maria can arrange visits to villages deeper into the surrounding countryside (one of the local datus is said to have 20 wives); ask about Mafil in barangay Tasimen. If you go, consider bringing something simple like noodles to share. Or closer by is T'bong village where you can visit a bamboo hut where weavers produce textiles in the traditional colours of white, red and black in T'nalak patterns are said to come in a dream inspired by Fu Dalu, the spirit of weavers. In general, weavers apprentice for six years and the average piece made from abaka material takes four months to complete. If you can, check out *Dreamweavers* (2000), a documentary about several T'boli artists and their practices and challenges in a rapidly modernising culture.

Lake Sebu

POP 76,200 / ELEV 300M

The watery bottom of a beautiful bowl, Lake Sebu is surrounded on all sides by hills and forests. Occasionally, dugout canoes slowly skim its placid surface; however, the picturesque scene is somewhat marred by the expanding ring of bamboo fish traps spreading inward from the shore (these are also negatively impacting the lake's health: overpopulation and industrialised feed leads to oxygen depletion and fish kill as a result). A large church sits on top of a hill and several other modern concrete buildings interrupt otherwise pristine views.

◉ Sights & Activities

Hire a **boat** (P500, 30 minutes) from any of the resorts for a swing around the lake (the light before sunset is beautiful); if alone, ask to join a group. Saturdays are the best time to visit, when tribespeople from surrounding communities descend on the town for the **weekly market**.

Seven Falls WATERFALL
A motorcycle (half-day with driver P300) can take you to **Hikong Alu** and **Hikong Bente** (also known as falls #1 and #2), two of the nearby Seven Falls (admission P20); the latter is an impressive sight and at 70ft the highest of the bunch. It's a short walk from where you park to both. A sometimes-operating superman-style **zipline**

(P300) takes you over three of the falls – views are magnificent.

T'boli Museum MUSEUM
(⊙7am-5pm) You can buy locally made handicrafts here, really nothing more than a small native-style house selling the same weavings and brassware items found at roadside souvenir stalls

✦ Festivals & Events

Helobung Festival CULTURAL
Held in the second week of November to commemorate the founding of the municipality, this festival is really a celebration of T'boli culture. There's traditional chanting, dancing, bangka racing as well as horse fights – locally known as the sport of royalty – where two stallions struggle over a mare in heat. For what it's worth, the fight is no longer to the death.

⊨ Sleeping & Eating

Several resorts that cater to Filipino tourists from Cotobato, General Santos and Davao overlook the lake. Another choice is SIKAT which offers homestays and accommodation in its headquarters' longhouse in town.

Punta Isla RESORT $
(☑0919 485 2910; www.puntaislaresort.com; r incl breakfast P950; ⊛) This resort offers lovely views from its **restaurant** (try the *tilapia kinilaw* but avoid the dry and rock-hard fried chicken) and room (simply furnished)

balconies. Groups of locals occupy the wood pavilions lining the lake at lunchtime and the resort puts on T'boli dance and music performances when enough guests are in house. Owned by Lake Sebu's mayor.

❶ Getting There & Away

Reaching Lake Sebu via public transportation involves several transfers. From General Santos (or Cotobato) catch a bus or van to Marbel (Koronadal City; P107, one hour), then transfer to a bus or van to Surallah (P29, 30 minutes) and finally hop in a van (P40, 45 minutes) for the final leg. Waits for departures aren't long.

If staying by the lake, don't get off at the first stop at a terminal in Lake Sebu despite the pleas of motorcycle 'taxi' drivers. The final stop is further along and within walking distance of lakeside resorts.

ZAMBOANGA PENINSULA

Zamboanga & Around

📞 062 / POP 807,100

When the sun sets in the Philippines, this city, whose otherwise banal skyline is punctuated by several minarets, is one of the last places to see it go. While Zamboanga City is geographically the end of the line, historically it's been a first step, from Islam's arrival to the islands in the 1400s to waves of migrants from the Sulu archipelago. Even though the city is 70% Muslim, most women don't wear headscarves and modern fashions are as strong here as elsewhere. The most commonly spoken language is Chabacano, a Spanish-Creole mix made up of Malay grammar and unconjugated Spanish verbs. The possible origin of the city's exotic-sounding name is threefold: it may come from the 16th-century Malay word *jambangan,* meaning 'land of flowers'; from *samboangan,* a 'docking point', identified on an early Spanish map; or from *sabuan,* the wooden pole used by local tribespeople to navigate their *vintas* (wooden boats with traditional brilliantly coloured angular cloth sails) over the coastal flats.

Often in foreign newspapers' datelines for reports of violence anywhere in Mindanao, Zamboanga has seen its share of the conflict over the years. Most significantly, a large contingent of MNLF forces laid siege to the city for three weeks in September 2013. Over 100,000 civilians were forced to flee (nearly half were still awaiting relocation at the time of research) and more than 10,000 homes and buildings destroyed in intense street fighting, including the majority of the homes in **Rio Hondo**, a Muslim village built out over the water east of Fort Pilar. Many buildings still standing are pockmarked with bullets and damage from mortars.

The Philippine Army's Southern Command (Southcom) is headquartered here, along with a contingent of US Special Forces soldiers.

◉ Sights

⭐ **Fort Pilar Museum**   MUSEUM
(⊙ 8.30am-noon & 1.30-5pm Sun-Fri) FREE At the southeastern end of town near the waterfront is this solid and squat building, partially restored to maintain its historic character. Inside is a museum with several impressive and recently renovated galleries. The marine exhibit includes some sophisticated displays and across the inner courtyard is a terrific ethnographic gallery on the boat-dwelling Sama Dilaut (otherwise known as the Badjao, or sea gypsies). Walk around the ramparts for 360-degree views of Zamboanga City and the busy ocean.

Other galleries include an exhibition of 18th- and 19th-century prints and the new 'Southern Philippines: Portal and Nexus of Barter Trade & Exchange'. The fort's checkered past is also worth noting: founded by the Spaniards in 1635; attacked by the Dutch in 1646; deserted in 1663; reconstructed in 1666; rebuilt in 1719; stormed by 3000 Moros in 1720; cannonaded by the British in 1798; abandoned by the Spaniards in 1898; occupied by the US in 1899; seized by the Japanese in 1942; and, finally, claimed by the Philippines in 1946.

Santa Cruz Island   ISLAND
Great Santa Cruz Island is around 7km off the Zamboanga waterfront, and is home to only a few dozen families from the Samal tribe. Visitors come to see the 2km-long pinkish beach, coloured from finely crushed red coral. You can swim here, but it's on a busy shipping channel and currents are strong. Bangkas (round-trip P2500 for up to six people) leave from in front of Paseo del Mar.

Zamboanga

Map labels:

Col Edwin Andrews Air Base (1km); Hana Sono (1.5km); ⬤; Mano-Mano na Greenfield (2km)

Alavar Seafood House (1.2km)

Santa Cruz Market (900m); Bus Terminal (1km)

Aleson Shipping Lines

Gov Alvarez Ave

Yakan Weaving Village (7km); La Vista Del Mar (7.5km)

Buenavista St

Santa Maria Sucabon Creek

Mayor Jaldon St

La Purisma St

Nunez St

Campaner St

Alejo Alvarez St

Mayor Ledesma St

Varela St

Calixto St

Almonte St

Barcelona St
Urdaneta St
R Reyes St

Gov Lim Ave

Jeepneys to Taluksangay

Veterans Ave

R Lustte St

Tomas Claudio St

Don P Lorenzo St

Pilar St

Corcuera St

Plaza Pershing

J S Alano St

Plaza Rizal

Department of Tourism

Gov Lim Ave

General V Alvarez St

Zamboanga General Hospital

Legionnaire St

City Hall

Valderoza St

Rizal St

P Burgos St

City Tourism Office

Boats to Santa Cruz

Fort Pilar Museum

Basilan Strait

Ferry Terminal

Paseo del Mar

200 m
0.1 miles

Zamboanga

◎ Top Sights

🛏 Sleeping

⊗ Eating

🎎 Festivals & Events

Fiesta de Nuestra Señora
Virgen del Pilar
RELIGIOUS

Although a Christian festival, it's a time for parades, dances, markets and food fairs enjoyed by the whole community and a big **regatta** brings *vintas* out on the water. Held 10 to 12 October.

🛏 Sleeping

Grand Astoria Hotel
HOTEL **$**

(☏ 062-991 2510; www.grand.astoria.ph; Mayor Jaldon St; s/d from P850/1200; ❄ @ 🛜) This efficiently run Zamboanga institution is often booked by groups for seminars, conventions, weddings and the like. Ask for one of the recently renovated rooms. Airline ticketing offices and a restaurant on the ground floor.

Marcian Business Hotel
HOTEL **$$**

(☏ 062-991 0005; www.marcianhotels.com; Mayor Cesar Climaco Ave; s/d P1520/1800; ❄ 🛜) Gleaming tile floors, spacious bathrooms with top-of-the-line shower heads, and beautifully designed boutique-style rooms make this the city's best midrange choice. Located at a busy intersection, the Marcian is a refuge from the noise and smog.

Lantaka Hotel
HOTEL **$$**

(☏ 062-991 2033; Valderoza St; s/d from P950/1200; ❄ 🛜 🏊) The upside to this long-standing Zamboanga institution is its waterfront location and sea-facing pool and lounge area. Downsides can be many depending on your wing and room. Older ones are in need of attention and service can be fusty. The old-school restaurant serves standard Filipino and generic international dishes.

✖ Eating

The most happening nighttime spot for restaurants and general lounging is **Paseo del Mar**, a waterfront development near Fort Pilar. **Mindpro City Mall** (⊙9am-7pm) and **Southway Mall** (⊙9am-7pm) have food courts and several fast-food joints; **KCC Mall**, the largest in the city, was due to open some time in 2015.

Mano-Mano na Greenfield FILIPINO $
(☑062 992 4717; Governor Ramos St, barangay Santa Maria; mains from P70) Housed in a large flashy version of the native-style outdoor pavilion, Mano-Mano specialises in grilled pork spareribs and baby back ribs. About 1km north of the Edwin Andrews Air Base. Its Paseo del Mar location gets extremely crowded.

★**Alavar Seafood House** SEAFOOD $$
(☑062 981 2483; barangay Tetuan; mains P200) Seafood, of course, is the specialty here – choose the species, size and cooking method from a menu of delicacies. What sets Alavar apart is the beautiful trellis-covered backyard. Enjoy a lantern-lit dinner serenaded by the loud squawking from an aviary of exotic birds. It's a P30 tricycle ride northeast of the city centre.

Curacha or spanner crab, one of the city's specialties, is steamed with Alavar's own sauce. A lot of work for not much meat but the taste is worth the struggle.

La Vista Del Mar FILIPINO, SEAFOOD $$
(mains P175) One of the more pleasant places to eat is this outdoor restaurant, inside the resort of the same name, just past the Yakan Weaving Village (taxi P100) west of the city. An American military outpost is next door.

🛍 Shopping

Yakan Weaving Village CRAFTS
(Calarian) About 7km out of Zamboanga, heading west, the Yakan Weaving Village is really no more than a collection of six or seven stalls selling some high-quality Yakan weavings, such as table runners and place mats, a little brassware and lots of ordinary mass-produced batik. Yakan are the indigenous people of nearby Basilan Island, and their woven designs are characterised by bright colours and geometric designs.

ℹ Information

The PNB and Bank of the Philippine Islands (BPI) around the plaza area and the Metrobank on La Purisima St have ATMs.

There are internet cafes scattered around the city centre east of Mayor Jaldon St and north of Plaza Pershing.

Bureau of Immigration (BOI; ☑062-991 2234; Radja Bldg, Gov Camins Ave) Provides visa extensions.

Department of Tourism (DOT; ☑062-993 0030; Valderrosa St; ⊙8am-noon & 1-5pm Mon-Sat) Attached to the Lantaka Hotel; the director Mary June Bugante is extremely helpful.

ℹ Getting There & Away

Few travellers venture to Zamboanga overland and most arrive by plane. However, for the intrepid and patient who want to travel throughout northern Mindanao before visiting the city, it's possible to get either a fast ferry (four hours) or bus (eight hours) in the town of Pagadian in the far north of Zamboanga del Sur. If you go by road only travel during the daytime.

Philippine Airlines, Cebu Pacific and 2GO all have offices in a building attached to the Lantaka Hotel.

AIR

PAL and Cebu Pacific fly between Manila and Zamboanga (1½ hours) several times daily; the latter also flies to Cebu (one hour) and Davao several times a week (one hour), and to Jolo and Tawi-Tawi in the Sulu archipelago. Cebu Pacific might fly to Malaysia, either Kota Kinabalu or Sandakan, in the near future.

The airport is 2km from the centre of Zamboanga. Catch a public tricycle (P10), jeepney (P8) or taxi (P150).

BOAT

George & Peter has a weekly trip to Cebu (P1000, 29 hours); and 2GO goes twice weekly to Manila (P1600, 48 hours) and Dumaguete (P1200, 12 hours).

Weesam Express (☑062-992 3986; www. weesam.ph) goes to Isabela (P175, 45 minutes, four daily) on nearby Basilan island and Jolo (P800, 3½ hours, 8.30am); the ticketing office is at the pier. **Aleson Shipping Lines** (☑062-991 2687; www.aleson-shipping.com; 172 Veterans Ave, Zamboanga) and **Ever Lines Shipping Inc** (☑062-991 0293; Mutual Bldg, 47 Valderrosa St) have trips to Sulu and Tawi-Tawi.

Palawan

Best Beaches

➜ North Cay Island (p412)

➜ Nacpan & Calitang
Beaches (p398)

➜ Secret Beach (p405)

➜ Malcapuya Island (p412)

➜ Sabang (p389)

Best Places
to Stay

➜ Sangat Island Reserve
(p409)

➜ Flower Island Beach
Resort (p395)

➜ El Nido Overlooking (p400)

➜ Al Faro Cosmio Hotel (p409)

Why Go?

Nothing defines Palawan more than the water around it. With seascapes the equal of any in Southeast Asia, and wildlife terrestrial and aquatic, the Philippines' most sparsely populated region is also the most beguiling. Because of its silhouette – a long sliver stretching 650km all the way to Borneo – there's a certain liberating logic to travel here.

Centrally located Puerto Princesa (Puerto) is the culinary capital and primary gateway to nearby rural and oceanfront tranquillity. The majority of travellers go north to El Nido or Coron town, base camps for island-hopping, snorkelling and diving adventures in the Bacuit Archipelago and Calamianes group.

The coastline serves as an alternative highway ferrying travellers in bangkas between fishing villages, tourist-friendly towns and a maze of uninhabited islands. In the south where the topography is more rugged it's possible to explore jungle-clad mountains, though facilities are decidedly rustic.

When to Go
Puerto Princesa

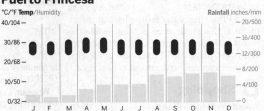

Mar–early May
The best time for sea travel.

June–Oct The southwest monsoon, with heavy rain, at least in the afternoon.

Nov–Feb Cooler and drier; a popular time to go.

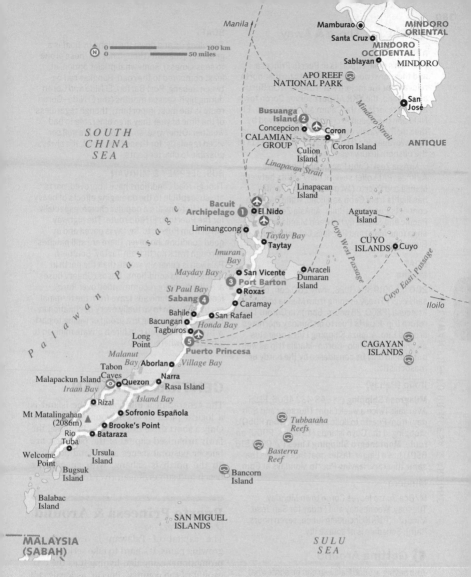

Palawan Highlights

1 Snorkel your way in and out of lagoons – nature's aquariums – in the **Bacuit Archipelago** (p403).

2 Wriggle through the portholes of WWII-era wrecks while diving around **Busuanga Island** (p405).

3 Move to the slow village pace, from hammock to beach and back again, in **Port Barton** (p392).

4 Make the most of a day in **Sabang** (p389), from floating through the cavernous darkness of the underground river to chilling on the beach at sunset.

5 Breeze through the countryside outside **Puerto Princesa** (p380) on a motorcycle.

ⓘ Getting There & Away

AIR

Palawan's main airport is in Puerto Princesa and there are two smaller airports further north relevant for the majority of travellers. On Busuanga Island, the **YKR Airport** serves Coron town and the resorts of the Calamian Archipelago. El Nido and the Bacuit Archipelago are served by the small privately owned Lio Airport and Island Transvoyager, Inc (ITI), which caters to guests of the offshore luxury resorts.

AirAsia Zest, Cebu Pacific and Philippine Airlines (PAL) offer several daily flights between Manila and Puerto (1¼ hours); Cebu Pacific has flights from Cebu and Iloilo, while PAL also connects Puerto and Iloilo. AirAsia Zest, Cebu Pacific and SkyJet fly between Manila and Busuanga (one hour) and PAL flies between Cebu and Busuanga.

BOAT
Manila

2GO (☑ 0919 894 3926; www.2GO.com.ph) sails every Friday evening from Manila to Puerto Princesa (P800, 28 hours, 6pm) via Coron. The return trip departs Puerto on Sunday mornings around 1am. Atienza Shipping Lines operates an unreliable El Nido–Coron–Manila trip as well but should only be considered by the hardy or masochistic.

Iloilo (Panay)

Milagrosa Shipping (☑ 048-433 4806; Rizal Ave) sails twice a week (3pm Thursday and Sunday) from Puerto to Iloilo (30 hours, from P950), stopping in the Cuyo Islands (13 hours, P900) en route. **Montenegro Shipping Lines** (☑ 0919 516 6501) has a bigger, faster boat that follows the same itinerary, leaving Puerto Mondays at 6pm.

Mindoro

M/Bca *Bunso* leaves Coron town Monday, Tuesday, Wednesday and Friday for San Jose, Mindoro (P1000 including lunch, seven hours, 8am). Schedule is of course iffy.

ⓘ Getting Around

Journeying around Palawan can be somewhat unpredictable, more so during the low season. Schedules are fluid and vehicles can be rickety and prone to breakdowns.

AIR

PAL and **Air Juan** (☑ 0939 901 8797; www. airjuan.com) fly between Puerto and Busuanga (1¼ hours); the latter also flies from Puerto to the Cuyo Islands twice weekly (10kg baggage allowed).

BOAT

Travelling up and down the island by boat is a generally pleasant (though not for those prone to seasickness), somewhat pricier option, at least compared to the road. Bangkas run between Sabang, Port Barton, El Nido and Coron during high-season months (the El Nido–Coron route is the most important), though regardless of the time of year they are vulnerable to bad weather. Otherwise, some routes are still serviced regularly; for those that aren't, it's always possible to charter boats.

BUS, JEEPNEY & MINIVAN

Though road conditions have improved, parts are susceptible to the damaging effects of heavy rains. Minivans are a popular choice, especially for the Puerto to El Nido route. The highway north from Puerto to Taytay is paved and in good condition; however, there are still patches of rough track north from Taytay. Southern Palawan is generally worse than the north in terms of road conditions. Buses (Cheery buses are slightly more recommended over Roro), jeepneys and minivans leave from the terminal north of Puerto to virtually every destination in Palawan. If travelling in a group or willing to part with extra cash, you can hire a private minivan to almost anywhere.

CENTRAL PALAWAN

The geographical midpoint of the island is a logical place to begin your explorations. Only a short drive from Puerto Princesa, the fairly urbanised capital of the province, are bucolic pastoral scenes and island-hopping. To the north is Sabang, with an alluring beach and subterranean river tour.

Puerto Princesa & Around
☑ 048 / POP 222,700

The capital of Palawan is experiencing growing pains. It's hard to take seriously the promotional campaign hyping it as the eco-capital of the country. 'Puerto', as locals call it, has traffic jams, and concrete buildings abound. It does have a thriving restaurant scene, and a number of worthwhile day trips, including island-hopping to remote beaches and drives through stunning countryside. Filipinos are coming in droves to book trips to the subterranean river in Sabang. More and more, however, travellers are choosing it primarily as a way station to destinations elsewhere on Palawan.

Central Palawan

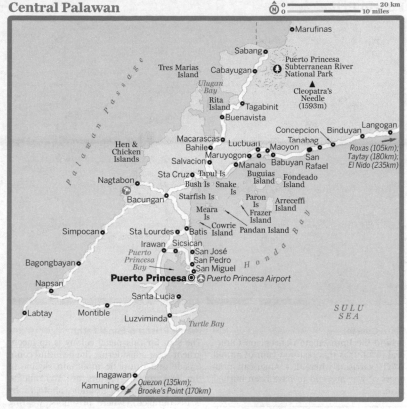

⊙ Sights & Activities

Several sights within the vicinity of Puerto are often visited as part of a day-long 'city tour' (P600), which caters primarily to Filipinos from Manila; each sight in itself isn't especially thrilling, so renting a motorbike doing a version of the tour on your own is a better option. Acrobatic long-snouted spinner dolphins can be seen in the surrounding waters (tours per person P900).

The Palawan Butterfly Garden, Irawan Eco-Park, Palawan Wildlife Rescue & Conservation Center and Iwahig Prison & Penal Farm are all located along the South National Hwy (it heads north out of town until turning west around the butterfly garden).

Island Divers (☎ 048-433 2917; www.islanddiverspalawan.com; Manalo Ext, Bgy Bancao-Bancao) offers diving in and around Honda Bay.

Most people visit the Underground River in Sabang by booking a tour (P1300 to P1500) with a travel company here.

⊙ Puerto Princesa

Palawan Heritage Center   MUSEUM
(Provincial Capitol Bldg; admission P50; ⊙ 9am-4.30pm Mon-Fri) This museum, designed and also operated by the provincial government, has a number of touch-screen videos, and even a hologram, which outline Palawan's history and explain the contemporary economic and environmental challenges it faces.

Palawan Museum   MUSEUM
(Mendoza Park, Rizal Ave; admission P20; ⊙ 9am-noon & 1.30-5pm Mon-Sat) Housed in the old City Hall building adjacent to Mendoza Park, this museum has two floors of ageing exhibits about the ethnological and archaeological significance of Palawan, most with interesting accompanying explanations in English.

Puerto Princesa

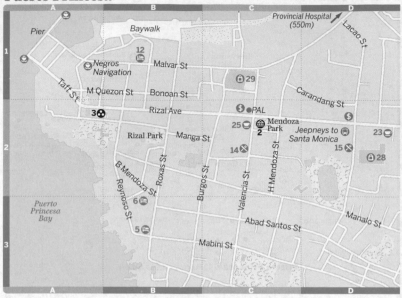

Plaza Cuartel
RUIN

Behind the Immaculate Concepcion Cathedral (c 1872) is this restored ruin of an old WWII garrison where 154 American prisoners of war are said to have been burned alive.

⊙ Out of Town

Palawan Wildlife Rescue & Conservation Center
WILDLIFE RESERVE

(Crocodile Farming Institute; admission P40; ⊘8.30-11.30am & 1.30-4.30pm Mon-Sat) This wildlife reserve is a complex of concrete buildings and outdoor pens that house hundreds of crocs, from newly hatched to scary behemoths. Guided tours leave every 30 minutes. Towards the back, in a densely forested area, other animals and birds eke out an existence in neglected aviaries and cages.

Nagtabon Beach
BEACH

This beach, on the northern side of the isthmus, has several hundred metres of white sand and shallow water good for swimming. Jeepneys from San Jose terminal (they leave around noon) aren't a convenient option so best to go by motorbike or rental car or van. The road is rough once it leaves the highway.

Iwahig Prison & Penal Farm
SITE

The sign for this penal colony is an incongruent sight considering the beautiful countryside and dramatic mountain skyline in the background. Visitors are welcome to enter the extensive grounds (photography is discouraged), where prisoners, wearing differently coloured T-shirts depending on whether they are minimum-, medium- or maximum-security inmates, live, work and roam freely.

Palawan Butterfly Garden
GARDENS

(27 Bunk House Rd, Santa Monica; admission P50; ⊘8am-5pm) An outdoor space near Santa Monica village where you can see different species of fluttering butterflies. Before entering, you can watch a short video that explains the life cycle of these delicate creatures. Now 'tribal' dance performances are offered to groups.

Irawan Eco-Park
ADVENTURE TOUR

(☏ 0912 542 2687, 048-434 1132; irawan_ecopark@ yahoo.com; zipline P800, canopy skywalk P250) Here you'll find a few ziplines of different lengths in a protected forest area along the Irawan River. It has a nice cafe, and the booking office in Puerto is at the Lotus Garden Restaurant on Rizal Ave.

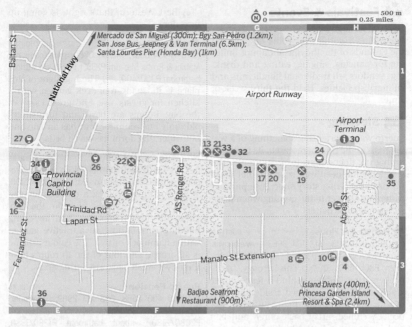

Puerto Princesa

◎ Sights
1 Palawan Heritage Center E2
2 Palawan Museum C2
3 Plaza Cuartel A2

◎ Activities, Courses & Tours
4 Pasyar Developmental Tourism H3

◎ Sleeping
5 Ancieto's Pension B3
6 Banwa Art House B3
7 Casa Linda Inn F2
8 Hibiscus Garden Inn G3
9 Mercedes B&B H2
10 One Manalo Place H3
11 Pagdayon Traveler's Inn F2
12 Puerto Pension B1

◎ Eating
13 Bilao at Palayok G2
14 Bruno's Swiss Food C2
15 Heavenly Desserts by Dorothy D2
16 Ima's Vegetarian E2
17 Kainatô G2
18 Kalui F2
19 La Terrase G2

20 Lou Chaolong Hauz G2
21 Thant-Tam Chaolong G2
22 Ugong Rock Seafood & Grill F2

◎ Drinking & Nightlife
23 Cafe Itoy's D2
24 Crossing Bridge Café H2
25 Divine Sweets C2
26 Kinabuchs Grill & Bar E2
27 Tiki Restobar E2

◎ Shopping
28 NCCC Mall D2
29 Public Market C1

◎ Information
30 Airport Tourist Information
Counter H2
31 Bureau of Immigration G2
32 Floral Travel & Tours G2
33 Inland Tours and Travel G2
34 Palawan Tourism Promotions &
Development Office E2
35 Sanctuary Travel & Tours H2
36 Tubbataha Management Office E3

Kim's Hot Springs

SPRINGS

Kim's (P400 for four hours for up to eight people) is conveniently located along the National Hwy, not far north of the turn-off for Honda Bay. The pools themselves are basically a covered shed with piping hot water; there's a garden and restaurant as well.

✨ Festivals & Events

Baragatan Festival CULTURAL
Palaweños from all over come together on the grounds of the Provincial Capitol Building for dancing, singing, eating and drinking; vendors sell traditional handicrafts and culinary specialties. Held the third week of June.

🛏 Sleeping

Puerto was experiencing something of a water crisis at the time of research: its reservoir drying up, fluctuations in pressure and the supplemental deep well source is not good for drinking. Long story short, use purified water and shower in the evening when pressure tends to be better.

★ **Banwa Art House** HOSTEL $
(☏ 0915 260 3113, 048-434 8963; www.banwa.com; Liwanag St; dm P350, d with/without bathroom P800/600; @ 🛜) This groovy backpackers' spot, hidden behind a fence down a side street in a cramped residential part of town, is nicer inside than you might expect. A chilled, artsy back porch and bar and lounge area is the highlight, and the wood-floored rooms (two dorm rooms are gender-segregated) are clean and warm.

Burgers (P185), pasta (P130) and other food served. Somewhat difficult to find, it's just off Roxas St.

Casa Linda Inn INN $
(☏ 0917 749 6956, 048-433 2606; casalindainn@gmail.com; Trinidad Rd; s/d with fan P550/650, with air-con P850/1000; ❄ 🛜) The meticulously maintained garden courtyard and pergola makes Casa Linda feel like a country refuge. The surrounding wood-floored rooms are clean and simply furnished, though thinly panelled walls mean noise can be a nuisance. There's a restaurant on-site, convenient for early morning pre-trip breakfasts.

Rotating ceiling fans might not provide enough relief from the heat; ask for one of the limited number of standing floor fans.

Pagdayon Traveler's Inn INN $
(☏ 0927 506 5321, 048-434 9102; Pagdayon Rd; d P950-1100; ❄ 🛜) This place is best described as modestly upscale native. Tile-floored rooms have small TVs, large closets and small, individual balconies, and the owners and staff are quietly professional and efficient. It's just down a narrow dirt road near the airport.

A Best Western, that's right, is going up next door.

Ancieto's Pension GUESTHOUSE $
(☏ 048-434 6667; mchona0860@gmail.com; cnr Mabini & Roxas Sts; dm P235, r P860, s/d without bathroom P300/400; 🛜) The highlight of this place is its shady roof-deck garden with a kitchen for guests' use, and great views of the bay. Rooms are basic and furnishings old; only one room for four has air-con and hot water; the dorm has seven beds.

Hibiscus Garden Inn INN $$
(☏ 048-434 1273, 0908 862 7403; www.puertoprincesahotel.com; Manolo Ext; r P2300-2800; ❄ 🛜) For those seeking a quiet sanctuary, well-managed Hibiscus will do the job. Large tile-floor rooms are in a low-slung building surrounding an attractive garden with a hammock or two. The colour scheme is all orange and four of the 10 rooms have their own small backyard sitting areas.

Puerto Pension HOTEL $$
(☏ 0915 406 8568, 048-433 2969; www.puertopension.com; 35 Malvar St; incl breakfast s/d P2080/2180, without bathroom P1280/1380; ❄ 🛜) An impressive-looking four-storey wood-and-bamboo building, located not far from the town pier, with sweeping views of the bay from the top-floor restaurant. Everything is here, including small flat-screen TVs and mini refrigerators in some rooms – but there's only just enough space to slide around the bed.

A small fenced-off area now has a Jacuzzi and massage area for couples (P1000).

Mercedes B&B HOTEL $$
(☏ 0916 714 5220; www.mercedesbb.com; P Abrea St; d incl breakfast P1400; ❄ 🛜) A handful of simple, modern rooms that front a mostly barren yard (with a hammock or two) only a short walk from the airport.

★ **Palo Alto Bed & Breakfast** B&B $$$
(☏ 0917 542 9782; www.paloalto.ph; Kawayanan St, Bgy San Pedro; r incl breakfast P3000-3500; ❄ 🛜) Surrounded by tall trees down a dirt road 5km north of town, Palo Alto is a refuge from the city's traffic and noise. The beautifully built two-storey building surrounds a U-shaped garden and the simple but modern rooms have flat-screen TVs and nice bathrooms. A shady pool area is just across a narrow alley in another part of the property.

Much of Palo Alto is made from the recycled ipil of a decommissioned power plant (logging of this dark wood is now banned in the Philippines). Free transfers from the airport and into town, own travel agency on the premises and disabled-friendly.

One Manalo Place   BOUTIQUE HOTEL **$$$**
(☑ 048-434 1280; www.onemanaloplace.com; Manolo St, Bgy Bancao Bancao; r incl breakfast P3200-4500; ✳ 🛜 ☒) The back of a mini-mall complex is not where you'd expect to find Puerto's nicest (maybe only) boutique hotel. Double rooms sport tile floors, little 'lanai' courtyards and high-end bathrooms. The gym which overlooks the pool (nonguests can swim for P250) is hands-down the best place to work out in Puerto.

Aplaya, a nice seafood restaurant, is in the hotel and Jukebox, a popular KTV spot, and a spa are in the attached plaza.

**Princesa Garden Island
Resort & Spa**   RESORT **$$$**
(www.princesagardenisland.com; Bgy Bancao-bancao; r incl breakfast from P6800; ✳ 🛜 ☒) The only real beach holiday resort in Puerto, even if it technically doesn't occupy any beachfront. Six connecting pools (the back porches of some rooms open directly into these), an artificial sandy area, palm trees and mangroves do the job. Tastefully done, boutique-style rooms with private patios and either Jacuzzis or gardens are probably the most luxurious in the city.

Three restaurants, including one with a Thai menu, are open; three more are planned for the future. Located down a dirt road along the water only 2km southeast of the airport.

Hotel Centro   HOTEL **$$$**
(☑ 048-434 1111; www.hotelcentro.ph; National Hwy, Barangay San Pedro; r incl breakfast from P5500; ✳ 🛜 ☒) Combining business class and resort luxury, Centro features the usual bells and whistles such as a gym and a spa. While its facade looks something like a corporate office building, the outdoor pool is one of the nicest around. It's north of town on the National Hwy, not far from Robinson's Place.

🍴 Eating

Puerto is easily the best place to eat in Palawan. In terms of volume there's no competition, but the city also surprises in terms of variety. A slew of restaurants is located on Rizal Ave between the airport and the National Hwy, within walking distance of a number of hotels.

The city has a number of **chaolong restaurants**, small informal eateries serving up a Filipino version of *pho* (spicy noodle soup with chicken, beef or pork) with a side of French bread. The restaurants are a lingering reminder of a thriving community of Vietnamese refugees who mostly settled in 'Viet Village' 13km north of the city. Other than a restaurant serving *chaolong*, it's now

PALAWAN PUERTO PRINCESA & AROUND

HONDA BAY

Compared with the islands in the Bacuit Archipelago, Honda Bay may be a poor stepchild; however, this is a bit of an unfair comparison and a day spent **snorkelling** and **island-hopping** is worth doing if you're in the area for more than a night.

A regular tour (P1500 per person) allows you to visit three islands, usually **Cowrie Island**, **Pandan Island** and the aptly named **Snake Island**, a winding strip of white sand that changes shape with the tides. Package tours are available from travel agencies and hotels in Puerto, and cost around P1100, which includes snorkelling, transport and lunch, and usually lasts from 8am to 4pm. To do it yourself, make your way to Santa Lourdes pier, 11km north from the city centre (P30 for a multicab; a tricycle will cost you P500 round trip), and ask around – a boat for up to six people should be around P1500 plus P50 entrance fee. Keep in mind that other than a shack on Snake Island selling a handful of provisions and grilled fish, there are no restaurants or stores. Cowrie and Pandan charge nominal entrance fees.

The only established place to spend the night in the islands is on Arreceffi Island at the luxurious **Dos Palmas Island Resort & Spa** (☑ in Manila 02-637 4226; www.dospalmas.com.ph; full board per person from P6500; ✳ 🛜 ☒). There's a spa, an infinity pool and a fully functioning dive centre. It's a 50-minute bangka ride from Santa Lourdes pier and non-overnight guests can spend the day (adult/child P1800/900 incl transportation, lunch and use of facilities).

a ghost town. **Lou Chaolong Hauz** (mains P50; ⊙8am-4am) and **Thant-Tam Chaolong** (Rizal Ave; mains P50-60; ⊙24hrs) are near one another on Rizal Ave out towards the airport; the latter has another location just before the intersection with the National Hwy.

Behind the market area along the waterfront is **Baywalk,** a mostly concrete expanse with sunset views and more than a half dozen informal **barbecue tents** (5pm to midnight) with outdoor seating.

Robinson's Place (p387) has the usual assortment of fast food, upscale mall eateries and large grocery.

Ima's Vegetarian
VEGETARIAN $

(Fernandez St; dishes P80-130; ⊙11am-9pm Sun-Thu, 11am-3pm Fri, 6.30-9pm Sat; 🖋) 🍴 Run by a couple dedicated to healthy living through better eating, all of Ima's rice and veggie dishes (the bean burrito and vegan cheese pizza can be recommended) are sans additives and preservatives.

Heavenly Desserts by Dorothy
CAFE $

(Lacao St; mains P100-185; ⊙9am-9pm, closed Sun; 🖼) A homey, charming spot with excellent cakes and muffins, plus an all-day breakfast menu (omelette P115) and burgers, pad thai and pastas. You can kick back with a frappucino and peruse year-old magazines in a comfy couch.

Gypsy's Lair
FILIPINO, MEXICAN $

(Mercado de San Miguel, National Hwy; mains P120; ⊙8am-11pm Sun-Thu, 9am-midnight Fri & Sat; 🖥) In a strip mall a few kilometres north of Rizal along the National Hwy is this postage-stamp-sized bohemian-style restaurant with live acoustic music most nights. Offers excellent desserts like ice *biko*, basically sweet sticky rice with homemade ice cream.

★Kalui
FILIPINO $$

(🖉048-433 2580; 369 Rizal Ave; mains from P225; ⊙11am-2pm & 6-11pm Mon-Sat; 🖼) Kalui has a lovely Balinese ambience – wooden floors,

colourful paintings, sculptures and masks adorn the walls, and there's a general air of sophistication. Choose from a few varieties of seafood, all served with veggies, a seaweed salad and rice plus there's a delightful fruit-mix dessert, served in a hollowed-out coconut. Reservations recommended, especially for dinner and groups. Shoes are stashed in cubby holes before entering the restaurant.

★Badjao Seafront Restaurant
FILIPINO, SEAFOOD $$

(🖉048-433 9912; badjaoseafront@yahoo.com; Abueg Sr Rd, Barangay Bagong Sikat; mains P195-400; ⊙11am-10pm; 🖥🖼) Perched over the water at the end of a raised boardwalk over mangroves, Badjao's sea and mountain views are truly mesmerising. A long lunch gnawing on whole grilled fish and other seafood (crabs, shrimp, squid etc) is a great way to spend an afternoon. Only downsides are some biting flies and service is slow when busy.

Ugong Rock Seafood & Grill
SEAFOOD $$

(Rizal Ave; mains P110-350; ⊙10am-midnight; 🖥) Choose your protein from the display trays (crabs, prawns, lobster, mussels, squid and several types of fish), the method of cooking, and a sauce, and a short time later you'll be feasting on your creation. Best to share a variety of dishes at one of the picnic tables; other choices on the menu include noodles and crocodile *sisig*.

Centrally located, with a fan-cooled outdoor pavilion with a couple of TVs.

Kainatô
FILIPINO $$

(Rizal Ave; mains P160-285) Attractively decorated with paintings and wood carvings, Kainatô is welcoming place serving the most Filipino specialties of any restaurant in town.

Bilao at Palayok
FILIPINO $$

(Rizal Ave; mains P140-225) Serves a variety of Filipino favourites, including *sinigáng*

TUBBATAHA REEFS

A 10- to 12-hour boat ride from Puerto Princesa, Palawan, are the Tubbataha Reefs, a marine protected reserve often compared to the Galápagos Islands. It was declared a Unesco World Heritage Site in 1993 and is home to hundreds of species of seabirds and fish, including mantas, whale sharks and the full gamut of pelagic marine life.

The season for visiting Tubbataha runs from mid-March through mid-June. The only way to visit is on one of the half-dozen or so live-aboards operating from Puerto Princesa. The average cost for a week-long trip is US$2100 to US$2600. Contact the Tubbataha Management Office (p388) in Puerto Princesa for more information.

(tamarind-based soup), *adobo* (pork stewed in vinegar and garlic) and grilled fish. This very pleasant eatery has a small pond, waterfall and soft music.

La Terrase   FILIPINO, FRENCH **$$$**
(Rizal Ave; mains P200-630; ⊘11am-11pm; 🐾) This is a sophisticated open-air dining room with a small menu of pasta, seafood and grilled meats (including pan-grilled organic duck breast). Attention is paid to organic and locally sourced ingredients. Sandwiches are available 2.30pm to 6pm.

Bruno's Swiss Food   EUROPEAN **$$$**
(Valencia St; mains P550; ⊘Mon-Sat) For those craving Swiss, Polish and German sausage, imported steaks and European beers and wines. A small grocery on one side and a few tables on the other. Good place to stock up for a picnic.

🍷 Drinking & Nightlife

A slew of informal bars and karaoke shacks, along with a few restaurants good for drinks, are lined up along the road between the airport and National Hwy.

★ Kinabuchs Grill & Bar   RESTOBAR
(Rizal Ave; ⊘5pm-2am) This is where a good chunk of Puerto goes at night. It's a large open-air property with several billiard tables, big-screen TVs and an extensive menu (mains from P100), though most people come for the cheap beer and lively atmosphere. Adventurous eaters can try the *tamilok*, basically a woodworm that's said to taste like an oyster.

Tiki Restobar   BAR
(cnr Rizal Ave & National Hwy; mains P160; ⊘7pm-2am) A large place in the middle of town, Tiki features bar games, beer buckets and – often – revellers shimmying on the dance floor to live music.

Crossing Bridge Café   CAFE
(Rizal Ave; ⊘6am-8pm, closed Sun; 🐾) Just outside the airport entrance, an outdoor spot perfect for an iced coffee, cookies-and-cream frappucino or small meal (mains P160 to P225) while waiting for your flight.

Divine Sweets   CAFE, INTERNATIONAL
(Valencia St; mains P150; ⊘7am-10pm; 🐾) A contemporary cafe with excellent pastries and cakes, as well as a full food menu.

Cafe Itoy's   CAFE
(Rizal Ave; ⊘6am-11pm; 🐾) Long-running coffee joint on the main drag with a shady back terrace. Pancakes and honey (and frozen butter) are good for breakfast.

🛍 Shopping

A few handicraft shops on Rizal Ave between the airport and AS Rengel Rd sell mainly generic imitation native masks and statues of the type found everywhere from Nairobi to Bangkok.

Public Market   MARKET
(Burgos St; ⊘9am-5pm) Piles of colourful tropical fruit and vegetables and fish stacked like sardines make up the tableau here.

Robinson's Place   MALL
(National Hwy; ⊘10am-9pm Mon-Thu, to 10pm Fri-Sun) Noteworthy because it's the first 'real' mall in all of Palawan, with restaurants and cinema; about 5km north of Rizal Ave.

ℹ Information

INTERNET ACCESS
Several internet cafes are located along Rizal Ave, between the airport and Jollibee restaurant.

MEDICAL SERVICES
Palawan Adventist Hospital (☎048-433 2156; National Hwy, Barangay San Pedro)
Provincial Hospital (☎048-433 2621; Malvar St)
Salvador P Socrates Government Center (Kilusang Ligtas Malaria; ☎048-434 6346; PEO Rd, Barangay Bancao-Bancao) For malaria issues only; can perform blood tests.

PALAWAN PUERTO PRINCESA & AROUND

MONEY

Important note: in all of Palawan only Puerto and Coron town on the far-north island of Busuanga have ATMs (well, Brooke's Point has a Landbank). Plan appropriately. There are several banks, plus a handful of moneychangers along Rizal Ave.

TOURIST INFORMATION

City Tourism Office (048-434 4211; www.visitpuertoprincesa.com; Puerto Princesa Airport; 6am-5pm) Has a desk in the airport terminal and an office just outside to the right.

Palawan Tourism Promotions & Development Office (048-433 2968; www.palawan.gov.ph; ground fl, Provincial Capital Bldg, Rizal Ave; 8am-noon & 1-5pm Mon-Fri) Extremely helpful staff. Ask for Rosalyn Palanca or Marabelle Buni.

Subterranean River National Park Office (048-723 0904; www.puerto-underground-river.com; City Coliseum, National Hwy, Bgy San Pedro; 8am-4pm Mon-Fri, 8am-noon & 1-5pm Sat & Sun) Standard Subterranean River permits (adult/child P150/100) issued here for those not booking with an agency; can usually purchase a day in advance but if travelling independently, don't show up in Sabang without one. Line up at counters one or two; it's best to avoid Fridays and weekends. The office is about 2km north of the centre.

Tubbataha Management Office (082-434 5759; www.tubbatahareef.org; 41 Abad Santos St) Provides information on trips to Tubbataha Reefs Natural Park.

TRAVEL AGENCIES

Floral Travel & Tours (048-434 2540; floral_travel@yahoo.com; Rizal Ave)

Inland Tours and Travel (048-434 1508, 0908 891 3347; www.inland-tours.com; 399 Rizal Ave; 7.30am-7pm) Booking agent for Lexus Shuttle for minivans to Sabang and El Nido.

Sanctuary Travel & Tours (048-434 7673; sanctuarytours@yahoo.com; Rizal Ave)

VISAS

Bureau of Immigration (BOI, 048-433 2248; 2nd fl, Servando Bldg, Rizal Ave; 8am-5pm Mon-Fri) Provides visa extensions.

Getting There & Away

AIR

Cebu Pacific has daily flights to Puerto Princesa from both Manila and Cebu, while PAL, Tigerair and AirAsia Zest have several daily flights from Manila only. Cebu Pacific also has thrice weekly flights to Iloilo on Panay.

Air Juan has flights to Busuanga (Thursday and Sunday) and the Cuyo Islands (Wednesday and Friday). Best to book a week in advance.

Malaysian airline MASwings temporarily suspended its Puerto to Kota Kinabalu flights; check to see if they're running again.

A larger, more modern terminal is expected to be operational by the end of 2016 with plans for direct flights from China and Korea.

BOAT

2GO Travel has weekly vessels from Puerto to Manila (P1500, 1am Sunday) via Coron.

BUSES & JEEPNEYS

All public buses, jeepneys and the majority of minivans operate from the San Jose terminal (otherwise known as the 'New Public Market'), 7km north of Puerto city centre off the National Hwy (tricycle is P50 per person or P140 or so if alone, multicab P13). It's a bit of a chaotic situation with makeshift sheds serving as terminals for individual companies.

The majority of departures are from 7am to 9am. There are other departures, some even late into the afternoon; however, it's best to show up as early as possible since vehicles don't leave until full – be prepared to wait and wait... Roro and Cherry buses are hit and miss in terms of quality and comfort. Note that routes, operators, departure times and fares change all the time.

CAR & MOTORCYCLE

If you've got the cash, hiring a car or van and a driver is a good way to get around, and with a big enough group it can be a reasonable option – try **Plong Car Rental** (0919 726 036, 048-723 1098; www.palawanselfdrivecarrental.com; 13 Capitol Commercial Complex) or a recommend-

BUSES FROM PUERTO PRINCESA

DESTINATION	COST	DURATION (HR)	FREQUENCY
Brooke's Point	P250	4	6 daily, 3am-9pm
El Nido	P380-480	6-9	4am to 10pm, every 2hr
Port Barton	P280	3½	7am, 9am (San Isidro bus)
Quezon	P200	3	hourly, 7am-5pm
Roxas	P150	2½	every 30min or so
Sabang	P200	2¼	7am, 9am, noon (D'Christ bus)
Taytay	P300	4½	4am-9pm

ed travel agency. The following are standard fares for a six-person van and driver: Narra (P3500), Sabang (P3500), Port Barton (P5500) and El Nido (P12,000).

MINIVANS

An increasing number of travellers fly into Puerto and immediately board 10- to 12-person minivans north for El Nido (P600 to P700, six hours). Some of the companies, including Lexus, also service Sabang (P350, two hours, 7.30, 8.30, 10am, 3pm, 5pm). Most offer airport or hotel pick-up though they often still stop at the bus terminal; last trip of the day is around 5.30pm. Eulen Joy and Fort Wally have sheds just outside the airport exit to the right.

Daytrippers (☎0917 848 8755; www.daytrippers.com)

Eulen Joy (☎0921 984 8150; eulenjoyexpress@yahoo.com)

Fort Wally (☎0917 276 2875, 048-434 2004; fortwallytransportation@yahoo.com)

Lexus Shuttle (☎0910 497 5610, 048-723 0128; Robinson's Place)

ℹ Getting Around

The fixed rate for a tricycle from the airport to any destination in central Puerto is P50; to San Jose bus terminal it's P120. Or you can simply walk out the driveway to Rizal Ave and flag one down for the standard fare (P8 for every 2km).

Multicabs (mini-jeepneys) clog the city's arteries; it's P10 for any ride, including from the centre of town to Robinson's Place.

A day spent riding a motorbike through the countryside around Puerto is a day well spent. **San Francisco DV's** (☎ mobile 0949 745 5013; mariodiego60@yahoo.com) and a number of other places along Rizal Ave near the airport advertise rentals and charge between P250 and P550 per day.

Sabang & Around
☎048

A wide beach dramatically framed by mountains and warm calm waters, Sabang certainly has more to offer than simply its most famous attraction. The dubious selection of Sabang's underground river as one of the 'seven wonders of the world' notwithstanding, the river is worth seeing if in the area. Perhaps the closest thing we can compare it to is a bumper-boat ride through a theme-park haunted house, albeit one punctuated with the sounds of dripping water and fluttering birds. After the hordes of day trippers who occupy the beachside picnic huts are ferried back to Puerto, it's impossible not to feel as if you were intruders in your own little paradise.

⊙ Sights & Activities

A few **snorkelling** spots are near Sabang, including Panganan Cave, Pilomena and Garcia islands (P800 per person, minimum four). **Fishing** expeditions can be arranged with Miguel Legaspi (0926 230 9137) at the little shed next to Green Verde Resort in the middle of Sabang beach, with other local boatmen or Daluyon Resort. Around half a dozen informal massage huts line the pathway along the Sabang beach; another whitesand beach lies just across the Poyuy-Poyuy River. A canopy walk around 5km from town was due to be finished late 2014.

Puerto Princesa Subterranean River National Park   BOAT TOUR
(www.puerto-undergroundriver.com; formerly St Paul Subterranean River) While the subterranean river is actually over 8km in length, standard tours only take you about 1.5km

EXPLORING SOUTHERN PALAWAN

Few people head south of Puerto, but for those who seek an adventurous alternative to more famous attractions elsewhere, the south offers rough but potentially rewarding travel. Highlights include **Tabon Caves**, near the town of Quezon; the daily market and beaches around **Narra**; and exploring **Mt Matalingahan** (2086m), the highest in Palawan, near the extremely remote town of **Rizal**.

into the river (the round trip is 45 minutes; beyond this point, navigation becomes difficult). The limestone cave that the river passes through is one of the longest navigable river-traversed tunnels in the world. In 2010 a team of Italian spelunkers discovered the million-year-old fossilised remains of a dugong (sea cow) on a part of the cave wall not currently open to the public.

The boat from Sabang pier drops you off on a beach near the entrance to the cave (a few crab-eating monkeys and monitor lizards roam the area); from there you walk five minutes to the actual entrance and are assigned a boat for the trip into the cave. This second boat fare is included in your permit fee. Along the way, your guide, with the help of a spotlight, will point out various features of the caves (this usually means one-liners and double entendres like 'we call that formation Sharon Stone' rather than geological facts).

Jungle Trail   HIKING

After visiting the subterranean river, energetic souls might want to return to Sabang on foot over the 5km-long Jungle Trail. Starting from the ranger station near the subterranean river, the Jungle Trail initially climbs very steeply over some overgrown limestone karsts before dividing into two paths. The right fork is the Jungle Trail (there's another ranger station where you can rest), and the left is the Monkey Trail (closed for many years now; talk was it would reopen in 2015).

You can also walk the Jungle Trail in the opposite direction from Sabang, but keep in mind that the trail officially closes at 3pm, it's not well marked and you need to purchase your park permit from the information office in Sabang.

Poyuy-Poyuy River   BOAT TOUR

(P150; ☉ 8am-4pm) This community-driven project involves paddling with a guide a few kilometres up the mangrove-lined, brackish Poyuy-Poyuy River. The trip takes less than an hour and is best done in the early morning when the birdlife (parrots, hornbills, herons etc) is more active. Otherwise, you might spot a few baby pythons and mangrove snakes. From January through May the water is clear and you can see to the bottom.

Follow the overgrown path at the northern end of the beach to the small office along the river.

Ugong Rock   HIKE

Around 20km from Sabang near barangay Tagabinet is the trailhead for the 7km hike to Ugong Rock, a karst formation with commanding views of the surrounding countryside. Ropes and wooden bridges allow you to explore the somewhat tricky path through strangely shaped tunnels and chambers – guides (P100) and permits (P100) are issued at the trailhead. It's possible to camp out overnight in an area village but you must bring your own tent.

The nearby zip-line is P500. A round-trip tricycle to the trailhead costs P700.

Sabang Zipline   ZIPLINE

(✍ in Puerto Princesa 048-434 2341; P550; ☉ 8am-5pm) Transport by jeep, raft and then short walk to this 800m long zipline on the other side of the mangroves at the eastern end of the beach. Ticket office is at the wharf.

🛏 Sleeping & Eating

Other than at the two high-end resorts (rumour was Accor and SM planned to build beachfront hotels in the near future), there is no hot water in Sabang and electricity runs only from around 6pm to 11pm. A few places along the beach offer very basic fan-cooled, cold-water rooms (P500 to P800), including Green Verde, Tabon, Tribal Lodge and Mary's, maybe the worst of the bunch. Most accommodations serve food and there are a couple of simple restaurants (fried chicken P160) near the pier; expect frustratingly slow service.

Dab Dab Resort   BUNGALOW $

(✍ 0949 469 9421; cottage P800; 🛜) This place, on the far side of the pier down a small dirt path, is an appealing haven. There's no beach here, only a rocky shoreline, but the seven hardwood cottages with nipa roofs are much nicer than those on the beach. Each is equipped with a ceiling fan, private porch and hammock. Ask for the friendly manager Mila Ponteras.

Simple meals (P180) can be provided in the equally attractive restaurant and lounge area.

Bambua Nature Cottages　　　LODGE **$**
(☑ 0927 420 9686; www.bambua-palawan.com; s/d without bathroom P250/450, cottage P800, r P1250) Get up close and personal with Sabang's magnificent rainforest in this garden lodge about a 15-minute walk south of town along the main road. There's a variety of rooms to choose from, many with stunning views.

★ Daluyon Resort　　　RESORT **$$$**
(☑ 048-723 0889; www.daluyonresort.com; r incl breakfast from P5500; ❈ ⊛ ≋) ✔ The Daluyon goes to show that luxury doesn't have to damage the aesthetic vibe of a beautiful locale, though you can't miss the two-storey thatched-roof cottages that peek out from behind towering palm trees. Inside, the rooms are all contemporary high end, from the flat-screen TVs to bathroom fixtures. The Daluyon has the best **restaurant** (mains P300 to P600) in Sabang.

Lounge chairs on the beach and in the pool area have some shade, though room balconies are great places to take in the views. All of Daluyon's vegies come from its organic farm.

Sheridan Beach Resort　　　RESORT **$$$**
(☑ 048-434 1449; www.sheridanbeachresort.com; r incl breakfast P7000; ❈ @ ⊛ ≋) This contemporary, somewhat generic resort, the newest addition to Sabang's beachfront, wouldn't be out of place in Boracay. An air of exclusivity, though not in itself a bad thing, feels a little out of place here. The only downside to the tastefully designed rooms is that they either face the large pool or each other in an outdoor corridor, rather than the beach.

❶ Getting There & Away

BOAT
During high season (November to May) bangkas chug from Sabang up to El Nido (P1800 per person, six hours) almost daily (7am and 1pm), with drop-offs in Port Barton (P1200 per person, 2½ hours). It's also easy to charter a boat on your own, which you'll have to do in the low/wet season (June to October); typical asking prices for six-passenger boats are P9000 for Port

Barton and P12,000 for El Nido. Assuming good weather, the trip to Port Barton is a pleasant and convenient choice; the long passage to El Nido can be trying.

BUS, JEEPNEY & MINIVAN
The turn-off to Sabang along the main highway is in Salvacion, from where it's a scenic 35km drive over a winding, sealed road.

Puerto
Most travel agencies, guesthouses and hotels in Puerto offer all-inclusive tours to the subterranean river and this is how the majority of day trippers arrive. Otherwise, the most comfortable transport option are the air-con minivans (P350, two hours) that make hotel pick-ups or leave from Puerto's San José bus terminal at 7am, 2pm and 4pm daily. They leave Sabang to return to Puerto at 7.30am, 1pm, 2pm, 4.30pm and 6pm. These fill quickly so book as early as possible.

There are two or three other departures a day that use a combination of jeepneys and buses (P200, three hours), and leave Puerto's bus terminal at 7am, 9am and noon; on the return trip, these leave Sabang at 7am, 10am, noon and 2pm (note that these are approximate times only).

North
Lexus Shuttle minivans ply the route north from Sabang to El Nido (P750, five to six hours, 7.30am, 8.30am, 1pm, 2pm, 4.30pm) and you can be dropped at the junction for Port Barton in San José (P600, 3½ hours) or Taytay.

Other options for reaching Port Barton or El Nido by road include a jeepney (P80), van (P120) or tricycle (P1000) to Salvacion (45 minutes to one hour) and wait for a passing bus, jeepney or van heading to Roxas, Taytay or El Nido (four hours); for Port Barton, you then need to get off at the highway junction at San José and hop on a tricycle or motorbike (P400, one hour). It's possible to arrange a private van for Port Barton (P5000, three hours) and El Nido (P7000, five hours). Look for Ed Garcia (☑ 0926 689 9812) where the road dead ends at the pier in Sabang.

NORTHERN PALAWAN

Many travellers make a beeline for this region and find it difficult to move on. Endowed with a bending and twisting coastline lined with secluded coves and beaches and labyrinthine offshore islands, it's seventh heaven for beachcombers and underwater adventurers alike. El Nido and Coron Town are the primary gateways to the area.

Port Barton & Around

POP 4400

Essentially a two-road town (Rizal and Boni-facio Sts run north–south for a few hundred metres) where the jungle drops precipitous-ly into the bay, Port Barton offers simple pleasures. It's the kind of place where, after just a few strolls down the beach, you don't want to share the tranquillity with outsid-ers. Several islands with good beaches and snorkelling aren't far offshore, as are rows and rows of buoys, the sign of working pearl farms. Jellyfish can be a problem for swim-mers at the town beach.

◉ Sights & Activities

Island-hopping **snorkelling trips** (half/full day for up to four people P700/P1400) with stops at various reefs and islands are at least the equal of similar trips in Honda Bay. The nearby **mangroves** (P700 for two, three

hours) and **Bigaho Waterfall** (P1500 for up to four) are also worth visiting. Friend-ly local boatman Jensen Gabco (☑ 0921 626 9191) can be recommended.

Long Beach
BEACH

One of the longest undeveloped beaches in the country is the 14km white-sand Long Beach on the mainland near San Vicente. Rumours that an airport with internation-al connections and Boracay-like hotels are imminent have lingered for nearly a decade.

Pamuayan Falls
WATERFALL

Cool off here after the 4km walk from town. Because the path is poorly marked you'll likely need to hire a guide (P200 to P400 de-pending on the number of people); the trail-head begins just past the Greenviews Resort.

Scuba Diving
DIVING

There are several reef, wall and wreck dives in the area, best done in the morning for the nice sunlight. **Easy Dive** (☑ 0918 402

North Palawan

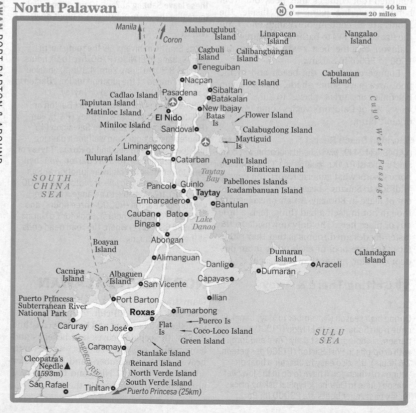

7041; www.palawaneasydive.com), at the southern end of the beach, and **Port Barton Divers** (☎0929 628 0425; www.portbartondivers.com) next to Jambalaya (it also has a shop in Puerto Princesa and is affiliated with Sea Dog Divers in El Nido), are both in ramshackle native style houses. Both offer three boat dives including equipment and lunch for around P3500.

🛏 Sleeping

🛏 Port Barton

A half-dozen or so resorts are located along the beachfront in town; some have hot water.

Ausan   COTTAGES $
(☎0929 444 0582; www.ausanbeachfront.com; cottages P550, r P950, q P2550; ❄🔊) An expanding group of cottages, Ausan caters to Filipino families as much as foreign travellers. Choose from several wood-floor cottages with colourful masonry in the bathooms and a few larger 'themed' rooms with trippy-looking wall murals and stonework. The creativity of the latter are undermined by chintzy furniture and satellite TVs.

No restaurant open at the time of research but future plans called for one as well as 24-hour electricity (currently 7am to midnight).

★Greenviews Resort   BUNGALOW $$
(☎0929 268 5333; www.palawandg.clara.net; r from P1000; 🔊) Solid hardwood bungalows, with simple, well-made furnishings, modern hot-water bathrooms and private porches, surround a large, nicely landscaped garden. The all-wood restaurant (mains P180 to P400) is on the 2nd floor of the beachfront house – expect slow service, especially when groups are in, but beautiful ocean views more than compensate. Live acoustic music Monday, Wednesday and Friday nights in high season.

The Greenviews owners have a property with a waterfall within hiking distance; they also rent kayaks, and have their own dive shop and their own boat for island-hopping.

Deep Moon Resort   RESORT $$
(☎0917 449 9212; www.deepgoldresorts.com; cottages P800-1500; ❄🔊) This resort at the southern end of the village is the only place in Port Barton where your front door opens directly onto the beach, at least as far as a

couple of A-frames with clean tile floors and modern bathrooms go. Otherwise, there a several more cottages and rooms set further back.

The larger beach A-frame (P1500) is especially recommended for its big stone bath and large porch. Hot-water shower available at night outside next to the restaurant. Japanese and other Asian fare (P60 to P250) is served up in the handsome all-wood lounge and restaurant area. Formerly Swissippini, then Ysobelle's, then Deep Gold, this place might be known to others by one of these names.

Elsa's Beach House Cottages   COTTAGES $$
(☎0908 271 4390; r P1000-1200; 🔊) This collection of spacious cottages towards the southern end of the beach has attractive hardwood floors and stone-and-bamboo walls – the only drawback is they face an inner garden and not the beach. At the time of writing, nine other rooms were going up in a row towards the back of the property. Extending out from the owner's home is a handsomely designed pavilion restaurant.

Summer Homes Beach Resort   MOTEL $$
(☎0946 995 7608; www.portbarton.info/summerhomes; r/cottage from P950/2000; ❄@🔊) Summer Homes spurns the native look with colourfully painted, fan-cooled, well-kept concrete cottages set on a manicured lawn. The back-row rooms are more basic than sea-facing ones.

🛏 Offshore Islands

Thelma & Toby's Island Camping Adventure (☎0999 486 3348, 048-434 8687; www.palawancamping.com; per person incl full board P1300; ☺mid-Nov–late-Apr) offers the rare opportunity to camp and live like a local islander.

You can ask to be dropped off at any of the following resorts when travelling by boat between other mainland destinations. Otherwise, transfers from Port Barton or San Vicente can be arranged with the hotel in advance or from boat operators in Port Barton or San Vicente. Average cost is P1500 one way for two to four people.

Coconut Garden Island Resort   RESORT $
(☎0918 370 2395; www.coconutgarden.palawan.net; Cacnipa Island; s/d P760/990, cottage P1250-1750) On the way to Port Barton from Sabang by boat, this resort occupies a truly lovely white-sand beach on Cacnipa Island. Several buildings, including a restaurant, a

handful of A-frame cottages and a row of basic rooms, are built up along a rise – all with ocean views and outdoor sitting areas.

Electricity is solar powered so a few rooms have lights 24 hours and one cottage has a hot shower. A caveat: not every room has a fan.

Blue Cove Tropical Island Resort   RESORT $$
(☑ 0908 562 0879; www.bluecoveresort.com; Albaguen Island; cottage with fan/air-con P1500/3000; ❄🛜) On Albaguen Island, a half-hour bangka ride from Port Barton, the Blue Cove's handful of cottages, basic in design and tucked underneath overhanging palms set back from the beach, are a miniretreat from the world. A charming beachside restaurant and bar also serves lunching day trippers.

Secret Paradise Resort   RESORT $$$
(☑ 0928 339 9446; www.secretparadiseresort.com; r P4500-9000; 🛜) 🏖 Stress seems to slide away at this tranquil hideaway, on a pretty little bay not far from San Vicente. The British owners, dedicated to conservation, have created a mini protected marine area with good snorkelling in front of several white-sand beaches. Several cottages are ideally spaced for maximum privacy, and a few rooms share a building with the restaurant.

✖ Eating

All of the resorts have their own restaurants which are open to nonguests.

★ Jambalaya Cajun Cafe   CAFE $$
(☑ 0915 315 3842; mains P200-300; ⊙ 7am-9pm; 🛜) A homey and quirky vibe and a great beachfront location makes Filipina-owned Jambalaya the place to hang in Port Barton. Of course jambalaya (the New Orleans cajun version of paella, P300) is the specialty; milkshakes (available all day thanks to the generator) and imported coffee are also on the menu. In addition, there's a book exchange and board games.

Only three tables and a funky treehouse-like platform with pillows for lounging means reservations are recommended for dinner in the high season. The 'mega mix cereal bowl' made with 10 healthy ingredients is a great breakfast.

Ayette's Bamboo House Restaurant   FILIPINO $
(mains P99-300; ⊙ 6.30am-9.30pm) Near the Caltex station, Ayette's is a friendly family-run place with several tablecloth-clad picnic tables and a few small nipa huts in the yard. Seafood dishes such as the fish curry and shrimp *sinigáng* are especially good. Happy hour means P35 San Miguel beers.

❶ Information

The town has electricity from around 6pm to midnight. Most of the accommodations have wi-fi, though usually only during the hours when there's power. There's no bank; a few resorts accept Visa and MasterCard.

A **Tourist Assistance Center** (☑ 0909 878 9102; ⊙ 8am-5pm) of limited utility has its headquarters on the 2nd floor of a wooden structure in the middle of the beach, near the Caltex station; set prices for various boat trips are posted.

❶ Getting There & Away

BOAT

During the November to May high season, it's possible to be dropped off in Port Barton on the regular scheduled boats between El Nido (P1500, five hours, 6am) and Sabang (P1200, 3½ hours). However, these boats are not allowed to pick up passengers, so if you want to leave Port Barton on one, you can be picked up on nearby Cacnipa Island. It's also easy to charter a boat on your own (ask at the Tourist Assistance Center) or join up with a group already doing the same; however, you might have to wait several days, at least during the low season. An association of sorts fixes the prices for most of the island-hopping and longer trips. To Sabang, a small boat that holds four people is P5000; on a larger boat that can hold up to eight, the rate is P6000. To El Nido, a small/large boat is around P8000/12,000. To San Vicente (45 minutes), a town along the mainland coast to the north, it's P700 per person.

BUS, JEEPNEY & MINIVAN

The 22km roadway between Port Barton and the highway at San José is improved and primarily paved though still rocky in parts. In good weather the trip is a scenic and thrifty mode of transport.

During the peak season San Isidro Express runs one daily air-con minivan (P250, three hours, 2pm) to Puerto.

A jeepney (an old, oversized one with forward-facing seats) runs daily from Port Barton to Puerto (P250, five hours, departs around 9am). It leaves from the waiting shed near the Bamboo House Restaurant. Minvans for six people can be hired to Puerto (P4500 to P5000, three hours) and El Nido (P7000, four to 4½ hours). Ask at Greenviews or Ausan.

Between Port Barton and Roxas, there is one jeepney a day (P150, 1½ hours, departing from the waiting shed between 8am and 9am), with the same schedule in the other direction. From Roxas you can grab a bus or minivan further north.

It's also possible to 'charter' a motorcycle or tricycle (P400, one hour) to or from the highway junction at San José (tricycles can be dangerous on downhill sections); you can also ride the regular morning jeepney (P100, one hour). From here, catch onward transport (buses and vans) north to Taytay and El Nido, or south to Sabang (you'll have to transfer again at the junction at Salvacion) and Puerto.

Taytay & Around

048 / POP 70,800

Formerly the capital of Palawan, today Taytay (*tye*-tye), a sleepy (comatose on Sundays) coastal town and primarily a way station for travellers, is distinguished by an impressive relic of the area's colonial history. Built on the very edge of town, the thick walls of Santa Isabel Fort (Kutang Santa Isabel) guarded against attacks from Moro pirates. On the right by the entrance is a marker indicating that it was first erected by the Augustinian Recollects (an order of Catholic priests) in 1667. Inside the enclosure is a well-maintained grassy garden and sweeping views of the bay.

More than a 20-minute drive south of town is Lake Danao (Manguao), the largest freshwater lake in Palawan. There are some trails for walking or mountain biking, and wildlife, including monkeys, monitor lizards and rare birds, abounds. Dugongs and elusive Irrawady dolphins can be spotted in the Malampaya Sound.

🛏 Sleeping

🛏 Taytay

Casa Rosa HOTEL $$
(☑0920 895 0092; www.casarosataytay.com; r without bathroom P500, cottages incl breakfast P1200-1500; ❄🛜) Located on a hill behind the town hall, with expansive bay views, this is the only recommended place to stay if you're stuck for a night in Taytay. Five cottages and two rooms – the former with terracotta floors and spacious bathrooms – and a nice little restaurant (mains P150 to P250).

🛏 OffShore Islands

Most guests transfer to these resorts from Taytay's airport or pier for an additional cost. Another option for all three is by boat from Batakalan, a tiny fishing village on the mainland about a 45-minute rough ride

directly east of El Nido. There's one daily jeepney from El Nido (P90, 1½ hours), or a tricycle (P750) or minivan can be hired.

Dilis Beach Resort RESORT $$
(☑0929 376 6100; www.dilisbeachresort.com; r/cottage per person incl meals P1500/2000) Located on Icadambanuan Island, at the south end of Taytay Bay, Dilis is a little offshore paradise. It has seven cottages, some fronting a white-sand beach, and two other modern rooms in a house set at the top of a hill. Food is especially good for such a modest operation.

★ **Flower Island Beach Resort** RESORT $$$
(☑ in Manila 0917 504 5567, mobile 0918 446 5473; www.flowerisland-resort.com; fan/air-con cottages incl all meals per person P4500/6100; ❄🛜) 🌿 Warning: leaving this idyllic low-key resort can induce severe depression. You might never have it so good again – the staff are warm and friendly, the native-style cottages such a perfect mix of modern comforts and rustic charm, and the small beach is of the whitest sand. Full moons induce skinny dipping with a rum and Coke in hand.

Guests can also bed down in the five-storey hilltop tower which has aerial views of the sea. Tours of the pearl farm factory nearby, which is owned by the same people as the resort, are fascinating. Affiliated with the Save Palawan Seas Foundation. Boat transfer fees are P4000 for four to six people one way from Taytay or P3000 to Batalakan (from there they can arrange a van for P2500 to El Nido).

Apulit Island RESORT $$$
(☑ in Manila 02-844 6688; www.elnidoresorts.com; cottages per person incl all meals from P10,000; ❄🛜🛏) This exclusive resort has rows of deluxe cabanas built directly over the water, which at night is illuminated by spotlights, turning it a translucent green. The offshore island nature reserve means there's nearby coral and marine life, perfect for snorkelling, and a range of other water-based activities.

❶ Getting There & Away

AIR
Taytay's Cesar Lim Rodriguez Airport (also known as Sandoval), located at the northern end of Taytay Bay about 30km from town over a rough road, wasn't receiving ITI flights when we were there. If operating, it's primarily for guests of Apulit Island Resort.

BOAT

For boats to and from El Nido (P2500, three hours) and other west-coast towns, you must use the pier at Embarcadero (also known as Agpay), an 8km tricycle ride (P150) from town. Other trips, like to the offshore resorts, leave from the pier next to the fort in town.

BUS, JEEPNEY & MINIVAN

You can usually find a seat on one of the buses, jeepneys and minivans stopping in Taytay on their way between Puerto (P220, five to six hours) and El Nido (P150, 1½ hours). Grab a bench and coffee at the Taytay terminal while waiting for connections. The road north is now mostly paved, although there are still patches of rough gravel and dirt. A tricycle is P50 to P60 from the Taytay terminal to the town pier.

El Nido

🏖 048 / POP 36,200

The ordinariness (and some might say the ugliness) of El Nido only heightens the contrast between the mundane and the sublime. Spanish for 'the nest', El Nido is the gateway to the fabulous Bacuit Archipelago. The town, sandwiched between towering limestone karst cliffs and Bacuit Bay, is cluttered with buildings that creep onto the beach and businesses that cater to tourists. Centre stage is the looming Cadlao Island just offshore.

Taking a room in town means being close to restaurants and beachside bars, but also closer to the everyday sights and sounds; otherwise, you can stay in one of the nearby communities, or splash some cash for accommodation in the archipelago itself. Something of a French invasion is occurring among accommodation, restaurant and other tourism-related businesses.

⊙ Sights

The Makinit hotspring, basically a very hard-to-find swampy creek with water scalding to the touch, is not worth a visit.

Nagkalit-kalit Waterfalls   WATERFALLS

Several kilometres after you've turned off the main road heading north from El Nido, you will pass by a house signposted Nagkalit-kalit Waterfalls; from here it's a 45-minute walk through several rivers (wear waterproof shoes) to the small pool at the base of the falls, which you can swim in. Ask at the house for a guide (P300), who you'll need to find the falls.

Balay Cuyunon   MUSEUM

(Sibaltan Museum; Sibaltan) You can take a guided tour (in English) of this well-preserved traditional Cuyonese home to learn about ordinary village life. Located on the east side of the mainland and not the easiest to reach via public transportation, consider a night in a native-style room to experience this community's daily rhythms. Admission by donation.

Activities

As things become more congested, more travellers are looking to find less standardised ways of exploring the area. With a little planning, flexibility and time you can still find quiet and beautiful out-of-the-way spots.

Although often overlooked, the inland area around El Nido offers several interesting trips for the active and adventurous. El Nido Boutique & Art Café is a one-stop-shop for **hiking, mountain-biking** and **cliff-climbing** (P350, one hour) trips; half-day treks to **Cadlao Island** are popular. **Stand-up paddleboarding** (P900), **windsurfing** (P1500) and **kitesurfing** are also now possible. The latter is done off the east coast of the mainland from November to April; get in touch with Qi Palawan (p398).

Island-Hopping

The most popular activity in El Nido is island-hopping and snorkelling in the Bacuit Archipelago. There are standard itineraries advertised by seemingly every shopfront and hotel; those that don't can certainly arrange matters regardless. Prices are also standard, although some charge extra for snorkelling gear, and all include lunch (grilled fish, rice, salad, fruit and coffee). Tour A, which takes in various lagoons and beaches, is P1200; Tour B, covering Snake Island, caves and Pinabuyutan Island, is P1300; Tour C, heading to Tapiutan Island, Matinloc Island and Secret Beach, is P1400; and the new Tour D, which is basically a Cadlao Island trip with stops at three to four beaches, is P1200. El Nido Boutique & Art Café (p401) is especially recommended. Some operators, include the Art Cafe, are encouraging more kayaking to limit the environmental impact of tourism.

Stop by **Tao Philippines** (📞 0915 509 4488; www.taophilippines.com) and consider taking a highly recommended overnight island-hopping tour.

Every person entering the Bacuit Archipelago must pay a P200 Eco-Tourism Development Fee (ETDF) meant to fund conservation projects; the small ticket is valid

El Nido

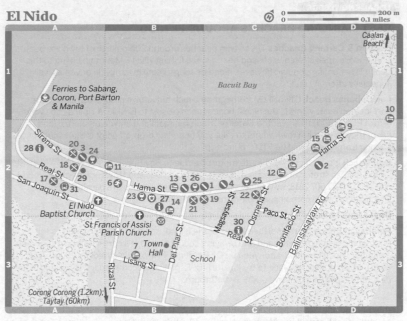

El Nido

for 10 days and can be purchased from most hotels or boat operators.

Many people are choosing to rent a kayak (half-day/day P450/700) and doing their own more limited island-hopping. The standard rate for renting snorkel gear is P100 each for mask and fins.

Diving
Along with a construction boom, El Nido has experienced a diving boom. Over a dozen shops now operate in town and nearly two dozen dive sites beckon, from shallow reefs to deep wall and drift dives, making it a popular destination for PADI certification courses.

LOCAL KNOWLEDGE

BEST MAINLAND BEACHES AROUND EL NIDO

Nacpan & Caitang Beaches These twin beaches around 20km north of town are beautiful, undeveloped stretches of sand near a small fishing village. Mountain biking to this beach is becoming popular; however, it can be tough going in a tricycle or van as well, especially after any rain.

Las Cabanas Beach Officially Maremegmeg beach but known around town for the resort located nearby, this is the nicest beach that's closest to El Nido. A zipline (one way/ return P500/900) flies over the water between the mainland and an offshore island. Every tricycle driver in town wants to take you here. The drop-off point is 3km south of Corong Corong – should be P150 round-trip.

Duli Beach It's a difficult 45-minute motorbike ride to Bgy Bucana and this jungle-backed stretch of white sand. Nearby, between Duli and **Dagmy Beach**, is **Verde Safari** (0917 507 2818; www.verdesafari.com; Bgy Teneguiban; up to 8 people P13,500), which offers beach camping, a rock-climbing wall and day visitors.

Dagal Dagal Beach Only a 15-minute tricycle ride or 30-minute walk from Las Cabanas.

Palabayan Beach On the northeast side of the island, near Bgy San Fernando, is this photogenic beach of white sand and swaying coconut trees. It's certainly worth spending a night or two at husband-and-wife-run **Qi Palawan** (www.qipalawan.com; r P6000-7250;), which is also the place to try kitesurfing. Especially recommended is the 2nd-floor beachfront villa with massive open-air bathroom.

Highlights include South Miniloc's cabbage coral and school of yellow snapper; North Rock's barracuda, spade fish and interesting rock formations; Twin Rocks for turtles and stingrays; and for advanced divers, Helicopter Island's 50m long natural tunnel. The average cost for two boat dives with equipment is P2800. The following are official PADI members and especially recommended:

Tabanka Divers   DIVING
(0905 225 3464; www.tabanka-divers.com; Ogie's Beach Pension, Hama St) German-Filipino owned, Tabanka is run by the professional and passionate Oliver Bachmann. Three dives P3800 and three-day PADI open-water courses for P19,900.

Palawan Divers   DIVING
(0916 552 1938; www.palawandivers.com.ph; Hama St) Well-oiled and friendly. Planning on opening a free-diving school and sailing safaris to Coron for divers.

Submariner Diving Center   DIVING
(0905 484 1764; ronny.oliwka@hotmail.com; Hama St) Recommended dive shop in El Nido.

Sea Dog Divers   DIVING
(0916 777 6917; barringtonwhiteley@gmail.com; Rizal St) Recommended dive shop in El Nido.

Deep Blue Seafari   DIVING
(0917 803 0543; www.deepblueseafari.com; Hama St) Offering highly recommended four

day, three night diving 'safaris' between El Nido and Coron from mid-October to mid-August (P34,000 per person). Nights are spent camping or in beach cottages for groups on islands along the way.

Sleeping

Most of El Nido's beachfront space is a claustrophobic hodgepodge of small buildings and construction sites. With nary another inch of sand to spare, hotels – aesthetics be damned – are going up quickly along the inland side of Hama St. The further west you go, the narrower the beach becomes and the more bangkas block your way. Hot water is uncommon in budget and even midrange accommodation (and best not to brush teeth with tap water as it generally comes from deep wells), while electricity runs from around 2pm to 6am; many hotels have generators for backup. Rumour was 24-hour electricity would arrive in 2015. Low-season rates are on average 30% to 40% less than those listed in our reviews.

If you want to escape the tourist scene, consider places in quiet Caalan Beach, accessible from the walkway at the eastern end of El Nido beach (possible to swim here at high tide). Corong Corong, a waterfront village a few kilometres south (tricycle ride from town P15), is experiencing its own hotel construction boom. It's worth noting, though, that its sandy beach covered with overhanging palm trees is about the width of a beach towel.

Camping on offshore islands is illegal; however, you can camp on the mainland at Sibaltan on the east coast and north at Verde Safari (p398). When we visited it was possible to 'squat' on the beach at Las Cabanas – this could change. Alternatively, you can stay in one of the top-end resorts in the bay.

El Nido

Ogie's Beach Pension
HOTEL $

(OG's; ☑0916 707 0393; ogspensionne@yahoo.com; cnr Hama & Del Pilar Sts; s/d P950/1200, without bathroom P750/950; ✳🛜) Situated right in the middle of the beach, from the outside Ogie's looks like a small vacant office building, so the clean but basic rooms are a mild surprise. Unfortunately, there are a few annoyances, such as some toilets lacking seats. It's mostly concrete throughout, including the large, primarily unfurnished 2nd-floor sitting area with ocean views where breakfast is served.

El Nido Sands Inn
GUESTHOUSE $

(☑0999 452 5843; Sirena St; dm/d without bathroom P300/600; 🛜) The simple clapboard rooms, all with shared bathrooms lacking toilet seats, are arguably El Nido's best budget deal. The lone dorm has just three sturdy bunk beds and they are first come, first serve – good luck. Nice wood floor and public balcony with views. It's near the pier.

Our Melting Pot Hostel
HOTEL $

(OMP; ☑0906 412 7861; ourmeltingpotbackpackers@gmail.com; Real St; dm incl breakfast P550; 🛜) Low-maintenance hardcore budget travellers who don't mind crowded sleeping conditions will be happy here. Hot water and sheets provided, while privacy is supplied by thin curtains on the bunks. One private single with a fan available.

Entalula
HOTEL $$

(☑0920 906 6550; www.entalula.com; s/d incl breakfast P2700/3000; ✳🛜) Entalula has what are perhaps the finest of the beachfront stand-alone cottages, with private porches, wood floors and nice bathrooms behind sliding doors. Ten other rooms are in a two-storey building set back from the beach that also doubles as the owner's home (you can join the family in watching sports on TV).

Balay Paragua
INN $$

(☑0912 387 6337; paragua_23@yahoo.com; Lisang St; r with fan/air-con incl breakfast P1300/2300;

✳🛜) A particularly tasteful refuge away from the chaos of Hama St, this seven-room two-storey inn has attractive wood and bamboo rooms. The 2nd-floor porch has a few small tables where coffee is served and there's one little A-frame budget room across the street above a *sari-sari* store and booking office.

Rosanna's Beach Cottages
HOTEL $$

(☑0920 605 4631; rosannascottaages_elnido@yahoo.com.ph; Hama St; r incl breakfast P2500; ✳🛜) Expanded and grown up, Rosanna's has a full-on modern atrium lobby. However, rooms in this new building have mismatched linens and hotel-style furniture; sea-facing ones are definitely preferred. Best are the four older rooms with private beachfront porches and hardwood floors. Across the street, a modern annex with six rooms is good for groups. Solar-powered hot-water showers.

Chislyk Cottages
BUNGALOW $$

(☑0918 243 3780; gladysmisajon@yahoo.com; cottage with fan/air-con P1000/1500; ✳🛜) Several small bamboo and concrete cottages share an almost stamp-sized beachfront; however, each has its own porch – a big amenity in this price range. Warm and attentive manager; instant coffee and tea served in the morning. Downside is the water has a sulfur smell.

Tandikan Cottages
COTTAGES $$

(☑0920 318 4882; tandikan_elnido@yahoo.com; Hama St; cottages with fan/air-con incl breakfast P1200/1800, q P3000; ✳🛜) Four basic, clean and well-made concrete and woven-mat bamboo cottages with thatched roofs. Each has a small porch, though only two face the beach. Another four rooms were being built when we visited.

El Nido Garden Beach Resort
RESORT $$$

(☑0915 489 9009, 048-723 0127; www.elnidogardenresort.com; r incl breakfast P5300; ✳🛜🍴) Because it's located at the far eastern end of El Nido, where there's a seawall instead of sand, this resort has improvised its own unique beach. Bungalows are built of concrete, stone and wood, and have high-end touches in the bathrooms. All surround a nicely landscaped garden and pool.

El Nido Beach Hotel
HOTEL $$$

(☑048-723 0887; www.elnidobeachhotel.com; Hama St; r incl breakfast P3500-4000; ✳🛜) You can't miss this two-storey, modern hotel. It occupies a long stretch of sand on the eastern edge of the beach.

⚓ Caalan Beach

La Salagane HOTEL $$
(📱0916 648 6994; www.lasalagane.com; r incl breakfast from P2500; ❋🛜) Essentially apartments, the extremely attractive and warm rooms in this two-storey building feel like a home away from home and are great for long stays (another La Salagane hotel is in town).

Makulay Lodge & Villas GUESTHOUSE $$
(📱0917 257 3851; makulayelnido@yahoo.com; r/apt from P1000/2700; 🛜) Occupying a small rise, immediately after you round the corner from town, Makulay offers convenience, privacy and wonderful views from the hilltop apartments and a newly carved out small sandy area with lounge chairs. The more utilitarian ground-floor rooms have their own kitchens and open onto a small outdoor sitting area.

Golden Monkey Cottages COTTAGES, HOTEL $$
(📱0929 206 4352; www.goldenmonkeyelnido.com; cottages P2400-5400, r P5400; ❋🛜) Greatly expanded, a handful of nipa cottages share the lushly landscaped property with a modern three story buildling. Breakfast included and electricity available 10am to 6am.

Kalinga Beach Resort COTTAGES $$
(📱0921 570 0021; sunset@kalingabeachresort. com; r P1800; ❋🛜🏊) A few nicely constructed bungalows with individual porches; fan and air-con rooms available. A small plunge pool was being built at the time of our visit. Only a large, awkwardly furnished family room faces the waterfront.

Cadlao Resort RESORT $$$
(📱0917 589 7069; www.cadlaoresort.com; r incl breakfast P7900; ❋🛜🏊) Half a dozen cottages, each with its own porch, face a landscaped garden with towering palm trees. No beach and a rocky shore; however, stunning sunset views of Cadlao Island from the infinity pool are more than enough. The most upscale place on the mainland. Nonguests can eat at the pleasant open-air **restaurant** (mains P250 to P400).

⚓ Corong Corong & Around

Greenviews Resort COTTAGES $$
(📱0921 586 1422; www.palawan-greenviews.com; Corong Corong; s/d with fan P1900/2400, with air-con P2200/2700; ❋🛜) Like its sister property in Port Barton, Greenviews looks like it was put together by highly skilled craftsmen.

From the hardwood floors, to the room furniture, to the wonderfully designed benches in the 2nd-storey restaurant, everything is a cut above the quality found elsewhere. Hot water in the modern bathrooms.

The British-Filipina couple who own Greenviews have a 10-hectare farm with a small waterfall good for swimming nearby. Guests are encouraged to visit.

Island Front Cottages COTTAGES $$
(📱0999 994 1309; www.islandfrontcottage.com; Corong Corong; r with fan/air-con incl breakfast from P1500/2000; ❋🛜) Somehow these overly decorated, colourful bamboo rooms, set in a cramped, wild garden, find a way to charm, with a mishmash of colours and carved wooden knick-knacks. Though it's on the beach there's little space for more than a bath towel.

★ El Nido Overlooking COTTAGES $$$
(www.elnido-overlooking.com; Corong Corong; d P3700, q P9000; ❋🛜🏊) Million-peso views are everywhere you look. No competition, if beachfront isn't the be-all and end-all for you, it's the place to stay in El Nido. It's up a steep hill and steps to the four villas featuring terracotta floors, high ceilings, teak decks with hammocks and flat-screen TVs. Also has a small infinity pool and lounge area.

The four person 'family villa' has its own pool and massive outdoor space. The generator here kicks in a few hours of extra electricity from 7am to 10am. Arnaud, the French owner, is building a small resort of similar style just down the hill on the beach in Corong Corong.

Las Cabanas Beach Resort COTTAGES $$$
(📱0917 887 8808; www.lascabanasresort.com; d/tr incl breakfast P5000/6000) Five large cottages, spread out in a large nicely landscaped garden, front the beach and have great views. With luggage it's best accessed by boat; otherwise it can be reached by following the footpath off the main road about 3km south of town and then walking a few hundred metres along the beach.

Dolarog Beach Resort RESORT $$$
(www.dolarog.com; s/d incl breakfast & dinner from P6000/10,400; ❋🛜) Although it's technically on the Palawan mainland, Dolarog Beach Resort is really only accessible by a half-hour bangka ride from town. Lining a small white-sand beach is a variety of fan and air-con cottages with hardwood floors and charming porches. A modern, low-slung building

WATER WORLD: OVERNIGHT TRIPS BETWEEN EL NIDO & CORON TOWN

Stepping aboard the bangka is stepping into another world. One whose daily rhythms are governed by the sun, napping and doing cannonballs off your boat and whose rituals involve being told to 'Attack!' the buffet of freshly caught seafood. Spot some seaweed while snorkelling and voila, it's a side dish at dinner. Zigzagging through the Bacuit Archipelago, Linapacan, Culion and the Calamianes on a Tao Philippines (www.taophilippines.com; offices in El Nido & Coron Town)' bankga expedition is easily the highlight of any trip to northern Palawan or perhaps all of the Philippines. It offers a rare opportunity to experience and interact with people and communities, unmediated by the mass tourism industry. Travellers stay in beachside nipa huts in remote fishing villages, albeit one of these has a karaoke bar and, somewhat surprisingly, most have a makeshift basketball court. Evenings are spent sipping rum drinks, watching the sunset or maybe a little homemade poi performance, star gazing and wondering how you can ever re-enter the everyday world again.

On the way you might learn about some of the education, nutrition, health advocacy and sustainable livelihood programs run by Tao, a socially conscious company that recently created the nonprofit Tao-Kalahi Foundation; it also built 100 fibreglass boats for area fishermen who lost theirs from Typhoon Haiyan/Yolanda.

These increasingly popular Coron to El Nido expeditions run between October and June (it has overnight trips around El Nido and Coron in August and September). All-inclusive costs are great value at P25,000 per person for the regular five day/four night trip. You can also opt for its 'paraw' trips on a uniquely constructed sail boat or the 'Flying Fish', a private three day/two night motorboat trip between El Nido and Coron (on demand and only in peak season).

Tao has small offices in El Nido and Coron Town and a larger base of operations at the Tao House near the Corong Corong public high school. You'll need a dry bag of around 30L (you can purchase these at Tao, Art Café in El Nido or various shops in Coron Town).

has several 'garden rooms', though these have less character. Daily island-hopping trips are included in the rates.

Beach Shack COTTAGES $$$

(☑ 0917 577 7513; bb_1352@yahoo.com; r P3500; ❄ 🛜) These three stand-alone hot-water cottages with white woven bamboo walls, wood floors, large porches with sliding doors and corrugated tin roofs occupy prime real estate on Las Cabanas beach. No daytime privacy because it's equally popular for its casual open-air eatery (7am to 8pm) with a bit of a Miami beach vibe. Just to the left of where the path from the road ends at the beach.

🍴 Eating

A number of stand-alone restaurants catering specifically to foreigners are found along Hama St; these have generic international and Filipino menus. Of the hotels, La Salagane (p402) has the best restaurant.

IBR FILIPINO $

(Hama St; mains P85; ⊙ 24hr) A Filipino greasy spoon where backpackers (often nursing a hangover) and locals chow down on soups and rice and meat dishes. Streetside fan seating and an air-con dining room in back.

Blue Azul Restaurant INTERNATIONAL $

(Real St; mains P140; ⊙ 6am-10pm; 🛜) Falafel, shwarma and pad thai are just a few of the offerings found here.

El Nido Boutique & Art Café INTERNATIONAL $$

(Sirena St; mains P220; ⊙ 6.30am-11pm; 🛜) Everyone ends up here at some point. Rightfully so. The large 2nd-storey dining room is a warm and relaxed place to eat, drink and get your bearings. Especially good are the salads (using lettuce and arugula from its own organic farm), homemade bread, seafood curry, pizza, pineapple upside down cake and chocolate and mango tarts. It has a bar and live music five nights a week.

La Plage FRENCH $$

(Corong Corong; mains P275) Something of a secret, this French-owned beachfront restaurant in Corong Corong has a small menu and relaxed vibe fitting for its beachfront location.

V & V Bagel CAFE, INTERNATIONAL $$

(Hama St; bagels P200-250; ⊙ 7.30am-8.30pm; 🛜) Certainly pricey, but New York city bagels by way of France are a nice change of pace. Other breakfast items are on the menu and the cheesecake is recommended.

Squido's Restaurant INTERNATIONAL $$
(Hama St; mains P150) Reminiscent of traveller spots in southern Thailand, Squido's has a widescreen TV that is never turned off and a varied menu. **Squido's Hilltop**, up a steep flight of steps around 1.5km north of town, has sunset views and live music most nights; buffet food and service are lacklustre.

★**Trattoria Altrove** ITALIAN $$$
(☑0947 775 8653; Hama St; mains P390; ⊘5-10pm) This Slovenian-owned place does the best pizza in El Nido, made with imported mozzarella in the street-level brick oven. A dozen types of pasta (P230), plus T-bone steak and other meat dishes are on the menu. During the high season especially it gets very crowded; you're in for a long wait if not there before 6.30pm or so. The handsome, wood-floor dining room and balcony with prime people-watching is on the 2nd floor.

Mezzanine El Nido ITALIAN $$$
(Sirena St; mains P250-400; ⊘11am-midnight; ☎) Stylish and sophisticated, the loungey 2nd-floor restaurant has waterfront views and a half-dozen varieties of pizza. Recommended dishes on the menu are seafood risotto, mussels and homemade ice cream (P160).

🍷 Drinking & Nightlife

Sea Slugs (mains P160; ⊘to 11pm or later) – an unfortunate name but it does get the speed of service about right – and Ogie's (p399) are great places to spend an evening when the sun goes down, the tiki torches are lit and the duelling acoustic guitar performances begin. The food – standard pasta, chicken and fish – however, can't live up to the ambience.

Full-moon parties are taking off during the high season at Swiss-owned **V-Bar** on Seven Commandos Beach. Boats (P200 return) pick-up and drop-off partiers from town (in front of Marber's restaurant on the beach).

★**Pukka Bar** BAR
(mains P150-300; ⊘4pm-3am; ☎) One of the most happening beachfront spots, especially after midnight, Pukka has live reggae, tables on the beach and a menu of Filipino fare, pizza, ribs and more. It also offers five small, well-kept backpacker rooms.

La Salagane BAR
(Sirena St; ⊘7am-10.30pm) Best of the hotel bars, sophisticated La Salagane makes its own uniquely flavoured rums. The food (mains P250 to P400) here is also recommended.

Water Hole BAR
(Hama St) Locals and tourists rub elbows at this low-key drinker's bar where a rum and Coke runs to P80. Facing the street, but the woven mat bamboo adds some character.

Asylum Bar BAR
(Hama St; ⊘8pm-2am) As the night wears on, the soundtrack moves from karaoke to discotheque, and feet and sometimes fists fly – good thing the police station is next door. This noisy, smoke-filled, mostly local place has cheap drinks, though you'll want to avoid the CR (bathroom).

ℹ Information

Keep in mind that there are no banks or ATMs in El Nido (rumor was BPI would open one once 24-hour electricity arrived). Most hotels and restaurants offer wi-fi and there are several internet cafes along Hama and Sirena Sts. Hama St is full of streetfront booking and travel agencies.

City Tourism Office (☑0917 788 7024; www.elnidotourism.com; Real St; ⊘8am-8pm Mon-Fri, to 5pm Sat & Sun) Staff are eager to help.

El Nido Boutique & Art Café (☑0920 902 6317; www.elnidoboutiqueandartcafe.com; Sirena St; ⊘6.30am-11pm; ☎) A one-stop shop for all your travelling needs (the travel center desk is open from 7am to 8pm). It will change money (no cash advances on credit cards); help you make international and domestic telephone calls; handles ITI and other airline bookings and onward boat transport (5% commission on some bookings). Importantly, it offers every imaginable water and land tour in the area. Also a book exchange, clothing, gear and souvenir store, and internet cafe (per hour P100); wi-fi for customers.

El Taraw Ticketing Agency (☑0918 648 6765; boyet_dandal@yahoo.com; Sirena St) Can book all airlines.

ℹ Getting There & Away

AIR

ITI (☑in Manila 02-851 5674; www.itiair.com) is the only airline flying into El Nido's privately run Lio Airport, 7km north of town (a tricycle there will cost P150 to P200). Seats on its new 50-seater planes are for guests of Bacuit Bay's El Nido Resorts; however, if space is available nonguests can book through El Nido Boutique & Art Café (p402) (in person or via email; from Manila flights, only five days in advance). Three flights daily between Manila and El Nido (P6750) and promo fares often available (P5000 to P6000). Luggage allowance of 10kg is strictly enforced; anything over incurs a stiff penalty. Drinks and snacks are served in the waiting shed at the airport.

BOAT

The most important boat service for visitors to northern Palawan is the El Nido–Coron connection. Oversized motorised bangka boats (M/Bca *Overcomer*, M/Bca *Bunso* and M/Bca *Jessabel* operate different days of the week) leave daily in good weather at around 7.30am (P1800 including lunch, coffee and soft drinks, seven to eight hours), though delays are common. Don't assume daily departures during the low season.

A bangka for hire costs around P15,000 to Coron.

There are infrequent boats to Sabang (P8500 to P13,000, seven hours) with drop-offs in Port Barton (P6000 to P12,000, 4½ hours). Costs depend on size of the boat and number of people.

The masochistic with plenty of time on their hands can consider **Atienza Shipping Lines** (☑ 0999 881 7266), which travels from El Nido to Manila (P1700, 29 hours, 7.30am Tuesday) via Liminangcong, Taytay and Coron.

BUS, JEEPNEY & MINIVAN

The majority of visitors to El Nido arrive on minivans from Puerto (P600, five-plus hours). To Roxas it's P450 where you can change for a jeepney to Port Barton. Contact any of the companies listed here or El Nido Boutique & Art Café in advance to book a seat (you can pay via PayPal on Art Café's website). Privately hired vans are another option; to Puerto it's around P8000 to P10,000.

Slower and less comfortable buses run south with stops in Taytay (P200 to P250, 1¼ hours) and Roxas (P250 to P300, six hours) before arriving in Puerto (P450 to P600, seven to eight hours). **Cheery Bus** and **Roro Bus** have departures every two hours from 7am to 9pm; the former alternates between ordinary and air-con.

There's one daily jeepney to Batakalan pier (P60, one hour, departs noon), from where you can arrange a pick-up to one of the off-island resorts on the eastern side of Palawan near Taytay. A tricycle costs around P750.

All transportation now leaves from the terminal across from the public market in Corong Corong. Vans will make pick-ups from hotels in town but frustratingly usually end up also stopping at the terminal.

Daytripper (☑ 0917 848 8755; www.daytripperpalawan.com) Slightly larger minivans than average (P800 to P950) with only two daily departures to Puerto (8am and 9am).

Fort Wally (☑ 0917 276 2875)

Lexus Shuttle In addition to Puerto, Lexus has two daily departures to Sabang (P900, 5.30am and 11am); you switch to a waiting vehicle in Salvacion, around 15km south of Roxas.

Win Eulen Joy Liner (☑ 0919 716 2210)

ⓘ Getting Around

Four-wheel-drive Jeeps, also available for rental, are a good option for those wanting to explore the Palawan mainland at their leisure.

Bacuit Archipelago

The crystalline waters of Bacuit Bay are a fantasyscape of jagged limestone islands, mesmerising from any vantage point, whether from underwater, from the air or lying on a beach. Easily the rival of southern Thailand or Halong Bay in Vietnam, the islands hide so many white-sand beaches, lagoons and coves, not to mention hundreds of species of fish and coral, that you'll be overwhelmed.

Miniloc Island

Miniloc Island is perhaps the most interesting of the islands of the archipelago. The real attractions here are Big Lagoon, Small Lagoon and Secret Lagoon, three of the more photographed sights in all of Palawan.

Big Lagoon is entered by an extremely shallow channel (you may have to swim into the lagoon and leave the boat outside). Inside, surrounded by jungle-clad karst walls, is an enormous natural swimming hole.

To enter Small Lagoon, you can swim through a hole in a rock wall or paddle through in a kayak at low tide – be sure to leave before the tide changes, otherwise you might not be able to squeeze back through. Inside is a wonderful hidden world, complete with a small cave that you can explore.

BEDDING DOWN IN THE BACUIT

Miniloc Island Resort (☑ in Manila 02-894 5644; www.elnidoresorts.com; r with full board from US$312; ❄ ✈), **Lagen Island Resort** (r incl breakfast from US$345, r with full board from US$400; ❄ @ ✈ ✖) and **Pangalusian Island Resort** (villa incl breakfast from US$560) are luxury, honeymoon-level resorts located on three different private islands amid idyllic settings in the Bacuit Bay. Miniloc cottages have a comparably native feel and Pangalusian is the newest and poshest. All are owned and operated by the same company, **Ten Knots Travel Office** (☑ 0917 207 2742; www.elnidoresorts.com; Real St, El Nido), located in El Nido. Rates include all meals and transfers to and from El Nido airport.

Bacuit Archipelago

N 0 — 5 km
0 — 2.5 miles

SOUTH
CHINA
SEA

Caverna Island
Coron; Manila
Cauayan Island
Emmit Island
Calitang Beach (20km)

Tambalanang Island
Mitre Island

Balinaod Bay

Binangculang Bay

Tapiutan Island
Inambuyod Island
Ubugon Cove
Cadlao Island
Bukal Island
Lio Airport

Tapiutan Strait
Mantinloc Shrine
Dilumacad Island (Helicopter Island)
Pasandigan Cove
Paradise Beach

Calmung Bay
Caalan Beach

Matinloc Island
Ipil Beach
El Nido

Seven Commandos Beach
Corong Corong

Secret Beach
Lapus-Lapus Beach

Miniloc Island
Small Lagoon
Big Lagoon
Corong Corong Bay
Las Cabanas Beach Resort

Miniloc Island Resort
Shimzu Island
Bacuit Bay
Depeldet Island
Las Cabanas Beach
Dolarog Beach Resort

North Guntao Island
Paglugaban Island
Entalula Island
Popolcan Island
Pinagbuyutan Island

South Guntao Island
Pangalusian Island
Pangalusian Island Resort
Malapacao Island

Guintungauan Island (Turtle Island)
Tabunan (Pangauanen)
Komokotuang Island
Snake Island
Lagen Island Resort
Manlalec

Vigan
Cudugnon Cave
Cathedral Cave
Lagen Island
Pungtud Island

Pinasil Island
Ninepin Island

Dibuluan Island

Saddle Island

Camago Is

Peaked Island
Needle Rocks
Anato Is
Bebeladan
Camago

Mt Maateg (345m)

Tuluran Island
Liminangcong
Endeavor Strait
Cataoba River

Taytay (58km)
Catarban

Matinloc & Tapiutan Islands

Like the back of a half-submerged stego-saurus, Matinloc Island snakes some 8km along the western edge of the Bacuit Archipelago. Along with neighbouring Tapi-utan Island, it forms the narrow **Tapiutan Strait**, the walls of which offer some of the best snorkelling in the archipelago. Like-wise, there is some excellent snorkelling and some good beaches on the eastern side of Matinloc.

The adventurous will surely want to check out tiny Secret Beach, which can only be entered by swimming through a keyhole slot in the western wall of Matinloc (generally can't be accessed in August and September during the southwest monsoon or *habagat*). But be warned: the entrance is lined with extremely jagged rocks and coral – *do not* even think of swimming through if there are any waves around as an accident could well be fatal.

Cadlao Island

Cadlao Island is like a mini-Tahiti miraculously relocated to the Bacuit Archipelago. In addition to being a wonderful piece of eye candy for those staying on the beach in El Nido, it's also home to lovely Cadlao Lagoon (also known as Ubugun Cove). This lagoon offers some good snorkelling in the shallow coral gardens that lie off the beach at the head of the bay. More and more people are kayaking out here on their own from El Nido.

Other Islands & Beaches

Every island in the archipelago has secret spots that await the adventurous explorer. Tiny Pinasil Island holds Cathedral Cave, an aptly named cavern with soaring limestone columns and wall-climbing monitor lizards, which call to mind the gargoyles of an actual cathedral. If you plan on exploring the cave, be sure to bring shoes and be careful walking on the sharp rocks. Dilumacad Island (Helicopter Island) has a fine beach on its eastern shore, which is topped only by the wonderful Seven Commandos Beach on the Palawan mainland. Snake Island, connected to the mainland by a narrow, winding strip of sand during low tide, offers striking panoramic views from the top.

CALAMIAN GROUP

This group of islands in the far north of Palawan has a frontier edge. Heading north to Busuanga Island, where Coron Town, the largest settlement in the Calamian group, is located, you'll pass through Linapacan Island, Culion Island, and other small islands where groups of huts hug the foreshore of beautiful beaches. Otherwise, you'll find nothing – no roads, and not even any lights after the sun goes down.

Underwater it's a different matter. More than two dozen Japanese navy WWII-era ships lie at the bottom of the sea, sunk by US Navy aircraft on 24 September 1944. More than half a dozen of these are accessible to experienced divers.

There's also endless undeveloped white-sand beaches, excellent coral for snorkelling, dense rainforests and mangrove swamps, and the crystal-clear lakes of Coron Island.

Coron Town & Busuanga Island

048 / POP 42,900

Approaching Coron Town from the water, it's not uncommon to wonder whether the long journey was worth it. There's no beach and the waterfront is a mishmash of half-done buildings, ramshackle houses and the mostly empty expanse of a misguided landfill project (part of this is referred to as Lualhati Park). This, the commercial and population centre of the Calamian group and main town on Busuanga Island, shouldn't be judged by appearances alone. It's best thought of as a gateway and base for other adventures on and around Busuanga Island, whether they be wreck diving, snorkelling, island-hopping or off-road motorbiking. Outside town, Busuanga is extremely rural. Some of the land has been given over to farming and small communities, with nothing more than a single *sari-sari* (small shop) hugging the rough dirt road that loops around the perimeter of the island.

From the late 1930s to the outbreak of WWII, there was a manganese mining boom and large-scale deep-sea fishing took off a decade later; however, these days tourism is Coron Town's big business. Environmental issues and concerns, including a controversial new power plant, appear to be trumped by the onward rush of development. After sweeping through the central Visayas, Typhoon Yolanda (internationally known as 'Haiyan') arrived on Busuanga at night with 200mph winds and a storm surge, destroying buildings, displacing families from their homes for months and killing over a dozen people in the Coron Town area.

Sights & Activities

Diving

This is a world-class destination for wreck diving. At least 10 Japanese warships and merchant ships, including the *Akisushima* (the only one with large calibre guns), a flying boat tender, the *Kogyo Maru*, the *Irako*,

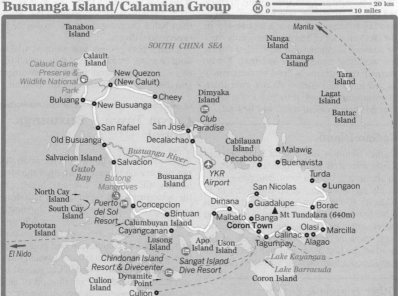

the *Tangat* wreck, the *Olympia Maru*, the *Lusong* gunboat and the *Okikawa* (long wrongly identified by most authorities as the *Tae Maru*), can be found in the waters off Busuanga. Most of the wrecks are at least a 45-minute to two-hour boat ride from Coron Town. The depths at which the wrecks are found vary from shallow to quite deep, so there are diving opportunities for beginners and experienced divers. The best wreck dives for beginners are the *Lusong* (also easily snorkelled) and *East Tangat*, at 9m and 22m, respectively. The visibility, which was around 18m to 20m several decades ago, is now down to 3m to 5m at some sites, largely because of polluted runoff.

Lake Barracuda on Coron Island is a popular dive site, less for what's visible than for the sensation of shifting temperatures underwater.

Dive operators mostly charge P2800/ P3400 for two/three dives including equipment. Some companies offer overnight 'safaris' to Apo Reef, another one of the best diving destinations in the country.

Coron Divers   DIVING
(☑ 0918 653 9854; www.corondivers.com.ph; National Hwy; 🚶) A recommended dive shop in Coron Town.

Sea Dive   DIVING
(☑ 0917 808 6700; www.seadiveresort.com) Part of the hotel complex of the same name. Ask about the status of planned three- to four-night diving safari tours.

Discovery Divers   DIVING
(☑ 0920 901 2414; www.ddivers.com) Based on Decanituan Island (aka Discovery Island); also maintains a shop in town.

DiveCal   DIVING
(☑ 0918 285 2060; www.divecal.com) Associated with Dive Link Resort.

Rock Steady Dive Center   DIVING
(☑ 0919 624 0034; www.rocksteadydivecenter.com) A recommended dive shop in Coron Town.

Other Activities

Even if you're here to dive and you've already checked out Coron Island, it's worth spending a day or two on a bangka exploring other nearby islands (around P1200 per person, or you can try negotiating a fee for an entire boat of four to six people). Hotels and tour companies in town can arrange trips; otherwise, walk down to the pier behind the central market where boats congregate (the boat association lists prices here).

Exploring the Busuanga countryside on a motorbike is an exhilarating journey past small villages, forests and lush farmland. Some stretches call for off-road experience. Several places rent motorbikes including **Boyet's Motorcycle Rental** (☑0928 292 9884; National Hwy), which charges P600 to P800 for the day.

One of the more interesting areas in which to kayak is near **Butong**, a mangrove area that cuts through a small peninsula north of the town of Concepcion on Busuanga Island.

Siete Pecados
SNORKELLING

(admission P100) Snorkelling at this small protected sanctuary not far offshore from Makinit Hot Springs, is a reminder of what has been destroyed elsewhere – the coral here is a wonderland of colours and shapes.

Makinit Hot Springs
SPRINGS

(admission P150; ⊙6am-10pm) An activity that is often included in a bangka day trip is a soak in the soothing-to-scalding waters 5km east of town and not far from Siete Pecados; it's a developed site easily accessible by tricycle from Coron Town (round trip P200 to P300); no entry after 8pm.

Mt Tundalara
HIKE

Hiking to the top of 640m Mt Tundalara, the highest point in northern Palawan, is an endurance test, especially in the midday heat. It takes around 2½ hours each way. To get to the trailhead, take a tricycle to Mabingtungan, around 3km north of Coron Town.

☞ Tours

Multiday Coron–El Nido expeditions run by **Tao Philippines** (www.taophilippines.com; National Hwy) are highly recommended.

Calamianes Expeditions Eco Tour
OUTDOORS

(☑0920 254 6553; www.corongaleri.com.ph; San Augin St) Rents tents (per night P200), mountain bikes and kayaks as well as arranges day and overnight trips. A shop with good gear is attached.

Showtime Adventures
OUTDOORS

(☑0927 372 8846; www.showtimeadventuretours.com) Run by the entrepreneurial Betan Pe (just ask for him around town). Trips, including fishing, overnight kayaking and even horseback riding excursions.

Tribal Adventures
ADVENTURE TOUR

(☑0917 819 3049; www.tribaladventures.com; National Hwy; kayaks from P500) Recommended tour operator for kayaking and mountain biking tours.

🛏 Sleeping

At the time of writing, a hotel building boom was well underway; some might say a building bubble was about to burst. As an alternative to sleeping in Coron Town, you can stay on one of the islands; some are only minutes away, while others are more substantial commutes.

Coron Town

★ Sea Dive Resort
HOTEL $

(☑0920 945 8714; www.seadiveresort.com.ph; d P450-1200; ✳🛜) There's no more convenient address in Coron Town than this multistorey building that juts into the bay. The higher up you go, the nicer the rooms become, though all of them are simple and clean with hot-water bathrooms. Noise from your neighbours is the only downside. Has a deservedly popular, open-air restaurant, and there's a bar out back.

The dive shop here is a hive of activity and the front desk is a good source of information for island-hopping and onward transportation. Ask about their beach house in Cheey in northern Busuanga.

Krystal Lodge
BUNGALOW $

(☑0908 357 3309; www.krystallodge.blogspot.com; r P400-800, cottage P1200; 🛜) Bunk down like locals in these all-bamboo bungalows perched over the water. It's worth the extra pesos for uniquely charming cottages with their own bars and sitting areas. When the friendly proprietor is in she can arrange a projector for outdoor movie nights. Breakfast and kitchen for guests available.

Coron Backpacker Guesthouse
HOSTEL $

(☑0919 388 6028; coronbackpacker@gmail.com; d P500; 🛜) This place has nine basic doubles in a shack over the water near the centre of town. The common area is pleasantly rustic, with a kitchen and lots of reading material.

KokosNuss Garden Resort & Restaurant
BUNGALOW $$

(☑0919 776 9544; www.kokosnuss.info; National Hwy; r with fan & shared/private bathroom P600/1500, cottages with air-con P1700; ✳🛜) This leafy, expanding compound, a 20-minute walk from town, has a variety of rooms that surround a slightly overgrown garden with plenty of shade, not to mention a goat or two. Rooms range from modern rondavel cottages with bright, painted murals (these might bring to mind a Hobbitt hole) to fan-cooled A-frame rooms in a bamboo structure.

Coron Town

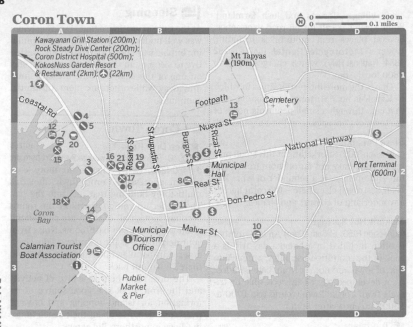

Ask to look at several rooms before choosing; at least one rondavel has a shower curtain for a bathroom door. The kitchen here prepares a mean BLT sandwich.

Princess of Coron Austrian Resort HOTEL **$$**
(☎ 0919 236 1430; www.princessofcoron.com; 6 Nueva St; r P2500; ❄ 🛜 🌐) This hotel blends into a hillside above town about as seamlessly as you'd expect an Austrian resort would. The white stucco main building has large rooms with gleaming tiled floors and spacious bathrooms. A couple of A-frame cottages in the front are good for families; kids can cool off in the small pool.

Island's View Inn HOTEL **$$**
(☎ 0917 547 6039; www.islandsviewinn.com; Don Pedro St; r incl breakfast P1500-2200; ❄ 🛜) Rooms here are sparkling clean, with flat-screen TVs, hot water and a 3rd-floor outdoor restaurant and lounge area.

Coron Ecolodge HOTEL **$$**
(☎ 0906 455 6090; www.coronecolodge.com; Calle Real; r P1600; ❄ 🛜) Neither especially eco nor lodge-like, this hotel has basic, modern rooms with old furntiure. Upsides are it's not smack in the middle of the noisy centre of town, a professional front desk and the pleasant cafe attached.

Corto del Mar Hotel
HOTEL $$$

(☑0936 312 4754; www.cortodelmar.com; r P5000-6000; ✳☎☒) Unfortunately situated at the end of a narrow road lined with *sari-sari* stores, is this tastefully done large Spanish-style building. The modern rooms, however, can feel a little musty. The restaurant is worth a visit for its pizza.

Coron Gateway Hotel
HOTEL $$$

(☑0915 846 9326; www.corongateway.com; Market Pier; r P3900-6000; ✳☎) While the back wall is hard up against market stalls and the front faces essentially a barren expanse of dirt, Gateway has the most luxurious accommodation in town. Many rooms have a large Jacuzzi tub separated from the rest of the room by a sliding door. The top floor sustained some damage from Typhoon Haiyan.

⌂ Busuanga Island

Elsie's Guest House, Al Faro, Busuanga Bay Lodge and Puerto del Sol are located in Bgy Concepcion around Dipuyai Bay, a safe haven for yachts and home of the Busuanga Bay Yacht Club. The bay also has a river and mangrove forest that can easily be explored by kayaks. At the mouth of the bay there is excellent snorkelling and diving on the reefs and the wreck of the *Okikawa Maru*, a Japanese oil tanker.

Elsie's Guest House
GUEST HOUSE $

(☑0936 904 4453; elsietrinadad01061983@ yahoo.com; r P500-1000) ✐ Run by Elsie, a charming host, former dive master and excellent cook from Bicol, this native-style house is nestled into the hillside of Dipuyai bay with wonderful west-facing views. Two rooms: one with private bathroom and TV, and a smaller one with a shared bathroom.

Most of the vegetables and herbs Elsie uses are homegrown and her seafood is delivered fresh. Lights, TV and kitchen refrigerator are all solar-powered. Although Elsie's is close to the main road between Coron and Salvacion it's only reachable by a short boat ride or kayak paddle. Arrange a transfer with Elsie in advance.

Ann & Mike's Bar & Restaurant
NIPA HUTS $

(☑0929 582 4020; r with shared bathroom P750) Ann & Mike's in Concepcion has two good-looking nipa cottages and a pleasant little eatery.

Pier House Lodging
HOTEL $$

(☑0912 362 2470; www.pierhouselodging.ph; r P1500-2500; ☎) A unique-looking white-stucco lodging house in Concepcion, that has a bar, a restaurant and large tile-floor rooms. It can feel deserted in low season.

★ Al Faro Cosmio Hotel
HOTEL $$$

(☑0908 865 8987; www.alfaropalawan.com; r incl breakfast P3200-3700; ☎☒) A touch of the Mediterranean and a dash of Disney-like fairy-tale architecture, this wonderfully situated place is perched on a hilltop overlooking Dipuyai Bay. Rooms are light and airy during the day, cozy at night and have private balconies where you can ponder your luck. It's a friendly, laid-back place but active types will be well cared for.

Puerto del Sol Resort
RESORT $$$

(☑0908 889 0866; www.puertodelsolresort.com; cottage with fan/air-con P2800/4200; ✳☎) The Puerto de Sol is a Mediterranean-style resort perched on a hillside with views of the bay. It's close to several wrecks, as well as inland activities such as horseback riding and hiking. The white-stucco cottages and large windows add to the light-filled atmosphere. Discovery Divers has a shop here.

Busuanga Bay Lodge
RESORT $$$

(☑in Manila 02-625 8627; www.busuangabaylodge. com; r P7800-11,700; ✳@☎☒) A luxurious white-washed Caribbean-style resort whose centrepiece is a large restaurant pavilion and whose cottages are furnished in a low-key stylish fashion. It has all the facilities: infinity pool, spa, dive centre, wine cellar, gym, marina for yachties. Airport transfers are an extra P2500 for five. Surprisingly, for its seeming remoteness it's popular with functions and conferences. When we were there it was all booked out by doctors on a pharmaceutical company's shindig.

⌂ Other Islands

Most of these resorts' room rates include transfers from the Busuanga airport or Coron Town, but it's worth confirming. Sangat and Chindonan are close to a good number of wrecks suitable for diving.

★ Sangat Island Dive Resort
RESORT $$$

(☑0917 522 7965; www.sangat.com.ph; cottages per person incl transfers & 3 meals US$103-150; ☎) ✐ Pulling up at the beach here feels like discovering the cool kid's secret hideout. Less than 40 minutes by speedboat from Coron Town, and perfect for R&R or action, Sangat has a full-service dive centre, kayaks and jet skis. Several native-style bungalows front a nice white-sand beach and two others are perched atop small hills tucked into the encroaching jungle.

For those seeking more privacy, there's a large villa around the corner accessed via a footbridge with an outdoor shower in a rock cave. And for the ultimate in off-the-grid-world-be-damned solitude, try the 'Robinson Crusoe' cottage (two weeks US$1000) on a 100m-long beach a short boat ride from Sangat. Kayaks, two-way radios and provisions can be provided. Groups can camp out here in tents as well. Ask to visit the hot springs concealed by a thicket of mangroves on the other side of the island or stop at Sangat's wild boar farm.

Club Paradise　　　　　BEACH RESORT $$$
(☑ in Manila 02-838 4956; www.clubparadisepalawan.com; per person incl 3 meals P5500-8500; 🅰🛜🏊) This resort on Dimyaka Island, north of Busuanga, lives up to its name (however, it was undergoing an ownership change during our visit). A true four-star resort, evident in everything from the beautiful variety of cottages (basically a high-end designer's version of the Filipino hut) to the sumptuous buffet meals.

Chindonan Island Resort & Divecenter　　　　BUNGALOW $$$
(☑ 0929 312 1594; www.chindonan-diveresort.com; per person incl breakfast & dinner P3800; 🅰🛜) This Danish-owned place has nearly a dozen spacious modern stucco rooms perched halfway up a hilltop on an island between Culion Town and Sangat. All have large terraces with sea-facing views – one with aircon. Diving can be arranged and the bar and restaurant are on the concrete pier; also, a small beach, a mix of gravel and sand.

✖ Eating

Most of the places to stay, including all the resorts located offshore or elsewhere on Busuanga, have their own restaurants. The one at Sea Dive Resort (p407) is the best in town, as much for its great location and social vibe as for the well-rounded menu. A bunch of fairly interchangeable barbecue and casual Filipino eateries are on the National Hwy between St Augustin and Rizal Sts. Cashews, especially *bandi*, the sugary treat made from cashews, are sold everywhere.

★**Bistro Coron**　　　INTERNATIONAL, FRENCH $$
(Coron Town; mains P200-500; ⊙ 8am-midnight) This place has an extensive menu including specials such as a version of *setoise* (soup with shrimp, fried diced bread and fish chunks), and Hungarian, Italian and Swiss sausages.

Kawayanan Grill Station　　FILIPINO, SEAFOOD $$
(National Hwy; mains P150; ⊙ 11am-late; 🛜) The new location of this festive outdoor restaurant (the one in the centre of town closed) serves the usual Filipino fare and seafood plus more exotic dishes such as boiled goat innards and sting ray – in outdoor nipa huts. Gets going, especially weekend nights when DJs occasionally spin.

La Sirenetta　　FILIPINO, INTERNATIONAL $$
(mains P250; ⊙ 11am-10pm; 🛜) The four pillars at the end of a long pier, in the shape of the eponymous sirens, bring a little Vegas kitsch to town. An eclectic menu with European flavours; it's also good for sunset drinks. Slow service.

Dali Dali　　　　　　　KOREAN $$
(mains P250; ⊙ 10am-10pm) Three tables and a counter, that's all there's room for at this authentic Korean spot. Ramen, bulgogi and tofu are on the menu.

Amphibi-ko　　　　　　JAPANESE $$
(National Hwy; mains P140; ⊙ 11am-10pm) On the top floor of the hotel (rooms tend to be small and musty) of the same name, Amphibi-ko is the best (and only) Japanese restaurant in town.

🍷 Drinking & Nightlife

No Name Bar　　　　　　　BAR
(National Hwy; ⊙ 7am-2am; 🛜) Open to the street with a mini thatch-roofed 'cabana' bar, No Name has more character than other spots. Cheap drinks (rum and Coke P45) and meals, from breakfast to burgers, are served.

Coffee Kong　　　　　　　CAFE
(National Hwy; ⊙ 7am-10.30pm; 🛜) As close to a big-city coffee shop as it gets in Coron. Excellent espresso drinks, tea and muffins; waffles offered for breakfast.

Blue Moon　　　　　　　　BAR
(National Hwy; ⊙ 10am-late) A bucket of beer goes for P25.

CORON ISLAND

This island, only a 20-minute bangka ride from Coron Town, has an imposing, mysterious skyline that wouldn't be out of place in a *King Kong* film. Flying over Coron, you see that what lies inland, on the other side of the fortresslike, jungle-clad, rocky escarpments, is inaccessible terrain pockmarked with lakes, two of which, Lake Kayangan (admission P250) and Lake Barracuda (admission P100), are Coron's primary attractions.

Accessible by a steep 10-minute climb, the crystal-clear waters of Lake Kayangan are nestled into the mountain walls. Underwater is like a moonscape; there's a wooden walkway and platform to stash your things if you go for a swim. Don't expect privacy or quiet, though, as the lagoon where bangkas unload passengers looks like a mall parking lot at noon.

Lake Barracuda is of more interest to divers for its unique layers of fresh, salt and brackish water and dramatic temperature shifts, which can reach as high as 38°C. It's accessible by a short climb over a jagged, rocky wall that ends directly in the water.

Other common stops are Banol Beach (admission P100), a small sandy area with shelter from the sun, and Twin Lagoons (admission P50).

The entire island is considered the ancestral domain of the Tagbanua, who are primarily fishermen and gatherers of the very lucrative *balinsasayaw* (bird's nests). Concerned about the impact of tourism, the Tagbanua have limited access to a handful of sights.

A day-long bangka trip to all of these sites is around P1500 for up to four people (this doesn't include admission fees for sights on Coron Island, or snorkelling gear, which is generally P250). Remember to carry enough small bills, as all fees are collected as you dock at each site (there's talk of possibly imposing a single island-wide admission fee). Virtually every hotel and resort can arrange a trip, as can every tour company in town (trips to fewer sites are advertised for P650 to P750 per person).

ℹ Information

BPI (National Hwy) and Metrobank accept most foreign ATM cards; **Allied Savings Bank** (cnr Don Pedro & Burgos Sts) fewer types. The majority of hotels offer wi-fi access and there are a couple of internet cafes on the National Hwy near St Augustin St.

Coron District Hospital (National Hwy)
Municipal Tourism Office (📱 0927 419 3805; corontourismoffice@gmail.com; Market; ⊙ 8am-5pm) The city and provincial tourism offices here are fairly uselsess; located in the mostly unoccupied municipal building next to the public market.

ℹ Getting There & Away

AIR
PAL, Cebu Pacific, AirAsia Zest and SkyJet fly to Manila out of the YKR airport on the north side of Busuanga Island around 25km from Coron Town. Cancellations and delays because of bad weather aren't uncommon.

It's a half-hour (P150) minivan ride between the airport and Coron Town (the road was being improved); vans meet incoming flights. In the other direction, most depart two hours before flights from in front of airline offices or hotels that offer transfers.

BOAT
During the high season, medium-sized bangka boats leave for El Nido from the main pier around 1.5km east of the town centre every day if the weather is good (P1800 including lunch, seven hours); less frequently in the low season. Most hotels and every streetfront agency can book. Otherwise, you can hire a boat for around P15,000 for up to six people.

2GO has ferry services from Coron to Manila (P1800, 14 hours, 4.30pm Sunday) and Puerto Princesa (P1500, 14 hours, 8am Saturday). And *M/V May Lilies* of **Atienza Shipping Lines** (📱 0939 912 6840) travels between Manila and El Nido with a stop in Coron; departs Coron for Manila (P1000, 20 hours) at 6.30pm Tuesday. There are better options so there's not much reason to take this boat.

You can get to San José on Mindoro with the *M/Bca Bunso* (P1000 including lunch, seven hours, Monday, Tuesday, Wednesday and Friday). Shops in town advertise the P1000 price but if you find the captain in advance you probably can pay P800. Schedule is of course iffy.

Bangka boats to virtually every destination within the Calamian group leave from a spot behind the Gateway Tavern Hotel. Offical rates are posted on a sign here; however, some negotiation is expected. Sample fares include P2500 for Malcapuya Island and P3000 for Calumbuyan

Island. Tour companies, as well as hotels, generally offer lower fares.

A daily boat goes to Culion Town (P180, 1½ hours, 1pm).

ℹ Getting Around

A jeepney to Salvacion leaves Coron at 11am daily (P80, 1½ hours).

Minivans are also available for tours around Busuanga. A sample round-trip fare is P2500 for Concepcion.

Tricycles around town, including to the main pier, are P10.

Culion Island & Around

Culion Island, one of the largest in the Calamian group, has excellent snorkelling around **Dynamite Point** on the northeastern tip. **Malcapuya Island**, about halfway down off the eastern side, has a nice beach; nearby **Banana Island** also has a pretty beach on the eastern side and good snorkelling on the west. A full-day boat tour from Coron Town out this way should run between P3000 and P3500. **Two Seasons**, a high-end resort, is on the northern tip of nearby Bulalacao Island.

In Culion Town you can visit the **Culion Museum & Archives** (☑0928 281 2276; admission P250; ⊙9am-noon & 1-4pm Mon-Fri) located on the hospital grounds. A half-hour film and several large rooms filled with photos and artifacts tell the poignant and little-known story of the leper colony that was opened here in 1906, once one of the largest in the world. The interior of the **La Immaculada Concepcion Church**, formerly a Spanish fort built in the mid-1700s, is worth a peek, and a hike up to where the eagle symbol is carved into the hills (created in 1926 by leper patients as a tribute to Philippine health services) offers panoramic views of town and the nearby islands.

Easily the nicest place in Culion Town is the modern **Hotel Maya** (☑0939 254 2744; s/d P7000/1100; ✱🛜), owned and operated by enthusiastic students of Ateneo-Loyola College. **Tabing Dagat Lodging House & Restaurant** (☑mobile 0908 563 1590; r with fan/air-con P590/790; ✱) has light-filled rooms with small balconies in barangay Balulua.

The town only has electricity between noon and midnight. A daily boat (P180, 1½

hours, 1pm) goes from Coron Town to Culion Town; to Coron Town it leaves at 7.30am.

Other Calamian Islands

Almost directly west of Busuanga's Concepcion is **Calumbuyan Island**; the northeast side has one of the best reefs (admission P100) for snorkelling in the area. The caretaker who protects the site can provide coffee, as well as permission to spend the night (P400 including admission) sleeping in a basic hut, a hammock or tents you bring on your own.

A good snorkelling and diving spot is the reef near the southwestern tip of **Lusong Island**; the shallowest wreck, the *Lusong* gunboat, found off the southern edge, is also prime snorkelling territory.

A white sandy beach and magnificent sunsets make a trip out to **North Cay Island** worth the hassle; the reef on the north side is well preserved. It's possible to stop here as part of an island-hopping trip, but if you have the foresight and time, arrange an overnight stay in the island's caretaker home; bring your own supplies, other than fish, which can be provided.

Just off the northwestern tip of Busuanga is **Calauit Island**, home to the **Calauit Game Preserve & Wildlife National Park** (☑0921 215 5482; admission per person P350, 2hr guided tour P1000). Megafauna commonly seen on safari in Kenya, such as giraffe, zebra, impala etc, can be viewed in their, um, adopted habitat, thanks to Ferdinand Marcos' efforts in 1976 to help save African wildlife, alongside several species endemic to Palawan (an alternative explanation offered is that Marcos' son Bong Bong wanted animals to shoot).

Whether arranged as an organised tour (P2400 per person) or done independently, it's a gruelling day-long journey (three plus hours by van from Coron Town). Boats from Macalachao, 7km north of Bululang (there's a 350m white-sand beach here) on Busuanga, can be hired for P350 round trip (10 minutes each way). It's possible to spend the night just outside the park in a basic room for P250, or to camp with your own tent. The waters off Caluit Island are also a habitat for the dugong, commonly known as sea cows, an endangered species and the only herbivorous mammal; it's rare, however, to spot them.

Understand the Philippines

The Philippines Today

Mega-malls metastasize while downtown streets flood. Macau-like casinos open up in Manila while tribes skirmish in Kalinga. Deep poverty persists while the overall economy booms. Politics and corruption go together like rum and karaoke. Storms – both weather related and of the international-diplomatic variety – come in waves. Through it all, ordinary Filipinos pull through, recover, embrace their loved ones and hope for better times ahead.

Best on Film

Norte, the End of History (2014) A character's struggle against an inexorable tide of forces; an epic masterpiece.

Imelda (2004) Fascinating look into the psyche of Imelda Marcos.

Metro Manila (2013) Part twisty, crime drama; part immersive look at the big city.

Serbis (2008) Critically acclaimed film about a family-run porn-movie house in Angeles.

Best in Print

Pacific Rims: Beermen Ballin' in Flip-Flops and the Philippines' Unlikely Love Affair with Basketball (Rafe Bartholomew) As riotous as the title implies.

Playing with Water – Passion and Solitude on a Philippine Island (James Hamilton-Paterson) This timeless account of life on a remote islet sheds much light on Filipino culture.

The Tesseract (Alex Garland) A thrilling romp through Manila's dark side by the author of the cult backpacker hit, *The Beach*.

Scandals

Known by acronyms like DAP or single-word appellations like Nopales or Malampaya, political-corruption scandals are to the Philippines what football is to Brazilians – a lens through which to interpret the national character. Even while former president Arroyo (and current Congressional representative) is under 'hospital arrest' awaiting a resolution of charges of plunder, talk of impeaching President Aquino was bandied about in the summer of 2014. A flurry of accusations surrounding the Disbursement Acceleration Program (DAP) – essentially a way for Aquino to bypass the legislature and, according to him, fast track a much needed stimulus package – was coming to a head. In a discouraging tit-for-tat Aquino threatened to impeach the Supreme Court justices who ruled DAP unconstitutional.

Before DAP, confidence in Aquino had already diminished thanks to a series of high-profile events including the Zamboanga siege; attack on farm workers at Hacienda Lucita; the Luneta hostage taking; the handling of relief operations after the Bohol earthquake and Typhoon Haiyan (known locally as Typhoon Yolanda); cuts in social services; and a failure to meet expectations in improving transportation and power infrastructure. Aquino is not the only figure embroiled in scandals, however. The ongoing Nopales investigation, in which an influential businesswoman is accused of channeling kickbacks to prominent opposition leaders, is a smorgasbord of wrongdoing.

Resistance Movements

Some of the longest lasting resistance movements in the world, of indigenous peoples and communist and Muslim rebel groups, continue to fracture society. While most actual fighting doesn't impact the daily lives of ordinary urban Filipinos, newspaper headlines tell a story of not infrequent clashes. Observers comment that as long as dramatic income inequality, poor education and a thoroughly unresponsive political system exist, there's little hope that resistance groups will lay down their weapons.

Most importantly, perhaps, is the resolution of the ongoing conflict in Mindanao. After more than 17 years of negotiations and cycles of violence, yet again, there's some hope for peace. Pending a referendum, a semi-autonomous Muslim region called the Bangsamoro could be created. Even if there is a political solution, and several splinter groups vow not to recognise the agreement if passed, the island's resources – gold, copper, nickel, iron, chromite and manganese, reserves of crude oil and natural gas – will likely insure some version of struggle will continue.

Disaster & Recovery

Situated in both the typhoon belt and the Pacific Ring of Fire, the Philippines is continuously ravaged by mother nature. As a result, Filipinos are resolute and adept survivors. Storms and natural disasters are part of the daily fabric of life, but 2013 was a particularly tragic year. Only three weeks after a 7.2 earthquake, the strongest in over two decades, struck near Bohol, Typhoon Haiyan (known locally as Yolanda) swept through the central Visayas on 7 November.

The world witnessed scenes of apocalyptic destruction and suffering. Widely estimated between 15,000 and 25,000, the death toll is more than three times the figure given by the government. Nevertheless, many of the communities have rebuilt and businesses, including tourist-related ones, have reopened. Some towns appear 'normal' while others, like many south of Tacloban in Leyte remain utterly devastated.

Geopolitics

In 2013, the Philippine economy grew faster than any other Asian economy after China. Government revenues increased primarily by raising tariffs on cigarettes and liquor, and simultaneously pursuing tax evaders and corrupt officials. However, nearly 10% of the economy is still based on remittances – money sent home by overseas Filipino workers.

Despite some positive trends, the country's location – in China's backyard, if you will – makes its economic momentum vulnerable. Territorial conflicts with the emerging superpower, mainly in the West Philippines and South China Sea, periodically flare up. Aquino signed a new 10-year defence agreement with President Obama and the US, and in the summer of 2014 the Chinese government temporarily suspended many flights between the two countries. While there is a need for focus on development, health and education, jockeying for influence and big-power politics no doubt will continue to distract.

POPULATION: **107.7 MILLION**

AREA: **300,000 SQ KM**

GDP: **US$272.2 BILLION**

GDP GROWTH: **6.8%**

UNEMPLOYMENT: **7.4%**

INFLATION: **2.8%**

if the Philippines was 100 people

28 would be Tagalog
13 would be Cebuano
9 would be Ilocano
8 would be Bisaya
8 would be Hiligaynon
6 would be Bikol
3 would be Waray
25 would be Other

belief systems
(% of population)

82.9 Catholicism
5 Islam
2.3 Iglesia
4.5 Other Christians
5.3 Other

population per sq km

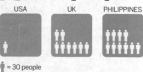

USA   UK   PHILIPPINES

≈ 30 people

History

Ancient Filipinos stuck to their own islands until the 16th century, when Ferdinand Magellan claimed the islands for Spain and began the bloody process of Christianisation. Filipinos revolted and won after the Spanish executed national hero José Rizal in 1896, only to have the Americans take over, whereupon they revolted again and lost. Out of the bloody ashes of WWII rose an independent republic, albeit one that would elect hardliner Ferdinand Marcos as president. His overthrow in the 1986 'People Power' revolution is the defining moment of modern Filipino history.

A History of Being 'Different'

History of the Philippines: From Indios Bravos to Filipinos by Luis H Francia and Under the Stacks by Saul Hofileña Jr are impressionistic accounts of Filipino history from the 'beginning'.

The islands' first colonisers arrived by boat from the north, south and west, establishing a loose network of settlements that had little contact with each other. Thus, from early on the idea of a Filipino 'identity' was a tenuous one. If you were to arrive in North Luzon 1000 years ago, you would have confronted the Ifugao tending to their spectacular rice terraces, which still wow tourists today around Banaue. It is thought the ancestors of the Ifugao were part of a wave that arrived some 15,000 years ago from China and Vietnam.

If you arrived 1000 years ago in southern Luzon or the Visayan lowlands, you would have encountered mostly animists of Malay origin, while in the southern regions of Mindanao and Sulu, Islam would already be spreading by way of immigrants from Brunei. Meanwhile, the archipelago's original inhabitants, the Negritos (also called Aeta, Dumagat or Ati), were sprinkled all over the place, much as they are today.

Rarely sedentary, the disparate communities of the Philippines roamed around hunting, gathering, fishing and growing a few basic crops such as rice. They formed small 'barangays' – named after the *balangay* boats in which the Malays arrived – under the leadership of a *datu* (chief). These simple barangays represented the highest form of political unit. The 'country', if you could call it that, possessed neither a centralised government nor a common culture or religion.

Into this diverse jumble strode the Spanish, with the singular mission to unite the Philippine islands around Christianity. Remarkably, they

TIMELINE	45,000 BC	AD 100–200	AD 100–1000
	'Tabon Man', the oldest discovered inhabitant of the 7000 islands, leaves a bit of his skull in a cave on Palawan, shedding light on the Philippines' deep, dark pre-history.	The Chinese become the first foreigners to trade with the islands, which they call Mai. Thus begins a long history of Chinese economic and cultural influence in the Philippines.	Malays in outrigger *balangay* boats arrive in several waves, becoming the islands' dominant ethnic group. The archipelago's eight main languages derive from various Malay tongues spoken by these immigrants.

would largely succeed, and over the next several centuries a semblance of a unified Filipino identity, bearing traces of both Spanish and traditional culture, began to emerge.

Catholicism Arrives

In the early 16th century, Islam was beginning to spread throughout the region. Barangays as far north as Manila had been converted, and all signs pointed to the archipelago adopting Islam on a wide scale. But on 16 March 1521 Portuguese explorer Ferdinand Magellan changed the course of Philippine history by landing at Samar and claiming the islands for Spain. Magellan set about giving the islanders a crash course in Catholicism and winning over various tribal chiefs. Having nearly accomplished his goal, Magellan was killed in battle against one of the last holdouts, Chief Lapu-Lapu of Mactan Island off Cebu.

Determined to press its claim after conceding the more strategically important Moluccas (Spice Islands) to Portugal, Spain sent four more expeditions to the Philippines: Ruy Lopez de Villalobos, commander of the fourth expedition, renamed the islands after the heir to the Spanish throne, Philip, Charles I's son. Philip, as King Philip II, ordered a fresh fleet led by Miguel Lopez de Legazpi to sail from Mexico to the islands in 1564 with strict orders to colonise and Catholicise. In 1565 Legazpi returned to the scene of Magellan's death at Cebu and overran the local tribe. An agreement was signed by Legazpi and Tupas, the defeated *datu*, which made every Filipino answerable to Spanish law.

Legazpi, his soldiers and a band of Augustinian monks wasted no time in establishing a settlement where Cebu City now stands; Fort San Pedro is a surviving relic of the era. Legazpi soon discovered that his pact with Tupas was meaningless because the chief had no authority over the islands' myriad other tribes. So Legazpi went about conquering them one by one.

After beating the local people into submission, Legazpi established a vital stronghold on Panay (near present-day Roxas) in 1569. The dominoes fell easily after that, the big prize being Manila, which he wrested from Muslim chief Rajah Sulayman in 1571. Legazpi hastily proclaimed Manila the capital of Las Islas Filipinas and built what was eventually to become Fort Santiago on Sulayman's former *kuta* (fort).

The new colony was run by a Spanish governor who reported to Mexico. But outside of Manila real power rested with the Catholic friars – the *friarocracia* (friarocracy). The friars attempted to move people from barangays into larger, more centralised *pueblos* (towns). They built imposing stone churches in the centre of each *pueblo* (dozens of these still stand) and acted as sole rulers over what were essentially rural fiefdoms.

The Philippines is the fourth-largest producer of pineapples in the world and 87% of the country's total are grown in two regions in Mindanao.

A Country of Our Own (2004) takes the controversial view that the Philippines will never be a strong nation because it has never had a unified soul, but author David C Martinez offers some possible solutions.

1100	1521	1565	1762
Traders from China, India, Japan, Vietnam, Cambodia, Thailand and other countries are regularly trading with Philippine islands. The Chinese establish trading posts along the Luzon coast.	Ferdinand Magellan lands at Samar and claims the country for the Spanish, but soon after is murdered by Chief Lapu-Lapu on Mactan Island off Cebu.	Legazpi lands in Cebu and forces the local chieftain to sign an agreement making every Filipino answerable to Spanish law. Within 10 years Spain controls most of the Philippines.	Great Britain occupies Manila for two years before being chased out. The incident demonstrates the weakness of the Spanish regime and marks the start of a united, nationalist Filipino spirit.

The Philippine Revolution

The following four baroque churches are UNESCO World Heritage Sites: Church of Santo Tomas de Villanueva in Miag-ao; Church of San Agustín at Paoay; the Church of the Immaculate Conception of San Agustín in Itramuros (Manila); and the Church of Nuestra Señora de la Asuncion in Santa Maria.

As Spain grew weaker, and as the friars grew ever more repressive, the natives started to resist. Several minor peasant revolts marked the end of the 18th century. Poorly funded and helplessly localised, they were easily quashed. But in the 19th century the face of the resistance would change as a wealthy class of European-educated mestizos (Filipinos of mixed Spanish or Chinese blood) with nationalist tendencies began to emerge. Known as *ilustrados*, the greatest and best known of the lot was Dr José Rizal, doctor of medicine, poet, novelist, sculptor, painter, linguist, naturalist and fencing enthusiast.

Executed by the Spanish in 1896, Rizal epitomised the Filipinos' dignified struggle for personal and national freedom. 'I am most anxious for liberties for our country', he wrote just before facing the Spanish firing squad. 'But I place as a prior condition the education of the people so that our country may have an individuality of its own and make itself worthy of liberties'.

By killing such figures, the Spanish were creating martyrs. Andres Bonifacio led an aggressive movement known as the Katipunan, or KKK, that secretly built a revolutionary government in Manila, with a network of equally clandestine provincial councils. Complete with passwords, masks and coloured sashes denoting rank, the Katipunan's membership (both men and women) peaked at an estimated 30,000 in mid-1896. In August, the Spanish got wind of the coming revolution and the Katipunan leaders were forced to flee the capital.

Depleted, frustrated and poorly armed, the Katipuneros took stock in nearby Balintawak, a barangay of Caloocan, and voted to launch the revolution regardless. With the cry 'Mabuhay ang Pilipinas!' (Long live the Philippines!), the Philippine Revolution lurched into life following the incident that is now known as the Cry of Balintawak.

After 18 months of bloodshed, most of it Filipino blood, a Spanish-Filipino peace pact was signed and the revolutionary leader General Emilio Aguinaldo agreed to go into exile in Hong Kong in December 1897. Predictably, the pact's demands satisfied nobody. Promises of reform by the Spanish were broken, as were promises by the Filipinos to stop their revolutionary plotting.

Meanwhile, another of Spain's colonial trouble spots – Cuba – was playing host to an ominous dispute between Spain and the USA over sugar. To save face, Spain declared war on the USA; as a colony of Spain, the Philippines was drawn into the conflict. Soon after, an American fleet under Commodore George Dewey sailed into Manila Bay and routed the Spanish ships. Keen to gain Filipino support, Dewey welcomed the return of exiled revolutionary General Aguinaldo and oversaw the Philip-

1815	1850	1871	1872
The last Spanish galleon sails between Manila and Acapulco, marking the end of Manila's lucrative monopoly on global trade with Mexico, and hence much of South America.	The sugar and tobacco industries thrive, creating a class of wealthy mestizos. The *ilustrados*, who studied abroad and brought ideas about independence back to the Philippines, emerge from this class.	Army-appointed Spanish King Amadeo I appoints hardliner General Rafael de Izquierdo as governor of the Philippines in an effort to stamp out rising nationalist sentiment in the archipelago.	Izquierdo's execution of Padre José Burgos and two other popular Filipino priests on suspicion of harbouring mutinous intentions reawakens the nationalist spirit spawned during the British occupation 100 years earlier.

pine Revolution phase two, which installed Aguinaldo as president of the first Philippine republic. The Philippine flag was flown for the first time during Aguinaldo's proclamation of Philippine Independence in Cavite on 12 June 1898.

The Philippine–American War

With the signing of the Treaty of Paris in 1898, the Spanish–American War ended and the USA effectively bought the Philippines, along with Guam and Puerto Rico, for US$20 million. A fierce debate raged in the US over what to do with its newly acquired territory halfway across the world. Hawks on the right clamoured to hold onto the islands for strategic and 'humanitarian' reasons, while 'anti-imperialist' liberals attacked the subjugation of a foreign peoples as morally wrong and warned that the battle to occupy the Philippines would drag on for years (about which they were correct).

US President William J McKinley originally opposed colonisation before caving in to hawks in his Republican party and agreeing to take over the islands. Echoing the imperialists, McKinley opined that because Filipinos 'were unfit for self-government', he had no choice but to take over the islands and 'civilise' them. Filipinos led by Aguinaldo had other ideas. They set up a makeshift capital in Malolos, outside Manila, in open defiance of the Americans. The Americans, in turn, antagonised the Filipinos and war broke out in February 1899.

The expected swift American victory didn't materialise, as the guerrilla campaign launched by Aguinaldo and rebels such as Gregorio del Pilar and Apolinario Mabini proved remarkably effective at neutralising American military superiority. Aguinaldo was captured in March 1901, but still the war dragged on. As it did, and as casualties on both sides mounted, the American public's opposition to the war grew. Resentment peaked in September 1901 in the aftermath of the Balangiga Massacre. It was only on 4 July 1902 that the US finally declared victory in the campaign, although pockets of guerrilla resistance continued to dog the Americans for several more years. Some 200,000 Filipino civilians, 20,000 Filipino soldiers and more than 4000 American soldiers died in the war from combat or disease.

The American Era

The Americans quickly set about healing the significant wounds their victory had wrought. Even before they had officially won the war, they began instituting reforms aimed at improving the Filipinos' lot, the most important of which was a complete overhaul of the education system. Whereas the Spanish had attempted to keep Filipinos illiterate and ignorant of Spanish, the Americans imported hundreds of teachers to the

HISTORY THE PHILIPPINE–AMERICAN WAR

The Spanish documentary *Returning to the Siege of Baler* (2008) recounts how 50 Spaniards holed up in Baler's church held out for 11 months against 800 Filipinos during the Philippine Revolution.

The 1904 World's Fair: The Filipino Experience (2005) is a page-turning account by Jose D Fermin of the 1100 Filipinos who were taken to the St Louis World's Fair in the US and displayed under zoolike conditions as examples of colonial triumph.

1892	1899	1901	1935
José Rizal returns home one year after his *El Filibusterismo*, which skewered the Spanish, is published. He forms La Liga Filipina, a social reform movement, and is banished to Mindanao.	William Grayson, an American army private from Nebraska on night patrol near Manila, fires the first shot in the Philippine–American War. The shot kills a drunk Filipino noncombatant.	The Americans capture revolutionary leader General Emilio Aguinaldo, who later urges his countrymen to accept US rule. His countrymen don't listen, and the war drags on another 1½ years.	Manuel L Quezon, a wealthy mestizo, wins the first national presidential election, marking the establishment of the Philippine Commonwealth. True Philippine independence will have to wait until after the war.

country to teach reading, writing, arithmetic – and English. Within 35 years the literacy rate among Filipinos had risen from a miniscule percentage to almost 50%, and 27% of the population could speak English.

Besides schools, the Americans built bridges, roads and sewage systems. They brought the recalcitrant Moros in Mindanao to heel and Christianised the Cordillera tribes of the north – two groups the Spanish had tried and failed to influence. And they instituted an American-style political system that gradually gave more and more power to Filipinos. The Americans also made a gesture considered unprecedented in the history of imperialism: they openly promised the Filipinos eventual independence.

Critics describe American benevolence during this period as a thinly veiled carrot disguising America's true goal of establishing economic hegemony over the islands. Whatever the motive, the US endorsed the Commonwealth of the Philippines in 1935, along with the drafting of a US-style constitution and the first national election. On paper at least, democracy and freedom had at last come to the Philippines. Unfortunately, WWII would ensure that they would be short-lived.

> The American military practised for the Vietnam War in the Philippines in the 1950s under the command of General Edward Landsdale, the model for Graham Greene's *The Quiet American.*

READING LIST

There has been a treasure trove of books published about the unique relationship between the US and the Philippines.

➡ *In Our Image: America's Empire in the Philippines,* by Stanley Karnow. Definitive work on America's role in the Philippines.

➡ *Benevolent Assimilation: The American Conquest of the Philippines 1899–1903,* by Stuart Creighton Miller. Eye-opening account of the Philippine–American War and how the US media treated that war.

➡ *America's Boy: A Century of United States Colonialism in the Philippines,* by James Paterson-Hamilton. Absorbing look at Marcos' symbiotic relationship with the US.

➡ *Vestiges of War: The Philippine–American War & Aftermath of an Imperial Dream,* by Angel Velasco Shaw and Luis H Francia. Multidisciplinary anthology that provides critical perspective on both countries' national narratives in relation to one another.

➡ *By Sword and Fire: The Destruction of Manila in World War II,* by Alphonso Aluit. Blow-by-blow account of the battle that flattened Manila, and America's role in it.

➡ *Retribution: The Battle for Japan,* by Max Hastings. Critically acclaimed WWII tome devotes much ink to the Philippines campaign and skewers Colonel MacArthur.

➡ *Asia's Cauldron: The South China Sea and the End of a Stable Pacific,* by Robert Kaplan. Has a chapter on the consequences of America's colonial burden with regards to a rising China.

1942	1945	1946	1969
75,000 American and Filipino troops surrender to Japan at Bataan – the largest surrender of troops in US history. The Bataan Death March ensues, and one month later Corregidor falls.	In battles to retake the Philippines, Manila is destroyed and 150,000 civilians killed. Many are the victims of doomed Japanese troops. The Pearl of the Orient would never be the same.	Japanese General Tomoyuki Yamashita, whose orders to abandon Manila were defied by his subordinates, is tried as a war criminal and hanged by order of General MacArthur.	Ferdinand Marcos becomes the first Philippine president to win two terms in office, even as resentment over Marcos' increasingly heavy-handed rule and the Philippines' involvement in Vietnam simmers.

The Destruction of Manila

When Japan bombed Hawaii's Pearl Harbor in 1941, other forces attacked Clark Field, where General Douglas MacArthur was caught napping, despite many hours' warning, setting off a string of events that would lead to the Japanese occupying the Philippines from 1942 to 1945.

In 1944 MacArthur honoured his now-famous pledge to return, landing at Leyte, determined to dislodge the Japanese. The main battleground in this onslaught was Manila, where defenceless residents suffered horrifically in the ensuing crossfire during February 1945. By the time MacArthur marched into the city, the combination of Japanese atrocities and American shelling had killed at least 150,000 civilians, and a city that had been one of the finest in Asia was destroyed.

A fierce debate rages to this day about who was to blame for the destruction of Manila. The vast majority of civilian casualties resulted from US artillery fire. But many argue that by failing to abandon Manila and declare it an open city, the Japanese gave MacArthur little choice. Whatever the truth, Manila belongs in a category with Warsaw, Hiroshima and Hamburg as cities that suffered the most damage in WWII.

Terror in Manila: February 1945 (2005) by Antonio Pérez de Olaguer is an unflinching account of Japanese atrocities during the battle for Manila. It's based on oral histories by Spanish survivors.

The Marcos Era

In 1965 Ferdinand Marcos, a dashing former lawyer from a prominent Ilocos political family, was elected the Philippines' fourth post-WWII president under the seductive slogan 'This nation can be great again'. At first it indeed was a new era, and Marcos and his even more charismatic wife Imelda went about trying to bring back some of Manila's pre-war energy. Imelda drove projects such as the Cultural Center of the Philippines. By 1970 widespread poverty, rising inflation, pitiful public funding and blatant corruption triggered a wave of protests in Manila. When several demonstrators were killed by police outside the presidential Malacañang Palace, Marcos' image as a political saviour died with them.

Citing the rise of leftist student groups and the communist New People's Army (NPA), Marcos imposed martial law on the entire country in 1972. Normally a constitutional last resort designed to protect the masses, martial law was declared by Marcos to keep himself in power (the constitution prevented him from running for a third term) and to protect his foreign business interests. Under martial law, a curfew was imposed, the media was silenced or taken over by the military, international travel was banned and thousands of anti-government suspects were rounded up and put into military camps. An estimated 50,000 of Marcos' opponents were jailed, exiled or killed. Marcos would not lift martial law until 1981.

Ferdinand Marcos died in exile in 1989 and his shoe-happy wife, Imelda, soon returned to the Philippines. Despite evidence that she and

Imelda Marcos ran unsuccessfully for president in both 1992 and 1998 while still under investigation for some 900 counts of corruption and other crimes. She ran successfully for Congress in 1995, in 2010 and again in 2013 at the age of 84.

1972	1980	1981	1983
As resentment of Marcos rises, the embattled president imposes martial law and jails thousands of teachers, journalists, union leaders and opposition leaders, including Benigno 'Ninoy' Aquino Jr.	Ninoy Aquino is released from custody to undergo a triple bypass operation in the United States. He remains in exile for more than three years.	Martial law is lifted on the eve of a visit by Pope John Paul II, who criticises Marcos' human rights record. Shortly after, a rigged election hands Marcos another six-year term.	Aquino is shot dead at Manila's airport as he disembarks from a flight returning him from exile in the USA. Two million mourners pour onto the streets to accompany Aquino's funeral cortege.

her husband helped themselves to billions of dollars from the treasury, Imelda lives freely in Manila and was elected to her second term in Congress in 2013.

The Birth of People Power

People Power was born in the streets of Manila in February 1986. As the whole world watched, millions of Filipinos, armed only with courage and religious faith, poured out onto the streets to defy the military might of the Marcos regime.

Despite Marcos' unpopularity in the mid-1980s, People Power might never have happened were it not for the assassination of immensely popular opposition figure Ninoy Aquino. With his death, Filipinos felt they had lost their hope for a peaceful return to democracy. Some two million mourners followed Ninoy's funeral cortege as it slowly wound its way through the streets of Manila for over 12 hours.

The decline and fall of the Marcos dictatorship came swiftly after that. By 1986 even the USA, which had backed Marcos all those years against communism in Southeast Asia, began to withdraw its support. In the face of mounting criticism abroad and rising unrest at home, Marcos called for snap elections on 7 February 1986. Corazon 'Cory' Aquino, Ninoy's widow, became the (reluctant at first) standard bearer of the opposition at the instigation of the Roman Catholic Church. Marcos came out the winner of the election, but the people knew Cory had been cheated, and they were no longer to be silenced.

On 26 February a massive sea of humanity gathered around Camp Aguinaldo and Camp Crame, along Epifanio de los Santos Ave, better known as EDSA, where two of Marcos' former ministers, Juan Ponce Enrile and Fidel Ramos, had taken refuge after defecting to the side of the people. They sang, chanted, prayed, shared food and drink, both among themselves and with government troops, who refused to fire into crowds and eventually went over to the side of the people. By nightfall the restless crowds were threatening to storm the palace. At this point the US stepped in and advised Marcos to 'let go'. Hurriedly the Marcoses boarded a US aircraft and flew to Hawaii and into exile.

The Filipino people had staged the world's first successful bloodless revolution, inspiring others to do the same across the world.

Same Old, Same Old...

The first decade of the 21st century was a tumultuous one in Philippine politics. It began with an impeachment trial that saw millions of Filipinos take to the streets to oust President Joseph Estrada over corruption allegations – the country's second 'People Power' revolution in 15 years. Estrada gave way to his vice president, Gloria Macapagal-Arroyo,

'Jihadists in Paradise' is a riveting *Atlantic Monthly* article by Mark Bowden about Abu Sayyaf rebels' seizure of a Palawan resort and subsequent 18-month detainment of two American missionaries.

Inside the Palace (1987) by Beth Day Romulo documents the rise and fall of the Marcoses – a couple made for drama.

1986	1989	1991	1997
The bloodless EDSA I Revolution, aka People Power, chases Marcos from the Philippines. Ninoy's widow, Corazon ('Cory'), who had lost the presidential election to Marcos days earlier, becomes president.	A coup attempt against Cory Aquino sees hundreds of foreigners taken hostage in condos and hotels in Makati. Alleged US involvement in suppressing the siege stokes rising anti-American sentiment.	Mt Pinatubo erupts, rendering the American military base at Clark unusable. The Philippine Senate votes to end the US military presence at Philippine bases permanently.	The Indigenous People's Rights Act (IRPA) led to law empowering tribal groups to acquire a certificate of ancestral domain title. It's long and complicated, and as a result, most ancestral lands aren't officially 'owned'.

THE MAGUIDANAO MASSCRE & THE MEDIA

It was the election-related crime that shocked the world: in the run-up to the 2010 gubernatorial elections in Maguindanao, Mindanao, 58 people were gunned down at a campaign event for an opposition candidate. Thirty-four of the victims were members of the media.

The alleged perpetrators were associated with the region's dominant Ampatuan clan, led by patriarch and incumbent governor (at the time) Andal Ampatuan Sr. His son, Andal Jr, who was running to replace him, is alleged to have masterminded the shootings.

A conviction in such a high-profile case was always far from certain in the Philippines, where clans like the Ampatuans tend to operate with impunity. President Aquino vowed to achieve justice in the case; however, as of August 2014 and amid charges of bribery, the prosecution had only rested its case against 28 of 114 accused.

Despite – or perhaps because of – the Philippines' vocal free press, the killing of journalists is common. The country ranked third (after Iraq and Somalia) in the Committee to Protect Journalists' 2014 'impunity index' – one more reason the legal proceedings have been closely watched.

whose nearly 10 years in office were also dogged by scandals, including alleged improprieties in her 2004 re-election and in 2007 congressional elections, the misuse of P366 million of public funds as well as general accusations of plunder and corruption.

In the 2010 presidential elections, the country found the fresh face it was looking for in the form of Benigno 'Noynoy' Aquino III, the previously squeaky-clean son of Corazon Aquino, hero of the first People Power revolution in 1986. Riding a wave of national grief after his mother's death in 2009, Aquino won a landslide victory with 42% of votes, emerging from a pack of candidates which included former president Estrada.

The Aquino administration did make some headway towards potentially ending several decades of armed conflict in parts of the southern islands of Mindanao and the Sulu archipelago. In the summer of 2014 the government and the Moro Islamic Liberation Front (MILF), one of the major rebel groups seeking an autonomous Muslim homeland, agreed to the basic framework for this entity called the Bangsamoro. Of course, other groups object, and periodic violence still continue apace.

The Fall of Joseph Estrada: The Inside Story (2001) is a highly readable account by Amando Doronila of the rise and crash of the actor who tried to be president during the late 1990s.

1999	2007	2013	2013
As all-out war rages with the Moro Islamic Liberation Front (MILF), President Estrada signs the controversial Visiting Forces Agreement, which allows American troops back to train Filipino forces.	Renegade soldiers on trial for plotting a coup in 2003 escape their courtroom and take over Manila's Peninsula Hotel in another attempted coup against Arroyo.	Moro National Liberation Front (MNLF) forces lay siege to Zamboanga City in Mindanao for three weeks. The resulting fighting with the Philippine Army destroys buildings and displaces 100,000 people.	Super Typhoon Haiyan (known locally as Yolanda) sweeps through the central Visayas in November, killing an estimated 15,000 to 25,000 people and destroying coastal communities.

People & Culture

It's impossible to deny it: Filipinos have a zest for life that may be unrivalled on our planet. The national symbol, the jeepney, is an apt metaphor for the nation. Splashed with colour, laden with religious icons and festooned with sanguine scribblings, the jeepney flaunts the fact that, at heart, it's a dilapidated pile of scrap metal. No matter their prospects in life, Filipinos face them with a laugh and a wink. Whatever happens...'so be it'.

The National Psyche

Altar of Secrets: Sex, Politics, and Money in the Philippine Catholic Church (2013) is journalist Aries Rufo's damning account of the leadership of the country's predominant religion.

The fatalism of the Filipino people has a name: *bahala na,* a phrase that expresses the idea that all things shall pass and in the meantime life is to be lived. *Bahala na* helps shape the carefree, welcoming nature of the Filipino people – and their tolerance. Travellers of any race, creed or sexual orientation are uniformly received with the utmost warmth and courtesy.

Family and religion are the two most important forces in Filipino society. The close-knit Filipino family unit extends to distant cousins, multiple godparents, and one's *barkada* (gang of friends). Almost without exception, all members of one's kinship group are afforded the utmost loyalty; respect for elders is paramount.

Filipino families, especially poor ones, tend to be large. It's not uncommon for a dozen family members to live together in a tiny apartment, shanty or nipa hut. Because of this, personal space is not the issue for Filipinos that it is for Westerners. Foreign visitors to Philippine resorts are often amazed – or appalled – when a family of 10 takes up residence in the room next door, complete with pets, videoke machine and cooking equipment.

The most basic political unit, the barangay, is merely an extension of the family-based community unit that defined the social structure in pre-Hispanic times. The idea of working together for the common good, virtually nonexistent at the national level, is alive and well at the barangay level, where it's known as *bayanihan*. Originally a rural entity, the barangay today is no less relevant in urban shanty towns, where a healthy cooperative spirit is essential for survival.

Suggested Websites

Vibal Foundation (http://vibalfoundation.org) Info on modern and classic Filipino literature

NCCA (www.ncca.gov.ph) Outstanding website on arts and ethnic groups

Another thread in the fabric of Filipino society is the overseas worker. At any given time well more than one million Filipinos are working abroad, and combined they send home tens of billions of dollars. The Overseas Filipino Worker (OFW) – the nurse in Canada, the construction worker in Qatar, the entertainer in Japan, the cleaner in Singapore – has become a national hero.

Faith & Superstition

More than 80% of Filipinos are Roman Catholic. While the separation of church and state is formalised in the Filipino constitution, the Catholic Church deeply influences national and local politics. A subtle hint from the church can swing a mayoral race and mean millions of votes for presidential or congressional candidates.

Filipinos may be overwhelmingly Catholic, but they can sin with the best of them. Drinking is a popular pastime (cheap local brandy is the favourite poison), adultery and prostitution are rampant, and grudges are often settled with bullets.

To the chagrin of the Catholic Church, Filipinos are also a superstitious lot. In urban areas, faith healers, psychics, fortune-tellers, tribal shamans, self-help books and evangelical crusaders can all help cast away ill-fortune. In the hinterland, it's a given that caves and forests are inhabited by spirits, ghosts and *aswang* (vampire-like figures who eat unborn children).

Melting Pot

Ethnologically, the vast majority of Filipinos are related to Malaysians and Indonesians, with substantial Chinese influence as well as a smattering of colonial American and Spanish blood thrown into the mix. The most influential group of immigrants has traditionally been the Chinese. Chinese-Filipino mestizos have dominated commerce, and to a lesser extent politics, in the archipelago since the Spanish era.

There are also close to 100 cultural minority groups in the Philippines, depending on your definition, and 170 or so different languages and dialects are spoken in the archipelago. In general ethnic minorities can be divided into three main, blurred groups: Negrito, Igorot and Manobo.

The critically acclaimed documentary *Give up Tomorrow* (2011) looks at the wrongful conviction of a Cebu man on double rape/murder charges.

The Negrito

Often referred to as the aborigines of the Philippines, the Negrito are represented by the Aeta, Ati, Eta, Ita and Dumagat peoples. Now thought to number as few as 20,000, Negrito people are generally the most racially victimised of the Filipinos. Negrito mainly live in extremely poor conditions on the coastal fringes of North Luzon and in the highlands of Mindoro, Negros, Samar, Leyte and Panay, where the famously festive Ati are said to have initiated the present-day Ati-Atihan festivals in Kalibo and surrounding towns.

PROSTITUTION IN THE PHILIPPINES

The sex business in the Philippines grew up around the American military bases at Clark and Subic Bay, reaching its heyday during the late Marcos era. The Americans were booted out in 1991, but prostitution remains rampant around their former bases and in most major cities. Various estimates put the number of sex workers in the country at about 400,000, with up to 20% of those underage. Although prostitution is officially illegal, the police, many of whom are paid off by the sex industry operators, tend to turn a blind eye.

The Asia-Pacific office of the **Coalition Against Trafficking in Women** (☏02-426 9873; www.catwinternational.org) is in Quezon City, Manila. Its website has information about prostitution in the Philippines, and several useful links. In Angeles, the **Renew Foundation** (www.renew-foundation.org) works to keep former sex workers and trafficked women off the streets by teaching them alternative work skills and providing safe shelter.

Of particular concern is the problem of child prostitution. A culture of silence surrounds child sex abuse in the Philippines. While *hiya* (shame) plays a big role in the silence, for the most part this silence is bought. There's big money in paedophilia, both for ringleaders who arrange meetings between paedophiles and children, and for law enforcers who get paid to ignore it.

ECPAT Philippines (☏02-441 5108; www.ecpatphilippines.org) in Quezon City works to promote child-safe tourism and to end the commercial sexual exploitation of children through child prostitution, child pornography and the trafficking of children for sexual purposes. To report an incident, contact ECPAT, the **Philippine National Police Women en and Children's Division** (☏0919 777 7377) or the **Human Trafficking Action Line** (☏02-1343).

The Igorot

The Cordillera region of Luzon is home to the mountain-dwelling tribes collectively known as the Igorot. They include the Apayao (or Isneg), Kalinga, Ifugao, Benguet, Bontoc and Tingguian (or Itneg). While generally considered unbowed by outside pressures, many Igorot traditions were suppressed first by the Spanish and then by the Americans. However, most Igorot rituals, fashions and beliefs remain in some form and some rural villagers continue to live much as their ancestors did, tending to rice terraces and living off the land.

The Manobo

Don't Stop Believing (2013) is an inspiring documentary about Journey frontman Arnel Pineda's rise from Manila's streets to rock and roll stardom.

The term Manobo is used to describe the major indigenous groups of Mindanao. Of these groups, five regard themselves as Muslim – the Badjao, Maguindanao, Maranao (or Maranaw), Tausag (or Tausug) and Samal. Regarded as the least Islamic of the Muslim groups, the animist Badjao are the 'sea gypsies' of the Sulu seas. Maguindanao people are the largest of all the Muslim groups, famed for their skills as musicians and weavers. Maranao people are the traditional owners of Lake Lanao, and are among the Philippines' most ingenious craftspeople. Tausag people were the earliest Filipino Islamic converts back in the 15th century and as such were the ruling class of the Jolo Sultanate. Samal people are the poorest of the Muslim groups, having long been the loyal subjects of the Tausag dynasties. The main non-Muslim indigenous groups of Mindanao are the Bukidnon, Bagobo, Mandaya and Mansaka peoples.

Arts

Music

Filipinos are best known for their ubiquitous cover bands and their love of karaoke, but they need not be in imitation mode to show off their innate musical talent.

Dating from the late 19th century, the *kundiman* genre, with its bittersweet themes of love, fate and death, remains one of the best-loved modes of musical expression in the Philippines. Traditional musical instruments used in *kundiman* include the *kudyapi,* a hauntingly melodic lute, and the *kulintang,* a row of small gongs mounted on a *langkungan,* a resonating platform.

Mindanao artist Kublai Ponce-Millan's nine statues of indigenous Filipinos playing musical instruments in St Peter's Sq, Vatican City, was the first time a non-Italian artist was allowed to participate in the Vatican's annual nativity scene display.

Filipino rock, known as OPM (Original Pinoy Music), had its heyday in the '70s, when blues-rock outfits like the Juan de la Cruz Band, Anakbayan and Maria Cafra ruled the roost. They looked and sounded the part, with big hair, bandanas and endless, soulful electric-guitar riffs. The Juan de la Cruz Band is credited with inventing Pinoy rock by busting out lyrics in Tagalog – the first big act to do so. From those humble origins evolved Eraserheads, the country's first modest international success. This four-man band, known as the Philippines' Beatles, rose to prominence in the early '90s with catchy guitar-heavy alternative rock. There's also the Philippines' U2 – The Dawn, a vaguely New Age '80s band – and the Philippines' Elvis, '60s actor-singer Eddie Mesa. Another legend is Freddie Aguilar, whose 'Anak', a song about parent-child relations, propelled him to fame at the beginning of the People Power revolution in the 1980s.

In the 2000s, three bands dominated the OPM scene, singing in both English and Filipino. This trio was led by the sometimes sweet, sometimes surly diva Kitchie Nadal, who continues to tour internationally. The eponymous band fronted by the singer Bamboo rose to prominence with a heady mixture of political invective and ballads laden with angst-ridden garage rock. Rounding out the big three, the agreeable

KARAOKE

Many Westerners would sooner have their wisdom teeth removed without anaesthetic than spend an evening listening to inebriated amateurs pay homage to Celine Dion and Julio Iglesias. But when Filipinos want to unwind, they often do it with karaoke – or 'videoke' as it's known throughout the Philippines.

Filipinos are unabashed about belting out a tune, whenever and wherever, alone or in company. They pursue the craft without a hint of irony, which means that criticising or making fun of someone's performance is decidedly taboo, and may even provoke violence.

With all that videoke going on it can be awfully hard to find peace and quiet in certain tourist hot spots. If loud, unmelodious singing grates like fingernails on a blackboard, stick to resorts run by foreigners, which tend to be less videoke-friendly.

Rivermaya, formerly fronted by Bamboo, made minor waves internationally with its 2005 hit 'You'll Be Safe Here'.

These days OPM is waiting for its next big thing, whom you might find playing at Quezon City's '70s Bistro or Conspiracy Bar, or at Outpost in Cebu. Two names to look out for are Mumford & Sons–esque folk rockers Ransom Collective, and jazzy vocalist Jireh Calo.

One veteran band worth checking out in the bars of Manila is Kalayo, which plays a sometimes-frantic fusion of tribal styles and modern jamband rock. The 11-piece band uses a plethora of bamboo reed pipes, flutes and percussion instruments, and sings in dialects as diverse as Visayan, French and Bicol.

Architecture

Long before the Spanish arrived, the simple, utilitarian nipa hut defined Filipino architecture. The most basic nipa hut is made of wood and bamboo, with a roof of palm thatch – cool and breezy in hot weather and easily repaired if damaged by typhoons.

The Spanish brought new forms of architecture, such as the *bahay na bato* (stone house) and squat, fortresslike 'earthquake-baroque' churches. But the basic design of the nipa hut endured. By the 19th century, Filipinos of means were building hybrid residences that mixed Spanish and Asian styles with elements of the nipa hut. These composite structures, distinguishable by their capiz-shell windows and huge upstairs *sala* (living room), remain the most elegant and distinctive architectural specimens the Philippines has to offer.

Maria Virginia Yap Morales' *Balay Ukit: Tropical Architecture in Pre-WWII Filipino Houses,* explores late-19th- and early-20th-century building styles that exhibit this hybrid style, the vast majority of which have been destroyed or abandoned, overwhelmed by quicker, cheaper and generic concrete structures. The Spanish colonial city of Vigan is the best place to view these houses, although you will sometimes stumble across fine examples in the most remote barangays.

Theatre

Filipino theatre evolved from marathon chants and epic legends, such as the Unesco-recognised Ifugao *hudhud,* sung in the rice fields around Kiangan in North Luzon to alleviate boredom while planting and harvesting. In the 17th century the Spaniards introduced *sinakulos* – passion plays depicting the life and death of Christ – to convert the locals to Christianity. Other early forms of theatre were the *moro-moro,* which glorified the Christian struggle against Muslims in the 19th century, and

Po-on is an easy intro to Filipino author F Sionil Jose, with all the tropes of Filipino literature: evil Spanish priests, heroic *ilustrados,* passive resistance and armed struggle. It's the first in a five-part series.

Eye of the Fish is an interesting collection of essays by Manila-born, New York–raised journalist Luis H Francia that is a good introduction to the various issues facing the Philippines and its people today.

a light, localised musical form known as *zarzuela,* which was used to protest American occupation at the outset of the 20th century.

When the Americans arrived, English became the language of the national theatrical scene. The journalist, novelist and playwright Nick Joaquin wrote his signature work, *Portrait of a Young Artist as a Filipino,* in 1951. Other important playwrights of the 20th century were Rolando Tinio, whose Filipino adaptations of English-language classics such as Shakespeare's tragedies remain unparalleled in their field; and Rene Villanueva, best known for his children's books but also highly regarded as a playwright.

Contemporary playwrights blend tradition with the issues of the day. The Philippine Educational Theater Association (PETA; www. petatheater.com) has an excellent development program for up-and-coming playwrights.

Aswang – mythical vampire-like figures who eat unborn children – have been the subject of at least one American cult horror flick. Any rural Filipino will tell you in a matter-of-fact manner about the many *aswang* living in their local forests.

Painting & Sculpture

The most recognisable form of artwork in the Philippines is centuries old and, in fact, wasn't conceived as artwork: the *bulol,* the sacred wood figures carved by the Ifugao, have for centuries been used to guard rice fields. The names of the sculptors were rarely recorded, but elder Ifugao can often identify the sculptor of original *bulol* based on the statue's style. Reproductions of these powerful statues flood souvenir shops across the country.

Modern Filipino sculpture is epitomised by Guillermo Tolentino's neoclassical masterpiece in Caloocan City, the resplendent *Monumento,* honouring the revolutionary hero Andres Bonifacio. Another name visitors may notice is Jose Mendoza, whose sculptures adorn the streets of Makati.

Painting in the Spanish era was dominated by the two unchallenged masters of Filipino art: Juan Luna and Felix Resurreccion Hidalgo. Luna's vast *Spoliarium* and Hidalgo's *Antigone* stunned European art circles when they won gold and silver medals at the prestigious 1884 Madrid Exposition.

The early 20th century saw the rise of the masters Fabian de la Rosa and Fernando Amorsolo. De la Rosa's work is distinguished by disciplined composition and brushwork, while Amorsolo painted quintessential rural Philippine scenes and subjects in a free-flowing, impressionist style.

Vicente Manansala, Arturo Luz, Anita Magsaysay-Ho, Fernando Zobel and Hernando Ocampo were among the great Filipino modernists who emerged after WWII. Zobel toyed with cubism before becoming the country's foremost abstractionist. The brilliant ethnic-Chinese painter Ang Kiukok, who studied under Manansala, opened eyes with his violent cubist paintings of fighting cocks, stray dogs and tormented lovers.

Ghosts of Manila (1994) by James Hamilton-Paterson is a chilling yet entertaining 'docufiction' of life, death and the corrupt chains binding Filipinos in Manila's slums.

The contemporary Filipino art scene is ever abuzz. The conceptual artist David Cortez Medalla, based in Britain, has pioneered avant-garde art movements such as minimalism and performance art. In addition to being well received internationally, artist-with-a-conscience Benedicto Cabrera ('Bencab') has dedicated considerable effort to the development of contemporary art, and created Tam-awan village, an artists retreat in Baguio.

Dance

Filipino dance is as rich and varied as the islands themselves. The national folk dance is the *tinikling,* which involves a boy and a girl hopping between bamboo poles, held just above the ground and struck together in time to music or hand-clapping. Some say this dance was inspired by the flitting of birds between grass stems or a heron hopping through the rice paddies. A version of the *tinikling* is the breathtaking *singkil,* where two dancers representing a Muslim princess and her lady-in-waiting weave in and out of four poles struck together at increasing speed.

Two of the best known and most successful Filipino folk-dance troupes are the Bayanihan National Folk Dance Company, which first wowed the world in 1958 at the Brussels Universal Exposition, and the Ramon Obusan Folkloric Group, founded in 1972. Both are resident companies of the Cultural Center of the Philippines.

Many Filipino ballet talents have won international recognition abroad, among them Maniya Barredo, former prima ballerina of the Atlanta Ballet, and Lisa Macuja, who played Giselle with the Kirov Ballet in Russia. Macuja now runs her own ballet company, Ballet Manila.

The 'yo-yo', which means 'come back' in Tagalog, was invented by a Filipino-American. The original yo-yo was a studded weapon attached to 6m ropes.

Sport

Sport in the Philippines is dominated by one man: lightweight boxer Manny Pacquiao, widely considered the best pound-for-pound prizefighter in the world. Pacquiao, who emerged from poverty in Mindanao to win title belts in five different weight classes, is a tremendous source of national pride for Filipinos. He ran successfully for Philippine congress in 2010, but continues to dominate opponents in the rings.

An even quirkier national hero takes the form of stocky, bespectacled Efren 'Bata' ('The Kid') Reyes, one of the world's best nine-ball billiards players. The other big sport, besides cockfighting, is basketball. Most midsized towns have at least one concrete court with a corrugated-iron roof, and you'll find at least a crude interpretation of a court in even the poorest, most remote barangays. The overwhelmingly popular Philippine Basketball Association (PBA) draws many former US college stars.

Football (soccer) is growing rapidly in popularity as the national team, Azkals, has improved markedly in recent years and now competes with the best teams in Asia.

In 1942 Filipino statesman Carlos P Romulo became the first Asian to win a Pulitzer Prize, for a series of articles on pre-WWII Asia.

Cockfighting

Cockfighting is to the Philippines what baseball is to the USA or rugby is to New Zealand. A couple of times a week, mostly male crowds pack their local cockpit (usually dubbed a 'sporting arena') and watch prized roosters fight to the death.

Before each fight, the noise level rises to a crescendo as bets are screamed out to middlemen in a scene reminiscent of a stock exchange. A hush falls over the crowd as the clash begins. The birds, fitted with lethal three-inch ankle blades, wander around aimlessly for a few moments before being reminded by their handlers that there's an adversary in the vicinity. The actual fight, once it finally begins, is short and brutal. The winner is whisked away to a team of waiting surgeons, who stitch up any gaping wounds and dose the bird with antibiotics. The loser usually makes his way into the cooking pot.

The practice has its critics, both in the Philippines and abroad. But as of yet animal-rights groups have made little progress stemming a pastime that is so deeply ingrained in the country's culture.

Food & Drink

Kain na tayo – 'let's eat'. It's the Filipino invitation to eat, and if you travel in the Philippines you will hear it over and over and over again. The phrase reveals two essential aspects of Filipino people: one, that they are hospitable, and two, that they love to, well, eat. A melange of Asian, Latin, American and indigenous cooking, Filipino culinary traditions – hybridised and evolving – reflect the country's unique colonial history and varied geography.

Influences & Reputation

Filipinos are constantly eating. Three meals a day just isn't enough, so they've added two *meryenda*. The term literally means 'snack', but don't let that fool you – the afternoon *meryenda* can include something as filling as *bihon* (fried rice sticks) or *goto* (Filipino congee) plus *bibingka* (fluffy rice cakes topped with cheese).

Influences include American (burgers, fast food); Chinese (*pansit, lumpia*, anything soy based, stir frying); Mexican (tamales); and Spanish (*bringhe*, a version of paella most closely associated with Pampanga; any dishes sautéd with garlic, tomatoes and onions; flans; sofritos; and fiesta foods).

Filipino food has a somewhat poor reputation in both the West, where Filipino restaurants are rare, and the rest of Asia, where the cuisine is considered unimaginative and unrefined. This perplexes Filipinos, who are convinced their home-cooked comfort food (which is usually a different deal entirely to that served up abroad) is the greatest thing in the world. Of course, locally grown ingredients and the abundant amount of time required for cooking aren't usually available in the foreign incarnations.

Just as euphemisms like 'farm-to-table' and 'artisanal' have become commonplace to the point of cliché elsewhere, a new generation of Filipino chefs, restauranteurs and organic farmers are creating their own networks of like-minded foodies.

The usual complaints about Filipino food are that it's too heavy, too salty and – especially – too sweet. Sugar is added in abundance to everything, from the hamburgers at Jollibee to locally rendered Thai food. But if you know what to order, or know a good cook, you'll find delights aplenty to satisfy the most discriminating tastebuds.

Typical Dishes

If there were a national dish, it would undoubtedly be *adobo* – pork, chicken or just about any meat stewed in vinegar and garlic. It's delicious done right, but can be awfully salty and greasy if done wrong. Other dishes you'll find with striking regularity include *sinigáng* (any meat or seafood boiled in a sour, tamarind-flavoured soup), *kare-kare* (oxtail and vegetables cooked in peanut sauce), *crispy pata* (deep-fried pork hock or knuckles) and *pansit* (stir-fried noodles). *Ihaw-ihaw* eateries, serving *inihaw* (grilled meat or fish), are everywhere. *Lechón* (suckling pig roasted on a spit) is de rigueur at Filipino celebrations. Common appetisers include *lumpia* (small spring rolls, usually vegetarian) and the truly delicious *kinilaw* (Filipino-style ceviche).

Then there's the ubiquitous Filipino breakfast – rice (preferably garlic rice) with a fried egg on top, with *tapa* (salty beef strips), *tocino* (honey-cured pork), *bangus* (milkfish) or *longganiza* (sausages) on the side. For dessert, try *halo-halo,* a glass packed with fruit preserves, sweet corn, young coconut and various tropical delights topped with milky crushed ice, a dollop of crème caramel and a scoop of ice cream.

Home Cooking

Ordinary home cooking is a different affair from restaurant food. Vegies are more prevalent and families might serve chicken once a week. Grilling or frying fish like *galunggong* (mackerel-like fish) or farmed *bangus* in vinegar and garlic is much more common. *Panga,* the jaw of a tuna, sort of the dark-meat equivalent, is fairly meaty and popular. No meal is complete without rice of course, but *pansit* is also usually served.

Regional Specialities

In a country of such cultural, ethnographic and geographic diversity, it's no surprise that there's an equally diverse array of regional specialities. And staples such as *longganiza, lechón* and even *balút* (boiled duck egg containing partly formed embryo) are rendered in different ways. Of the regional cuisines, the spicy food of Bicol is probably most amenable to Western palettes, while Filipinos consider Pampanga province in central Luzon the country's food capital.

Bicol

Bicolano cooking involves many varieties of *sili* (hot chlili pepper) and *gata* (coconut milk); anything cooked in *gata* is known as *ginataán*. Perhaps most well known is Bicol *exprés,* a spicy mishmash of ground pork, *sili,* baby shrimps, onion, garlic and other spices cooked in coconut milk. Look for vendors sellling *pinangat,* green *gabi* (taro) leaves wrapped around pieces of fish, shrimp and/or pork. Another Bicol favourite is *candingga,* diced pork liver and carrots sweetened and cooked in vinegar.

Best Cookbooks

Memories of Philippine Kitchens: Stories and Recipes From Far and Near (Amy Desa & Romy Dorotan)

The Coconut Cookery of Bicol (Honesto C General)

Philippine Food & Life (Gilda Cordero-Fernando)

FOOD & DRINK HOME COOKING

EXOTIC EATS

The Philippines is a good place for culinary daredevils. Start off with the obvious one: *balút* (or 'eggs with legs' as it's also known) is a boiled duck egg containing a partially developed embryo, sometimes with tiny feathers. The WOW Philippines tourism website offers the following instructions for eating *balút:* 'Lightly tap on the wider end of this boiled duck egg and gently peel off some of the shell. Season with a little rock salt and enjoy sipping out the flavourful soup. Once done, peel off more of the shell to reveal a yolk at hard-boiled consistency, and a nearly developed duck embryo.'

Once you've crossed *balút* off your list, other foods won't seem quite so exotic. *Aso* or *asusena* (dog meat) is said to be tastier than any other red meat, though we can only report this based on hearsay. It's immensely popular in the Cordillera Mountains of North Luzon (as is 'Soup No 5' or bull-ball soup), where just about anything is fair game for the alimentary canal.

In some provinces, people will cook anything *adobo*-style (stewed in vinegar and garlic) – rat, cat, bat, frog, cricket, *bayawak* (monitor lizard), you name it. To work up the courage to consume any of these, down a few shots of *lambanog* (roughly distilled palm wine). Beetles, fried or floating in soup, and steamed tree-ant nests are two other gastronomic specialities found in the Philippines, though these are becoming harder to find.

In comparison, *sisig* – sizzling grilled bits of pig jowl – seems downright tame. We mention it because it's a favourite Filipino bar snack and it really is tasty, though it won't do your cholesterol level any favours. *Sisig* is the cousin of *bopis* – pig's lungs, chopped and fried.

With all of these dishes and other main courses, you can expect to find *natong* or *laing,* a chopped, leafy green vegetable commonly served on its own as a side dish. And finally in the dessert department, *pili* nut, an alleged aphrodisiac, is popping up in cookies, pastries, marzipan, pies and ice cream. For more on Bicolano cooking, see the boxed text p166.

Negros
Inasal (also the name of a fast-food chain) – basically grilled or roasted chicken marinated in lemongrass, annatto, *calamansi* (a local citrus) and garlic – has become something of a national dish and is most associated with Bacolod.

Pampanga
Dishes are often sweet and cooked with fermented sugar while shellfish is frequently fermented in rice sauce. *Pinaupong manok,* steamed chicken stuffed with vegetables, is a Pampanga speciality beloved throughout the country.

Ilocos
To some, Ilocano cooking is a vegetarian's paradise. Its version of *pinakbét* with eggplant, tomatoes, okra and *ampalaya* (bitter melon) – cooked in layers in a pot like a vegetable lasagne or terrine – is possibly the most well-known in the country. Their specific version of fish paste is called *bagoong* and goat or pig bile is sometimes used to flavour dishes.

Batanes
If you make it to these islands in the far north, be sure to try the following: *uved* balls, a surprisingly tasty dish (given the ingredients) made with bananas, mixed with minced pork and pig's blood; and *vunes,* which looks like a brown mess, but is actually chopped-up taro root stalks cooked with garlic.

Cordillera
A warning, rather than encouragement: they eat pretty much everything in the Cordillera. Unless of course you get excited at the idea of eating python, a bundle of frogs and dog meat.

Mindanao
Northern Mindanao, around Cagayan de Oro, is known for its *kinilaw* (ceviche), which is spiced with *tabon tabon,* a fruit native to northern Mindanao. Local foodies claim their city's *lechón baboy* (roasted pig), stuffed with lemongrass and other herbs and spices, is the tastiest. *Adobo* in Zamboanga is made with cream coconut, and *bulad* (dried fish), while popular everywhere in the country, comes in an especially large amount of varieties in southern Mindanao.

Fruits & Vegetables
If you find you aren't getting enough fruits and greens in the Philippines (and many do), buy them at outdoor fruit stands, street markets or, in bigger cities, supermarkets. Fruits and vegetables come in an astonishing variety, and anything grown domestically is dirt cheap. The only common vegetarian dish is *pinakbét:* a tasty melange of pumpkin, string beans, eggplant, okra and other vegies, seasoned with garlic, onions, ginger, tomatoes, shrimp paste and, sometimes, coconut milk. If you don't eat shrimp paste, ask for it not to be used.

Exotic tropical fruits such as durian, mangosteens, rambutans, jackfruit and longans, which will be familiar to those who have travelled elsewhere in Southeast Asia, are grown seasonally here. Walnut-sized

Camaro (fried crickets cooked in salt, vinegar and soy sauce) eating contests are held in Pampanga, where the dish is traditionally served.

Those square plots you see in Manila Bay and in rivers, lakes and ponds throughout the country are fish farms growing mainly tilapia and *bangus* (milkfish), the primary sources of animal protein for the majority of Filipinos.

lanzones, similar to longans but more sour, are a local speciality. *Santol* look like oranges, but have white pulp with the texture of wet fur. The Davao area is known for growing the country's best tropical fruit, including delicious mangosteens, stinky durian and succulent pomelos.

Temperate vegetables such as lettuce, carrots and broccoli are grown at high altitudes and sold in markets nationwide. Somewhat exotic vegetables grown locally include *kamote* (sweet potatoes), *ube* (purple yam), *ampalaya* (a bitter gourd) and *sayote* (chayote).

Lastly, the Philippines really, truly does have the best mangoes in the world. Period.

Vegetarians & Vegans

If you're vegetarian or vegan, you'll have a hard time eating out in the meat-mad Philippines. It's hard to find soy-based products outside of big cities, where Chinese merchants and restaurants sell tofu, soy milk etc. Beans in general don't figure prominently on the menu in the Philippines, thus, getting adequate protein can be tricky. If you feel this is going to be a problem, then it's wise to stock up on these products before leaving Manila or Cebu.

Most places, even *turu-turò* (basic eateries), offer some version of stir-fried vegetables, but many vegetables are cooked with (or simply include) bits of meat. Meat stock is commonly used in kitchens, and it's nigh impossible to get chefs to change their cooking methods, especially in villages. In larger towns you'll find small shops that sell bread, cereals and milk, and in bigger cities like Manila, Cebu or Davao you'll find well-stocked supermarkets. All that said, if you eat fish and eggs, you'll have no problem in the Philippines, and steamed rice is always an option!

The chef at the upscale Manila restaurant Goose Station created a tasting menu inspired by independence leader José Rizal's life and writings.

Fiesta Food

Each village, town and city in the Philippines has its own fiesta, usually celebrated on the feast day of its patron saint, as determined by the Catholic calendar. Historically every household was expected to prepare food and serve it to anybody who appeared at the door. Nowadays, food is still prepared but on a greatly diminished scale, and only people who have been invited show up at the buffet table. The fare on such occasions varies regionally, but generally consists of pork, beef and chicken dishes, sometimes with some fish and seafood thrown in.

Kaldereta (beef or sometimes goat-meat stew), *igado* (stir-fried pork liver), fried chicken and, of course, *lechón* are some of the dishes you can

---

CUSTOMS & HABITS

➡ An everyday meal in the Philippines is a fairly informal occasion, though it can take on the trappings of a formal Western-style dinner in the houses of the rich.

➡ Boiled rice is the centrepiece of any meal.

➡ All dishes are usually served family-style on large plates in the middle of the table.

➡ *Calamansi* (a type of citrus) juice mixed with soy sauce is a commonly offered condiment.

➡ Generally Filipinos eat with a fork and a spoon (the latter is meant to double as a knife) and napkins tend to be super-thin and small – many visitors find both a little hard to get used to.

➡ 'For a while': an expression used in all settings but in restaurants could mean your food is minutes or hours away from being served.

➡ Menus, especially in informal restaurants and rural areas, are platonic versions of what could be served at any one time. It's not unusual for a good number of items to be unavailable.

expect to find at a fiesta. Sweet rice cakes, usually local delicacies, are served as dessert. Birthdays and other private parties are usually celebrated with a big plate of *pansit*, though nowadays this has been widely replaced by spaghetti, the local version of which will strike most Westerners as being unduly sweet. A birthday cake and ice cream are a must, especially at children's parties.

Drinks

Nonalcoholic Drinks

Tap water in much of the Philippines is fine, in other parts purified water is strictly recommended. Some cities, such as Davao, boast extremely safe water, while others, such as Puerto Princesa, caution against drinking theirs. To be safe, ask locals and expats for advice or stick to boiled water, or bottled water, which is cheap (except in restaurants where it costs on average four times as much). Many restaurants try to push expensive bottled water on you; if you don't want it, request 'service' water or bring in your own – all but the most expensive and formal places are usually fine with this.

It's a mixed bag for coffee drinkers. Three-in-one packets are dirt cheap, quick and often the only option; however, the taste is overly sweet and weak. Meanwhile, in Manila and other large cities as well as in touristy resort areas, you can find plenty of Starbucks-like imitators serving good ground coffee. A handful of serious cafes with state-of-the-art machinery roasting single origin beans are also in Manila. Otherwise, European-owned accommodation and restaurants tend to prioritise espresso drinks.

Tea is served in Chinese restaurants; elsewhere, soft drinks rule. *Buko* juice, said to be good for staving off dehydration, is young coconut juice with bits of translucent coconut meat floating in it. It's usually sold in the nut, but you'd best stick to the type that comes in presealed cups or bottles. *Guayabano* (soursop) juice is sweet and refreshing. The popular little local citrus known as *calamansi* or *kalamansi* is used to make a refreshing cordial or gets added to black tea. Wondrous curative powers are ascribed to it, so take a sip...

> The longest barbecue on record, measuring 8000m and using 50,000kg of fish, was held in Pangasinan in April 2014.

Alcoholic Drinks

At around P30 a bottle, San Miguel ('San Mig') pale pilsner and light beer enjoys a virtual monopoly on the local brew market, although pricier imports do provide some competition. In Manila, there's something of a minor craft beer revolution. However, with the exception of meek rival Beer Na Beer, most domestic beers you see on store shelves are San Miguel products, including the wildly popular Red Horse Extra Strong (alcohol content: 7%; chance of bad karaoke post–Red Horse: 100%).

Palatable brandies, whiskies and gins are produced domestically. Tanduay Rum (P40 to P80 for a 500mL bottle) is a perfectly drinkable travelling companion – and a handy antiseptic! Rural concoctions include *basi*, a sweet, portlike wine made from sugar cane juice. *Tuba* is a strong palm wine extracted from coconut flowers; in its roughly distilled form it's called *lambanog*. Local firewater packs a punch – your stomach (if not your head) will thank you in the morning if you partake of the *pulutan* (small snacks) always served with alcohol.

> The eclectic Filipino dessert *halo-halo* is appropriately translated as 'mix-mix'.

Where to Eat & Drink

Turu-Turò The basic Filipino eatery is a *turu-turò* (literally 'point point'), where customers can order by pointing at the precooked food on display. These come in many guises, from small roadside canteens to huge enterprises.

Food Carts & Vendors These have a wide range of mostly snacks on offer. Kebabs and fish or squid balls are popular, usually fried in boiling oil and served on skewers. Mobile vendors may also sell *balút* (carried in a basket) and a sweet bean-curd snack known locally as *taho*.

Restaurants It's worth trying well-prepared, authentic Filipino cuisine from a popular chain such as Gerry's or Dencio's. Restaurants serving international fare, including excellent Japanese, Korean and Chinese (Thai and Italian are probably next-most common) are found in all large cities. Malls are comfortable air-conditioned places to find both fast food and more upscale Filipino chain eateries.

Cafes International and Filipino coffee-shop chains are becoming more and more common; most malls have at least one. Besides hot and cold espresso drinks, cakes and pastries, they usually offer a menu of light fare.

Markets Some cities boast special outdoor food markets where clusters of vendors serve regional and national specialities; notable examples are in Vigan, Legazpi, Dumaguete and Cagayan de Oro.

Fast Food Filipinos love their fast food, and these places are sometimes the only modern, air-con eating options available. Chowking, Jollibee and Greenwich Pizza are seemingly ubiquitous.

The mascot for the fast-food chain Jollibee is an insect in a blazer who loves to dance; the adventures of Jollibee and his sidekicks are chronicled in a TV series called *Jollitown*.

FOOD & DRINK EAT YOUR WORDS

Eat Your Words

Names of dishes often describe the way they are cooked, so it's worth remembering that *adobo* is stewed in vinegar and garlic, *sinigáng* is sour soup, *ginataán* means cooked in coconut milk, *kilawin* or *kinilaw* is raw or vinegared seafood, *pangat* includes tomatoes in a light broth, and *inihaw* is grilled meat or fish (*ihaw-ihaw* denotes eateries that specialise in grilled food). The word for 'spicy' is *maangháng*.

MENU DECODER

adobo	often called the national dish; chicken, pork or a mixture of both, marinated in vinegar and garlic and stewed until tender
adobong pusít	squid or cuttlefish cooked adobo-style
arróz caldo	Spanish-style thick rice soup with chicken, garlic, ginger and onions
aso	dog; eaten with relish (or just plain) by North Luzon's hill tribes
bachoy	popular concoction of broth, onion, rice noodles, beef, pork and liver
balút	boiled duck egg containing a partially formed embryo
calamares	crispy fried squid
crispy pata	deep-fried pork hock or knuckles
goto	rice porridge made with pork or beef innards
halo-halo	various fruit preserves served in shaved ice and milk
lechón	spit-roast whole pig served with liver sauce
lechón kawali	crispy fried pork
lomi	type of noodle dish
lumpia	spring rolls filled with meat and/or vegetables
mami	noodle soup; similar to *mee* in Malaysia or Indonesia
menudo	pork bits sautéd with garlic and onion and usually garnished with sliced hot dog
pansit bihon	thick- or thin-noodle soup
pinakbét	mixed vegetable stew
pochero	hotpot of beef, chicken, pork, Spanish sausage and vegetables, principally cabbage
rellenong bangus	fried stuffed milkfish
sisig	eg. pork sisig: sizzling grilled bits of pig jowl
tapsilog	a modern compound combining three words: *tapa* (dried beef), *sinangag* (garlic fried rice) and *itlog* (fried egg); usually eaten for breakfast
tocino	cured pork made with saltpetre

Environment

The environment of the Philippines has two very different faces: one is a spectacular tropical-island-topia, home to a global treasure of endemic species; the other is one of the world's top conservation priorities, due to the many grave threats to its health. The visitor might begin by understanding both, then focus on finding the diamonds in the rough, safe in the knowledge that selective ecotourism can not only be tremendously rewarding here, but also do an enormous amount of good.

The Land

The Mindanao Trench in the Philippine Sea, at 10,497m, is the second-deepest spot in the world's oceans.

The Philippines is the world's second-largest archipelago, with 7107 islands – although when asked how many, locals commonly joke 'at what tide?' This vast network, stretching some 1810km from the tip of Batanes to the Sulu archipelago, is the defining characteristic of the country, shaping it socially, politically and economically. Only its next-door neighbour, Indonesia, offers a larger string of pearls. In fact, combine the two and you could hop to a different island every day for over 50 years!

While the Philippine islands range from tiny coral islets to the sprawling, amoeba-like giants of Luzon and Mindanao, they are all tropical. Think jungle-clad, mountainous interiors, arcs of sandy beach, aquamarine waters and coral reefs. Winding interior roads are typically lined by tin-roofed shacks; rice paddies fill the lowlands and form scenic terraces above; outrigger fishing boats dot simple fishing villages. Concrete provincial cities, clogged with traffic and wrapped in spaghetti-like power lines, are linked by a complex, ever-changing ferry network.

Wildlife

Millenniums of geographical isolation from the rest of Southeast Asia has resulted in the evolution of thousands of species found nowhere else on earth, leading biologists to dub the archipelago 'Galápagos times 10'. In fact, new species are still being discovered at a remarkable rate.

Some statistics tell the tale: the Philippines has 191 species of mammals, of which 16 were only discovered in the last 10 years. More than 100 of these are endemic – even more than in Madagascar. Some 600 species of bird also call the Philippines home, nearly 200 of which are endemic – only much larger Indonesia and Brazil have more unique varieties. Reptiles are represented by about 235 species, some 160 (68%) of which are endemic. The country is also home to approximately 13,500 species of plant; only four countries can boast more. Scientists estimate that 30% to 40% of those species are unique to the Philippines.

The story is the same underwater. The Philippines is part of the 'Coral Triangle', the global centre for marine biodiversity. At the same time, it has a higher concentration of species per unit area than anywhere else in this region, making it the very 'centre of the centre'.

However, while the Philippines is renowned for its underwater life, it's not well known for terrestrial wildlife-spotting. This is because the ecotourism infrastructure doesn't exist and the animals themselves are elusive, particularly in the face of ongoing development.

Animals

As you would expect from such a hotspot of biodiversity, the Philippines contains some extraordinary animals. The poster mammal is the lovable, palm-sized tarsier, a primate found mainly on the island of Bohol, and easiest seen at the Tarsier Sanctuary (p313). The Philippines proudly lays claim to the world's smallest hoofed mammal – the rare Philippine mouse deer of Palawan – one of four deer species on the islands. Other furry favourites include the Palawan bearcat, or binturong, which looks like a black raccoon, and the small but charming Visayan leopard, with its big dark eyes.

The most impressive land mammal is the *tamaraw,* a dwarf water buffalo found in Mindoro's Mt Iglit-Baco National Park. A century ago their population numbered 10,000; today only a few hundred remain. More common are the eight species of fruit bat (flying fox) that dwell in caves across the country, at least by day. Those visiting Boracay need only look up at dusk to spot the nightly bat migration, including that of the giant golden-crowned flying fox, which has a 1.7m wingspan.

There are a few places around the country where you might spot whales if your timing is right, such as the channel between Negros and Cebu. However, you're more likely to spot dolphins. Less well known are dugong (known locally as *duyong*), a type of sea cow once found in great numbers in Philippine waters but now relatively rare. Two places where you can spot them (if you're lucky) are in Malita, Mindanao, and off Busuanga Island, in northern Palawan.

The national bird is the enormous Philippine eagle. Less than a few hundred survive in the wild, mostly in the rainforests of Mindanao, Samar, and the Sierra Madre Mountains of North Luzon. They are more easily seen at the Philippine Eagle Research & Nature Center (p371) in Calinan, outside of Davao. Further south, the Sulu hornbill is one of several extraordinary hornbills on the islands, part of a genus known for its blazing beaks. The Palawan peacock pheasant is also a remarkable bird: the males of this species have a metallic blue crest, long white eyebrows and large metallic blue or purple 'eyes' on the tail. Now nearing endangered status, these ground-dwellers are found only in the deepest forests of Palawan.

Among the reptiles, geckos are ubiquitous. There are also 10 species of flying lizard, which glide from tree to tree using a flap of skin on either side of their body. More elusive is the rare sailfin dragon, which is just as advertised, with a sail-like fin standing atop its back. Rarest of all is the endangered, and enormous, Philippine crocodile, which can be seen in Sierra Madre Natural Park. There's also a wide variety of venomous and nonvenomous snakes, including pythons, sea snakes (which can be seen

ENVIRONMENT WILDLIFE

A 21ft-long crocodile, one of the largest in the world, was captured in 2011 near Bunawan, Mindanao.

BEST WILDLIFE-SPOTTING

Python (Danjugan Island, off Negros) Yes, monster pythons do eat bats in mid-air.

Whale Shark (Oslob, Cebu) A once-in-a-lifetime chance to see – and swim with – the largest fish in the sea.

Tarsier (Bohol) You've got a good chance of spotting this adorable creature on an organised night trek.

Fruit Bat (Monfort Bat Cave p370, Samal Island, off Mindanao) Just you, and 2.5 million of them.

Dugong (off Busuanga Island, Palawan) Is it a whale, or a seal? This strange hybrid is worth the search.

Philippine Eagle (Mt Apo, Mindanao) What better place to spy this majestic bird than the tallest peak in the Philippines?

when snorkelling), and the Philippine cobra, which can spit its venom 3m; pack an umbrella.

Of course, divers and snorkellers also flock to the Philippines to see any of the islands' 2500-plus species of fish. Some of the larger denizens include whale sharks, which are typically seen in Donsol or, more commonly now, at Oslob, Cebu; and thresher sharks, which use their enormous tails to herd their prey. Sea turtles are often a common sight while snorkelling, with a resident tribe lying off the beach at Apo Island.

Plants

While the pretty yellow-flowered *nara* is the national tree of the Philippines, the unofficial national plant must surely be the nipa palm, whose leaves form the walls and roofs of nipa huts all over the country. The national flower is the highly aromatic *sampaguita,* a variety of jasmine. For both quality and quantity, you can't beat the some 900 endemic species of orchid, including the *waling-waling (Vanda sanderiana)* of Mindanao and the red-spotted star orchid *(Rananthera mautiana).* Another favourite is pitcher plants; climbers may stumble upon rare examples of these as they explore at remote elevations, such as on Mt Guiting-Guiting (p272) on Sibuyan Island.

Ecotourism

With so many natural wonders spread out among so many beautiful islands, you might think that the Philippines would have a highly developed ecotourism industry. And below the water, you might be right. In southern Negros alone, new dive resorts are sprouting like hotels in Boracay. Even remote resorts have dive centres now. Along with this upsurge has come the ongoing creation of dozens of marine reserves. Palawan has more than 60; southern Negros over a dozen. This has led to a marked increase in marine life in places like Hundred Islands National Park and Apo Reef Natural Park. However, make no mistake about it: there is still an ongoing battle to protect marine reserves from local fisherfolk, who frequently invade them at night. It can be very distressing to snorkel at Carbin Reef, part of Panay's flagship Sagay Marine Reserve, and not see a single fish larger than your finger.

The world's biggest pearl was found by a Filipino diver in the waters off Palawan in 1934. It weighed over 6kg and was valued at US$42 million.

While ecotourism on land is no less challenged, it is far less advanced, due primarily to a lack of basic infrastructure. At first glance, the Philippines would appear to have a robust national park system. As of 2012, there were 240 protected areas covering almost 12% of the country. However, few actually meet the international definition of a national park. According to Conservation International, two-thirds have human settlements, and one quarter of their lands have already been disturbed or converted to agriculture. Only a select few parks have features such as offices, trail maps, established campsites or any facilities at all. Just consider the country's largest protected area, the 4766-sq-km Northern Sierra Madre Natural Park on Luzon: it contains roughly half of the Philippines' remaining primary forest, yet lacks an established trail network. You'll need serious jungle-trekking skills and an excellent local guide to penetrate it.

This lack of infrastructure extends to local tour companies. Only a handful of enterprises offer the spelunking, jungle-trekking, rappelling, kayaking, wildlife and mountain-bike tours for which the Philippines is tailor-made. Consequently, one has to be downright careful when trying to find a trekking company or guide, or when planning an outdoor expedition of any kind. The necessary accreditation, training, emergency procedures, accountability and professional organisation are simply not there. Having said that, the undeveloped nature of the ecotourism industry does mean that the opportunity exists to blaze your own trail – as long as you do it wisely. When assessing key factors like local weather conditions, remember that your guide's opinion may be driven more by economics than safety, given that a guide's wage is less than $2 a day. If you're not sure where to turn, visit local tourism offices, which are generally excellent.

Two interesting new ecotourism models deserve mention. One has arisen in Oslob, Cebu, where the local fishing village now makes its living taking tourists out to see and snorkel with whale sharks. The model has been criticised by some because the fishermen attract the sharks by feeding them, creating the marine equivalent of a bird feeder, but others state that no sharks have been hurt, visitors are lining up to do it and many consider it a highlight of a lifetime, while fishing pressure is reduced and no one is hunting sharks for their fins.

A second is the combination of ecotourism with adventure sports. In Tibiao, Panay, the local municipality has turned the area around the Tibiao River into the Tibiao EcoAdventure Park (p231; TEA Park). There are two tour companies, basic accommodation, kayaking, hiking and ziplining, all aimed primarily at luring visitors from Boracay. If this municipal model proves profitable, expect it to be replicated elsewhere.

Environmental Damage

Take an extraordinary environment of 7107 tropical islands, add 100 million people, many of whom live well below the poverty line, and manage this society with a notoriously dysfunctional and corrupt political system, and what do you get? A long list of environmental ills, including deforestation, soil erosion, improper waste disposal, air and water pollution, overfishing, destructive fishing and coral reef loss. Not all the damage is self-inflicted, however. The Philippine environment is also suffering from some well-known external pressures, from plastic bottles floating ashore from the rest of Southeast Asia to the many impacts of climate change.

There is an ongoing battle between the many sources of these problems, and the many conservation organisations, both governmental and non-governmental, arrayed against them. The environment of the Philippines today is basically the product of this conflict, whose shifting front line is everywhere to be seen.

In 2014, Unesco delisted several World Heritage Sites in the Philippines, including Panglao Island, Mt Apo and Taal Volcano, for environmental violations.

Deforestation

Over the course of the last century the forest cover of the Philippines has dropped from 70% to under 20%, with only about 7% of its original, old-growth, closed-canopy forest left. At current levels of deforestation, the country's forests will be extinct by 2100. Nevertheless, an astonishing 75% of Philippine forest is still classified as production forest. In addition to severe soil erosion, this trend is particularly concerning because Philippine forests are the last home for so many endemic species.

Unregulated logging, massive farming expansion, and urbanisation have all taken their toll. Indigenous people's claims on upland regions have been ignored by urban elites. The government has regularly granted logging concessions of less than 10 years, with loggers having no incentive to replant. Much of what's left of Philippine forests is only safeguarded by high altitudes, as they're difficult to reach.

Mining

A related issue is mining. There are an estimated 500,000 small-scale mines operating in more than 30 Philippine provinces, many of them illegal, and many also using toxic mercury. At the other end of the scale are the huge mining conglomerates, which continue to lobby the government for more access. The government claims that adequate safeguards are in place to prevent the social and environmental damage that has dogged past mining projects, such as the Marcopper disaster in 1996, which poisoned an entire river system. However, if anything challenges this claim, it is the ongoing, unpunished killings of environmental activists – at least 16 under the Aquino administration – by forces under military control, some of them particularly public. In 2007, Sibuyan Island councilman Armin Marin was shot dead on camera, surrounded by scores of witnesses, while leading a picket of anti-mining advocates. After five years of investigations and court hearings, the accused, a plain-clothed mining security officer, was given a three-year sentence for 'criminal negligence', then released early.

Pollution

According to the WWF only about 10% of waste in the Philippines is treated or disposed of in an environmentally sound manner. Not surprisingly, water pollution is a growing problem for the country's groundwater, rivers, lakes and coastal areas. Only a third of Philippine river systems are considered suitable for the public water supply. Poor management, including bad planning and a lack of regulatory enforcement, is largely to blame.

Coastal Degradation

With a coastal ecosystem that stretches for almost 20,000km, the Philippines has become one of the earliest victims of climate change. The combination of high sea temperatures, acidification and unseasonable storms has done enormous damage to the country's reefs. Centuries-old coral is dying almost overnight. The World Bank recently estimated that only about 1% of Philippine coral reefs remains pristine, while more than 50% are unhealthy. Snorkellers around Puerto Galera and Boracay now face a coral graveyard; pearl farms are increasingly unproductive.

Coastal development has further damaged the marine environment, including mangroves and seagrasses. Population growth has driven increasing needs for construction materials and living space; excavation, dredging and land reclamation have followed. Mangroves have further suffered at the hands of the aquaculture industry, which has reduced mangrove stands over 60% in the past century.

As the population of fishing villages has expanded, overfishing has depleted fish stocks. Meanwhile, local fishing communities continue to employ destructive methods like dynamite, cyanide and chlorine. The result is a completely unsustainable fishing industry. According to the Asian Development Bank, certain areas in the Philippines have seen a 90% drop in trawler hauls, in what should otherwise be one of the world's most productive fisheries.

CONSERVATION ORGANISATIONS

The following websites contain information related to the environmental concerns facing the Philippines.

Coral Cay Conservation (www.coralcay.org) Works to protect coral reefs and other tropical forests.

Haribon Foundation (www.haribon.org.ph) One of the forerunners of the Philippine environmental movement; its mission is to protect the country's biodiversity. Active in preserving habitats of endangered species and other areas.

Negros Forests & Ecological Foundation Inc (www.negrosforests.org) Works to protect various Philippine habitats, focusing on Negros.

Biodiversity Management Bureau (www.bmb.gov.ph) Links to the various conservation projects of the Philippine government.

Survival Guide

Directory A–Z

Accommodation

The top end includes big city Shangri-Las (including the actual one in Manila) to extravagant private island resorts where guests arrive by helicopter or float plane. The very bottom end includes cold water, windowless cells with paper-thin walls and neither fan nor air-con. Of course, the vast majority are somewhere in between.

It's worth noting the very real divide between accommodation that caters to Filipino tourists and those that target foreigners. The former tend to be concrete with family-sized rooms, air-con and little attention to aesthetics. Whereas, the latter, or at least those owned by foreigners and most often Europeans, are usually more sophisticated and tastefully done and utilise native style features like thatched roofs. Accommodation geared particularly to the increasing number of travellers from China and Korea also continues to grow.

Beachfront accommodation might be considered most important in an archipelago of thousands of islands. Unfortunately, because there are no zoning codes to speak of, nor town planning, beautiful natural settings are often marred by haphazard and slipshod construction and congestion. That being said, from homestays to modern, boutique hotels, there's something for everyone in the Philippines.

Resorts These range from the ultraluxurious on private islands, the rival of any in Southeast Asia, to basic fan-cooled nipa huts (dwellings made from the leaves of nipa palm trees). European-owned ones tend to be more aesthetically sophisticated.

Hotels Many cater to the domestic market, which means generic concrete construction, air-con and multiple beds for families, whereas five-star hotels in Manila are over-the-top palatial affairs. International chains are in the big cities.

Pensionnes Sort of a catch-all term referring to less expensive, independently-owned hotels.

Hostels Those that focus on foreign travellers tend to be more comfortable than ones for primarily young Filipinos; beds in the latter are generally shorter.

Costs & Seasons

Within the budget ($) category, rooms for less than P500 are generally dorms or private fan-cooled rooms with a shared cold-water bathroom. Rooms between P700 and P1000 usually have a fan and private bathroom. Anything higher (and some within this range) should have both air-conditioning and a private bathroom.

High-season rates are from November to May. While prices in resort areas go down around 20% to 50% in the low season, they may double, triple or even quadruple during the 'super peak' periods of Holy Week (Easter), around New Year and, in some areas, around Chinese New Year.

Booking Ahead

As more and more Filipinos travel it's becoming more difficult to just walk in and find a room in certain resort areas and touristy towns. Booking ahead is always a good idea in the high season, essential in 'super peak' season and not a bad idea on weekends and holidays during the low season. That said, if you don't book ahead, even in the high season, you'll find something eventually.

Deposits

Many resorts, especially at the top end, require a deposit, often nonrefundable if you cancel less than two weeks prior to your arrival (generally from 20% to 50%). Annoyingly, a few still ask you to wire or direct-deposit the money into a Manila bank account. PayPal and credit cards are now more common.

Discounts & Promos

Promo rates Especially during off-peak periods, hotels often offer 'promo rates' that they won't tell you about unless you ask. So always ask.

Walking in In many resort areas, the 'walk-in' (ie no reservation) rate is substantially cheaper than the reservation rate. Conversely, in some hotels the reservation rate is actually cheaper than the walk-in rate. It helps to ask.

Websites Popular Asian online booking sites, especially Agoda. com, offer significant discounts on rooms all over the country.

Fan v air-con Some midrange places have two-tiered pricing for the same room. Even if not formally offered, you can say no to the air-con and request a fan for cheaper rates.

Children

Filipinos are simply crazy about kids, and are rather fond of parents, too – you and your offspring will be the focus of many conversations, and your children won't lack for playful company.

➡ You can buy disposable nappies (diapers) and infant formula in most towns and all cities, but be sure to stock up on such things before heading off the beaten track.

➡ Many hotels and resorts offer family rooms (this is how Filipinos travel), and can provide cots on request.

➡ Discreet breastfeeding in public is acceptable in all areas except some conservative Muslim areas in the south.

➡ It is almost impossible to arrange a taxi with a child seat.

➡ Many restaurants can provide a high chair upon request.

➡ See Lonely Planet's *Travel with Children* for further useful advice about travel with kids.

Customs Regulations

➡ Firearms and pornography are forbidden.

➡ You can bring up to 2L of alcohol and up to 400 cigarettes (or two tins of tobacco) into the country without paying duty.

➡ Foreign currency of more than US$10,000 and local currency of more than P10,000 must be declared upon entry or exit.

Electricity

220V/60Hz

Embassies & Consulates

The **Philippines Department of Foreign Affairs** (DFA; www.dfa.gov.ph) website lists all Philippine embassies and consulates abroad, and all foreign embassies and consulates in the Philippines.

Some of the countries requiring their citizens to

have visas for entry have embassies in Manila, including China, Egypt and India.

Australian Embassy (☑02-757 8100; www.philippines. embassy.gov.au; 23rd fl, Tower 2, RCBC Plaza, 6819 Ayala Ave, Manila)

Canadian Embassy Cebu City (☑032-254 4749; 45-L Andres Abellana St); Manila (☑02-857 9000; Levels 6-8, Tower 2, RCBC Plaza, 6819 Ayala Ave)

Dutch Embassy Cebu City (☑032-346 1823; Metaphil Building, Tipolo, Mandaue); Manila (☑02-786 6666; www. philippines.nlembassy.org; 26th fl, Equitable PCI Bank Tower, 8751 Paseo de Roxas, Makati)

French Embassy (☑02-857 6900; www.ambafrance-ph.org; 16th fl, Pacific Star Bldg, cnr Gil Puyat & Makati Aves, Manila)

German Embassy Cebu City (☑032-236 1318; Ford's Inn Hotel, AS Fortuna St); Manila (☑02-702 3000; www.manila. diplo.de; 25/F Tower 2, RCBC Plaza, 6819 Ayala Ave)

Indonesian Consulate (☑082-297 2930; www.kemlu. go.id/davaocity; General Ecoland Subdivision, Matina, Davao)

Malaysian Consulate (☑082-221 4050; mwdavao@ kln.gov.my; 3rd fl, Florentine Bldg, A Bonifacio St, Davao; ⊗8am-4pm Mon-Fri)

New Zealand Embassy
(02-891 5353; www.nzembassy.com/philippines; 23rd fl, BPI Buendia Centre, 360 Sen Gil Puyat Ave, Manila)

UK Embassy Cebu City (032-346 0525; 4 Palmera St, Villa Terrace, Greenhills Rd, Casuntingan, Mandaue); Manila (02-858 2200; 120 Upper McKinley Rd, McKinley Hill)

US Embassy (02-301 2000; www.manila.usembassy. gov; 1201 Roxas Blvd, Manila)

Food

See the Food & Drink chapter, p430, for details on Filipino cuisine.

Gay & Lesbian Travellers

➡ *Bakla* (gay men) and *binalaki* or *tomboy* (lesbians) are almost universally accepted in the Philippines.

➡ There are well-established gay centres in major cities, but foreigners should be wary of hustlers and police harassment.

➡ Remedios Circle in Malate, Manila, is the site of a June gay-pride parade and the centre for nightlife.

➡ Online gay and lesbian resources for the Philippines include **Utopia Asian Gay & Lesbian Resources** (www. utopia-asia.com).

Insurance

➡ A travel-insurance policy to cover theft, loss and medical problems is a good idea.

➡ Some policies specifically exclude 'dangerous activities', which can include scuba diving, motorcycling and even trekking.

➡ Check that the policy covers ambulances and an emergency flight home.

➡ Worldwide travel insurance is available at www. lonelyplanet.com/travel-insurance. Buy, extend and claim online anytime – even if you're already on the road.

Internet Access

➡ Theoretically, internet access is available in much of the Philippines. In reality, it's frequently not working, inconsistently working or very slow, for example in Manila where networks are overloaded.

➡ Bank on P25 per hour for internet access, double that in very remote areas.

➡ Fewer and fewer hotels and resorts have computers for guests to use, whereas wi-fi is becoming more ubiquitous in accommodation, cafes and some restaurants. That said, don't count on it to function. Quality is hit or miss.

➡ The @ symbol indicates that a hotel has an internet-enabled computer for guests to use. The 🛜 symbol indicates that a hotel (or other establishment) has wi-fi, more often in the lobby area and in rooms close to the server. Ask in advance if it's important for you to have in-room access. Wi-fi is free of charge unless otherwise indicated.

➡ You can hook your laptop up to Smart or Globe networks by buying a prepaid USB dongle for around P3000; check out the Smart and Globe websites for promo deals for international wi-fi.

➡ If you have an internet-enabled mobile phone you can get online through the regular wireless networks of both Globe and Smart.

Legal Matters

➡ Drugs are risky. Being caught with marijuana for personal use can mean jail time.

➡ Should you find yourself in trouble, your first recourse is your embassy, so make a point of writing down the phone number.

➡ Small bribes remain a common way of getting out of traffic infractions.

Maps

➡ For a map of the entire country, the best of the lot is probably Nelles Verlag's 1:1,500,000 scale *Philippines* (US$20), which is available internationally.

➡ For local travel, E-Z Maps (P100) and **Accu-Map** (www. accu-map.com) produce excellent maps covering most major islands, large cities and tourist areas. They are widely available at hotels, airports, bookshops and gas stations.

➡ To buy (or see online) highly detailed topographical maps of virtually any region contact the government's mapping agency, **Namria** (02-887 5446; www.namria. gov.ph; Lawton Ave, Fort Bonifacio, Makati, Manila).

Money

The unit of currency is the peso (P), divided into 100 centavos. Banknotes in wide circulation come in denominations of 20, 50, 100, 200, 500 and 1000 pesos. The

---

EATING PRICE RANGES

The following price ranges refer to the cost of the average main course. Unless otherwise stated the 12% VAT tax is included in the price.

$ less than P120

$$ P120–250

$$$ more than P250

most common coins are 1, 5 and 10 pesos. ATMs are widely available and credit cards are accepted at hotels, restaurants and some shops in all but remote areas. For info on tipping, see p21.

ATMs

➡ Getting crisp P500 and P1000 peso bills out of the myriad ATM machines that line the streets of any decent-sized provincial city usually isn't a problem.

➡ Some regions, such as a large chunk of Palawan, do not have ATMs.

➡ The Maestro-Cirrus network is most readily accepted, followed by Visa/Plus cards, then by American Express (Amex).

➡ The most prevalent ATMs that accept most Western bank cards belong to Banco de Oro (BDO), Bank of the Philippine Islands (BPI) and Metrobank.

➡ Most ATMs charge P200 per withdrawal and have a P10,000-per-transaction withdrawal limit; Citibank allows P15,000 while HSBC ATMs in Manila and Cebu let you take out P40,000 per transaction.

Cash

➡ Cash in US dollars is a good thing to have in case you get stuck in an area with no working ATM. Other currencies, such as the euro or UK pound, are more difficult to change outside of the bigger cities.

➡ 'Sorry, no change' becomes a very familiar line in the provinces. Stock up on coins and P20, P50 and P100 notes at every opportunity.

Credit Cards

➡ Major credit cards are accepted by many hotels, restaurants and businesses.

➡ Businesses often charge extra (generally 4% to 6%) for credit-card transactions.

➡ Sometimes, signal problems in out of the way locations mean cards can't be used until the machines are back online.

➡ Refunds on credit cards, even for large companies such as Philippine Airlines, can take many months to be processed.

➡ Most Philippine banks will let you take out a cash advance on your card.

Opening Hours

Banks 9am–4.30pm Monday to Friday (most ATMs operate 24 hours)

Bars 6pm–late

Embassies & Consulates 9am–1pm Monday to Friday

Post Offices 9am–5pm Monday to Saturday

Public & Private Offices 8am or 9am to 5pm or 6pm, with a lunch break from noon to 1pm, Monday to Friday

Restaurants 7am or 8am to 10pm or 11pm

Shopping Malls 10am–9.30pm

Supermarkets 9am to 7pm or 8pm

Post

On average, it takes a week or so for mail sent from the Philippines to reach the US or Europe. Mail sent from abroad to the Philippines is slower and less reliable; you're better off using FedEx or UPS.

Public Holidays

Government offices and banks close on public holidays, although most shops and malls stay open. Maundy Thursday and Good Friday are the only days when the entire country closes down – even most public transport stops running, and some airlines ground their planes. Chinese New Year (31 January to 15 February) and Golden Week (29 April to 5 May), a Japanese holiday period, are times of heavy travel.

New Year's Day 1 January

People Power Day 25 February

Maundy Thursday Varies; around March or April

Good Friday Varies; the day after Maundy Thursday

Araw ng Kagitingan (Bataan Day) 9 April

Labour Day 1 May

Independence Day 12 June

Ninoy Aquino Day 21 August

National Heroes Day Last Sunday in August

All Saints' Day 1 November

End of Ramadan Varies; depends on Islamic calendar

Bonifacio Day 30 November

Christmas Day 25 December

Rizal Day 30 December

New Year's Eve 31 December

Muslim Holy Days

Most Muslim holy days are observed only in the Muslim parts of Mindanao, though some are now also national holidays.

Hari Raya Haji Varies; depends on Islamic calendar

Hijra New Year Varies; depends on Islamic calendar

Maulod En Nabi (Prophet's Birthday) Varies; depends on Islamic calendar

Ramadan Varies; depends on Islamic calendar

Hari Raya Puasa (Feast of the Breaking of the Fast) Begins on the last evening of Ramadan and may last for three days.

Safe Travel

➡ The Philippines certainly has more than its share of dangers. Typhoons, earthquakes, volcano eruptions, landslides and other natural disasters can wreak havoc on your travel plans – or worse if you happen to be in the wrong place at the wrong time.

➡ To keep track of the weather situation check out the following: www.typhoon2000.ph (mapping and good for forecasting); www.pagasa.gob.ph (government run); www.passageweather.com; and www.myweather2.com.

➡ Keep an eye on the news and be prepared to alter travel plans to avoid trouble spots.

➡ Mindanao (the central and southwest regions in particular) and the Sulu Archipelago are sometimes the scenes of clashes between the army and separatist groups.

➡ Manila in particular is known for a few common scams targeting tourists.

Telephone

The Philippine Long Distance Telephone Company (PLDT) operates the Philippines' fixed-line network. Local calls cost almost nothing, and long-distance domestic calls are also very reasonable.

International calls can be made from many hotels (for a hefty price) or from any PLDT office. PLDT offers flat rates of US$0.40 per minute for international calls (operator-assisted calls are much more expensive).

Mobile Phones

Filipinos are consistently ranked as some of the biggest users of mobile phones in the world and smartphones are increasingly popular. Text messaging is a national pastime and often the best way to book accommodation and make plans with Filipino friends. It's worth popping into the closest mall to buy a local SIM card for a nominal charge – these can be used in almost all phones.

Text messaging rates within the Philippines are generally only P1 or P2. Businesses, including accommodation places, frustratingly change their numbers frequently. They also tend to indicate which network they're part of – usually Globe or Smart. The quality of reception and service varies throughout the country and if you plan on travelling in one particular region it's worth asking what locals recommend.

Roaming with your home phone is another, though likely very expensive, option.

Phone Codes

For domestic long-distance calls or calls to mobile numbers dial 0 followed by the city code (or mobile prefix) and then the seven-digit number. Useful dialling codes from land lines:

Philippines country code ☑63

International dialling code ☑00

PLDT directory ☑187 nationwide

International operator ☑108

Domestic operator ☑109

Phonecards

➡ Prepaid phonecards for the new local number you acquired with the SIM card are widely available from hotels, sari-sari stores and phone kiosks, and are usually in denominations of P100 or P200.

➡ PLDT cards such as 'Budget' (for international calls), 'Pwede' and 'Touch' cards can be used to make calls from any PLDT landline or from card-operated PLDT phones located in hotel foyers, commercial centres and shopping malls. Calls to the US using the Budget card cost only P3 per minute; other international destinations cost slightly more. 'Pwede' and 'Touch' cards allow dirt-cheap domestic calls from any PLDT landline or payphone.

Time

The Philippines is eight hours ahead of Greenwich Mean Time/Universal Time Coordinated (GMT/UTC), meaning when it's noon in Manila, it's 11pm the previous night in New York (midnight during daylight savings); 4am the same day in London; 1pm the same day in Tokyo; and 2pm the same day in Sydney (3pm during daylight savings).

TRAVELS WITH MY LIFE JACKET

The Philippines' maritime transport record reads like a litany of disasters: MV St Thomas Aquinas sinks in 2013: 114 people dead; MV Princess of the Stars capsizes in 2008: 437 dead, and so on. Some boats stock life jackets, but often in insufficient quantities, since poorly maintained boats are frequently filled beyond capacity. Life jackets, where they do exist, are often little more than glorified orange collars and safety demonstrations are rare. Filipinos are fatalistic about boat travel, but I find the idea of drowning due to other people's incompetence highly objectionable. After two colleagues of mine nearly died during stormy crossings aboard Filipino boats, I acquired a state-of-the-art (well, OK, polystyrene chunks sewn up in some orange cloth) life jacket, which proceeded to accompany me to the Batanes and all over Southern Luzon. The one place I was particularly grateful to have it was during the crossing of the 'typhoon highway' between Catanduanes and Caramoan, as you'll never find a life jacket aboard a fisherman's bangka. The life jacket was left behind during my last crossing between Marinduque and Lucena, where it (slightly) swelled up the boat's own sparse stock.

Anna Kaminski

Toilets

➡ Toilets are commonly called a 'CR', an abbreviation of the delightfully euphemistic 'comfort room'.

➡ Other than at some bus terminals and ports public toilets are virtually nonexistent, so head to a fast-food restaurant should you need one.

➡ Some downmarket hotels don't have toilet seats.

➡ In Filipino, men are *lalake* and women are *babae*.

➡ Filipino men will often avail themselves of the nearest outdoor wall – hence the signs scrawled in many places: 'Bawal Ang Umihi Dito!' ('No Pissing Here!').

Tourist Information

➡ The official organ of Philippine tourism is the **Philippine Department of Tourism** (DOT; www.itsmorefuninthephilippines.com; www.visitmyphilippines.com).

➡ The main DOT centre is in Manila and you'll find regional DOT offices – varying from mildly helpful to completely useless – in popular destinations throughout the Philippines. Most DOT offices should at least be capable of setting you up with accommodation. The better ones can also help find guides or hire vehicles, while a few actually run adventure tours, such as whale-shark tours in Donsol, spelunking in Tuguegarao (North Luzon) and diving at Apo Reef through the tourist office in Sablayan (Mindoro Occidental).

Travellers with Disabilities

➡ Steps up to hotels, tiny cramped toilets and narrow doors are the norm outside

of four-star hotels in Manila, Cebu and a handful of larger provincial cities.

➡ Lifts are often out of order, and boarding any form of rural transport is likely to be fraught with difficulty.

➡ On the other hand, most Filipinos are more than willing to lend a helping hand, and the cost of hiring a taxi for a day, and possibly an assistant as well, is not excessive.

Visas

Citizens of nearly all countries will receive a 30-day visa free of charge upon their arrival. If you overstay your visa you will face fines, and airport officials may not let you pass through immigration. Your passport must be valid for at least six months beyond the period you intend to stay.

Visa Extensions

To renew your 30-day visa for another 29 days or beyond you must apply for an extension from any office of the **Bureau of Immigration** (BOI; www.immigration.gov.ph). Most regional hubs and touristy areas such as Boracay have BOI offices; a full list of the regional offices can be found on the BOI website. If done more than a week prior to expiration, the first visa extension costs P3030; if less than a week, a P1010 penalty is applied. It may or may not be possible to extend retroactively (and pay at least the P1010 fine) upon departure

at the airport – we wouldn't chance it. Longer extensions are possible, with correspondingly higher fees; see the BOI website for details.

The visa renewal process is generally painless, with one notable exception: the massive BOI office in Manila. You can pay a travel agent about P1000 to go to the Manila BOI office for you. If you insist on going it alone, bring proof of identity and expect long lines.

You can also receive the 29-day extension (for the same fee as above) immediately upon arrival at airports in Manila and Cebu. Immigration officers will direct you to an office – it shouldn't take more than a half hour to process.

Another option is to secure a three-month visa before you arrive in the Philippines. These cost US$30 to US$45 depending on where you apply. Multiple-entry visas valid for up to six or 12 months are also available.

Onward Tickets

You must have a ticket for onward travel to enter the Philippines if you plan to receive a 30-day visa on arrival. While Philippine immigration inspectors rarely ask to see this onward ticket, most airlines will refuse entry on flights headed to the Philippines without proof of onward travel. A photocopy of your onward ticket will not suffice; you need to show the actual ticket or e-ticket. If you do not have one, the

PRACTICALITIES

Newspapers & Magazines The Philippines has a vocal and vibrant press, with about 20 major national and regional English-language newspapers to go along with scores of regional publications. The best of the broadsheets are the *Philippine Daily Inquirer* (www. inquirer.net), *Business World* (www.bworldonline.com) and *Business Mirror* (www.businessmirror.com.ph). Other big national dailies include the *Philippine Star* (www.philstar. com) and *Manila Bulletin* (www.mb.com.ph). The *Philippine Center for Investigative Journalism* (www.pcij.org) and *Rappler* (www.rappler.com), a multimedia site operating since 2012, are excellent sources for breaking news.

Radio Manila radio stations worth listening to: Monster Radio RX 93.1 for contemporary popular music and Jam 88.3 for more indie and alternative.

TV About seven major channels broadcast from Manila (including ABS-CBN and GMA), sometimes in English, sometimes in Tagalog. Most midrange hotels have cable TV with access to between 20 and 120 channels, including some obscure regional channels, a couple of Filipino and international movie channels, and the big global news and sports channels such as BBC and ESPN.

Weights & Measures The Philippines is metric, but inches, feet and yards (for textiles) are common in everyday use for measuring things. Weights are normally quoted in kilograms and distances in kilometres.

airline will make you purchase a one-way ticket out of the Philippines, departing within 30 days from your date of arrival. When you get to Manila, you are free to exchange this ticket – for a hefty fee, of course.

If you're applying for a longer-term visa through a Philippine embassy or consulate abroad, you should also have proof of onward travel, although in this case a photocopy of your itinerary from your travel agent may suffice (call the embassy to clarify).

Volunteering

Coral Cay Conservation (www.coralcay.org) Works to protect coral reefs and other tropical forests.

Gawad Kalinga (📞in Manila 02-533 2217; www.gk1world. com/ph) GK's mission is building not just homes but entire communities for the poor and homeless. Volunteers can build houses, teach children or get involved in a host of other activities.

Habitat for Humanity (📞02-846 2177; www.habitat.

org.ph) Builds houses for the poor all over the country, concentrating on disaster-affected areas.

Hands On Manila (www. handsonmanila.org.ph) This organisation is always looking for volunteers to help with disaster assistance and other projects throughout the Philippines.

Haribon Foundation (📞02-421 1209; www.haribon.org.ph) A longstanding conservation organisation focused on scientific research and community empowerment programs.

Rise Above Foundation (📞032-255 1063; www.riseabove-cebu.org; 252 I Limkakeng St, Happy Valley Subd, Cebu City) Housing, education, vocational training projects in Cebu. We've had positive feedback from recent volunteers.

Springboard Foundation (📞02-821 5440; www.springboard-foundation.org) Not a volunteer organisation, per se, but has ties to many charity organisations doing volunteer work in the Philippines.

Volunteer for the Visayas (📞0917 846 6967; www. visayans.org) Runs various

volunteer programs around Tacloban, Leyte.

World Wide Opportunities on Organic Farms (📞0908 608 4369; www.wwoof.ph) There are several WWOOF sites in the Philippines, including the Julia Campbell Agroforest Memorial Park and the Enca Farm, both in North Luzon.

WWF Philippines (www. wwf.org.ph) To get involved with biodiversity and species-conservation projects contact WWF Philippines.

Women Travellers

Foreign women travellers will generally have few problems in most of the Philippines, although they might get more attention than they're used to, particularly if travelling solo outside major tourist areas. This isn't necessarily particular to the Philippines, but it's probably a good idea to check on the reputation of guides if booking overnight trips.

In conservative Muslim areas in Mindanao it's best to dress appropriately – this means long pants and tops.

Transport

GETTING THERE & AWAY

Most people enter the Philippines via one of the three main international airports:

Manila Ninoy Aquino International Airport (NAIA), by far the most popular and best connected to the rest of the country

Cebu A good option if you are heading to the Visayas (or Camiguin and Siargao in northern Mindanao since direct flights are only from Cebu)

Clark Budget flight hub north of Manila

A handful of international flights also go straight to Kalibo, near Boracay, Iloilo City on the island of Panay and Davao in southern Mindanao. Flights between Malaysia and Puerto Princesa, Palawan and Zamboanga City might resume again in the near future and a handful of charters regularly fly to Laoag City in North Luzon.

The only feasible non-flight option is by ferry to Zamboanga (Mindanao) from Sandakan in the Malaysian state of Sabah.

Flights, tours and train tickets can all be booked online at lonelyplanet.com/bookings.

Entering the Country

Entering the country through any of the main ports is a breeze. Most nationalities are issued a free 30-day visa.

Air

Book well in advance if you plan to arrive in the Philippines during December – expat Filipinos flood the islands to visit their families during Christmas and New Year. The lead-up to Chinese New Year in late January or early February can also get congested.

Airports

Ninoy Aquino International Airport (NAIA; ☎02-877 1109; www.miaa.gov.ph) The busiest international airport in the country and where you're most likely to fly into and out of. Even after the long-awaited opening of NAIA Terminal 3 (as of August 2014 Delta, KLM, Emirates, Singapore Airlines and Cathay Pacific had moved operations here), the airport generally receives negative reviews from travellers.

Mactan-Cebu International Airport (MCIA; ☎032-340 2486; www.mactan-cebuairport.com.ph; ☎) Cebu's Mactan-Cebu International Airport is second only to Manila in terms of air traffic, but way ahead in terms of user-friendliness. Note that the airport is actually on Mactan Island, 15km east of Cebu City.

Diosdado Macapagal International Airport (Clark Airport, DMIA; www.clark-airport.com) Clark Airport is near Angeles, a two-hour bus ride north of downtown Manila.

CLIMATE CHANGE & TRAVEL

Every form of transport that relies on carbon-based fuel generates CO_2, the main cause of human-induced climate change. Modern travel is dependent on aeroplanes, which might use less fuel per kilometre per person than most cars but travel much greater distances. The altitude at which aircraft emit gases (including CO_2) and particles also contributes to their climate change impact. Many websites offer 'carbon calculators' that allow people to estimate the carbon emissions generated by their journey and, for those who wish to do so, to offset the impact of the greenhouse gases emitted with contributions to portfolios of climate-friendly initiatives throughout the world. Lonely Planet offsets the carbon footprint of all staff and author travel.

DEPARTURE TAXES

In order to alleviate congestion and long lines, as of 1 October 2014 international passengers no longer have to pay a P550 departure tax; it is being subsumed into airline tickets. Expect some hiccups, and authorities say full implementation, whatever that means, won't be in effect until some time in 2015.

Several low-cost Asian airlines fly here: Asiana, Cebu Pacific, Tigerair, Dragonair, Jin Air and AirAsia Zest servicing Incheon, Hong Kong, Singapore, Macau, Kuala Lumpur and Kota Kinabalu; Qatar Airways flys to Doha.

Francisco Bangoy International Airport For now, only SilkAir has flights to Singapore; routes to Malaysia might begin operating.

Kalibo International Airport Useful direct flights to Kalibo, near Boracay from Beijing, Kunming, Hong Kong, Seoul, Shanghai and Singapore.

Airlines

Besides the international airlines which come up on any internet flight search, several Philippines and regional carriers are worth checking out for flights into and out of the country. Mergers have stabilised things somewhat, however, the situation, especially in terms of routes, is fluid and dynamic.

AirAsia Zest (02-855 3333; www.zestair.com.ph) Now known as AirAsia Zest, after the merger of the two airlines. Hubs in Manila, Cebu and Kalibo (the jumping-off point for Boracay) with direct flights to Kota Kinabalu, Macau, Incheon and Jinjiang, China. Direct flights between Manila and Miri, Malaysia (northern Sarawak), although service is seasonal.

Cebu Pacific (02-702 0888; www.cebupacificair.com) Discount flights from Manila to an ever-growing list of Asian cities, including Bangkok, Siem Reap, Phuket, Bali, Guangzhou, Hanoi, Jakarta, Kota Kinabalu, Kuala Lumpur, Saigon, Shanghai and Singapore, and several cities in the Middle East. Flies to Hong Kong and Singapore from Cebu City and even Incheon, Pusan and Singapore from Iloilo City.

Jetstar (1-866 397 8170; www.jetstar.com) Discount Australian airline with flights from Manila to Singapore and Osaka.

Philippine Airlines (PAL; 02-879 5601; www.philippineairlines.com) International flights of the country's flagship carrier use Terminal 2 in Manila.

Tigerair (02-884 1524; www.tigerair.com) Hubs in Manila, Clark, Kalibo and Cebu with connections to a number of regional cities.

Sea

Although there are plenty of shipping routes within the Philippines, international services are scarce. The only route open to foreigners at the time of writing was a ship from Zamboanga to Sandakan in the Malaysian state of Sabah. Keep in mind that travel in the Zamboanga region is considered risky.

More than a dozen international cruise ships dock at Manila's South Harbor port, most from China, Japan and Hong Kong. Cebu, Puerto Princesa, Caticlan and Subic are ports that might see more cruise ships in the future.

GETTING AROUND

Air

PAL Express (formerly known as Airphil Express) and Cebu Pacific are the main domestic carriers and in general have the newest planes. AirAsia Zest (the new name after the two separate airlines merged) and Tigerair are alternatives worth considering. Due to the dynamic situation be sure to check your ticket to confirm which terminal you'll fly out of in Manila.

You can always dispense with lines and crowds – and reach some areas not serviced by commercial flights – by chartering your own plane with Sky Pasada.

Also keep in mind the following tips when booking domestic flights:

➡ Pay attention to baggage allowances; some routes are more restrictive than others. Luggage is weighed and fines levied at check-in counters at the airport. Have Philippine pesos on hand for this.

➡ If you book a month or so in advance, you'll rarely pay more than P1200 (about US$28) for a one-way ticket. There are some exceptions: Boracay and especially El Nido tend to be more expensive, and all airlines jack up rates during peak domestic travel periods (Chinese New Year, Easter and Christmas).

➡ On most airlines, you won't pay a premium for one-way tickets or save money by byuing a round-trip ticket.

➡ Flight routes are skewed towards Manila and (to a lesser extent) Cebu. If you want to fly between any other cities you'll likely have to purchase two tickets: one to Manila/Cebu, and then a separate onward ticket.

➡ Don't plan too tight a schedule for connecting flights – flight delays are a fact of life in the Philippines.

➡ Typhoons and adverse weather often ground planes from June to November. Some routes are more susceptible than others.

➡ Many domestic flights depart painfully early in the morning, as there's more turbulence in the afternoons as air heats up.

Airlines

AirAsia Zest (☑in Manila 02-742 2742; www.airasia.com) Services Tacloban, Tagbilaran, Puerto Princesa, Kalibo and Davao out of Manila and Cebu.

Cebu Pacific (☑02-702 0888; www.cebupacificair.com) The airlines' yellow and orange colour scheme and cartoon logo are ubiquitous at most Philippines airports. Connects the greatest number of destinations within the country and has the most departures daily.

Fil Asian Airways (Mid-Sea Express; ☑032-851 0984; www.filasianair.com) In addition to Cebu, Davao, Manila and Zamboanga, it has flights to less serviced desitnations like Masbate, Ormoc and Tagbilaran.

ITIAIR (☑02-851 5664; www.itiair.com; ITI Hangar No 5-03-127, Andrews Ave, Pasay) Serves El Nido from Manila; primarily for guests of the offshore El Nido Resorts.

Northsky Air (☑in Tuguegarao 078-304 6148; www.northskyair.com) Charters and scheduled flights connecting Tuguegarao (North Luzon) with Batanes, Maconacon and Palanan (the last two are in Isabela province in North Luzon).

PAL Express (PAL; ☑02-879 5601; www.philippineairlines.com) Philippine Airlines' domestic partner carrier. Domestic flights use both Terminals 2 and 3 in Manila.

Sky Pasada (☑in Cebu 032-912 3333; www.skypasada.com) Flies from Manila to Baguio, Batanes and Boracay, between Bacolod and Boracay, and has two short flights out of Tuguegarao in North Luzon as well as charter flight services elsewhere.

Skyjet Airlines (☑in Manila 02-863 1333; www.skyjetair.com) Flies to Batanes (Basco airport), Coron (Busuanga airport), Manila, Boracay (Caticlan airport), Kalibo and Baler.

Tigerair (www.tigerair.com) After a merger with Seair, more recently brought under Cebu Pacific umbrella.

Bicycle

Away from the traffic and exhaust fumes of major cities, cycling can be a great way to get around quieter islands.

➡ You can take bicycles on domestic flights (you may have to partially disassemble the bicycle), but take heed of the baggage allowance on small planes.

➡ If there's room, you can stow your bike on a bus or jeepney, usually for a small charge.

➡ Depending on where you are, mountain bikes can be hired for P300 to P700 per day, with price very much linked to quality.

➡ In the big cities you will find bicycle shops where you can purchase brand-new bikes of varying quality. Outdoor gear shops (most malls have at least one) are good places to enquire about local biking clubs and events.

Boat

The islands of the Philippines are linked by an incredible network of ferry routes, and prices are generally affordable. Ferries are usually motorised outriggers (known locally as bangkas), speedy 'fastcraft' vessels, car ferries (dubbed ROROs – 'roll-on, roll-off') and, for long-haul journeys, vast multidecked passenger ferries. It's worth highlighting the mega company **2GO Travel** (www.travel.2go.com.ph), the result of the merger of Cebu Ferries, Supercat, Negros Navigation and Superferry. 2GO serves the majority of major destinations in the Philippines.

Most ferry terminals have a small fee (P20 on average); Manila's is P95.

Check out real-time locations of the larger ferries plying the waters at www.marinetraffic.com. The website www.schedule.ph is not comprehensive but it's a good place to start for schedules.

Bangkas The jeepneys of the sea, also known as pumpboats. They are small wooden boats with two wooden or bamboo outriggers. Bangka ferries ply regular routes between islands and are also available for hire per day for diving, snorkelling, sightseeing or just getting around. The engines on these boats can be deafeningly loud, so bring earplugs if you're sensitive to noise. They also aren't the most stable in rough seas, but on some islands they're preferable to travelling overland. Time schedules should be taken with a grain of salt.

'Fastcraft' These are passenger only, and are mainly used on popular short-haul routes; they cut travel times by half but usually cost twice as much as slower RORO ferries. One modern convenience used to excess on these spiffy ships is air-conditioning, which is permanently set to 'arctic' – take a sweater or fleece.

ROROs (car ferries) Popular on medium-haul routes, especially along the so-called 'Nautical Highway' running from Manila to Davao in southern Mindanao. ROROs are slow but in good weather are the most enjoyable form of ocean transport, as (unlike most fastcraft) they allow you to sit outside in the open air and watch the ocean drift by.

Passenger Liners Multidecked long-haul liners, which carry up to 4000 passengers as well as cars. They are pretty reliable but you'll need to be prepared for changes in itineraries due to adverse weather conditions or maintenance.

Tickets

➡ Booking ahead is essential for long-haul liners and can be done at ticket offices or travel agencies in most cities.

➡ For fastcraft and bangka ferries, tickets can usually be bought at the pier before departure.

➡ Passenger ferries offer several levels of comfort and cost. Bunks on or below deck on 3rd or 'economy' class should be fine, as long as the ship isn't overcrowded. First

FERRY SAFETY

For the most part, ferries are an easy, enjoyable way to hop between islands in the Philippines, but ferry accidents are not unknown. Bad weather, lax regulations and maintenance, equipment breakdowns, overcrowding and a general culture of fatalism are to blame. It's best to follow your instincts – if the boat looks crowded, it is, and if the sailing conditions seem wrong, they are. Bangkas during stormy weather are especially scary. It's always worth checking that life jackets are on board (one of our authors, admittedly somewhat paranoid, brought her own; see the boxed text p446).

Sulpicio Lines alone has had four sinking incidents involving at least 150 casualties each since 1987, including that year's sinking of the *Doña Paz*, in which almost 4500 people are believed to have perished – it's still the largest peacetime maritime disaster in history. Nearly 800 passengers were lost in June 2008 when a Sulpicio Lines ferry went down off Romblon in Typhoon Frank. In 2009, Sulpicio Lines changed its name to Philippine Span Asia Carrier Corp (PSACC) and refocused on cargo shipping. However, in August 2013, one of its freight ships collided with a 2GO passenger vessel just outside Cebu, killing more than 116.

All of this is to say that it's best to ask locals for advice regarding the most recent news and advice concerning boat travel.

class nets you a two-person stateroom.

➜ Before purchasing your ticket, it pays to ask about 'promo rates' (discounts). Student and senior citizen discounts usually only apply to Filipino citizens.

Bus & Van

➜ Philippine buses come in all shapes and sizes. Bus depots are dotted throughout towns and the countryside. Most buses will stop if you wave them down.

➜ Bus 'terminals' also run the gamut. Some are well-secured large garage-like structures with destinations clearly signposted and even ticket booths; others are nothing more than a few run-down sheds with drivers clamouring for business.

➜ More services run in the morning – buses on unsealed roads may *only* run in the morning, especially in remote areas. Night services, including deluxe 27-seaters, are common between Manila and major provincial hubs in Luzon, and in Mindanao.

➜ Air-con minivans (along with jeepneys) shadow bus routes in many parts of the Philippines (especially Bicol, Leyte, Cebu, Palawan and Mindanao) and in some cases have replaced buses altogether. However, you may have to play a waiting game until the vehicles are full.

➜ Minivans are a lot quicker than buses, but also more expensive and cramped.

➜ As in most countries, it pays to mind your baggage while buses load and unload.

➜ Reservations aren't usually necessary, however they're essential on the deluxe night buses heading to/from Manila (book these at least two days in advance, if possible, at the bus terminal).

Car & Motorcycle

Driving is a quicker option than relying on jeepneys and other public transport, but it's not for the faint of heart. The manic Filipino driving style is on full display in Manila, and driving the congested streets of the capital definitely takes some getting used to.

International car-rental companies are in the larger cities, however these are exactly the places you probably don't want to drive in. But if you want to get out of the city you have to begin somewhere – rates start at around P3000 per day. Gas costs P56 to P64 per litre.

Defensive driving is the order of the day: even relatively quiet provincial roads are packed with myriad obstacles. Right of way can be confusing to determine and obedience to stop signals is followed selectively. Most drivers roll into intersections before or without checking for oncoming traffic (just such a situation resulted in this author's own motorcycle accident).

It's best to avoid driving at night if you can, not least because tricycles, jeepneys and even large trucks are often without lights (many drivers believe that driving without lights saves petrol), not to mention potential robberies in political trouble spots.

Motorcycle

Small and midsized islands like Camiguin, Siquijor and Bohol beg to be explored by motorcycle. You can even ride down to the Visayas via the 'Nautical Highway' – the system of car ferries that links many islands – and enjoy pleasant riding on larger islands like Cebu and Negros.

Most touristy areas have a few easy-to-find shops or guesthouses renting out motorcycles – usually in the form of Chinese- or Japanese-made motorcycles (75cc to 125cc). The typical rate is P300/P500 per half-day/day, but you'll likely be asked for more in particularly popular resort areas. Ask for a helmet; these aren't always automatically included.

In more remote areas, just ask around – even if there's no rental shop, you can always find somebody willing to part with their motorcycle for the day for a fee.

Driving Licence

Your home country's driving licence, which you should carry, is legally valid for 90 days in the Philippines. Technically, you are supposed to have an International Driving Permit for any period longer than this, and some car-rental companies may require you to have this permit when hiring vehicles from them.

Insurance

Philippine law requires that when renting a car you have third-party car insurance with a Philippines car-insurance company. This can be arranged with the rental agency. You are required to have a minimum of P750,000 of insurance.

Road Rules

Driving is on the right-hand side of the road. With the exception of the expressways out of Manila, most roads in the Philippines are single lane, which necessitates a lot of overtaking. Local drivers do not always overtake safely. If an overtaker coming the other way refuses to get out of your lane, they're expecting you to give way by moving into the shoulder. It's always wise to do so.

Local Transport

Jeepney

The first jeepneys were modified army jeeps left behind by the Americans after WWII. They have been customised with Filipino touches such as chrome horses, banks of coloured headlights, radio antennae, paintings of the Virgin Mary and neon-coloured scenes from action comic books.

➡ Jeepneys form the main urban transport in most cities and complement the bus services between regional centres.

➡ Within towns, the starting fare is usually P8, rising modestly for trips outside of town. Routes are clearly written on the side of the jeepney.

➡ Jeepneys have a certain quirky cultural appeal, but from a tourist's perspective they have one humongous flaw: you can barely see anything through the narrow open slats that pass as windows. The best seats are up the front next to the driver.

Light Rail

Some parts of Manila are served by an elevated railway system, akin to rapid transit metro (see p91 for details).

Taxi

Metered taxis are common in Manila and most major provincial hubs. Flagfall is P40, and a 15-minute trip rarely costs more than P150. Airport taxi flagfall is usually P70.

Most taxi drivers will turn on the meter; if they don't, politely request that they do. If the meter is 'broken' or your taxi driver says the fare is 'up to you', the best strategy is to get out and find another cab (or offer a low-ball price). Rigged taxi meters are also becoming more common, although it must be said that most taxi drivers are honest.

Alternatively, arrange a taxi and driver for the day – from P2000 to P4000 – through your hotel or another trustworthy source.

Though it's not common, there have been cases of taxi passengers being robbed at gun or knife point, sometimes with the driver in cahoots with the culprits or the driver himself holding up the passengers.

Get out of a cab straight away (in a secure populated area, of course, not in the middle of nowhere or in a slum area) if you suspect you're being taken for a ride in more ways than one.

Tricycles, Kalesa & Habal-Habal

Found in most cities and towns, the tricycle is the Philippine rickshaw – a little, roofed sidecar bolted to a motorcycle. The standard fare for local trips in most provincial towns is P8. Tricycles that wait around in front of malls, restaurants and hotels will attempt to charge five to 10 times that for a 'special trip'. Avoid these by standing roadside and flagging down a passing P8 tricycle. You can also charter tricycles for about P300 per hour or P150 per 10km if you're heading out of town.

Pedicabs Many towns also have nonmotorised push tricycles, alternately known as pedicabs, *put-put* or *padyak*, for shorter trips.

Habal-habal These are essentially motorcycle taxis with extended seats (literally translated as 'pigs copulating,' after the level of intimacy attained when sharing a seat with four people). *Habal-habal* function like tricycles, only they are a little bit cheaper. They are most common in the Visayas and northern Mindanao. In some areas they are known simply as 'motorcycle taxis'.

Kalesa Two-wheeled horse carriages found in Manila's Chinatown and Intramuros, Vigan (North Luzon) and Cebu City (where they're known as *tartanillas*).

Train

The *Bicol Express* train route south from Manila to Naga in southeast Luzon – the only functioning railway line in the country – was suspended at the time of writing.

Health

Health issues and the quality of medical facilities vary enormously depending on where and how you travel in the Philippines. Many of the major cities are very well developed – indeed Manila and Cebu are 'medical tourism' destinations, where foreigners flock for affordable yet competent health care in modern hospitals. Travel in rural areas is a different story and carries a variety of health risks. For that matter, the average islander who practises small-scale farming and fishing can't afford modern medical care. As a result, some seek treatment from *mananambals* (folk healers) who are generally associated with Highlands people (the island of Siquijor is particularly well known for this).

Some travellers worry about contracting infectious diseases when in the tropics, but infections are a rare cause of serious illness or death in travellers. Pre-existing medical conditions and accidental injury (especially traffic accidents) account for most life-threatening problems.

Treat our advice as a general guide only; it does not replace the advice of a doctor trained in travel medicine.

BEFORE YOU GO

➡ Philippine pharmacies are usually well stocked with sterilised disposable syringes, bandages and antibiotics, but it doesn't hurt to bring your own sterilised first-aid kit, especially if you're going to be travelling off the beaten track. Contact-lens solution and spare contacts are readily available in cities.

➡ Pack medications in their original, clearly labelled containers. A signed and dated letter from your physician describing your medical conditions and medications, including generic names, is also a good idea. If you have a heart condition, bring a copy of your ECG taken just prior to travelling.

➡ If you take any regular medication bring double your needs in case of loss or theft. Philippine pharmacies generally require a doctor's prescription to issue medications. It can be difficult to find some of the newer drugs, particularly the latest anti-depressant drugs, contraceptive pills and blood-pressure medications.

Insurance

➡ Even if you are fit and healthy, don't travel without health insurance – accidents happen.

➡ Declare any existing medical conditions you have (the insurance company will check if your problem is pre-existing and will not cover you if it is undeclared).

➡ You may require extra cover for adventure activities such as rock climbing or scuba diving.

➡ If you're uninsured, emergency evacuation is expensive; bills of more than US$100,000 are not uncommon.

➡ Ensure you keep all documentation related to any medical expenses you incur.

Recommended Vaccinations

Specialised travel-medicine clinics are your best source of information; they stock all available vaccines and will be able to give specific recommendations. The doctors will take into account factors such as past vaccination history, the length of your trip, activities you may be undertaking and underlying medical conditions.

➡ Visit a doctor six to eight weeks before departure, as most vaccines don't produce immunity until at least two weeks after they're given.

➡ Ask your doctor for an International Certificate of Vaccination (otherwise known as the 'yellow booklet'), listing all vaccinations received.

➡ The only vaccine required by international regulations is yellow fever. Proof of vaccination will only be required if you have visited a country in the yellow-fever zone within the six days prior to entering Southeast Asia.

Medical Checklist

Recommended items for a personal medical kit:

➡ antibacterial cream, eg Mupirocin

➡ antibiotics for diarrhoea, eg Norfloxacin, Ciprofloxacin and Azithromycin for bacterial diarrhoea; Tinidazole for giardiasis or amoebic dysentery

➡ antibiotics for skin infections, eg Amoxicillin/ Clavulanate or Cephalexin

➡ antifungal cream, eg Clotrimazole

➡ antihistamine for allergies, eg Cetirizine for daytime and Promethazine for night

➡ anti-inflammatories, eg Ibuprofen

➡ antiseptic, eg Betadine

➡ antispasmodic for stomach cramps, eg Buscopan

➡ contraceptives

➡ a decongestant, eg Pseudoephedrine

➡ DEET-based insect repellent

➡ diarrhoea treatment – consider an oral rehydration

solution, eg Gastrolyte; diarrhoea 'stopper', eg Loperamide; and anti-nausea medication, eg Prochlorperazine

➡ first-aid items such as scissors, safety pins, Elastoplasts, bandages, gauze, thermometer (electronic, not mercury), tweezers, and sterile needles and syringes

➡ indigestion medication, eg Quick-Eze or Mylanta

➡ iodine tablets (unless you are pregnant or have a thyroid problem) to purify water

➡ laxative, eg Coloxyl

REQUIRED & RECOMMENDED VACCINATIONS

The World Health Organization (WHO) recommends the following vaccinations for travellers to Southeast Asia:

Adult diphtheria and tetanus Single booster recommended if none has been given in the previous 10 years. Side effects include a sore arm and fever.

Hepatitis A Provides almost 100% protection for up to a year; a booster after 12 months provides at least another 20 years' protection. Mild side effects such as headache and a sore arm occur in 5% to 10% of people.

Hepatitis B Now considered routine for most travellers. Given as three shots over six months. A rapid schedule is also available, as is a combined vaccination with hepatitis A. Side effects are mild and uncommon, usually headache and a sore arm. Lifetime protection occurs in 95% of people.

Measles, mumps and rubella Two doses of MMR required unless you have had the diseases. Occasionally a rash and flu-like illness can develop a week after receiving the vaccine. Many young adults require a booster.

Polio Only one booster is required as an adult for lifetime protection.

Typhoid Recommended unless your trip is less than a week. The vaccine offers around 70% protection, lasts for two to three years and comes as a single shot. Tablets are also available, however the injection is usually recommended as it has fewer side effects. A sore arm and fever may occur.

Varicella If you haven't had chickenpox, discuss this vaccination with your doctor.

These are recommended only for long-term travellers (more than one month):

Japanese B Encephalitis Three injections in all. Booster recommended after two years. A sore arm and headache are the most common side effects.

Meningitis Single injection. There are two types of vaccination: the quadrivalent vaccine gives two to three years' protection; meningitis group C vaccine gives around 10 years' protection. Recommended for long-term travellers aged under 25.

Rabies Three injections in all. A booster after one year will then provide 10 years' protection. Side effects are rare – occasionally a headache and sore arm.

Tuberculosis A complex issue. Adult long-term travellers are usually recommended to have a TB skin test before and after travel, rather than vaccination. Only one vaccine is given in a lifetime.

➡ migraine medication (your personal brand), if a migraine sufferer

➡ paracetamol for pain

➡ Permethrin (to impregnate clothing and mosquito nets) for repelling insects

➡ steroid cream for allergic/itchy rashes, eg 1% to 2% hydrocortisone

➡ sunscreen

➡ thrush (vaginal yeast infection) treatment, eg Clotrimazole pessaries or Diflucan tablet

➡ Ural or equivalent if you're prone to urine infections

Websites

World Health Organization (WHO; www.who.int/ith) Publishes a superb book called *International Travel & Health*, which is revised annually and is available free online.

MD Travel Health (www.mdtravelhealth.com) Provides complete travel health recommendations for every country and is updated daily.

Centers for Disease Control and Prevention (CDC; www.cdc.gov) Good general information and country-specific warnings.

Further Reading

➡ *Healthy Travel – Asia & India* (Lonely Planet) Handy pocket size, packed with useful information.

➡ *Travellers' Health* by Dr Richard Dawood.

➡ *Travelling Well* (www.travellingwell.com.au) by Dr Deborah Mills; now in its 18th edition (2013).

IN THE PHILIPPINES

Availability of Health Care

Good medical care is available in most major cities in the Philippines. It is difficult to find reliable medical care in rural areas, although there will usually be some sort of clinic not too far away. Your embassy and insurance company are also good contacts.

If you think you may have a serious disease, especially malaria, do not waste time – travel to the nearest quality facility to receive attention. It is always better to be assessed by a doctor than to rely on self-treatment.

Infectious Diseases

Chikungunya Fever

This less common viral infection poses only a small risk to travellers in the Philippines, mainly in the Visayas. Sudden pain in one or more joints, fever, headache, nausea and rash are the main symptoms.

Cutaneous Larva Migrans

This disease is caused by dog hookworm; the rash starts as a small lump, then slowly spreads in a linear fashion. It is intensely itchy, especially at night. It is easily treated with medications and should not be cut out or frozen.

Dengue Fever

This mosquito-borne disease is by far the most prevalent of the diseases you have a chance of contracting in the Philippines. It's especially common in cities, especially in metro Manila and it's the leading cause of hospitalisations of children in the country. While not usually fatal, dengue can kill; of more than 42,200 cases diagnosed in the first six months of 2013, 193 resulted in death. There is no vaccine available so it can only be prevented by avoiding mosquito bites. The mosquito that carries dengue can bite day and night. Symptoms include high fever, severe headache and body ache (dengue was previously known as 'breakbone fever'). Some people develop a rash and experience diarrhoea. There is no specific treatment, just rest and paracetamol – do not take aspirin as it increases the likelihood of haemorrhaging. See a doctor to be diagnosed and monitored.

Travellers are advised to prevent mosquito bites by taking these steps:

➡ Use a DEET-containing insect repellent on exposed skin. Wash this off at night, as long as you are sleeping under a mosquito net. Natural repellents such as citronella can be effective, but must be applied more frequently than products containing DEET.

➡ Sleep under a mosquito net impregnated with Permethrin.

➡ Choose accommodation with screens and fans (if not air-conditioned).

➡ Impregnate clothing with Permethrin in high-risk areas.

➡ Wear long sleeves and trousers in light colours.

➡ Use mosquito coils.

➡ Spray your room with insect repellent before going out for your evening meal.

Filariasis

This is a mosquito-borne disease that is very common in the local population, yet very rare in travellers. Mosquito-avoidance measures are the best way to prevent this disease.

Hepatitis A

A problem found throughout the region, this food- and water-borne virus infects the liver, causing jaundice (yellow skin and eyes), nausea and lethargy. There is no specific treatment for hepatitis A; you just need to allow time for the liver to heal. All travellers to Southeast Asia should be vaccinated against hepatitis A.

Hepatitis B

The only sexually transmitted disease that can be prevented by vaccination, hepatitis B is spread by body fluids, including sexual contact. In some parts of Southeast Asia up to 20% of the population are carriers of hepatitis B, and usually are unaware of this. The long-term consequences can include liver cancer and cirrhosis.

Hepatitis E

Hepatitis E is transmitted through contaminated food and water and has similar symptoms to hepatitis A, but is far less common. It is a severe problem in pregnant women and can result in the death of both mother and baby. There is currently no vaccine, and prevention is by following safe eating and drinking guidelines.

Japanese B Encephalitis

While a rare disease in travellers, at least 50,000 locals are infected each year in Southeast Asia. This viral disease is transmitted by mosquitoes. Most cases occur in rural areas and vaccination is recommended for travellers spending more than one month outside of cities. There is no treatment, and a third of infected people will die while another third will suffer permanent brain damage.

Malaria

For such a serious and potentially deadly disease, there is an enormous amount of misinformation concerning malaria. Malaria is caused by a parasite transmitted by the bite of an infected mosquito. The most important symptom of malaria is fever, but general symptoms such as headache, diarrhoea, cough or chills may also occur. Diagnosis can only be made by taking a blood sample.

According to the Centers for Disease Control and Prevention (CDC), in the Philippines there is no malaria risk in Bohol, Boracay, Catanduanes, Cebu, Manila or other urban areas. The risk of side effects from anti-malarial tablets probably outweighs the risk of getting the disease in these areas.

In general, malaria is only a concern if you plan to travel below 600m in extremely remote areas such as southern Palawan. Before you travel, seek medical advice on the right medication and dosage for you. Note that, according to the CDC, chloroquine is not an effective antimalarial drug in the Philippines.

Measles

Measles remains a problem in some parts of Southeast Asia. This highly contagious bacterial infection is spread via coughing and sneezing. Most people born before 1966 are immune as they had the disease in childhood. Measles starts with a high fever and rash and can be complicated by pneumonia and brain disease. There is no specific treatment.

Rabies

This uniformly fatal disease is spread by the bite or lick of an infected animal – most commonly a dog or monkey. You should seek medical advice immediately after any animal bite and commence post-exposure treatment. Having pre-travel vaccination means the post-bite treatment is greatly simplified. If an animal bites you, gently wash the wound with soap and water, and apply iodine-based antiseptic. If you are not pre-vaccinated you will need to receive rabies immunoglobulin as soon as possible.

Schistosomiasis

Schistosomiasis is a tiny parasite that enters your skin after you've been swimming in contaminated water. Travellers usually only get a light infection and hence have no symptoms. Schistosomiasis exists in the Philippines but it's not common and is confined to a few areas well off the tourist trail. On rare occasions, travellers may develop 'Katayama fever'. This occurs some weeks after exposure, as the parasite passes through the lungs and causes an allergic reaction – symp-

toms are coughing and fever. Schistosomiasis is easily treated with medications.

Tuberculosis

Tuberculosis (TB) is rare in short-term travellers. Medical and aid workers, and long-term travellers who have significant contact with the local population, should take precautions. Vaccination is usually only given to children under the age of five, but adults at risk are recommended pre- and post-travel TB testing. The main symptoms are fever, cough, weight loss, night sweats and tiredness.

Typhoid

This serious bacterial infection is spread via food and water. It gives a high and slowly progressive fever and headache, and may be accompanied by a dry cough and stomach pain. It is diagnosed by blood tests and treated with antibiotics. Vaccination is recommended for urban areas, not just smaller cities, villages or rural areas.

Typhus

Murine typhus is spread by the bite of a flea while scrub typhus is spread via a mite. These diseases are rare in travellers. Symptoms include fever, muscle pains and a rash. Avoid these diseases by following general insect-avoidance measures. Doxycycline will also prevent them.

Traveller's Diarrhoea

Traveller's diarrhoea is by far the most common problem affecting travellers. In over 80% of cases, traveller's diarrhoea is caused by a bacteria (there are numerous potential culprits), and therefore responds promptly to treatment with antibiotics. Treatment with antibiotics will depend on your situation – how sick you are, how quickly you need to get better, where you are etc.

Traveller's diarrhoea is defined as the passage of

more than three watery bowel actions within 24 hours, plus at least one other symptom such as fever, cramps, nausea, vomiting or feeling unwell.

Treatment consists of staying well hydrated; rehydration solutions like Gastrolyte are the best for this. Antibiotics such as Norfloxacin, Ciprofloxacin or Azithromycin will kill the bacteria quickly.

Loperamide is just a 'stopper' and doesn't get to the cause of the problem. It can be helpful, for example if you have to go on a long bus ride. Don't take Loperamide if you have a fever, or blood in your stools.

Amoebic Dysentery

Amoebic dysentery is very rare in travellers but is often misdiagnosed by poor-quality labs in Southeast Asia. Symptoms are similar to bacterial diarrhoea, ie fever, bloody diarrhoea and generally feeling unwell. You should always seek reliable medical care if you have blood in your diarrhoea. Treatment involves two drugs: Tinidazole or Metronidazole to kill the parasite in your gut and then a second drug to kill the cysts. If left untreated complications such as liver or gut abscesses can occur.

Giardiasis

Giardia lamblia is a parasite that is relatively common in travellers. Symptoms include nausea, bloating, excess gas, fatigue and intermittent diarrhoea. The parasite will eventually go away if left untreated but this can take months. The treatment of choice is Tinidazole, with Metronidazole being a second-line option.

Environmental Hazards

Air Pollution

Air pollution, particularly vehicle pollution, is a major problem in the Philippines' largest cities, especially Manila. If you have severe respiratory problems speak with your doctor before travelling to any heavily polluted urban centres. This pollution can also cause minor respiratory problems such as sinusitis, dry throat and irritated eyes. If troubled by the pollution, leave the city for a few days and get some fresh air.

Diving

Divers and surfers should seek specialised advice before they travel to ensure their medical kit contains treatment for coral cuts and tropical ear infections. Divers should ensure their insurance covers them for decompression illness – get specialised dive insurance through an organisation such as **Divers Alert Network** (DAN; www.diversalertnetwork.org). Have a dive medical before you leave your home country – there are certain medical conditions that are incompatible with diving, and economic considerations may override health considerations for some dive operators.

Heat

For most people it takes at least two weeks to adapt to the hot climate. Swelling of the feet and ankles is common, as are muscle cramps caused by excessive sweating. Prevent these by avoiding dehydration and excessive activity in the heat. Take it easy when you first arrive. Don't eat salt tablets (they aggravate the gut), although drinking rehydration solution or eating salty food helps. Treat cramps by stopping activity, resting, rehydrating with double-strength rehydration solution and gently stretching.

Heatstroke is a serious medical emergency. Symptoms come on suddenly and include weakness, nausea, a hot dry body with a body temperature of over 41°C, dizziness, confusion, loss of coordination, fits and eventually collapse and loss of consciousness. Seek medical help and commence cooling by getting the person out of the heat, removing their clothes, fanning them and applying cool wet cloths or ice to their body, especially to the groin and armpits.

Prickly heat is a common skin rash in the tropics, caused by sweat being trapped under the skin. The result is an itchy rash of tiny lumps. Treat by moving out of the heat and into air-con for a few hours and by having cool showers. Creams and ointments clog the skin so they should be avoided. Locally bought prickly-heat powder can be helpful.

Insect Bites & Stings

Bedbugs don't carry disease but their bites are very itchy. They live in the cracks of furniture and walls and then migrate to the bed at night to feed on you. You can treat the itch with an antihistamine. Lice inhabit various parts of your body but most commonly your head and pubic area. Transmission is via close contact with an infected person. Lice can be difficult to treat and you may need numerous applications of a lice shampoo such as Permethrin. Pubic lice are usually contracted from sexual contact.

Ticks are contracted after walking in rural areas. If you have had a tick bite and experience symptoms such as fever or muscle aches, a rash at the site of the bite or elsewhere, you should see a doctor. Doxycycline prevents tick-borne diseases.

Leeches are found in humid rainforest areas and are very common in the Philippines. They do not transmit any disease but their bites are often intensely itchy for weeks afterwards and can easily become infected. Apply an iodine-based antiseptic to any leech bite to help prevent infection.

Bee and wasp stings mainly cause problems for people who are allergic to them. Anyone with a serious bee or wasp allergy should carry an injection of adrenaline

DIVING EMERGENCIES

Recompression Chambers

There are four stationary recompression chambers in the Philippines.

St Patrick's Hospital Medical Center (☎0915 506 7621; www.divemed.com.ph; Batangas Hyperbaric Medicine & Wound Healing Center, St Patrick's Hospital Medical Center, Lopez Jaena St, Batangas City, Luzon) The only privately owned recompression chamber in the Philippines.

Cebu Doctor's University Hospital (☎0918 807 3837; Osmena Blvd) Cebu's recompression chamber. Contact Memerto Ortega.

PCSSD Armed Forces Hyperbaric Unit (☎02-920 7183; APF Medical Centre, V Luna Rd) In Quezon City, Manila.

Philippine Commission of Sports Scuba Diving (☎0915 219 6611; TIEZA Building, P Burgos St, Mandaue City, Cebu City) A chamber in the Cebu area.

Evacuation and Search & Rescue Services

The Philippine Air Force, the Coast Guard and private operators such as Subic Seaplanes can assist with evacuations. However, their range is limited and you can't expect them to miraculously appear in the middle of places like the Sulu Sea.

Philippines Air Force Search & Rescue (☎02-854 6701, 853 5013, 853 5008; Villamor Air Base, Pasay City, Manila)

Subic Seaplanes (☎047-252 2230, mobile 0919 325 1106; www.seaplane-philippines.com; Subic Bay Freeport Zone, Zambales)

(eg EpiPen) for emergency treatment. For others, pain is the main problem – apply ice and take painkillers.

Most jellyfish in Southeast Asian waters are not dangerous, just irritating. An exception is box jellyfish, which are extremely dangerous and can be fatal. They are not common in Philippine waters but they do exist, so ask around to make sure there have been no recent sightings in areas where you'll be swimming.

First aid for jellyfish stings involves pouring vinegar onto the affected area to neutralise the poison. Do not rub sand or water onto the stings. Take painkillers, and anyone who feels ill in any way after being stung should seek medical advice.

Parasites

Numerous parasites are common in local populations in Southeast Asia, however, most of these are rare in travellers. The two rules to follow if you wish to avoid parasitic infections are to wear shoes and to avoid eating raw food, especially fish, pork and vegetables. A number of parasites, including strongyloides, hookworm and cutaneous *larva migrans,* are transmitted via the skin by walking barefoot.

Skin Problems

Fungal rashes are common in humid climates. There are two common fungal rashes that affect travellers. The first occurs in moist areas that get less air, such as the groin, armpits and between the toes. It starts as a red patch that slowly spreads and is usually itchy. Treatment involves keeping the skin dry, avoiding chafing and using an antifungal cream such as Clotrimazole or Lamisil. *Tinea versicolor* is also common. It causes small, light-coloured patches, most commonly on the back, chest and shoulders. Consult a doctor.

Cuts and scratches become easily infected in humid climates. Take meticulous care of any cuts and scratches to prevent complications such as abscesses. Immediately wash all wounds in clean water and apply antiseptic. If you develop signs of infection (increasing pain and redness) see a doctor. Divers and surfers should be particularly careful with coral cuts as they can become easily infected.

Snakes

Southeast Asia is home to many species of both poisonous and harmless snakes. Assume all snakes are poisonous and never try to catch one. Always wear boots and long pants if walking in an area that may have snakes. First aid in the event of a snakebite involves pressure immobilisation via an elastic bandage firmly wrapped around the affected limb, starting at the bite site and working up towards the chest. The bandage should not be so tight that the circulation is cut off, and the fingers or toes should be kept free so the circulation can be checked. Immobilise the limb with a splint and carry the victim to medical attention. Do not use tourniquets or try to suck the venom out. Antivenene is available for most species.

Language

Tagalog, Pilipino, Filipino – the various language names might cause confusion, but they reflect the political history of the lingua franca across the 7000-island archipelago of the Philippines. Although not the mother tongue of every Philippine citizen, Filipino is spoken as a second language throughout the country (with over 165 other languages), and is an official language used for university instruction and in most legal, business and governmental transactions (the other official language being English). It belongs to the Malayo-Polynesian language family and has around 45 million speakers worldwide.

Filipino is easy to pronounce and most sounds are familiar to English speakers. In addition, the relationship between Filipino sounds and their spelling is straightforward and consistent, meaning that each letter is always pronounced the same way. If you read our coloured pronunciation guides as if they were English, you'll be understood just fine. Note that ai is pronounced as in 'aisle', ay as in 'say', ew like ee with rounded lips, oh as the 'o' in 'go', ow as in 'how' and ooy as the 'wea' in 'tweak'. The r sound is stronger than in English and rolled, and the ng combination – which is found in English words such as 'sing' or 'ringing' – can appear at the beginning of words. Filipino also has a glottal stop, which is pronounced like the pause between the two syllables in 'uh-oh'. It's indicated in our pronunciation guides by an apostrophe ('), and in written Filipino by a circumflex (ˆ), grave (`) or acute (´) accent over the vowel that's followed by a glottal stop.

In our pronunciation guides the stressed syllables are indicated with italics. The markers 'pol' and 'inf' indicate polite and informal forms respectively.

BASICS

Good day.	Magandáng araw pô. (pol)	ma·gan·dang a·row po'
	Magandáng araw. (inf)	ma·gan·dang a·row
Goodbye.	Paalam na pô. (pol)	pa·a·lam na po'
	Babay. (inf)	ba·bai
Yes.	Opò. (pol)	o·po'
	Oo. (inf)	o·o
No.	Hindí pô. (pol)	heen·dee' po'
	Hindî. (inf)	heen·dee'
Thank you.	Salamat pô. (pol)	sa·la·mat po'
	Salamat. (inf)	sa·la·mat
You're welcome.	Walá pong anumán. (pol)	wa·la pong a·noo·man
	Waláng anumán. (inf)	wa·lang a·noo·man

How are you?
Kumustá po kayó? (pol) koo·moos·ta po ka·yo
Kumustá? (inf) koo·moos·ta

Fine. And you?
Mabuti pô. Kayó pô? (pol) ma·boo·tee po' ka·yo po'
Mabuti. Ikáw? (inf) ma·boo·tee ee·kow

What's your name?
Anó pô ang pangalan ninyó? (pol) a·no po' ang pa·nga·lan neen·yo
Anó ang pangalan mo? (inf) a·no ang pa·nga·lan mo

My name is ...
Ang pangalan ko pô ay ... (pol) ang pa·nga·lan ko po' ai ...
Ang pangalan ko ay ... (inf) ang pa·nga·lan ko ai ...

WANT MORE?

For in-depth language information and handy phrases, check out Lonely Planet's *Filipino Phrasebook*. You'll find it at **shop.lonelyplanet.com**, or you can buy Lonely Planet's iPhone phrasebooks at the Apple App Store.

Do you speak English?
Marunong ka ba   ma·*roo*·nong ka ba
ng Inglés?   nang eeng·*gles*

I don't understand.
Hindí ko   heen·*dee* ko
náiintindihán.   na·ee·een·teen·dee·*han*

ACCOMMODATION

Where's a ...?	*Násaán ang ...?*	na·sa·*an* ang ...
campsite	*kampingan*	kam·*pee*·ngan
guesthouse	*bahay-*	ba·hai·
	bisita	bee·*see*·ta
hotel	*otél*	o·*tel*
youth hostel	*hostel para*	hos·tel pa·ra
	sa kabataan	sa ka·ba·*ta*·an

Do you have	*Mayroón ba*	mai·ro·*on* ba
a ... room?	*kayóng*	ka·*yong*
	kuwartong ...?	koo·*war*·tong ...
single	*pang-isahan*	pang·ee·sa·han
double	*pandala-*	pan·da·la·
	waha	wa·han
twin	*may kambál*	mai kam·*bal*
	na kama	na *ka*·ma

How much is	*Magkano ba*	mag·*ka*·no ba
it per ...?	*para sa*	*pa*·ra sa
	isáng ...?	ee·*sang* ...
night	*gabí*	ga·*bee*
person	*katao*	ka·*ta*·o
week	*linggó*	leeng·*go*

air-con	*erkon*	er·kon
bathroom	*banyo*	ba·nyo
toilet	*kubeta*	koo·*be*·ta
window	*bintanà*	been·*ta*·na'

DIRECTIONS

Where's the (market)?
Násaán ang   na·sa·*an* ang
(palengke)?   (pa·*leng*·ke)

How far is it?
Gaano kalayo?   ga·*a*·no ka·*la*·yo

What's the address?
Anó ang adrés?   a·*no* ang a·*dres*

Could you please write it down?
Pakísulat mo?   pa·*kee*·soo·lat mo

Can you show me (on the map)?
Maáari bang   ma·*a*·a·ree bang
ipakita mo sa   ee·pa·*kee*·ta mo sa
akin (sa mapa)?   a·keen (sa *ma*·pa)

LANGUAGE EATING & DRINKING

SIGNS

Pasukán	Entrance
Labásan	Exit
Bukás	Open
Sará	Closed
Bawal	Prohibited
CR	Toilets
Lalaki	Men
Babae	Women

It's ...	*Iyón ay ...*	ee·*yon* ai ...
behind ...	*nasa*	na·sa
	likurán	lee·koo·*ran*
	ng ...	nang ...
in front of ...	*sa harapán*	sa ha·ra·*pan*
	ng ...	nang ...
near (...)	*malapit*	ma·*la*·peet
	(sa ...)	(sa ...)
next to ...	*katabí*	ka·ta·*bee*
	ng ...	nang ...
on the corner	*nasa kanto*	na·sa kan·to
opposite ...	*katapát*	ka·ta·pat
	ng ...	nang ...
straight ahead	*diretso*	dee·*ret*·so

Turn ...	*Lumikó*	loo·mee·*ko*
	sa ...	sa ...
at the traffic	*ilaw-*	ee·low·
lights	*trápiko*	tra·pee·ko
left	*kaliwâ*	ka·lee·*wa'*
right	*kanan*	*ka*·nan

EATING & DRINKING

I'd like to	*Gustó kong*	goos·to kong
reserve a	*mag-reserba*	mag·re·*ser*·ba
table for ...	*ng mesa*	nang *me*·sa
	para sa ...	*pa*·ra sa ...
(eight)	*(alás-otso)*	(a·*las*·ot·so)
o'clock		
(two) people	*(dalawáng)*	(da·la·*wang*)
	tao	*ta*·o

I'd like the menu.
Gustó ko ng menú.   goos·*to* ko nang me·*noo*

What would you recommend?
Anó ang mairere-   a·*no* ang ma·ee·re·re·
komendá mo?   ko·men·*da* mo

What's in that dish?
Anó iyán?   a·*no* ee·yan

I don't eat (red meat).
Hindî akó   heen·*dee'* a·*ko*
kumakain ng (karné).   koo·ma·*ka*·een nang
(kar·*ne*)

Cheers!
Tagayan tayo!   ta·*ga*·yan *ta*·yo

That was delicious!
Masaráp!   ma·sa·*rap*

Please bring the bill.
Pakidalá ang tsit.   pa·kee·da·*la* ang tseet

Key Words

bottle	bote	*bo*·te
breakfast	almusál	al·moo·*sal*
cafe	kapiteryá	ka·pee·ter·*ya*
cold	malamíg	ma·la·*meeg*
dinner	hapunan	ha·*poo*·nan
drink	inumin	ee·*noo*·meen
fork	tinidór	tee·nee·*dor*
glass	baso	*ba*·so
grocery	groseryá	gro·ser·*ya*
hot	mainit	ma·ee·*neet*
knife	kutsilyo	koot·*seel*·yo
lunch	tanghalian	tang·ha·*lee*·an
market	palengke	pa·*leng*·ke
plate	pinggán	peeng·*gan*
restaurant	restoran	res·*to*·ran
spoon	kutsara	koot·*sa*·ra
vegetarian	bedyetaryan	bed·ye·*tar*·yan
with ...	may ...	mai ...
without ...	walâ ...	wa·*la'* ...

Meat & Fish

beef	karné	kar·*ne*
chicken	manók	ma·*nok*
duck	bibi	bee·bee
fish	isdâ	ees·*da'*
lamb	tupa	*too*·pa
meat	karné	kar·*ne*
mussel	paros	*pa*·ros
oysters	talabá	ta·la·*ba*
pork	karnéng baboy	kar·*neng* ba·*boy*
prawn	sugpô	soog·*po'*
tuna	tulingán	too·lee·*ngan*
turkey	pabo	*pa*·bo
veal	karnéng bulô	kar·*neng* boo·*lo'*

Fruit & Vegetables

apple	mansanas	man·*sa*·nas
bean	bin	been
cabbage	repolyo	re·*pol*·yo
capsicum	bel peper	bel *pe*·per
cauliflower	koliplawer	ko·lee·*pla*·wer
cucumber	pipino	pee·*pee*·no
fruit	prutas	*proo*·tas
grapes	ubas	oo·bas
lemon	limón	lee·*mon*
mushroom	kabuté	ka·boo·*te*
nuts	manê	ma·*ne'*
onion	sibuyas	see·*boo*·yas
orange	kahél	ka·*hel*
pea	gisantes	gee·*san*·tes
peach	pits	peets
pineapple	pinyá	peen·*ya*
potatoes	patatas	pa·*ta*·tas
spinach	kulitis	koo·*lee*·tees
tomato	kamatis	ka·*ma*·tees
vegetable	gulay	*goo*·lai

Other

bread	tinapay	tee·*na*·pai
butter	mantekilya	man·te·*keel*·ya
cheese	keso	*ke*·so
egg	itlóg	eet·*log*
garlic	bawang	*ba*·wang
honey	pulót-pukyutan	poo·*lot*-pook·*yoo*·tan
ice	yelo	*ye*·lo
oil	mantikà	man·*tee*·ka
pepper	pamintá	pa·meen·*ta*
rice (cooked)	kanin	*ka*·neen
salt	asín	a·*seen*
soup	sopas	*so*·pas
sour cream	kremang maasim	*kre*·mang ma·a·*seem*
sugar	asukal	a·*soo*·kal
vinegar	sukà	*soo*·ka'

Drinks

beer	serbesa	ser·*be*·sa
coffee	kapé	ka·*pe*
juice	katás	ka·*tas*
milk	gatas	*ga*·tas

tea	*tsaá*	tsa·*a*
water	*tubig*	*too*·beeg
wine	*alak*	*a*·lak

EMERGENCIES

Help!	*Saklolo!*	sak·*lo*·lo
Go away!	*Umalís ka!*	oo·ma·*lees* ka
Call ...!	*Tumawag ka ng ...!*	too·*ma*·wag ka nang ...
a doctor	*doktór*	dok·*tor*
the police	*pulís*	poo·*lees*

There's been an accident.
May aksidente. mai ak·see·*den*·te

I'm sick.
May sakít akó. mai sa·*keet* a·ko

It hurts here.
Masakít dito. ma·sa·*keet* dee·to

I'm allergic to (antibiotics).
Allergic akó sa a·*ler*·jeek a·ko sa
(antibayótikó). (an·tee·ba·yo·tee·ko)

I'm lost.
Nawawalâ akó. na·wa·wa·*la'* a·ko

Where are the toilets?
Násaán ang kubeta? na·sa·an ang koo·*be*·ta

SHOPPING & SERVICES

I'd like to buy ...
Gustó kong bumilí goos·to kong boo·mee·*lee*
ng ... nang ...

I'm just looking.
Tumitingín lang too·mee·tee·*ngeen* lang
akó. a·ko

Can I look at it?
Puwede ko bang poo·we·de ko bang
tingnán? teeng·*nan*

How much is it?
Magkano? mag·*ka*·no

That's too expensive.
Masyadong mahál. mas·ya·dong ma·*hal*

Can you lower the price?
Puwede mo bang poo·we·de mo bang
ibabâ ang presyo? ee·ba·*ba'* ang pres·yo

There's a mistake in the bill.
May malí sa kuwenta. mai ma·*lee* sa koo·*wen*·ta

bank	*bangko*	*bang*·ko
internet cafe	*ínternet kapé*	een·ter·net ka·pe
post office	*pos opis*	pos o·*pees*
public telephone	*teléponong pampúbliko*	te·*le*·po·nong pam·*poob*·lee·ko

NUMBERS

1	*isá*	ee·*sa*
2	*dalawá*	da·la·*wa*
3	*tatló*	tat·*lo*
4	*apat*	*a*·pat
5	*limá*	lee·*ma*
6	*anim*	*a*·neem
7	*pitó*	pee·*to*
8	*waló*	wa·*lo*
9	*siyám*	see·*yam*
10	*sampû*	sam·*poo'*
20	*dalawampû*	da·la·wam·*poo'*
30	*tatlumpû*	tat·loom·*poo'*
40	*apatnapû*	*a*·pat·na·*poo'*
50	*limampû*	lee·mam·*poo'*
60	*animnapû*	*a*·neem·na·*poo'*
70	*pitumpû*	pee·toom·*poo'*
80	*walumpû*	wa·loom·*poo'*
90	*siyamnapû*	see·yam·na·*poo'*
100	*sandaán*	san·da·*an*
1000	*isáng libo*	ee·*sang* lee·bo

tourist office	*upisina ng turismo*	oo·pee·*see*·na nang too·*rees*·mo

TIME & DATES

What time is it?
Anóng oras na? a·*nong* o·ras na

It's (10) o'clock.
Alás-(diyés). a·*las*·(dee·yes)

Half past (10).
Kalahating oras ka·la·*ha*·teeng o·ras
makalampás ang ma·ka·lam·*pas* ang
(alás-diyés). (a·*las*·dee·yes)

am	*ng umaga*	nang oo·*ma*·ga
pm (12–2pm)	*ng tanghalì*	nang tang·*ha*·lee'
pm (2–6pm)	*ng hapon*	nang *ha*·pon
yesterday	*kahapon ng*	ka·*ha*·pon nang
today	*sa araw na itó*	sa a·row na ee·*to*
tomorrow	*bukas ng*	*boo*·kas nang
Monday	*Lunes*	*loo*·nes
Tuesday	*Martés*	mar·*tes*
Wednesday	*Miyérkoles*	mee·*yer*·ko·les
Thursday	*Huwebes*	hoo·*we*·bes
Friday	*Biyernes*	bee·*yer*·nes
Saturday	*Sábado*	sa·ba·do

Sunday	Linggó	leeng·go
January	Enero	e·ne·ro
February	Pebrero	peb·re·ro
March	Marso	mar·so
April	Abríl	ab·reel
May	Mayo	ma·yo
June	Hunyo	hoon·yo
July	Hulyo	hool·yo
August	Agosto	a·gos·to
September	Setyembre	set·yem·bre
October	Oktubre	ok·too·bre
November	Nobyembre	nob·yem·bre
December	Disyembre	dees·yem·bre

TRANSPORT

Public Transport

Which ... goes to (Bataan)?	Alíng ... ang papuntá sa (Bataan)?	a·leeng ... ang pa·poon·ta sa (ba·ta·an)
boat	bapór	ba·por
catamaran	catamaran	ka·ta·ma·ran
ferry	ferry	pe·ree

Is this the ... to (Baguío)?	Itó ba ang ... na papuntá sa (Baguío)?	ee·to ba ang ... na pa·poon·ta sa (ba·gee·o)
bus	bus	boos
jeepney	dyipni	jeep·nee
megataxi	mega-taksi	me·ga·tak·see
train	tren	tren

When's the ... (bus)?	Kailán ang ... (bus)?	ka·ee·lan ang ... (boos)
first	unang	oo·nang
last	hulíng	hoo·leeng
next	súsunód na	soo·soo·nod na
A ... ticket (to Liliw).	Isáng tiket ... na (papuntá sa Liliw).	ee·sang tee·ket ... na (pa·poon·ta sa lee·lew)
1st-class	1st class	pers klas
2nd-class	2nd class	se·kan klas
one-way	one way	wan way
return	balikan	ba·lee·kan

What time does the (bus) leave?
Anóng oras áalís ang (bus)?
a·nong o·ras a·a·lees ang (boos)

What time does the (boat) get to (Samal)?
Anóng oras darating ang (bapór) sa (Samal)?
a·nong o·ras da·ra·teeng ang (ba·por) sa (sa·mal)

Does it stop at (Porac)?
Humihintó ba itó sa (Porac)?
hoo·mee·heen·to ba ee·to sa (po·rak)

Please tell me when we get to (Tagaytay).
Pakisabi lang sa akin pagdating natin sa (Tagaytay).
pa·kee·sa·bee lang sa a·keen pag·da·teeng na·teen sa (ta·gai·tai)

I'd like to get off at (Rizal).
Gustó kong bumabá sa (Rizal).
goos·to kong boo·ma·ba sa (ree·sal)

Please take me to (this address).
Pakihatíd mo akó sa (adrés na itó).
pa·kee·ha·teed mo a·ko sa (a·dres na ee·to)

bus stop	hintuan ng bus	heen·too·an nang boos
ticket office	bilihan ng tiket	bee·lee·han nang tee·ket
train station	istasyón ng tren	ees·tas·yon nang tren

Driving & Cycling

I'd like to hire a ...	Gustó kong umarkilá ng ...	goos·to kong oo·mar·kee·la nang ...
4WD	4WD	por·weel·draib
bicycle	bisikleta	bee·seek·le·ta
car	kotse	kot·se
motorbike	motorsiklo	mo·tor·seek·lo

Is this the road to (Macabebe)?
Itó ba ang daán patungo sa (Macabebe)?
ee·to ba ang da·an pa·too·ngo sa (ma·ka·be·be)

Can I park here?
Puwede ba akóng pumarada dito?
poo·we·de ba a·kong poo·ma·ra·da dee·to

The (car) has broken down at (San Miguel).
Nasiraan ang (kotse) sa (San Miguel).
na·see·ra·an ang (kot·se) sa (san mee·gel)

I have a flat tyre.
Plat ang gulóng ko.
plat ang goo·long ko

I've run out of petrol.
Naubusan akó ng gasolina.
na·oo·boo·san a·ko nang ga·so·lee·na

bike shop	tindahan ng bisikleta	teen·da·han nang bee·seek·le·ta
mechanic	mekániko	me·ka·nee·ko
petrol/gas	gasolina	ga·so·lee·na
service station	serbis istesyon	ser·bees ees·tes·yon

GLOSSARY

arnis de mano – pre-Hispanic style of stick-fighting (more commonly known simply as *arnis*)

bagyo – typhoon

bahala na – you could almost call this the 'national philosophy'; in the days before the advent of Christianity, god was called bathala by ancient Filipinos; the expression *bahala na* is derived from this word and expresses faith (God will provide) as well as a kind of fatalism (come what may); it's somewhere between an Australian 'no worries' and Kurt Vonnegut's 'so it goes', but less individualistic than either: all things shall pass and in the meantime life is to be lived, preferably in the company of one's friends and – most importantly – family

bahay na bato – stone house

balangay – artfully crafted seagoing outrigger boat

balikbayan – an overseas Filipino returning or paying a visit to the Philippines

balisong – fan or butterfly knife

bangka – a wooden boat, usually with outriggers and powered by a cannibalised automotive engine; a pumpboat

barangay – village, neighbourhood or community, the basic sociopolitical unit of Filipino society

barkada – gang of friends

barong – a generic term to describe the Filipino local shirt (for men) that is the 'national costume'; it usually has a heavily embroidered or patterned front

Barong Tagalog – traditional Filipino formal shirt (the barong was originally for men only; it refers only to the shirt), with elaborate embroidery or patterning down the front; made of jusi or pinya

baryo – Filipiniation of the Spanish word barrio (neighbourhood). Now known as a barangay.

bayanihan – Filipino tradition wherein neighbours would help a relocating family by carrying their house to its new location. More generally, the word has come to mean a communal spirit that makes seemingly impossible feats possible through the power of unity and cooperation

BPI – Bank of the Philippine Islands

butanding – whale shark

carabao – water buffalo, sometimes called a kalabaw

CBST – Community-Based Sustainable Tourism

CR – Comfort Room (toilet)

fronton – *jai alai* court

GROs – 'Guest Relation Officers' are officially glorified waitresses; unofficially they are sex workers

haribon – the Philippine eagle, an endangered species; haribon literally means 'king of birds'

ilustrado – a 19th-century Filipino of the educated middle class

jai alai – a fast-paced ball game, and one of the more popular sports in the Philippines

jeepney – a brightly painted vehicle that looks like an extended jeep, fitted with benches, adorned with everything but a kitchen sink and crammed with passengers

jusi – fabric woven from ramie fibres; used to make a barong

kalesa – horse-drawn carriage

kundiman – a melancholy genre of song originating in Manila (and the Tagalog region); one of the country's most loved musical idioms

lahar – rain-induced landslide of volcanic debris or mud from volcanic ash, common around Mt Pinatubo

mestizo – Filipino of mixed (usually Chinese or Spanish) descent. A Filipino of mixed Asian ancestry other than Chinese is not called a mestizo.

MILF – Moro Islamic Liberation Front

MNLF – Moro National Liberation Front

Moro – Spanish colonial term for Muslim Filipinos, once derogatory but now worn with some pride

nara – a hardwood tree, the Philippine national tree

nipa – a type of palm tree, the leaves of which are used for making nipa huts, the typical house in rural areas

NPA – New People's Army

paraw – traditional outrigger with jib and mainsail

pasyon – Christ's Passion, sung or re-enacted every Holy Week

Philvolcs – Philippine Institute of Volcanology & Seismology

Pinoy – a term Filipinos call themselves

pinya – fabric woven from pineapple fibres; commonly used to make a *barong*

PNP – Philippine National Police

poblasyon – town centre

sabong – cockfighting

sala – living room

santo – religious statue

sari-sari – small neighbourhood store stocked with all kinds of daily necessities; *sari-sari* literally means 'assortment'

swidden farming – the cultivation of an area of land that has been cleared through the use of slash-and-burn agricultural practices.

Tagalog – the dominant dialect of Manila and surrounding provinces, now the basis of the national language, Filipino

tamaraw – an endangered species of native buffalo, found only in Mindoro; one of the most endangered animals in the world

tinikling – Philippine national folk dance

tricycle – a Philippine rickshaw, formerly pedal-powered but now predominantly motorised

v-hire – local van/minibus

Behind the Scenes

SEND US YOUR FEEDBACK

We love to hear from travellers – your comments keep us on our toes and help make our books better. Our well-travelled team reads every word on what you loved or loathed about this book. Although we cannot reply individually to your submissions, we always guarantee that your feedback goes straight to the appropriate authors, in time for the next edition. Each person who sends us information is thanked in the next edition – the most useful submissions are rewarded with a selection of digital PDF chapters.

Visit **lonelyplanet.com/contact** to submit your updates and suggestions or to ask for help. Our award-winning website also features inspirational travel stories, news and discussions.

Note: We may edit, reproduce and incorporate your comments in Lonely Planet products such as guidebooks, websites and digital products, so let us know if you don't want your comments reproduced or your name acknowledged. For a copy of our privacy policy visit lonelyplanet.com/privacy.

OUR READERS

Many thanks to the travellers who used the last edition and wrote to us with helpful hints, useful advice and interesting anecdotes:

Alan Bowers, Angela Chin, Anton Rijsdijk, Barry Thompson, Bert Theunissen, Brian Bate, Bruno Michelini, Chris Urbanski, Christopher Atwood, Claudia Mueller, Conrad Wenham, Dan Roux, Daniel Johnson, David Bonsor, Debbie Foster, Donavan Albert, Erwin Meijer, Floortje Snels, Guido Nijssen, Hagai Benkuzari, Harrie Boin, Ian Drever, Inna Nesnova, Iven Immer, Jamil Reyes, Jan Hijman, Jan Ivarsson, Jason Baker, Jen Broadbent, Jennifer Richardson, Jenny Kim, Jessica Horber, Joanna Nelson, Joe Bryant, Juerg Buetler, Kamila Divisova, Katharina Asghari , Katrina Smith, King Pia, Laurence Poesy, Marc Iwen, Maria Fatima Bonus, Michael Young, Michal Rudziecki, Nicole Sarkis, Noah Impekoven, Rob Dunn, Robert Holt, Ruth Mosser, Suzanne Mingoa-Licuanan, Sekeun Daniel Yu, Simon Dabbs, Tanya Bonte, Thomas Sarosy, Vera Chiodi and Will Nahum.

AUTHOR THANKS

Michael Grosberg

Thanks to Kublai Millan and Min Ponce for their hospitality and warmth; Sunil and Ramesh for their advice and thoughts; Andy Pownall; Gerry Deegan; all you sea urchins – you know who you are, and Jim Boy, Zaza and Eddie; Alexander Lumang and Ronald Blantucas for the lift with accompanying sports talk; Maurice Noel 'Wing' Bollozos for his insight on Camiguin; Romy Besa for food talk; Mark Katz for health advice; and Carly Neidorf and Booners for their love and support.

Greg Bloom

For this edition, Johnny Weekend, Windi and Anna (my eight-year-old daughter) all did hard time as my research assistants. Anna exhibited particular patience in reviewing every resort on Siquijor. Thanks to Michelle and Noel for the royal treatment in San Jose. Thanks to Gavin for the Tacloban hookups, and to the tourist office in Tacloban. Thanks to Susan for the lift out of Guiuan. Thanks to cold San Miguel Pale Pilsen. Thanks to that dude in Catarman who knew everything about Northern Samar.

Trent Holden

A big shout out to all the cool Manileños I met this trip, and for all your invaluable tips and suggestions. Lots of love to all my family (including the latest addition, my nephew Campbell) and my girlfriend and partner in crime, Kate. Finally huge thanks to Laura Crawford for giving me the chance to work on another edition for the Philippines, plus my

BEHIND THE SCENES

fellow authors and the in-house team who all worked hard behind the scenes on this book.

Anna Kaminski

Many thanks to Team Philippines, not least to Laura for entrusting me with three chapters, my co-authors for all their helpful input and Greg in particular for all his advice and warm hospitality. A huge *salamat* to all who helped me en route, including Rafael Oca and Rafael Dionisio from Circle Hostel (plus Paul Melicor), Robert Baradi for handing in my lost wallet, Ela from Bombo Radyo Baguio for tracking me down, the super-helpful proprietress of Midtown Inn in Virac, tourism officers in Basco and Sabtang, Kiki for sharing her experiences, Kinad for the Cordillera knowledge, Ephraim for incomparable motorbike skills, MJ and Jerome Avenue of Bicol Adventure ATV, and the good people of East Point Hotel by the Sea.

Paul Stiles

My thanks goes out to Curtis for great company and cartography, Paul for inside access to Boracay, Ray for organising everything, and the many dedicated people in the Philippines Department of Tourism, Region VI, who helped me cover a huge area in a limited amount of time. *Mabuhay!*

ACKNOWLEDGMENTS

Climate map data adapted from Peel MC, Finlayson BL & McMahon TA (2007) 'Updated World Map of the Köppen-Geiger Climate Classification', *Hydrology and Earth Systems Sciences*, 11, 163344.

Cover photograph: Rice farmer looking over the mountains, Philippines. Per-Andre Hoffman/Getty

THIS BOOK

This edition of Lonely Planet's *Philippines* guidebook was written by Michael Grosberg, Greg Bloom, Trent Holden, Anna Kaminski and Paul Stiles. Greg, Michael and Trent also worked on the previous edition, along with Adam Karlin. This guide was produced by the following:

Destination Editor
Laura Crawford

Product Editor
Kate Mathews

Senior Cartographer
Julie Sheridan

Book Designer
Mazzy Prinsep

Assisting Editors Nigel Chin, Andrea Dobbin, Kate Evans, Justin Flynn, Victoria Harrison, Kate James, Andi Jones, Jodie Martire, Jenna Myers, Tracy Whitmey, Simon Williamson

Assisting Cartographers
Hunor Csutoros, Gabe Lindquist

Cover Researcher
Naomi Parker

Thanks to Anna Harris, Martin Kemp, Claire Naylor, Karyn Noble, Katie O'Connell, Martine Power, Ellie Simpson, Samantha Tyson, Diana Von Holdt, Lauren Wellicome, Dora Whitaker

Index

INDEX B-C

NOTES

Map Legend

Sights
- Beach
- Bird Sanctuary
- Buddhist
- Castle/Palace
- Christian
- Confucian
- Hindu
- Islamic
- Jain
- Jewish
- Monument
- Museum/Gallery/Historic Building
- Ruin
- Shinto
- Sikh
- Taoist
- Winery/Vineyard
- Zoo/Wildlife Sanctuary
- Other Sight

Activities, Courses & Tours
- Bodysurfing
- Diving
- Canoeing/Kayaking
- Course/Tour
- Sento Hot Baths/Onsen
- Skiing
- Snorkelling
- Surfing
- Swimming/Pool
- Walking
- Windsurfing
- Other Activity

Sleeping
- Sleeping
- Camping

Eating
- Eating

Drinking & Nightlife
- Drinking & Nightlife
- Cafe

Entertainment
- Entertainment

Shopping
- Shopping

Information
- Bank
- Embassy/Consulate
- Hospital/Medical
- Internet
- Police
- Post Office
- Telephone
- Toilet
- Tourist Information
- Other Information

Geographic
- Beach
- Hut/Shelter
- Lighthouse
- Lookout
- Mountain/Volcano
- Oasis
- Park
- Pass
- Picnic Area
- Waterfall

Population
- Capital (National)
- Capital (State/Province)
- City/Large Town
- Town/Village

Transport
- Airport
- Border crossing
- Bus
- Cable car/Funicular
- Cycling
- Ferry
- Metro/MRT/MTR station
- Monorail
- Parking
- Petrol station
- Skytrain/Subway station
- Taxi
- Train station/Railway
- Tram
- Underground station
- Other Transport

Note: Not all symbols displayed above appear on the maps in this book

Routes
- Tollway
- Freeway
- Primary
- Secondary
- Tertiary
- Lane
- Unsealed road
- Road under construction
- Plaza/Mall
- Steps
- Tunnel
- Pedestrian overpass
- Walking Tour
- Walking Tour detour
- Path/Walking Trail

Boundaries
- International
- State/Province
- Disputed
- Regional/Suburb
- Marine Park
- Cliff
- Wall

Hydrography
- River, Creek
- Intermittent River
- Canal
- Water
- Dry/Salt/Intermittent Lake
- Reef

Areas
- Airport/Runway
- Beach/Desert
- Cemetery (Christian)
- Cemetery (Other)
- Glacier
- Mudflat
- Park/Forest
- Sight (Building)
- Sportsground
- Swamp/Mangrove

Caramoan peninsula, immersing herself in Ivatan culture and (sort of) mastering wakeboarding. Anna also wrote the Diving in the Philippines chapter for this guide.

Paul Stiles

Boracay & Western Visayas When he was 21, Paul bought an old motorcycle in London and drove it to Tunisia. That did it for him. Since then he has explored 60 countries. With a passion for exotic islands, he's covered Madagascar, Borneo, and five Hawaiian Islands for Lonely Planet, and lived for four years at the base of El Teide, the tallest volcano in the Atlantic Ocean. For this book he happily overdosed on islands, covering 14 of them in five weeks. Paul also wrote the Environment essay for this guide.

OUR STORY

A beat-up old car, a few dollars in the pocket and a sense of adventure. In 1972 that's all Tony and Maureen Wheeler needed for the trip of a lifetime — across Europe and Asia overland to Australia. It took several months, and at the end — broke but inspired — they sat at their kitchen table writing and stapling together their first travel guide, *Across Asia on the Cheap*. Within a week they'd sold 1500 copies. Lonely Planet was born.

Today, Lonely Planet has offices in Franklin, London, Melbourne, Oakland, Beijing and Delhi, with more than 600 staff and writers. We share Tony's belief that 'a great guidebook should do three things: inform, educate and amuse'.

OUR WRITERS

Michael Grosberg

Coordinating Author, Palawan, Mindanao This is the 5th edition of the Lonely Planet *Philippines* guide that Michael has worked on – the 1st was also his very first Lonely Planet assignment. Combined with other trips for work and pleasure, he's traversed much of the country from Batanes in the far north to General Santos in the south. At the end of every trip he's exhausted, sunburned and usually sustaining an injury (this time, a strained rotator cuff from a motorbike accident) but always itching to return. His most cherished experiences travelling in the Philippines involve unexpected moments of warmth and hospitality from people he meets along the way. Michael has worked on more than 35 Lonely Planet guidebooks and lives in Brooklyn when not on the road.

Read more about Michael at:
lonelyplanet.com/members/michaelgrosberg

Greg Bloom

Mindoro, Cebu & Eastern Visayas Greg divides his time between Phnom Penh and Manila, writing, editing, taking photos and dispensing travel advice. This is his fourth stint on Lonely Planet's *Philippines*. He has also written the Philippines chapter for Lonely Planet's *Southeast Asia* guide, as well as working on many other titles. His 10-plus years of covering the Philippines have brought both highs (diving Apo Reef) and lows (being ejected from a jeepney in Palawan). When not writing about Southeast Asia, Greg might be found snouting around Russia or patrolling Asia's ultimate frisbee fields. Greg also wrote the Welcome To and Top 15 chapters and the People & Culture essay for this guide.

Read more about Greg at:
lonelyplanet.com/members/gbloom4

Trent Holden

Manila, Around Manila As a huge fan of energetic, gritty, chaotic megacities, Trent feels right at home whenever he visits Manila and is convinced it's Asia's coolest city. So it was with great delight that he got to tackle it and unveil its hidden charms for Lonely Planet. A Melbourne writer based in London, Trent has worked on 20 guides for Lonely Planet, covering destinations across Asia and Africa. It's his second time covering the Philippines. You can catch him on Twitter @hombreholden. Trent also wrote the Outdoor Activities chapter.

Anna Kaminski

North Luzon, Southeast Luzon During this particular Pinoy venture Anna has been very lucky. Her wallet had been lost and found, she managed to avoid every single typhoon while travelling in typhoon season and she'd travelled further than ever before – as far as the remote Batanes. Six weeks and countless jeepney, bus, tricycle, bangka, RORO, fastcraft and motorbike rides later, her most treasured experiences include overnighting with Kalinga tribespeople, exploring the pristine

OVER PAGE MORE WRITERS

Published by Lonely Planet Publications Pty Ltd
ABN 36 005 607 983
12th edition – May 2015
ISBN 978 1 74220 783 4
© Lonely Planet 2015 Photographs © as indicated 2015
10 9 8 7 6 5 4 3 2 1
Printed in China